EXPLORING YOUR WORLD

THE ADVENTURE OF GEOGRAPHY

Prepared by the Special Publications Division
NATIONAL GEOGRAPHIC SOCIETY
Washington, D.C.

Carved by waves over centuries, cliffs edge the Pacific Ocean near La Jolla, California. A wide-angle camera lens reshapes the bird's-eye view enjoyed by a hang-gliding pilot and pet.

At home in the earth's highest mountains, Sherpa porters and their yaks trek near Himalayan peaks of Sagarmatha National Park in Nepal. Sherpas are famous for their mountain climbing skills.

Windmills rise from fields where storm tides once lashed the low-lying Netherlands. For centuries, Netherlanders have held back the North Sea with dikes and have pumped water off land with windmills.

Skyscrapers viewed from the Staten Island ferry symbolize Manhattan's commercial and financial might. For more than 300 years, New York City has reaped the benefits of its location near rivers and the ocean.

Buildings ablaze with light tower above pedestrians in Tokyo, Japan, where crowding makes open space increasingly rare.

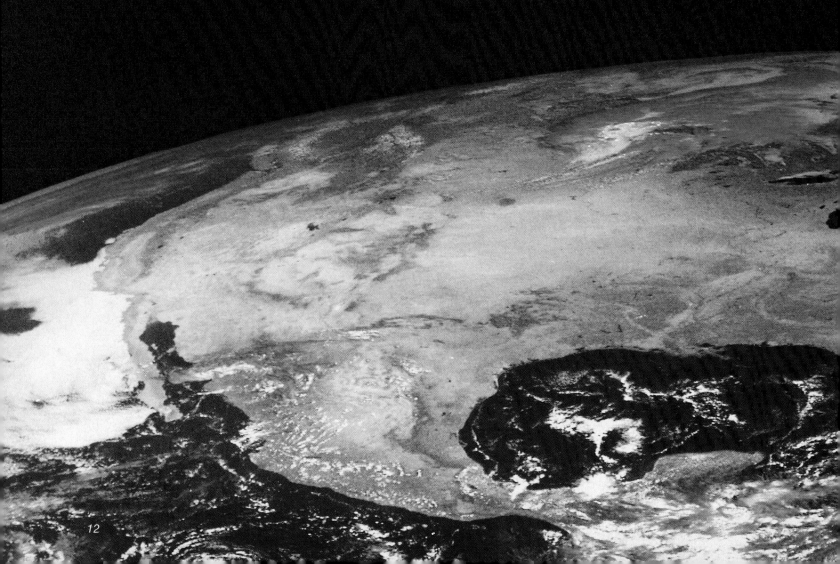

EXPL
YOUR

THE ADVENTU

ORING WORLD

RE OF GEOGRAPHY

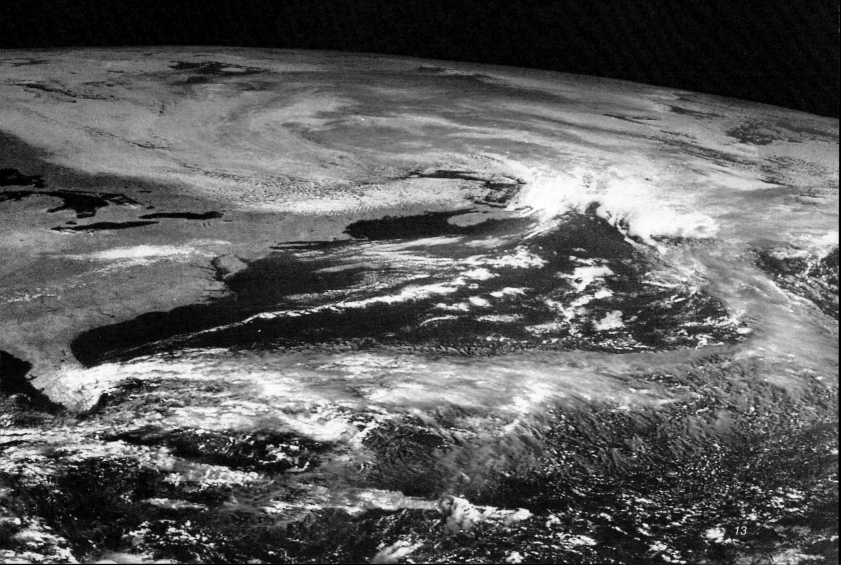

EXPLORING YOUR WORLD: THE ADVENTURE OF GEOGRAPHY

Published by
The National Geographic Society

Prepared by
The Special Publications Division

Gilbert M. Grosvenor
*President and
Chairman of the Board*

Melvin M. Payne
Thomas W. McKnew
Chairmen Emeritus

Donald J. Crump
Director

Philip B. Silcott
Associate Director

Bonnie S. Lawrence
Assistant Director

Alice T. M. Rechlin, Ph.D.
Staff Geographer

Sue Appleby Purcell
Educational Consultant

Owen R. Anderson
Executive Vice President

Robert L. Breeden
*Senior Vice President,
Publications and
Educational Media*

Peter B. Stifel, Ph.D.
Geology Consultant

John C. Kammerer
Hydrology Adviser

J. Murray Mitchell, Ph.D.
Climatology Consultant

Robert O. Petty, Ph.D.
Biology Consultant

Lynda Bush, Ph.D.
Reading Consultant

Staff for this book

Margery G. Dunn
Managing Editor

Debra Guthrie Haer
Assistant Managing Editor

Catherine O'Neill
Gene S. Stuart
Assistant Editors

Toni Eugene
Susan Tejada
Contributing Editors

H. Robert Morrison
Peggy D. Winston
Editorial Consultants

Leslie Allen
Joseph Alper
Jennifer Davidson
Jacqueline Geschickter
Ann Nottingham Kelsall
Susan McGrath
Catherine O'Neill
Judith E. Rinard
Gene S. Stuart
Peter Winkler
Writers

Marjorie R. Dana
Ann DiFiore
Thomas F. Howard
Thomas A. Outler
Christopher More Petite
James M. Popkin
Thomas B. Winston
Contributing Writers

Carol R. Curtis
Marisa J. Farabelli
Sandra F. Lotterman
Eliza Morton
Editorial Assistants

Dennis R. Dimick
Illustrations Editor

Susan A. Bender
Erin Taylor Monroney
Illustrations Researchers

Artemis S. Lampathakis
Illustrations Assistant

George V. White
*Director, Manufacturing
and Quality Management*

Vincent P. Ryan
*Manager, Manufacturing
and Quality Management*

David V. Showers
Production Manager

Lewis R. Bassford
Production Project Manager

Kathleen M. Cirucci
Timothy H. Ewing
Senior Production Assistants

Kevin P. Heubusch
Production Assistant

Sharon Kocsis Berry
Catherine G. Cruz
Lisa A. LaFuria
Dru Stancampiano
Marilyn Williams
Staff Assistants

Lynette R. Ruschak
Art Director

Robert Hynes
Principal Illustrator

Ross Culbert
 Holland & Lavery, NYC
Map Design

Corinne Szabo
Layout Assistant

John D. Garst, Jr.
Virginia L. Baza
Isaac Ortiz
Peter J. Balch
Donald L. Carrick
Robert W. Cronan
Sven M. Dolling
Susan I. Friedman
Elizabeth G. Jevons
Gary M. Johnson
Carl J. Mehler
Mark S. Nardini
Joseph F. Ochlak
Daniel J. Ortiz
Martin S. Walz
Publications Art

Carolinda E. Hill
Research Editor

Elisabeth B. Booz
Victoria D. Garrett
Alyson L. Greiner
Gail N. Hawkins
Patricia Bragan Kellogg
Kimberly Anne Kostyal
Thomas A. Outler
Christopher N. Scaptura
Elizabeth P. Schleichert
Jacqueline N. Thompson
Diana L. Vanek
David W. Wooddell
Researchers

Susanne E. Früh
Alison J. Kahn
Ann Nottingham Kelsall
Jane L. Matteson
Gregory A. McGruder
Suzanne Nave Patrick
Jayne Wise
Contributing Researchers

Marjorie R. Dana
Elizabeth A. Frankenberg
Lucy Y. Herring
Jeffrey D. Osterman
Barbara A. Schwartz
Deborah L. Stewart
Geography Interns

Anne K. McCain
Indexer

George I. Burneston, III
Assistant Indexer

Cover, regular edition: Top row (left to right): The Mittens,
Monument Valley, Utah/Arizona; Dent du Géant (Giant's
Tooth), French Alps; giraffe, East Africa. Middle row: Devil's
Marbles, Northern Territory, Australia; Hong Kong harbor;
geisha, Kyoto, Japan. Bottom row: Panama Canal; sunset,
Kenya; drying corn, Hebei Province, China.

Pages 12–13: A weather satellite image shows most of the
United States and Mexico under fair skies. Right: Celebrating
their diversity, New Yorkers enjoy an international festival along
Manhattan's Ninth Avenue.

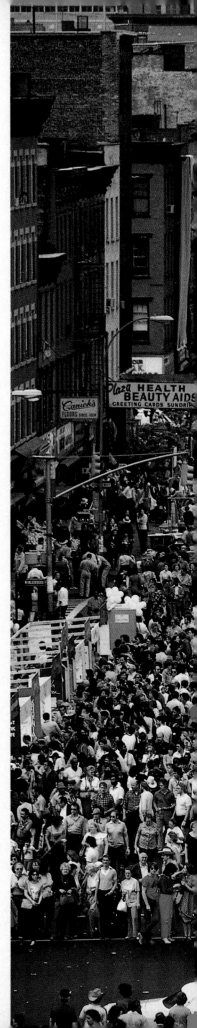

CONTENTS

PAGES 12–13: EARTH SATELLITE CORP.
LEFT: NICHOLAS DEVORE III / PHOTOGRAPHERS ASPEN

First row: astronaut in space; vendor, India; freshwater marsh, United States; immigrant farm workers, Canada; volcanic eruption, Hawaii, U.S. Second row: zebra, Kenya; terraced rice fields, Japan; Inuit children, Canada; grain, U.S.; boy with a tilapia, Zaire; blowing snow, U.S. Third row: Popocatépetl volcano, Mexico; Song dynasty manuscript, China; gold coins, Austria; old-growth forest, U.S.; motorbike riders, Thailand. Fourth row: commodity traders, U.S.; tropical coast, Western Samoa; farm activity, U.S.; young girl, Bolivia; sand dunes, Peru. Fifth row: offshore oil drilling platform, U.S.; badlands, U.S.; aurora borealis, U.S.; overseas-bound cars, Japan.

FOREWORD

I vividly remember my excitement as a child each time an explorer visited our home. As I listened to one fascinating story after another, I came to see geography as an African plain full of wildlife, or the teeming, fragile web of life in a rain forest, or a polar region where only the howling wind seemed alive. Geography illuminated the world for me.

Many people do not have the opportunity to travel widely, but everyone can—and should—feel the wonder of learning about the earth and its peoples. As President of the National Geographic Society and as a parent, I have made geography education my top priority. I am trying to see to it that everyone discovers that geography is fun, that it is exciting, and, most important, that it is necessary.

In the future, the peoples and places of the world will be even more interdependent than they are today. Local events will more frequently have global consequences. Tomorrow's leaders must understand the worldwide effects of environmental hazards, trade imbalances, religious conflicts, and a host of other issues that are grounded in geography.

With these things in mind, the staff of *Exploring Your World: The Adventure of Geography* has spent more than three years working with educators and experts in many fields to produce this unique volume. Between its covers is an unparalleled amount of geographic information for students of all ages, conveyed through text, photographs, maps, and art.

This book invites readers to explore the "hows" and "whys" of our planet—its processes and interrelationships—as well as the "wheres." Though its nature has changed, exploration has become perhaps even more exciting since the Society was founded in 1888 for "the increase and diffusion of geographic knowledge." Now, as the Society moves into its second century, *Exploring Your World* reaffirms our commitment to nurturing thoughtful citizens of tomorrow's world.

Gilbert M. Grosvenor
President and Chairman of the Board

WHAT IS GEOGRAPHY?

Imagine a typical morning. You might wake to the music of a British rock band on your Japanese clock radio. Perhaps the shirt you put on was made in Hong Kong. The oranges for the juice you drink at breakfast may have come from Brazil. The wheat for your cereal was probably grown on North America's Great Plains.

Do you have time to read an article in the newspaper (perhaps made from Canadian wood pulp) about air pollution in the United States? How rushed you are may depend on how far you live from your school or your job. Finally, just as you step outside, it starts to rain. A low pressure system that formed thousands of kilometers away sends you running back inside for your Taiwanese umbrella.

As these examples show, each of us is linked in many ways to other parts of the world. Thinking geographically means thinking about such links. As a field of knowledge, geography is the study of the earth's surface and the processes that shape it; of places and their connections to other places; and of the relationships between people and environments. Just as important, geography is a point of view, a way of looking at the world in terms of its interconnections.

To begin thinking geographically, you need to have curiosity about the world and how it functions. Geography has much more to do with asking questions and solving problems than it does with memorizing facts and figures. The same kinds of questions you might ask yourself about places are also starting points for geographers.

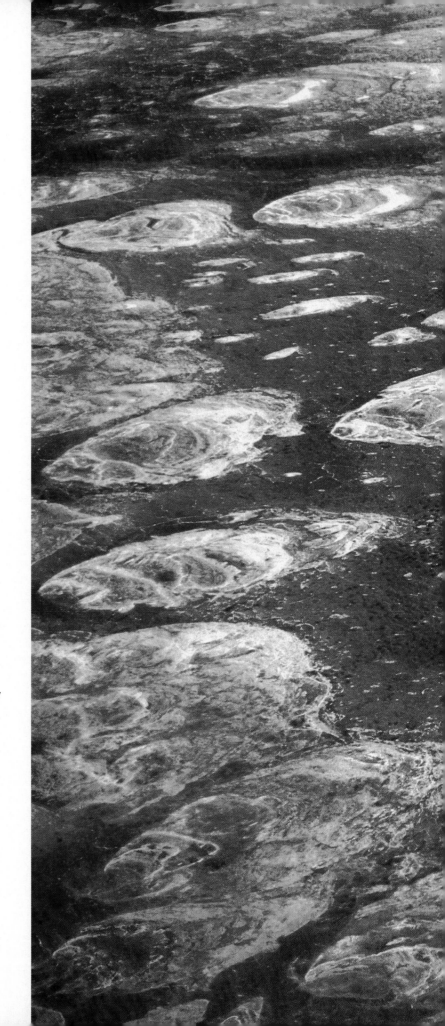

The waters of Lake Natron, stained red by a bloom of algae, spread beneath a low-flying plane in the East African country of Tanzania.
N.G.S. PHOTOGRAPHER GEORGE F. MOBLEY

For instance, a label tells you that your shirt was made in Hong Kong. Where is Hong Kong? As a beginning geographer, you would first locate Hong Kong on a map. What is Hong Kong like? And how is it that some of the clothing we wear might come from so far away? To answer these questions, you would consider the physical and human factors that distinguish Hong Kong from other places. For example, you would want to know what economic and political characteristics have placed Hong Kong in the world market. You would also want to know what factors have made trading with Hong Kong desirable and affordable. The movement of goods, as well as of people and information, from one place to another is a major interest of geographers.

Geographers study the ways that people interact with their environments. After reading the newspaper article about air pollution, you might wonder about the effects of such pollution both locally and worldwide. How might it be damaging lakes and forests—and endangering people's health? Is it affecting global climate? Geographers seek answers to these and similar questions.

Dividing the earth into regions—areas that have certain things in common—helps geographers see the world in terms of similarities and differences. For instance, the wheat for your cereal was grown on the Great Plains, a region of North America extending from Canada deep into the United States. A geographer would want to know what characteristics the provinces and the states of the Great Plains share, and what physical and economic conditions make the region suitable for growing wheat.

Geography is one of the oldest sciences. Among the earliest geographers were Greeks who lived more than 2,000 years ago. In fact, the term "geography" comes from a Greek word that means writing about the earth. Writing about or describing the earth has always been an important aspect of geography. It was particularly so in past centuries, as explorers, mapmakers, scientists, and others charted previously unknown areas and features of the world.

By the time geography became an independent discipline in the late 18th and early 19th centuries, much of the earth had been explored and much of it had been mapped. Since then, geographers have concentrated on explaining the similarities and differences among places and on analyzing the physical and human processes that shape them. In addition, geographers study spatial patterns—the ways people, places, and things are distributed over the surface of the earth.

Early geographers were often explorers who served rulers seeking to colonize new lands and establish trade routes. Present-day geographers also address practical needs. They help plan the layout of new suburbs and the revitalization of cities. They help manage and conserve natural resources. They study voting patterns and the spread of diseases. Some of them are teachers; others are skilled in cartography, the science and art of mapmaking. Geographers can be found in dozens of other occupations as well. Aspects of their work often overlap other fields of study, such as geology, biology, anthropology, and history. What sets geography apart, though, is its emphasis on the "where" of things and on the human and environmental characteristics that explain spatial patterns around the world.

Geography's scope expands not only as we learn more about the world but also as our perspective changes. The known world of prehistoric people, for example, was considerably smaller than that of educated Europeans living 500 years ago. Today, we can see the earth as a whole in satellite images. From space, it resembles a fragile Christmas tree ornament, small enough to cup in a hand.

In a sense, we do hold the world and its future in our hands. The dangers of nuclear and toxic wastes, the population explosion, the depletion of natural resources, and other critical problems of our time are global in nature. Even regional events—a miners'

Women and children fill jugs with water pumped from a well in the Sahel, a semiarid region of Africa just south of the Sahara.
GEORG GERSTER/ZUMIKON, SWITZERLAND

strike, a good harvest, the building of a highway—often have far-reaching effects. One of the most valuable things geography can give us is an understanding of the global consequences of events at particular places.

About This Book

The number and diversity of geographic terms covered in *Exploring Your World* reveal the earth as an incredibly varied and complex planet. Among the 334 entries, arranged alphabetically, you will find BIOSPHERE and BRIDGE, CAPITALISM and COMPASS, RELIGIONS and RING OF FIRE.

The book's extensive system of cross-referencing underscores the many interconnections that exist in the world and the many concerns its peoples share. All of the entries end with the words "See also" and a list of related entries found elsewhere in the encyclopedia. These cross-references are a kind of road map through networks of related topics. After reading about climate, for instance, you might go on to ATMOSPHERE, DESERT, FOREST, GRASSLAND, GREENHOUSE EFFECT, ICE AGE, ICE SHEET, MOUNTAIN, OCEAN, POLAR REGIONS, SEA LEVEL, SEASONS, TUNDRA, VEGETATION REGIONS, or WEATHER. If you choose to read next about the greenhouse effect, you will in turn be referred to POLLUTION, and from POLLUTION to CONSERVATION, FOSSIL FUEL, OZONE LAYER, and SMOG.

The book's index is a kind of road map, too. In it, the titles and page numbers of all the entries appear in **boldfaced** type. The index also includes hundreds of subtopics covered in the entries.

Metric measurements are used throughout the encyclopedia, with the equivalent customary measurements given in parentheses. In some cases, the measurements are precise. In others, they are approximations, and so both metric and customary figures are rounded. The metric system is now standard in almost all countries and is coming into greater use in the United States. ∎

By-product in a land of plenty, trash piles up for shredding at a Florida facility. Limited disposal space, ecological hazards, and concern about dwindling natural resources cause people to seek new ways of dealing with wastes.
ALEX WEBB/MAGNUM

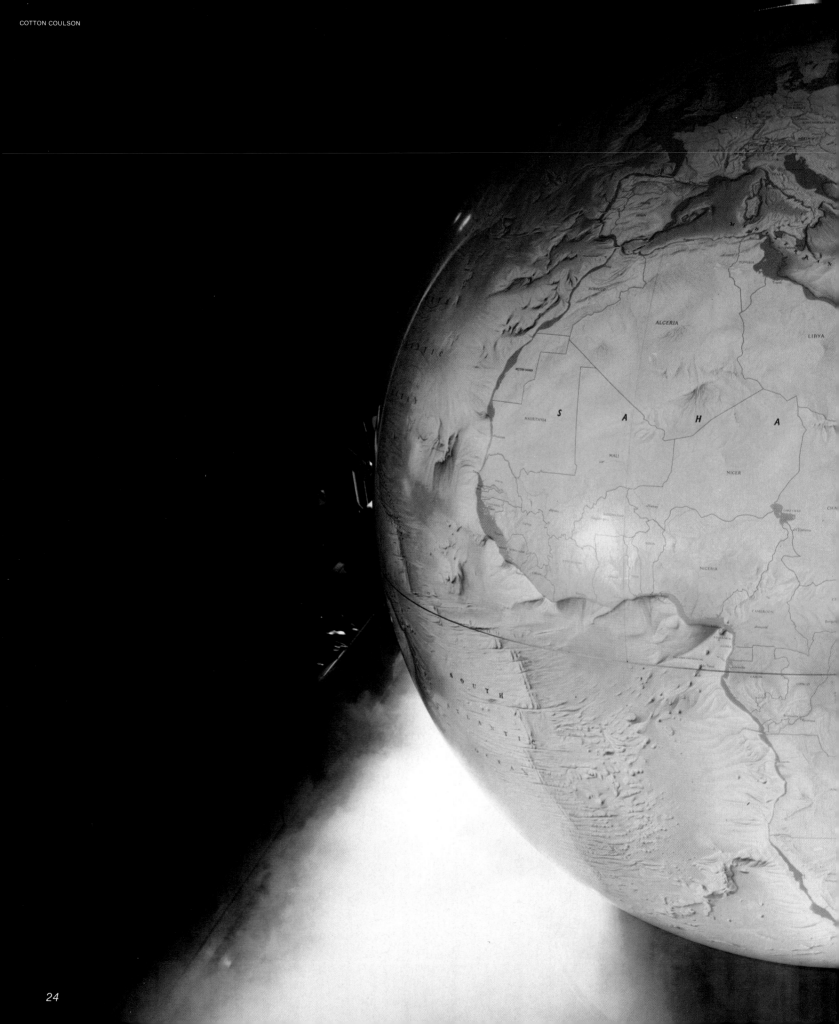

A world of information spins into focus on National Geographic's giant globe. It shows political boundaries along with mountains and other features of the land and the ocean floor.

Climbers reach an icy ledge in New Zealand's Southern Alps, where remote peaks, glaciers, and rivers still challenge explorers and scientists.

GORDON W. GAHAN

28

Splendor of the past endures in an Egyptian pyramid. Camels have provided desert transport in parts of Africa and Asia since ancient times.

Sleek jetliners taxi at the Dallas-Fort Worth International Airport in Texas. Air transportation links peoples and places throughout the world.

An aurora borealis shimmers in a starry sky over Canada. Inside an observation bubble, a researcher studies the light display, an atmospheric phenomenon.

Fireworks burst into splinters
of light as Parisians celebrate
the French national day—
Bastille Day, July 14. Arches
of the Eiffel Tower frame
the spectacle.

WILLIAM ALBERT ALLARD

35

AGRICULTURE

When you hear the word "agriculture," you may picture a farmer on a tractor planting a field of corn, apple trees bending under the weight of ripe fruit, or barnyards full of cows, hogs, or chickens. You might not think of a beekeeper tending hives, vegetables being grown in water instead of in soil, or someone harvesting trout raised in a pond. Yet, each of these activities is a form of agriculture.

Agriculture is the art or science of cultivating the soil, growing crops, and raising livestock. It can include activities such as the preparation of plant and animal products for human use and their distribution to markets. These products, as well as the agricultural methods people use, may vary from one part of the world to another.

Agriculture provides most of the food we eat, as well as cotton, wool, and much more. Tree farming gives us wood for construction and for paper products. Agriculture has been a vital part of human existence for thousands of years. Over centuries, the growth of agriculture contributed to the rise of civilizations.

▲ Caring for his herd of cattle, a Kansas farmer rescues a Hereford calf from winter cold.
◄ A Montana farmer levels a load of harvested wheat pouring from a combine. Agriculture includes growing crops and raising livestock.

Before agriculture became widespread, people spent most of their lives in the search for food—hunting wild animals and gathering wild plants. About 10,000 years ago, people gradually began learning how to cultivate cereal and root crops, and slowly settled down to a life based on farming.

By 2,000 years ago, much of the earth's population had become dependent on agriculture. Scholars are not sure why this shift to a settled existence took place. It may have happened because of an increase in population, changes in climate, or a variety of other changing circumstances.

When people began growing crops, they also began herding and breeding wild animals. Adapting wild plants and animals to human use is called domestication.

The first domesticated animals were dogs used in hunting. Sheep and goats were probably domesticated next. People also domesticated cattle and pigs. Most of these animals had once been hunted for hides and

meat. Some now were also sources of milk, cheese, and butter. Eventually, people used domesticated animals such as oxen for plowing, pulling, and transportation.

Agriculture enabled people to produce surplus food. They could use this extra food when crops failed or trade it for other goods. Food surpluses freed many people to perform tasks unrelated to farming.

Agriculture kept formerly nomadic people near their fields and led to the development of permanent villages. These became linked through trade. New economies were so successful in some areas that cities grew and civilizations developed. The earliest civilizations based on intensive agriculture arose near the Tigris and the Euphrates Rivers in Mesopotamia and along the Nile in Egypt.

As human knowledge and technology have developed over thousands of years, agricultural methods have improved. The time line on pages 38–43 summarizes landmarks in agriculture from 9000 B.C. to the present.

▼ *The time line beginning on this page and continuing on the following five pages describes major developments in agriculture from about 9000 B.C. to the present.*

In southwestern Asia, wheat and barley were cultivated, and sheep and goats were domesticated. Dogs had been domesticated in Europe by about 10,000 B.C.
By 9000–7000 B.C.

Agriculture developed in parts of the Americas. Domesticated crops included beans, corn (maize), cassavas, squashes, potatoes, and peppers.
7000–3000 B.C.

The Huang (Yellow) River Valley was an area of early farming in northern China. Millet was a staple crop there. Rice, which may have originated in India, was cultivated throughout much of Asia by 5000 B.C.
6000 B.C.

Before 7000 B.C.
Grain agriculture developed in Egypt.

6500 B.C.
Cattle were domesticated in Greece.

About 5500 B.C.
In Mesopotamia, simple irrigation began and led to increased agricultural production, eventually contributing to the rise of cities.

For thousands of years, technological advances in agriculture were very slow. Farmers cultivated small plots of land by hand, using crude axes to clear away trees and hoes and pointed digging sticks to break up and till the soil.

Over time, improved farming tools of stone, bone, and iron were developed. In addition, new methods of storage evolved. People began stockpiling foods in bins, jars, and clay-lined pits for use in times of scarcity. They also began making clay pots and other vessels for carrying and cooking food.

Around 5500 B.C., farmers in Mesopotamia, in southwestern Asia, developed simple irrigation systems. By channeling water from streams onto their fields, farmers were able to settle in areas once thought to be unsuited to agriculture. In Mesopotamia, and later in Egypt and China, the building and maintaining of more refined and dependable irrigation systems encouraged people to work together in an organized way.

Perhaps as important as irrigation was the gradual development of improved varieties of plants. For example, a new variety of wheat became known in southwestern Asia or in Egypt by 6000 B.C. It was hardier than previous cereal grains; its hulls could be more easily removed; and when mixed with leaven, it could be made into raised bread, whereas earlier grains produced only flatbreads. People could grow this wheat in irrigated fields.

The Romans, several thousand years later, adopted the best agricultural methods of the people they conquered. They brought wheat varieties from southwestern Asia and northern Africa to Rome, and adapted them to their land. They wrote manuals about the methods of farming they observed.

During the Middle Ages, the workhorse was brought into northern Europe. At first, its strength seemed less than that of the ox. But a new kind of collar harness, introduced from China, nearly quadrupled the horse's working efficiency. In many parts of Europe,

Llamas were domesticated in South America. The animals were used as beasts of burden and as sources of wool and meat in some Andean areas.
By 3500 B.C.

Grain agriculture formed the basis of the Harappan civilization in the Indus River Valley in present-day Pakistan and India.
About 2500 B.C.

3000 B.C.
The water buffalo was domesticated in India and became an important draft animal.

A.D. 800
The open-field system of planting was common in western Europe. Village land was divided into two or three large fields, and crops were rotated in each field yearly, with one field left unplanted.

the horse replaced the ox as a plow animal.

Many medieval farmers used an open-field system of agriculture. This was a system of alternating planting in their fields. One field would be planted in spring and another in autumn, and one would be left unplanted, or fallow. This system preserved nutrients in the soil, increasing crop production.

In the 15th and 16th centuries, explorers introduced new varieties of plants and agricultural products into Europe. From Asia they carried home coffee, tea, and indigo, a plant that yields blue dye. From the Americas they took plants such as potatoes, tomatoes, corn (maize), beans, peanuts, and tobacco. Some of these became staples and expanded people's diets in parts of Europe.

The 18th and 19th Centuries

A period of important agricultural development began in Great Britain and in the Low Countries (present-day Belgium, Luxembourg,

and the Netherlands) in the early 1700s and lasted more than a century. Over time, agricultural inventions dramatically increased food production in Europe, the United States, Canada, and some other countries. One of the most important of the developments was an improved seed drill invented by Jethro Tull about 1701 in England. Until that time, farmers had sowed seeds by hand. Tull's seed drill bored rows of holes into which seeds were dropped. By the end of the 18th century, seed drilling was widely practiced. Most of the world was not affected by these developments and, for the most part, continued to use centuries-old ways of farming.

Many machines were developed in the United States. The cotton gin, invented by Eli Whitney in 1793, reduced the time needed to separate cotton fiber from seed. In the 1830s, Cyrus McCormick's reaper, a great improvement over earlier harvesting tools, helped modernize the grain-cutting process. At about the same time, John and Hiram Pitts

Explorers introduced plants and agricultural products from Asia and the Americas into Europe. Coffee, tea, and indigo were carried back from Asia. Potatoes, tomatoes, corn (maize), and beans were among the plants brought from the Americas. Some of these plants expanded peoples' diets in parts of Europe.
1400s–1500s

Jethro Tull introduced the seed drill to English farmers. This device, which cut furrows and dropped in seeds, ended the slow, laborious task of sowing seeds by hand for many people.
1701

In the United States, Eli Whitney invented the cotton gin, a machine that separated fiber from seed much more quickly than people could do it by hand.
1793

Early 1700s
New crop rotation methods evolved in Europe's Low Countries and in England, improving previous systems. Charles Townshend popularized a four-field system in Norfolk County, England. He found that turnips could be rotated with wheat, barley, clover, and ryegrass to make soil more fertile and increase yields.

Late 1700s
In England, Robert Bakewell pioneered the selective breeding of cattle and sheep to produce meatier animals.

invented a horse-powered thresher that shortened the tedious process of separating grain and seed from chaff and straw. John Deere's steel plow, introduced in 1837, made it possible to work the tough midwestern prairie soil with much less horsepower. The plow was designed to keep the heavy black soil from clinging to it.

Along with new machines, there were several important advances in farming methods. By selective breeding of animals—breeding those with desirable traits—farmers increased the size and productivity of their livestock. The Leicester sheep, for example, developed in England through selective breeding, gave both quality meat and long, coarse wool.

New crop rotation methods evolved in both the Low Countries and England in the early 18th century. Many of these were adopted over the next century or so throughout Europe. For example, the Norfolk four-field system, developed in England, proved quite

◄ *Using a digging stick, a Tarahumara Indian woman of Mexico plants corn by hand. Such traditional agricultural practices date back for centuries and survive in many American Indian cultures. For them, corn plays a major role in daily life and in rituals.*

In the United States, John Deere patented the steel plow. It was stronger, sharper, and more efficient than wooden or iron plows. Heavy damp soil did not stick to it as readily.
1837

The results of Gregor Mendel's studies in heredity were published in Austria. In experiments with pea plants, Mendel learned how traits were passed from one generation to the next. His work paved the way for improving crops through genetics.
1866

1834
In the United States, the first practical reaper, or grain harvesting machine, was patented by Cyrus McCormick.

1842
In England, Sir John Bennet Lawes founded the first factory to manufacture superphosphate. This marked the beginning of the chemical fertilizer industry.

1850s–Early 1900s
Railroad and steamship lines were expanded, opening up new markets. Improved methods of refrigeration and canning made possible the long-distance shipping of perishable agricultural products.

► *A New Zealand farmer tends his flock. His country has the world's highest lamb and mutton production, with vast grazing lands supporting millions of sheep. In many countries, sheep are a source of meat, wool, milk, and cheese.*

The first gasoline-powered tractors were built. They gradually replaced steam-powered tractors and draft animals in many parts of the world.
Early 1890s

Better nutrition, disease control measures, and breeding practices greatly improved livestock production in many countries.
1920s

The U. S. Rural Electrification Administration was established. Electricity became more readily available in rural areas.
1935

1890s
The combine harvester, which combined the cutting and threshing of grain crops, came into widespread use in California. It gradually spread to other western states. The combine reduced the amount of labor needed to harvest one hectare (2.5 acres) of wheat from 37 to 6.25 man-hours.

Late 1920s
Scientists improved the seeds from which farmers grew corn. The best qualities of several kinds of seeds were combined. Fertilizers helped farmers produce more from each plant.

successful. It involved the yearly rotation of several crops, including wheat, turnips, barley, clover, and ryegrass. This added nutrients to the soil, enabling farmers to grow enough to sell some of their harvest without having to leave any land unplanted.

20th-Century Developments

In the early 1900s, an average farmer in the United States produced enough food to feed himself, his wife, their three children, and two other people. Many of today's farmers can feed a family of five and nearly a hundred other people. How did this great leap in productivity come about? It happened largely because of scientific advances and the development of new sources of power.

By the late 1950s, most farmers in developed countries were using both gasoline and electricity to power machinery. Tractors had replaced draft animals and steam-powered machinery, and farmers were using machines in every stage of cultivation and in many areas of livestock management.

Electricity had become a power source on farms in Japan and Germany in the early 1900s. By 1960, most farms in the United States and other developed countries were electrified. Electricity lighted farm buildings and powered machinery such as water pumps, milking machines, and feeding equipment. Today, electricity controls entire environments in livestock barns and poultry houses, and also runs the farmer's computer.

Traditionally, farmers have used a variety of methods to protect their crops from pests and diseases. They have put herb-based poisons on crops; handpicked insects off plants; practiced rather unscientific breeding of hardy varieties of crops; and rotated crops to try to control insects.

Now, many farmers, especially in developed countries, rely on chemicals to control pests that range from insects to animals such as rabbits and mice, as well as weeds and

Machines and increased productivity in industrialized countries sharply reduced the number of people working in agriculture. Through scientific advances and improved management techniques, farmers produced more food than ever before.
1945–About 1970

Researchers in California first spliced, or introduced, a gene from one organism into another, and the age of genetic engineering began. Genetic engineering offers the possibility of making plants and animals hardier, more resistant to disease, and more productive.
1970s–Present

1939
DDT was introduced, marking the beginning of agriculture's heavy use of chemical pesticides in developed countries. The U. S. banned DDT in 1972 because it was harming the environment.

1950s–1960s
Several developing countries, such as India and the Philippines, experienced the green revolution. High-yield grains were introduced, greatly increasing production and local supplies.

Early 1980s
In developed countries, farmers began using computers to keep farm accounts; to monitor crop prices and weather conditions; to help decide when to irrigate and plant; and to automate the application of fertilizers and pesticides.

HISTORY OF AGRICULTURE

disease-causing organisms—bacteria, viruses, and fungi. Though crop losses have declined dramatically, a heavy reliance on chemicals has disturbed the environment, often destroying helpful species of animals along with harmful ones and posing a health hazard to humans, especially through contaminated water supplies. To correct this, scientists are seeking safer agricultural chemicals and new natural controls. Some farmers already use natural controls and rely less and less on chemicals.

For thousands of years, farmers relied on natural materials such as manure, wood ash, ground bones, fish or fish parts, and bird wastes called guano to replenish or increase nutrients in the soil.

In the early 1800s, scientists discovered which elements were most essential to plant growth: nitrogen, phosphorus, and potassium. Later, fertilizer containing these elements was manufactured in the U.S. and in Europe. Now, many farmers use chemical fertilizers

▲ *Africans show off their goats. Many people in developing countries are subsistence farmers, raising food for home use and selling any surplus.*

▼ *Pigs in Thailand scramble to a meal at feeding time. In global terms, they have become one of the most important food-producing animals.*

because they greatly increase crop yields, and because manure and other organic fertilizers are no longer widely available.

Technology in Agriculture

For centuries, people have bred new types of plants and animals by random experimentation. But only in this century have we fully understood what determines the results of breeding. Inside every cell are genes, hereditary material that determines many of the characteristics of an organism.

With greater knowledge of what characteristics organisms inherit and how these traits are transmitted, people can scientifically select characteristics they want to reproduce in order to improve varieties of plants and animals. New technology has revolutionized the selective breeding process. For example, breeders use artificial insemination to produce dairy cows that give more milk.

Beginning in the 1970s, scientists found that they could rearrange genes in cells and add new ones to promote disease resistance and productivity in crops and livestock. This process is called genetic engineering. For example, a new gene can be used with strawberry plants to increase their resistance to cold and thus extend their growing season.

The development of livestock vaccines and more nutritious feeds has brought advances in animal husbandry, the raising of domesticated animals. Today's farm animals are faster growing and more productive than were their ancestors. An egg-producing chicken in a poultry house, for instance, lays about 250 eggs a year. Until the 1950s, a typical hen produced 50 to 150 eggs a year.

Agriculture includes such forms of cultivation as hydroponics and aquaculture. Both involve farming in water. Hydroponics is the growing of plants in nutrient solutions. Just 0.4 hectare (1 acre) of a nutrient solution can yield more than 50 times the amount of lettuce grown on the same amount of soil.

Aquaculture—primarily the cultivation of fish and shellfish—was practiced in China,

▼ *Bounty of fresh milk overflows a pail on a farm in Iceland. Rural families in many different areas may keep one or two cows to supply them with milk. Worldwide, people drink nearly half the milk produced, processing the rest into foods such as butter and cheese.*

▲ *Draped in a protective veil, a Chinese beekeeper tends hives. People have kept bees since ancient times. Honey is prized as a food; beeswax is used for candles and other products.*

India, and Egypt thousands of years ago. It is now practiced in lakes, ponds, the ocean, and other bodies of water throughout the world. Some forms of aquaculture, such as shrimp farming, have become important industries in many Asian and Latin American countries and in the southern United States.

The Green Revolution

During the 1950s and 1960s, scientists developed new strains of high-yield wheat and rice. They introduced them into Mexico and parts of Asia. As a result, production of grain soared in these areas. Able to grow large quantities of grain, countries such as India, Indonesia, and the Philippines have accumulated grain surpluses in most years. This bold experiment in agriculture has been called the green revolution.

With the successes of the green revolution came unexpected problems. To produce high yields, the new "miracle" strains required chemical fertilizers, pesticides, and irrigation. In most countries, small farmers slowly adopted the new technology. Some, however, could not afford it. They could not compete with larger, wealthier farmers. Ultimately, they lost their land.

Agriculture in Developing Countries

Most of the world's farmers live in developing countries in Africa, Asia, and Latin America. Many of them cultivate small plots of land as their ancestors did hundreds or even thousands of years ago.

Most farmers cannot afford the technology that would increase their crop yields. Often the soil they farm is eroded or depleted. They have only themselves and their animals for power, and they depend solely on rain, seasonal flooding, or both, to water their plots. They produce far less per person than farmers using more advanced technology. These people are called subsistence farmers. They use the bulk of the food they produce for themselves and their families, unlike commercial farmers, who only grow crops to sell.

◀ In a Texas feedlot, cattle eat feed selected scientifically to fatten them for market. Feedlots mean big business in many developed countries.

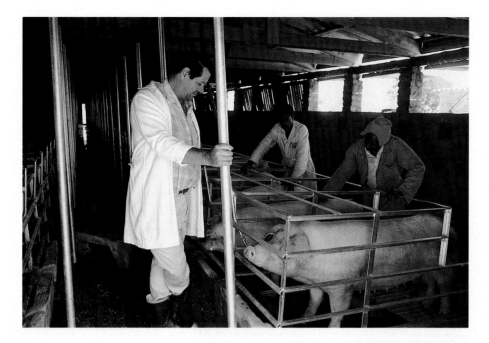

▲ In Africa, a farmer inspects breeding sows cared for to ensure healthy piglets. Such large farm operations worldwide use modern scientific technology.
► A California poultry farm reduces labor with machines that feed chickens and collect and package eggs.
▼ One man at an Israeli farm cooperative uses machines to milk several cows at a time. Machines have revolutionized the dairy industry.

Different Methods of Cultivation

Agricultural methods often vary widely around the world, depending on climate, terrain, traditions, and available technology.

In coastal West Africa, farmers, usually women, plant corn (maize) soon after the first rains of the growing season. They often use an ancient method of clearing called slash-and-burn. First, the farmer cuts all the brush in her plot. When this vegetation dries, she sets fire to it. The heat from the fire makes the soil easy to turn, and the burned vegetation fertilizes it. The farmer then sows kernels of corn saved from the previous year's harvest.

Between rows of corn, the farmer plants other staple crops: legumes such as cowpeas, or root crops such as yams and cassavas. This practice of growing several crops in the same plot is called intercropping. By covering most of the ground with vegetation, intercropping prevents moisture loss and soil erosion from seasonal rains.

Rain supplies water for the growing plants. The farmer weeds her plot with a hoe. At harvesttime, she and her family pick the corn, husk it, and spread the ears in the sun to dry. They grind the dried corn into meal to make porridge. The average corn yield is 1.3 tons per hectare (20 bushels per acre).

Traditionally, the farmer uses the same plot for several years, until its fertility declines. Then she moves to another plot, leaving the first to lie fallow for up to ten years. Now, however, fallow periods are being reduced and permanent cultivation is becoming more common because of demands on the land from an increasing population.

Agricultural methods used in the corn belt region of the United States are very different. Soon after harvesting the corn in autumn, a farmer in Iowa works any leftover vegetation, or stubble, into the soil. In the spring, he works the soil again, using an implement with rows of sharp-edged steel discs, called a disc harrow. The discs cut into the soil, breaking it into smaller pieces and supplying it with air. Next, a tractor-pulled planter sows rows of seed. It makes furrows in the soil, drops in kernels of high-yield corn, and covers them with soil. After the corn seeds have sprouted, another machine injects liquid fertilizer into the soil. The farmer then controls weeds and

loosens the soil with a tractor-pulled cultivator during the growing season.

The Iowa farmer may plant about 40 hectares (100 acres) in corn alone. The practice of specializing in a single crop is known as monoculture. To harvest the crop, the farmer uses a mechanical harvester that picks the ears of corn and shells them into a bin. A harvest often yields about 8 tons of corn per hectare (125 bushels per acre), and an average harvester can pick at the rate of 1.6 hectares (4 acres) an hour. Most of the corn is used to feed livestock and poultry.

Differences in Animal Husbandry

From alpacas in Peru to zebus in India, billions of domesticated animals around the world are raised and cared for in a variety of ways. In many countries, domesticated animals are an important source of food.

In Nigeria, for example, 80 percent of the cattle belong to members of the Fulani tribe. The Fulani are pastoral nomads. They move with their herds from one grazing area to another. The cattle feed on scrub and grasses in land unsuitable for farming. The Fulani rely on cattle for milk, their principal food, and rarely slaughter their animals for meat.

Throughout the United States, beef cattle

▲ *Old farming ways prevail in many developing countries. An Ethiopian man shoulders a plow that animals will pull in a land often parched by drought.*
◄ *Cattle in India pull a bamboo harrow. Draft animals often power traditional farm implements in poor rural areas of the world.*

◄ *Timeless rhythm of swinging scythes marks a grain harvest in Turkey. The sharp-bladed tools came into wide use in the Old World during the eighth century, making harvesting more efficient. Scythes continue in use only in some areas. Harvesting machines such as combines have replaced them in most developed countries.*

◄ *Southeast Asians gather rice seedlings to transplant in larger fields. Intensive manual labor produces abundant rice, the staple food of half the world's population.*
▼ *An Irish lad displays a pail of potatoes. Once Ireland's most famous food, the tubers are now grown mostly in gardens for home consumption.*

are bred to grow quickly and to yield large quantities of meat. When they are five to twelve months old, the animals are shipped to feedlots. There, they are kept in pens and fed grain and vitamin supplements until they reach market size.

Many families throughout the world keep chickens to supply their households with eggs and meat. The birds forage for food in farmyards and backyards. They eat whatever they find: seeds, insects, household scraps, surplus grain.

In many developed countries, poultry production has become a major agricultural industry. Chickens are bred either for eggs or for meat. One poultry house may contain more than a million birds. Often, machines automatically provide feed and water, collect the eggs, and remove waste.

The Future of Agriculture

Experts think the world's population may double from 5 billion to 10 billion in the next 50 to 60 years. Food production must keep pace with population growth. This is an enormous challenge, but many agricultural experts are convinced it can be met.

Since 1945, the problem has been not food shortages but unequal distribution of the world's food supply. The ratio of population to arable land—land suitable for farming—has favored some countries, such as the United States, more than others, such as India. Some experts believe that government policies in both developed and developing countries have further hindered equal food distribution. Droughts, floods, and other disasters continue to cause local food shortages.

About 450 million people—or nearly 10

▼ *A Peruvian Indian girl lays corn out to dry in the traditional way. Corn has served as a staple food for most Indians of the Americas for centuries.*

percent of the world's population—are considered by some experts to be seriously undernourished, or without enough food. Most of them live in poverty in developing countries. Much of the population increase in the next 50 years will occur in these countries, where hunger is already a serious problem.

Sending food from countries with surpluses to those with shortages will not solve the problem of world hunger. Poor countries do not have the money to buy all the food they need, and they do not want to depend forever on the charity of other countries. In fact, continuing donations of food may discourage countries from trying to develop their own agricultural programs.

Experts believe that the hunger problem will be solved only when all countries have the means to grow their own food or can earn the money to buy it through international trade.

Continued application of agricultural science may help developing countries reach this goal. Through selective breeding and genetic engineering, scientists are developing new high-yield varieties of crops that will not require as many pesticides or as much fertilizer and water, and will grow in colder or warmer climates. In addition, they are trying to develop crops that will take nitrogen from the air and generate it in the ground—as peas and beans do naturally. Such crops would

reduce the need for using costly fertilizers.

Agricultural science alone, however, cannot solve all the problems associated with hunger. Farmers in developing countries could produce more if given the incentive. For example, governments could establish higher prices for crops, help farmers learn new agricultural methods, and lend money for new technology such as high-yield seeds, fertilizers, and farm equipment. Food distribution could be improved by building better roads, storage facilities, and more advanced communications systems. Ways to increase incomes and lower poverty levels in developing countries need to be found. This will help more people to buy food.

The challenges of feeding the hungry

◄ A machine sprays pesticide on a potato field in Canada. Chemicals improve crops, but they also pollute water and leave harmful traces in foods.

cannot be met unless the world's land and water are safeguarded. Agricultural practices in both developed and developing countries have led to a severe loss of valuable topsoil, water, and other resources.

Many countries need better programs for replanting forests. Careless cutting of forests has increased runoff, which carries away topsoil. Overpopulation has pushed a growing number of farmers onto lands too fragile to sustain cultivation without heavy soil erosion. Demands for food have led to increased irrigation worldwide. In some areas, irrigation has caused water tables to drop and wells to go dry. Agricultural chemicals that increase production often contaminate soil and groundwater, and disrupt food chains.

Agriculture does not have to harm the environment. By protecting the land, water, and air and by sharing knowledge and resources, people may yet find solutions for the problem of world hunger.

SEE ALSO CIVILIZATION, CONSERVATION, DEVELOPMENT, DOMESTICATION, ECONOMY, FARMING, FOOD, GRAINS, GROWING SEASON, HERDING, IRRIGATION, LAND USE, POPULATION, *and* SOIL.

▲ *Pivoting sprinklers sweep fertile circles in a once-barren region of Oregon. While creating arable farmland or increasing productivity, some types of irrigation may lower water tables and can add harmful salts to the soil.*
▶ *In Kansas, a researcher examines a hardy grain crossbred at the Land Institute. Scientists work to develop new crop varieties and improve world food production.*

AIR

Air is the invisible mixture of gases surrounding the earth. Nitrogen and oxygen make up about 99 percent of dry air. Carbon dioxide, essential to plant life, makes up less than .04 percent. Most oxygen has been generated by plants during photosynthesis, the process in which energy from sunlight changes water and carbon dioxide into food for the plants. Most other gases were spewed from the earth's interior by early volcanoes.

SEE ALSO ATMOSPHERE.

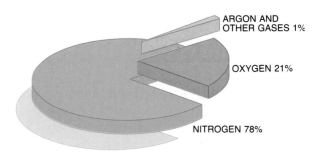

ARGON AND OTHER GASES 1%

OXYGEN 21%

NITROGEN 78%

AIR MASS

An air mass is a large volume of air that is mostly constant in temperature and humidity. Air masses can extend thousands of kilometers and can reach up to the stratosphere. They form over large surfaces with uniform temperatures and humidity, called source regions. These are usually associated with the anticyclonic flow of the polar and subtropical high pressure regions. Low wind speeds permit air to remain stationary long enough to take on the characteristics of the source region. Meteorologists name air masses according to where they form. Tropical air masses are born in low-latitude areas and are warm, while polar air masses take shape in high-latitude regions and are cold. Maritime air masses develop over water and are humid, while continental air masses arise over land and are dry. Thus, an air mass that develops over northern Canada is called a continental polar and is cold and dry. One that forms over the tropical ocean is called a maritime tropical and is warm and humid.

SEE ALSO ANTICYCLONE, FRONT, *and* WEATHER.

ALLUVIAL FAN

An alluvial fan is a fan-shaped or cone-shaped deposit of alluvium—gravel, sand, and smaller materials. Fans are commonly found near the bases of mountains in arid areas. Water flowing swiftly down a mountain picks up sand and other sediment. Where the outflow reaches a wide valley or a plain, it spreads out, depositing the alluvium. As deposits accumulate, an alluvial fan develops.

SEE ALSO COASTAL PLAIN *and* WEATHERING AND EROSION.

ALPHABET

An alphabet is a set of letters, arranged in a specific order, that are used to write a language. Each letter represents a spoken sound. Combinations of letters can represent syllables or words. Alphabets are only one of many kinds of writing systems.

The earliest writing systems used pictographs, or picture writing. Each picture stood for a thing or an idea. Some cultures developed pictographs into hieroglyphs, symbols that represented sounds, syllables, or words. Ancient Egyptians and the Maya of Mexico and Central America used hieroglyphs.

The first known alphabetic system developed around 1500 B.C. in the eastern Mediterranean area. Invented by Semitic people, it resembled hieroglyphs in many ways. By 1000 B.C., Phoenicians had adopted and refined this alphabet, and were spreading its use along their trade routes. The Greeks added vowels to the Phoenician alphabet and brought it into general use by 500 B.C. The word "alphabet" comes from the first two letters of the Greek alphabet, *alpha* and *beta*.

The Romans derived their Latin alphabet from the Etruscan alphabet, which was based on the Greek. The late Roman alphabet had 23 letters. During the Middle Ages, the letters *j, u,* and *w* came to symbolize the letter sounds as we know them, bringing the modern Western alphabet to its present total of 26 letters. This alphabet is used for writing most European languages, including English.

SINAI-SEMITIC	PHOENICIAN	GREEK	ROMAN	MODERN
℧	⅄	A	A	A
⊏	Ⴘ	B	B	B
∟	ヿ	Γ	C	C
	△	Δ	D	D
	⇗	E	E	E
Ⴤ	Ⴤ		F	F
	⅃		G	G
୪	⊟	H	H	H
	⅂	I	I	I
				J
Ψ	⅄	K	K	K
⅂	↓	Λ	L	L
⟋⟋⟋	Ϻ	M	M	M
	Ϥ	N	N	N
⊙	O	O	O	O
◇	⅂	Π	P	P
	φ		Q	Q
⬡	⅄	P	R	R
⌣	W	Σ	S	S
✕	✕	T	T	T
	Ⴤ		V	U
				V
				W
⇌	╪	Ξ	X	X
	Ⴤ	Y	Y	Y
═	Ⅰ	Z	Z	Z

◄ *This chart shows the evolution of the modern Western alphabet. Early alphabets used consonant letters based on picture writing. The Greeks first used letters representing vowels. The system refined as the 26-letter alphabet we use today developed over a period of more than 3,500 years.*
► *Ten different scripts record the same name—that of Aristotle, an ancient Greek scholar. Chinese uses word symbols; Japanese, Hindi, and Thai use syllables; other scripts employ alphabet letters. All can record sounds of any language.*

Russian and many other Slavic languages are written in the Cyrillic alphabet, which is thought to be based on Greek handwriting of the ninth century.

Since alphabets have letters symbolizing single sounds rather than ideas, they have fewer characters than other writing systems and can be learned more quickly. A single alphabet can be used to write many languages covering a wide geographic area. Alphabets have played an important role in written communication throughout history, making government and trade more efficient and permitting the spread of culture and knowledge. The modern Western alphabet has been used to record languages never written before and has aided the spread of literacy worldwide.

SEE ALSO LANGUAGE, LITERACY, *and* TRANSPORTATION AND COMMUNICATION.

ALTIMETER

An altimeter is a device that measures altitude. It is an important instrument for airplane pilots. It works on the principle that air pressure decreases as altitude increases. A simple altimeter includes a sealed metal chamber with some air removed, a spring, and a pointer that shows altitude in meters or feet. The chamber expands as air pressure decreases and contracts as it increases, bending the spring and moving the pointer.

SEE ALSO ALTITUDE *and* ATMOSPHERIC PRESSURE.

ALTITUDE

Altitude, like elevation, is distance above sea level. Elevation refers to height on the surface of the earth, and altitude refers to height in the atmosphere.

Altitude also is the vertical angle between the horizon and the sun or some other heavenly body. For example, if a star is directly overhead, its altitude is 90°. If it has set or is about to rise, its altitude is 0°.

SEE ALSO ELEVATION *and* NAVIGATION.

▲ *With ink and brush, a Korean scribe writes Chinese characters, the oldest script still in use. Chinese writing developed more than 4,000 years ago. It is the only major writing system without an alphabet. Today it includes more than 50,000 characters, each representing a word or a concept. The Japanese and Koreans used Chinese script for centuries, but developed simplified writing systems as well.*

A NAME IN TEN SCRIPTS	
ROMAN	**ARISTOTLE**
GREEK	ΑΡΙΣΤΟΤΕΛΗΣ
CYRILLIC	АРИСТОТЕЛЬ
AMHARIC	አርስጣጣሲስ
ARABIC	ارسطوطاليس
HEBREW	אריסטו
CHINESE	亞里士多德
JAPANESE	アリストテレス
HINDI	अरिस्टोटल
THAI	อริสโตเติ้ล

ANEMOMETER

An anemometer is an instrument that measures wind speed. The most common type consists of three or more hemispherical cups attached to a vertical rod. The wind turns the cups, which spin the rod. These rotations are counted either mechanically or electrically. The stronger the wind, the faster the anemometer rotates. Because there are many wind gusts and lulls, wind speed is usually averaged from the anemometer's recordings over a short period of time. An anemometer is usually paired with a wind vane, which indicates wind direction.

SEE ALSO WEATHER *and* WIND.

ANTARCTIC

The Antarctic is a cold, remote region, most of which is encompassed by the Antarctic Circle. The Circle (see figure below) is the line of latitude about 66½ degrees south of the Equator. The continent of Antarctica, which is mostly covered by a massive ice sheet, makes up much of the Antarctic region. Lichens and mosses are among the few kinds of vegetation that can grow there. The surrounding ocean waters, however, teem with fish and other marine life. Scientists from many countries conduct research in Antarctica, but few people stay there year-round.

SEE ALSO CONTINENT *and* POLAR REGIONS.

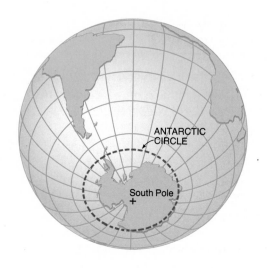

ANTHROPOLOGY

One of the broadest fields of study today is anthropology. The name comes from two Greek words that together mean "the study of humans." Anthropologists try to understand human nature through research into our development, behavior, and relationships to environments. In doing so, they investigate and describe the different peoples of the world. Anthropology can be divided into two main branches: biological anthropology, sometimes called physical anthropology, and cultural anthropology.

Biological anthropologists investigate the development of the physical and skeletal characteristics and the genetic makeup of

▲ *Archaeological workers sift for clues on Samana Cay in the Bahamas. Columbus came ashore in these islands in 1492; findings suggest he may have landed here.*
► *Giant stone heads, once part of a Greek tomb, stand near the Euphrates River in Turkey. Archaeologists can learn much about the society of an ancient kingdom here from these 2,000-year-old sculptures.*

humans. Seeking origins, they study fossils of humanlike species, as well as modern physical types. They compare humans with other primates, such as apes and monkeys.

Cultural anthropologists study the lifeways of people both ancient and modern. Whenever possible, they directly observe people and their ways of living.

One of the largest subdivisions of cultural anthropology is ethnology. Ethnologists concentrate on analyzing and comparing different cultures. They look for the special characteristics of a particular population or activity. They try to find out how certain customs develop and why societies need them to function successfully. They also try to interpret how people respond to their physical environment. Ethnologists investigate all peoples. For example, ethnologists specializing in urban anthropology study the ways people in cities interact with one another and cope with their environment. Often the field of ethnology overlaps with sociology and geography.

The Work of Archaeologists

A well-known subdivision of cultural anthropology is archaeology, the study of the material remains of peoples and cultures of the past. These remains can vary from a few tiny seeds to enormous stone temples and palaces. They provide archaeologists with information about the experiences and activities of people who lived before.

▼ *Wearing nose plumes, earlobe disks, and beads, an Indian chief in a Brazilian rain forest displays adornments favored by his tribe. Ethnology, a branch of anthropology, analyzes and compares cultures throughout the world.*

Together, biological anthropologists and archaeologists have discovered evidence that modern humans, *Homo sapiens sapiens*, lived in Europe and North Africa at least as early as 30,000 B.C. People lived in North America by at least 13,000 B.C., having arrived from Asia across the land bridge that once connected the two continents.

Archaeology traces developments and changes in cultures and the rise of early civilizations. Without it, lives of ancient peoples who left no written records would remain mysteries. Historical archaeology and ethnohistory use written records of cultures to determine the significance of archaeological discoveries and to add details to them. Other fields, such as physics and chemistry, help archaeologists. For instance, radioactive carbon can be used to determine the age of materials up to 40,000 years old. Aerial and satellite photography aids archaeologists by revealing sites, habitats, and terrain.

Experts in anthropological linguistics analyze and compare languages and trace their development and distribution through time. Today, people make and use tape recordings to study rural dialects and city slang.

Applied anthropology aims to spread knowledge of social groups and an understanding of their cultures and concerns. It offers practical help and guidance to governments and other organizations that control or influence public life.

SEE ALSO CULTURE *and* LANGUAGE.

ANTICYCLONE

Anticyclones are large weather systems in which air tends to spin clockwise in the Northern Hemisphere and counterclockwise in the Southern Hemisphere. They are areas of high barometric pressure and are called high pressure systems or highs. Cyclones, or lows, have low pressure at their centers and spin in the opposite direction. The satellite image below reveals both high pressure and low pressure areas over North America.

Anticyclones may form wherever air sinks—the condition that produces high pressure areas. As descending air blows outward from the high pressure area, the Coriolis effect deflects it to the right in the Northern Hemisphere, causing clockwise rotation. An approaching anticyclone generally brings clearer, more settled weather, since sinking air is usually stable.

Anticyclones can be warm or cold. During the summer, warm highs from the subtropics can stall over land areas, creating heat waves. Cold winter highs, formed in the high latitudes, often bring cold waves.

In the Northern Hemisphere, you can tell if an anticyclone is coming if you stand with your back to the wind. The high pressure area will be behind your right shoulder. If the area is to the west, a high is probably on the way.

SEE ALSO AIR MASS, ATMOSPHERIC PRESSURE, CORIOLIS EFFECT, CYCLONE, WEATHER, *and* WIND.

AQUIFER

An aquifer is a layer of water-bearing rock through which groundwater moves. Water-bearing rocks are permeable; they have interconnected openings through which liquids and gases can pass. Rock such as sandstone, and loose deposits of sand and gravel, for example, can form the water-bearing layers. An aquifer receives water from rain or melted snow that drains into the ground at the earth's surface. In some areas, the water passes through the soil; in others, it enters through joints and cracks in rock outcrops. The water moves downward until it meets less permeable rock through which it cannot pass easily. Aquifers act as reservoirs for groundwater. Water from aquifers sometimes flows out in springs. Wells drilled into aquifers provide water for drinking, agriculture, and other uses.

There are two types of aquifers. An unconfined aquifer is underlain by less permeable rocks and is only partly filled with water. The top of the zone filled with water is called the water table. The water table rises or falls depending on the amount of water entering and leaving the aquifer. A confined aquifer lies between two layers of less permeable rocks and is filled with water.

SEE ALSO GROUNDWATER, OASIS, ROCK, SPRING, *and* WATER TABLE.

▼ *Aquifers occur in nearly all regions of the United States. On the map below, green areas show major aquifers where wells can yield at least 189 liters (50 gallons) of water per minute. Yellow areas do not contain major aquifers. Some aquifers, such as those in northwestern Ohio (purple box), consist of consolidated, or solid, rock, with cracks or pore spaces. Unconsolidated deposits, consisting of loose sediments, form aquifers in other areas—such as coastal regions of Virginia and North Carolina (red box).*

MAJOR AQUIFERS IN THE U. S.

■ CONSOLIDATED AQUIFER

■ UNCONSOLIDATED AQUIFER

ARCHIPELAGO

An archipelago is a group of closely scattered islands in any large body of water. The word originally referred to the arm of the Mediterranean Sea between Greece and Turkey known as the Aegean Sea. In Greek, this body of water was called *Aigaion pelagos*. Later the word "archipelago" was applied to any sea studded with many small islands. Today it has come to refer to the islands themselves.

Many archipelagoes are of volcanic origin. Japan is an archipelago consisting of four large islands and some 3,000 smaller ones. In several places in the Japanese archipelago, volcanoes are still active. The Hawaiian Islands, a typical archipelago, consist mainly of the tops of a submerged volcanic mountain chain. The greatest numbers of archipelagic islands are found in the central and south Pacific Ocean. Among them are the Fiji Islands and the many islands that make up Kiribati and French Polynesia.

SEE ALSO ISLAND, SEA, *and* VOLCANO.

▼ *Like stepping-stones in the sea, the 10 islands that make up the Santa Barbara archipelago extend 240 kilometers (150 mi) along the California coast.*

▼ *Spanning a vast area of the Pacific Ocean, the Hawaiian Islands form an archipelago that includes more than 130 volcanic and coral islands. Some are no more than reefs that barely break the surface of the ocean.*

ARCTIC

The Arctic is the frigid region at the earth's extreme north. Most scientists define the region as the area within the Arctic Circle (see figure below), which is the line of latitude about 66½ degrees north of the Equator. Within the circle are the Arctic Ocean and the northern parts of Scandinavia, the Soviet Union, Canada, Alaska, and Greenland. Eskimos and other peoples have thrived for centuries in the harsh region, living off fish, seals, and other animals. Though some forests lie near the Arctic Circle, plant life is limited primarily to tundra vegetation such as mosses and lichens. The Arctic is rich in oil and in other resources such as nickel and copper.

SEE ALSO POLAR REGIONS *and* TUNDRA.

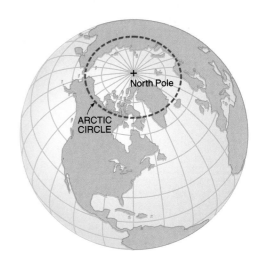

AREA

Geographers use the term "area" to refer to any particular portion of the earth's surface. It may be as small as a picnic area or a neighborhood, or as large as a continent or an ocean. When an area has some unifying characteristic, such as the same vegetation or climate, it is more accurately called a region.

Area is also an exact measure of the size or extent of a surface with specific boundaries. For example, California has an area of 411,013 square kilometers (158,693 sq mi).

SEE ALSO BOUNDARY, MEASUREMENT, REGION, *and* ZONE.

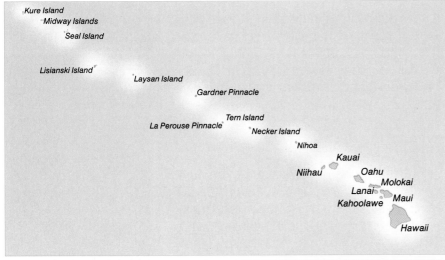

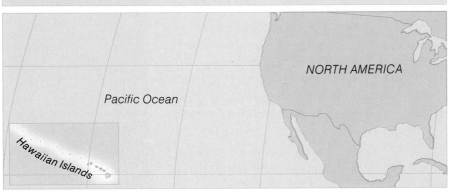

ASH

Volcanic ash is made up of fragments of lava less than two millimeters (.08 in) across. Coarse ash looks and feels like grains of sand, and very fine ash is powdery. Ash forms as lava is thrown into the air during an explosive eruption. Gases in the lava expand and shatter it into tiny particles called ash. When Mount St. Helens, in Washington State, erupted in 1980, a column of ash from the volcano rose 19 kilometers (12 mi) into the air.

SEE ALSO CONE, ERUPTION, LAVA, *and* VOLCANO.

▲ *Volcanic ash blown out during eruptions of Galunggung blankets a village in Indonesia.*

ATLAS

The title page of some early collections of maps carried a picture of Atlas, the giant in Greek mythology who supported the world on his shoulders. In 1595, a collection of maps prepared by the Flemish cartographer Gerardus Mercator was published with the word "atlas" in the title. This was the first time the term was applied to a collection of maps. Eventually, "atlas" came to be used for any book of maps.

Atlases contain a great deal of information about the earth. Besides showing maps of all the countries and continents, a world atlas may provide facts about the countries and maps of major cities. There are many kinds of specialized atlases, such as road atlases, geologic atlases, and historical atlases.

SEE ALSO CARTOGRAPHY *and* MAPS AND GLOBES.

ATMOSPHERE

We live at the bottom of an invisible ocean called the atmosphere, a mixture of gases that include water vapor, and dust. Nitrogen and oxygen account for 99 percent of the gases in dry air, with argon, carbon dioxide, helium, neon, and other gases making up the rest. The atmosphere is so spread out that we barely notice it, yet its weight is equal to a layer of water 10.4 meters (34 ft) deep covering the earth. The bottom 30 kilometers (19 mi) of the atmosphere contain about 98 percent of its mass.

Scientists believe that our present atmosphere evolved from gases spewed out by early volcanoes. At that time there would have been little or no free oxygen. Oxygen may have been added to the atmosphere by primitive plants during photosynthesis. Later, more advanced forms of plant life would have added more oxygen to the atmosphere. Photosynthesis, the process plants use to make food and oxygen out of carbon dioxide and water, may account for most of the oxygen in the atmosphere. Present levels were reached only after millions of years.

The atmosphere acts as a gigantic filter, keeping out most ultraviolet radiation while letting the sun's warming rays through to heat the earth and the lower atmosphere. Solar heat is the fuel that makes the atmosphere function as a giant weather machine.

Layers of the Atmosphere

The atmosphere has a layered structure. From the earth upward, the layers are the troposphere, the stratosphere, the mesosphere, the thermosphere, and the exosphere, which merges with the thin gases of interplanetary space. The boundaries between the layers are not sharply defined, and they vary with latitude and season.

Weather occurs in the troposphere. On average, this layer extends to an altitude of about 10 kilometers (6 mi), ranging from less than 6 kilometers (4 mi) at the Poles to

► *The setting sun beams through layers of clouds in the troposphere, the region of the atmosphere closest to the earth. It is where weather occurs.*

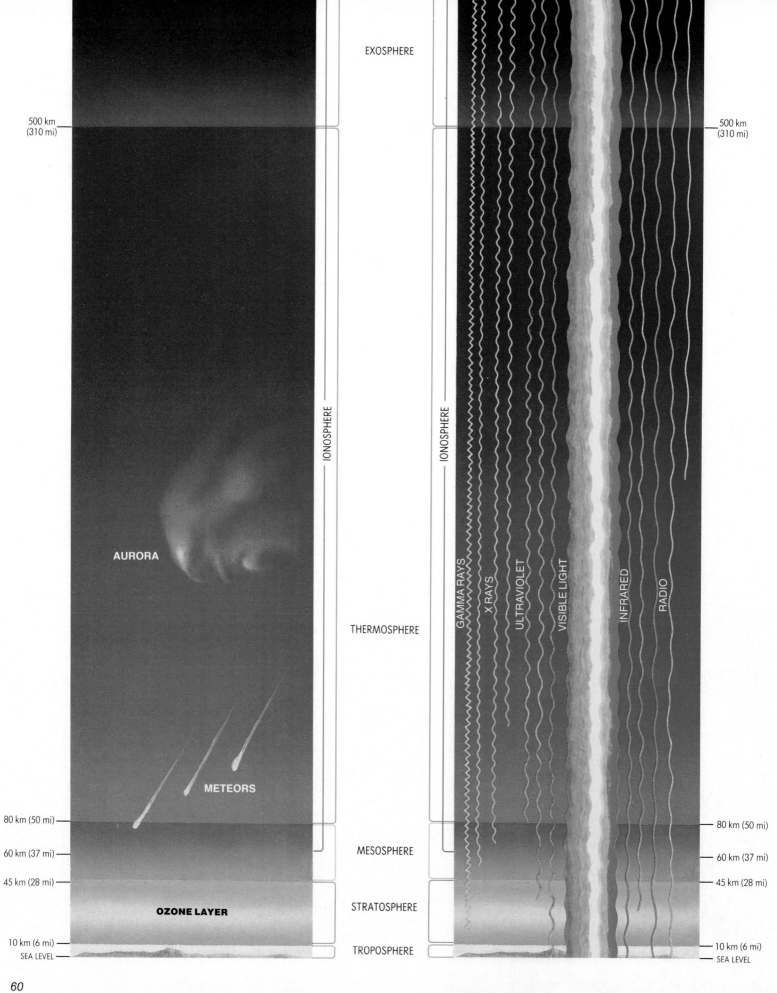

EXOSPHERE

500 km
(310 mi)

500 km
(310 mi)

IONOSPHERE

IONOSPHERE

THERMOSPHERE

GAMMA RAYS
X RAYS
ULTRAVIOLET
VISIBLE LIGHT
INFRARED
RADIO

AURORA

METEORS

80 km (50 mi)

80 km (50 mi)

MESOSPHERE

60 km (37 mi)

60 km (37 mi)

45 km (28 mi)

45 km (28 mi)

STRATOSPHERE

OZONE LAYER

10 km (6 mi)

10 km (6 mi)

TROPOSPHERE

SEA LEVEL

SEA LEVEL

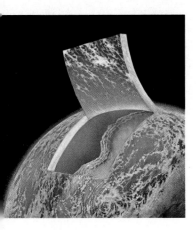

▼ *This painting shows how thin the atmosphere is compared to the size of the earth. The portion shown represents an altitude to about 500 kilometers (310 mi), the region where the exosphere begins. The lifted section reveals part of South America.*

◄ *Layers form in the atmosphere as a result of temperature changes that occur at various altitudes. The boundaries are approximate, as they vary with season and latitude. Weather occurs in the troposphere, which cools as altitude increases, helping clouds to form. Temperature rises in the stratosphere because of the ozone layer, which absorbs most ultraviolet radiation. The mesosphere is the coldest region, while the thermosphere is the warmest and thickest. The thermosphere warms because it absorbs X rays and shortwave ultraviolet radiation. Visible light, some ultraviolet and infrared radiation, and radio waves, all part of the electromagnetic spectrum, pass through all these layers.*

more than 16 kilometers (10 mi) at the Equator. The top of the troposphere is higher in summer than in winter. Because the troposphere contains most of the atmosphere's water vapor, clouds form almost exclusively in this layer. Temperature decreases rapidly in the troposphere as altitude increases.

The sun's rays pass easily through the troposphere, but it does absorb heat that is radiated from the earth into the atmosphere. Various trace gases in the troposphere, such as carbon dioxide, water vapor, and methane, trap this radiated heat. The warming of the atmosphere through heat absorption is known as the greenhouse effect.

The boundary between the turbulent troposphere and the calm stratosphere is called the tropopause. It is not continuous, but has an overlapping, leaflike structure. Fast-moving winds called jet streams travel in the area of the tropopause.

Scientists used to think that the atmosphere's temperature continued to drop with increasing altitude. Measurements made with weather balloons and rockets showed that this is not so. In the lower stratosphere, just above the tropopause, temperature remains nearly constant. As altitude increases in the stratosphere, temperature also increases.

The Stratosphere and Beyond

Strong horizontal winds blow in the stratosphere, but there is little turbulence, which is why commercial jet pilots like to fly in this layer. Because the stratosphere is very dry, clouds are rare there. Those that do form are thin and wispy. They are called nacreous, or mother-of-pearl, clouds because their colors look like those inside a mollusk shell.

The stratosphere is crucial to life on earth because it contains small amounts of ozone. This gas absorbs some of the sun's ultraviolet radiation, which would otherwise severely harm all living things. By absorbing ultraviolet radiation, ozone warms the stratosphere.

About 50 kilometers (30 mi) above the earth, temperatures begin to fall again. This marks the end of the stratosphere and the beginning of the mesosphere. The mesosphere has the coldest temperatures in the atmosphere, ranging from about -2°C (28°F) to about -138°C (-216°F). It also has the highest

clouds. In clear weather, you can sometimes see them as silvery wisps immediately after sunset. They are called noctilucent, or night-shining, clouds.

The thermosphere is above the mesosphere. Here, at altitudes of about 90 to 500 kilometers (56 to 310 mi), widely scattered molecules of gas absorb X rays and shortwave ultraviolet radiation. This propels the molecules to great speeds. Because of this, temperatures in the thermosphere can rise to 1000°C (1830°F) or more.

The thermosphere largely corresponds to the ionosphere. Here, electrically charged molecules reflect radio waves back to the earth, making the region important to long-distance communication. The atmosphere continues to thin in the exosphere. Then, somewhere above 500 kilometers (310 mi), it merges with interplanetary space.

SEE ALSO AIR, ATMOSPHERIC PRESSURE, CLIMATE, CLOUDS, EARTH, GREENHOUSE EFFECT, OZONE LAYER, SUN, WATER CYCLE, *and* WEATHER.

ATMOSPHERIC PRESSURE

Atmospheric pressure is the force exerted on a unit area, such as a square centimeter, by the mass of the atmosphere as gravity pulls it to earth. It is commonly measured with a mercury barometer, a glass tube in which the height of a column of mercury fluctuates as the weight of the atmosphere changes. At sea level in the mid-latitudes, standard atmospheric pressure is 1,013 millibars, or 760 millimeters (29.92 in of mercury), at a temperature of 15°C (59°F). Atmospheric pressure drops as altitude increases. It is also an indicator of weather. Pressure drops when a cyclone, or low pressure system, approaches an area. In an average low, it falls to about 995 millibars (29.4 in of mercury). Anticyclones, or high pressure systems, cause the pressure to rise. In a moderate high, pressure reaches about 1,030 millibars (30.4 in of mercury).

SEE ALSO AIR, AIR MASS, ANTICYCLONE, BAROMETER, CYCLONE, *and* WEATHER.

ATOLL

An atoll is a coral reef in the open ocean that appears as a low ring-shaped island or ring of islets. The reef surrounds a body of water called a lagoon. Channels between islets connect a lagoon to the ocean. Atolls are found mainly in the tropics, and are most common in the Pacific Ocean.

Atolls form in several stages and only where undersea volcanoes occur. First, a volcano erupts on the ocean floor, piling up lava. As the volcano continues to erupt, the pile of lava grows higher and eventually breaks the surface of the water. The top of the volcano becomes an island.

In the next stage, tiny sea animals called corals begin to build a limestone reef around the island just below the water's surface. Then, over millions of years, the now-quiet volcano erodes and, because of its great weight, sinks into the seafloor. The sea level may also rise. As the volcano sinks, the corals build the reef higher. Eventually, only a small portion of the volcano remains above the surface. In time, even that disappears. The ring-shaped reef remains, just below the surface.

In the final stage of an atoll's formation, ocean waves break apart pieces of the reef and toss them back on top of it. There, the waves break down the coral into grains of sand. Sand and other material deposited by the waves pile up on the reef, eventually forming an island or islets.

SEE ALSO CORAL REEF, ISLAND, LAGOON, VOLCANO, WAVES, *and* WEATHERING AND EROSION.

▲ *The coral reef that forms Wailagi Lala Atoll in the southwest Pacific once encircled a volcano. Over time, the volcano sank, leaving the atoll.*

AURORA

An aurora is a colorful light display that shimmers in the dark polar sky. Named for the Roman goddess of dawn, the lights in the earth's upper atmosphere shift gently and change shape like softly blowing curtains. The display is visible almost every night to people within or near the Arctic and Antarctic Circles, which are about 66½ degrees north and south of the Equator. In the north the display is called aurora borealis or northern lights and in the south, aurora australis or southern lights. A few times a year, residents in the lower latitudes also see the light show.

The activity that creates auroras begins on the sun. As we stand on the earth and look out into space, we are at the bottom of an invisible ocean of air called the atmosphere. The layers of the atmosphere are full of electrical and chemical activity, much of which is related to the sun.

The sun is a ball of superhot gases made up of electrically charged particles. The particles, which continuously stream from the sun's surface, form solar wind. As solar wind approaches the earth, it meets the earth's magnetic field, the invisible magnetic envelope that forms a thick protective shield around the planet. Most of the solar wind is blocked by the magnetic field, but in a process that scientists still do not fully understand, some of the particles become trapped for a time in ring-shaped holding areas. These areas, beyond the earth's atmosphere, are centered on the earth's geomagnetic poles. The geomagnetic poles are not the same as the geographic North and South Poles. The geomagnetic poles, which mark the axis of the earth's magnetic field, lie about 1,300 kilometers (800 mi) from the geographic Poles.

The charged particles that enter the ring-shaped areas are speeded up, and some leak into the earth's upper atmosphere. There, the particles collide with atoms of oxygen and nitrogen, and the energy released causes a colorful glowing halo around the

geomagnetic poles—an aurora. Depending on the altitude at which the collisions take place and the kind of atoms struck, the colors of an aurora will vary. If oxygen atoms are struck, the glow may be red or yellow-green. If the particles hit nitrogen atoms, blue lights will fill the sky.

The halo of color can be seen at lower latitudes at times of intense magnetic activity on the sun. During these times, flares of gas erupt on the sun, increasing the force of the solar wind. As the sun spins on its axis, huge streams of particles sweep like jets from a rotating sprinkler. The intensity of the solar wind causes more activity in the earth's upper atmosphere, and the width of the halo increases so that people living at lower latitudes can see the beautiful light display. If particularly strong blasts of solar wind penetrate several layers of the atmosphere, a palette of pink, yellow, blue, and red colors will paint the sky. During times of intense solar activity, the energy released by the charged particles scatters radar signals, disrupts radio transmissions, and garbles long-distance telephone conversations.

To find out more about the mysterious light displays, scientists have launched satellites specially designed to study auroras. Even without a full understanding of what causes an aurora, people can enjoy the colorful spectacle.

SEE ALSO ATMOSPHERE, LATITUDE, MAGNETISM, POLAR REGIONS, POLES, *and* SUN.

▲ *Scientists observe the aurora australis, or southern lights, from inside the dome at Siple Station, in Antarctica. Auroras result when charged particles from the sun collide with atoms in our atmosphere.*

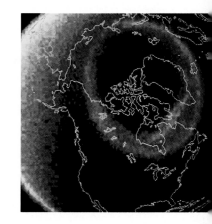

▲ *As sunlight bathes the Eastern Hemisphere, at left, it is nighttime in the Western Hemisphere. A satellite camera that records ultraviolet light captured the aurora borealis ringing the north geomagnetic pole. A computer drew in the continent lines. In the polar regions, auroras are visible on almost any clear night.*

◄ *Icy-blue aurora borealis, also called northern lights, ripples gently above slender pines sheltering a log cabin in the Alaskan woods. Auroras are rarely seen at low latitudes.*

AVALANCHE

During an avalanche, a mass of snow, rock, ice, soil, or other material slides swiftly down a mountainside. Avalanches of rocks or soil are often called landslides. Snowslides, the most common kind of avalanche, can sweep downhill faster than the fastest skier. A few avalanches have reached speeds of more than 300 kilometers per hour (200 mph). Some snow avalanches are small slides of powdery, dry snow that move as formless masses. Others carry giant blocks of snow weighing thousands of tons.

A snow avalanche begins when an unstable mass of snow breaks away from a slope and shatters. The snow picks up speed as it moves downhill, producing a river of snow and a cloud of icy particles that rises high into the air. The moving mass picks up even more snow as it rushes downhill. A large, fully developed avalanche can weigh as much as a million tons.

During winter, repeated snowfalls build a snowpack composed of many layers. The layers may vary in thickness and in texture, depending on the type of snow crystals within them. The bonds holding the layers together may be weak. Melted snow that refreezes may cause a slick coating of ice to form on the surface of a layer. The slick layer may not hold a new snowfall, and the new snow may slide off. During spring thaw, melted snow seeps through a snowpack, making the surface of an underlying layer slippery. Added weight or vibration can easily send the layers above it hurtling downhill.

Snow avalanches are most likely to occur after a fresh snowfall adds a new layer to a snowpack. If new snow quickly piles up during a storm, the snowpack may become overloaded, setting off a slide. Earthquakes may also start avalanches. Skiers may set them off when they cross unstable areas of snow. Just one skier can cause enough vibration to trigger an avalanche.

In the mountains of the western United States, there are some 100,000 avalanches each year. They occur on steep slopes with deep snow, the kind that some skiers favor.

Many ski areas employ avalanche control teams to lessen the danger by starting slides before skiers head for the slopes. At some ski areas, patrols use explosives to set off avalanches. Or they may blast hazardous slopes with cannon to shake loose large, new accumulations of snow.

In the high mountains of Canada and Switzerland, special troops are in charge of avalanche control. Many Swiss mountain villages protect homes from snowslides by building structures to anchor snowpacks, thus helping to prevent avalanches.

An avalanche is one of the most powerful events in nature. A fractured mass of snow may flow down a slope or become airborne. As a heavy mass descends rapidly, it may compress the air below it, producing a powerful blast wave that can blow a house apart, breaking windows, splintering doors, and tearing off the roof. Wet, slower-moving

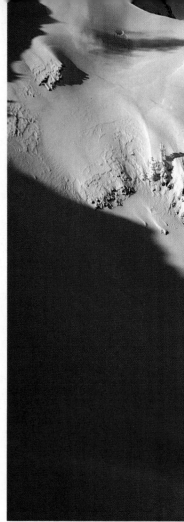

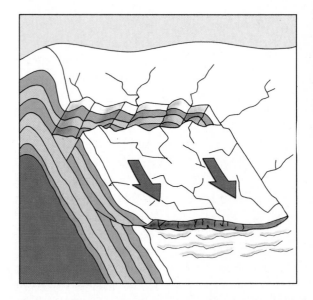

◄ During an avalanche, a great layered block of snow breaks away from a mountainside. A heavy snowfall, a change in temperature, an earthquake, or vibrations caused by a skier may make a large slab of snow pull away from a slope and head downhill. Once the snow starts sliding, it shatters into many separate blocks. The snow blocks break up into ever smaller pieces. Some of the pieces rise into the air as a moving cloud of icy particles. The cloud races downhill at high speed, pushing a large mass of air ahead of it.

avalanches usually do not cause blast waves.

Avalanches strike suddenly and can be deadly. In the Andes in 1970, a massive avalanche of rocks and ice destroyed the town of Yungay, Peru, killing 18,000 people.

SEE ALSO LANDSLIDE *and* SNOW.

AXIS

An axis is an invisible line about which a body rotates, or spins. Each of the planets in our solar system, for example, rotates on its axis. The axes of Mercury, Venus, and Jupiter are almost perpendicular to their orbital planes. The axes of the other planets are tilted to varying degrees. Earth's axis is tilted about $23\frac{1}{2}$ degrees from the perpendicular to the planet's orbital plane (see figure below). Since Earth is always tilted in the same direction as it orbits the sun, the sun's vertical rays strike different latitudes throughout the year, moving between the Tropic of Cancer and the Tropic of Capricorn. This makes the sun appear to follow a yearly pattern of northward and southward motion in the sky.

The North and South Poles lie at the ends of Earth's axis of rotation. Earth, spinning from west to east, makes one complete rotation on its axis in about 24 hours.

SEE ALSO EARTH, ORBIT, PLANETS, ROTATION, SEASONS, SOLAR SYSTEM, *and* TROPICS.

▲ *In Utah's Wasatch Range, an avalanche hurtles down a steep mountainside into Big Cottonwood Canyon.*
► *A stand of evergreens serves as a natural barrier that shields Andermatt, a village in Switzerland, from devastating avalanches.*
▼ *Fencelike steel barriers above the Swiss town of Wengen help prevent avalanches by stabilizing the snow.*

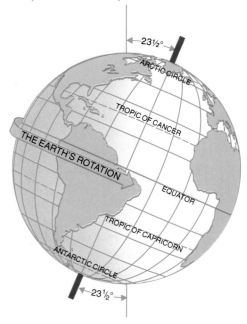

23½°
ARCTIC CIRCLE
TROPIC OF CANCER
THE EARTH'S ROTATION
EQUATOR
TROPIC OF CAPRICORN
ANTARCTIC CIRCLE
23½°

BAROMETER

In the 1640s, an Italian mathematician, Evangelista Torricelli, invented the first barometer, an instrument that measures atmospheric pressure. It became an important forecasting tool, since changes in atmospheric pressure usually indicate changes in the weather. A mercury barometer consists of a glass tube sealed at one end. The tube is filled with mercury, and its open end is submerged in an open dish of mercury. The mercury in the tube then falls to a level in balance with the weight of the atmosphere above the dish. The mercury column's height indicates the atmospheric pressure. The aneroid barometer is the barometer found commonly in homes. It has a sealed metal chamber, with some air removed, that expands and contracts with changes in atmospheric pressure. A pointer, linked to the chamber, moves along a scale as the chamber changes in size.

SEE ALSO ATMOSPHERIC PRESSURE *and* WEATHER.

BASIN

A basin is a depression in the earth's surface. Some basins are filled with water; others may be dry most of the time. Major types of basins include river drainage basins, basins formed by tectonic activity, and those formed by other natural processes. The drainage of a basin may be exterior, leading to the ocean. Or a basin may have interior drainage, resulting in a low area surrounded by higher land.

River Drainage Basins

A river drainage basin is an area drained by a river and its tributaries. Every river has its own drainage area and is part of a network of streams that make up a river system's entire drainage basin.

Some drainage basins are very large. The Mississippi basin, for example, extends from Canada to the Gulf of Mexico over an area of more than 3 million square kilometers (1.2 million sq mi). The Amazon basin in South America is the largest drainage basin in the world. It stretches 6,437 kilometers (4,000 mi) from the Andes in Peru to the Atlantic Ocean. It drains an area roughly three-fourths the size of the contiguous United States.

Tectonic and Other Processes

Tectonic activity and natural processes of weathering and erosion, such as the movement of glaciers, may also form basins. When disturbances in the earth's crust cause downfolds or faulted depressions in the surface, a feature called a structural basin may form.

Tectonic activity can result in a depression in the earth's crust that has interior drainage. This type of basin—normally found in arid regions—has insufficient water to drain its own area into the ocean. Death Valley, in California, is a basin of interior drainage. At 86 meters (282 ft) below sea level, it is the lowest point in the Western Hemisphere. The water draining into it from intermittent streams evaporates or seeps into the ground.

A lake basin may be formed in a valley that is blocked by rocks and other debris from a landslide or by hardened lava from a volcanic eruption. A temporary lake basin may be made by a glacier when it deposits a moraine—a ridge of rocks and debris—in a stream's path. The moraine may act as a dam,

▲ *The branching system of tributaries in the Mississippi River basin drains water from 31 states and 2 provinces, and empties into the Gulf of Mexico. The river has built up a vast delta.*

trapping water and forming a lake. Ice may block a mountain valley and form a lake basin in the same way.

Lake basins may also be carved out by glaciers as they move down valleys or across the land. When the glaciers retreat, the depressions remain. Ice sheets carved the basins of New York State's Finger Lakes.

Ocean Basins

Ocean basins are the largest depressions on the earth. They exist because the granitic rock that makes up continents is lighter and higher than the heavy basaltic rock that underlies the ocean. Edges of the continents form the sides of the ocean basins.

Tectonic activity—seafloor spreading and subduction—constantly changes the ocean basins. Seafloor spreading forms new oceanic crust along the Mid-Ocean Ridge. Older seafloor is destroyed by subduction, mostly around the edges of the Pacific.

SEE ALSO GLACIER, LAKE, OCEAN, PLATE TECTONICS, RIVER, ROCK, SEAFLOOR SPREADING, WATERSHED, *and* WEATHERING AND EROSION.

▲ *Flanked by mountains, the Valley of Mexico formed as ancient volcanic eruptions and repeated earthquakes caused the surface of the earth to fold and buckle, forming a huge basin. Once the site of several lakes, the basin is now one of the planet's most populous places.*
◄ *Coasts, such as this rocky shore in Maine, form the edges of the vast ocean basins.*
► *In Death Valley, a basin in California, the evaporation of an ancient lake left behind salt crystals at the Devil's Golf Course.*

BAY

A bay is similar to a gulf. Both are bodies of water partially surrounded by land. A bay, however, is generally smaller and less enclosed, and its mouth, where it meets the ocean or a lake, is typically wider than that of a gulf. In naming bays and gulfs, people have not always made these distinctions. For example, the Persian Gulf, in the Middle East, is much smaller than Hudson Bay, in Canada.

Bays are usually formed when the ocean overflows a coastline that has eroded or sunk because of movement in the earth's crust. A type of bay known as a ria is actually an estuary that has been taken over by the ocean. Rias are often called "drowned rivers." Chesapeake Bay, the largest bay on the Atlantic coast of the United States, is also one of the world's largest rias. It is the drowned mouth of the Susquehanna River.

Other well-known coastal bays include New York Bay and San Francisco Bay in the United States; the Bay of Fundy in eastern Canada; the Bay of Biscay in Western Europe; the Bay of Bengal in Asia; and Botany Bay in Australia. Bays are also found along the shores of lakes. Georgian Bay, for example, is a prominent bay in Lake Huron, one of North America's Great Lakes.

Because their waters are relatively calm and protected, most bays make excellent

▲ Hudson Bay and the smaller James Bay reach 1,290 kilometers (800 mi) into North America.

◄ Breakers curl onto a beach at Prion Bay, a ria, or drowned river mouth, in Tasmania, Australia.
► Rugged islands rise in Amalik Bay in Alaska's Katmai National Park, a roadless wilderness haven for wildlife.
▼ Shrouded in fog, Golden Gate Bridge spans the entrance to San Francisco Bay, one of the world's largest landlocked harbors. Size and ease of access make the bay a magnet for shipping and recreation.

harbors, and major port cities are located on them. Very small bays are often called coves. In them, boats can find safe anchorage and shelter from storms.

Some bays have been greatly changed by human activity. Much of San Francisco Bay, for example, has been filled in to make more land for building. People are trying to restore and protect Chesapeake Bay, which has been polluted by sewage, wastes from industries, and chemicals used in agriculture.

SEE ALSO COAST, ESTUARY, GULF, *and* HARBOR.

BAYOU

A bayou is a marshy creek or a swampy backwater of a river or a lake. Bayous generally occur in nearly flat areas with poor drainage, such as parts of some floodplains and deltas. They are common in the southern United States along the Gulf coast, including lowland areas near the Mississippi River.

The term "bayou" is derived from a Choctaw Indian word meaning "river" or "creek"; it was adopted by French-speaking people who settled along the bayous of Louisiana. Bayous are usually shallow and sometimes heavily wooded. Many local economies are based on the variety of fish and game living in and around bayous.

SEE ALSO DELTA, LAKE, *and* RIVER.

▲ *Surrounded by lush vegetation, a fisherman in a type of canoe called a pirogue dangles his line in the slow, shallow waters of a Louisiana bayou.*

BEACH

A beach is a narrow, gently sloping strip of land that lies along the edge of the ocean or a lake. Materials such as loose sand, pebbles, rocks, and seashell fragments cover beaches. Most beach materials are the products of weathering and erosion on land. The weathered materials are carried to the ocean or a lake by streams.

Materials that build beaches also result from the action of waves that wear away the rocks and sediments exposed along the shore. Some materials come from the ocean or lake bed and are moved ashore when waves churn up the bottom.

Beaches are constantly changing. The materials that form them are shifted and rearranged by the waves, currents, and winds that continually sweep along the shore. These forces may erode much of a beach during harsh winter storms, when strong winds and waves pull sand from the shoreline and carry it away. In summer, small waves may carry sand back in to shore and build the beach up again.

Human activities and settlements also alter beaches. In many areas where buildings line beaches, engineers have erected seawalls to hold back the ocean. In other places, large quantities of beach sand have been removed for use in making concrete.

People also try to protect beaches from erosion. Along many sandy beaches, walls of wood or concrete known as groins have been built out into the water to catch sand carried in by waves and thus build up the shore. In some places, machinery is used to dredge sand from the seabed just offshore and return it to the beach. Miami Beach, in Florida, was restored by this method.

Varieties of Beaches

There are many kinds of beaches. Some along rocky coastlines are narrow and crescent-shaped. They lie at the heads of protected coves between cliffs and are often called pocket beaches. Many such beaches are found along the coast of Normandy, in France. Other beaches are broad and straight and may extend along a shore for many kilometers.

Barrier beaches are found on low offshore

▲ *Volcanic boulders worn smooth by the ocean rim a campsite on the island of Kauai in Hawaii. Sand along the shoreline comes from rocks that were weathered by ocean waves.*

► *The low, windswept beach of Assateague Island stretches along the coastlines of Maryland and Virginia. This barrier island protects the mainland from the battering of ocean waves.*

BEAUFORT SCALE

The Beaufort scale is a wind scale on which the force of the wind is indicated by a series of numbers from 0 to 12. Brief descriptions accompany each number. The scale is named for Sir Francis Beaufort of the British Royal Navy. In 1805, he devised a method of describing wind force according to procedures for setting sails on a warship. An illustrated version of the scale is shown below.

SEE ALSO WEATHER *and* WIND.

islands called barrier islands. Many barrier islands stretch along the Atlantic and Gulf coasts of the United States. These narrow islands form barriers between the ocean and lagoons or sounds, thus protecting the mainland from the battering of ocean waves.

Beach Composition

Beaches vary according to the kinds of material that cover them. Many people think of sandy beaches as having light-colored sand, such as those along the coasts of North America. Yet in different parts of the world there are sandy beaches of many colors, from pure white to jet black.

White sand is formed by waves breaking up coral, a material produced by small sea animals called corals. Black sand, found on a few beaches in Hawaii and on other Pacific islands, results from the action of waves pulverizing dark, hardened lava called basalt. There is also pink sand, created by the surf breaking up shell and coral fragments, and green sand, formed by the weathering of a grayish-green basalt that contains the greenish mineral olivine.

Some beaches are not sandy at all. They are covered with flat pebbles called shingles or rounded rocks known as cobbles. Such beaches are common along coasts of the British Isles.

SEE ALSO COAST, DUNE, ISLAND, OCEAN, WAVES, *and* WEATHERING AND EROSION.

BEAUFORT SCALE			
BEAUFORT NUMBER	EFFECTS ON LAND	WIND SPEED	EFFECTS DESCRIBED
0		CALM less than 1 kph 1 mph	Smoke rises vertically.
1		LIGHT AIR 1-5 kph 1-3 mph	Smoke drift shows wind direction.
2		LIGHT BREEZE 6-11 kph 4-7 mph	Wind can be felt on face; ordinary wind vane moves.
3		GENTLE BREEZE 12-19 kph 8-12 mph	Light flag is extended; wind moves leaves and twigs.
4		MODERATE BREEZE 20-28 kph 13-18 mph	Paper and leaves are lifted; small branches move.
5		FRESH BREEZE 29-38 kph 19-24 mph	Small trees sway; crests form on small waves on lakes.
6		STRONG BREEZE 39-49 kph 25-31 mph	Umbrellas are hard to use; large branches move.
7		MODERATE GALE 50-61 kph 32-38 mph	Trees sway; walking in the wind is difficult.
8		FRESH GALE 62-74 kph 39-46 mph	Twigs break off of trees.
9		STRONG GALE 75-88 kph 47-54 mph	Wind damages buildings; roof tiles blow off.
10		WHOLE GALE 89-102 kph 55-63 mph	Wind uproots trees; causes more building damage.
11		STORM 103-118 kph 64-73 mph	Wind causes widespread damage; very rare.
12		HURRICANE 119-220 kph 74-136 mph	Devastation occurs.

BEDROCK

Bedrock is the solid rock beneath surface materials such as soil and gravel. Bedrock also underlies sand and other sediments on the ocean floor. Exposed bedrock can be seen on some mountaintops, along rocky coastlines, in stone quarries, and as the caprock of plateaus. As bedrock is slowly altered by water, ice, and plant roots, it breaks into many small pieces that eventually form soil. Sometimes the forces of weathering and erosion remove the materials that cover the bedrock, allowing water and wind to break it down more rapidly and carry the loose materials away. During the ice ages, when huge glaciers moved across parts of the earth, large areas of ancient bedrock were scraped bare of overlying materials.

SEE ALSO CONTINENT, GLACIER, PLATEAU, ROCK, SOIL, *and* WEATHERING AND EROSION.

BIOME

Many scientists use the classifications "biome," "vegetation region," and "ecosystem" to divide the earth into ecological communities. Sometimes these terms are used interchangeably. Generally, however, when scientists use "biome," they are classifying communities according to the plant and animal life within them. When using "vegetation region," they are classifying areas primarily by plant life. When using "ecosystem," they are classifying areas by how living organisms and their environment function as a unit.

Temperature, soil, and the availability of light and water help determine the life that will exist in a biome. Scientists differ about the number and kinds of biomes. Some use broad classifications, such as forest biome or grassland biome. Others use narrower classifications. Each kind of forest, for example, may be considered a biome. Boundaries between biomes are not always sharply defined. For instance, there may be transition zones that lie between grassland and forest biomes.

SEE ALSO ECOSYSTEM *and* VEGETATION REGIONS.

BIOSPHERE

The biosphere is made up of those parts of the earth where life exists. Scientists describe the earth in terms of spheres. The solid outer part of the earth is the lithosphere. The atmosphere is the layer of air that extends above the lithosphere. The earth's water—on the surface, in the ground, and in the air—makes up the hydrosphere. Since life exists on and in the ground, in the air, and in the water, the biosphere overlaps these spheres. Although the biosphere measures about 20 kilometers (12 mi) from top to bottom, most life exists on and in the lithosphere and in the upper 120 meters (400 ft) of the hydrosphere.

Origin of the Biosphere

There is evidence that the biosphere has existed for more than three billion years. The earth's distance from the sun makes the planet neither too hot nor too cold to support life as we know it. Early life-forms that survived without oxygen evolved into higher organisms that used sunlight to make simple sugars and oxygen out of water and carbon dioxide, a process called photosynthesis. Over a long period of time, the atmosphere developed a mix of oxygen and other gases that would sustain new forms of life. The energy plants receive from the sun is part of the cycle that makes life possible. Animals feed on plants

▼ *Burrowing into the soil, an earthworm opens passages that allow air and water to reach plant roots. Earthworms are vital to sustaining life in the lithosphere, or land, portion of the biosphere.*

▼ *Farmers work in rice fields near Bai, a town in China. The food people grow helps support life. Land, air, water, and energy from the sun help make the production of food possible. Living and nonliving things in the earth's ecosystems are interdependent.*

ATMOSPHERE

H₂O

O₂

CO₂

HYDROSPHERE

LITHOSPHERE

and on other animals. Bacteria and other small organisms decompose, or break down, dead animals and plants. Nutrients released from decomposed plant and animal matter in the soil are absorbed by growing plants. This exchange of food and energy makes the biosphere a remarkably efficient self-supporting and self-regulating system.

The biosphere is sometimes thought of as one large ecosystem—a complex community of living and nonliving things functioning as an ecological unit. More often, however, the biosphere is considered to be made up of many ecosystems. People play an important part in maintaining the flow of energy within these ecosystems. Sometimes, however, people disrupt the flow. For example, oxygen levels decrease and carbon dioxide levels increase when people clear forests or burn fossil fuels such as coal and oil. Oil spills and industrial wastes threaten life in the hydrosphere. The future of the biosphere will depend on how people interact with the other living things within the zone of life.

SEE ALSO ATMOSPHERE, BIOME, EARTH, ECOSYSTEM, FOOD CHAIN, HYDROSPHERE, LITHOSPHERE, POLLUTION, *and* WATER CYCLE.

▲ *Extending from the earth's land areas (lithosphere) and water areas (hydrosphere) into the air (atmosphere), the biosphere is the planet's thin layer of life. A flow of energy is sustained by the cycling of molecules of water (H_2O), oxygen (O_2), and carbon dioxide (CO_2) through the biosphere, making it a self-supporting ecosystem.*

BLUFF

A bluff is a cliff, or steep wall of rock or soil, that borders a river or its floodplain. Bluffs may form along a river where it meanders, or curves from side to side. Water flowing faster on the outside of the curve erodes, or wears away, the lower part of a riverbank. No longer supported, the upper part of the bank breaks off, leaving a high, steep wall.

Erosion also produces bluffs along the edges of a floodplain. Over thousands of years, a meandering river gradually shifts from side to side across its floodplain. Where the meanders, or loops, of the river reach its valley walls, water may carve bluffs.

A bluff differs from an escarpment, another kind of cliff. An escarpment does not form near a river; it usually separates two relatively level sections of land.

SEE ALSO CLIFF, ESCARPMENT, FLOODPLAIN, RIVER, VALLEY, *and* WEATHERING AND EROSION.

▲ *In Alaska, the Charley River snakes past rocky bluffs. Bluffs form on a river's outside curves where fast-flowing water erodes the banks.*

BOG

A bog is a wetland of soft, spongy ground consisting chiefly of partially decayed plant matter called peat. Bogs are generally found in cool northern climates. They often develop in poorly draining lake basins formed by glaciers during the most recent ice age. A lake slowly fills with plant debris, and sphagnum moss and other vegetation grow out from the lake's edge and eventually blanket the surface. The bog becomes choked with vegetation, and decaying material forms a thick, spongy layer of peat. Peat, a fossil fuel, is generally considered the first stage in the long transformation of plant material into coal.

SEE ALSO FOSSIL FUEL, LAKE, *and* WETLAND.

▲ *This bog in Michigan, now reflecting clouds, eventually will be choked with vegetation.*

BOUNDARY

The term "boundary" most commonly refers to an imaginary line separating one country from another. There are also boundaries between smaller political units, such as states, provinces, and counties. Political boundaries are always human devices for partitioning areas, but they often follow physical features, such as rivers or mountains. For part of its length, the boundary between the United States and Mexico follows the Rio Grande. The boundary between France and Spain follows the crest of the Pyrenees. The area on either side of a boundary is known as a border or, in some cases, a frontier.

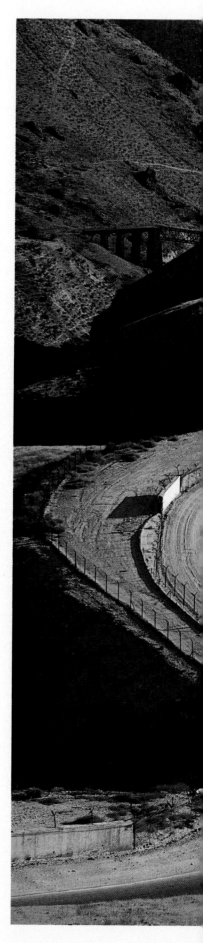

◄ *Double fences provide extra security along the boundary between Jordan, at left, and Israel. Such protected borders often reflect tension between countries.*
► *A stone marker in the Rocky Mountains indicates the boundary between Canada, at right, and the United States. The two countries share the world's longest undefended border, stretching 6,416 kilometers (3,987 mi).*

▲ *Looming above the French town of Chamonix, rugged peaks of the Alps divide France and Italy. The political boundary between the two countries follows the mountain chain.*

Geographers are concerned with other kinds of boundaries as well. For example, there are linguistic boundaries between areas where different languages are spoken, economic boundaries between different marketing centers, and social boundaries between different neighborhoods. Usually these kinds of boundaries are not sharply defined the way political ones are; rather, they represent transition zones.

SEE ALSO AREA, COUNTRY, NATION, REGION, STATE, *and* ZONE.

BRIDGE

Bridges are structures that allow vehicles and people to cross areas that otherwise would be obstacles to travel. The first bridge was probably a tree trunk across a stream.

Bridges are defined by their design and construction materials. The major bridge designs are girder, or beam, arch, suspension, and truss. Cantilever and movable bridges are modifications of these four designs. The choice of design depends on the length of the span, the conditions of the terrain, and the nature of the traffic. The design helps determine what types of materials are used—for example, wood, steel, or reinforced concrete.

Since a bridge must support its own weight as well as the traffic on it, support systems are crucial. The supports of a girder bridge, which often look like giant connected "T's," distribute the weight vertically. Arch bridges use one or more giant arches to support the weight of the bridge above. The arch of the Sydney Harbour Bridge in Australia required 33,566 tons of steel.

Suspension bridges include the primitive footbridges of birch, bamboo, twisted vines, or cane still used in parts of China, India, Africa, and South America. They are suspended by cables tied to tree trunks or posts, and often sway and sag as travelers cross them. Modern suspension bridges use flexible

steel-wire cables. Anchored to foundations of concrete and steel, the cables are in a constant state of tension and pull the foundations inward. Two cables, each containing 27,572 wires, support the Golden Gate Bridge across San Francisco Bay in California.

Truss, or lattice, bridges are arrangements of horizontal, vertical, and strengthening diagonal girders.

SEE ALSO RIVER *and* TRANSPORTATION AND COMMUNICATION.

▲ *In Portland Harbor, Oregon, a vertical lift bridge rises to let ships through. Beyond, another kind of movable bridge, called a bascule bridge, stands open.*
▶ *Supporting the roadway, giant cables of San Francisco's Golden Gate Bridge pass over the tops of twin towers. Each tower is as tall as a 65-story building.*

▲ *Peruvian villagers cross the swirling Apurímac River on a suspension bridge of hand-spun rope.*
▶ *Skilled engineers, ancient Romans built the foundations of this bridge at Benevento, in Italy.*

BUTTE

Buttes are tall, steep-sided towers of rock. These rock formations were formerly part of a flat section of raised rock known as a mesa, and an even more extensive area of raised land called a plateau.

As streams gradually cut through a plateau, flat-topped, rocky areas, known as outliers, are left standing alone. A large outlier is called a mesa; a tower-like outlier is known as a butte.

Buttes usually occur in arid regions, such as those in Mexico, Spain, and the southwestern United States. In these regions, infrequent heavy cloudbursts erode, or wear away, the sides of buttes. Because the hard uppermost layers of buttes, called caprock, resist weathering and erosion, the formations stay the same height as the original plateau or mesa of which they were part. Weathering and erosion, most often by water rushing through gullies, gradually cause the exposed sides to wear away. Buttes slowly become slender spires of rock. Eventually, the spires topple.

SEE ALSO MESA, PLATEAU, *and* WEATHERING AND EROSION.

▲ *Two buttes known as the Mittens reach skyward in Monument Valley on the Utah-Arizona border.*

SOME NOTABLE BRIDGES OF THE WORLD			
Kind	Name	Length of Main Span	Country
Suspension	HUMBER	1,410 meters (4,626 ft)	United Kingdom
Suspension	VERRAZANO NARROWS	1,298 meters (4,260 ft)	United States
Suspension	BOSPORUS	1,074 meters (3,524 ft)	Turkey
Cantilever	QUEBEC RAILWAY	549 meters (1,800 ft)	Canada
Steel Arch	SYDNEY HARBOUR	503 meters (1,650 ft)	Australia
Cable-stayed	SECOND HOOGHLY	457 meters (1,500 ft)	India
Continuous Truss	ASTORIA	376 meters (1,232 ft)	United States
Concrete Arch	GLADESVILLE	305 meters (1,000 ft)	Australia
Concrete Arch	AMIZADE	290 meters (951 ft)	Brazil

CALDERA

The circular depression around a volcano's vent is called a crater. The largest depressions, which can be several kilometers wide, are called calderas. A caldera forms after an eruption blasts away a volcano's summit or causes it to collapse inward. Oregon's Crater Lake fills a caldera about 10 kilometers (6 mi) wide. It resulted from an eruption that occurred nearly 7,000 years ago. The basin formed by the caldera later filled with water.

SEE ALSO CRATER, LAKE, *and* VOLCANO.

CALENDAR

A calendar is not only a chart with an arrangement of months, weeks, and days but also a system for organizing time. Our calendar evolved over thousands of years as people studied the earth and the sky.

Early tribes of hunters may have watched the skies for repeating signs that would help them predict cycles of events. The yearly appearance of stars in the same patterns may have told them when migrating animals would appear or when winter was coming.

More than 4,000 years ago in Sumer, the first known written calendars were created using solar and lunar observations. These calendars told people the time for planting and irrigating and for making sacrifices to their gods. Through the years, the Chinese, the Maya, and other societies devised different systems for making calendars, most of them complicated and all of them well suited to the needs of the people who invented them. Each society had its own standard for measuring the length of the calendar unit we call a week. The ancient Greeks divided their month into three ten-day periods. The Romans preferred a unit of eight days, the time from one market day to the next. The seven-day week may have originated in the Hebrew custom of observing a day of rest every seventh day.

The year, the month, and the day are natural divisions of time. The year corresponds to the time it takes the earth to orbit the sun—about 365¼ days. The moon's cycle of phases takes about 29½ days. The 24-hour day is based on the time it takes the earth to make one turn on its axis. One difficulty in designing a calendar is that the year is not an exact multiple of months or of days. The Babylonians dealt with the problem by making some months 29 days long and others 30 days long, and by adding an extra month to some years to keep the calendar in step with the seasons.

The Egyptians used a 365-day year. In 46 B.C., the Roman dictator Julius Caesar took the Egyptian calendar and added a day every four years to account for the extra fourth of a day it takes the earth to complete each orbit of the sun. Even with these leap years, the Julian calendar was about 11 minutes off the true solar year. As time passed, the discrepancy grew between the calendar and the date determined by astronomical readings.

▲ Sunrise in Wyoming's Bighorn Mountains lights up an ancient calendar ring. By observing the sun and certain more distant stars in relation to cairns, or piles of rocks, around the ring, Indians could track the arrival and passage of summer.
◄ Zodiac signs and the phases of the moon decorate the June page of a 15th-century Julian calendar. Ornate pages depict activities typical of each of the 12 months.

In 1582, Pope Gregory XIII announced a reformed calendar, now called the Gregorian calendar in his honor. First, he cut the year 1582 by ten days. Then, though he continued the practice of leap years, he declared that centurial years, such as the year 1600, would be leap years only if they were divisible by 400. This adjustment brought the calendar more in step with the earth's rotation and the seasons. Pope Gregory's calendar is the one commonly used today, and the difference between it and the true solar year is reduced to less than one day in 3,000 years.

SEE ALSO EARTH, MOON, *and* SEASONS.

◄ *The Maya date 9.7.17.12.14, equivalent to our A.D. 590, is carved in figures, bars, and dots around a ball player on this stone disk found in Mexico. The Maya planned religious rites, recorded hundreds of years of history, and calculated dates for future events with a sophisticated calendar that used these symbols as numbers.*

CANAL

A canal is an artificial waterway. There are two types of canals. Navigation canals are used by ships and other vessels. Water conveyance canals carry water from one place to another. This type includes irrigation and drainage canals. Canals range in size from shallow ditches to passages wide and deep enough to accommodate large ships.

The first canals were ditches dug to channel water from rivers to farmland. The building and maintaining of irrigation canals encouraged people to work together in an organized way. This helped lead to the rise of civilizations in Mesopotamia, Egypt, China, and the Americas. The Egyptians built canals as early as 3000 B.C. The pharaoh, or king, controlled the flow of water. In Egypt and elsewhere, canals were so important that armies were used to protect them, and bureaucracies were set up to oversee them.

Canals have continued to play a vital role in agriculture, particularly in lands with sparse or seasonal rainfall. California's All-American Canal, for example, carries water 130 kilometers (80 mi) from the Colorado River to the arid Imperial Valley, now a major agricultural area.

Navigation Canals

People have built navigation canals since ancient times. Some link bodies of water separated by land. Such canals can trim days or weeks from a voyage by creating a more direct route. The Canal du Midi in France enables ships to travel from the Mediterranean Sea to the Bay of Biscay by way of the Garonne River, thus eliminating the long voyage around the Iberian Peninsula.

Other canals, such as the James River and Kanawha Canal and the Chesapeake & Ohio Canal in the United States, were built parallel to rivers. Sections of some rivers have been canalized—made into canals—so that vessels can avoid waterfalls, rapids, and other obstacles to navigation.

For centuries, animals were used to tow barges through canals. Horses or mules on a

▲ *The city of Amsterdam, in the Netherlands, relies on a network of more than a hundred canals, which drain the land and serve as thoroughfares.*

▶ *One gondola passes another on a narrow canal in Venice. More than 150 canals lace this Italian city, which is made up of some 120 islands.*

towpath beside the canal were tied by long ropes to the barge, which moved as the animals plodded along. Today, barges are pulled by tugboats or pushed by towboats.

Until the 1800s, canals provided the chief means of transporting large quantities of heavy goods inland. In Europe, merchants relied on networks of canals linking rivers and trading centers. In the United States, canals were vital in shipping goods from eastern ports to western settlements and in opening eastern markets to western agriculture.

The Erie Canal, in New York State, runs between Albany, on the Hudson River, and Buffalo, on Lake Erie. Vessels could move up the Hudson from New York City, reach Lake Erie by canal, and go farther on other waterways. Opened in 1825, the Erie Canal contributed to New York City's growth as a port and inspired the building of more canals. There were more than 4,800 kilometers (3,000 mi) of canals in the U.S. by 1840. Soon, however, railroads began to dominate transportation, and the use of canals began to decline.

In some parts of Europe and North America and in the Soviet Union and China, canals still play an important role. The Netherlands, for example, ships 20 percent of its freight on canals, the highest percentage for any country in Western Europe.

The Grand Canal in China is a system of canals and navigable sections of major rivers, including the Huang (Yellow) and the Yangtze. Stretching some 1,600 kilometers (1,000 mi), it is the longest artificially created

▲ A boat crosses a roadway on an aqueduct bridge near Stratford, England. British canals have become popular for vacation cruises.

▶ *One of the world's busiest canals, the Panama Canal links the Atlantic Ocean and the Pacific Ocean (in the distance) through the Isthmus of Panama. Ships traveling in either direction use the Miraflores Locks, in the foreground.*

▼ *Two freighters pass the control house at the Miraflores Locks. Raising or lowering the water in a lock takes vessels from one level to another.*

▲ *A freighter travels north through the Suez Canal, which connects the Mediterranean and the Red Seas. Opened in 1869, the canal stretches north and south across the Isthmus of Suez, in Egypt. Like the Panama Canal, the Suez Canal is too narrow for some modern ships, including the largest supertankers.*

waterway in the world. It is also a vast irrigation project that provides water for half of the country. Construction of the waterway began more than 2,400 years ago, and it has been rebuilt and extended over the centuries.

Because of changes in land elevation, vessels moving through canals may have to be raised or lowered from one water level to another. This is done by means of locks. A lock is a large rectangular chamber formed by placing two gates across the canal. One gate is opened to let the vessel in. Once the gate is closed again, water is allowed to flow into or out of the lock until the water level matches that of the canal's next stretch. When the vessel is at the desired level, the second gate opens, and the vessel moves on.

The first locks may have been developed more than 2,200 years ago in Egypt. Probably the first European lock was built near Brugge (Bruges), in present-day Belgium, in the 1100s. The first one in the United States was built at Little Falls, New York, in 1793.

New technology has modernized some locks. At the Ronquières lock in Belgium, boats on the Brussels-Charleroi Canal enter a giant steel tank that moves along rails up a slope. In 20 minutes, a boat arrives at a level 67 meters (220 ft) higher than the starting point. Tanks can also be used to lift boats vertically. Opened in 1976, a vertical lift at Scharnebeck, in West Germany, raises barges 38 meters (125 ft) in three minutes.

Navigation canals offer many advantages, such as shortcuts for ships and inexpensive transportation of bulk goods.

The Suez Canal and the Panama Canal are the world's most famous ship canals. Both take large oceangoing vessels. Opened in 1869, the Suez Canal allows ships to go from the Mediterranean Sea to the Indian Ocean by way of the Red Sea, thus eliminating the long voyage around Africa. The Panama

▼ *The Colorado River supplies water to the southwestern United States. Aqueducts carry its waters to Los Angeles, and a canal brings irrigation water to California's Imperial Valley.*

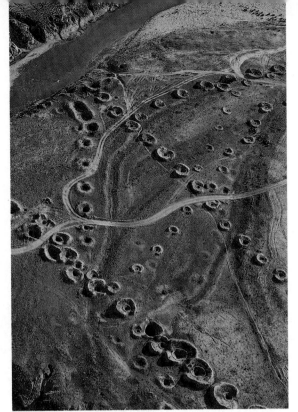

◀ *Viewed from an aircraft, lines of manholes indicate the paths of irrigation tunnels in a desert in southern Iran. The strong sunlight here would evaporate water in surface canals. The ancient Persians may have developed such tunnels, called qanats, more than 2,000 years ago. The technique spread to Afghanistan, Egypt, and China.*
▼ *Workers dig a shaft leading into a qanat.*

Canal, opened in 1914, links the Atlantic and Pacific Oceans through the Isthmus of Panama. It cuts 12,600 kilometers (7,800 mi) from the voyage between New York and San Francisco. Sailing around South America may cost a ship ten times more in fuel and salaries.

The Nord-Ostee Kanal (Kiel Canal), in West Germany, allows some 90,000 vessels a year to pass between the Baltic and North Seas. A vessel enters the canal about every six minutes.

Grain, coal, ores, and other goods needed in large quantities are the staples of modern canal shipping. Though slower, sending goods by canal is usually less expensive than transporting them by truck or train.

Old canals that are no longer economical for shipping have become popular for holiday cruises. In Europe, the canals of Venice and Amsterdam, which serve those cities as thoroughfares, draw crowds of tourists.

SEE ALSO IRRIGATION, ISTHMUS, *and* TRANSPORTATION AND COMMUNICATION.

◀ *Iranian laborers remove silt from a qanat some 25 meters (82 ft) below ground. Such tunnels, often several kilometers long, channel water for domestic use as well as for irrigation.*

CANYON

A canyon is a deep, narrow valley with steep sides. "Canyon" comes from the Spanish word *cañón,* which means "tube" or "pipe." The terms "canyon" and "gorge" are often used interchangeably to describe a deep, narrow valley. But a canyon is almost always wider and longer than a gorge.

Canyons develop most often in mountain or plateau areas where rocks are relatively hard, the climate is arid, and streams cascade down steep slopes. As erosion takes place, rushing water picks up and transports quantities of sand and rocks. Carried by moving water, this debris scrapes along a streambed, carving out an ever deeper channel. Gradually, a canyon forms.

Types of Canyons

Some canyons, such as Utah's Zion Canyon on the Colorado Plateau, have steep walls. These kinds of canyons develop where the rock is relatively resistant and rainfall is

▲ *Rock climbers prepare to descend a steep cliff face in Utah's Canyonlands National Park. Over millions of years, the Colorado River etched these curving canyons in the rock of a high plateau.*
► *A lone hiker contemplates the vast Grand Canyon in Arizona. The canyon rims are as much as 29 kilometers (18 mi) apart. Far below snakes the Colorado River, carving ever deeper into the rock.*

infrequent yet heavy. The canyon sides remain steep because they weather, or crumble, very little.

The walls of some canyons, such as the Grand Canyon in Arizona, become V-shaped. In these canyons, layers of hard and soft rock alternate. The hard rock layers resist weathering, but the softer layers of rock beneath them crumble easily.

As the V-shaped canyon forms, the processes of weathering and erosion act on both types of rock. Plant roots grow in cracks, helping to break the stone apart. In winter, freezing water expands in cracks, breaking off more bits of rock. During brief, heavy rains, water rushes down the canyon walls, loosening rocks and transporting them to the bottom of the canyon.

▲ *A hiker fords a stream at the bottom of Samaria Gorge in Crete. Gorges, like canyons, are deep, narrow valleys—but canyons are usually wider.*

▼ *Waimea, nicknamed the "Grand Canyon of the Pacific," winds 23 kilometers (14 mi) through the Hawaiian island of Kauai.*

Because the layers of soft rock weather and erode more readily than the hard layers do, a series of ledges and slanting slopes results. The ledges form terraces that resemble giant steps in the rock. As more rocks crumble and fall, the canyon grows wider at the top than at the bottom.

The Grand Canyon, for example, has a narrow floor, but is wide at the top. Its width from rim to rim varies from 8 to 29 kilometers (5–18 mi). Scientists estimate that it has taken millions of years for the Colorado River to carve the Grand Canyon. In one place the canyon measures 1.6 kilometers (1 mi) deep from rim to river.

By studying the exposed layers of rock in a canyon wall, experts learn about the history of the earth. Fossils, the remains of ancient plants and animals, that are found in the rocks help scientists trace the development of life on the earth.

Some of the deepest canyons lie beneath the ocean. These canyons cut into the continental shelves and slopes—underwater extensions of the continents. Some were carved by rivers that flowed during periods when the sea level was lower, and the continental shelves were exposed. Canyons can develop under water when powerful ocean currents sweep bits of rock and soil, called sediment, across the continental shelves. Just as rivers erode land, these currents carve deep canyons in the ocean floor.

SEE ALSO CONTINENTAL SHELF, FOSSIL, GORGE, PLATEAU, RIVER, ROCK, SEA LEVEL, VALLEY, *and* WEATHERING AND EROSION.

CAPE

A cape is a point of land that extends into a river, a lake, or the ocean. Some capes, such as the Cape of Good Hope in South Africa, are parts of large landmasses. Others, such as Cape Hatteras in North Carolina, are parts of islands. Some capes form as coastal currents meet in shallow water, sweeping sand into pointed shapes offshore. Others form as rivers deposit gravel and other material in shallow water. Many capes are shaped by waves that wear away soft coastal rock, leaving hard rock cliffs jutting out from shore. Some, such as Cape Cod in Massachusetts, are formed along coasts by glacial deposits.

SEE ALSO CLIFF, COAST, GLACIER, RIVER, and WEATHERING AND EROSION.

▲ Near Africa's southern tip, the Cape of Good Hope stretches into the Atlantic Ocean, forming False Bay.

▼ Cliffside apartment houses perch on Cape Foulweather, where Pacific surf buffets the Oregon coast.

CAPITAL

The capital of a country is the city where the government is located. In a few countries, such as the Netherlands, government functions are divided between two cities. There are two kinds of capitals: permanent and introduced. A permanent capital is part of its country's historic core area and is often the country's most populous and important city. Paris, in France, and Lima, in Peru, are examples of permanent capitals. An introduced capital is one built to replace an old capital and perform new functions. Brazilians built their introduced capital, Brasília, mainly to open their country's interior to settlement. States and other smaller political units also have capitals serving as seats of government.

SEE ALSO CITY, COUNTRY, *and* GOVERNMENT.

CAPITALISM

Capitalism is an economic system based on private ownership and control of businesses. Individuals make economic decisions, determining what to produce and how much to charge for it, and the public may sometimes buy shares in companies. Countries with largely capitalist economies include the United States, Canada, and Japan.

Competition drives a capitalist economy. Buyers can choose from a variety of goods, so sellers compete by offering goods of a quality and price demanded by buyers. Ideally, both buyer and seller gain from each transaction. The interactions between buyers and sellers are known collectively as the market. In the 1700s, Scottish economist Adam Smith argued that the market acts as an "invisible hand" guiding the economy to produce better results for all participants. Capitalist economies sometimes suffer declines in business activity. Today, governments are often active in capitalist economies, regulating businesses or even owning some of them. The combination of private enterprise and government regulation is called a mixed economy.

SEE ALSO ECONOMY *and* INDUSTRY.

CARTOGRAPHY

Cartography is the science and art of making maps. In its widest sense, it includes all the stages of mapmaking, from data gathering to printing. Almost every kind of information about the earth can be shown on a map. The task of the cartographer is to present this information clearly and accurately.

As a science, cartography must be as precise as possible. It deals with the geometric qualities of the earth, such as shapes, areas, distances between places, and directions. Cartographers use mathematical formulas to project the earth's spherical surface onto a flat surface. The choice of projection and the scale to which the map is drawn depend on the purpose of the map. As an art, cartography requires skillful use of design and color to communicate information.

In the 20th century, two technological developments revolutionized cartography. One is remote sensing—the use of aerial photography, satellite imaging, and radar—which gives cartographers much information about our world. The other is the use of computers, which perform much of the detailed work that cartographers used to do by hand.

SEE ALSO CHART *and* MAPS AND GLOBES.

▼ *A cartographer paints a relief map showing the ocean floor near Antarctica. Charts based on depth soundings supplied the data.*

▼ *Outlines of buildings provide a panoramic key to the Old City of Jerusalem. By referring to the map, the man can pick out landmarks and other points of interest. His hair and clothing identify him as a Hasid, a member of an ultra-Orthodox Jewish sect.*

CAVE

A cave, or cavern, is an underground chamber that opens to the surface and is often large enough for a person to enter. A network of caves connected by passages is called a cave system. Carlsbad Caverns, a cave system in New Mexico, has at least 34 kilometers (21 mi) of passages. One of the caves in the system is so big that it could accommodate 11 football fields.

Most caves form in rock, such as limestone, marble, or dolomite, that dissolves in a mixture of rainwater and carbon dioxide. Rainwater absorbs carbon dioxide from the air, forming a very weak acid. This acidic water seeps down into tiny cracks in rock below the soil. Cracks and spaces in the rock fill with water until the area is saturated. The surface of the saturated area is called the water table. Below the water table, water flows horizontally and eventually drains into streams. As it flows, the acidic water dissolves surrounding rock and carries it away.

Over thousands of years, the flowing water hollows out channels, or tunnels, in the rock. In time, the water table may drop below the level of a tunnel. Then the tunnel fills with air and becomes a cave.

Water that trickles into caves contains dissolved limestone, or calcium carbonate. The water evaporates, leaving minerals that build up into formations called dripstone. Minerals in the water determine a formation's color, and the way the drops flow affects its shape. Water dripping from the roof of a cave deposits calcium carbonate that may form stalactites, icicle-shaped pieces of dripstone that hang from the ceiling. When water drips onto a cave floor, the minerals it deposits may build up into spires called stalagmites.

Lava, Sea, and Ice Caves

During a volcanic eruption, the surface of a lava flow eventually cools and hardens. Below the rigid surface, hot lava may continue to flow. In rare cases, the hot lava drains away, leaving a hollow tube of hard lava behind. Lava tube caves can cover a large area. Kazimura Cave, in Hawaii, contains some 12 kilometers (7.5 mi) of lava tube passages.

Sea caves form where water pounds against coastal cliffs. Waves hurl sand and gravel against the cliffs, gradually wearing away parts of the rock, especially where it is relatively soft or fractured.

Caves also form in large masses of ice called glaciers. As some of the ice melts, water drains through the glacier, hollowing out ice caves.

Cave Inhabitants

Darkness prevents plant growth in caves, so cave dwellers must obtain all their nourishment from the outside or from other residents. Some creatures, such as bats, shelter in caves but hunt for food outside. A few kinds of animals, including fish, cockroaches, millipedes, and beetles, never venture outside their cave homes. They live on waste material, such as bat guano, produced by other cave dwellers.

Thousands of years ago, many people used caves as shelters. Archaeologists have uncovered fossil remains, stone tools, weapons, and wall paintings in caves in Europe,

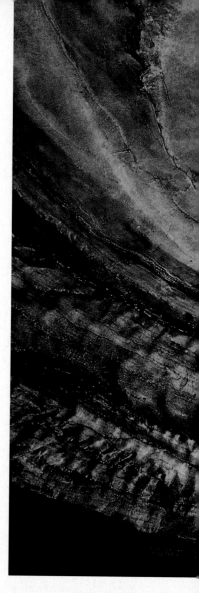

▲ Booth's Amphitheater, a massive chamber in Kentucky's Mammoth Cave, arches above a visitor. The chamber is named for Edwin Booth, a 19th-century actor who performed Shakespeare here. The Mammoth Cave system has some 480 kilometers (298 mi) of mapped passages.
◄ On Bonaire, an island off the coast of Venezuela, a cave explorer inches through a narrow passage. Bonaire's caves, which contain Arawak Indian drawings, attract many visitors.

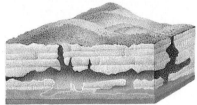

▲ Caves form where acidic rainwater seeps into cracks in underground rocks such as limestone or dolomite. Gradually, the water dissolves the rock, enlarging the cracks and forming tunnels. These spaces fill with air and become caves when the water table drops below the level of the tunnel.

► When water laden with minerals seeps into caves, it can build fantastic shapes like the ones in this painting. Where the water drips from the ceiling, it may fashion bacon draperies (1) or icicle-shaped stalactites (2). From the cave floor, the water droplets build up spires of limestone called stalagmites (3). Columns (4) form where stalactites and stalagmites join. When the water splashes into pools (5), the minerals in it may form coatings around grains of sand. Eventually, the layers of minerals create small spheres known as cave pearls (6).

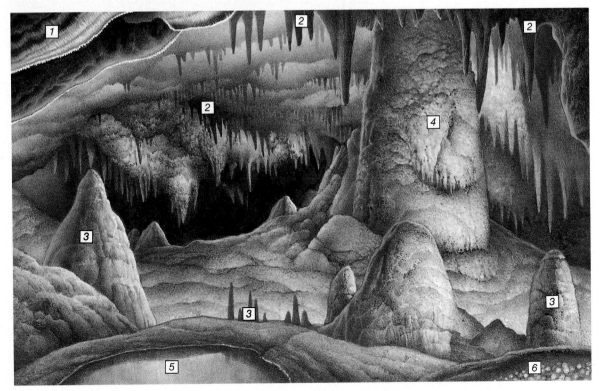

Africa, and western Asia. In the French cave of Lascaux, for example, Ice Age artists painted images of horses, deer, and other animals on the rock walls. In some parts of the world, people still use caves as homes. Caves in Matera, a town in Italy, have been continuously inhabited since prehistoric times.

The study of caves is known as speleology. People who explore caves are called cavers or spelunkers.

There are some 17,000 known caves in the United States. Many more remain to be explored. More than 100 caves are open to the public, and some 15 have been designated as national parks or monuments.

SEE ALSO GLACIER, LAVA, WATER TABLE, *and* WEATHERING AND EROSION.

CENSUS

A census is a count of the population of a country, usually conducted by its government. It records the number of people and data such as age, sex, and occupation. Censuses have many uses, such as helping governments to plan for the future. The U.S. government conducted its first census in 1790 and undertakes a new one every ten years.

SEE ALSO POPULATION.

CHANNEL

A channel is a wide strait or waterway between two landmasses that lie close to each other. The English Channel, for example, runs between the southern coast of England and the northern coast of France.

The word "channel" is also used to describe the part of a river that is deepest and carries the most water.

In shallow water, a channel is a passageway that is deep enough for ships. Many channels leading into harbors are natural breaks in reefs. Others, such as Ambrose Channel leading into New York harbor, have been artificially deepened.

SEE ALSO HARBOR, RIVER, *and* STRAIT.

CHART

A chart is a special kind of map that is used in ship and airplane navigation. Sea captains and airplane pilots may encounter areas with many dangers and few signs to show the way. A chart will locate the dangers and point out features that can be used to choose the best route. A nautical chart emphasizes features of interest to sailors, such as the depth of the water and the locations of buoys and lighthouses. An aeronautical chart emphasizes features pilots are concerned about, such as mountains and runways.

SEE ALSO MAPS AND GLOBES *and* NAVIGATION.

▲ *Thousands of years ago, an eruption spewed out the lava that built this cave near Susua Volcano in Kenya. The surface of the lava cooled and hardened; hot lava within the flow drained away, forming a cave.*

◄ *An ice fountain glistens in a cave high in the Austrian Alps. Cold keeps the limestone walls of this cave sheeted with ice year-round.*

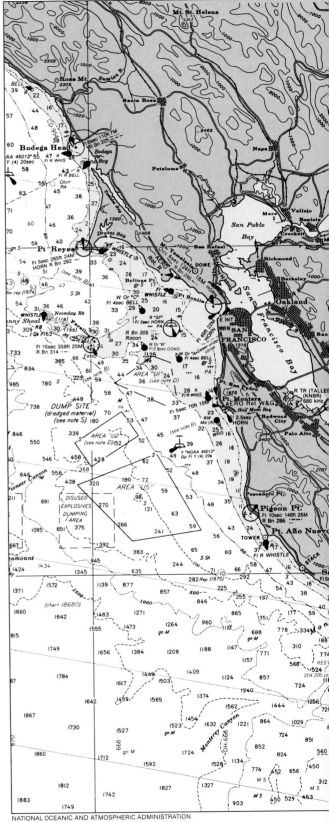

NATIONAL OCEANIC AND ATMOSPHERIC ADMINISTRATION
THIS REPRODUCTION IS NOT TO BE USED FOR NAVIGATION.

▲ *A nautical chart of waters off San Francisco, California, indicates depths in fathoms. Radio signals from shore can increase navigational accuracy when used with such charts.*

CITY

For most of human history, people lived in natural environments that provided them with means of survival. Some people even adapted to climatic extremes such as Arctic cold, tropical heat, and high elevations. Today, some two billion people—about 40 percent of the world's population—live in an almost entirely artificial environment. By the year 2000, experts say, it will be home to a clear majority of the people in developed countries. This important new environment has been said to mark a major step in human evolution. It is the city.

Definitions of the term "city" vary, but generally a city is a large settlement whose inhabitants carry on a variety of activities that are not related to agriculture. In some parts of the world, the term has a more specific meaning as well. In the United States, localities with populations of 2,500 or more are defined as urban, which means "characteristic of a city." In Japan, a settlement must have a population of at least 30,000 to be considered a city; in Sweden, a densely settled population of 200 is sufficient. In the United Kingdom, "city" is a title given to towns that historically served as religious centers or were honored by a special act of the crown. For most purposes, though, the term "city" can be used to describe almost any urban center in the world.

▲ Travelers pack a Tokyo commuter train in the world's fastest, most crowded subway system.
► Growing upward and outward, São Paulo, in Brazil, leads South American cities in population, industrial production, traffic, and air pollution.

Characteristics of Cities

All cities share certain characteristics. They are densely populated, and their inhabitants hold a wide variety of jobs requiring specialized skills. City dwellers depend upon one another for services and for survival in a complex way of life. Communication and cooperation among residents are essential if a city is to function smoothly.

Discoveries and inventions such as electricity, the telephone, and the automobile have played major roles in the growth of modern cities. Because of technology, metropolitan centers have more influence over rural areas than in the past. In developed countries, radio, television, and the telephone quickly link cities to smaller settlements and isolated farms. Highways, air routes, railroads, and waterways connect cities to one another and to the countryside. Most of the wealth and political power of a country are concentrated in its largest cities, as are its social, cultural, and commercial activities. For food, however, cities have always been dependent on rural areas, where farming technology makes the existence of cities possible.

Cities of all sizes offer their residents many advantages. Job opportunities are many and varied. Cultural opportunities often include concerts and museums. Apartment buildings provide housing near workplaces, and public transportation is often available.

Cities also have disadvantages, such as overcrowding, noise, pollution, rising land prices, poverty, slums, and, often, high crime rates. People living in urban areas usually have more demanding schedules and experience more stress than those living in rural areas. Two symbols of city life are the traffic light and the time clock.

The range of incomes and social classes is usually much greater in cities than in rural areas. In addition, cities often have a greater variety of ethnic groups. Differences in beliefs and attitudes among groups can cause disagreements and conflicts that are not as common in smaller settlements.

In spite of living close to other people, individuals in all classes, income groups, and ethnic groups sometimes feel lonely and isolated in cities. Neighborhoods within cities, however, can give people security and a

sense of belonging. This is especially true of neighborhoods occupied by ethnic groups that share interests and traditions. Such neighborhoods usually include large numbers of relatives and friends.

Cities have grown at an amazing rate since the industrial revolution of the 18th and 19th centuries. In 1810, for example, no city in the United States had a population of more than 100,000. In 1988, 74 U.S. urban areas had populations of half a million or more.

To illustrate how recently the artificial environment called a city arose, two experts make this comparison: "If the time humankind has spent on earth were compared to a 24-hour day, then only in the last half hour have there been settlements of more than a

▲ *Aberdeen harbor in Hong Kong provides a contrast in living standards. Floating junks and sampans serve as homes for the city's poor. Luxury high-rise apartment buildings house the wealthy.*
► *Rebuilt in the old style, blocks of row houses in Rotterdam, in the Netherlands, replace those leveled by bombs during World War II.*
▼ *Children play in the yard of a tenement near Miami, Florida. Such housing is common in many U.S. urban areas.*

hundred people. Only a few minutes have elapsed since towns and cities first emerged, and large-scale urbanization has been going on for less than 60 seconds."

Ancient Cities

The first great human environmental revolution occurred when people domesticated animals and plants about 10,000 years ago. This led to the rise of agriculture and settled life. Villages and towns soon developed, and by around 3000 B.C. there were cities. The rise of cities marked an environmental revolution as important as the earlier agricultural one and as far-reaching as the industrial revolution many centuries later.

The first urban centers evolved in lower

▲ A vendor (top) in Los Angeles, California, sells news in Spanish. Publications in native languages help urban ethnic groups to maintain their identity. Above, women shop for clothing in Paris, France. Cities offer a rich variety of goods and services.

▼ *In Iraq, the ruins of a ziggurat mark the site of the Sumerian city of Ur, one of the world's first urban centers. Built about 2100 B.C., the brick structure had three tiers and a shrine. It stood at the city's center near palaces and storehouses.*

Mesopotamia and then in the Nile Valley of Egypt. By about 2500 B.C. cities flourished in the Indus Valley on the Indian subcontinent. They developed along the Huang (Yellow) River in China by 1500 B.C. Cities did not arise in the Americas until about 500 B.C.; the first were in what is now Mexico.

All early cities shared certain characteristics that made them different from smaller settlements. Each developed in a productive agricultural environment where not all people needed to be farmers. Much of the population was not involved in food production. People became specialists such as soldiers, priests, and craftsmen; some were skilled in metallurgy, the science and technology of metals. Only a few people were literate—able to read and write. They formed an elite, a small but powerful minority, who encouraged the arts and helped manage commerce and administration. Usually the city's ruler governed with absolute authority and was also the high priest in a powerful religion.

Many cities were planned and laid out along a grid, a network of intersecting lines. Temples and palaces—examples of the world's first great urban architecture—usually occupied the center, and defensive walls often surrounded the entire city. All cities were centers of religion, government, and commerce. Far-ranging trade routes made them centers of wealth, and some, such as Babylon, became centers of empires. Few, however, had populations of more than 20,000.

The early cities were experiments in a new way of life. Every one of them failed. War, drought, the breakdown of trade systems, or a combination of such misfortunes brought about their collapse. Their economies were so fragile and their very existence so tenuous that they could not survive major disasters.

Gradually, technology improved and new cities emerged. New, larger empires developed around the Mediterranean Sea and in Asia. Great trade routes, such as those of the Phoenicians and, later, the Romans, spread

▲ *The Americas' first planned city, Teotihuacan, in Mexico, housed as many as 200,000 people about A.D. 500. Pyramids, temples, and palaces flanked a wide avenue.*
▼ *The Parthenon and other temples crown the Acropolis of Athens. The city's architecture and plan influenced those of later Western centers.*

Under imperial Rome, urbanism—the city way of life—spread to northern Europe. The Romans built road systems and planned cities from Asia Minor to the British Isles. The city of Rome itself was centered on the forum, a concentration of buildings used much as those of the Athenian agora were. Rome's population may have reached one million around A.D. 100. The ruling class lived in palaces with plumbing and central heating. The masses lived in shabby apartment buildings sometimes several stories high. Such apartments, a Roman innovation, were the first high-density dwellings in the Western world. They were crowded and unsanitary tenements that attracted two types of people still with us today—the land speculator and the slum landlord.

As the Roman Empire declined, so did city life in Europe. Some Mediterranean cities continued to prosper, among them Constantinople and Venice. Cities flourished in Asia and in the Americas. Teotihuacan in present-day Mexico, for example, was a totally

▲ An aerial view of Marrakech, in Morocco, reveals a vast jumble of red-clay dwellings, mosques, and other structures in a maze of narrow, winding streets. Founded in 1062, this African city reached its peak in the 1400s. Above, Albarracín, in Spain, typifies medieval European cities. A wall protects it; a church rises in the center; a hilltop fortress stands guard.

civilization as well as goods and contributed to the rise of cities from China to North Africa and present-day Spain.

Athens, in Greece, became a powerful city-state. During its golden age in the fifth century B.C., it had a population of perhaps 150,000. Later cities of the Western world adopted its city plan, which included an agora—a gathering place for commerce and public meetings—surrounded by schools, libraries, and theaters. Athens was the first ancient city to survive the collapse of its power. It endured as an artistic and intellectual center through the period of the Roman Empire, from the first century to the fifth century A.D.

▲ Since the Middle Ages, the Cathedral of Notre Dame has graced the city of Paris. This masterpiece of Gothic architecture was begun in the 1100s; Paris has been a capital since A.D. 507.

planned city of avenues, religious and administrative buildings, housing complexes, and workshops. It eventually covered 20 square kilometers (8 square miles)—an area larger than that of imperial Rome—and may have had a population of 200,000 in A.D. 500.

The Middle Ages and Afterward

European city life flourished again in the 11th century as a result of success in long-distance trade. Because of a new and powerful merchant class, more cities and towns were founded in the 12th and 13th centuries than at any other time between the end of the Roman Empire and the industrial revolution. Led by the merchants, who became the middle class of later centuries, many communities gained independence and self-rule.

Medieval cities were often walled and had a cathedral and a marketplace at their center, but they seldom grew according to a plan. For most people, urban life meant crowded dwellings, narrow lanes, and unsanitary conditions. Because of plagues, wars, disruption of trade, and uprisings of crafts-

men and laborers, the growth of European cities declined in the 14th and 15th centuries.

During the High Renaissance, from about 1500 to 1600, and the following centuries up to 1800, European cities changed dramatically. Urban and rural areas were united into states ruled by monarchs.

One city became the capital of each centralized European power, and all urban areas grew rapidly. City dwellers looked to ancient Athens and Rome for basic ideas about planning and architecture. To accommodate the new government bureaucracies, the first office buildings were constructed. Broad boulevards were laid out for the enjoyment of wealthy citizens and for the movement of troops. Open squares, palatial houses, and splendid gardens were built for aristocrats. The new capital of the United States, Washington, D.C., was laid out by a French engineer in the 1790s; his plan called for wide circles and broad avenues. Grand designs for cities reached their peak with the rebuilding of central Paris in the mid-1800s.

In European cities, living space for the working classes was limited. They were

▲ Rows of brick dwellings sprawl on the outskirts of Birmingham, the United Kingdom's leading industrial center. A power plant looms beyond.

► Heading for the subway, workers in Toronto, Canada, pass gleaming office towers, examples of imaginative architecture in a thriving city.

crowded together in cramped medieval sections of cities or in congested suburbs. As populations increased, urban overcrowding became a problem that still exists today.

From the Industrial Revolution to Today

The industrial revolution involved radical changes in industry and technology. These changes began in Great Britain in the 1700s and later spread to the rest of Europe and to North America and Australia.

Old cities became new industrial cities as factories were built near their centers. They continued as hubs of commerce and finance. In contrast to earlier times, many wealthy people moved to the outskirts of cities, leaving the centers largely to the poor. This trend continues today in many Western cities.

Urban populations increased as new jobs attracted people from rural areas. The population of Manchester, England, for example, grew from 6,000 in 1685 to about 303,000 in 1851. Unlike farming, factory work provided a steady income. Wages were very low, however, and working conditions were deplorable. Even ten-year-old children labored 10 to 14 hours a day in dirty, unsafe factories. Manufacturing produced waste dumps and caused severe air and water pollution. Living conditions were very bad. Families often lived

▲ *High-rise buildings soar in Sydney, Australia's largest city. Since the 1950s it has boomed as one of the world's newest industrial cities.*
▼ *Types of urban architecture spanning a century meet in San Francisco, where skyscrapers rise beyond Victorian-style houses.*

in dank cellars or overcrowded, unsanitary tenements; diseases killed many thousands of people. Infant death rates were high. Life expectancy in urban areas was low. In 1893, male workers in Manchester had an average life expectancy of 28 years; in nearby rural areas, men lived on average about 52 years.

Despite the plight of factory workers, increasing amounts of manufactured goods, along with new technology, improved the quality of life for the general population. Growing numbers of people entered the middle class. In the Western world, largely agricultural societies were transformed into largely industrial ones.

Countries where most of the people live in cities are called urban nations. Great Britain became the world's first urban nation in

▶ *Billboards in Tokyo advertise an American movie and an English musical based on a French novel. Such cross-cultural influences are common in all large cosmopolitan cities.*
▼ *Visitors view paintings by Old Masters in a gallery of the Louvre in Paris. The city is one of the world's foremost cultural centers, and the Louvre is one of the greatest art museums.*

the late 1800s after becoming industrialized. By 1900 Australia, too, was an urban nation. The United States and most other developed countries did not become urban nations until later in the 20th century.

The United Nations estimates that the world's urban population has tripled since 1950. It is now more than two billion. By the mid-1980s, some 250 urban complexes had populations of more than a million. As a result of rapid growth, some cities are now so large

▶ *Filled to capacity, Dodger Stadium in Los Angeles becomes an entertainment center for 56,000 baseball fans. Winning home teams boost civic pride among urban dwellers.*

▲ Miniature golf among fanciful fish and dinosaurs delights a child in sunny Panama City, Florida. Amusement parks near urban centers dot the United States and have spread to other parts of the world.

cities. They commute to the cities for jobs, shopping, and cultural events, and to use urban services such as hospitals. A city with suburbs is called a metropolitan city. A metropolitan area includes the city and the surrounding built-up area.

In recent decades, wealthy and middle-class people have tended to live in suburbs. Large numbers of poor people live in the inner city, the area around the central business district. Some housing in the inner city may be in slums, areas with decaying buildings where low-income and unemployed people live. When all residents are considered together, however, people in the metropolitan areas of the United States, Canada, and Western Europe have the highest living standard of any people in history.

During the industrial revolution, factories were built in the center of cities. Today, new industries tend to be in the countryside, in complexes called industrial parks. These industries are cleaner, safer, and in more pleasant surroundings than those of the 19th century. There are other advantages as well. Highways and transportation networks have made these industries easily accessible, and rural land for large building sites is cheaper than urban land. Moving jobs into rural areas helps relieve congestion in industrial cities. Workers usually live in nearby towns, villages, and suburbs, and have living standards that are in many ways better than those of factory owners in the 19th century.

that they have merged with others to become one vast urban area. Terms such as "world city," "megalopolis," and "conurbation" have been invented to describe such areas.

One megalopolis in the United States stretches along the East Coast from Massachusetts to Virginia and includes Boston, Washington, D.C., and all cities in between. Almost 40 million people—about one-sixth of the country's population—live in this megalopolis, which occupies only one-fiftieth of the country's total land area. This works out to a population density of 232 people per square kilometer (about 600 people per square mile)—twice the population density of any state outside the area.

Huge urban areas exist in many other parts of the world. Among the largest are Dortmund-Essen-Düsseldorf in West Germany and the London-Liverpool Corridor in England. The world's largest urban complex extends from Tokyo to Osaka-Kobe in Japan. In 1988 it included more than 50 million people.

Since the 1940s, large numbers of people have moved into communities near big

▲ In Buenos Aires, Argentina, children scan an exhibit in a district known for its artists. Urban art displays can bring joy and cultural enrichment to passersby.

Cities in Developing Countries

Industrialized countries dominate international politics, finance, commerce, and technology. They are centers of influence and change. Developing countries, however, have roughly three-fourths of the world's population and about half of the world's cities. These cities have grown more rapidly than those in developed countries, and many have become larger as well. They are called emerging cities. Most of them are comparable to European cities in the early stages of industrialization. They have a mixture of large factories and small-scale enterprises, which are often carried on in people's homes.

Many emerging cities, such as those in India, are in countries that were once controlled by foreign powers. Now the countries have gained independence, and their urban areas have been left to develop on their own. They may grow without an overall plan. Most traffic is pedestrian along narrow, twisting streets. The city center usually consists of a market and religious buildings, such as temples or mosques. Some emerging cities, such as Jakarta, in Indonesia, have become centers of international trade and have bustling central business districts. All of these cities are densely populated.

Thousands of poor people from the countryside arrive in emerging cities each day looking for work. Few have the skills needed for city jobs. Most simply exchange rural poverty for urban poverty.

Emerging cities are unable to provide low-cost housing. As a result, millions of the world's urban poor are squatters, people who live on property without legal right or payment of rent. Squatter settlements built of scrap materials often spring up near garbage dumps and even in city parks. In Lima, Peru, squatters make up at least a quarter of the population; in Caracas, Venezuela, about 35

▲ Cars creep bumper-to-bumper along a multi-lane freeway in Los Angeles. Smog, caused partly by traffic fumes, is a problem in many cities.

▶ Neon signs and street lamps light up the Ginza in Tokyo. By day this is a major shopping district; after dark it becomes a lively center of nightlife.

percent. The poorest of the poor have no shelter at all. In Bombay, India, at least 100,000 people are "pavement dwellers" and pay for the right to sleep on a stretch of sidewalk.

In many emerging cities, governments cannot provide enough food, clean water, sewers, and health care. In one Bombay slum, for example, there were only 162 public water taps for nearly half a million people in 1987. Hunger, poor sanitation, and disease take their toll, just as they did in European cities during the industrial revolution.

Experts see these problems as part of the evolution of cities. They believe emerging cities are developing into industrial centers as

▼ A policeman in Chengdu, China, directs traffic, mainly bicycles and city buses. Hundreds of bikes a minute pass through this downtown intersection, the city's busiest.
▼ Rush-hour traffic in Varanasi, India, moves at the speed of a slow bicycle. Though vehicle types may vary, most cities have rush hours and traffic jams.

Western cities did. Urbanism, they say, is a worldwide trend without a foreseeable end.

Today, three out of every four people in the U.S. live in metropolitan areas. New York City and its suburbs form the country's largest metropolis with a population of 18 million. In Japan, one of every four people lives in or around Tokyo, the world's largest metropolis with a population of about 26 million. Experts predict that by the year 2000, Tokyo and Mexico City, the capital of a developing country, will be vying for first place as the largest metropolis, with populations approaching 30 million. By then, perhaps about three billion people will be living in urban areas worldwide.

Government officials, city planners, architects, and environmentalists are among those experts who seek solutions to urban problems and try to anticipate future ones. No city is an ideal place to live, but most cities have plans for improving housing and social services and for solving traffic problems.

▲ *Traffic clogs an avenue of grain merchants in an old part of Delhi, India, where handcarts, bicycle rickshas, trucks, and people cause chaos.*

▼ *A mountain of shredded garbage keeps growing at a landfill near Miami, Florida. Waste disposal is a major problem for city officials.*

Planned communities called new towns have been built to help relieve city congestion. Some new towns, such as Columbia, Maryland, and Reston, Virginia, were designed to be self-contained, providing both jobs and comfortable housing for residents. That goal has yet to be fully achieved.

New cities have also been built. Brazil and Pakistan, for example, have constructed new capitals—Brasília and Islamabad—in sparsely settled areas.

In developed countries, old, deteriorating sections of some cities have been restored or completely rebuilt. This has happened in U.S. cities such as San Francisco and Boston and in European cities such as London and Paris. In some cases, old structures have been put to new uses: Warehouses, for example, have been turned into apartments, and former factories now contain restaurants, shops, and art galleries.

Although the costs will be high, city planners hope the future will bring urban environments that will provide convenience, safety, and general well-being for all their residents.

SEE ALSO AGRICULTURE, CAPITAL, DENSITY, ECONOMY, FOOD, GOVERNMENT, INDUSTRY, LAND USE, NEIGHBORHOOD, POPULATION, TRANSPORTATION AND COMMUNICATION, *and* URBAN AREA.

▲ *Circles of nearly identical houses line geometrically spaced roads in Sun City, a totally planned community in Arizona.*
▼ *A French resort on the Mediterranean occupies land that once was marshy wilderness. Pyramid-shaped apartment blocks allow maximum sunshine.*

CIVILIZATION

Civilization is a complex way of life that came about as people began to develop urban settlements. The term comes from the Latin word *civis,* citizen. All civilizations have shared certain basic characteristics. These include large population centers; monumental architecture and developed art styles; political and religious systems for administering territories; a complex division of labor; and the division of people into social classes.

The earliest civilizations developed after 3000 B.C., when the rise of agriculture allowed people to have surplus food and economic stability. Farming populations advanced beyond village life and achieved civilization first in Mesopotamia, then in Egypt. Civilization thrived in the Indus Valley by 2500 B.C., in China by 1500 B.C., and in Mexico by 1200 B.C.

Civilizations expand through trade, war, and exploration, and many have flourished and then failed. Experts believe that misuse of the environment may have helped cause the collapse of some civilizations and that modern societies' use of natural resources will affect future civilizations.

SEE ALSO AGRICULTURE, ANTHROPOLOGY, CITY, CULTURE, *and* NATURAL RESOURCE.

CLIFF

A cliff is a very steep, vertical, or overhanging face of rock, earth, or ice. Agents of weathering and erosion, including wind, ocean waves, rivers, and ice, cut cliffs. Rivers sometimes carve steep-walled canyons. Ocean waves batter coastlines and form cliffs. Cliffs also occur where glaciers grind against valley walls. Laden with sand and gravel, water or ice wears away rock, leaving an almost vertical wall. The stormy English Channel has sculptured cliffs along the white chalk coast at Dover, in England. These cliffs are a conspicuous landmark for people sailing across the channel.

SEE ALSO BLUFF, ESCARPMENT, *and* WEATHERING AND EROSION.

CLIMATE

"Climate" refers to all weather conditions for a given location over a period of time. The term "weather" refers to the state of the atmosphere over short periods of time. Weather can change from hour to hour, from day to day, from month to month, or even from year to year. For periods of 30 years or more, however, meteorological records reveal that distinct weather conditions prevail over different parts of the world. Each set of conditions forms a climate type, and the area covered by a particular type is called a climate region.

Some parts of the world are hot and rainy nearly every day; they have a tropical wet climate. Others are cold and snow-covered most of the year; they have a polar climate. Between the icy Poles and the steamy tropics are the many other climates that help make the earth a unique planet.

Features of Climates

Average temperature and precipitation are important features of a climate. So, too, are the day-to-day, day-to-night, and seasonal variations in temperature and precipitation. San Francisco, California, and Beijing, China, for example, have similar yearly temperature and precipitation averages, but there the similarity ends. San Francisco's winters are not much cooler than its summers; Beijing is hot in summer and cold in winter. San Francisco's summers are dry and its winters are wet; the wet and dry seasons are reversed in Beijing. Climate features also include windiness, humidity, cloud cover, and fogginess.

A climate is something like a personality: It is usually constant, but there may be surprises. Just as someone with a cheerful disposition will sometimes become sad, so an area with a generally mild climate will occasionally experience extremes of temperature or rainfall. But because climates are mostly constant, living things can adapt to them. The enormous variety of life on earth results in

► *Palm trees shade thatched houses on Savai'i Island in Western Samoa. Its wet, warm tropical climate has virtually no distinct seasons, and temperatures vary only within a small range.*

◄Dogs pull a sled across a snow-swept frozen lake north of the Arctic Circle in Canada. In this tundra climate, winters are long and weather is often severe. Summers are short and cool.

large part from the variety of climates that exist today and the climate changes that have occurred during the earth's history.

Climate has influenced the development of cultures and civilizations. People everywhere have adapted in various ways to the climates in which they live. It is probably not a coincidence that ancient agricultural civilizations, such as those in Greece and India, flourished where the climate was mild.

Today, farmers are still in tune with the climate. They plant certain crops according to the expected amount of rainfall and the length of the growing season. This season includes the time between the last frost of spring and the first frost of autumn. When the weather does not follow the typical climate pattern, it can mean hard times for farmers and higher food costs for consumers.

Types of Climates

The most widely used system for classifying climates was proposed in 1900 by Wladimir Köppen, a Russian-born meteorologist and climatologist working mostly in Germany. Köppen observed that the type of vegetation in a region depended largely on climate, and he used this fact as the starting point for his classification scheme. Studying temperature and precipitation data, he and other scientists continued to refine the designation of climate regions. The climate map on pages 108–109 is based on their classification system.

According to this system, there are six climate groups: tropical, dry, mild, continental, polar, and that of high elevations. These climate groups are further divided into climate types. There are two types in the tropical group, for example: tropical wet, and tropical wet and dry, in different seasons.

All climates are the product of many factors, including latitude, elevation, topography, vegetation density, distance from the ocean, and location on a continent. The rainy tropical climate of West Africa, for example, results from the region's equatorial location and its position on the western side of the

TROPICAL (WESTERN BRAZIL)

DRY (EGYPT)

CONTINENTAL (SOUTH DAKOTA)

POLAR (NORTHERN CANADA)

◄ *The lush forests of the tropics, the barren sands of desert areas, the grasses of continental climates, and the ice of polar regions are typical of the earth's varied climate regions.*

continent. A constant amount of sunlight keeps temperatures in the area warm and steady. At the same time, the continuous presence of the intertropical convergence zone (ITCZ), where the trade winds of the Northern and Southern Hemispheres meet, brings a steady supply of rising moist air and almost daily rains.

Places with a tropical wet climate, such as Hawaii and equatorial West Africa, have the most predictable weather on earth. It rains

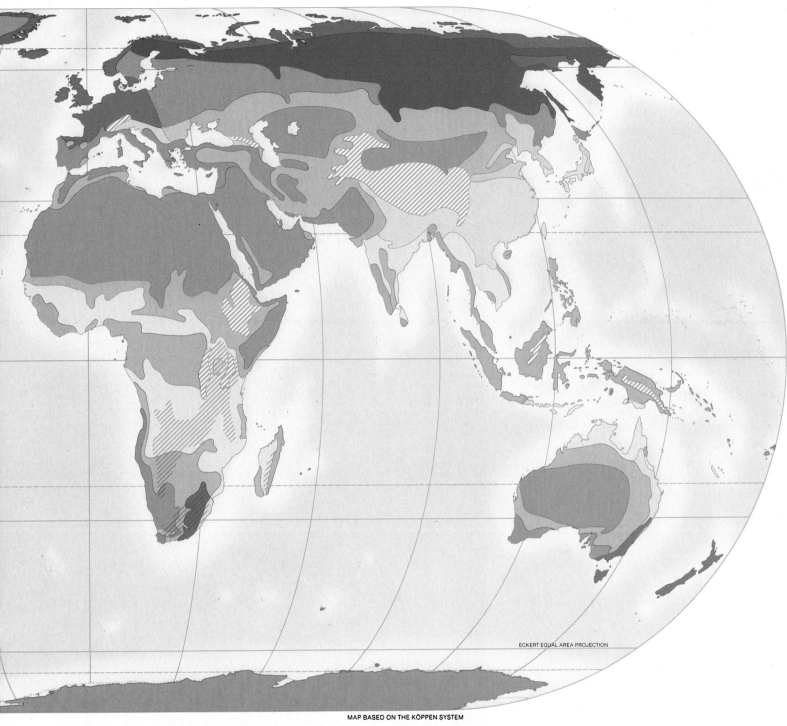

ECKERT EQUAL AREA PROJECTION

MAP BASED ON THE KÖPPEN SYSTEM

nearly every afternoon. Annual rainfall exceeds 150 centimeters (59 in), and the temperature varies more during a day than it does in a year. The coolest temperature, about 20° to 23°C (68°–73°F), occurs just before dawn. Afternoon temperatures usually reach 30° to 33°C (86°–91°F). Seasons are barely distinct because the average monthly temperature varies from 25° to 28°C (77°–82°F).

Tropical wet climates exist in a band extending about 10 degrees on either side of the

WORLD CLIMATE MAP

TROPICAL CLIMATES
Tropical Wet
Tropical Wet and Dry

DRY CLIMATES
Semiarid
Arid

MILD CLIMATES
Marine West Coast
Mediterranean
Humid Subtropical

CONTINENTAL CLIMATES
Warm Summer
Cool Summer
Subarctic

POLAR CLIMATES
Tundra
Ice Cap

HIGH ELEVATIONS
Highlands
Uplands

▲ This map shows the earth's climate regions. Throughout the world, plant growth is largely dictated by climatic conditions such as ranges and extremes of temperature and amounts of precipitation.

▶ *Rain forest covers slopes surrounding a rugged peak on Viti Levu, an island in Fiji. Dense rain forests characterize tropical wet climates.*
▼ *Workers in Cameroon clear rain forest, a source of fine woods. Mahogany and ebony are two of many species found in the tropical wet climate. Much of the country's valuable wood is exported.*

Equator. This part of the globe is always under the influence of the moisture-laden ITCZ, the intertropical convergence zone. The zone follows a pendulum-like path during the course of a year, moving back and forth across the Equator in step with the sun.

The areas just beyond the wet tropics come under the ITCZ's influence only part of the year. They have a tropical wet and dry climate with three seasons: cool and dry, when the ITCZ is in the opposite hemisphere; hot and dry, as the ITCZ approaches; and hot and wet, from the time the ITCZ arrives until it crosses the Equator again. Life in these regions depends on the wet season's rains. During years when rains are light, both people and animals suffer. Havana, Cuba; Calcutta, India; and Africa's Serengeti Plain are in the wet and dry tropics.

Regions lying within the dry climate group occur where precipitation is low, including cool, high latitudes. There are two dry climate types: arid and semiarid. Although rainfall is limited in a dry climate, there are few parts of the world where it never rains. Most arid regions receive 10 to 30 centimeters (4–12 in) of rain each year, and semiarid ones receive enough to support extensive grasslands. Temperatures in both arid and semiarid climates show large daily and seasonal variations. The hottest spots in the world lie within arid climates. The temperature in the North African town of Azizia, Libya, reached 58°C (136°F) on September 13, 1922—the highest weather temperature ever recorded.

One of the driest places on earth is the Atacama Desert of Chile, on the west coast of South America. There, the town of Arica averages less than .05 centimeter (.02 in) of rain a year. Rising cold water in the ocean keeps such arid coastal regions cool enough to be fog-covered much of the time. Fog forms in a stable atmosphere, where rainfall is unlikely. Nearby inland mountains trap high-pressure systems, whose sinking air further reduces the chance of rain.

Arid regions of the subtropics, such as Africa's Sahara and Australia's outback, lie between the ITCZ and mid-latitude low pressure systems. There, air sinks most of the time, making it nearly impossible for rain clouds to form.

In the mid-latitudes, arid and semiarid climates occur when moist air is blocked by

▲ Monsoon rain floods a street in Delhi, India. Monsoons, seasonal winds that bring heavy rains, provide water essential to crops in lands where half the world's people live.

▼ A giraffe stands near a baobab tree in Kenya's Tsavo National Park. Tall grasses, shrubs, and scattered trees are typical vegetation in a tropical wet and dry climate.

mountains in the heart of a continent. Denver, Colorado, and the Great Plains of the United States have this type of dry climate.

The climate groups known as mild and continental lie between about 25 and 70 degrees latitude. They are also called the temperate regions, and both are marked by distinct cold seasons.

Areas with a continental climate have colder winters, longer-lasting snow, and shorter growing seasons, and are the transition zones between mild and polar climates. Because of the year-round battle between tropical and polar air masses in mild and continental climates, the annual temperature variation exceeds the day-to-night variation.

In these parts of the world, climate is influenced mostly by latitude and by a region's position on a continent. For example, the mild climate type called Mediterranean, found on the west coasts of continents between 30 and 40 degrees latitude and along the shores

of the Mediterranean Sea, has a warm summer and a short and mild but rainy winter. Many people enjoy the Mediterranean climate of areas such as central California. Subtropical high pressure, with sinking air, dominates the summers, producing clear skies, cool nights, and little rain. The city of Jerusalem, near the eastern Mediterranean, once had no rain in July for more than 100 years. In winter, westerly winds blow in from the ocean. They

▲ A rancher with a team of horses crosses rolling Montana hills. The type of grassland in this semiarid climate is known as shortgrass prairie.
◄ A prairie dog in South Dakota surveys its surroundings. Such semiarid climate regions of the mid-latitudes are usually at the center of continents, protected by mountains and far from the ocean's moisture.

bring rain but keep the temperatures mild.

The type of mild climate known as humid subtropical is usually found on the eastern sides of continents. In cities such as Savannah, Georgia; Shanghai, China; and Sydney, Australia, the hot, humid summers are oppressive, and winter cold spells can be severe. Precipitation is spread evenly through the year and totals 76 to 165 centimeters (30–65 in). Hurricanes and other violent storms are common.

Weather on both sides of a continent becomes generally cooler as latitude increases. The marine west coast climate, a type of mild climate typical of cities such as Seattle, Washington, and Wellington, New Zealand, has a longer, cooler winter than does the Mediterranean climate. Drizzle falls about two-thirds of winter days, and temperatures average about 5°C (41°F). Rain also falls during the mild summers, since the dominance of subtropical high pressure is not complete.

The three types of continental climate—warm summer, cool summer, and subarctic—occur only in the Northern Hemisphere. While the summers are usually warm, even hot at times, it is here that we find true winters with low temperatures and snow. Cold winds, sweeping in from the Arctic region and driven by large continental high-pressure systems, dominate the winter weather. People living in these climates have grown accustomed to the

▲ *A single palm tree marks the remains of a house abandoned to shifting desert sands near the I-n-Salah Oasis in Algeria. Though rainfall is sparse in arid climates, underground water enables trees and other plants to grow in oases.*
◄ *Joshua trees stand among brush in the Mojave Desert in California. This type of vegetation is common in North American deserts.*

▼ *Moss-draped trees and ground-covering ferns thrive in the Hoh Rain Forest in Washington State. Heavy rainfall of the marine west coast climate supports the lush growth.*

▶ *Humid subtropical climates, like that of the Okefenokee Swamp region of Georgia, nurture abundant and varied plant life. Here, cypress trees grow among lily pads.*

harsh weather, but those unprepared for such cold may suffer. Many of Napoleon's soldiers, for example, died in bitter cold as they retreated from Russia in the winter of 1812.

The range of weather in continental climate regions makes them among the most spectacular on earth. In autumn, for instance, vast forests put on their annual show of brilliant color before shedding their leaves as winter approaches. Thunderstorms and tornadoes, among the most powerful forces in nature, form chiefly in spring and summer as the conflict between arctic and tropical air masses reaches its peak.

Found toward the Poles within the Arctic and Antarctic Circles are the two polar climate types, tundra and ice cap. In tundra regions, summers are short, but plants and animals are plentiful. Temperatures can average as high as 10°C (50°F) in July. Wildflowers dot the landscape, and flocks of birds return to feed on insects and fish. Whales feed on the microscopic creatures in the nutrient-rich waters. Eskimos and other peoples have lived in the tundra for thousands of years.

Except for the hardiest mammals and birds, few living things exist in the ice cap regions of the Arctic and Antarctic. Temperatures rarely rise above freezing, even in

summer. The ever present ice helps keep the weather cold by reflecting most of the sun's energy back into the atmosphere. Skies are mostly clear and precipitation is low all year.

There are two high elevation climate types. They are called upland and highland. Upland climates occur on high plateaus, and highland climates occur on mountains. Climbing a lofty mountain can be like moving toward the Poles. On some mountains, such

▼ *A shepherd tends his flock in the Spanish region of Aragon. The grasses and small trees growing here are characteristic of the Mediterranean climate's mild winters and dry summers. Changes in global wind patterns account for the climate's normally dry summers.*

as Kilimanjaro in Africa, the climate is tropical at the base and polar at the peak, and usually the climate differs from one side of the mountain to the other.

No climate, of course, is uniform. Small variations, called microclimates, exist in every climate region. Most are caused by topographic features such as lakes, vegetation, and cities. In a large urban area, for example, streets and buildings absorb great amounts of solar energy, raising the average temperature of the city above the averages of more open areas nearby. The Great Lakes cause profound microclimatic effects. Cities on the southern side of Lake Ontario, for example, are cloudier and receive much more snow than do those on the northern shore.

Changes in Climate

Weather may vary from day to day, but climates change slowly over hundreds or thousands of years or more. The presence of polar ice caps suggests that the earth today is still in an ice age. Many scientists believe we are in an interglacial period, when warmer temperatures have caused the ice caps to recede to Antarctica and to numerous Arctic islands. Many centuries from now, the glaciers may advance again.

There is evidence that the climate was very different not so long ago in geologic terms. Fossil shells of ancient marine creatures called goniatites were found in the Sahara. They indicate that ocean covered much of that region about 400 million years ago.

Other evidence from a variety of sources supports the idea that the earth's climate has changed many times. Certain leaf fossils, for example, may indicate that plants now growing only in the tropics were once widespread over the earth. On the other hand, fossils and landforms such as moraines—ridges of rocks and other debris deposited by glaciers— suggest that ice caps have covered large areas of the Northern and Southern Hemispheres at least four times during the past 500 million years. The most recent ice age began about two million years ago, and the ice caps began retreating only 18,000 years ago.

Scientists believe that the changing tilt of the earth's axis and shape of the earth's orbit around the sun play a role in long-term

◀ Corn and oats grow side by side in eastern Iowa, which has a continental climate. Warm summers, plentiful rainfall, and rich soil combine to make this a productive farming area.
▼ Fog rises from a lake in Ontario, Canada. This continental climate region has mild, cool summers and year-round rains that sustain forests.

◀ Black spruce trees stand against the wind in Manitoba, Canada. A long, severe winter is the dominant season in the subarctic climate. With warm, short summers, the climate has some of the world's widest annual ranges of temperature.

▶ *An array of flowering plants brightens the landscape near Hudson Bay. The tundra climate marks the transition from milder continental climates to the ice cap.*
▼ *Frost rims leaves of bearberry, cloudberry, and heather, vegetation common in the tundra.*

▼ *In Canada's Northwest Territories, an Inuit pulls his catch from a hole cut through the ice. Even in the severe polar climates, people and animals adapt and thrive. The average temperature on the ice cap rarely rises above freezing.*

climate changes. Though we think of those planetary factors as constant, they change slowly over time and may affect how much of the sun's energy reaches different parts of the world in different seasons of the year.

Climate changes occur over shorter periods as well. Such changes may be caused by fluctuations in the sun's energy output. Small deviations in the amount of sunlight that reaches the earth can have an effect on global temperatures. One theory that has been popular for more than a century, though it is yet unproved, is that the earth's climate is related to the number of sunspots on the sun's surface. Scientists have noticed that an unusually quiet period of sunspot activity coincided with the Little Ice Age of the 16th and 17th centuries. This was determined through studies made of the rings of trees that were more than 300 years old. The thickness of the annual rings is related to the amount of the trees' annual growth, which in turn is related to climate changes.

Some climate changes are almost predictable. One results from the warming of the surface waters of the tropical eastern Pacific Ocean. The warming is called El Niño—The Child—because it tends to begin around Christmas. In normal years, trade winds blow steadily across the ocean from east to west, dragging warm surface water along in the same direction. This results in a shallow layer of warm water in the eastern Pacific and a buildup of warm water in the west. Every few years, normal winds falter and ocean currents reverse. Warm water deepens in the eastern Pacific. This, in turn, produces dramatic climate changes. Rain diminishes in Australia and southern Asia, and freak storms may pound Pacific islands and the west coast of

► *Hikers cross Mackinnon Pass in New Zealand at an elevation of about 1,000 meters (3,300 ft). Various highland climates exist in lofty mountain ranges throughout the world.*

the Americas. Within a year or so, El Niño ends, and climate systems return to normal.

Climate in the Future

Many scientists are concerned that human activities are causing dangerous changes in the earth's climate. Temperatures around the world have risen slightly since the late 1870s, and the five warmest years in the past 130 occurred in the 1980s. This warming trend may be a sign that the greenhouse effect is increasing.

The greenhouse effect is the mechanism by which carbon dioxide, water vapor, and other gases in the atmosphere absorb some of the sun's heat as it is radiated back from the surface of the earth. This keeps the earth warm. A change in the composition of the atmosphere could alter the greenhouse effect,

▼ *Poppies color a valley in the Canadian Rockies. Since microclimates exist at different elevations, there is often a wide variety of plant life on one mountainside.*

▼ *Hayden Peak in Colorado looms above a stand of golden aspen. Because of the changing elevation, this is one of many local climates in the Rocky Mountains.*

▲ Pollution from a Mexican oil refinery billows into the air, clouding a sunset. The release of more carbon dioxide and other gases into the atmosphere may increase the greenhouse effect and, as a result, add to global warming.

▲ The earth's climate changes constantly but slowly. Water covered the Sahara some 400 million years ago. This fossilized sea shell, called a goniatite, was found in the desert.
► Cypress trees, perhaps 4,000 years old, survive on underground water at the edge of the Sahara. About 10,000 years ago, rainfall was more abundant here and cypress trees thrived.

however, and slowly make the earth warmer.

The burning of fossil fuels by industries and automobiles and the destruction of tropical forests have increased the amount of carbon dioxide in the atmosphere by more than 20 percent over the past 100 years. The amounts of methane, produced by decomposing plant and animal matter, and chlorofluorocarbons, used in refrigeration and in aerosol sprays, are also increasing. As the proportion of these gases in the atmosphere

rises, so does the temperature of the earth. The temperature will continue to rise unless preventive steps are taken.

Climatologists worry that the global temperature will increase so much that the polar ice caps will begin melting within the next several decades. The sea level would rise, causing heavy flooding of coastal areas. More precipitation would fall in some places and far less in others. Regions where crops now grow could become deserts.

Experts agree that we must reduce the amounts of "greenhouse gases" released into the atmosphere. Cutting back on our use of fossil fuels would help, and so would developing substitutes for chlorofluorocarbons.

The climate has changed many times during the earth's history, but the changes have occurred slowly, over thousands of years. Only in this century have human activities begun to influence the climate—and only recently have we begun to understand what the consequences may be.

SEE ALSO ATMOSPHERE, BIOSPHERE, DESERT, EARTH, FOREST, GRASSLAND, GREENHOUSE EFFECT, ICE AGE, ICE SHEET, MOUNTAIN, OCEAN, POLAR REGIONS, SEA LEVEL, SEASONS, TUNDRA, VEGETATION REGIONS, and WEATHER.

CLOUDS

In most of the world, it is a rare day when there are no clouds in the sky. From day to day, from moment to moment, the look of the sky changes as clouds form and move. Although clouds can differ greatly in size, shape, and color, they all consist of visible masses of tiny water droplets or ice crystals.

Although the liquid water and the ice are clear, clouds look white because the droplets and crystals scatter sunlight. When clouds block the sun, they appear gray or black.

Clouds form when air cools below its dew point. The dew point is the temperature at which air becomes saturated, or filled with moisture. Because its capacity to hold water is limited, air is very much like a sponge. Warm air can hold more water vapor than cold air can, and lowering the temperature of a mass of air is like squeezing a sponge. How hard you need to squeeze a sponge to wring water from it depends on how much water it contains. A full sponge drips with the slightest pressure, whereas a damp sponge requires a good squeeze. Similarly, moist air becomes cloudy with only slight cooling, whereas dry air must be cooled more to form clouds. With further cooling or additional moisture, the ice or water particles that make up clouds can grow together into bigger particles that fall to earth as precipitation.

Water droplets in clouds are microscopic, averaging .01 millimeter (.0004 in) in diameter. Raindrops, which form from droplets, range from less than 5 millimeters (0.2 in) to less than 1 millimeter (.04 in) in diameter and contain millions of times more water.

We usually think of rainwater as pure, but in fact each cloud droplet has a tiny impurity, called a condensation nucleus, at its center. Salt particles from the ocean, meteor dust, windblown sand grains, and pollutants all act as seeds around which water condenses to form droplets. If the atmosphere is cold enough, the droplets either start out as, or freeze into, ice crystals.

You probably rely on weather reports to help you decide whether to dress for rain when you go out. But sometimes you can make your own weather forecasts by observing the types of clouds in the sky.

▲ *Massive storm clouds rise over Sydney, Australia. This type of cloud formation, cumulonimbus with a cirrus anvil, means a sweeping thunderstorm.*
▶ *A cumulonimbus cloud builds above the horizon while two bison graze in sunshine. Unstable air feeds the cloud's growth.*

CLOUDS AND THE WEATHER

The ten types of clouds in the picture below never appear in the sky at the same time. The artist painted them together to show their relative sizes and positions in the atmosphere. Meteorologists name clouds according to a system developed around 1800 by British biologist Luke Howard. He classified clouds into three main groups: cirrus, stratus, and cumulus.

Cirrus clouds are wispy, curly, or stringy. They usually signal fair weather ahead. **Stratus** clouds are stratified, or layered, often blanketing the entire sky with a uniform cover. **Cumulus** clouds are lumpy or heaped. The weather they bring depends on their height and size.

The prefix *cirro-* refers to clouds that lie more than 6 kilometers (20,000 ft) above the earth, such as **cirrocumulus** and **cirrostratus** clouds. *Alto-* denotes clouds whose bases are between 2 and 6 kilometers (6,500–20,000 ft) above the earth, such as **altocumulus** and **altostratus** clouds. Clouds that produce rain take the prefix *nimbo-* or the suffix *-nimbus,* as in **nimbostratus** or **cumulonimbus.**

Puffy **cumulus** clouds form when thermals, up-

drafts of warm air, cool as they rise to altitudes of about 1 kilometer (3,300 ft). The higher the clouds are, the drier the atmosphere and the fairer the weather will be. Cumulus clouds can grow into **cumulonimbus** clouds, or thunderheads, by midafternoon. Such cumulonimbus clouds also occur along cold fronts. As evening approaches, cumulonimbus clouds usually shrink and gradually become **stratocumulus** clouds, which rarely produce rain.

Clouds in the stratus group often form at the boundary of a warm front. Warm, moist air is forced up over cold air, producing clouds across the entire front. **Stratus** clouds form when stable air does not permit cumulus ones to develop. They often blanket the sky as a gray layer stretching from horizon to horizon and can measure hundreds of kilometers in length and width. If precipitation falls from these clouds at all, it is usually in the form of drizzle or light snow. **Nimbostratus** clouds bring continuous precipitation that can last for many hours.

SEE ALSO AIR MASS, ATMOSPHERE, CONDENSATION, EVAPORATION, FRONT, PRECIPITATION, THUNDERSTORM, WATER CYCLE, *and* WEATHER.

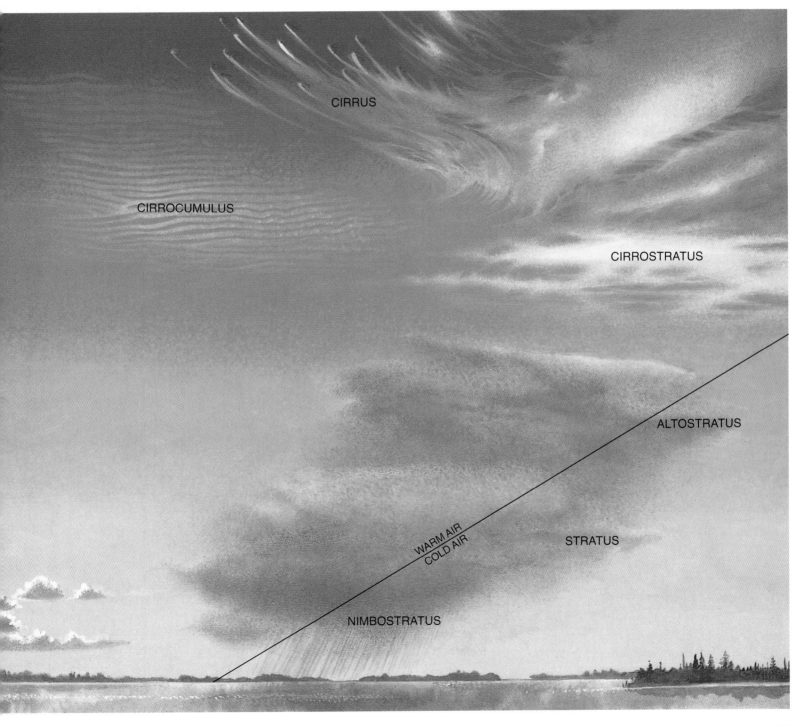

COAL

Coal, a fossil fuel, is a dark substance formed from plants that died millions of years ago. Plant matter settled in layers at the bottom of swamps and other wetlands where the lack of oxygen kept it from decaying completely. Over time, pressure from accumulating layers caused the vegetation to harden into coal. For centuries, coal has been burned and used as fuel. Deposits of this fossil fuel can be found on every continent.

SEE ALSO BOG, ENERGY, FOSSIL FUEL, MINING, POLLUTION, *and* WETLAND.

▲ *Coal, considered the most abundant fossil fuel, piles up at a strip mine in Montana.*

COAST

The edge of land that borders the ocean along a continent or an island is called the coast, or seacoast. Some coasts are smooth and straight, with wide, gently sloping beaches. Others are rugged and irregular, with steep, rocky cliffsides and jagged points that jut out into the water. Still other coasts are low-lying marshes or coral reefs.

Most people think of coasts as fixed, enduring boundaries that mark the land's end. Yet all coasts are constantly changing in an endless battle with the ocean.

Since ancient times, people have found abundant food and hospitable climates along coasts. Throughout history, coasts have been gateways to exploration, trade, and settlement. Most of the world's major cities lie along seacoasts or along rivers leading to coasts.

In some areas, however, rugged coastal features such as cliffs and reefs have raised barriers to exploration and settlement.

Nearly two-thirds of the world's people live in coastal areas. Today, coasts attract people because of their cosmopolitan cities, their scenic beauty, and recreational activities such as swimming, fishing, and boating.

The Diversity of Coasts

Many factors—including fluctuating sea levels, the action of glaciers, the forces of weathering and erosion, and the types of rock that make up shorelines—have combined to produce earth's great variety of coasts.

Over the last two million years, scientists believe, world sea level has risen and fallen many times. At the peak of the most recent ice age, about 18,000 years ago, the sea level was perhaps 100 meters (330 ft) lower than it is today. This drop in sea level happened because tremendous amounts of water were frozen in the glaciers that covered much of the land. When the earth warmed and glaciers melted, the sea level rose.

In some places where the drop in sea level had left the land exposed, rivers had cut deep valleys. The rising ocean flooded the rivers and valleys, creating great estuaries and bays. One such bay is the Chesapeake, on the East Coast of the United States.

Along mountainous coasts, the heavy ice of the glaciers cut and dug deep, narrow U-shaped valleys in the coastline. When the glaciers melted, the sea level rose, flooding the channels and creating fjords such as those along Norway's coast.

Coasts have been shaped not only by changes in sea level but also by changes in the land itself. Because of movement within the earth's crust, coastal land in some places is sinking, while in others it is rising.

Rivers help shape coasts by carrying silt and other sediments to the ocean. Some rivers, such as the Mississippi in the U.S. and the Nile in Egypt, build up huge deposits at their mouths, creating fertile coastal lands called deltas. Waves, tides, and currents sweeping along some coasts may move great amounts of sand, forming sandbars, spits, and extended beaches.

While some coasts are built up by the

▲ *Pacific surf sweeps against cliffs on the island of Hawaii. Steep coastlines like this one often occur on recently formed volcanic islands, where ocean waves have not worn down the shore into flat, sandy beaches.*
▶ *Blackbeard Island, a barrier island off the coast of Georgia, lies between Sapelo Sound and the Atlantic Ocean. The action of tides and violent storms constantly changes the shape of this stretch of coast.*

deposition of materials such as sand and silt, other coasts are shaped by the forces of weathering and erosion, which break down and wear away rocks. The chief agent of erosion along coasts is ocean waves. Waves pound against coastal rocks relentlessly, day after day, year after year. Storm waves can have tremendous power. When a big breaker crashes against a rock face, it compresses air in cracks in the rock. When the wave recedes, the trapped air expands explosively, sometimes shattering the rock.

Ocean waves hurl sand, gravel, pebbles, and even boulders against the coast. These materials slowly carve cliffsides or caves along the shore. The chemical action of the seawater in waves and spray helps break down coastal rock by slowly dissolving the soluble minerals it contains.

Whether a coastline is being built up or worn down, the kind of rock exposed along it may influence its shape. For example, relatively soft rock, such as the chalk of the cliffs at Dover, England, erodes easily and forms steep, smooth sides. However, when very hard rock such as granite is also present, the combination of rock types results in irregular coastlines where resistant rocks jut out and less resistant rocks are eroded, forming indentations such as coves or bays.

SEE ALSO BEACH, DELTA, FJORD, GLACIER, RIVER, ROCK, SEA LEVEL, WAVES, *and* WEATHERING AND EROSION.

COASTAL PLAIN

A coastal plain is a large area of low, flat land lying next to the ocean. Coastal plains form in three ways. Many begin as part of a continental shelf, the undersea land that forms a continent's edge. As the level of the ocean slowly drops, uncovering part of the shelf, a coastal plain emerges. A coastal plain can also form when forces inside the earth raise part of a shelf above the ocean's surface. A coastal plain can develop where a river deposits rock, soil, and other sedimentary materials in the ocean. Layers of this sediment build up and become a plain when they emerge from the ocean.

Near the seaward edge of a coastal plain, water often pools in low-lying areas and wetlands develop. In wetlands such as the Everglades in Florida, waterfowl and other wildlife thrive.

SEE ALSO ALLUVIAL FAN, COAST, CONTINENTAL SHELF, PLAIN, *and* WEATHERING AND EROSION.

COMMUNICATION

Communication is the process by which people exchange information. There are many ways to communicate, including speaking, writing, and using sign language or body language. The sharing of information among individuals and small groups is called interpersonal communication. The sending of information to large audiences is called mass communication. Books, magazines, newspapers, and radio and television broadcasts are used for mass communication.

Means of communication vary throughout the world. In developed countries, communications systems are often highly advanced, involving the use of satellites and computers. People in developing countries often use simpler, nonelectronic methods of communication, such as relaying information by messenger. In all lands, communication is vital to the orderly functioning of society.

SEE ALSO ALPHABET, LANGUAGE, *and* TRANSPORTATION AND COMMUNICATION.

COMMUNISM

Communism in its strictest sense is an economic system based on the idea that the members of a society should own all property together and that wealth should be distributed according to individuals' needs. In communist countries, economic and political systems are combined. The state owns almost all land, decides what to produce, sets prices, and limits individual economic freedom.

Communism as a political force was first advocated by Karl Marx and Friedrich Engels in *The Communist Manifesto*, published in 1848. Poverty, they argued, would spur workers to rebel and abolish private property. In 1917, Russian revolutionaries established the first communist state, known today as the Soviet Union. In the 1980s, a third of the world's people were living under communist regimes in China, Poland, Vietnam, and elsewhere.

SEE ALSO ECONOMY *and* GOVERNMENT.

COMPASS

A compass is a device that indicates direction. It is one of the most important instruments in navigation. A magnetized needle that is free to move will line up with the earth's magnetic field, so that one end points to magnetic north and the other to magnetic south. The earliest compass may have been a magnetized needle stuck through a piece of wood floating in a dish of water. Later, a needle was mounted on a pivot and placed in the middle of a card that showed the cardinal points — north, south, east, and west.

There are many modern forms of the compass. A familiar one is the orienteering compass, which is helpful on camping and hiking trips and for map reading. It has a clear plastic base, a freely spinning magnetized needle, and a movable 360-degree dial. In a compass you may have seen on the dashboard of a car, the needle and card are attached and move together under a fixed pointer in a small clear dome.

SEE ALSO DIRECTION, NAVIGATION, *and* POLES.

CONDENSATION

Condensation is the process by which water vapor becomes liquid water. It is the reverse of evaporation. It occurs when air is cooled below its dew point or becomes saturated through evaporation. In nature, condensation occurs on microscopic particles called condensation nuclei. The best nuclei for this are hygroscopic, meaning they have a special attraction for water. Soil and particles of sea salt are among the most common hygroscopic particles in the atmosphere. When water vapor condenses, it gives off heat. This heat, called latent heat, warms the air, increasing its buoyancy and making it rise. If the air is humid, water will continue to condense as the air rises and cools, releasing still more heat. In an unstable atmosphere, rapid condensation helps generate severe storms such as thunderstorms and tornadoes.

SEE ALSO CLOUDS, DEW, EVAPORATION, PRECIPITATION, *and* WATER CYCLE.

▲ *Beads of dew, formed by condensation during a cool night, cling to a spider's web hanging between tall blades of grass in the early morning.*

CONE

A cone forms as eruptions pile up material around a volcanic vent, or opening. Alternating layers of lava, ash, and broken rock build composite cones. Cinder cones are somewhat smaller and are made up largely of lava fragments called cinders.

SEE ALSO ERUPTION, MOUNTAIN, *and* VOLCANO.

CONSERVATION

The earth's natural resources include air, water, soil, minerals, fuels, plants, and animals. Conservation is the practice of caring for resources so that all living things can benefit from them now and in the future.

People often waste natural resources. Animals are overhunted. Forests are cleared, exposing the land to wind and water damage. Fertile soil is exhausted and lost to erosion because of poor farming practices. Fuel supplies are depleted. Water and air are polluted. If resources are carelessly managed, many will be used up. Some of them, including fossil fuels such as coal, oil, and natural gas, cannot be replenished for our use, regardless of how they are managed. If used wisely and efficiently, however, such resources will last much longer. Through conservation, people can end wasteful practices and manage natural resources wisely.

In many parts of the world, populations have grown enormously in the past two centuries and continue to multiply rapidly. The world's billions of people use up resources quickly as they consume food, build houses, produce goods, and burn fuel for transportation. The continuation of life as we know it depends on the careful use of natural resources to ensure their quality and availability.

The need to conserve resources often conflicts with other needs. For some people, a wooded area may be a good place to put a farm. A timber company may want to harvest the area's trees for construction materials. A business may want to build a factory or a shopping mall on the land. All these needs are valid, but sometimes the plants and animals that live in the area are forgotten. The benefits of development need to be weighed against the disadvantages to animals that may be forced to find new homes to survive.

People are becoming more aware of the interconnections within the earth's ecosystems. For example, the destruction of forests increases soil erosion, destroys wildlife, and

◄ *Severe soil erosion in this Washington State wheat field (top) results from cultivating up and down a slope. Strip-cropping, as practiced in the Nebraska fields at left, reduces erosion.*

▼ *Phosphate detergent foams in a California river. Phosphates promote the growth of algae. Oxygen levels fall, harming fish and other aquatic life.*

causes dangerous increases in carbon dioxide. To be effective, conservation efforts must take these interactions into account. Development and conservation can coexist in harmony. It is, in fact, impossible to sustain development without conservation of resources.

Methods of Conservation

Soil conservation is vital to food production. Poor farming methods, such as repeatedly planting the same crop, deplete nutrients in the soil. Soil erosion by water and wind increases when farmers plow up and down hills. One soil conservation method is contour strip-cropping. Several crops, such as corn, wheat, and clover, are planted in alternating strips across a slope or across the path of the prevailing wind. The different crops planted in this pattern help slow erosion.

Harvesting all the trees from a large area, a practice called clear-cutting, increases the chances of losing productive topsoil to wind and water erosion. Selective harvesting, the practice of removing individual trees or small groups of trees, leaves other trees standing to anchor the soil.

Trees can be conserved if paper products are recycled. People in China and Mexico reuse much of their wastepaper. If half the world's paper were recycled, much of the worldwide demand for new paper would be fulfilled, thus saving many of the earth's trees. By protecting existing forests from uncontrolled harvesting and by planting trees and

other vegetation, people can prevent excessive erosion and help preserve wildlife habitats and global rainfall patterns.

Plants and wildlife are threatened by livestock overgrazing on grasslands and by the dredging and filling of wetlands. Some governments have established parks where such ecosystems exist, protecting many species and their habitats. Efforts are being made to abolish hunting and fishing practices that may cause the extinction of some species.

Conservation efforts ensure not only the availability of a resource but also its quality.

▼ *At a wildlife refuge, a peregrine falcon gets an identifying band. Bird banding programs enable scientists to monitor the welfare of a species.*

▲ *Hong Kong customs agents sort through piles of cheetah pelts that were seized at Kai Tak Airport. Illegal trade in skins threatens the survival of not only the cheetah but also of other wild animal species.*

Pollution of the air and water has far-reaching effects. The water cycle's purification process is hampered when water is polluted. Limiting the production of hazardous wastes and controlling their disposal are essential to the protection of water supplies.

The burning of fossil fuels for transportation and industry has contaminated the air we breathe, and fallout commonly called acid rain has damaged lakes and forests and the life within them. Using alternative nonpolluting energy sources such as the sun and the wind reduces chemical pollutants in the air and water. By using other resources, people can conserve nonrenewable energy resources, such as oil and natural gas.

Earth's supply of known mineral resources is in jeopardy. Of the mineral deposits that have been located and mapped, many have been depleted. Yet junkyards filled with rusting cars are a common sight, as are roadways littered with aluminum cans. Less wasteful mining methods and the recycling of materials will help conserve mineral resources. In Japan, for example, car manufacturers recycle many raw materials used in making automobiles. In the United States, nearly one-third of the iron produced comes from recycled automobiles.

Conservation Groups

Businesses, international groups, and some governments are involved in conservation efforts. The United Nations encourages the establishment of national parks around the world. Governments enact laws defining how land should be used and which areas should be set aside as wildlife preserves and parks. Governments also enforce laws designed to protect the environment from pollution, such as those requiring installation of pollution control devices.

Private groups around the world are dedicated to conservation. Members support causes such as saving rain forests, protecting threatened animals, and cleaning up the air. The International Union for the Conservation of Nature and Natural Resources (IUCN) is an

▼ *Mount McKinley looms in the distance as caribou graze in the vast wilderness of Alaska's Denali National Park and Preserve. Grizzly bears, timber wolves, and other animals roam freely in the protected parkland.*

▶ *Clearing trees from rain forests, as a man does here in Brazil, increases erosion and threatens the future of millions of plant and animal species.*

▼ *Teenagers practice conservation by recycling newspapers. Recycling helps preserve forests. Fewer trees need to be cut to produce new paper.*

alliance of governments and private groups that was founded in 1948 to protect wildlife. The IUCN soon turned its attention to wildlife habitats as well, and in 1980 the group proposed a world conservation strategy. Its goals were to maintain ecological processes and systems and to protect plants and animals. Many governments have used the IUCN model to develop conservation strategies for their countries. In addition, the IUCN monitors

▼ *Abandoned cars, trucks, and buses, just a few of the millions of vehicles Americans junk yearly, crowd a lot in Michigan. Much of the metal in them could be recovered and reused.*

newspapers and aluminum cans are just a few examples. Riding bikes, walking, carpooling, and using public transportation help conserve fuel and reduce the amount of pollutants released into the environment. Individuals can plant trees to create homes for birds and squirrels. At grocery stores, people can request paper bags, which are recyclable and less polluting than plastic bags. If each of us would conserve in small ways, the result would be a major conservation effort.

SEE ALSO ENERGY, FOREST, LAND USE, NATURAL RESOURCE, POLLUTION, SOIL, *and* WATER.

▼ *Ignoring a "No Dumping" sign, people have littered the area shown below with cans and trash. Recycling empty cans, as the two children are doing, helps conserve aluminum and reduce the pollution associated with its production. Industry analysts believe that almost 80 percent of all aluminum used could be recycled.*

the status of endangered wildlife, threatened national parks and preserves, and other environments around the world.

Local organizations can make major contributions to conservation. In India, the Chipko Movement, which is dedicated to saving trees, was started by villagers in the state of Uttar Pradesh. *Chipko* means "hold fast." The villagers flung their arms around trees to keep loggers from cutting them down. They won, and Uttar Pradesh banned the felling of trees in the Himalayan foothills. The movement has since expanded to other parts of India.

Individuals can do many things to help conserve resources. Turning off unnecessary lights, repairing leaky faucets, and recycling

CONTINENT

A continent is one of the earth's principal divisions of land. The term comes from a Latin word that means "continuous mass of land." By convention, there are seven continents. From largest to smallest, they are Asia, Africa, North America, South America, Antarctica, Europe, and Australia. When geographers identify the land areas they consider part of a continent, they usually include all the islands associated with the landmass.

"Continent," however, has more than just a physical definition. To some people, the term has a cultural connotation. Europe and Asia, for example, which are actually parts of one enormous landmass often referred to as Eurasia, are culturally diverse. On the whole, though, the various cultural groups of Europe have more in common with one another than they do with those of Asia. Thus, many geographers divide Eurasia between Asians and Europeans along a line running from the northern Ural Mountains south to the Caspian Sea, then west to the Dardanelles.

All together, the continents add up to a great deal of land, totaling about 148 million square kilometers (57 million sq mi). Even so, the surface area of the ocean is more than twice that of the continents combined. These proportions can be seen easily if you look at a globe. The expanses of blue that usually represent water are far more extensive than the areas of brown and green that often represent land and vegetation.

The ocean, which covers almost three-fourths of the earth, is divided by the continents. Its various sections have been given different names. The continents make up most of the earth's land surface, which covers more than one-fourth of the planet. A very small portion of the total land area is made up of islands that are not located near the large landmasses. New Zealand, French Polynesia, the Samoa Islands, and the Hawaiian Islands are examples of land areas that are not considered part of any continent.

You can find each continent on the map below. On this map, as on most others, the coastlines do not indicate the actual boundaries of the continents. There are gently sloping areas called continental shelves that extend outward under the water, often stretching far into the ocean. If the underwater shelves were included in the total land area, the continents would make up more than one-third of the earth's surface.

▼ *Large landmasses called continents, including the islands that are associated with them, make up more than one-fourth of the earth's surface. This map shows the locations of all the continents. Individual physical maps of the continents appear on the following pages.*

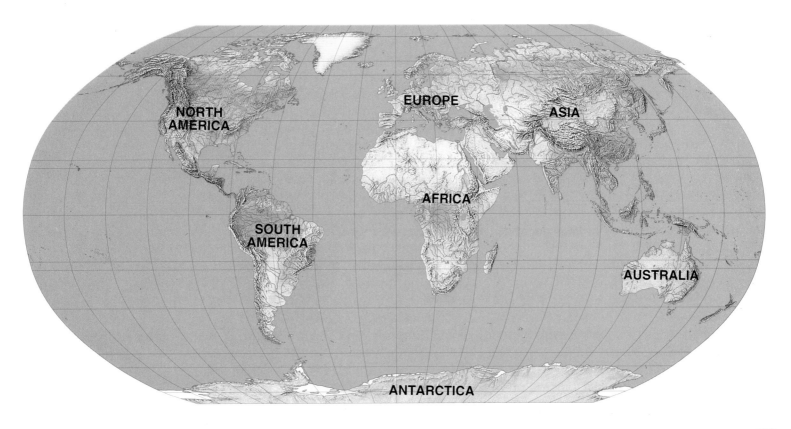

Building the Continents

Scientists speculate that the earth formed some 4.6 billion years ago from a great swirling cloud of dust and gas. Some of the material in the cloud came together and formed the earth. The continuous bombardment by space debris and the pull of gravity contributed to the heating of the planet's interior. As the heat increased, some of the earth's rocky materials melted and rose to the surface, where they cooled and formed a crust. Heavier elements sank toward the earth's center. Eventually, the earth came to have three main layers: the core, the mantle, and the crust.

As the interior developed, gases released from it mixed together, creating a steamy atmosphere around the planet. According to one theory, water vapor condensed and eventually covered most of the crust with a primitive ocean.

The crust and the top portion of the mantle form a rigid shell around the earth that is broken up into huge sections called plates. The heat from inside the earth causes constant movement of the plates. The plates are moving slowly today, just as they have been doing for hundreds of millions of years. Geologists believe that the interaction of the plates in a process called plate tectonics contributed to the building of the continents.

Studies of rocks found in stable, ancient areas of North America have revealed that the oldest known pieces of the continents began to form nearly four billion years ago. At that time, geologists think, only a small fraction of the earth's crust was made up of continental material. They theorize that the rocky material had built up along the boundaries of adjoining plates during a process called subduction. During subduction, earth's huge plates collide, and the edge of one plate slides beneath the edge of another.

When oceanic crust—crust that forms the ocean basins—slid down toward the mantle, the crust melted in the earth's intense heat. Once melted, the rock became lighter. Called magma, it rose through the overlying plate and burst out as lava. When the lava cooled, it hardened into igneous rock.

Gradually, the igneous rock built up, and small volcanic islands appeared above the surface of the ocean. Over time, these islands grew bigger, partly as a result of more lava flows and partly from the buildup of material scraped off descending plates. When plates carrying islands subducted, the islands did not descend into the mantle. Their material fused with that of islands on the adjoining plate, resulting in ever larger landmasses—the first continents. The building of volcanic islands and continental material through plate tectonics has taken millions of years, and it is a process that continues today.

Wandering Continents

If you could visit the earth as it was many millions of years ago, you would find an unfamiliar place. The continents have not always been where they are today. About 480 million years ago, most of them were scattered chunks of land lying along or below the Equator. Millions of years of continuous movement changed their positions greatly, and by some 240 million years ago, almost all of the world's landmasses were joined in a single, huge continent. Geologists call this supercontinent Pangaea, which means "all lands" in Greek.

By about 200 million years ago, the forces of plate tectonics that helped form Pangaea caused the supercontinent to begin to break apart. As the plates moved, the continental crust along the plate boundaries split, and large segments separated. The pieces of Pangaea that began to move apart were the beginnings of the continents we have now.

A landmass that would become Europe, Asia, and North America separated from another mass that would split up into the other continents. In time, Antarctica and Australia, still joined together, broke away from South America and Africa and drifted southward. India broke away and for millions of years moved northward as a large island before colliding with Asia. Gradually, the different landmasses moved to their present positions.

The positions of the continents are always changing. North America and Europe are moving away from each other at the rate of about 2.5 centimeters (1 in) per year. If you could visit the planet in the distant future, you might find that part of California had separated from North America and become an island and that Africa had split in two along the Great

Bering
Sea

ALEUTIAN ISLANDS

NORTH AMERICA

AREA
24,258,000 square kilometers
(9,366,000 sq mi)

POPULATION
(1988 estimate)
416,000,000

HIGHEST POINT
(above sea level)
Mount McKinley (Denali), Alaska
6,194 meters (20,320 ft)

LOWEST POINT
(below sea level)
Death Valley, California
-86 meters (-282 ft)

Arctic
Ocean

Chukchi
Sea

Bering Strait

180°

160°W

140°W

120°W

100°W

80°W

QUEEN
ELIZABETH
ISLANDS

80°N

20°W

Greenland
(DENMARK)

40°W

Baffin
Bay

60°W

60°N

Beaufort
Sea

Alaska
(U. S.)

Mt. McKinley
(Denali)

Gulf of
Alaska

Victoria
Island

Baffin

Island

ARCTIC CIRCLE

Davis
Strait

Labrador
Sea

MacKenzie River

Great
Slave
Lake

C

A

N

A

D

A

Hudson
Bay

Coast Mountains

R

O

C

K

Y

G

R

E

A

T

SHIELD

CANADIAN

Island of
Newfoundland

Gulf of
St. Lawrence

Vancouver
Island

M

o

u

n

t

a

i

n

s

P

L

A

I

N

S

Lake
Winnipeg

Missouri River

Lake
Superior

St. Lawrence River

40°N

Cascade Range

Coast Ranges

Cape Mendocino

Sierra Nevada

Great
Salt
Lake

Colorado River

GREAT
BASIN

Death
Valley

Lake
Michigan

Lake
Huron

Lake
Ontario

Appalachian Mountains

Lake
Erie

Cape Cod

U

N

I

T

E

D

S

T

A

T

E

S

Ohio River

Cape Hatteras

Mississippi
River

Atlantic
Ocean

Pacific
Ocean

Gulf of California

Baja California

Rio Grande

Western Sierra Madre

Eastern Sierra Madre

COASTAL PLAIN

Mississippi
River Delta

TROPIC OF CANCER

BAHAMAS

TROPIC OF CANCER

20°N

TROPIC OF CANCER

Gulf of
Mexico

Straits of Florida

W E S T

I N D I E S

CUBA

Hispaniola

Puerto
Rico (U. S.)

YUCATAN
PENINSULA

JAMAICA

HAITI

DOMINICAN
REPUBLIC

M E X I C O

BELIZE

HONDURAS

Caribbean Sea

GUATEMALA

EL SALVADOR

NICARAGUA

0   KILOMETERS   1000

0   MILES   600

CHAMBERLIN TRIMETRIC PROJECTION

COSTA
RICA

PANAMA

SOUTH AMERICA

Rift Valley. It is even possible that yet another supercontinent may form someday.

Continental Features

The surface of the continents has changed many times in a complex sequence of mountain building, weathering and erosion, and buildup of sediment, accompanied by continuous slow plate movement. During the earth's history, the rocks that form the continents have been shaped and reshaped many times. Great mountain ranges have risen and then have been worn away by the forces of weathering and erosion. Ocean waters have flooded huge areas and then gradually withdrawn from the land. Massive ice sheets have come and gone, sculpturing the surface of the land in the process.

Today, the continents have great mountain ranges, vast plains, extensive plateaus, and complex river systems. The landmasses' average elevation above sea level is about 840 meters (2,750 ft).

Although each is unique, all the continents share two basic features: old, geologically stable regions and younger, somewhat more active regions. In the younger regions, mountain building has occurred recently in the continent's geologic history. In general, a continent has a central, relatively flat area bordered or crossed by mountain ranges.

The power for mountain building comes from plate tectonics. One way mountains form is through the collision of masses of crust on two plates. The impact creates wrinkles in the crust, just as a throw rug rumples when you push against one end of it. Scientists believe such a collision several million years ago thrust up the Himalayan range, when the plate carrying India slowly and forcefully shoved the landmass of India into Asia, which was riding on another plate.

The most prominent features of the continents are their mountain belts, as a relief map reveals. Recently formed mountains rise near the western coasts of North and South America. Steep, young mountains also extend eastward across Europe and into Asia. Older mountain systems are also found on the continents, including the Appalachians in North America and the Urals on the border between Europe and Asia.

Even older than these ancient, eroded mountain ranges are relatively flat, stable areas of the continents called shields. Each continent has at least one. A shield is an area of ancient crust that formed during the earth's early history. Some of the shields may be the roots or cores of ancient mountain ranges that were completely eroded away over millions of years. Shields are generally found in the interiors of continents, where they form vast plains or low plateaus and hills.

The Canadian Shield makes up about a quarter of North America. For hundreds of thousands of years, sheets of ice up to 3 kilometers (2 mi) thick coated the Canadian Shield. The moving ice wore away rock overlying ancient rock layers, exposing some of the oldest formations on the earth. When you stand on the oldest part of the Canadian Shield, your feet rest on rocks that formed more than 3.5 billion years ago.

North America

North America, the third largest continent (map on pages 130–131), extends from the tiny Aleutian Islands in the northwest to Panama's border with Colombia in the south. The continent includes the island of Greenland in the northeast. In the far north, the continent stretches halfway around the world, from Greenland to the Aleutians. But at Panama's narrowest part, the continent is just 50 kilometers (31 mi) across. Thousands of bays and inlets help give North America the longest coastline of any continent.

Young mountains—including the massive Rockies, North America's largest chain—rise in the west. Some of the earth's youngest mountains are found in the Cascade Range of Washington, Oregon, and northeastern California. Some peaks there began to form only about a million years ago—a wink of an eye in earth's long history. North America's older mountain ranges rise near the east coast of the United States and Canada.

In between the mountain systems lie wide plains. Deep, rich soil blankets large areas of the plains in Canada and the United States. Much of the soil was formed from material deposited during recent ice ages. During these times of widespread glaciation, vast ice sheets and fast-moving winds scoured the

SOUTH AMERICA

AREA
17,823,000 square kilometers
(6,881,000 sq mi)

POPULATION
(1988 estimate)
286,000,000

HIGHEST POINT
(above sea level)
Aconcagua, Andes, Argentina
6,960 meters (22,835 ft)

LOWEST POINT
(below sea level)
Valdés Peninsula, Argentina
-40 meters (-131 ft)

NORTH
AMERICA

Caribbean Sea

Gulf of
Venezuela

Gulf of
Paria

VENEZUELA

*Lake
Maracaibo*

Magdalena River

L L A N O S

Orinoco River

GUYANA

SURINAME

FRENCH
GUIANA
(FRANCE)

Angel Falls

G U I A N A   H I G H L A N D S

COLOMBIA

Negro River

EQUATOR

ECUADOR

*Marajó
Island*

Amazon River

Gulf of
Guayaquil

A   M   A   Z   O   N

PERU

B   A   S   I   N

B   R   A   Z   I   L

São Francisco River

Andes

*Lake
Titicaca*

BOLIVIA

*MATO GROSSO
PLATEAU*

B   R   A   Z   I   L   I   A   N

*Lake
Poopó*

ALTIPLANO

Paraguay River

H   I   G   H   L   A   N   D   S

Pacific
Ocean

20° S

Atacama Desert

TROPIC OF CAPRICORN

GRAN CHACO

PARAGUAY

Paraná   River

Atlantic
Ocean

ARGENTINA

P   A   M   P   A   S

Uruguay River

*Cerro
Aconcagua*

URUGUAY

CHILE

*Río de
la Plata*

Samborombón Bay

San Matías Gulf

40° S

*Valdés
Peninsula*

*CHONOS
ARCHIPELAGO*

PATAGONIA

Gulf of
San Jorge

0	KILOMETERS	1200

0	MILES	800

CHAMBERLIN TRIMETRIC PROJECTION

Gulf of Penas

*Grande
Bay*

*FALKLAND
ISLANDS*
(U.K.)

Strait of Magellan

*TIERRA
DEL
FUEGO*

Cape Horn

80° W   60° W   40° W

ICELAND

ARCTIC CIRCLE

North Cape

Barents Sea

VESTERÅLEN

Inari

LOFOTEN

KOLA PENINSULA

Norwegian Sea

FINLAND

Gulf of Bothnia

NORWAY

SWEDEN

White Sea

Lake Onega

60°N

20°W

FAROE ISLANDS

Lake Ladoga

SHETLAND ISLANDS

Gulf of Finland

Rybinsk Reservoir

ORKNEY ISLANDS

Vänern

Lake Peipus

Lake Il'men'

BRITISH ISLES

HEBRIDES

Vättern

Atlantic Ocean

North Channel

Skagerrak

Kattegat

Baltic Sea

E U R O P E A N

Dnieper R.

North Sea

UNITED KINGDOM

S O V I E T

IRELAND

Shannon R.

Irish Sea

Great Britain

DENMARK

JUTLAND

N O R T H E R N

Vistula River

Celtic Sea

St. George's Channel

Thames R.

Strait of Dover

NETHERLANDS

Elbe R.

EAST GERMANY

POLAND

English Channel

CHANNEL ISLANDS

BELGIUM

WEST GERMANY

Kremenchug Reservoir

Seine R.

Dniester River

LUXEMBOURG

Loire R.

Rhine R.

CZECHOSLOVAKIA

Kakhovka Reservoir

Bay of Biscay

FRANCE

Danube R.

Carpathian Mountains

Cape Ortegal

SWITZERLAND

AUSTRIA

LIECHTENSTEIN

HUNGARY

Cape Finisterre

Garonne R.

Rhône River

A L P S

Lake Garda

ROMANIA

Pyrenees

Po River

ITALY

MONACO

SAN MARINO

Douro R.

SPAIN

ANDORRA

Gulf of Lions

Ligurian Sea

YUGOSLAVIA

Ebro R.

IBERIAN PENINSULA

Tiber R.

Adriatic Sea

BULGARIA

Black

PORTUGAL

Tagus R.

Cape Roca

Balearic Sea

Corsica

VATICAN CITY

Apennines

Bosporus

Gulf of Cádiz

Guadalquivir R.

Gulf of Valencia

Sardinia

A p e n n i n e s

TURKEY

Point Tarifa

Strait of Gibraltar

Alboran Sea

Tyrrhenian Sea

Strait of Otranto

ALBANIA

Sea of Marmara

Dardanelles

Aegean Sea

SPORADES

Mediterranean Sea

Strait of Sicily

Gulf of Taranto

IONIAN IS.

Ionian Sea

GREECE

0°

Sicily

Strait of Messina

PELOPONNESUS

Cape Taínaron

CYCLADES

AFRICA

MALTA

Sea of Crete

Crete

20°E

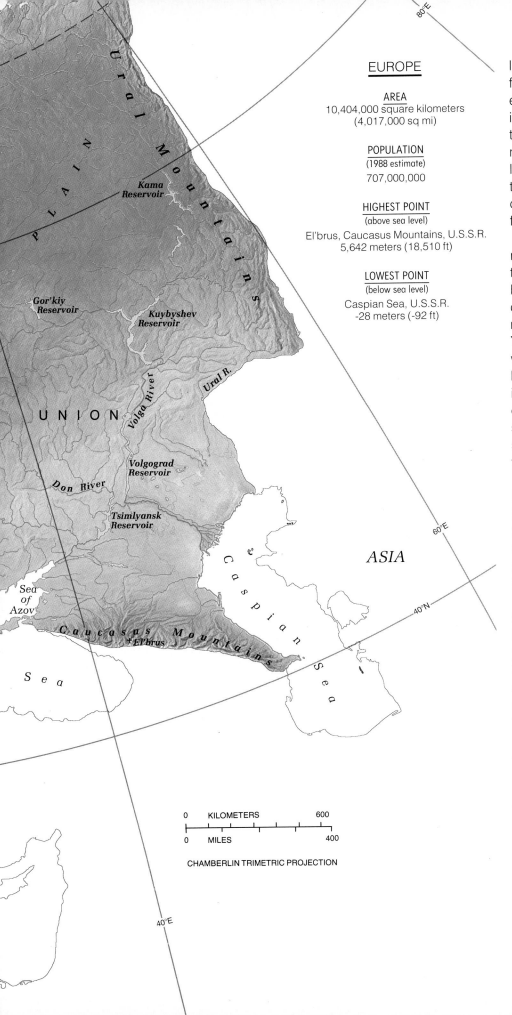

EUROPE

AREA
10,404,000 square kilometers
(4,017,000 sq mi)

POPULATION
(1988 estimate)
707,000,000

HIGHEST POINT
(above sea level)
El'brus, Caucasus Mountains, U.S.S.R.
5,642 meters (18,510 ft)

LOWEST POINT
(below sea level)
Caspian Sea, U.S.S.R.
-28 meters (-92 ft)

ASIA

```
0    KILOMETERS    600
0    MILES         400
```

CHAMBERLIN TRIMETRIC PROJECTION

landscape. Rocks and soil were picked up from one place, carried along, and deposited elsewhere. The most recent ice age reached its peak about 18,000 years ago. Afterward, the glaciers began to retreat, and streams of melted ice dropped more sediment on the land, building up layers of productive soil in the plains region. Grain grown in this region, called the breadbasket of North America, feeds a large part of the world.

North America contains a wealth of natural wonders. A great variety of landforms and types of vegetation can be found within its boundaries. North America holds magnificent canyons, such as the Grand Canyon in Arizona and Copper Canyon in northern Mexico. Yellowstone National Park has some of the world's most active geysers. Canada's Bay of Fundy has the greatest variation of tide levels in the world. The Great Lakes form the planet's largest area of fresh water. In California, some giant sequoias, the world's most massive trees, grow more than 76 meters (250 ft) tall and nearly 30 meters (100 ft) around.

Greenland, off the east coast of Canada, is the world's largest island, excluding Australia, which is sometimes called the island continent. Despite its name, Greenland is mostly covered with ice. Its ice is a remnant of the great ice sheets that once blanketed much of the North American continent.

Today, North America is home to the citizens of Canada, the United States (excluding Hawaii and some U.S. territories), the Danish province of Greenland, Mexico, Belize, Costa Rica, El Salvador, Guatemala, Honduras, Nicaragua, Panama, and the island countries and territories that dot the Caribbean Sea and the western North Atlantic Ocean.

South America

South America (map on page 133) is the fourth largest continent and extends from the southern border of Panama and the sunny beaches of the Caribbean Sea almost to frigid Antarctica. The continent's southernmost islands, in a group called Tierra del Fuego, are less than 1,125 kilometers (700 mi) from Antarctica. The Andes, the earth's longest mountain chain on land, stretches from Cape Horn, in the Tierra del Fuego islands, to Panama in the north. Many active volcanoes dot the

135

range. They are fueled by heat generated as a large oceanic plate off the west coast grinds beneath the plate carrying South America.

Tropical rain forests blanket a huge portion of northern South America. A vast river system, the Amazon, flows through the earth's most extensive rain forest. In volume, the Amazon is the largest river in the world. More water flows from it than from the next six largest rivers combined. Rain forests contain an enormous wealth of animal and plant life. Thousands of plant and animal species live in the Amazon basin. Many Amazonian plant species are sources of food and medicine. Scientists are trying to find ways to preserve this precious and fragile environment as people move into the Amazon basin and clear land for their settlements and for farming. The movement to settle in rain forests is accelerated by the high population growth rate in South America, particularly in Brazil. The population of Brazil almost equals that of all the other South American countries combined.

Europe

Europe (map on pages 134–135), the sixth largest continent, contains just seven percent of the earth's land. In total area, Europe is slightly larger than Canada. Europe has more than 30 countries and many of the world's major cities, including London, Paris, Rome, Madrid, and Moscow. The population of Europe is about the same as that of North and South America combined.

Most European countries have access to the ocean. The continent is bordered by the Arctic Ocean in the north, by the Atlantic Ocean in the west, by the Caspian Sea in the southeast, and by the Mediterranean and Black Seas in the south. The nearness of these bodies of water and the navigability of many of Europe's rivers have played a major role in the continent's history.

In the east, the Ural Mountains separate Europe from Asia. Another range, the Kjølen Mountains, extends along the northern part of the border between Sweden and Norway. To the south, the Alps form an arc stretching from Yugoslavia across Austria, Switzerland, and northern Italy into France. Youngest and steepest of Europe's mountains, the Alps resemble the Rockies of North America.

A large area of gently rolling plains extends from northern France eastward to the Urals. A climate of warm summers, cold winters, and plentiful rain helps make much of Europe's farmland productive.

Africa

Africa (map on page 137), the second largest continent, covers an area more than three times that of the United States. From north to south, Africa stretches about 8,000 kilometers (5,000 mi). It is 7,400 kilometers (4,600 mi) across at its widest part.

The Sahara, which covers much of North Africa, is the world's largest hot desert. The world's longest river, the Nile, flows more than 6,600 kilometers (4,100 mi) from its most remote headwaters in a stream south of Lake Victoria to the Mediterranean Sea in the north. A series of falls and rapids along the southern part of the river makes navigation difficult. Africa's other major rivers include the Zambezi, the Zaire (Congo), and the Niger.

Much of Africa is a plateau surrounded by narrow strips of coastal lowlands. Hilly uplands and mountains rise in some areas of the interior. The Great Rift Valley runs through East Africa from the Red Sea to Mozambique. It follows a series of rifts, or breaks, in the earth's surface that opened long ago. Lava poured out of the rifts, forming peaks such as Mount Kilimanjaro, Africa's highest mountain. Even though Kilimanjaro is not far from the Equator, snow covers its summit year-round.

In the Great Rift Valley, scientists can study plate tectonics in action. The continent is slowly tearing apart along the valley's rifts. In some places, the valley is several kilometers wide and hundreds of meters deep. The gap grows 10 centimeters (4 in) wider every hundred years. Eventually, part of East Africa may split off from the rest of the continent. The ocean would then flow between the two landmasses. The Red Sea has already filled a part of the Great Rift Valley system.

Asia

Asia (map on pages 138–139), the largest continent, stretches from the eastern Mediterranean Sea to the western Pacific. There are about 40 countries in Asia, including

AFRICA

AREA
30,271,000 square kilometers
(11,688,000 sq mi)

POPULATION
(1988 estimate)
623,000,000

HIGHEST POINT
(above sea level)
Mount Kilimanjaro, Tanzania
5,895 meters (19,340 ft)

LOWEST POINT
(below sea level)
Lake Assal, Djibouti
-156 meters (-512 ft)

EUROPE

ASIA

Mediterranean Sea

Strait of
Gibraltar

MADEIRA
ISLANDS
(PORTUGAL)

CANARY
ISLANDS
(SPAIN)

MOROCCO

Atlas Mountains

Gulf of
Gabes

TUNISIA

Gulf of
Sidra

ALGERIA

LIBYA

Libyan Desert

EGYPT

Nile River
Delta

Gulf of
Suez

WESTERN
SAHARA
(MOROCCO)

TROPIC OF CANCER

S

a

h

a

r

a

Lake
Nasser

*Nubian
Desert*

Red

20° N

MAURITANIA

MALI

NIGER

CHAD

S U D A N

Nile River

Sea

Cape
Verde

Senegal River

Niger River

Lake Chad

SENEGAL

GAMBIA

GUINEA-
BISSAU

GUINEA

BURKINA FASO

BENIN

S

u

NIGERIA

d

a

n

White Nile R.

Blue Nile R.

DJIBOUTI

Gulf of Aden

ETHIOPIA

*ETHIOPIAN
HIGHLANDS*

Lake
Assal

SIERRA
LEONE

CÔTE
D'IVOIRE

GHANA

Lake
Volta

SOMALI PENINSULA

LIBERIA

TOGO

*Niger River
Delta*

CAMEROON

CENTRAL
AFRICAN REPUBLIC

Lake
Turkana

SOMALIA

EQUATORIAL
GUINEA

SAO TOME
AND PRINCIPE

GABON

CONGO

Congo River

Lake Albert

UGANDA

KENYA

*KENYA
HIGHLANDS*

EQUATOR

Gulf of Guinea

C

O

N

G

O

Lake Edward

RWANDA

BURUNDI

Lake
Victoria

Kilimanjaro

Ungama Bay

EQUATOR

CABINDA
(ANGOLA)

Crystal Mountains

B

A

S

I

N

TANZANIA

Lake
Tanganyika

Indian
Ocean

Bengo Bay

ZAIRE

*KATANGA
PLATEAU*

Lake Malawi

COMOROS

Atlantic
Ocean

ANGOLA

MOZAMBIQUE

ZAMBIA

MALAWI

Zambezi River

*Victoria
Falls*

MOZAMBIQUE

Mozambique Channel

MADAGASCAR

ZIMBABWE

20° S

Namib Desert

NAMIBIA

BOTSWANA

*Kalahari
Desert*

SWAZILAND

TROPIC OF CAPRICORN

3

1

LESOTHO

*Declared independent by South Africa.
Thus far no other country has recognized
these homelands as separate nations.*

0   KILOMETERS   1200

0   MILES   800

CHAMBERLIN TRIMETRIC PROJECTION

St. Helena
Bay

SOUTH AFRICA

2

Orange River

Northern Karroo

2

1. BOPHUTHATSWANA
2. TRANSKEI
3. VENDA
4. CISKEI

Great Karroo

Cape of
Good Hope

20° W

0°

20° E

40° E

60° E

40° N

Japan, China, India, and most of the Soviet Union. More than half the earth's population lives in Asia. More than a third of the world's people live in India and China.

Most of Asia's people live in cities and fertile farm areas in or near river valleys, plains, and coasts. The plateaus in central Asia are largely unsuitable for farming and thus are thinly populated.

Asia accounts for almost a third of the world's land. The continent has a wide range of climate regions, from polar in the north to tropical in the south. Asia is the most mountainous of all the continents. It has the highest point on the earth, Mount Everest, which soars 8,848 meters (29,028 ft) in the Himalayan range. Dozens of Himalayan peaks are higher than any other mountains in the world.

Plate tectonics continuously pushes the mountains higher. As the landmass of India pushes northward into the landmass on the Eurasian plate, parts of the Himalayan range rise at a rate of about 2.5 centimeters (1 in) every five years. Asia contains not only the earth's highest mountains, but also the lowest place on the surface of the land, the shores of the Dead Sea. The land there lies 400 meters (1,312 ft) below sea level.

Australia

In addition to being the smallest continent, Australia (map on page 140) is the flattest and the second driest, after Antarctica. The entire island continent is one country.

A plateau makes up three-fifths of the continent's total area. Rainfall is light on the plateau, and few people have settled there.

ASIA

AREA
44,026,000 square kilometers
(16,998,000 sq mi)

POPULATION
(1988 estimate)
3,071,000,000

HIGHEST POINT
(above sea level)
Mount Everest, China-Nepal
8,848 meters (29,028 ft)

LOWEST POINT
(below sea level)
Dead Sea, Israel-Jordan
-400 meters (-1,312 ft)

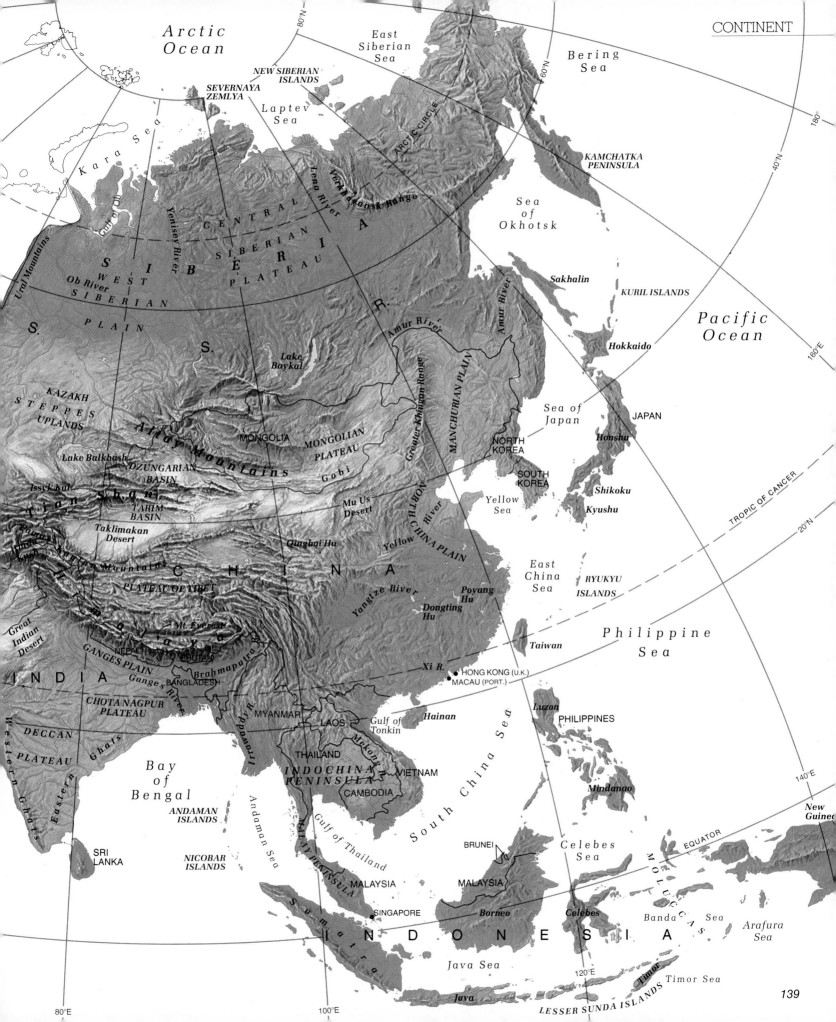

Arctic
Ocean

East
Siberian
Sea

Bering
Sea

**NEW SIBERIAN
ISLANDS**

**SEVERNAYA
ZEMLYA**

Laptev
Sea

80°N

60°N

40°N

180°

Kara Sea

Gulf of Ob

**KAMCHATKA
PENINSULA**

ARCTIC CIRCLE

Lena River

Verkhoyansk Range

CENTRAL

SIBERIAN

PLATEAU

Sea
of
Okhotsk

Ural Mountains

Yenisey River

S I B E R I A

Sakhalin

KURIL ISLANDS

Pacific
Ocean

S I B E R I A

Ob River

WEST

SIBERIAN

PLAIN

*Lake
Baykal*

R.

S.

Amur River

Amur River

Hokkaido

160°E

S.

KAZAKH
STEPPES
UPLANDS

MONGOLIA

MONGOLIAN
PLATEAU

Greater Khingan Range

MANCHURIAN PLAIN

Sea of
Japan

JAPAN

Lake Balkhash

Altay Mountains

Honshu

Issyk Kul

DZUNGARIAN
BASIN

Gobi

NORTH
KOREA

Tian Shan

TARIM
BASIN

Mu Us
Desert

SOUTH
KOREA

Shikoku

TROPIC OF CANCER

20°N

Pamirs

Taklimakan
Desert

Qinghai Hu

Yellow
Sea

Kyushu

Hindu Kush

Kunlun Mountains

C H I N A

YELLOW

NORTH CHINA PLAIN

Yellow River

East
China
Sea

**RYUKYU
ISLANDS**

Great
Indian
Desert

PLATEAU OF TIBET

Himalaya

Yangtze River

Poyang
Hu

Mt. Everest

Dongting
Hu

Taiwan

Philippine
Sea

NEPAL

BHUTAN

GANGES PLAIN

Brahmaputra

Ganges River

BANGLADESH

Xi R.

● HONG KONG (U.K.)
● MACAU (PORT.)

I N D I A

CHOTA NAGPUR
PLATEAU

Irrawaddy R.

MYANMAR

LAOS

Gulf of
Tonkin

Hainan

Luzon

140°E

Western Ghats

DECCAN

PLATEAU

THAILAND

Mekong

VIETNAM

PHILIPPINES

Eastern Ghats

Bay
of
Bengal

Andaman Sea

INDOCHINA
PENINSULA

CAMBODIA

South China Sea

Mindanao

New
Guinea

**ANDAMAN
ISLANDS**

Andaman Sea

Gulf of Thailand

EQUATOR

SRI
LANKA

**NICOBAR
ISLANDS**

MALAY PENINSULA

BRUNEI

Celebes
Sea

MOLUCCAS

MALAYSIA

MALAYSIA

Borneo

Celebes

*Banda
Sea*

*Arafura
Sea*

SINGAPORE

Sumatra

I N D O N E S I A

Java
Sea

Timor

Timor Sea

120°E

Java

LESSER SUNDA ISLANDS

80°E

100°E

139

AUSTRALIA

AREA
7,682,000 square kilometers
(2,966,000 sq mi)

POPULATION
(1988 estimate)
16,500,000

HIGHEST POINT
(above sea level)
Mount Kosciusko, New South Wales
2,228 meters (7,310 ft)

LOWEST POINT
(below sea level)
Lake Eyre, South Australia
-16 meters (-52 ft)

The Great Dividing Range, a long mountain chain, rises near the east coast and extends from northern Queensland through New South Wales and into Victoria. Most of Australia's people live along the coast south and east of the mountains.

Scientists who study animals consider Australia a living laboratory. When the continent began to break away from Antarctica more than 60 million years ago, it carried a cargo of animals with it. Isolated from life on other continents, the animals developed into creatures unique to Australia, such as the koala, the platypus, and the Tasmanian devil.

Antarctica

Located around the South Pole, Antarctica (map on page 141) is the windiest, driest, and iciest place on the earth. Antarctica is larger than either Europe or Australia, but unlike them, it has no permanent population. People who work there are scientific researchers and those who help them. Numerous bases have been established on the continent for studies in fields that include geology, oceanography, and meteorology.

Antarctica is almost completely covered with ice, with a maximum thickness of as

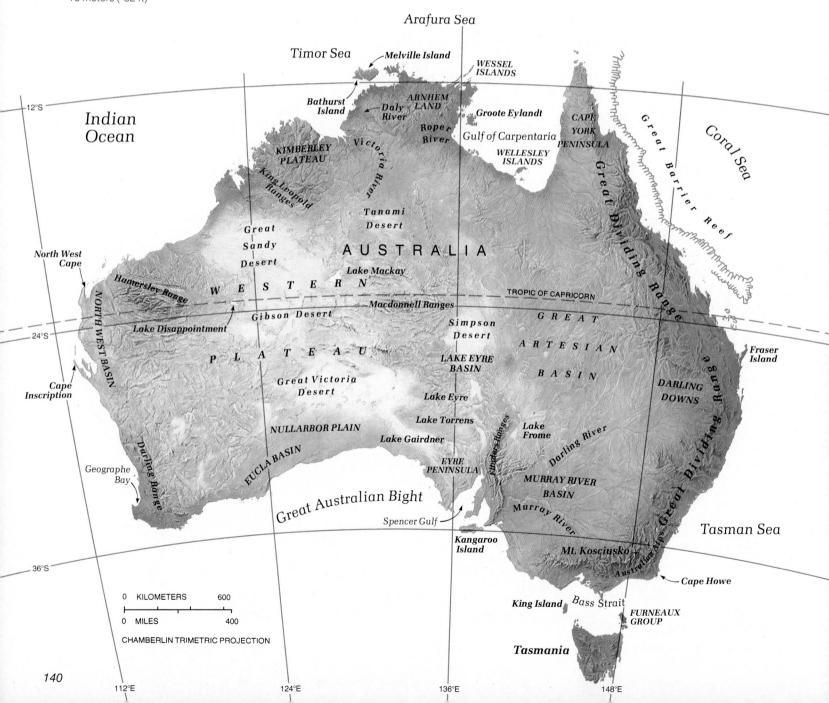

much as 3 kilometers (2 mi). In winter, Antarctica's area may double as pack ice builds up in the ocean around the continent. The climate is much colder than that of the Arctic. Temperatures in Antarctica plunge lower than -73°C (-100°F).

Like other continents, Antarctica has volcanic activity. The most active volcano is Mount Erebus, which is less than 1,400 kilometers (870 mi) from the South Pole. Its frequent eruptions are evidence of hot rock beneath the continent's icebound surface.

Antarctica is not divided into countries. No countries own land on the continent, although several have laid claim to territory there. International cooperation prevails as a result of a multinational treaty negotiated in 1959 and subject to review in 1991. One of the treaty's basic provisions is that the continent be used solely for peaceful purposes.

SEE ALSO ANTARCTIC, CLIMATE, CONTINENTAL DRIFT, CONTINENTAL SHELF, CULTURE, EARTH, GLACIER, ICE AGE, ISLAND, MOUNTAIN, OCEAN, PLAIN, PLATE TECTONICS, PLATEAU, POLAR REGIONS, POPULATION, RIFT VALLEY, RIVER, ROCK, VOLCANO, *and* WEATHERING AND EROSION.

ANTARCTICA

AREA
13,209,000 square kilometers
(5,100,000 sq mi)

HIGHEST POINT
(above sea level)
Vinson Massif, Ellsworth Mountains
5,140 meters (16,864 ft)

LOWEST KNOWN POINT
(below sea level)
Bedrock below ice
in Marie Byrd Land lies at
-2,538 meters (-8,327 ft)

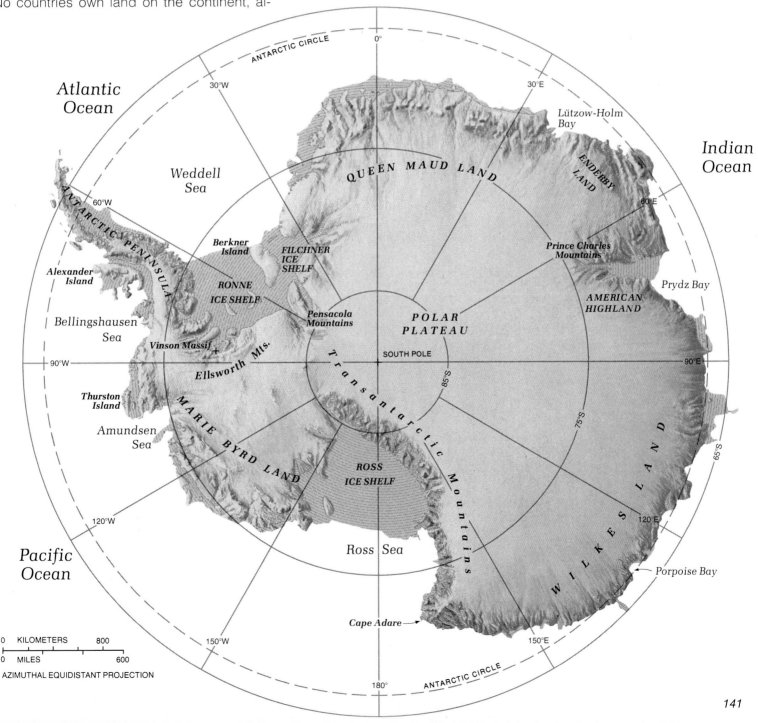

CONTINENTAL DIVIDE

A continental divide is an elevated boundary that separates rivers flowing toward opposite sides of a continent. The river systems on different sides of the divide empty into different parts of the global ocean.

A continental divide usually follows a mountain range or other high ground. In western North America, for example, the Continental Divide roughly follows a 4,800-kilometer (2,983-mi) path along the crest of the Rocky Mountains. The continental divide in South America runs along the Andes.

SEE ALSO DIVIDE, MOUNTAIN, RIVER, *and* WATERSHED.

▼ The Chinese Wall, a series of limestone cliffs high in the Montana wilderness, forms part of western North America's Continental Divide. The divide roughly follows the Rocky Mountains, separating rivers so that they flow toward opposite sides of the continent.

CONTINENTAL DRIFT

In the early 20th century, German scientist Alfred Wegener published a paper explaining his theory that the continental landmasses, far from being immovable, were drifting across the earth. He called this movement continental drift.

Wegener had noticed that the coasts of western Africa and eastern South America looked like the edges of interlocking pieces of a jigsaw puzzle. He was not the first to notice this, but he had a revolutionary explanation for the apparent fit. He was convinced that the two continents were once part of a large landmass that had split apart. He knew that the two areas had many geologic and biologic similarities. Rock formations and plant and animal fossils on one continent closely resembled those on the other.

Wegener believed that South America, Africa, and all the other continents had once been joined in a single supercontinent. The huge landmass is known as Pangaea, which means "all lands" in Greek. Over millions of years Pangaea broke into pieces that moved away from one another, slowly assuming their present positions.

At first, other scientists did not accept Wegener's theory. But throughout the 20th century, evidence has been gathered that supports continental movement. Underwater exploration has revealed that the seafloor is spreading. Along a network of ridges in the ocean, molten rock rises from within the earth and adds new seafloor to the edges of the old. As the seafloor grows wider, the continents on opposite sides of the ridges are carried away from each other.

Scientists now know that the seafloor and the continents rest atop massive slabs of rock called plates. The plates make up the earth's rigid shell, or lithosphere, and they are always moving and interacting in a process called plate tectonics. Over time, tectonic activity changes the earth's surface, rearranging and reshaping its landmasses.

SEE ALSO CONTINENT, CRUST, LITHOSPHERE, PLATE TECTONICS, *and* SEAFLOOR SPREADING.

► *This map shows the current locations of the continents. According to the theory of continental drift, they have not always been in these positions or had these familiar shapes. All the maps on this page show the continents in their present-day shapes.*

TODAY

► *The continents are gradually drifting around the earth. About 120 million years ago, South America and Africa were breaking apart, and North America was moving away from Europe.*

120 MILLION YEARS AGO

► *Geologists speculate that about 240 million years ago and at other times in the past, most of the landmasses were joined in a huge supercontinent.*

240 MILLION YEARS AGO

► *Throughout geologic history, the continents have repeatedly come together, then separated. Approximately 360 million years ago, they were slowly drifting toward one another.*

360 MILLION YEARS AGO

► *Some 480 million years ago, the continental landmasses were spread out across the planet. Most of them were in the Southern Hemisphere. Some, including North America and Australia, straddled the Equator.*

480 MILLION YEARS AGO

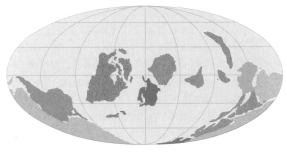

MOLLWEIDE PROJECTION

CONTINENTAL SHELF

A continental shelf is the underwater land that borders a continent. It extends from the shoreline to a drop-off point called the shelf break. From the break, the shelf descends toward the deep-ocean floor in what is called the continental slope.

Continental shelves are actually extensions of the continents. The width of the continental shelves varies. Along parts of California, for example, the continental shelf extends less than a kilometer. But along the northern coast of Siberia, in the Soviet Union, the shelf extends some 1,290 kilometers (800 mi). The average width of a continental shelf is 65 kilometers (40 mi).

Most continental shelves are broad, gently sloping plains covered by relatively shallow water. In some places, deep canyons and channels cut through the shelves. Water depth over the continental shelves averages about 60 meters (200 ft). Sunlight penetrates the shallow waters, and many kinds of plants flourish—from microscopic ones to giant seaweed called kelp. Upwelling ocean currents near shore and runoff from rivers bring nutrients that help plants grow.

Plants make the continental shelves rich feeding grounds for sea creatures. The shelves make up less than 10 percent of the total area of the oceans. Yet they are so fertile that most of the ocean's plants and animals live in their waters.

How Continental Shelves Formed

The continental shelves built up as rivers carried sediment—bits of rock, soil, and gravel—to the edges of the continents and into the ocean. The sediments gradually piled up in layers at the edges of the continents. At the same time, the remains of countless sea plants and animals began piling up. Over many millions of years, these materials formed the continental shelves.

Many continental shelves were once dry land. Some 18,000 years ago, at the peak of the most recent ice age, much of earth's water was frozen into huge masses of ice called glaciers. The sea level dropped, exposing the continental shelves. Scientists believe that at that time the sea level was perhaps 100 meters (330 ft) lower than it is today. They have found the bones and teeth of prehistoric land animals as well as the remains of grasses and seeds on shelves that are now underwater.

When the shelves were above water, rivers and glaciers moved over them and changed their surfaces. Rivers carved out channels. In places, the rivers deposited soil and rock, building up the land. As alpine glaciers moved downhill, they gouged out deep, U-shaped valleys. Now the valleys, filled with seawater, are known as fjords.

In many places, the shelves are smooth plains. In other areas, their edges are cut by enormous underwater canyons. Scientists think the canyons form as sand and mud from the land, moved by powerful ocean currents, cascade down the shelves. These underwater avalanches erode deep channels in the shelves. Some submarine canyons are nearly as deep as the Grand Canyon in Arizona.

SEE ALSO CANYON, COAST, CONTINENT, FJORD, GLACIER, OCEAN, *and* SEA LEVEL.

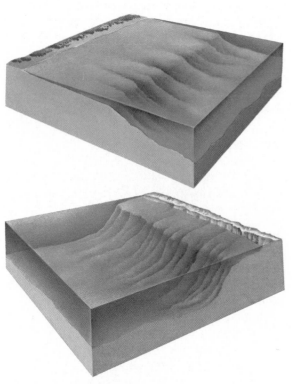

▲ *Continental shelves bordering the earth's large landmasses may be wide and slope gently toward the ocean floor (top). Or the shelves may be narrow, with abrupt drop-offs.*

CORAL REEF

In tropical ocean waters lie coral reefs, some of the world's most beautiful and complex natural formations. They are rocklike, multicolored ridges built by tiny sea animals called corals.

There are many different kinds of corals. The ones that build reefs are known as hard, or stony, corals. Their hard outer skeletons are what make up coral reefs.

Coral reefs grow slowly, usually at the rate of only a few centimeters each year. Some have formed over millions of years and measure hundreds of meters thick. The largest is the Great Barrier Reef off the northeast coast of Australia. It stretches in a broken chain for 2,000 kilometers (1,250 mi).

Coral reefs provide shelter for thousands of kinds of sea animals. As the reefs build up along coastlines or form new islands, they change the face of the earth.

How Coral Reefs Are Formed

A coral animal is known as a polyp. It grows no larger than a human fingernail and is often only the size of a pinhead. It has a simple, tubelike body with tentacles at one end.

Most corals reproduce by budding, a process of forming small buds that develop into new polyps. The polyps build hard, cup-shaped skeletons around their soft bodies. These protect them from enemies and, at the same time, form part of a coral reef.

Sometimes, corals reproduce from eggs. A larva hatches from an egg laid by an adult polyp. The larva drifts through the water until it reaches a spot it can attach itself to, usually part of an existing coral reef. The young polyp absorbs calcium from the water and produces a material called calcium carbonate. This hardens into coral limestone underneath the polyp, cementing it to the spot.

Corals usually live together in large colonies. Side by side, the polyps build their skeletons. As the animals die, more polyps build skeletons on top of theirs.

Different species of corals build formations in different shapes. Some look like branching trees or bushes, others like large domes, fans, or even deer antlers. The bodies

▲ *Always attached to land, fringing reefs grow outward from a coastline, forming a border along its edge. These reefs develop mostly in shallow waters around islands of volcanic origin.*
◄ *Extensive fringing reefs surround Yaroua, one of the islands in the Lau Group in Fiji.*

▲ *A barrier reef forms when an island subsides, separating the reef from the coast. The body of water between the reef and the island is called a lagoon.*
◄ *An aerial view of Fiji's Nairai Island reveals a barrier reef roughly parallel to the coast.*

▲ *Atolls form when a volcano subsides below the surface of the ocean, leaving the coral reef around it standing alone.*
◄ *Waturu, a coral atoll in the Maldive Islands, encircles a calm lagoon.*

of the living polyps are colored in vivid shades of pink, yellow, blue, purple, and green. They make the reef look like a flower garden.

Reef coral colonies grow only in shallow water, often no deeper than 46 meters (150 ft). This is because tiny plants live inside the bodies of the coral polyps. These algae are vital to the corals because they produce chemicals that help the polyps make calcium carbonate. Like other plants, the algae need sunlight to survive, and so the coral polyps will not grow in water deeper than the sunlight can penetrate.

Because the algae that live in coral thrive only in warm waters of approximately 21°C (70°F), coral reefs grow mostly in the ocean waters of the tropics.

In addition to warm water to grow in, the corals need water that is crystal clear. Water laden with silt and other sediments would suffocate the delicate coral polyps.

There are three kinds of coral reefs: fringing reefs, barrier reefs, and atolls.

A fringing reef forms along the edge of a coast and is attached to the land. It extends outward from the shore like a shelf just below the surface of the water.

A barrier reef is separated from the shore by a lagoon. The reef forms a barrier between the land and the open sea. Some barrier reefs consist of chains of smaller reefs separated by narrow waterways.

An atoll is a reef in the open sea that surrounds a lagoon. This kind of reef forms when a ring of coral builds up on the sides of an undersea volcano that has risen above the ocean surface. Weathering and erosion gradually wear away the volcanic peak; the peak also begins to subside, or sink down, into the ocean floor. The volcano subsides at a slow enough rate that the growth of the coral reef keeps pace at the surface, even though it builds up only a few centimeters each year. Over time, parts of the reef appear above the sea as a ring-shaped island or chain of islets.

As fringing and barrier reefs build up along coasts, they slow the fast-moving, powerful waves that crash into shore. The reefs protect the land from weathering and erosion.

When waves finally break down the hard coral of a reef, they pound it into fine sand. Such sand covers many tropical beaches and helps form new land.

▼ *Along Australia's northeast coast, the Great Barrier Reef—the world's largest reef formation—stretches some 2,000 kilometers (1,250 mi).*

Life in a Coral Reef

As it grows, a coral reef provides homes for a vast number of living creatures. Coral reefs are among the richest, most varied communities of life found anywhere in the ocean.

Several hundred kinds of corals grow on some reefs. They form huge stony forests that shelter as many as 3,000 species of other animals. These include tropical fish, turtles, crabs, clams, eels, octopuses, barracudas, sharks, and stingrays.

Many reef creatures, including the coral polyps themselves, are active only at night. During the day, the corals close up inside their skeletons to hide from predators such as starfish. After dark, the corals open and extend tentacles, which are covered with stinging cells. Waving in the water, the tentacles sting and catch plankton, tiny plants and animals that the polyps eat.

Other reef animals survive by blending in with their surroundings. Many tropical reef fish, for example, are brilliantly colored, matching the bright, vivid colors of the coral. These fish often have dark stripes, patches, or spots that help break up the outlines of their shapes, making it more difficult for predators to see the fish among the coral.

Coral Reefs and People

For centuries, coral reefs have supplied people with fish and other seafood. But today, some human activities are harmful to reefs. As people along coasts plow the earth to plant crops or bulldoze it to build homes and roads, they loosen the soil. Rain washes much of it into rivers, which carry it to the ocean. There, the soil forms a layer of sediment that suffocates and buries coral.

Many coastal cities dump sewage and other wastes into the ocean. Such pollution causes certain types of algae to grow so rapidly that they form thick mats that block the sunlight and promote the growth of oxygen-consuming bacteria. This can be fatal to a living coral reef.

Reefs have been harmed by underwater mining and oil drilling. Some have been damaged by explosives used to clear out channels in the seabed for ships to pass through.

People have overfished some reefs, killing tropical fish for sport or collecting them live to sell to aquarium dealers. Other reef creatures have been collected for their shells in such numbers that many are now rare.

To protect coral reefs, some countries have set aside parts of them as marine parks or scientific preserves. Such parks may be found off the Florida Keys, in the Virgin Islands, in American Samoa, and along Australia's Great Barrier Reef.

SEE ALSO ATOLL, ISLAND, LAGOON, OCEAN, VOLCANO, WAVES, *and* WEATHERING AND EROSION.

▲ A scuba diver examines a brain coral in Brewster's Reef near Miami, Florida. This type of coral, with its convoluted ridges and grooves, may grow to a diameter of about 2.5 meters (8 ft).
◄ Many ocean creatures make their homes in coral reefs. Here, small fish called blue chromis swim among branches of Gorgonian corals on a reef in the Caribbean Sea.

CORE

The earth is composed of three main layers: core, mantle, and crust. The solid, inner part of the core is thought to be made up of superhot, iron-rich material. The temperature there may be as high as 6600°C (12,000°F)—even hotter than the sun's surface. The pressure on the inner core is so intense that not even the high temperature can melt the material. The outer part of the core is probably molten iron and nickel. The entire core is about 7,000 kilometers (4,350 mi) in diameter, more than half the earth's diameter. Studies of the earth's interior using seismic tomography, a kind of earth X ray, suggest that the outer boundary of the core may be irregular, with topography like that of the earth's surface.

SEE ALSO EARTH *and* PLATE TECTONICS.

CORIOLIS EFFECT

Winds that blow over the earth do not usually travel directly from high pressure areas to low pressure areas, as you might expect. The actual paths of winds—and of ocean currents, too—are partly a result of the Coriolis effect, named after Gaspard de Coriolis, the 19th-century French mathematician who first explained it.

You could observe the effect on a small scale if you and a friend stood on a rotating merry-go-round and threw a ball back and forth. The ball would appear to curve instead of going straight. Actually, the ball would be traveling in a straight line, but you and your friend would be moving out of its path while it is in the air. A third person standing on the ground near the merry-go-round would be able to confirm that the ball travels a straight line. The same holds true for winds and currents. Because the earth rotates toward the east, winds and currents appear to bend to the right in the Northern Hemisphere and to the left in the Southern Hemisphere.

Fast moving objects such as airplanes and rockets are influenced by the Coriolis effect. Pilots take the effect into account when figuring compass bearings on long flights.

The map below illustrates the Coriolis effect. The solid lines indicate apparent direction; the dashed lines show actual direction.

SEE ALSO ANTICYCLONE, CURRENT, *and* WIND.

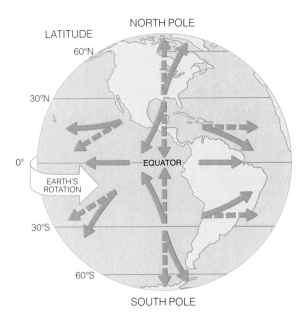

COUNTRY

A country is a recognized territory whose government is the highest legal authority over the land and the people living within its boundaries. Each country has not only distinct boundaries, but also a unique name and flag. All but the smallest countries issue their own money.

The number of countries multiplied rapidly after World War II ended in 1945. Portions of Africa and Asia, colonized by Europeans in the 18th and 19th centuries, were divided into new countries. Although not every country is a member of the United Nations, its roster reflects this change: There were 51 member countries in 1945 and 159 in 1989.

How many countries are there in the world? Some sources say 174; others say 164, or 214. The

► *This general reference map shows countries of the world. A star marks each country's capital, the city where the government is located. Water can separate the parts of a country, as in Indonesia and New Zealand. Some Pacific Ocean countries include more water than land within their boundaries. Countries may exercise control over land outside their boundaries. Denmark, for example, administers the Faroe Islands in the Norwegian Sea. A territory controlled by a country apart from it is called a dependency. The name of the country with which an outlying area is affiliated is given in parentheses.*

numbers vary because experts disagree about the status of some territories. An important yardstick is whether the governments of other countries formally recognize a territory as independent and self-governing. The four black homelands declared independent by South Africa have not been recognized by other countries. Ukraine and Byelorussia, Soviet socialist republics of the U.S.S.R., helped found the United Nations in 1945 and are the only parts of a country given separate representation in that organization.

"State" often has the same meaning as "country," although it is generally a more formal term. The term "nation" is frequently used as a synonym for "country." Nations, however, are groups of people with a common culture and may be divided by political boundaries. Countries are political territories and may contain more than one national group.

SEE ALSO BOUNDARY, GOVERNMENT, INTERNATIONAL ORGANIZATION, NATION, *and* STATE.

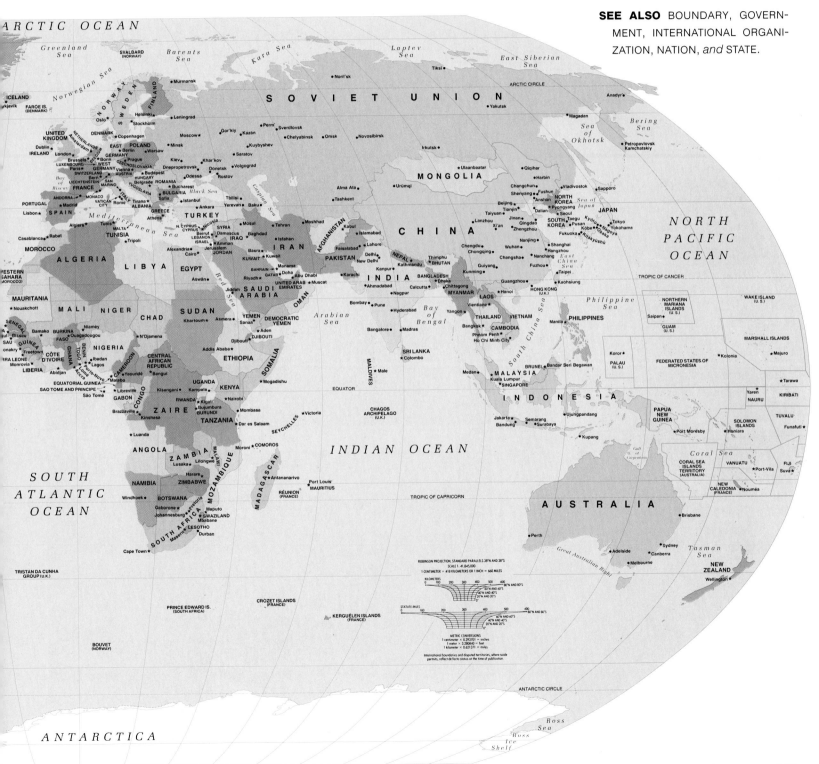

COUNTY

A county is a territorial division and a unit of local government in some countries. The functions of a county vary from country to country. In the United Kingdom, for example, counties are the main political subdivisions of the country, with responsibilities similar to those of the states of the United States. In the U.S., counties are usually the administrative units below the state level. Louisiana has parishes instead of counties, and Alaska has boroughs. The number and size of counties varies from state to state. Texas, with 254, has the most, while Delaware has only 3. Major county responsibilities in the United States include law enforcement, road maintenance, and sometimes public education.

SEE ALSO GOVERNMENT.

CRATER

A crater is a bowl-shaped depression, or hollowed-out area, produced by a volcanic eruption or by the impact of a meteorite.

The earth's moon has many craters. Most were formed when meteorites, bodies of solid matter from space, slammed into the lunar surface millions of years ago. The high-speed impact of a large meteorite compresses a wide area of rock and pulverizes it. Almost immediately after the strike, the rock rebounds. Enormous amounts of shattered material jet upward, leaving behind a wide crater. Most of the material falls around the rim of the newly formed crater.

A few meteorite craters are found on the earth's surface. One of the best known is Meteor Crater, near Winslow, Arizona. The crater, which is 1.3 kilometers (.75 mi) in diameter and 175 meters (575 ft) deep, was formed when a meteorite hit the earth many thousands of years ago. Meteorite craters are also found on some of the solar system's other planets and on their moons.

Volcanic craters occur at the tops of volcanoes and on their sides. Some craters are deep and have steep sides. Others are wide and relatively shallow.

A volcanic crater develops during a major eruption. Material around a volcano's vent is expelled, along with gases and lava from inside the volcano. If the ejected material falls away from the vent, a crater is formed. Over a long period of time, small nonexplosive eruptions may eventually fill a crater with new material. At Mount St. Helens, in Washington State, for example, a large crater formed when a major eruption in 1980 tore off 400 meters (1,300 ft) of the mountaintop. Soon after, smaller eruptions began piling up lava on the crater floor, slowly rebuilding the mountain.

SEE ALSO CALDERA, METEOROID, *and* VOLCANO.

▼ *Small craters pit cinder cones within a much larger crater atop Haleakala, a dormant volcano in Hawaii. The small cones built up long after the huge crater formed. The crater in the lower photograph formed very differently. Thousands of years ago, a meteorite slammed into the earth near Winslow, Arizona, leaving this depression, called Meteor Crater.*

CREVASSE

A crevasse is a deep, wedge-shaped opening in a moving mass of ice called a glacier. Crevasses usually occur in the upper 50 meters (160 ft) of a glacier, where the ice is brittle. Below that, a glacier is less brittle and moves plastically, sliding over uneven surfaces without cracking. But the more inflexible upper portion may split as it moves. Crevasses also occur when different parts of a glacier move at different speeds. When traveling down a valley, for example, a glacier moves faster at its midpoint than at its sides, which scrape against the valley walls. As the sections advance at different speeds, crevasses open in the ice.

Crevasses may stretch across a glacier, run along its length, or even crisscross it. Some crevasses have measured 20 meters (66 ft) wide and 45 meters (148 ft) deep.

SEE ALSO GLACIER, ICE, ICE SHEET, VALLEY, and WEATHERING AND EROSION.

▲ A crevasse halts a hiker trying to cross McBride Glacier in Alaska.
▼ Safety ropes secure a mountaineer as he climbs over a crevasse in the Himalayan range. Crevasses can be dangerous, especially when they lie hidden by a layer of snow.

CRUST

The rocky outermost layer of the earth is called the crust. The continents and the ocean basins are part of the crust. Under the ocean, the crust is about 5 kilometers (3 mi) thick. The average thickness of the continental crust is 35 kilometers (22 mi). The crust is composed largely of two kinds of rock, heavy basalt and lighter-weight granite. Oceanic crust is basalt; the continents are mostly granite. The crust and an underlying layer of brittle rock form the lithosphere, which is broken into huge sections called plates.

SEE ALSO CONTINENT, EARTH, LITHOSPHERE, OCEAN, PLATE TECTONICS, and ROCK.

CULTURE

There are thousands of different cultures in the world, and every human being is born into one. A culture is the entire way of life shared by a group of people. It is learned behavior passed from one generation to the next. Because of this, people within one group have the same language and similar customs, beliefs, ceremonies, and habits. They are accustomed to certain foods, types of housing, and kinds of clothing. A culture is also a plan for living that allows a society to function smoothly and fulfill its needs.

Environmental factors such as climate and terrain play a role in where cultures develop and affect how they grow. The customs of one culture often influence those of another. All cultures change through time. Most have evolved slowly over many centuries. In the modern world, however, the ease of communication and the spread of industry and technology often bring about rapid cultural changes. Today's technology is making cultural isolation a thing of the past.

Cultural geographers divide the world into cultural regions on the basis of similar language, religion, and history, and study how cultures differ from place to place.

SEE ALSO ANTHROPOLOGY, ETHNIC GROUP, LANGUAGE, and RELIGIONS.

CURRENT

A current is a flowing movement of water or air within a larger body of these substances. Water currents flow in rivers and in the ocean. Air currents flow in the atmosphere, the layer of air surrounding the earth.

Moving air is called wind. Air currents are winds that move in a riverlike flow in a certain direction. They range from gentle thermals, rising currents of warm air that help birds soar, to the rapid jet streams that circle the earth high in the atmosphere.

Air currents are caused by the uneven heating of the earth by the sun. As the sun beams down on the earth, it warms some areas, particularly the tropics, more than others. As the earth is heated, it warms the air just above it. The warmed air expands and becomes lighter than the surrounding air. It rises, creating a warm air current. Cooler, heavier air then pushes in to replace the warm air, forming a cooler air current.

A river current is the moving water in a river. The fastest river currents are channel currents, which often move from side to side in a river. Rivers flow from high points to lower ones, and eventually down to the ocean. The force of gravity, which makes the water flow downward, creates river currents.

Ocean currents are great streams of water flowing both near the ocean's surface and far below it. Prevailing winds that blow over parts of the ocean push the water along, creating surface currents. The spin of the earth from west to east causes the moving water to swerve to the right north of the Equator and to the left south of the Equator. This swerving, known as the Coriolis effect, sets surface currents flowing clockwise in circular patterns in the Northern Hemisphere and counterclockwise in the Southern Hemisphere.

Differences in seawater density in different areas also cause ocean currents. The water's density is determined by its temperature and salinity, or saltiness. The colder and saltier the water is, the denser and heavier it is. Cold, dense water tends to sink and flow under warmer, lighter water, creating a current.

SEE ALSO AIR, ATMOSPHERE, CLIMATE, CORIOLIS EFFECT, JET STREAM, OCEAN, RIVER, *and* WIND.

CYCLONE

Cyclones are large weather systems that rotate counterclockwise in the Northern Hemisphere and clockwise in the Southern Hemisphere. Because there is low pressure at the center of cyclones, these systems are also called lows. An anticyclone spins in the opposite direction from a cyclone, has high pressure at its center, and is called a high.

The passage of lows and highs is responsible for the world's constantly changing weather. Lows and highs are nature's agents for mixing cold air from the polar regions with the warm air of the tropics.

Areas of clouds and precipitation are usually associated with cyclones. As air streams come together and rise near the center of a cyclone, or low, the air cools and expands, often resulting in clouds and precipitation. In an anticyclone, or high, air sinks and flows outward, making it difficult for clouds to form. Because of this, highs are associated with clear skies.

Extratropical Cyclones

There are two major types of cyclones: extratropical and tropical. Extratropical cyclones form between about 30 and 75 degrees latitude. An average low of this type lasts from a few days to a couple of weeks, and ranges in size from a few hundred to several thousand kilometers across. Such lows travel at about 30 kilometers per hour (20 mph) in summer and 50 kilometers per hour (30 mph) in winter.

Extratropical cyclones are formed and get their energy from temperature differences between colliding warm and cold air masses. These cyclones arise from small irregularities in the polar front, the meeting place of warm westerly winds and cold easterly winds from the Poles. To the east of the low, southeasterly winds push warm air northward, while cold air moves in from the northwest. This activity produces a wavelike kink in the polar front. In satellite photographs, a developing cyclone shows up as a cloud pattern resembling a huge comma.

The advancing cold air mass, moving faster than the warm air mass, forces the

▲ *Precipitation from a nimbostratus cloud dims distant peaks in Alaska's lofty Brooks Range. Such weather is typical of cyclones, or low pressure systems.*
▶ *Heavy rain drenches railroad cars and a worker in Sacramento, California. Extratropical cyclones bring most precipitation in the mid-latitudes. Precipitation can range from a drizzle or a dusting of snow to a downpour or a blizzard.*

warm air to rise. The kink begins to curl in the way that a wave curls as it enters the shallows. In time, the cold air mass overtakes the warm air mass. The curl closes up on itself, forming a rotating cyclone.

Though most extratropical cyclones develop in the same way, they vary in strength depending on the supply of moisture available, local geographic features, time of year, temperatures, and other factors. The interactions of these factors produce the wide variety of weather brought about by cyclones. Some, for example, merely bring warm, muggy weather without precipitation to an area; others produce thunderstorms and tornadoes.

Cyclones in the Northern Hemisphere

▶ Survivors of the 1985 tropical cyclone that killed 10,000 people in Bangladesh walk past beached boats and a ruined footbridge.

▼ Most hurricanes form in summer and autumn, powered by heat from the ocean at its warmest. In this cutaway view, trade winds (1) govern a storm's course. As the developing storm begins a cyclonic rotation (2), moisture-laden air rises to form spiral cloud bands (3) that drop rain. Air flows toward the center and is whirled upward (4). Wind speed increases, reaching its maximum at the eye wall (5). When rising air reaches the top, it spreads (6), merging with high-altitude air currents. Some air that is now dry is forced down (7), creating an eye, the clear, calm area at the storm's center.

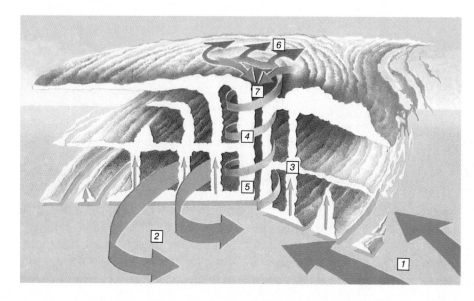

tend to move toward the northeast, but their movement is usually erratic. They may stop and start, speed up and slow down, and even loop around themselves.

One of the major problems in weather forecasting is predicting how cyclones and anticyclones will move across a region. The weather surrounding a low is often predictable, however. The weather to the north and east of the system is usually cool and cloudy, with more or less constant precipitation. To the south, the air is warm, humid, and hazy.

The area west of the cyclone has pleasant weather with cool, clear air.

Tropical Cyclones

Tropical cyclones always form over warm water, which acts as an energy source for these systems. They form exclusively between about 5 and 25 degrees latitude; they rarely develop over the South Atlantic Ocean or the southeastern Pacific Ocean because the water there is too cold. Tropical cyclones arise from turbulence in the intertropical convergence zone (ITCZ), where the trade winds of the Northern and Southern Hemispheres meet. Mild tropical cyclones are also called tropical depressions.

Of the many tropical depressions that form each year, only about 80 have strong enough winds to become tropical storms. Some gather more strength, turning into the destructive storms that people in different parts of the world call hurricanes, typhoons, or cyclones. They can destroy life and damage property and environments.

SEE ALSO ANTICYCLONE, CLIMATE, HURRICANE, OCEAN, PRECIPITATION, TORNADO, WEATHER, and WIND.

DAM

A dam is a structure built across a river to control the flow of water. Reservoirs, or artificial lakes, form behind some dams, and water can be released from them when needed. Since the early days of civilization, people have constructed dams to control rivers and to store water for irrigating farmland. Nearly 5,000 years ago, the first Egyptian pharaoh built a dam to store waters of the Nile River.

As in ancient Egypt, dams today provide water for irrigating farmland in dry weather. Dams store water for industry and home use and help produce hydroelectric power. The lakes behind many dams are used for recreation. Some dams do not store water. During times of heavy rain, they protect downstream areas from floodwaters.

There are several kinds of dams. A gravity dam is made of concrete or earth and rock. Its massive weight holds back the water. A concrete arch dam has a face that curves upstream. The force of the water against the face is transferred to the ends of the dam, bonding the structure to canyon walls. All dams have spillways—openings around or

▲ *A concrete arch 221 meters (726 ft) tall, Hoover Dam spans the Colorado River on the boundary between Arizona and Nevada.*
▼ *Water gushes through a spillway at Itaipú Dam, one of the largest hydroelectric plants in the world. The dam is a joint project of Paraguay and Brazil.*

through the dams that release excess water.

Although dams are useful, death and destruction may result if they collapse. During the 20th century, thousands of lives have been lost as a result of severe flooding caused when dams broke. Dam building is often controversial. Creation of a reservoir behind a dam, for example, may require the flooding of scenic and agricultural lands. Changing the water's natural flow sometimes destroys wildlife habitats.

SEE ALSO ENERGY, HYDROELECTRIC POWER, LAKE, RESERVOIR, *and* RIVER.

DATE LINE

The date line is a boundary running from the North Pole to the South Pole. It roughly follows the 180th meridian, which is halfway around the globe from the prime (0°) meridian. By international agreement, the calendar day begins at the date line. The area immediately west of the line is always a day ahead of the area immediately east of the line.

SEE ALSO LONGITUDE, PRIME MERIDIAN, *and* TIME AND TIME ZONES.

DELTA

A delta is the flat, low-lying plain that sometimes forms at the mouth of a river. The plain is composed of layers of clay, silt, sand, and gravel, known collectively as alluvium or sediment. The alluvium is deposited by a river when it slows down as it flows into a larger body of water such as a lake or the ocean. Sediment is also deposited when a river overflows its banks during floods.

The major types of deltas are arcuate, bird-foot, and estuarine. The arcuate, or fan-shaped delta, is the most familiar. Its outline resembles the triangular symbol for delta, the fourth letter of the Greek alphabet. The ancient Greeks first used the term "delta" to describe the arcuate delta of the Nile in Egypt.

A bird-foot delta has many channels that branch from the river's main channel. The Mississippi Delta, in Louisiana, is perhaps the best example of this kind of delta.

An estuarine delta is an extensive floodplain of salt flats and marshes that is confined by the shape of an estuary. The Rhône Delta in southern France, known as the Camargue, is an estuarine delta.

All deltas form in similar ways. As a river empties into a larger body of water such as a lake, a bay, or the ocean, it slows down. Before the river reaches its mouth, it may be affected by incoming tides, which also slow its current. Because the river moves more and more slowly, it tends to drop its sediment as it nears and flows into the larger body of water. The heavier, coarser material settles first. Smaller debris is carried farther downstream. The finest sediment is deposited beyond the river's mouth. As this alluvium accumulates, new land is formed.

How fast a delta forms depends in part on the amount of sediment the river carries. The Mississippi carries more than 200 million tons of sediment a year past the city of New Orleans into the Gulf of Mexico to form a fast-growing delta. New land may also form rapidly if the action of waves and currents is mild at a river's mouth. The Po River in Italy, for example, flows into the shallow Adriatic Sea. Former ports on the Adriatic have been cut off from the sea because of the quantities of silt the Po River carries to its delta.

Not all rivers have deltas. Although some major rivers, such as the Columbia in North America, carry huge loads of sediment, powerful ocean waves and currents sweep away the material as quickly as it is deposited. Others, such as the St. Lawrence in Canada, do not carry enough sediment to form deltas.

Deltas have always been important to people. Abundant wildlife and edible plants on deltas attracted early people. Branching waterways provided routes for trade and communication. Alluvium deposited by rivers built up fertile soil for crops. Some of the earliest civilizations, such as those of Egypt and Mesopotamia, arose on or near deltas. Today, deltas are among the most heavily populated areas in the world.

SEE ALSO ESTUARY, RIVER, SEDIMENT, *and* SILT.

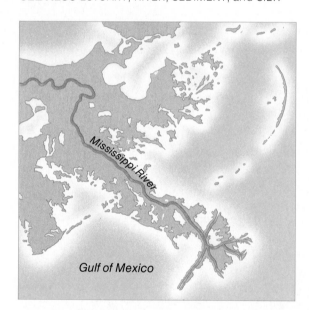

Gulf of Mexico

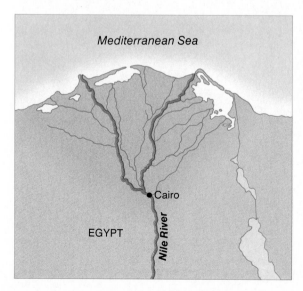

Mediterranean Sea

Cairo

EGYPT

Nile River

▲ *Cowboys called* gardians *round up wild horses in the salt flats of the Camargue, a delta in the south of France. The horses, as well as a variety of birds and other wildlife, thrive in the marshy delta formed by two branches of the Rhône River.*
◄ *Because of the shape of its many branching channels, the Mississippi River Delta is termed a bird-foot delta. The triangular Nile Delta, in Egypt, forms the more familiar arcuate, or fan-shaped, delta.*

DEMOCRACY

Democracy is a form of government in which power is held by the people and is exercised by them directly or through their elected representatives. A country with this form of government is commonly called a democracy. The term comes from the Greek words *dēmos,* people, and *kratos,* rule.

The first known democracy arose about 2,500 years ago in the Greek city-state of Athens. There, adult male citizens would assemble to make laws and to elect officials. A system in which the people make their own laws is called a direct democracy. Some New England towns and Swiss cantons practice direct democracy. Most democracies are representative, not direct. Citizens elect representatives to a legislature that acts on behalf of all the people. The chief executive, usually a president or a prime minister, is chosen by the people or by their representatives. Free elections and protection of citizens' rights are characteristics of a democracy. The United States is one of the world's most enduring democracies. India, with more than 800 million people, is the most populous.

SEE ALSO GOVERNMENT.

◀ *A river picks up sediments as it moves downstream toward its mouth. There, as the river nears a body of tidal or standing water, its current slows. The load of sand, silt, and clay it carries drops to the bottom. These diagrams show the formation of a delta. First, sediments build up along the river's main channel (top). The channel becomes blocked with the material, and the river seeks new branches called distributaries (center). A broad, fertile plain develops, and new land builds up (bottom).*

DENSITY

In geography, density is a measure of the number of people, other life-forms, or things of one kind within a specific area. The population, or arithmetic, density of a country is the average number of people per square kilometer or mile. It is calculated by dividing the number of people in the country by the land area of the country. Since climate, terrain, natural resources, and other factors vary within countries, populations are often unevenly distributed. Demographers, people who study population statistics, have devised ways of taking this into account. For instance, they may assess a country's physiological density—the number of people per square kilometer or mile of land that can be farmed.

SEE ALSO DISTRIBUTION *and* POPULATION.

DESERT

People often use the adjectives "hot," "dry," and "empty" to describe deserts, but these words do not tell the whole story. Although some deserts are very hot, with daytime temperatures as high as 54°C (130°F), other deserts have cold winters or are cold year-round. All deserts are arid, or very dry; rain falls on some of them as rarely as once in 50 years. Even so, flash floods take more lives in deserts than thirst does. And most deserts, far from being empty and lifeless, are home to a variety of plants and animals.

Most experts agree that a desert is an area of land that receives 25 centimeters (10 in) or less of precipitation a year. The amount of evaporation in a desert often greatly exceeds the annual rainfall. In all deserts, there is little water available for plants and animals.

Deserts are found on every continent. Desert and near-desert regions cover more than 49 million square kilometers (19 million sq mi), or about one-third of the earth's land area. About one billion people, one-fifth of the earth's population, live in these regions.

Though the word "desert" may bring to mind a sea of shifting sand, dunes cover only about 10 percent of the world's arid lands. Some deserts are mountainous. Others are dry expanses of rock, sand, or salt flats.

Kinds of Deserts

The world's deserts can be divided into five kinds—subtropical, coastal, rain shadow, interior, and polar—according to the causes of their dryness. Most deserts lie along the Tropic of Cancer, between 15 and 30 degrees north of the Equator, or along the Tropic of Capricorn, between 15 and 30 degrees south of the Equator. These are the subtropical deserts, which are caused by the circulation patterns of air in the earth's atmosphere. Hot, moist air rises near the Equator. As the air rises, it cools and drops its moisture as heavy

► Shade cast by a boulder in Egypt's Western Desert, part of the Sahara, offers relief from the heat of the sun. The highest official temperature ever recorded on the earth occurred in the Sahara: 58°C (136°F), on September 13, 1922.

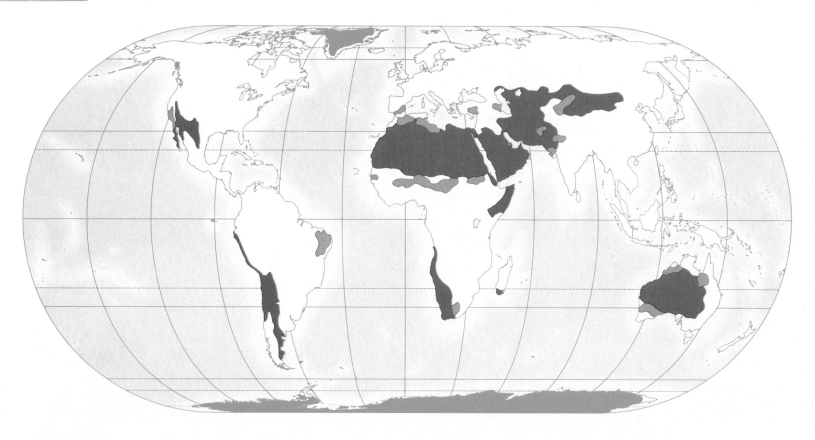

EXPANDING DESERTS

■ Hot Desert

▨ Areas with High Risk of Desertification

▨ Polar Desert

▲ *The world's largest deserts are in Africa, Asia, Australia, and Antarctica. Ever spreading, deserts do not have fixed borders. Through poor land use, people often hasten desertification. Desert and near-desert regions already cover about one-third of the earth's land surface.*

tropical rains. The resulting cooler, drier air moves away from the Equator. As it arrives in the vicinity of the subtropics, near the Tropics of Cancer and Capricorn, the air descends and warms. The descending air hinders the formation of clouds, so that little rain falls on the land below. The world's largest hot desert, the Sahara of North Africa, is a subtropical desert roughly the size of the United States. Other subtropical deserts are the Kalahari Desert in southern Africa and the deserts of Australia.

Coastal deserts are caused largely by cold ocean currents moving along the shoreline. Air blowing toward shore, chilled by contact with the water, produces a layer of fog that is carried onto the land. Though humidity is high, the atmospheric disturbances that normally cause rainfall are not present. A

coastal desert may be almost totally rainless yet often damp with fog. The Atacama Desert of Chile is a coastal desert. Some areas of the Atacama, one of the driest places on the earth, are often covered by fog, but precipitation is barely measurable.

Rain shadow deserts exist near the leeward slopes of some mountain ranges, the slopes facing away from prevailing winds. When moisture-laden air encounters a mountain range, it is forced to rise. The air cools and drops its moisture on the windward slopes, those facing into the wind. When the air moves over the crest and begins to descend the leeward slopes of the range, there is little moisture left. Descending air makes it difficult for clouds and precipitation to form. Rain shadow deserts often exist under these arid conditions. The deserts of Patagonia, in southern Argentina, for example, result in part because of their position near the leeward, or eastern, slopes of the Andes.

Interior deserts, which are found in the heart of Asia and deep within some other continents, exist because no moisture-laden winds reach them. The Gobi, in Central Asia, for example, lies hundreds of kilometers from the ocean. Winds that reach the Gobi have long since lost their moisture.

DESERT FACTS	
DRIEST DESERT:	Atacama Desert, Chile, parts of which receive an annual average of only .05 centimeter (.02 in) of moisture
LARGEST HOT DESERT:	Sahara, North Africa, 9 million square kilometers (3.5 million sq mi)
LARGEST POLAR DESERT:	Antarctica, 13 million square kilometers (5 million sq mi)
ANNUAL RATE OF DESERTIFICATION:	207,000 square kilometers (80,000 sq mi), an area almost equal to that of Kansas

Parts of the Arctic and the Antarctic are classified as deserts. Frozen regions that annually receive less than 25 centimeters (10 in) of precipitation are called polar deserts. They contain great quantities of water, but most of the moisture is locked in ice throughout the year. Thus, as with hot deserts, there is little water available for plants and animals.

The regions that are deserts today were not always so dry and harsh. Between 8000 and 3000 B.C., for example, a much milder, moister climate existed in the Sahara. Archaeological evidence of past settlements, including rock paintings, graves, and hand axes and other tools, is abundant in the middle of a wasteland where today primarily snakes and lizards thrive. Lime and olive trees, oaks, and oleanders once bloomed in the Sahara. Elephants, gazelles, rhinos, giraffes, and people used stream-fed pools and lakes. Similar lush conditions existed about 25,000, 60,000, and 200,000 years ago. Between the moist periods came periods of dryness much like today's. These climatic fluctuations appear to have occurred much earlier in the earth's history as well, perhaps as long as 720 million years ago. Most of today's deserts are about five million years old, which is young in terms of geologic history.

Desert Characteristics

Humidity—water vapor in the air—is near zero in most deserts. Light rains often evaporate in the dry air, never reaching the ground. Rainstorms sometimes come as violent cloudbursts. A cloudburst may bring as much as 25 centimeters (10 in) of rain in an hour.

The humidity is usually so low in deserts that not enough water vapor exists to form clouds. The sun's rays beat down through

▲ *Vast expanses of sand in the Arabian Peninsula's Rub al-Khali desert cover a wealth of oil, as do many other Middle Eastern deserts.*
▼ *Biologists explore an arid valley in Antarctica. Less than a centimeter of precipitation falls annually on the frigid continent, virtually all of which is a polar desert.*

cloudless skies and bake the land. The ground heats the air so much that air rises in waves you can actually see. These shimmering waves confuse the eye, causing travelers to see distorted images called mirages.

Temperature extremes are a characteristic of most deserts. In some deserts, temperatures rise so high that people die because of the heat. At night, these areas cool quickly because they lack the insulation provided by humidity and clouds. Temperatures can drop to 4°C (40°F) or lower; without protection, people may die from exposure.

Winds at speeds of about 100 kilometers per hour (60 mph) or more sweep through some deserts. With little vegetation to block it, the wind can carry sand and dust across continents. Windstorms in the Sahara hurl so much material into the air that African dust sometimes crosses the Atlantic Ocean and tints Florida sunsets yellow.

First-time visitors to deserts are often amazed by the unusual landscapes, which may include star-shaped dunes, towering

▲ Early morning fog from the Atlantic Ocean shrouds the dunes of the Namib, a coastal desert in southern Africa. With fog as its primary source of moisture, the largely uninhabited area has little vegetation.

◄ Life-giving waters from the high Andes flow through Quebrada Camiña, a river valley in Chile, resulting in an oasis in the midst of a desert. Irrigation allows crops to flourish in this oasis, which supports a small population.

bare peaks, flat-topped formations, and smoothly polished canyons. These features differ from those of wetter regions, which are often gently rounded by regular rainfall and softened by lush vegetation.

Water helps carve desert lands. During a sudden storm, water scours the dry, hard-baked land, gathering sand, rocks, and other loose material as it flows. As the muddy water roars downhill, it cuts deep channels, called arroyos or wadis. A thunderstorm, often too far away to be seen or heard, can send a fast-moving torrent of water down a dry arroyo. A flash flood like this can sweep away anything and anyone in its path.

Over time, water and wind wear away softer rock, and sometimes more resistant rock is carved into tablelike formations such as mesas and buttes. At the foot of these ta-blelands, the water drops its burden of gravel, sand, and similar alluvium, forming spreading deposits called alluvial fans. Many deserts have no drainage to the ocean. Rainwater collects in large depressions called basins. The

▲ *Saguaro cactuses in Arizona form a prickly forest in the Sonoran Desert. Cactuses conserve water by storing it in their trunks and branches.*

▼ *A dirt road cuts through an arid landscape in Australia's outback. Desert and near-desert regions make up about two-thirds of Australia.*

▲ *Dark boulders in a desert in Baja California, Mexico, have been worn smooth by wind and sand. Exposed to sandblasting for hundreds of years, some rock surfaces become deeply pitted.*

▶ *Sun-bleached stones lie scattered over the parched sands of northern Chile's Atacama Desert, where in some places rain does not fall for decades at a time.*

shallow lakes that form eventually evaporate, leaving playas, or salt-surfaced lake beds.

Wind is the primary sculptor of a desert's hills of sand, called dunes. Depositing sand behind obstacles such as boulders and shrubs, wind builds dunes that may rise as high as 180 meters (590 ft). Dunes migrate constantly with the wind. They usually shift a few meters a year, but a particularly violent windstorm can move a dune 20 meters (65 ft) in a single day. Dunes may bury everything in their path—rocks, fields, and even towns.

Desert Water

Rain is not the only source of desert water. Underground water sometimes rises to the dry surface, forming springs or seeps. A fertile green area called an oasis may exist near such a water source. About 90 major, inhabited oases dot the Sahara. They are supported by some of the world's largest supplies of underground water. Rivers that begin in distant, wetter regions flow through some deserts. The Colorado River, for example, slices through North America's Sonoran Desert. Lush vegetation, including grasses and trees, grows near these rivers, forming greatly elongated oases. Oases provide people and other animals with food, water, and shelter.

Life in the Desert

Desert plants grow widely spaced, allowing them to obtain as much of the scarce water around them as possible. This spacing gives some arid and semiarid regions a desolate appearance. Desert vegetation is usually xerophytic, from the Greek words meaning "dry" and "plant." The structure of xerophytic plants is adapted in various ways to obtain and conserve water.

Some desert plants, such as cactuses, have shallow, wide-spreading root systems. The plants soak up water quickly after a storm and store it in their cells. Saguaro cactuses expand like accordions to store water in the cells of their trunks and branches. A large saguaro is a living storage tower that can hold hundreds of liters of water.

Other desert plants have very deep roots. The roots of a mesquite tree, for example, can reach water more than 30 meters (100 ft) underground.

Xerophytic plants often have tiny leaves, so little water evaporates from their small surfaces. Cactuses have no leaves at all. They manufacture food in their green stems. Some cactuses and other desert plants have thorns that protect them from grazing animals.

Many desert plants are annuals, which means that they live only one season. Their seeds may lie dormant for years during long dry spells. When rain finally comes, the seeds sprout rapidly. Plants grow, bloom, produce new seeds, and die, often in a short span of time. A soaking rain can change a desert into a wonderland of flowers almost overnight.

Various kinds of insects, reptiles, birds, and mammals have adapted to the desert environment. Some avoid the sun by resting in the scarce shade. Many animals, such as the desert tortoise, escape the heat in cool burrows they dig in the ground. A tortoise's thick shell insulates the animal and reduces water loss. Other creatures, such as the sidewinder rattlesnake and certain kinds of lizards, have

developed ways to lift themselves above the hot sand as they travel—by twisting or leaping, or by moving swiftly on long legs.

Desert animals may travel long distances to find water, or they may get water from the food they eat. The tiny kangaroo rat drinks little or no water. It gets its moisture from the plants, insects, and seeds it eats.

Camels are also efficient water users. The animals do not store water in their humps,

▼ Curving ridges radiate from the center of this star-shaped dune in southern Africa's Namib Desert. Seasonal winds blowing from different directions form star dunes, some of which reach heights of 90 meters (300 ft).

► Strong prevailing winds shape seif dunes like these in Egypt's Western Desert. From the air, seif dunes may appear to be just ripples in the sand, but some grow 90 meters (300 ft) tall and six times as long.

► Fist-size rocks cap the horns of this miniature crescent dune. Also called a lee dune or barchan, a crescent dune forms in regions where the wind direction is almost constant. The horns of the crescent trail downwind as sand blows around the edges as well as over the top of the heap.

as people once believed. Camels store fat. During a shortage of food or water, the animals draw upon this fat. Hydrogen molecules in the fat combine with inhaled oxygen to form water. Camels have adapted in other ways to the desert heat. Their short coats help block the sun's heat. With their broad, thickly padded feet, camels walk easily on shifting sand.

Desert People

Many of the nearly one billion people who live in deserts rely on centuries-old customs to make their lives as comfortable as possible. In the hot, dry Middle East, many people wear long robes of loose cloth. Long-sleeved, full-length, and often white, the robes shield all but the head and hands from the sun. White robes reflect sunlight, and the loose fit allows cooling air to flow across the skin.

Tuareg nomads of the Sahara wrap long cloths loosely around their heads and across part of their faces. This protects them from wind, sand, heat, and cold.

Saharans build houses with thick earthen walls that provide insulation. Though temperatures outside vary greatly from day to night, temperatures inside do not. Tiny, high windows let in only a little light and help keep out dust and sand.

The nomads of Iraq live in tents of loosely woven cloth that blocks the sun but lets cool

▼ *In the Khutse Game Reserve, part of Africa's Kalahari Desert, San (Bushmen) use empty ostrich eggshells to store rainwater after a storm.*

▲ *A young San (Bushman) in Africa's Kalahari Desert uses a stick to extract bitter pulp from a tsama melon. There is little surface water, so this fruit is a major source of liquid.*
▶ *San huddle around a fire to ward off the dawn chill. For centuries, these nomadic people have survived in the desert by hunting and gathering. Today, few follow the nomadic life.*

◀ *In an Algerian desert town, shadows in a narrow passageway provide refuge from the burning sun. These houses have been painted white to reflect the sun's rays.*
▼ *Camels have traditionally been an important means of transport in the deserts of Africa and Asia. Here they carry grain to market in Niger. Camels store fat in their humps. When traveling long distances, the animals draw on the fat as a source of food and water. This allows them to travel many kilometers without becoming dehydrated.*

◀ *A hollow log serves as a drinking trough for these thirsty oxen in Burkina Faso. An earthenware pot attached to a line is lowered into the well, then pulled up hand over hand by the herdsman. This is a common scene in African deserts.*

breezes blow through. The nomads move frequently so that their flocks of sheep and goats will have water and grazing land.

To ease their lives, many people in some dry areas, such as Egypt and parts of California, rely on resources brought from other places—water piped from wetter regions and food trucked in from distant farmlands. Large areas of fertile desert soil are irrigated by water pumped from underground sources or brought by canal or aqueduct from distant rivers or lakes. A variety of crops can thrive in these irrigated oases.

Air transportation and the development of air-conditioning have made the sunny climate of warm-winter deserts more accessible and attractive to residents of colder climate regions, giving rise to resorts such as those in Palm Springs, California. Desert parks, such as Death Valley National Monument, in the southwestern United States, attract thousands of visitors each year.

Spreading Deserts

Human activity often contributes to the growth of desert lands. Over time, unwise farming and herding practices can destroy fragile grasslands at a desert's edge, as is occurring in North Africa's Sahel region. Damaging grasslands through overgrazing and cutting trees for firewood leaves the ground bare. Without vegetation to anchor the soil and to hold water, grasslands may become deserts. This process is known as desertification. Overuse of precious groundwater accelerates desertification. Deserts are now growing by millions of hectares a year.

Many countries are trying to reduce the rate of desertification. Trees and other vegetation are being planted to break the force of the wind and to hold the soil.

In China's Tengger Desert, researchers have developed another way to control wandering dunes. They anchor the drifting sand with a gridlike network of straw fences. Straw is poked partway into the sand, forming a pattern of small squares along the contours of the dunes. The resulting fences break the force of the wind at ground level, stopping dune movement by confining the sand within the squares of the grid.

Improving farming practices and limiting

► *Drifting with the wind, sand dunes slowly engulf a village in Egypt's Western Desert. Villagers have been forced to leave the disappearing oasis to find new homes. Desertification is increasing by millions of hectares annually.*
▼ *Massive sand dunes bury a house and its surrounding walls in Mauritania. Forced to find other shelter, food, and water, the family moved to the capital city of Nouakchott, 160 kilometers (100 mi) away.*

the number of grazing animals also can help slow the desertification of productive land.

Unique Natural Habitats

In literature and in legend, deserts are often described as hostile places to avoid. Today, in an increasingly crowded world, people value the resources in deserts. These regions offer open space, sometimes fertile soil, underground water, oil, and other natural resources. Some countries undertake expensive irrigation projects to make desert lands available for human use. In addition to the resources they offer, deserts are unique and fascinating parts of the natural world.

SEE ALSO AQUIFER, ATMOSPHERE, BUTTE, CANAL, CANYON, CLIMATE, DUNE, EROSION, GROUND WATER, IRRIGATION, OASIS, PLATEAU, POLAR REGIONS, PRECIPITATION, RAIN SHADOW, VEGETATION REGIONS, *and* WEATHERING AND EROSION.

DEVELOPMENT

Development is the process of changing from one condition to another. In an economic sense, the term refers to the change from a simple, or traditional, economy to a modern one. Traditional economies center on survival. The work of producing food, clothing, housing, and household goods is often done by each family. Developing countries, with largely traditional economies, often must rely on the extraction of raw materials to trade for finished goods. Modern economies rely on many different individuals and organizations performing specialized tasks. This results in a great variety of goods and services.

There is a broad range of development, from very traditional economies, such as those of Ethiopia and Bangladesh, to very modern ones, such as those of the United States, Japan, and West Germany. An economy's level of development is often measured by the value of goods and services the country produces. Indicators of a high level of development include mechanized industry, advanced technology, sophisticated systems of transportation and communication, an educated population, and a high life expectancy.

SEE ALSO AGRICULTURE, ECONOMY, INDUSTRY, POPULATION, TECHNOLOGY, TRADE, *and* TRANSPORTATION AND COMMUNICATION.

DEW

Dew is drops of moisture that collect on vegetation, on other objects, and on the ground during a clear, calm night. Water that forms on a glass of iced tea on a warm summer day is also dew. The ground and objects on it radiate heat on a cloudless night. If the ground becomes cool enough, the air immediately above it will also cool and become saturated, and water vapor will condense on the ground. The temperature at which water vapor condenses and dew forms is called the dew point. If the temperature is below freezing, frost forms instead of dew.

SEE ALSO CONDENSATION, FROST, *and* WEATHER.

DIKE

A dike is a wall or other barrier. It can be natural or artificial. A natural dike is a vertical sheet of rock. It forms when molten rock called magma cools as it forces its way toward the surface from deep within the earth. Dikes are often found in areas where volcanoes have been active.

Many natural dikes remain hidden deep underground. Others reach to the surface or are exposed by the forces of weathering and erosion. Natural dikes range in width from a few centimeters to several kilometers. One of the largest dikes known, in Zimbabwe, is 483 kilometers (300 mi) long and 8 kilometers (5 mi) wide.

Artificial dikes are barriers of earth, rock, concrete, or steel, often built to prevent flooding and to channel floodwaters into reservoirs. In the United States, artificial and natural dikes known as levees line the banks of the lower Mississippi River. These levees help protect settlements from floods. Since the 12th century, people in the Netherlands have been building dikes to claim land from the sea. Without these artificial dikes, much of the country would be under water.

SEE ALSO FLOOD, FLOODPLAIN, LEVEE, MAGMA, RIVER, *and* VOLCANO.

▲ *Molten rock cooled underground and formed this long dike in Colorado. Erosion wore away the rock that once covered it. Some dikes in this area are 30 meters (100 ft) high.*
▼ *A highway tops an artificial dike in the Netherlands, where more than 1,930 kilometers (1,199 mi) of dikes hold back the North Sea.*

DIRECTION

To know where places are in relation to one another, we need a system for telling direction. We often give directions in terms of ahead and behind, and left and right. These are sometimes enough when we are telling someone how to get somewhere. But we also need a system of direction by which we can survey the earth and make maps—a system that can be used by everyone everywhere.

One set of directions the world has in common is provided by the rising and setting of the sun. Because the earth rotates from west to east, the sun appears to rise in the east and set in the west.

When you face north, east is to your right, west is to your left, and south is behind you. This always holds true except at the Poles. North, south, east, and west are the four cardinal points. By using them, you can relate any place on the earth to any other place.

SEE ALSO COMPASS, MAPS AND GLOBES, NAVIGATION, *and* POLES.

DISTRIBUTION

Many of the things geographers study are found in some places, but not in others. They occur in certain distributions over the earth's surface. "Distribution" refers to the way something is spread out or arranged over an area. Recognizing distributions on a map is a starting point for many geographic studies. Geographers look for and try to explain any patterns that may appear.

Some distributions—of farmhouses in the countryside, for example—can be seen directly from an airplane. Others, such as the pattern of world population, can be seen only when marked on a map. In some areas there may be many people, in others almost none. To interpret such a map fully, we may need to know the distribution of climate regions, landforms, vegetation, and other related factors. Maps can reveal patterns of geographic data that might not be noticed otherwise.

SEE ALSO MAPS AND GLOBES *and* POPULATION.

DIVIDE

A divide is the elevated boundary between areas that are drained by different river systems. Water flowing on one side of a divide travels in one direction. On the other side, the water flows in a different direction. Divides range in height from a slight rise in the land to the crest of a mountain chain. A divide in northern Belgium, for example, is a low rise on a plain. The Continental Divide in western North America varies from slight rises in the land to the crest of the Rocky Mountains.

SEE ALSO BASIN, CONTINENTAL DIVIDE, RIVER, *and* WATERSHED.

DOME

A dome is a formation or structure that has a curved shape. Some domes develop when magma or forces deep within the earth push up surface rock layers. Lava domes form as lava hardens atop volcanic vents. Another kind of dome is shaped primarily by weathering and erosion, which cause curved sheets of rock to separate from a large rock mass. Salt domes result when rock salt rises through overlying sedimentary rock.

SEE ALSO LAVA, MAGMA, MOUNTAIN, ROCK, VOLCANO, *and* WEATHERING AND EROSION.

DOMESTICATION

Domestication is the process of adapting wild plants and animals for human use. Plant domestication began about 10,000 years ago, marking the beginning of agriculture. About the same time, people began to tame animals such as goats and sheep, mainly for meat, milk, and hides. Later, domesticated animals such as oxen were used for plowing and transportation. Today, people breed plants and animals scientifically to improve them as food sources or for other purposes.

SEE ALSO AGRICULTURE, FOOD, *and* HERDING.

▲ *A Minnesota cornfield withers in drought. During 1976 and 1977, drought affected 60 counties in the state. For some farmers, it was the worst of the century.*
► *Members of the Bella tribe dig for edible water lily roots in a parched riverbed. In this part of Africa, known as the Sahel, rivers commonly run dry after months of little rain. A drought lengthens this period and devastates the land.*

DROUGHT

A drought is a prolonged period of greatly reduced precipitation. Droughts can last a few weeks (in which case they are called dry spells) or months, or even years. They strike at more people than any other natural disaster. In 1877, for example, famine resulting from drought caused more than ten million deaths in China. In the 1970s and again in the 1980s, droughts devastated agriculture in Africa's Sahel region, leading to widespread starvation and the disruption of entire societies. The worst drought in U.S. history added to the economic hardships of the Great Depression of the 1930s. So little rain fell through most of the decade that winds swept away vast quantities of topsoil, turning much of the Great Plains into a dust bowl. Some parts of the country suffered the worst drought in 50 years during the summer of 1988.

The causes of drought are complex. In 1988, for example, fluctuations in ocean temperature, along with the shifting of the jet stream, caused a high pressure system to stall over the United States. This blocked the eastward progression of rain-producing low pressure systems. These same elements can combine to delay or prevent the onset of monsoons, seasonal wind changes that bring rain vital to farming in parts of Asia and Africa.

SEE ALSO AGRICULTURE, CLIMATE, FAMINE, FOOD, MONSOON, PRECIPITATION, *and* WEATHER.

DUNE

A dune is a mound of sand piled up by the wind. Dunes occur along some seashores and in some deserts. Many dunes are small humps; others may reach heights of 180 meters (590 ft). A dune begins to form when windblown sand is deposited in the sheltered area behind an obstacle. The sand pile grows as more grains accumulate. The amount of sand, the kind of land surface it covers, and the direction and force of the wind determine a dune's size and shape. As a dune is forming, it may move. Wind blows sand up and over the top of the mound. The sand slides down the far side of the dune, and the dune creeps forward.

SEE ALSO BEACH, COAST, DESERT, WEATHERING AND EROSION, *and* WIND.

▲ *The wind has piled up a series of huge, curving dunes that tower over a small settlement of herders' tents in the Gobi, a desert in Central Asia.*

DUST

Dust consists of tiny, dry particles of solid matter light enough for the wind to carry. Dust may include bacteria, pollen, smoke, ash, salt crystals from the ocean, and bits of soil and rock. When water condenses on dust particles in the air, raindrops may form. When strong winds sweep across dry, unprotected soil, dust storms occur. In some areas, windblown dust has settled into deposits called loess, which can be many meters deep.

SEE ALSO AIR, LOESS, SOIL, *and* WIND.

► An astronaut aboard Apollo 17 in
1972 photographed the earth from
40,000 kilometers (25,000 mi) out in
space. Blue ocean bathes much of the
planet. Clouds swirl above Antarctica
and parts of Africa and Asia.

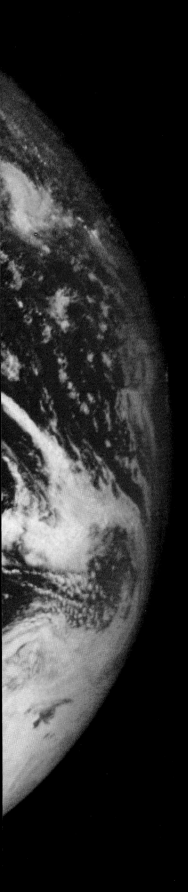

EARTH

One of the smaller members of the sun's family of nine known planets, the earth is a rocky body constantly moving around the sun in a path called an orbit. As far as scientists have been able to determine, our planet is the only one that can support life as we know it.

Earth is the third planet from the sun, after Mercury and Venus. An average distance of about 150 million kilometers (93 million mi) separates our planet from the sun. The earth is spherical in shape but not perfectly round. It has a slightly greater diameter at the Equator than it does from Pole to Pole. The earth measures 12,756 kilometers (7,926 mi) across at the Equator. The equatorial diameter of Jupiter, the largest planet in the solar system, is more than 11 times greater.

Earth and its moon follow a slightly oval-shaped orbit around the sun. Earth's year, the time the planet takes to travel once around the sun, is about $365\frac{1}{4}$ days long. Each journey around the sun, a trip of about 950 million kilometers (590 million mi), is called a revolution. Earth orbits the sun at a speed of 1,800 kilometers (1,120 mi) per minute.

At the same time that it revolves around the sun, the earth turns on its axis. It makes one complete turn, or rotation, in slightly more than 24 hours, causing the periods of light and darkness we call day and night. The part of the earth facing the sun is in daylight; the part facing away from the sun is in darkness. Earth spins from west to east, so the sun appears to rise in the east and set in the west.

Earth's axis of rotation is an invisible line running from Pole to Pole through the center of the planet. The axis is not perpendicular to the earth's orbital plane but is tilted $23\frac{1}{2}$ degrees from the perpendicular. Seasonal climate changes are due in part to the earth's tilt, which causes the periods of daylight and darkness and the angle of the sun's rays to vary at different latitudes throughout the year. Since the earth is always tilted in the same

direction, the latitude at which the sun appears directly overhead at noon changes as the earth orbits the sun. The sun appears to follow a yearly pattern of northward and southward motion in the sky. The direct rays of the sun reach their northernmost latitude at about $23\frac{1}{2}°$N, the Tropic of Cancer, and their southernmost latitude at about $23\frac{1}{2}°$S, the Tropic of Capricorn.

Earth's Beginnings

Scientists believe the earth formed about 4.6 billion years ago. One theory is that the planet began in a swirling cloud of dust and gas. Most of the material in the cloud came together and formed the sun. The rest continued to whirl about the sun, eventually compressing into planets, asteroids, and moons.

The theory suggests that the bombardment by space debris and the pull of gravity contributed to the heating of the earth's interior. As the heat increased, earth's rocky materials began to separate. The lighter ones floated upward and cooled into a thin crust. Heavier elements sank toward the earth's center. Eventually, three main layers formed: the core, the mantle, and the crust.

According to some scientists, as the earth's internal structure developed, gases released from the interior mixed together, forming a steamy atmosphere around the planet. Water vapor condensed, and rain began to fall. Water slowly filled up basins in the

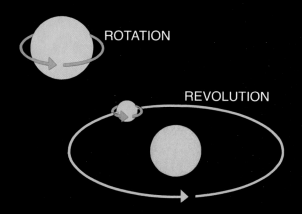

▲ The earth and the other planets in our solar system are in constant motion. Each rotates on an axis and at the same time revolves around the sun. The earth takes about 24 hours to complete one rotation. Each revolution around the sun takes the planet approximately $365\frac{1}{4}$ days.

earth's crust, forming a primitive ocean that covered most of the planet. Today, ocean waters cover nearly three-fourths of the earth.

The Spheres

Earth's physical environment is often described in terms of spheres: the atmosphere, or air; the hydrosphere, or water; and the lithosphere, or the earth's rocky shell. Parts of these three spheres make up the biosphere, which is the area of the earth where life exists.

The blanket of gases enveloping the earth is called the atmosphere. It provides air to breathe. It also acts as a filter, keeping out most ultraviolet radiation while letting the sun's warming rays through to heat the earth and the lower atmosphere. Solar heat is the fuel that makes the atmosphere function as a giant weather machine. The planet's average surface temperature is 15°C (59°F).

The hydrosphere is composed of the earth's water. The ocean, lakes, and streams contain most of the water supply. Water also is found in the ground, in a gaseous form in the air, and locked in ice. The water is constantly recycled. It evaporates from bodies of water, condenses in clouds, and returns to the planet's surface as precipitation.

The lithosphere is the earth's solid shell. The continents and the seafloors are part of the crust, which makes up the top portion of the lithosphere. The brittle upper part of the mantle is also part of the lithosphere.

Earth's Interior

No one has ever ventured below earth's crust. One way geologists have gathered information about what lies below the planet's surface is by studying seismic waves, or vibrations, associated with earthquakes.

When rocks in the crust shift, various kinds of seismic waves move away from the place where the shifting occurred and pass through the entire planet. As they move through materials of varying density, they change speed, arriving at the surface at different times. Scientific instruments record the arrival of the waves. From seismic data, geologists have learned much about the composition and thickness of the earth's layers.

Scientists believe the superhot core of

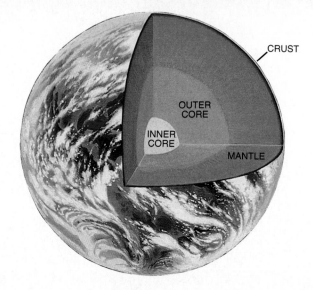

▲ Earth's surface seethes as red-hot lava flows from Etna, a volcano on the Italian island of Sicily. In the distance, lights of the coastal city of Catania glow. More than 200 eruptions have been recorded at Etna. Such volcanic activity is part of the planet's ongoing evolution.

CRUST

OUTER CORE

INNER CORE

MANTLE

indicate that the boundary between the outer part of the core and the mantle is bumpy and irregular, with high peaks and valleys.

Earth's Crust

Earth's crust is the planet's thinnest layer. It forms ocean basins and continents and encloses the other layers the way an eggshell encloses an egg. Under ocean waters, the crust's average thickness is about 5 kilometers (3 mi). The average thickness of continental crust is about 35 kilometers (22 mi).

Over millions of years, the crust has been shaped into a variety of landscapes, from flatlands to towering mountain ranges. Its highest point is Mount Everest, which soars 8,848 meters (29,028 ft) in the Himalaya, a range in Asia. Its deepest point is at the bottom of the Mariana Trench, 10,915 meters (35,810 ft) below the surface of the Pacific Ocean.

If there had never been movement within the earth's crust, weathering and erosion would have made the planet as smooth as a bowling ball. But the earth is an active planet. Its lithosphere is broken into enormous slabs called plates that collide, pull apart, and slide past one another. The interaction of the slabs is called plate tectonics. Along the Mid-Ocean Ridge, where plates pull away from each other, new crust is constantly formed as molten rock wells up from the mantle. At some plate boundaries, old crust subducts, or descends, into the mantle, where it melts. Crust is sometimes thrust up when plates collide, forming mountains. Because of plate tectonics, weathering, and erosion, the earth's surface undergoes slow but constant change.

SEE ALSO ATMOSPHERE, AXIS, BIOSPHERE, CLIMATE, CONTINENT, CORE, CRUST, EARTHQUAKE, HYDROSPHERE, LITHOSPHERE, MANTLE, OCEAN, PLANETS, PLATE TECTONICS, POLES, SEASONS, SEISMOLOGY, SOLAR SYSTEM, VOLCANO, WATER, WEATHER, *and* WEATHERING AND EROSION.

◄ *As this simplified diagram shows, the earth consists of a solid inner core, a liquid outer core, a thick mantle of heavy rock, and an outer layer called the crust.*
► *Earth has two kinds of crust. Oceanic crust is dense and relatively thin. Continental crust is lighter and thicker. The crust and the brittle upper mantle on which it rests form the rigid lithosphere.*

the planet may consist of a solid iron-rich center surrounded by an outer layer of liquid. The solid part is about 2,430 kilometers (1,510 mi) in diameter. The liquid layer around it is about 2,270 kilometers (1,410 mi) thick. A mostly solid mantle of heavy rock surrounds the core. It has a maximum thickness of about 2,900 kilometers (1,800 mi). Recent studies

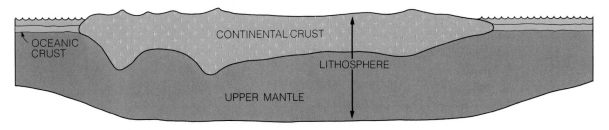

OCEANIC CRUST

CONTINENTAL CRUST

LITHOSPHERE

UPPER MANTLE

EARTHQUAKE

An earthquake is a shaking of the earth caused by the release of energy as rock suddenly breaks or shifts under stress. Most quakes are associated with faults—fractures in the earth's crust along which great masses of rock move. Not all faults are visible at the earth's surface. Movement along a fault is often so gradual that only sensitive scientific instruments can detect it. When the movement of rock under stress is sudden, however, it causes an earthquake. Energy, which was stored in the strained rock, is released as seismic waves, or vibrations. The waves move through the earth, causing a quake.

During a severe earthquake, movement along a fault causes the ground to move forward and backward, heave up and down, or shift from side to side. The surface of the ground may ripple as waves do in water. An earthquake this powerful happens only about every five years or so. But smaller quakes, most so weak that people usually do not notice them, occur every day.

Major earthquakes have dangerous side effects such as landslides and tsunami, seismic sea waves that sweep through the water at speeds of more than 800 kilometers per hour (500 mph). Tsunami can cause great destruction far from the sites of the earthquakes that trigger them.

▲ In 1980, a strong earthquake ruined houses in the Azores, an island group in the Atlantic Ocean. ◄ Walls collapsed in Huaraz, Peru, during one of the most destructive quakes on record in South America. It measured 7.8 on the Richter scale.

▼ *The effects of a 1976 earthquake in Guatemala are visible in Chichicastenango, where poles support the facade of Santo Tomás, a centuries-old church that suffered structural damage.*

makes up the earth's crust may seem hard and immovable, but it is actually somewhat elastic. When pushed or stretched by forces inside the earth, rock stores energy the way a coiled metal spring does. But rock cannot hold the energy forever. The stress builds up until the rock breaks apart or lurches forward along a fault, releasing stored energy.

The seismic waves produced by an earthquake travel rapidly outward in all directions the way ripples move outward when a pebble is dropped into a pond. Seismic waves release large amounts of energy in a short time. There are three kinds of seismic waves. Waves that move the fastest are called primary, or P, waves. Somewhat slower

▼ *A gasoline pump stands among the ruins of El Progreso after the 1976 earthquake in Guatemala, which left more than a million people homeless across the country. The quake caused the collapse of this bridge, a major transportation link. The earthquake occurred when one of the earth's plates, the rigid slabs that make up the earth's rocky shell, lurched suddenly past another.*

Most earthquakes occur along the edges of the earth's major plates. The earth's lithosphere, or shell, is made up of thick slabs of rock called plates. The plates are always moving and interacting in a process called plate tectonics. The huge slabs push against, pull away from, or grind past one another. Thus, fault zones are frequently associated with plate boundaries. The largest earthquake belt is where plates carrying the Pacific Ocean come in contact with plates carrying continents surrounding the Pacific. Another belt runs through the Himalaya, a mountain range in Asia, into the Mediterranean Sea. Earthquakes are also frequent along the Mid-Ocean Ridge, an immense mountain range that runs along the seafloor. Volcanoes occur in these geologically active areas, and earthquakes sometimes precede or accompany volcanic eruptions.

Sometimes earthquakes occur where stress builds up far from plate edges. As a result, the crust at that point is stretched or compressed until it breaks. The rock that

are secondary, or S, waves. The slowest waves are the long, or L, waves, which cause extensive damage as they move along the earth's surface.

All three kinds can be detected and recorded by a sensitive instrument called a seismograph. A seismograph is anchored to the ground. When the earth moves during an earthquake, a device suspended within the seismograph makes tracings on paper or film, producing a pattern of lines called a seismogram. The seismogram reveals how much energy was released during a quake. Scientists called seismologists analyze seismograms to find out where an earthquake began, how long it lasted, and how strong it was.

The place where an earthquake begins is called its focus. The focus may be hundreds of kilometers below the surface or relatively shallow. The point on the surface directly above the focus is called the epicenter.

The Richter scale, named for a seismolo-

gist who developed it during the 1930s and '40s, indicates an earthquake's magnitude— the amount of energy released. Readings of seismic waves determine a quake's position on the scale. The scale has no limits. To date, the smallest quakes have had a Richter reading of about minus 2. The largest ones have been between magnitudes 8 and 9.

Another system, the Modified Mercalli

▲ *A rescue worker searches for survivors in the rubble of a Mexico City building after violent earth tremors in September 1985. More than 200 buildings fell and several thousand people died.*
◄ *A member of the Mexican Red Cross, center, and others from international relief organizations were among the many workers who labored day and night to help the people of Mexico City.*

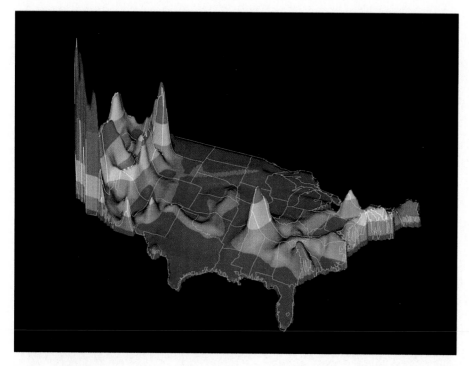

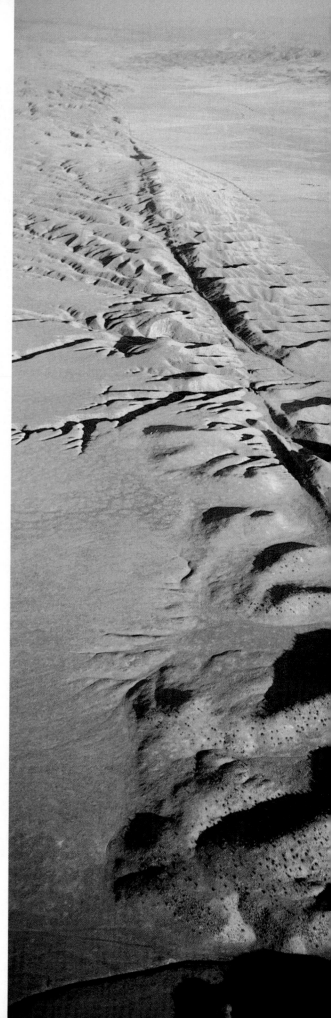

▲ *Using color and relief, this computer-drawn map shows where earthquakes are most likely to occur in the contiguous United States. Relatively low-risk areas are flat and colored dark-green; red peaks highlight high-risk areas. The West can expect more quakes than the East, but the potential for damaging ones is high in both regions.*

scale, measures the intensity of an earthquake—the effect it has on structures, on people, and on the earth's surface. Observations at the site help determine the quake's position on the scale, which uses Roman numerals I to XII. A XII represents the most destructive earthquake.

To monitor earthquakes worldwide, seismologists use a vast network of seismographs and other instruments. Because any sudden shift in the crust, even a small one, causes a quake, the network records nearly one million earthquakes a year. Most are never felt by people. In a small quake, the ground may vibrate as it does when a big truck rumbles by. On average, earthquakes exceeding magnitude 8 on the Richter scale occur about every five years. Called great earthquakes, they can cause widespread destruction.

A great earthquake struck Alaska late on March 27, 1964. The southern Alaska coast

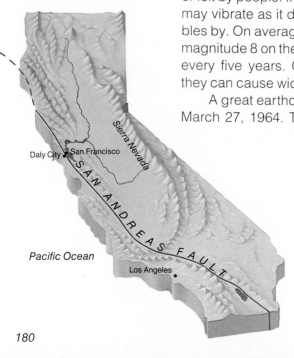

◄ *A sliver of California lies between the Pacific Ocean and the San Andreas Fault, a fracture zone where two of the earth's plates meet. Along this boundary, the great slabs of rock grind slowly past each other.*

◄ The San Andreas Fault slashes through California for more than 1,100 kilometers (700 mi). Movement along the fault and associated fractures causes some 10,000 earthquakes each year, most of them minor.

▼ At Daly City, California, the San Andreas Fault, in the distance, heads into the Pacific Ocean. The fault runs along the coast for several kilometers before slicing through land again north of the San Francisco Peninsula.

► In Los Angeles, artists paint a shattering vision of the future. The mural depicts the aftermath of the next big quake in southern California. While this vision is greatly exaggerated, experts do expect a devastating quake on the San Andreas Fault within the next 30 years.

is a geologically active area. A portion of the Pacific plate is subducting, or sliding, beneath the coast, which is on the North American plate. Many earthquakes are set off in this subduction zone.

In Anchorage and in the surrounding countryside, the ground rolled, and huge cracks opened in the earth. Buildings and roads collapsed, railroad tracks twisted, and landslides thundered into the ocean. The earthquake triggered tsunami in the Gulf of Alaska, and the seismic sea waves surged ashore at many places along the west coast of North America and at several other places around the Pacific. At its epicenter, the great quake measured 8.5 on the Richter scale and X on the Modified Mercalli scale. The main shock was felt in much of Alaska. More than a

◄ *Seeking to learn more about when and why the earth moves, the U.S. Geological Survey has set up sensitive equipment to monitor seismic activity along the San Andreas Fault. A field technician regularly checks the equipment, which gathers data about ground movement.*
▼ *Laser beams fired from a shed hit reflectors on both sides of the San Andreas Fault, helping scientists detect subtle shifts in the ground. Changes in the round-trip travel time of the laser beams signal movement along the fault.*

mographs, there are creepmeters that check for horizontal shifts along faults, tiltmeters that monitor changes in the slope of the land, and satellites that detect changes in the position of the earth's moving plates.

In 1975, Chinese scientists predicted a quake. Warnings were issued just hours before the quake occurred, and millions of people fled from their homes in a province of northeast China. Hundreds died, but experts believe that tens of thousands of people were saved by the warning.

A reliable method of predicting earthquakes may be found someday, but finding a way to prevent earthquakes may be impossible. For the present, experts believe the best protection against earthquakes is to avoid building houses and businesses in high-risk zones along faults. In the many earthquake-prone areas where people already live, protection efforts include reinforcing existing buildings and designing new structures to be earthquake-resistant.

San Francisco lies near the San Andreas Fault, one of the most geologically active places on the North American continent. A devastating earthquake destroyed much of the California city in 1906. If a similar quake occurs, San Franciscans hope to be more prepared. Today, many of the city's buildings are designed to withstand strong quakes without collapsing. Such precautions will not prevent an earthquake, but they may help save lives when the next one strikes.

SEE ALSO CRUST, EARTH, FAULT, LITHOSPHERE, PLATE TECTONICS, RICHTER SCALE, RING OF FIRE, ROCK, SEISMOLOGY, TSUNAMI, *and* VOLCANO.

hundred people were killed, most by tsunami, and thousands were left homeless.

Tragically, great earthquakes often claim many more victims than the one in Alaska did. History tells of quakes claiming hundreds of thousands of lives. About 830,000 died as a result of an earthquake in China in 1556.

Learning to predict earthquakes accurately is the goal of many scientists around the world. Even so, the ability to predict when and where earthquakes will strike remains limited. To study earthquakes, scientists use many sophisticated instruments. In addition to seis-

► *Workers install steel rods to reinforce the walls of a hotel in Los Angeles, California. Such safety measures are being taken to protect many older buildings in earthquake-prone areas of the state. Most new structures are designed to resist earthquakes.*

ECLIPSE

As the planets and their satellites orbit the sun, they cast cone-shaped shadows. When one body casts its shadow on another, the event is called an eclipse.

The moon revolves around the earth, and both bodies orbit together around the sun. As often as three times a year, always at the time of the full moon, the moon and the sun line up with the earth between them. The moon moves briefly through all or part of the earth's shadow, which is large enough to cover the moon. The lunar eclipse can be seen from the earth anywhere the moon has risen.

During a total lunar eclipse (see diagram below), the moon looks gray as it enters the shadow called the penumbra. After about an hour, the earth's deep shadow, or umbra, cuts across the edge of the moon and gradually covers its whole face. The moon is not black during an eclipse but is dimly lit. Light from the sun bends around the earth and reflects off the moon's surface, often making it look coppery red. Though lunar eclipses vary in length, they can last more than six hours. The total eclipse of the moon by the umbra, however, usually lasts less than two hours.

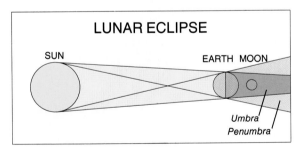

LUNAR ECLIPSE

SUN EARTH MOON

Umbra
Penumbra

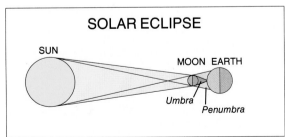

SOLAR ECLIPSE

SUN MOON EARTH

Umbra
Penumbra

▶ *From top to bottom, these photographs capture stages of a total solar eclipse. The moon passes between the earth and the sun, progressively hiding our view of the sun. The halo of light around the sun, called the corona, can be seen only when the sun is totally obscured by the moon (middle). After a few minutes, the sun reappears.*

The sun is about 390 times greater in diameter than the moon, but the two appear to be the same size because the sun is 390 times farther away. Two to five times a year the sun and the earth line up with the moon between them, and for a while the moon's shadow falls on the earth, causing an eclipse of the sun. A total eclipse of the sun (see diagram) is seen as total only along the narrow strip where the moon's deep shadow falls. The diameter of the umbra in a total solar eclipse is usually about 145 kilometers (90 mi). To viewers in the moon's penumbra, the event appears as a partial eclipse. Those outside the moon's shadow see no eclipse at all.

The moon's orbit causes the distance between the earth and the moon to vary. Sometimes when the moon passes between the sun and the earth, it is so far from the earth that the moon's umbra does not reach the planet. The moon does not hide the sun completely, so the moon appears to be a dark spot in the sun's center with a bright ring around it. This is called an annular eclipse.

In ancient times, many people found eclipses frightening. Today, most people understand them as regular and predictable events in the workings of our solar system.

SEE ALSO MOON, ORBIT, SOLAR SYSTEM, *and* SUN.

ECOLOGY

Ecology is a branch of science that examines the interrelationships of living things and their environment, or surroundings. Every living organism depends on living and nonliving things for its survival. Animals eat plants and other animals, and plants absorb energy from the sun and nutrients in the soil that come from decayed plants and animals. Scientists who study such interrelationships are called ecologists. Many ecologists specialize in studying the effects people have on the environment. Research on such subjects as air and water pollution and population growth helps ecologists identify ways to protect the earth and its plant and animal life.

SEE ALSO BIOSPHERE, ECOSYSTEM, ENVIRONMENT, FOOD CHAIN, *and* POLLUTION.

ECONOMY

Everyone needs goods and services: food, housing, clothing, health care, education, and much more. To get what they need or want, people develop arrangements for producing, distributing, and consuming goods and services. A set of such arrangements for a particular group is called its economy. A family or a business may be said to have an economy, but the term is most often applied to regions, countries, or the world. The global economy is huge. In 1987, for example, world trade in goods amounted to 2.4 trillion dollars, and trade in services totaled one trillion dollars.

Money and Prices

Individuals and businesses provide goods and services for their own use or to sell to others. Many people grow food and build houses for themselves. There was often no alternative in the past, and this is still the case in many parts of the world. Even in advanced societies, with countless goods and services to choose from, people may grow their own vegetables, build their own furniture, and repair their own cars. They do so to save money, to enjoy themselves, or to create something better than what they could buy.

▲ A Parisian market offers an array of fruit. The forces of supply and demand help set prices in free markets, from neighborhood stores to stock exchanges. Changes in prices affect economies.
◄ Traders on the New York Stock Exchange buy and sell shares of ownership in companies.

CANADA

ARGENTINA

CAMEROON

FRANCE

◄ Economic activities around the world: In Canada, an Inuit woman hangs caribou skins to dry. An Argentine worker smooths a pipe. Sacks of cacao beans, loaded onto a barge in Cameroon, can be used to make chocolate. A high-speed train races through French farmland.

No one can provide every necessary good and service. An early solution was to trade one good for another, a practice called bartering. But bartering can be impractical. Suppose you wanted to trade some chickens for a horse. How many chickens is a horse worth? What if the horse's owner wants something besides chickens?

A practical solution came with the development of money. Instead of trading chickens for a horse, you could give the horse's owner

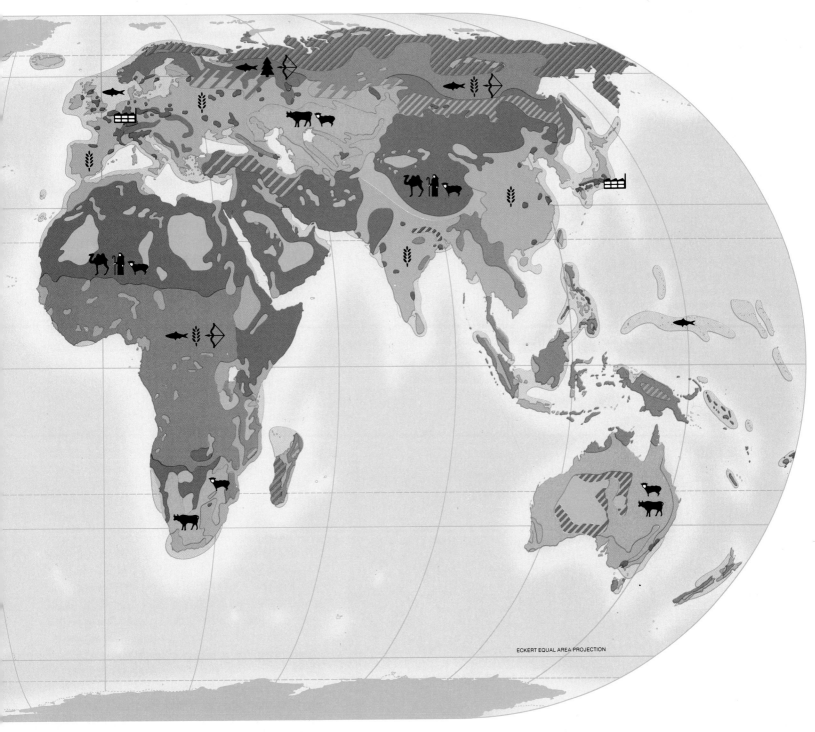

ECKERT EQUAL AREA PROJECTION

a specified amount of money, which he, in turn, could use to buy necessities. What makes money valuable is confidence that another person will accept it as payment for a good or service. Beads and shells have been used as money. Coins made of various metals are an ancient form of money; paper currency, checks, and credit cards are more recent.

The availability of money allows an individual or a business to focus on providing a particular good or service. Many individuals

PREDOMINANT ECONOMIES

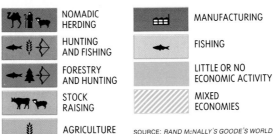

NOMADIC HERDING	MANUFACTURING
HUNTING AND FISHING	FISHING
FORESTRY AND HUNTING	LITTLE OR NO ECONOMIC ACTIVITY
STOCK RAISING	MIXED ECONOMIES
AGRICULTURE	

SOURCE: *RAND McNALLY'S GOODE'S WORLD ATLAS*
COPYRIGHT 1986, R.L. 89-S-129

▲ This map shows the different types of predominant economies in the world. A region's principal economic activity is determined by such factors as climate, natural resources, tradition, and technology. Agriculture is one of the most widespread economic activities.

◄ An Egyptian woman gets water at an oasis in the driest part of the Sahara. Groundwater flowing into this basin is chiefly used to irrigate crops.

many parts of the world, children are trained to do the same work as their parents. A key factor is the producer's evaluation of how much money a particular good or service will earn. Producers estimate how much they can sell, and at what price, to make a profit.

A producer asks several questions before setting a price for a good or a service: How much did it cost to provide? How great is the need for it? What competitors are there? How much money do customers have to spend? The price should be high enough to give the producer a profit, but low enough to attract customers. A piano maker, for example, might want to charge one million dollars, but few would pay this amount. On the other hand, many people might want to buy a hundred-dollar grand piano, but no producer could afford to sell one. At 20 thousand dollars, a piano is costly enough for producers to make a profit and not too expensive for some people to buy. The workings of the market set a price acceptable to both buyer and seller.

Distribution of Goods and Services

Selling is the customary method of distributing goods and services. Individuals use their money to pay for food, a home, utilities, and other goods and services. Companies and governments pay for the supplies and labor needed to do their work. Consumers

sell their skills, such as cooking, operating computers, or welding. Companies develop products or services to sell. The owners of a business hope to sell enough to make more money than it costs to run the business. The additional money, called profit, is the owners' compensation for putting money into the business. Money lent to a business in the hope of earning a profit is called investment.

Several factors determine what goods and services are available. Individuals often try to sell work they like doing or crafts they enjoy making. Custom can be important: In

▲ A Montana farmer plows a field to plant wheat, the world's leading grain crop.
► Cannery workers in Alaska unload live snow crabs from a fishing boat's holding tank. Harvesting the sea is a profitable business in many parts of the world. Food plays a crucial role in many countries' economies, including that of the United States.

(individual, business, or government) have different needs, desires, and incomes.

Few consumers have enough money to buy everything they want. Instead, consumers have to allocate their money among the different possibilities for spending it. As a result, every purchaser faces choices: a new car or a vacation? an expensive new suit or two inexpensive ones? Businesses may have to decide whether they will buy new equipment, use costlier materials, or hire more employees. Governments must decide how to allot funds for defense, administration, and services for the public.

A choice often requires a sacrifice. For example, spending more on computers may leave a business with less money to hire more people. Such a sacrifice is called an opportunity cost. Skipping a vacation may be the opportunity cost of buying a new car.

The deals between buyers and sellers are known collectively as the market. The market may be a small village or farm market, a neighborhood store, or an international financial market or stock exchange in which most buyers and sellers never see each other. Ideally, the market satisfies each producer and consumer. Scottish economist Adam Smith described the market as an ''invisible hand'' guiding the economy to benefit all participants. In his book *The Wealth of Nations*, published in 1776, Smith argued in favor of allowing individuals to pursue their own economic self-interest. He believed this would do more to create wealth and ensure freedom than government control could.

The market sometimes cannot prevent harm to individuals or to whole communities. For example, a factory may benefit producers and consumers, but if it dumps its wastes in a river, it harms the environment. Some people choose to have their governments impose regulations against polluting because they think the market does not adequately deal with the problem. The U.S. government, for example, has required emission controls on cars to limit the release of pollutants.

▼ *Employees count money at a commercial bank in Kinshasa, the capital of Zaire. Paper money is a convenient medium of exchange. Merchants accept it as payment, confident that they can exchange it for goods and services.*

▲ *Steam pours from funnels at a coke processing plant in Zimbabwe. Used in steel production, coke is what remains of coal after it is burned. Mining brings wealth to Zimbabwe. Copper, gold, asbestos, and nickel top the list of minerals mined there.*
▶ *The Santa Fe Railway sorts nearly 136,000 freight cars a month at this huge classification yard in Kansas City, Kansas, a major rail hub. In the late 1980s, trains moved more freight in the U.S. than did trucks, barges, or pipelines.*

▼ *Yugoslavian weavers make carpets by hand. Handmade goods, often costlier than manufactured ones, are prized for their quality.*

Every country's government plays some role in the economy. Governments levy taxes, issue currency, provide for national defense, and perform other functions that affect the economy. The extent to which a government regulates or owns businesses varies greatly. Using the role of the government as a basis, economies are divided into three types: capitalist, socialist, and communist.

In capitalist economies, private citizens own and operate most businesses. Individual producers decide what to sell and how much to charge for it. Consumers select goods and services offered by competing producers. Competition should keep quality high and prices fair, since producers who fail to please their customers will lose business. The United States, Canada, and Japan are examples of countries with largely capitalist economies.

Even in capitalist countries, however, governments are often active in the economy. Food standards, regulations against dishonest advertising, and assistance to the poor are examples of such government activity. The combination of private ownership and public regulation is called a mixed economy.

Socialist economies, such as those of Sweden, Norway, and Israel, feature government ownership of some industries. Western European governments took over, or nationalized, steel mills, railroads, and other industries after World War II ended in 1945. Some governments, notably those of the United Kingdom, France, and West Germany, have

▲ *Laborers in India carry baskets of sand to be used in construction. Industry in developing countries often relies on armies of workers to do burdensome tasks performed by machines in developed countries.*
◄ *Practicing welding, a Jordanian student acquires technical skills. Worker training gets high priority in developing countries attempting to industrialize.*

recently sold industries back to private owners and moved away from socialism.

In a communist economy, the government owns almost all property and businesses. State planners determine production priorities and set prices. Individuals can use their wages to buy goods and services, but their choices are often very limited. Some communist countries, including China and the Soviet Union, have begun experimenting with free enterprise.

GNP and GNP Per Capita

The total value of the goods and services a country produces in a year is called the gross national product (GNP). Each country's currency data is converted into U.S. dollars to make comparisons possible. For example, in 1987 France's GNP was 715 billion dollars and Ethiopia's was 5.5 billion.

Dividing the GNP of a country by its population yields a figure called GNP per capita. It reflects the value of the economic activity of a country and the income of its residents. In 1987, GNP per capita was 12,860 dollars in France and 120 dollars in Ethiopia.

National economies are often divided into two groups: developed and developing.

◄ Solar energy powers a telephone in the desert. Communication between buyers and sellers permits markets to exist almost anywhere.

▲ Tiny computer chips with giant memories enable the electronics industry to produce high-technology goods.
▼ Sleek, efficient, speedy, and profitable, Japanese bullet trains symbolize that country's economic success in rail transportation.

Japan, the United States, and other developed countries have high GNPs. Most of their inhabitants enjoy a high standard of living, with a wide variety of goods and services.

Developing economies are prevalent in countries where most people have a low standard of living, with few goods and services. Such countries contain roughly three-fourths of the world's population. Infant mortality is high in developing countries. But as these countries progress economically and living conditions improve, more infants survive the first year of life. For many years, developing

▲ *Yarns of many colors invite buyers at an open-air market in Ecuador, where the manufacture of textiles is important to the developing economy.*

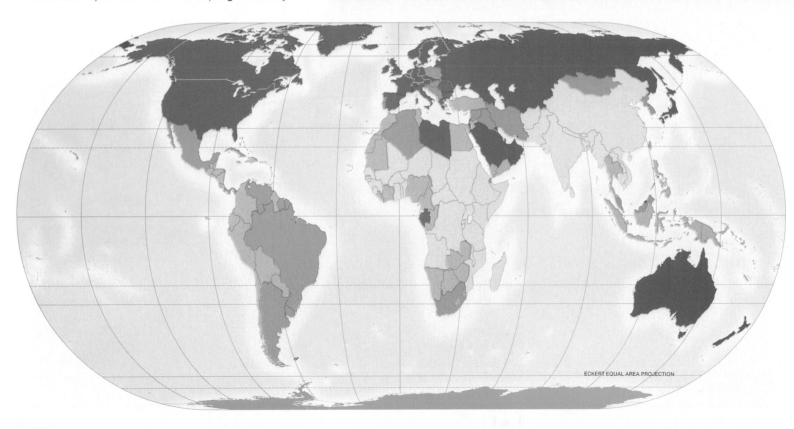

ECKERT EQUAL AREA PROJECTION

▲ Selling in bulk lets this discount warehouse in Anchorage, Alaska, offer goods at low prices.
◄ This map shows GNP per capita in countries around the world. GNP per capita is the part of the gross national product each person would have if GNP were divided equally. It helps measure a country's well-being.

GNP PER CAPITA
(Figures are in U. S. dollars)

■	$7,000 and over
■	$3,200-$6,999
■	$1,600-$3,199
■	$400-$1,599
■	$0-$399
■	No data available

SOURCES: *WORLD BANK ATLAS, 1987, AND HANDBOOK OF ECONOMIC STATISTICS, 1987.*

countries had a comparative advantage only in agricultural products such as sugar and coffee and in the sale of raw materials. Today, many of them produce and export manufactured goods as well. Some developing countries are increasingly able to make and sell cars, electronic equipment, and other goods competitively in the world economy.

SEE ALSO CAPITALISM, COMMUNISM, DEVELOPMENT, GOVERNMENT, INDUSTRY, POPULATION, SOCIALISM, TRADE, *and* TRANSPORTATION AND COMMUNICATION.

ECOSYSTEM

"Ecosystem," a contraction of "ecological system," is a term used in classifying the earth's natural communities according to how living and nonliving things and their environment function as a unit. Some people think of the biosphere, the portion of the earth occupied by the various forms of life, as one huge ecosystem. More often, however, the biosphere is subdivided into two kinds of ecosystems: aquatic (water) and terrestrial (land). A lake is an aquatic ecosystem consisting of water, rocks, plants, fish, and other living and nonliving things. A forest is a terrestrial ecosystem. When scientists study a forest ecosystem, they may examine the interrelationships of its soil, climate, water, plants, insects, birds, and other animals.

In an ecosystem, the primary function is the flow of energy and the cycling of nutrients. This takes place in food chains and usually requires three kinds of organisms: producers, consumers, and decomposers. Plants are producers. They store the sun's energy and convert it into food through a process called photosynthesis. Animals feed on plants and other animals; they are consumers. Bacteria and other small organisms that break down dead animals and plants are decomposers. Nutrients released from the decomposed material are absorbed by plants. The continuous flow of energy and food in an ecosystem allows it to sustain itself.

SEE ALSO BIOME, BIOSPHERE, ENVIRONMENT, FOOD CHAIN, *and* HABITAT.

ELEVATION

Elevation, like altitude, is distance above sea level. Altitude refers to height in the atmosphere, and elevation refers to height on the surface of the earth.

Elevations are usually measured in meters or feet. They can be shown on maps by contour lines, which connect points with the same elevation; by bands of color; or by numbers giving the exact elevations of particular points on the earth's surface.

Elevation influences climate, and where and how people live. Most of the world's people live on coastal plains at elevations of 150 meters (500 ft) or less. In Tibet, a region in central Asia, people live at elevations as great as 5,334 meters (17,500 ft). Above this elevation the climate becomes too cold for growing crops, and the air no longer contains enough oxygen to sustain human life.

SEE ALSO ALTITUDE, GROWING SEASON, SEA LEVEL, *and* TOPOGRAPHY.

EMIGRATION

Emigration is the movement of people from one country for the purpose of settlement in another. Reasons for emigration include lack of job opportunities and religious or political persecution. Sometimes people flee their native countries to escape famine, war, or natural disasters.

Large-scale emigration may help relieve problems of overpopulation, but it can also change the population structure of a country. Young adults and people with higher education are usually the most likely to seek opportunities in other lands. This drain often affects the most productive parts of a country's work force. Some countries restrict emigration.

In the 19th century, crop failures, population pressures, and religious discontent encouraged many Europeans to emigrate. The U.S. had the most newcomers; more than four million arrived between 1840 and 1860.

SEE ALSO IMMIGRATION, MIGRATION, *and* POPULATION.

ENERGY

Energy provides the power to make things happen. It moves children's muscles as they pedal bicycles. It heats and lights houses, offices, and factories. It powers tractors and subway systems. It runs movie projectors, office equipment, and industrial machinery. Energy lifts rockets into space and cooks dinners on the earth.

Scientifically defined, energy is the capacity to do work. The energy stored in food provides the fuel that the human body requires to live. Energy stored in coal, oil, and natural gas heats and cools homes and workplaces. The energy released when fuel is burned powers engines in automobiles and other vehicles. People enjoy the many benefits that the earth's energy resources provide. Often, however, they fail to consider that some of the resources used to provide these benefits are dwindling and cannot be renewed. Scientists have made significant progress with new technologies that help us harness alternative sources of energy, such as the wind and the sun. All of us, however, can help make nonrenewable resources last longer by using and demanding products that are more energy-efficient.

▲ *Men cut slabs of peat from a bog in Scotland. Long used to warm homes in some countries, peat consists chiefly of decaying plant matter.*
► *For centuries, people have harnessed the wind's energy. Moving air currents, still a source of energy today, are captured here by a wind turbine on the island of Hawaii.*

Where Energy Begins

When a man swings an ax to chop wood, he uses muscle energy. When he burns the logs he chopped, he converts energy stored in the wood into thermal energy, or heat. Where does the energy stored in wood come from? It begins in the sun.

Through photosynthesis, trees and other plants use the sun's energy to convert carbon dioxide and water into oxygen and the food they need to grow. When people burn wood from the trees, they are recovering energy that came from millions of kilometers away, in the superhot core of the sun.

The sun is the original source of most of the energy used on the earth. Solar energy results from a process called nuclear fusion. In the sun's core, particles of hydrogen gas constantly collide. When they collide, they fuse, or join together. The fusion, which occurs at extremely high temperatures, releases enormous amounts of energy in the form of heat and light. The heat and light radiate throughout our solar system.

Heat from the sun warms the atmosphere—the layer of air surrounding the earth. The heat causes movement in the atmosphere in the form of wind. The energy in wind can be harnessed to power sailboats and to turn windmills.

▲ *A power shovel scoops up coal at a Wyoming strip mine. Demand for coal is increasing as known reserves of oil and natural gas decrease.*

▼ *Production platforms tower above the North Sea near Scotland. Pipes extend down from the platforms to reach oil beneath the seafloor.*

WORLD ENERGY SOURCES, 1985

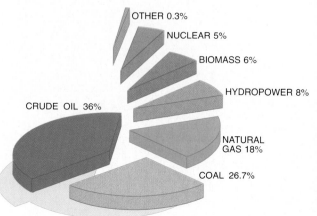

OTHER 0.3%

NUCLEAR 5%

BIOMASS 6%

HYDROPOWER 8%

CRUDE OIL 36%

NATURAL GAS 18%

COAL 26.7%

▲ *Crude oil and coal continue to be the energy sources used most often in the world today.*
▶ *Oil fields, such as this one in Oman, often flare off vast amounts of natural gas when pumping oil. Many of the world's known reserves of crude oil lie beneath the deserts of the Middle East.*

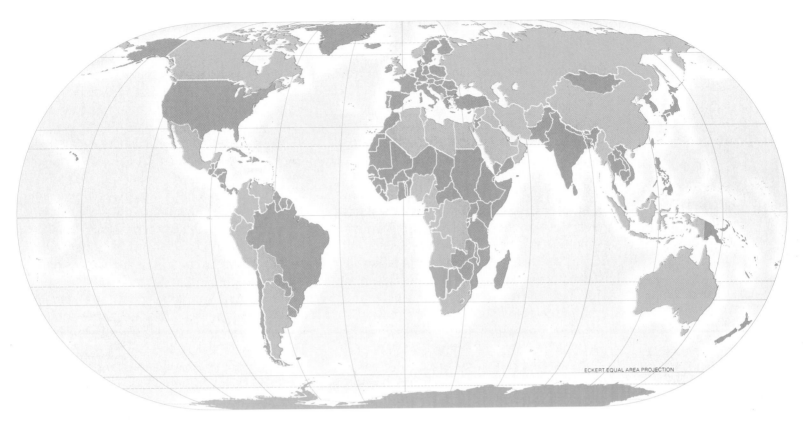

ECKERT EQUAL AREA PROJECTION

The sun's heat evaporates water, which becomes precipitation that in turn fills rivers. Many dams on rivers harness the water's energy and convert it into electricity.

Fossil fuels such as oil, coal, and natural gas also began with energy from the sun. Existing oil and gas formed from the remains of ancient plants and animals that were deposited with sediments on the seafloor. Over time, pressure from overlying sediments helped convert the remains into oil and gas and harden surrounding materials into rock. When burned, these fuels give up their energy as heat. If your house is heated with oil, you are retrieving energy that was stored in plants and animals millions of years ago. The sun's energy is not lost; it just changes form.

For most of human history, people have depended on wood and other resources such as wind and running water to retrieve the energy they need. More than one billion people in developing countries still depend directly on nature for their energy requirements and burn fuels such as animal dung and wood. Fossil fuels, which provide more than three-fourths of the energy consumed worldwide each year, have allowed many people to live comfortably and to produce goods faster and more efficiently.

Although fossil fuels have provided affordable energy for many years, we are now beginning to run out of them. Known reserves of oil and natural gas are dwindling. Though coal will still be available for several centuries, environmentalists are concerned about global climate changes that may result from the amounts of carbon dioxide released when coal is burned and about the land that is damaged when coal is mined. Fossil fuels are considered nonrenewable resources because they cannot be replenished before current supplies run out.

Scientists are experimenting with ways to make the supply of nonrenewable resources last longer. Two products that could help supplement supplies of gasoline, which is made from oil, are ethanol and liquefied coal. Corn, when converted into ethanol, can be blended with gasoline to make gasohol for cars and other machines with internal combustion engines. If economical methods for liquefying coal are discovered, coal also could help fulfill transportation energy needs formerly met primarily by gasoline.

Our ability to conserve fossil fuels and to harness other sources of energy, such as wind and water, will help determine whether we have enough energy for the future.

PRODUCTION AND CONSUMPTION OF COMMERCIAL ENERGY IN 1984

■	CONSUMPTION EXCEEDED PRODUCTION
▨	PRODUCTION EXCEEDED CONSUMPTION
■	DATA NOT AVAILABLE

▲ The map above shows which countries used more commercial energy than they produced and which countries produced more energy than they consumed in 1984. Commercial energy, the energy produced for sale rather than for direct use, comes primarily from nonrenewable resources such as oil and natural gas. By emphasizing energy efficiency, countries that use more energy supplies than they produce could achieve a closer balance between consumption and production.

Solar Energy

Energy coming directly from the sun is a tremendous resource. In less than an hour, enough solar energy reaches the earth to fill everyone's energy needs for a year. The problem lies in trying to collect and store the seemingly limitless supply economically.

If you have ever felt hot water running out of a hose that was left out in the sun on a summer day, you have felt the effect of solar energy at work. Using a similar process, scientists have developed solar energy systems for home and business use. In one system, the sun heats fluid running through pipes in a rooftop collector. As the heated fluid circulates throughout a structure, it radiates heat that warms the rooms. The solar-heated fluid can also transfer its heat to water, which can be stored until the hot water is needed.

Scientists are studying ways to convert solar power into enough electricity to supply a city's needs. One method is the "solar farm," such as Solar One in Barstow, California. Rows of special mirrors, called heliostats, direct the sun's heat and light to water in a small boiler atop a tower. The resulting steam powers a machine called a turbine, which in turn drives a generator to produce electricity.

A newer and more efficient solar technology is the one employed by a solar plant based in the Mojave Desert in California. Troughs of curved mirrors, guided by computers, use the sun's heat to warm synthetic oil to 390°C (735°F). The oil, which passes through vacuum-sealed tubes attached to the mirrors, heats water to produce steam that turns an electric turbine.

In space, satellites and space stations get their energy from solar cells that convert sunlight directly into electricity. These cells, called photovoltaics, are used on the earth, too. The cost of producing photovoltaics is declining as the technology is refined. In

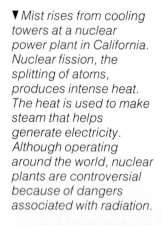

▼ *Mist rises from cooling towers at a nuclear power plant in California. Nuclear fission, the splitting of atoms, produces intense heat. The heat is used to make steam that helps generate electricity. Although operating around the world, nuclear plants are controversial because of dangers associated with radiation.*

► *Water flowing down a stream in Syria provides the energy to propel a primitive waterwheel. The wheel lifts water to an aqueduct that carries it away to be used for drinking and irrigation. Many modern hydroelectric plants provide people with drinking and irrigation water as well as electricity.*

developing countries, photovoltaics provide energy to a growing number of individual users. Although the use of the cells in developed countries is also increasing, it is still less expensive to bring electricity into homes and offices from a central location that uses conventional energy sources. However, many experts believe photovoltaics will be used increasingly to help supply electricity to people either directly or through power companies. The sun may one day provide large supplies of clean, affordable energy that can replace limited and polluting fossil fuels.

Wind Energy

Long ago, people learned to harness wind to move sailing ships. By about 3000 B.C., for example, the Egyptians were sailing ships upon the ocean. By 200 B.C., wind power was being used to turn the blades of windmills. Through a system of gears, the movement of the blades activated the stones that ground grain. Windmills were once widely used to pump water on U.S. farms.

Today, wind turbines modeled after early windmills are coming into use in parts of the world where winds are fairly constant. In some places, wind turbines can generate power efficiently enough to compete with other energy systems. A massive wind turbine in Hawaii, for example, supplies 1,200 homes with electricity.

At present, average annual wind speeds of 21 kilometers per hour (13 mph) are needed to operate wind turbines economically. Winds of this power are available in many parts of the world. As the technology improves, turbines may be able to operate efficiently at lower wind speeds. "Wind farms," where hundreds, or even thousands, of wind turbines are clustered together, contribute significantly to energy supplies in many areas. For example, in San Francisco, California, 15 percent of the city's electricity needs in 1988 were met by wind-generated electricity.

Geothermal and Water Energy

Geothermal energy is heat energy generated within the earth. Scientists believe the heat is produced by pressure and by atoms as they decay, or break apart. The intense interior heat causes some rocks to melt and form magma. In some places, magma lies fairly close to the surface. Layers of rock near magma become very hot. In areas where cracks have formed in the crust, water seeps down to the hot rock layers and is heated there by geothermal energy. Then the hot

▲ *Energy in flowing water is tapped to generate power at the Bonneville Dam in Oregon. Water from the Columbia River turns turbines that produce more than a million kilowatts of electricity each year.*

▼ The sun glitters from a circle of mirrors at Solar One, an experimental solar power plant in Barstow, California. The mirrors, called heliostats, rotate to reflect sunlight onto a black receiver that tops the tower in the center. The concentrated solar energy changes water within the receiver into superhot steam. The steam can be stored for future use or used immediately to drive generators that produce electricity.

water rises through the cracks toward the surface, where heat is usually released quietly through hot springs. In hot springs called geysers, intense pressure causes steam to force heated groundwater to the surface in powerful eruptions. For years, people who live near hot springs have used geothermal energy for bathing, home heating, and cooking.

In Iceland, a country that lies along the volcanically active Mid-Atlantic Ridge, the city of Reykjavik is almost entirely heated by a system that uses geothermal energy. Geothermal wells capture water heated by the hot rocks inside the earth and pipes circulate it throughout the city. Home heating in the city costs less and pollutes far less than it would if Icelanders used oil or coal. Reykjavik is known as one of the world's cleanest cities.

Geothermal power plants are located in areas where hot springs are found or where heated groundwater can be reached by tapping into natural cracks in the earth's crust.

New technology, however, developed by scientists at Los Alamos National Laboratory in New Mexico, can recover the heat energy in dry hot rocks. Water is pumped through wells drilled into the hot rocks, and the heated water is used to generate electricity. Such developments may make geothermal energy more available in the future.

Moving water can be used as an energy source, as millers have known for centuries. Water mills use moving water to turn wheels, just as windmills use wind. A hydroelectric power plant works on the same principle. Water, stored behind a dam, is released to flow through machines called turbines that drive generators to produce electricity. An increasing amount of the energy consumed worldwide is produced by hydroelectric plants.

Scientists are exploring ways to use the tides, a form of gravitational energy, to generate electricity. In France, a dam was built across an estuary, where a river empties into

the ocean. The dam has turbines that turn in either direction to take advantage of tides coming in and going out. Water turns the blades of the turbines, enabling the power plant to produce electricity.

Scientists in the United Kingdom are developing ways to harness the energy in ocean waves. If wave power can be tapped, seas around the British Isles could one day produce enough electricity to supply a large part of the area's energy needs.

Nuclear Energy

In the late 1930s, scientists discovered how to split the nucleus of an atom. The process, called nuclear fission, releases the energy that bound the nucleus. They found that as one atom of the radioactive element uranium splits, it triggers others to split. This is called a chain reaction. An uncontrolled chain reaction can cause an explosion, as with an atomic bomb. A controlled chain reaction within a nuclear reactor produces tremendous amounts of heat energy in a fraction of a second. The energy heats water, creating steam that turns turbine generators to produce electricity.

Nuclear energy is perhaps one of the most controversial energy sources in use today. Radioactive waste from the fission process can destroy cells in the bodies of people and other animals and contaminate plants and water. Radioactive waste must be stored safely for many thousands of years, until it is no longer dangerous. Although a nuclear plant cannot explode like a bomb, explosions associated with a sudden increase in generated power can occur unexpectedly in some nuclear plants, allowing the release of radioactive material into the air. This occurred in 1986 at Chernobyl, in the Soviet Union, causing illness and death and contaminating crops.

Nuclear physicists are working to improve the safety of nuclear reactors. They are also exploring a safer method of gathering the power locked in atoms. This process, called nuclear fusion, mimics the way energy is released in the sun. In fusion, the nuclei of hydrogen atoms fuse, or join, to form another element. In the process of fusing, they release energy. Fusion at high temperatures has been achieved only briefly in laboratories.

▲ Vacationing factory workers soak in a hot mineral bath at a spa in Romania. The water comes from a geothermal spring heated indirectly by magma, molten rock within the earth. Popular with ancient Romans, the spring has been used for more than 2,000 years.
◄ Water from geothermal wells warms the greenhouse where an Icelandic gardener grows roses for market.

Scientists also are working on ways to achieve fusion at room temperatures. Fusion may be less polluting than fission, and it could generate large quantities of energy.

Energy Efficiency

Scientists around the world are working on ways to harness alternative energy sources that are more affordable and cleaner than the fossil fuels we depend on now. A transition to alternative sources will not mean that people will have to give up their comforts. People want heat, light, and the other benefits that energy provides; they are not particularly concerned about which energy source is used to provide them. In the meantime, however, people can help conserve current energy supplies by using energy more efficiently. This means not only practicing energy conservation in homes and offices but also using products that consume less energy to provide the comforts they enjoy. If people take advantage of technological advances in energy efficiency, they can have the same comforts at a lower energy cost. If people demand more energy-efficient products and services, industries will be encouraged to provide them.

Efficiency improvements in car manufacturing have been impressive. Aerodynamic designs and lighter materials have made many cars on the market more fuel efficient. Several car manufacturers have developed prototypes made of lighter, stronger materials and with more efficient engines that get better than 30 kilometers per liter (70 mpg). If the public demands vehicles that are more energy efficient, the manufacturers will be willing to mass produce them.

There has been great technological progress in lighting efficiency. A new kind of fluorescent ceiling light has been developed that provides a pleasant lighting effect and is 25 to 40 percent more energy efficient than standard fluorescents. New minifluorescents that can replace standard incandescent light bulbs are 75 percent more energy efficient. Currently, minifluorescents are costly, but because they last ten times longer than incandescents, they pay for themselves in lower electricity bills and replacement costs. If all the incandescents and old fluorescents in the United States were replaced by these new

▲ The potential energy in the repetitive motion of ocean waves is tremendous. If efficiently harnessed, wave power, a renewable energy source, could fulfill energy needs in certain parts of the world.
◄ Corn is more than food. The grain can also be converted into ethanol, as is done at this Illinois factory. Ethanol blended with gasoline makes gasohol, which can be used to fuel cars, trucks, and other vehicles.

▶ *Workers at Princeton University in New Jersey build a high-temperature fusion test reactor. Fusion, the process that makes the sun burn, may one day be a practical energy source on earth.*
▼ *Scientists are searching for economical ways to convert coal into a liquid fuel that could be used to fulfill transportation needs.*

products, the amount of electricity consumed for lighting would be halved.

By conserving fossil fuels through the use of energy-efficient products and by continuing the development of technologies to harness alternative energy sources, people should be able to fulfill the energy needs of future generations.

SEE ALSO COAL, CONSERVATION, FOSSIL FUEL, GEOTHERMAL ENERGY, GEYSER, HYDROELECTRIC POWER, MINING, NATURAL GAS, NATURAL RESOURCE, NUCLEAR ENERGY, OIL, SOLAR ENERGY, TIDAL ENERGY, *and* WIND ENERGY.

ENVIRONMENT

An environment is the sum of the conditions that surround and influence an organism. The environment of a plant includes the soil in which it grows, the amount of sunlight and rain it receives, the temperature of the air surrounding it, and the animals that eat it. The environment of people and other animals includes not only the physical conditions that surround them but also the social or cultural conditions that influence them.

Changes in the environment can be beneficial. Technology, for example, has allowed people to create a more comfortable environment through the generation of electricity to heat and cool homes and offices. Insecticides help farmers protect their crops. Changes such as these may also destroy elements of the environment. Burning coal and other fossil fuels to generate electricity may pollute the air. An insecticide may make plants dangerous to eat, or pollute the air and nearby rivers.

Sustaining the earth's environment will require making difficult choices between the short-term benefits people enjoy and the long-term costs to the environment. The Environmental Protection Agency and other organizations in the United States work to protect the environment. The United Nations Environment Program, based in Nairobi, Kenya, operates internationally to preserve and improve the global environment.

SEE ALSO BIOME, BIOSPHERE, CONSERVATION, CULTURE, ECOSYSTEM, *and* POLLUTION.

EQUATOR

The Equator is an imaginary line around the middle of the earth. It is halfway between the North and South Poles, and divides the earth into the Northern and Southern Hemispheres. The Equator is the 0° line of latitude, the only line of latitude that is also a great circle. Except in high mountains, places along the Equator are warm year-round because they receive the sun's rays most directly.

SEE ALSO GREAT CIRCLE, HEMISPHERE, *and* LATITUDE AND LONGITUDE.

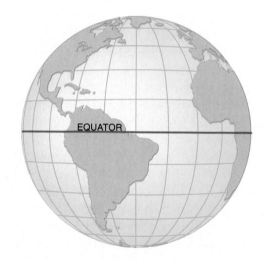

EQUINOX

An equinox occurs twice a year when the sun appears directly overhead to observers at the Equator. Then the periods of daylight and darkness are nearly equal worldwide. The earth, tilted on its axis, orbits the sun (see figure on page 481). Thus, the plane of the Equator is tilted with respect to the plane of the earth's orbit, and the sun appears to be either north or south of the Equator for most of the year. At equinoxes, however, the earth passes through the points at which the orbital and the equatorial planes intersect. In the Northern Hemisphere, the spring equinox occurs about March 21 and the autumn equinox about September 23. This is reversed in the Southern Hemisphere.

SEE ALSO SEASONS *and* SOLSTICE.

EROSION

Erosion is the movement of weathered materials—rock fragments and particles of soil broken down by water, ice, and temperature changes. Water, ice, wind, and gravity are the agents of erosion. They move these materials and change the shape of the land.

As rivers flow, they carve their own valleys. Where masses of moving ice called glaciers are present, they widen and deepen the valleys. Wind hurls sand against rocks, sculpturing them into different shapes. The pull of gravity and heavy rains and snows cause landslides and avalanches. Where any slope exists, surface material is moving slowly down it. Water, wind, and ice deposit rocks and similar debris, forming deltas, dunes, or piles of rocky material called moraines. Erosion is also at work beneath the earth's surface. Groundwater causes limestone to dissolve. The water then carries away the dissolved matter, sometimes forming caves.

The combined actions of weathering and

▲ *After wind erosion blankets pasture in Texas with sand, only wasteland remains.*
▼ *Rainwater erodes, or wears away, the earth's surface, sculpturing rocky spires like these in Utah's Bryce Canyon.*

erosion would eventually wear the surface of the earth into a smooth, low plain if it were not for the movement of the earth's plates. The plates, rigid slabs of rock that make up the earth's hard shell, are constantly shifting, building mountains and raising the land's surface in other ways.

People benefit from some effects of erosion. When rivers flood, their waters deposit fine sediments on the land, making the soil more fertile for growing crops. Erosion reduces the land's productivity, however, when wind and rain carry away topsoil, as has happened in many parts of the world. People often increase the unwanted effects of erosion by careless land use and poor farming methods. Plowing along the contours of the land and planting trees as windbreaks are examples of the many efforts people are making to limit erosion's damaging effects.

SEE ALSO AVALANCHE, CANYON, DELTA, DUNE, GLACIER, ICE, LANDSLIDE, MORAINE, PLATE TECTONICS, RIVER, SOIL, VALLEY, WAVES, WEATHERING AND EROSION, *and* WIND.

ERUPTION

The sudden release of liquid, solid, or gaseous material from an opening in the earth's crust is called an eruption. Some eruptions are explosive. They blow the tops off volcanoes and spew clouds of ash and steam high into the atmosphere. That is what happened at Mount St. Helens, in Washington State, in 1980. Other eruptions, though less violent, are still spectacular. At Hawaii's Kilauea volcano, lava often pours from cracks in the ground and spreads out over large areas.

SEE ALSO ASH, GEYSER, LAVA, *and* VOLCANO.

▲ *Ash-filled clouds billow from a volcano in Guatemala during an explosive eruption.*
▼ *In Iceland, glowing lava erupts from a newly formed volcanic cone.*

ESCARPMENT

An escarpment is a cliff, or steep rock face, that separates two comparatively level land surfaces. The sides of a plateau, formed by weathering and erosion, may be escarpments. A fault scarp is an escarpment formed by movements of the earth's crust. When land along a fault, or crack in the crust, moves up or down, the result may be a fault scarp.

SEE ALSO CLIFF, FAULT, PLATE TECTONICS, PLATEAU, *and* WEATHERING AND EROSION.

▼ *An escarpment rises above a settlement near the Sea of Galilee in Israel. Erosion often carves escarpments along plateau edges. The steep cliffs offer dramatic vistas.*

ESTUARY

An estuary is the broadened seaward end or extension of a river. Most estuaries contain a mixture of fresh water from the river and salt water from the ocean. Water levels in estuaries rise and fall with the tides. An estuary is sometimes a drowned river valley where the downstream parts of the valley have subsided below sea level, or the level of the ocean itself has risen.

SEE ALSO HARBOR, RIVER, *and* WETLAND.

▼ *Fed by Atlantic Ocean tides, the narrow finger of an estuary winds its way through a rich salt marsh in coastal South Carolina. On many coasts, estuarine areas like this provide ideal homes for a variety of birds and other wildlife.*

ETHNIC GROUP

A segment of a population united by its own culture is called an ethnic group. The word "ethnic" comes from the Greek word *ethnos,* meaning "people" or "nation," but today the definition is not as broad. Members of an ethnic group have a common ancestry and cultural tradition, and live as a minority within a larger society. Ethnic groups can provide members with a shared identity and religion, friendships, and business opportunities.

Ethnic groups originate in various ways. If political boundaries change, part of a majority population in one country may suddenly be cut off and become a minority in another country. This happened to the Armenians, whose ancient country is now divided among the Soviet Union, Turkey, and Iran. People with a common culture who migrate to another country may form an ethnic group there. The United States is home to many ethnic groups because of such migrations.

The process by which an ethnic group changes so that it functions within a larger society is called acculturation. The loss of all ethnic traits is called assimilation. Judging other groups by the standards and practices of one's own group is called ethnocentrism.

SEE ALSO CITY, CULTURE, IMMIGRATION, MIGRATION, NATION, *and* NEIGHBORHOOD.

EVAPORATION

Evaporation is the process by which liquid water becomes water vapor. The reverse is condensation. Water evaporating into the air from the ground, from plants, and from bodies of water provides the moisture that returns to earth as precipitation. In dry climates, local evaporation exceeds local precipitation. In wet areas the opposite is true. The evaporation rate depends on temperature, wind speed, and relative humidity. In a hot desert, where temperature is high and relative humidity is low, evaporation occurs rapidly.

SEE ALSO CLOUDS, CONDENSATION, PRECIPITATION, *and* WATER CYCLE.

F

FALL LINE

The geologic line that joins the points on roughly parallel rivers where waterfalls and rapids begin is called the fall line. The waterfalls are caused by differences in the continent's underlying rock structure as each river descends from uplands to lowlands.

In the eastern United States, there is a major fall line between the hard rock of the Appalachian Piedmont and the softer sediments of the Atlantic Coastal Plain. This fall line was important in early European settlement because it marked the limit of inland travel for ships. Eventually the waterfalls were seen as ready sources of power. Many cities, such as Trenton, New Jersey, on the Delaware River and Richmond, Virginia, on the James, developed along the eastern fall line.

SEE ALSO COASTAL PLAIN, RIVER, *and* WATERFALL.

FAMILY

A family is a group of closely related people. It is probably the oldest and most enduring of all the many kinds of groups into which people divide themselves.

The idea of who belongs to a family varies from culture to culture. The nuclear family is the basic social unit in most industrialized countries. It includes a father and a mother, or a single parent, and their children.

The usual family group found in most societies and frequently in agricultural countries is the extended family. It includes parents, their children, grandchildren, and other relatives. This arrangement provides a labor force to help work family land and perform household tasks. It ensures not only care for the elderly and the young but also social and economic support for all.

SEE ALSO CULTURE *and* POPULATION.

FAMINE

A famine is an extreme food shortage of long duration that affects all or most of the population within a region. Many famines occur when crops fail because of natural disasters such as droughts, floods, blights, and insect plagues. Other contributing factors may include war and political unrest. Famines occur in places without enough food reserves or ways of distributing food supplies.

The main effects of famine are disease and death resulting from lack of food. Widespread epidemics often devastate weakened and helpless famine-affected populations.

SEE ALSO AGRICULTURE, FOOD, *and* POPULATION.

▼ *Refugees from famine get food at a camp in Sudan. During the 1980s, drought caused famine in nearly half of the African continent. Before the drought, millions already suffered from undernutrition. Food production in many areas had not kept pace with population growth.*

FARMING

Farming is devoting land to growing crops and raising livestock. Nearly all of the world's food comes from farming. In developing countries, most people live on small subsistence farms and produce little more food than their families need. In developed countries, however, the opposite is often true. For example, only 2.5 percent of the people in the United States farm, but they produce large amounts of food. Modern technology helps make U.S. farming a big business.

SEE ALSO AGRICULTURE *and* FOOD.

▲ *A farmer in southern Alaska harvests grass with a forage chopper. Stored in a silo, the grass will provide feed for his herd of dairy cattle during the long winter.*

FAULT

A fault is a break in the earth's crust, or outermost layer, along which there has been movement. Solid rock on one side of a fault may move up, down, or sideways in relation to solid rock on the other side of the fault. Breaks in the crust where horizontal, or sideways, movement occurs are called strike-slip faults. Upward or downward movement occurs at dip-slip faults.

Slow movements along a fault cause subtle changes that may not be apparent for many years. Sudden movement is felt as an earthquake. Many earthquakes, including the one that devastated San Francisco in 1906, occur along the San Andreas Fault, a strike-slip fault in California that stretches more than 1,100 kilometers (700 mi). The fault marks the boundary between two huge, rigid slabs of rock called plates. Strike-slip faults associated with plate boundaries are also known as transform faults. Plate movement continues to put strain on the San Andreas Fault. The rocks on the west side of the fault are slowly sliding north in relation to the rocks on the east side.

SEE ALSO CRUST, EARTHQUAKE, ESCARPMENT, LITHOSPHERE, MOUNTAIN, PLATE TECTONICS, RIFT VALLEY, *and* VALLEY.

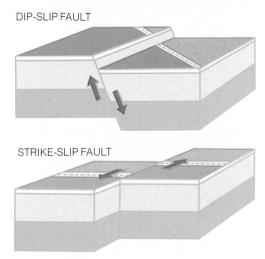

DIP-SLIP FAULT

STRIKE-SLIP FAULT

▲ *Movement along faults can create spectacular geologic formations. Faulting, weathering, and erosion over millions of years exposed these rocks in the Devil's Punchbowl in California's San Gabriel Mountains.*
▶ *Rock layers move up or down at a dip-slip fault (upper diagram). Along a strike-slip fault, blocks of rock slip sideways past each other.*
▼ *California's San Andreas Fault, a strike-slip fault, wrinkles the Carrizo Plain, about 160 kilometers (100 mi) north of Los Angeles.*

FERTILITY

As a geographic term, fertility has two meanings. One is the capacity of soil to sustain plant growth. Fertile soil is easily crumbled and contains large amounts of nutrients derived from minerals and decaying plant and animal matter. Chemical and organic fertilizers may increase soil fertility. Other factors, such as poor farming and grazing practices and erosion, have the opposite effect.

For demographers, people who study population statistics, fertility has another meaning. It is the number of live births occurring in a population. The general fertility rate is the number of live births per 1,000 women of childbearing age in a given year. Fertility rates are used to project future population growth. A related term, fecundity, refers to a population's capacity to reproduce. Fecundity rates are always higher than fertility rates.

SEE ALSO AGRICULTURE, POPULATION, *and* SOIL.

FIRE

Fire is the heat and light produced as a substance burns. Burning, a chemical reaction, occurs when temperatures are hot enough to cause a rapid union of oxygen with other materials, such as wood or coal. The reaction releases heat and carbon dioxide gas, which appear as a flame.

Through the ages, fire has given rise to legends explaining its origins. The ancient Greeks, for example, believed that the god Prometheus stole fire from the sun and gave it to mortals.

Fire has been an important tool for centuries. People have used it to provide heat and light, to make tools, to ward off dangerous animals, and to cook food. The ability to make a fire allowed people to spread out over the earth's surface and to live in areas where they otherwise would have died from the cold. As civilizations developed, many more uses for fire were found. For example, fire provides the energy to power combustion engines in cars and in other machinery, and it helps generate electricity to keep industries operating.

Fire has gained importance among ecologists as an influential force in the natural environment, along with moisture, temperature, wind, and soil. Although a fire in nature is destructive, it can be beneficial to an ecosystem. In a forest, for example, fire is nature's way of getting rid of deadwood and ground

▲ *A flaming torch provides light for this nighttime portrait of a man in the West Indies.*
▼ *For centuries, fire has provided light and heat for cooking, as it does here in Madagascar.*

debris. Their removal lets in more sunlight and opens more space on the forest floor for young trees to grow. Some trees, such as the lodgepole pine, require the heat of a fire to release their seeds. Seeds will germinate more readily in a fire-cleared forest or grassland. Grassland fires free grasses from competition with woody plants such as shrubs and saplings. Fires greatly hasten the return of minerals to the soil and stimulate new plant growth.

The ecological benefits of fire have led to the practice of controlled burning. When weather conditions are right, foresters carefully set a small, controlled ground fire to clear away forest debris. If a fire starts naturally at a later time, it thus will have less fuel to feed on. Fires can be used to clear ground for grazing cattle or for raising crops, to build new roads, to destroy unwanted plants and insects, and to improve some wildlife habitats. These same uses of fire, however, may also have a negative impact on an ecosystem. If trees are burned down, the soil is exposed to increased weathering and erosion.

In 1988, fires swept through Yellowstone National Park, which covers parts of Wyoming, Idaho, and Montana. About half of the park's 890,000 hectares (2.2 million acres) was affected, though much of this was not actually touched by flames. Since 1972, officials at Yellowstone, the oldest national park in the United States, had been allowing some lightning-caused fires to burn themselves out, letting nature clean out areas of deadwood. Natural fires were monitored, but not routinely put out. In 1988, however, the lack of rain, the massive accumulations of natural kindling that still remained in the forest, and gusting winds helped spread the fires in the park farther than was expected.

Although it will take many years for the forest to regenerate after these fires, the rebirth of this ecosystem has already begun. Sunlight now reaches the previously dark forest floor, and grasses and other plants have begun to grow. Some ecologists predict a great increase in plant species. Wildlife is expected to return in greater numbers.

From its benefits to the earth's ecosystems to its uses in industry, fire plays a vital and natural role in sustaining life on earth.

SEE ALSO ECOSYSTEM, FOREST, *and* GRASSLAND.

◄ *Fire sweeps across a Kansas grassland. Fires can prevent the invasion of woody vegetation and stimulate new growth, helping maintain grasses as the dominant plants.*

► *Smoke billows over the Sierra Nevada in California as a fire rages out of control in Kings Canyon National Park. Such blazes are common during the summer.*

▼ *A fire fighter helps contain a controlled fire in Oregon's Willamette National Forest. Such fires help clear deadwood and allow more sunlight to reach the forest floor.*

FJORD

A fjord is a long, narrow ocean inlet that reaches far inland. Fjords form in U-shaped valleys that were carved by great rivers of ice called glaciers. They may be thousands of meters deep. Fjords occur mainly in Norway, Alaska, Chile, New Zealand, Canada, and Greenland. One of the best known is Norway's Sognefjorden, which is more than 160 kilometers (100 mi) long; its walls tower up to 1,000 meters (3,280 ft) above the water's surface and extend the same distance below it. A fjord is usually deepest farther inland where the force of the glacier that formed it was greatest. Fjords are natural harbors, and they offer safe passage to ships along their calm, protected channels.

SEE ALSO COAST, GLACIER, *and* HARBOR.

▲ *Its U-shaped bottom hidden under deep water, this fjord on the coast of Norway displays a characteristically steep, smooth wall.*

FLOOD

A flood is the rising and overflowing of a body of water onto land that is not normally covered with water. One type of flood is the overflowing of inland streams or lakes caused by seasonal events or severe weather, including spring rains, melting snows, monsoons, hurricanes, and cloudbursts. These floods occur primarily along streams and their floodplains. Another type is coastal flooding caused by high winds and tides or by seismic sea waves called tsunami.

Floods are recurring events. Locally, small floods may occur year after year. Severe floods may happen every ten years on average, or only once in a century or more. The effects of a flood can range from preventing or relieving drought to causing widespread destruction.

Flooding can occur when the ground is

◄ *Following heavy rains, the Seine River, in France, often overflows and floods nearby villages. Such floods can cause extensive damage, destroying farm equipment and crops, and drowning farm animals.*
▼ *Residents of Bangkok take to boats or wade in the streets during annual flooding. Swollen by three months of monsoon rain, Thailand's principal river, the Chao Phraya, floods Bangkok each autumn.*

saturated and no longer able to absorb rain-water or when rain falls too fast to soak in. Floods can also occur when the ground is frozen in winter, or baked hard by summer sun. The result of these conditions is runoff—water that flows over the surface of the ground. Extensive runoff flowing into streams and lakes may cause them to flood.

Flash Floods

Some floods occur as a result of heavy rainstorms. These sudden floods, known as flash floods, can be extremely dangerous. Their surging waters strike with great speed and sometimes without warning.

On the evening of July 31, 1976, residents and campers along the Big Thompson River in Colorado took refuge during a rainstorm. Some 25 centimeters (10 in) of rain fell in four hours. Officials began to warn people of a possible flood, but there was no time. Within minutes, a wall of water 6 meters (20 ft) high roared through Big Thompson Canyon. The flash flood killed at least 139 people and swept away an entire town.

Few regions are completely safe from the threat of flash floods. In a desert, for example, a rainstorm can quickly fill a dry channel or gully, known as an arroyo, with a raging torrent of water.

Coastal Floods

The most far-reaching and disastrous floods have generally been caused by tropical storms, which form over the ocean. In different parts of the world they are called hurricanes, cyclones, or typhoons.

A tropical storm contains a huge amount of water, which is released as the storm moves toward the land. Sometimes the rain is accompanied by a storm surge, a mass of wind-driven seawater, that crashes ashore with tremendous force.

On September 8, 1900, for example, a hurricane drove a huge mass of water across the city of Galveston, Texas. The resulting flood was the greatest natural disaster in U.S. history, with a death toll of more than 6,000. In November 1970, a far greater catastrophe befell the Asian country that is now called Bangladesh. Some 300,000 people lost their

▶ Ice forms around parking meters in a flooded municipal lot in Chicago. The ice formed after high waves from Lake Michigan swept ashore.
▼ Wind-driven waves batter a building near Lake Michigan. Waterfront cities such as Chicago are particularly susceptible to flooding.

lives in floods caused by a cyclone sweeping in from the Bay of Bengal.

Seasonal Floods

Not all floods are harmful. Often, a flood is a seasonal occurrence that has beneficial effects. For centuries before the Aswan High Dam was built, the annual inundation, or flooding, of the Nile River watered and fertilized the soil of Egypt. The high waters carried sediments and nutrients, depositing them on the Nile's vast floodplain. Because of the long history of the river's life-giving waters, Egypt has been called "the gift of the Nile."

The monsoon that sweeps across Asia each year between May and September brings with it both life and destruction. This seasonal shift in wind direction often provides the only rainfall a region will have during an entire year. Without the torrential monsoon rains, drought and famine could devastate vast areas of the continent. Agriculture in much of Asia—and thus the survival of nearly 2.5 billion people—depends on the arrival of the wet monsoon. But when the rains come, the dry soil cannot absorb the water fast enough, and widespread flooding occurs. In China in 1887, for example, the Huang (Yellow) River overflowed during the monsoon, causing a flood that killed nearly one million people. Before modern flood prevention programs were set up, the

Huang caused so much destruction that the river became known as "China's Sorrow."

Flood Control

One way to minimize the disastrous effects of floods is by trying to exercise control over the earth's waters. Another way is to avoid building valuable structures on floodplains that are likely to be flooded. Common methods of flood control include the deepening of river channels so that they can hold more water, and the building of artificial banks or walls, called levees. Dams are built to regulate the flow of rivers and to hold excess water temporarily in storage reservoirs. In mountainous areas, limiting the cutting of trees and reforesting bare slopes can help reduce runoff into streams.

SEE ALSO DAM, DIKE, FLOODPLAIN, HURRICANE, LAKE, LEVEE, MONSOON, RIVER, *and* TSUNAMI.

▲ *Artificial embankments, or dikes, such as this one in the Netherlands, often make effective barriers that protect the land from rising sea levels. Hundreds of kilometers of dikes protect the Netherlands from ocean flooding.*

FLOODPLAIN

A floodplain is the flat area alongside the course of a stream that is subject to flooding. As the stream overflows, it deposits part of the sediment it has been carrying. A river may change its course significantly in a floodplain. It forms bends called meanders as alluvium— sand, silt, gravel, and clay—is repeatedly moved from some banks and deposited on others downstream. Floodplains may be broad: The Mississippi system's floodplain is as much as 130 kilometers (80 mi) wide.

SEE ALSO FLOOD, OXBOW LAKE, RIVER, *and* SEDIMENT.

▼ *Prominent features of a floodplain include terraces and ridges of sediment called levees. Oxbow lakes are meanders, or bends, that were once part of the main channel. A yazoo stream, named after a river that parallels the Mississippi, is a tributary prevented by levees from joining a main river.*

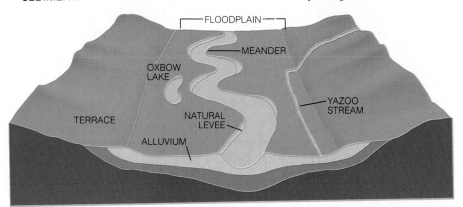

FOG

Fog is a cloud at ground level that reduces visibility to 1 kilometer (.62 mi) or less. It forms when low-lying moist air cools enough to make water vapor turn into water droplets. There are several types of fog. Radiation fog occurs when cloudless nighttime skies allow heat to radiate away from the ground. The air above the ground cools, and if the air contains enough moisture, fog forms. Radiation fog occurs mostly over land, usually in cool weather. Advection fog is fog that arises when humid air moves over cool ground or water. This type of fog is common in coastal areas, such as San Francisco Bay in California and along the coast of Chile. Fog is often a contributing factor in road accidents, airplane crashes, and ship collisions.

SEE ALSO CLOUDS, CONDENSATION, *and* MIST.

▲ *Dense fog shrouds a ship traveling across Lake Superior. The fog formed when moist inland air moved over cold lake water.*

FOOD

Food is one of the basic necessities of life. Food contains nutrients, nourishing substances essential for the growth, repair, and maintenance of body tissues and for the regulation of vital processes. Nutrients provide the energy our bodies need to function.

The energy value in food is measured in units called calories. Age, sex, weight, height, and level of activity determine the number of calories a person needs each day. In the United States, the average daily calorie requirement for a child aged 11 to 14 is 2,550, and for an adult, 2,700.

Kinds of Nutrients

Scientists divide nutrients into different groups: carbohydrates, fats, proteins, minerals, and vitamins.

Carbohydrates provide energy for the body. Nearly all the carbohydrates we eat

▲ A Greek woman displays her handiwork: loaves of rye bread. The nutrients in food, essential to good health, sustain human life.
◄ Part of the world's great bounty of food, fruits overflow crates in an Afghan market.

BARLEY (CEREAL GRAIN)

CARROTS (VEGETABLE)

STRAWBERRIES (FRUIT)

CHEESE (DAIRY PRODUCT)

BEEF (MEAT)

◄ The four major food groups include cereal grains; vegetables and fruits; dairy products such as milk and cheese; and meat, fish, poultry, eggs, and legumes. Many nutritionists recommend eating foods from each group for a balanced, healthful diet.

come from plants. They include starches, found in cereal grains and plants such as potatoes and yams, and sugars, found in fruits, vegetables, and milk. Sugarcane and sugar beets are grown specifically for their sugar content. Many of the starches and sugars we eat have been processed into products such as flour and white sugar used in cookies, cakes, breads, pastas, and pies.

Fats provide more than twice as much energy as carbohydrates do and also help

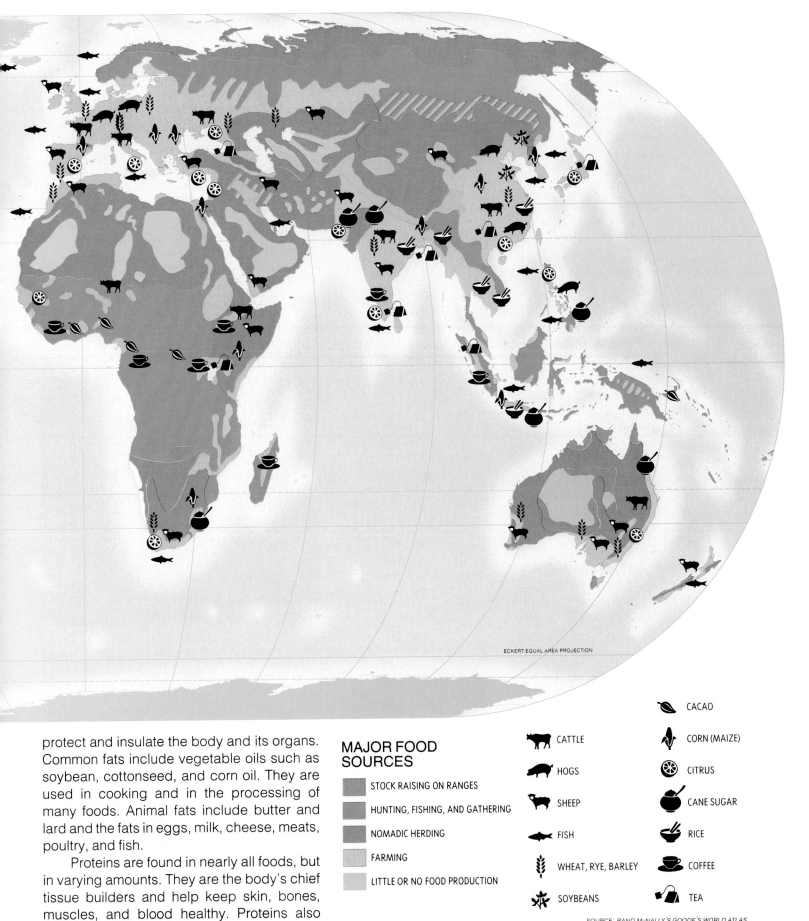

protect and insulate the body and its organs. Common fats include vegetable oils such as soybean, cottonseed, and corn oil. They are used in cooking and in the processing of many foods. Animal fats include butter and lard and the fats in eggs, milk, cheese, meats, poultry, and fish.

Proteins are found in nearly all foods, but in varying amounts. They are the body's chief tissue builders and help keep skin, bones, muscles, and blood healthy. Proteins also

MAJOR FOOD SOURCES

STOCK RAISING ON RANGES

HUNTING, FISHING, AND GATHERING

NOMADIC HERDING

FARMING

LITTLE OR NO FOOD PRODUCTION

CATTLE

HOGS

SHEEP

FISH

WHEAT, RYE, BARLEY

SOYBEANS

CACAO

CORN (MAIZE)

CITRUS

CANE SUGAR

RICE

COFFEE

TEA

ECKERT EQUAL AREA PROJECTION

SOURCE: RAND MCNALLY'S GOODE'S WORLD ATLAS
COPYRIGHT 1986, R.L. 89-S-129

help in the regulation of bodily processes such as the transporting of oxygen and nutrients into and out of cells, the clotting of blood, and the formation of antibodies, which help fight disease. The proteins in meat, fish, poultry, eggs, and dairy products provide all the balanced amounts of the proteins the body needs. Vegetable proteins, such as those found in grains, nuts, and some beans, also provide adequate amounts of proteins when eaten in proper combination.

Minerals and vitamins are called micronutrients because they are needed in very small quantities compared with carbohydrates, fats, and proteins. Minerals provide building materials for the body and help regulate its activities, much as proteins do. For example, calcium and phosphorus build strong bones and teeth; iron contributes to healthy blood; and iodine helps ensure a functioning thyroid gland. Vitamins help the body make full use of other nutrients by assisting the chemical reactions that make those nutrients work. For example, vitamin B_1, or thiamine, helps regulate the release of energy from carbohydrates, promotes a healthy appetite, and aids the functioning of the nervous system. Vitamin D helps in the growth and maintenance of healthy bones.

Other essentials for the body's health include water, oxygen, and fiber. Some scientists include water in the list of basic nutrients. Water makes up more than 50 percent of the body and is involved in most of its processes, such as the regulation of temperature, the transporting of nutrients into the cells, and the elimination of waste products from the cells. Oxygen is not a nutrient, since it is breathed in and not eaten, but it is essential to life. It permits the release of energy from food in the body. Fiber is indigestible material found in most plant foods. It adds bulk to the diet, helping to keep the intestines healthy. Fiber-rich foods include whole grains, dried beans, and fresh fruits and vegetables.

A healthful diet contains a balanced mix of different kinds of foods that together provide all the essential nutrients. Undernutrition results when the body does not get enough food to meet its needs. Many diseases and even death are caused by lack of food or hunger-related conditions. To have adequate amounts of nutrients, we need to select from a

▲ Navajo in New Mexico sort corn (maize), a food sacred to many Native American peoples. The three most important grains, in terms of world production, are wheat, rice, and corn.
► Workers on the island of Madagascar harvest rice, the main staple food for more than half of the earth's population.
▼ In Nepal, women use sickles to harvest wheat, the most abundantly produced cereal grain in the world. Wheat, often eaten as bread, serves as the principal food grain for most people living in regions with temperate climates.

range of foods: cereal grains; fruits and vegetables; legumes, meat, poultry, fish, and eggs; milk and dairy products. All come from plants or animals.

Cereal Grains

Cereal grains are the edible seeds of certain grasses. People have grown them since the beginnings of agriculture. The main food source for every major civilization has been a cereal grain. Today, the most commonly grown grains are wheat, rice, and corn (maize). Other important grains are sorghum, millet, barley, oats, and rye.

Worldwide, cereal grains are the most important staples—that is, they are eaten regularly in large amounts. They supply three-quarters of the calories and many of the carbohydrates and proteins consumed by the world's population. Cereal grains and the products made from them are food not only for people but also for livestock such as cattle, chickens, and hogs.

Throughout the world, more land is planted in wheat than in any other grain. Wheat is a chief ingredient in most breads, cookies, cakes, crackers, pastas, and some breakfast cereals. The Soviet Union, China, the United States, India, and Canada are the major wheat producing countries.

Rice, an Asian tropical grass, is the basic food for more than half the global population. More than 90 percent of the world's total rice crop is produced and consumed in southern and eastern Asia. Rice is also a staple for people in parts of Africa and Latin America. This cereal grain thrives in a warm, humid climate with heavy rainfall or with wet ground. It is often grown in flooded fields called paddies.

Hominy grits, corn bread, popcorn, and tortillas are all made with corn. Although corn (maize) is native to the Americas, it is now cultivated throughout most of the world and is a staple food in many areas. It grows in various soils and climates and at different elevations. U.S. farmers produce nearly half the world's corn; 80 percent of it is used to feed livestock.

Sorghum and millet are also commonly used as livestock feeds. These grains are also staple foods for people in parts of Africa and Asia, where they are used in breads, porridges, and cakes.

▶ *Some of these grains are grown as staple foods; all are economically important in various parts of the world. People use grains in making breads, porridges, breakfast foods, and alcoholic beverages, and also as nutritious animal feeds.*

Three other grains—barley, oats, and rye—are important in many regions. Barley thrives in a wide range of climates. It is used much as sorghum and millet are. One type of barley is the source of malt for making beer. Barley is also used in making vinegar, malt extract, and some beverages similar to milk. Pearl barley, the most popular form of this grain, is used in soups and other foods.

Oats and rye were domesticated much later than were other grains. They can survive cold better than wheat can and are grown farther north. Oats are used mainly as livestock feed, but also go into oatmeal and other breakfast cereals. Rye ranks second only to wheat as a bread flour; the two are often mixed together in breads. Bread made with rye alone, called black bread, is popular in many European countries.

Fruits and Vegetables

The term "fruit" has several meanings. To a botanist, it means the part of the plant that contains the seeds. According to this definition, fruits include most nuts, and vegetables such as cucumbers and tomatoes. To most of us, though, "fruit" means the often juicy, tart, or sweet seed-bearing treats that we enjoy as desserts or snacks. This kind of fruit is defined as the soft, edible, seed-bearing part of a perennial plant, a plant that lives for more than one growing season. Fresh fruits are rich in carbohydrates, vitamins, minerals, and roughage, or fiber. They can be preserved by freezing, canning, or drying.

Scientists classify fruits into groups according to the kind of climate they grow in. For example, temperate fruits grow best where there is a well-defined cold season, as in parts of Europe and the United States. Such fruits include apples, berries, grapes, pears, plums, and peaches. Subtropical fruits thrive where temperatures are mostly warm year-round, as in Florida and in parts of California, along the Mediterranean Sea, and in parts of Australia and Africa. Citrus fruits, such as

SORGHUM

BARLEY

OATS

RYE

lemons, oranges, and grapefruits, as well as dates, pomegranates, and some types of avocados are subtropical fruits. Bananas, pineapples, mangoes, and papayas are tropical fruits; they require a hot climate.

Vegetables are defined as the edible parts of herbaceous plants. These plants have stems that are softer and less woody than those of trees and shrubs. Most vegetables are annuals, living for only one growing season. Vegetables include the roots, leaves, stems, seeds, or bulbs of certain plants. For example, carrots, radishes, and beets are roots; cabbage, celery, lettuce, and spinach are leaves or leafstalks; heads of broccoli are flower stalks topped by thick clusters of flower buds; asparagus is a stem; cucumbers, eggplants, and tomatoes contain the seeds of the plant; garlic, leeks, and onions are bulbs. Vegetables are good sources of fiber, minerals, and vitamins.

Some plants, called tubers, have a specialized type of underground stem that can be eaten fresh as a vegetable or used as an ingredient in other dishes. In temperate regions, the potato is the most important tuber. The potato was first a staple to some Indians of South America; the Spanish introduced it into Europe in the 16th century. Today, the major potato-growing countries are the Soviet Union, China, and Poland. Important tropical tubers include yams, cassavas, and taros.

Legumes, Meat, Poultry, Fish, and Eggs

Legumes are plants that are cultivated for their edible seeds or seedpods. For example, peas, lima beans, soybeans, peanuts, and lentils are legumes. Scientists often include legumes with meat and the other foods in this group because they are eaten for their protein content. In addition, legumes supply iron, other minerals, and vitamins.

The term "meat" usually refers to the edible parts of mammals such as cattle, hogs, and sheep. Meat is a high-protein food and is rich in other nutrients as well.

The United States, the Soviet Union, and Argentina raise much of the world's beef cattle. Meat from very young calves is called veal. The major hog producers are China, the United States, the Soviet Union, and West Germany. Meat from hogs is called pork.

Popular, widely grown vegetables include cabbages, squashes, and radishes. Potatoes, cultivated as vegetables, are tubers, the large ends of the potato plant's underground stems. Often people eat dried beans, members of the legume family, as vegetables. Nutritionists frequently group legumes with meat, poultry, fish, and eggs because of their high protein content.

CABBAGES

BEANS

SQUASHES

RADISHES

POTATOES

Lamb is meat from sheep less than a year old. It is popular in the Middle East, Australia, the United Kingdom, and in other areas of the world. Mutton, meat from mature sheep, has a stronger flavor and a rougher texture than lamb. The Soviet Union, Australia, and New Zealand are the biggest producers of lamb and mutton. In some parts of the world, water buffalo, camels, goats, and yaks are sources of meat, as are wild animals such as rabbits and deer.

The term "poultry" refers to domesticated birds that are raised for meat and eggs. Chickens are an important food source for most of the world's people. Raising chickens is a major industry in many countries, including China, the United States, and the Soviet Union. Ducks, turkeys, geese, and guinea fowl are also raised for food in many parts of the world.

Fish and shellfish are popular foods in many places. Fish provide about 15 percent of the animal proteins consumed by the world's population, and they supply important vitamins and minerals as well. People eat fish raw or cooked, and preserve it by canning, freezing, drying, salting, smoking, or pickling. Most of the fish and shellfish people eat come from the ocean; the rest come from inland bodies of fresh water and from fish farms, where they are raised commercially. Abalone is a popular seafood on the West Coast of the United States and in Japan. Conch is eaten in the Florida Keys and in the West Indies. Eels, octopuses, squids, mussels, and shark fins are eaten in certain parts of the world.

Eggs are a source of proteins, fats, minerals, and vitamins. Boiled, fried, scrambled, or deviled, chicken eggs are popular around the world and are used in a variety of baked goods. People also eat the eggs of other birds, such as ducks and plovers, and those of reptiles, such as turtles and crocodiles. The eggs of certain fish, mainly sturgeon, are prepared as the delicacy known as caviar.

Milk and Dairy Products

In many parts of the world, most milk, cream, butter, and cheese are products of dairy cows. Goats, camels, reindeer, sheep, yaks, and water buffalo supply milk products in some areas. In much of Asia, people have

ORANGES

APPLES

CHERRIES

GRAPES

BANANAS

Whether in backyard plots or in vast orchards, millions of tons of fruits are grown each year. Fruits contain nutrients such as carbohydrates, vitamins, and minerals. Scientists classify fruits according to the climate they require. Apples, cherries, and grapes grow in temperate regions; oranges thrive in subtropical areas; bananas come from the tropics.

▶ Workers in a Chinese milk-processing plant check empty bottles for cleanliness. Milk contains many nutrients, including proteins, minerals, and vitamins. Since ancient times, people have used milk from animals such as cows, goats, and sheep in their diets.
▼ Popular in much of the world, milk is also processed into cheese, butter, yogurt, and other products. A soft cheese called Brie (below) ages to ripeness in France.

▲ A conveyer in a poultry plant moves chicken eggs past bright lamps for inspection and grading. As lights illuminate the shells, they reveal the contents. Eggs, high in proteins, also contain many minerals and vitamins.

traditionally consumed milk made of soybeans instead of animal milk. Elsewhere, milk and dairy products supply proteins, carbohydrates, fats, and essential vitamins and minerals. The Masai of East Africa consume large amounts of milk. People in the U.S., in parts of Europe, in the Middle East, and in India eat yogurt, a fermented milk food.

Foods Around the World

People's diets vary from one country to another and also within a country. The variations result partly from geographical differences. For example, people who live near the ocean tend to eat a lot of fish. People living in cool regions with short growing seasons depend on crops that mature quickly, such as potatoes. In warm, wet lowlands where the soil retains water, rice is often a staple.

Such geographical factors are less important today than they were a century ago, at least in developed countries. Improved transportation and communication, increased tourism, and growing numbers of immigrants in many cities have broadened people's tastes in food. New York, London, Paris, and Tokyo, for example, have a wide variety of ethnic restaurants. Improved methods of food processing, preservation, storage, and shipping allow many people to enjoy foods produced far from their homes. Spanish olive oil, French cheeses, and sardines from Norway, Portugal, and elsewhere are eaten in much of the developed world.

Local traditions and customs play a role in determining what foods people eat and how they are prepared. English tradition, for example, dictates that roast beef and Yorkshire pudding be eaten together. Many Asians serve rice with almost every meal.

Economic factors affect what people eat. In developed countries, many people have enough money to buy a variety of nutritious foods. But even in rich countries, there are many poor people who cannot buy these foods because resources are not evenly distributed throughout the population. And those who can afford good food may eat poorly. Studies have revealed that the diets of many people in developed countries are too rich in fats, salt, and refined sugar, and lack fresh produce and fiber.

In developing countries, where most people are poor, diets reflect the income level. People eat mostly grains and other starches, but often do not get enough food.

Religion sometimes plays a role in what people eat. Many Hindus are not permitted to eat beef because cattle are considered sacred. Many Jews and Muslims do not eat pork, shellfish, and certain other foods.

If you take a look at foods in different parts of the world, you will find a great variety. In the United States, for example, steak, hamburgers, chicken, and ice cream are popular. There are regional preferences, too: barbecue in the South, lobster in Maine, crabs in Maryland, and salmon in Washington State.

In Brazil, the national dish is *feijoada,* black beans cooked with meats and served with rice and kale or collard greens. The original recipe came from Argentina. Cassava meal, chili-pepper and lime-juice sauce, and sliced oranges accompany the beans and greens. Black beans, rice, and cassava meal are basic ingredients in Brazilian cooking. *Churrasco,* barbecued veal, pork, or beef, is a favorite food.

In the central African country of Zaire, boiled cassava root is a staple food. The leaves of the cassava, which resemble spinach greens, and a fiery pepper sauce called *pili-pili* are often part of the meal. Fresh-picked bananas, papayas, and pineapples are frequently eaten. Animal proteins from caterpillars, poultry, dried fish, monkeys, or crocodiles occasionally supplement the diet.

In France, people have traditionally placed great importance on food. Wine is a basic ingredient in French cooking, and wine or mineral water accompanies most meals. Delicately seasoned sauces, crusty breads and croissants, light pastries and soufflés, and a variety of meat dishes are common.

In the Soviet Union, soups are favored foods, especially borscht, or beet soup, and cabbage soup. Cabbage cooked in a variety

▶ An outdoor market in Rome, Italy, displays fresh poultry, domesticated birds raised for food. Chickens, the poultry most commonly eaten throughout the world, hang above plucked geese. ▼ Pork, like this in a French butcher shop, ranks among the world's most important meats. Both meat and poultry have high amounts of protein.

of ways is a staple, as are breads, potatoes, and kasha—cooked buckwheat, barley, or semolina. Blini, or buckwheat pancakes, are served with caviar, smoked fish, butter, and sour cream. Pickles, cucumbers, and onions are widely eaten.

In India, the highly spiced and seasoned cooking varies from region to region. Millions in this developing country are vegetarians— non-meat eaters. A festive meal in South India might include several vegetable dishes, rice,

▲ Beef and lamb await shipment in a New York City wholesale meat market. Usually people in developed countries eat more of these relatively expensive foods than do people living in less developed countries.

rayta, or yogurt salad, pickles, chutney, and fresh fruit.

In Japan, the arrangement and appearance of the food, the table setting, and the dishes are almost as important as the taste of the food itself. Serving dishes, for instance, should complement the food and please the eye. A traditional dinner consists of rice and soup, served with fish or meat, and vegetables. Green tea and perhaps rice wine or beer accompany the meal. Since Japan is surrounded by the ocean, fish is a mainstay of the diet. It is prepared in a variety of ways. Sashimi, for example, is raw fish dipped in seasoned soy sauce; tempura is prawns or slices of fish and vegetables dipped in batter and fried; and sushi is flavored rice patties covered with slices of raw or cooked fish and other condiments and dipped in soy sauce.

In the South Pacific, roast suckling pig is a favorite feast food. It is usually baked in an outdoor pit. Other foods include taros, sweet potatoes, yams, chickens, prawns, baby octopuses, and fish. Coconuts are used in everything from soups to desserts.

The World Food Supply

The world food supply is the total amount of food produced on earth. Since the late 1940s, grain supplies have fluctuated, but worldwide there has been a surplus, or more than enough food to feed everyone. Yet millions go hungry. Of the more than 5 billion people on earth, an estimated 450 million are undernourished, or lack enough food.

▲ *A freshly netted catch of shrimps cascades into a holding bin aboard a commercial fishing boat. The ocean teems with many varieties of edible, high-protein shellfish.*

▼ *Octopuses, popular food in Japan, tempt buyers in a Tokyo fish market. On average, people eat more fish and shellfish per person in Japan than in most other countries.*

▲ *Fishermen prize northern porgy, or scup, an Atlantic Ocean fish popular for panfrying. Fish supply only one percent of the world's food, but provide 15 percent of its animal protein.*

Each year, more than 14 million, most of them children, die of hunger-related diseases.

Why do so many starve when the world produces enough to feed everyone? One reason is that resources such as arable land, as well as food and the money to buy it, are not evenly distributed among the world's people. Most hunger is the result of poverty. Many people in developing countries are too poor to grow or buy the food they need. They are farmers, landless laborers, or the unemployed, living in rural poverty or urban slums.

Crisis situations contribute to hunger as well. In some countries, years of continuous war have severely disrupted food production and caused millions of people to flee their homes and become dependent on international food aid. Severe droughts, floods, and other natural catastrophes have contributed to the problem of hunger. And in many developing countries, especially in Africa south of the Sahara, the population is growing faster than the rate of food production.

The governments of these countries cannot afford to buy food for all their hungry people, and they do not want to depend always on wealthier countries for gifts of food. Some experts say that governments of both developing and developed countries do not have effective long-term policies for distributing food and for helping countries to increase their agricultural production.

To help solve the problem of hunger and increase worldwide food production, experts say, small farmers in many developing countries need incentives and assistance in learning new agricultural methods and in buying machinery and other improvements such as hardy seeds. Better transportation and communications systems and storage facilities would lead to improved food distribution.

In much of the developing world, growing populations are pushing farmers onto land not suited to agriculture, causing widespread environmental damage. Experts fear this trend will intensify, increasing the loss of valuable topsoil and the depletion of the earth's resources. In the future, efforts to expand the world's food supply must go hand in hand with efforts to protect the environment.

SEE ALSO AGRICULTURE, FAMINE, FARMING, MIGRATION, *and* POPULATION.

▲ *Children visit a Libyan supermarket with well-stocked shelves. The world has more than enough food for its people, but unequal distribution of resources often means that poorer countries lack adequate supplies.*

▼ *Empty vessels in a food line at a Sudanese refugee camp reflect the misery of drought and famine. Perhaps 450 million people in the world suffer from hunger; millions die annually from its related diseases.*

CANADA

UNITED STATES

MEXICO

CUBA
GUATEMALA
JAMAICA HAITI
HONDURAS
NICARAGUA
EL SALVADOR
COSTA RICA
PANAMA
ECUADOR
COLOMBIA
VENEZUELA
DOMINICAN REPUBLIC
PUERTO RICO
TRINIDAD AND TOBAGO

PERU
BOLIVIA
BRAZIL
PARAGUAY
CHILE
URUGUAY
ARGENTINA

IRELAND
UNITED KINGDOM
NETHERLANDS
BELGIUM
FRANCE
SWITZERLAND
PORTUGAL
SPAIN
ITALY

NORWAY FINLAND
SWEDEN
DENMARK
EAST GERMANY
POLAND
WEST GERMANY
CZECHOSLOVAKIA
AUSTRIA
HUNGARY
YUGOSLAVIA
ROMANIA
ALBANIA
GREECE
BULGARIA

SOVIET UNION

AFGHANISTAN
TURKEY
IRAN

SYRIA IRAQ
LEBANON
ISRAEL
JORDAN KUWAIT
SAUDI ARABIA
UNITED ARAB EMIRATES
OMAN
YEMEN
DEMOCRATIC YEMEN

MAURITANIA
SENEGAL
GAMBIA
GUINEA-BISSAU
GUINEA
SIERRA LEONE
LIBERIA
CÔTE D'IVOIRE
TOGO
BENIN
GHANA
BURKINA FASO
MOROCCO
MALI
ALGERIA
TUNISIA
LIBYA
NIGER
CHAD
NIGERIA
CAMEROON
GABON
CONGO
CENTRAL AFRICAN REPUBLIC
SUDAN
EGYPT
ETHIOPIA
SOMALIA
UGANDA
KENYA
RWANDA
BURUNDI
TANZANIA
ZAIRE
ANGOLA
ZAMBIA
ZIMBABWE
MOZAMBIQUE
MALAWI
NAMIBIA
BOTSWANA
SOUTH AFRICA
LESOTHO
MADAGASCAR

WORLD FOOD SUPPLY

Population, not land area, determines the size of the countries in this cartogram. Each small square on the background grid represents one million people. Countries with fewer than one million people are not shown.

For comparison, a familiar map of the world's land areas appears at right. On both maps, shades of color show differences in food supplies according to the average daily number of calories available per person. Generally, countries with low annual population growth rates have more food per person than countries with high growth rates.

STATISTICS PROVIDED BY POPULATION REFERENCE BUREAU, INC. AND FOOD AND AGRICULTURE ORGANIZATION OF THE UNITED NATIONS

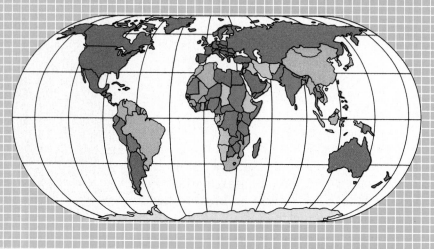

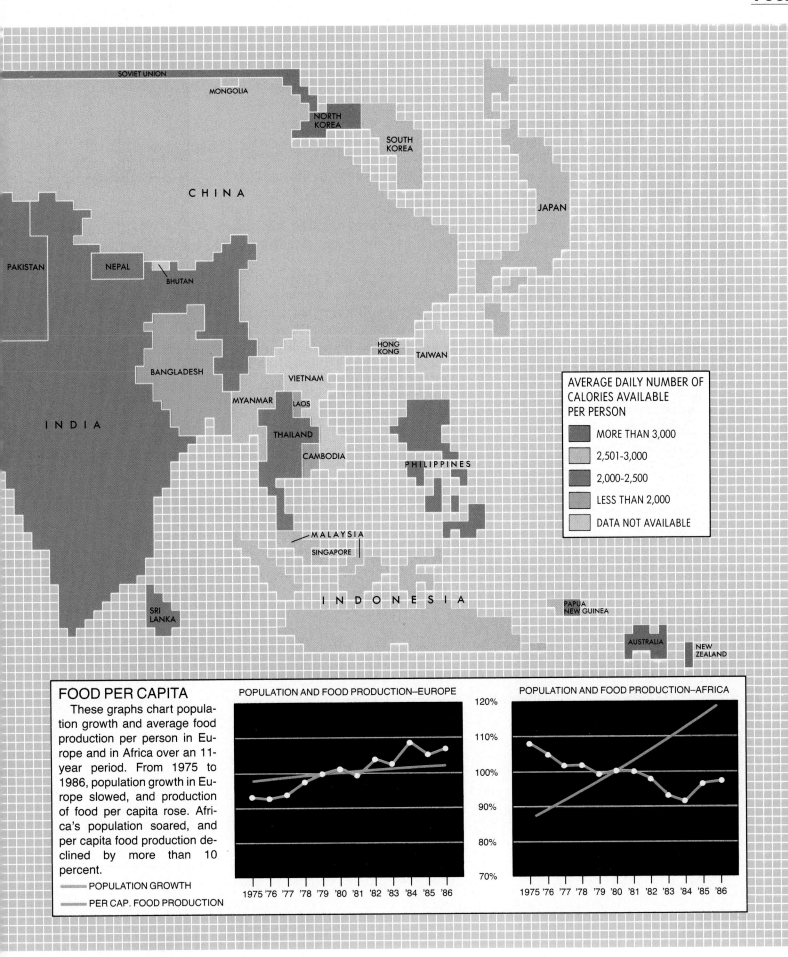

SOVIET UNION

MONGOLIA

NORTH KOREA

SOUTH KOREA

CHINA

JAPAN

PAKISTAN

NEPAL

BHUTAN

BANGLADESH

MYANMAR

VIETNAM

LAOS

HONG KONG

TAIWAN

INDIA

THAILAND

CAMBODIA

PHILIPPINES

MALAYSIA

SINGAPORE

SRI LANKA

INDONESIA

PAPUA NEW GUINEA

AUSTRALIA

NEW ZEALAND

AVERAGE DAILY NUMBER OF CALORIES AVAILABLE PER PERSON

MORE THAN 3,000

2,501-3,000

2,000-2,500

LESS THAN 2,000

DATA NOT AVAILABLE

FOOD PER CAPITA

These graphs chart population growth and average food production per person in Europe and in Africa over an 11-year period. From 1975 to 1986, population growth in Europe slowed, and production of food per capita rose. Africa's population soared, and per capita food production declined by more than 10 percent.

POPULATION GROWTH

PER CAP. FOOD PRODUCTION

POPULATION AND FOOD PRODUCTION—EUROPE

POPULATION AND FOOD PRODUCTION—AFRICA

120%

110%

100%

90%

80%

70%

1975 '76 '77 '78 '79 '80 '81 '82 '83 '84 '85 '86

1975 '76 '77 '78 '79 '80 '81 '82 '83 '84 '85 '86

FOOD CHAIN

A food chain is a feeding pattern in which energy from food passes from one level to the next in a sequence. All living things are linked in food chains, and there are millions of different chains in the world. The sun is the principal source of energy for all of them.

Each chain is made up of interrelated organisms in an ecosystem, or natural community. Organisms at one level feed on those at the preceding one and, in turn, provide energy for others. Organisms in the first link are called the producers and are usually green plants. Those in the other links are known as the consumers and are usually animals.

One common food pattern is called the grazing food chain. Grasses and other green plants using solar energy are the base of this food chain. They are eaten by herbivores, or plant-eating animals. Herbivores are con-sumed by carnivores, meat-eating animals, or by omnivores, animals that feed on both plants and animals. In a typical grazing food chain, a cow eats grass; the cow is then eaten by people. Energy from the grass is transferred to the cow. When a person consumes beef from the cow, some of the animal's energy is passed on.

In any food chain, a large amount of energy is not transferred because some food at every level is indigestible, and much energy is used in the process of living. Because of this energy loss, there are usually no more than six links in a chain.

Another common food chain, called the detritus food chain, begins with the remains of plants and animals. These remains are slowly broken down, or decomposed, by organisms such as bacteria and fungi. In this process, nutrients are returned to the soil and then used again by plants.

Food chains can have many different patterns and can be complex. Most organisms eat several kinds of food and therefore belong to more than one chain. Because of this, experts often refer to connecting food chains as food webs, networks that transfer energy within an ecosystem.

SEE ALSO ECOSYSTEM.

▼ *In this food chain, a short-horned grasshopper, which feeds on plants, falls prey to a bluegill fish. The bluegill provides a meal for a largemouth bass; the bass will become food for the fisherman.*

FOREST

If you step into a forest on a bright summer day, you will notice how quiet and cool it is. Trees block the wind, so the air is still. Leafy treetops shade the interior. Fallen leaves turn the forest floor into a springy carpet. The quiet forest reveals little of the life teeming within it. A diverse community—songbirds, mammals, insects, seedlings, and wildflowers—and climate, soil, and water form a complex ecosystem.

Strictly defined, a forest is a large area covered with trees grouped so that their foliage shades the ground. Most forests need at least 75 centimeters (30 in) of rainfall a year. Areas that receive consistently less rain do not support extensive forests.

Every continent except Antarctica has forests. Millions of years ago, they covered more than 60 percent of the earth's surface. Natural causes, such as radical changes in climate and the movement of glaciers, along with people-related causes, such as the clearing of trees for firewood and to make room for farms and settlements, have destroyed half of the world's original forestlands.

Profile of a Forest

Viewed from the outside, a forest may look like a tangle of greenery. This is because

▲ Needleleaf evergreens, like the spruce and fir in the boreal forests of Canada's Jasper National Park, flourish in the cold climate of the far north.
◄ Coastal redwoods, the world's tallest trees, dwarf a visitor to California's Redwood National Park. The trees soar as high as 110 meters (360 ft).

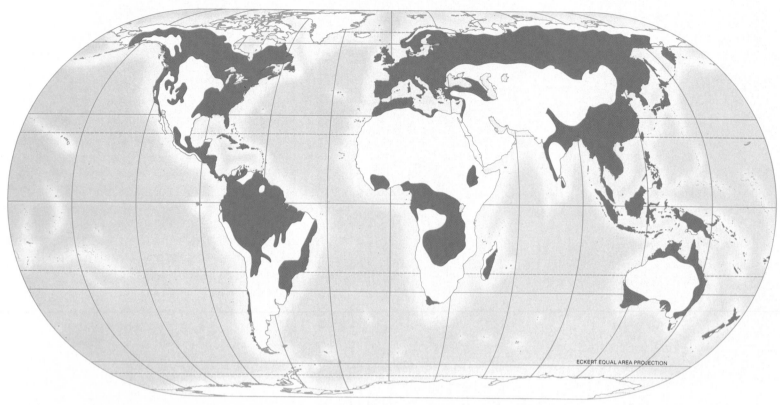

▲ *About 30 percent of the earth's land surface is covered by forests.*
▼ *Mosses and ferns hang from trees in Washington State's Hoh Rain Forest, which yearly receives 380 centimeters (150 in) of precipitation.*

plants on the edge of a forest grow outward, competing for the sun's light. All green plants use sunlight as fuel to produce the food they need to grow—a process known as photosynthesis. Vegetation may be less dense just a few meters inside a forest, where little sunlight may penetrate.

In most mature forests there are several layers of foliage, formed by plants of varying heights. The forest canopy is the highest layer, made up of the crowns, or tops, of the tallest trees. Below the canopy is the understory, composed of smaller trees and immature canopy trees. A layer of shrubs, woody plants branching out from a single stem, grows below the understory. An herb layer made up of ferns, mosses, wildflowers, and other soft-stem plants covers the forest floor.

The floor itself makes up the lowest layer of the forest structure. Countless insects, earthworms, and microscopic organisms live here. Feeding on fallen leaves and animal wastes, they help decompose the debris, releasing nutrients into the soil that are necessary for plant growth. The animals move through the soil, opening it up to water, air, and seeds. These largely unseen residents, vital to the health of a forest, contribute to its diversity and growth.

Kinds of Trees and Forests

There are many ways to categorize the kinds of trees in a forest. Some people group trees by the nature of their leaves. Needleleaf trees, for example, usually have long, needle-like leaves. Most needleleaf trees are cone-bearing, or coniferous, as well. Broadleaf trees have wider, flat leaves.

Trees are also categorized by how often they lose and grow leaves. Trees that are leafless for a season are called deciduous trees. Those that shed and replace some leaves while remaining green all year are called evergreen trees. A tree that constantly sheds and replaces its large, flat leaves and is green year-round is called a broadleaf evergreen.

Different systems are used to categorize the kinds of forests. One system classifies forests according to the type of trees found most often in them—broadleaf deciduous forest, for example, or coniferous evergreen forest. Another system classifies forests into categories according to climate and the kinds of trees commonly found there. Tropical rain forests, tropical deciduous forests, temperate deciduous forests, temperate evergreen forests, and boreal, or needleleaf evergreen, forests are the five kinds of forests in this system.

Tropical rain forests are found mainly near the Equator, where the climate is warm and wet year-round. The largest continuous rain forest covers the Amazon basin in northern South America. Central America, Africa, and Southeast Asia also have extensive tropical rain forests.

The chief characteristic of rain forests is their mixture of trees. While a square kilometer of a temperate deciduous forest in eastern North America might have 25 or fewer tree species, an area of the same size in a rain forest may have as many as a thousand tree species. Most trees in a tropical rain forest are broadleaf evergreens. Each tree supplies a niche for smaller plants—ferns, vines, and mosses. The surface of the rain forest floor, however, is relatively bare because of the limited sunlight and the rapid decay of debris in the tropical climate. Frequent rains leach minerals from the soil. Thus, the soils in these forests are generally infertile and shallow.

Tropical rain forests are home to about

▲ At autumn's peak, a sugar maple leaf turns fiery scarlet.
◄ Vivid-hued deciduous trees, like these aspens in New Mexico's Santa Fe National Forest, lose their leaves each fall.
▼ A mixed deciduous forest in Bulgaria is typical of European forests, where there are often fewer species than in North America.

50 percent of all the plant and animal species on the earth, some of which could live no-where else. Food, including plants and insects, is plentiful in the lush canopies of tropical rain forests, so this layer attracts most of the forests' animals, such as monkeys, birds, bats, and reptiles.

Tropical deciduous forests occur in India, southern Africa, and parts of Central and South America. These forests can be similar to rain forests in appearance and in animal life, but they occur in regions where rainfall is more seasonal. During the dry season, many of the trees shed their leaves.

Temperate deciduous forests grow across eastern North America, western Europe, and eastern Asia. These regions have a temperate climate, with warm summers and cold winters. Most trees there are broadleaf and deciduous. Though there may be many tree species in the temperate deciduous forests, two or three species, such as maple,

◄ Coconut palm trees in a tropical rain forest form a lush canopy above women on one of the Marquesas Islands in the South Pacific. Tropical rain forests thrive in wet equatorial climates.
▼ Massive tree roots, called buttress roots, grow several meters above ground in a Costa Rican rain forest. Large trees in rain forests typically extend only a shallow root system into the nutrient-poor soil and rely on buttress roots as support for their colossal trunks.

beech, and ash, often dominate these forests.

Many flying and climbing animals, such as birds, bats, squirrels, and raccoons, live in temperate deciduous forests. These forests are also homes for bears and deer.

Temperate evergreen forests vary enormously in their kinds of plant life. In some, needleleaf trees dominate. Others have mainly broadleaf evergreen trees. Some Pacific coastal forests have a mixture of these kinds of trees. Temperate evergreen forests are common in the coastal areas of temperate regions that have mild winters and heavy rainfall, such as the Gulf coast and northwestern coast of the United States. Frogs, snails, and other animals that live near water abound in these forests.

Boreal forests are the needleleaf evergreen forests that stretch like a dark green ribbon across the far northern areas of Europe, Asia, and North America. These high-latitude forests, sometimes called taiga, have extremely cold winters and short, cool summers. Because of the short growing season, there are fewer forest layers in the boreal forests than in the temperate and tropical forests. Boreal forests, made up primarily of spruce and fir, usually have one canopy layer, no understory, and a sparse shrub layer. Mosses and lichens grow thickly on the forest floor and on the branches and trunks of the trees.

Many animals live in the boreal forests, including rabbits, wolves, deer, and moose. Insects abound in the summer. Some animals there are migratory. They move farther south during the winter to warmer climate regions where food is plentiful and return north in the spring. Others hibernate for the winter.

These forest classifications are broad, and some forests, called mixed forests, have characteristics of more than one kind. Some forests are transitional forests. Deciduous trees, for example, gradually may take over a forest that was primarily made up of evergreen trees. Sometimes the transition is managed by people who change the nature of a forest by cutting down one kind of tree to encourage the growth of a more commercially valuable kind.

► *Mountains of wood chips—some 200,000 tons—stored at Japan's Honshu Paper Mill will be used in making paper.*

▲ *A logger in Lander, Wyoming, uses horsepower to help him thin a stand of stunted, overcrowded lodgepole pines.*

▼ *A riverboat chugs past piles of lumber awaiting transport out of Brazil's Amazon rain forest region.*

▲ Part of a tropical rain forest has been destroyed in Borneo, Malaysia, to make room for a cacao plantation.

▼ The burning of this Brazilian rain forest exposes the fragile soil to heavy rains that wash away nutrients.

◄ In developing countries, the immediate need for food often conflicts with the long-term need to preserve forests. Here, a woman in Zaire plants manioc in a burned-out clearing. Corn plants grow beside the felled trees.

The Value of Forests

Forests provide the world with many resources, both economic and environmental. Wood is the principal product of a forest. Worldwide, people use about three billion tons of wood a year—enough to cover the city of Detroit to the height of a ten-story building. A little more than half of this wood is burned as fuel. The rest is used mostly as lumber. Almost 200 million tons of wood a year are turned into pulp for making paper.

Forests also yield rattan and wicker, often used in making furniture; latex, used in making rubber; turpentine; cork; and a variety of gums, tannins, and resins, used in industry.

Forests provide environmental benefits. They help recycle the planet's oxygen, nitrogen, and carbon, which are vital to sustaining life. They are habitats for many plant and animal species. Forests influence temperature by cooling areas covered by thick canopies. Trees anchor topsoil with their roots.

Forests play an integral part in recycling the earth's water supply. Trees help slow water runoff, allowing more water to be absorbed into the soil. Some of the water becomes groundwater that feeds lakes and streams. The roots of the trees also absorb the water. Some of the moisture transpires through the leaves of the trees and evaporates. Later, the cycle begins anew when moisture condenses in the atmosphere and precipitation falls to the ground.

Destruction of Forests

People began clearing forests some 10,000 years ago, when they started settling down to a life based on farming. Most of the loss occurred in temperate regions as forests were replaced by cropland and pasture. Recently, that trend has changed. Temperate forests in much of Europe, Asia, and North America are protected by law. Many tropical forests are not protected, however, and they are shrinking rapidly.

▶ Seedlings of temperate evergreen trees are carefully cultivated in a Washington State nursery. When mature, the seedlings will be transplanted. Such projects help the lumber industry meet its growing need for timber.

Every minute, about 11 hectares (27 acres) of tropical rain forest are destroyed—an area equivalent in size to 20 football fields. Experts fear that in less than 50 years much of the world's rain forests will be gone. Some of the trees are being used as sources of lumber and pulp. Many of the trees are being cleared for agriculture and for settlements. Nutrients are quickly depleted, however, after a few seasons of cultivation in the shallow soil. Then more forest is destroyed for cultivation.

Many forests in temperate regions are protected from overcutting, and they regenerate faster than trees can in the worn out soil of the tropics. But temperate forests are being damaged by another enemy—pollution. Acid rain and other forms of pollution are killing trees across thousands of square kilometers in North America and Europe. The pollution, carried by wind and rain, may come from industrial areas hundreds of kilometers away.

The need for firewood also poses a serious threat to the earth's forests, especially in developing countries. People cut trees and burn the wood to cook their food and to heat their homes. When trees, which anchor soil, are cut down, topsoil washes away, and the land often becomes unproductive.

Burning the trees also contributes to pollution of the air and releases more carbon dioxide into the atmosphere. As carbon dioxide levels increase, more heat radiated from the earth is absorbed. This may cause unpredictable changes in the world's climate.

Saving the Forests

Efforts to save the world's forests have focused on management and replanting. Forests can supply vast amounts of timber without being depleted as long as the annual harvest does not exceed annual growth. As trees mature, growth slows down and eventually stops. Removing the older trees and encouraging new growth by leaving seed trees or replanting ensures a vigorous and growing forest. There are also areas where forests are

crowded, stunting tree growth. The thinning of these areas enables the trees that remain to grow faster and straighter. In the United States, the Forest Service practices these and other methods of forest management in national forest areas. The Forest Service tries to make sure that forest growth exceeds the amount of timber cut or destroyed by disease, fire, or insects each year. Many countries have enacted laws regulating which forest tracts can be cut and which must be protected. By designating some forests as wilderness areas, many countries preserve the ecological value of their forests. By leaving some forest areas untouched and using others selectively and intelligently, people will be able to help the earth's forests survive.

SEE ALSO ATMOSPHERE, CLIMATE, FIRE, GREENHOUSE EFFECT, POPULATION, RAIN FOREST, TIMBERLINE, *and* VEGETATION REGIONS.

▲ In Zaire, forests are cleared for coffee trees, one of the country's most profitable crops.
▼ Planting seedlings of fast-growing trees helps replace harvested areas of forests.

FOSSIL

Fossils are the preserved remains or traces of ancient animals and plants. A fossil can be a complete organism or a part of one—even a fragment of bone, shell, feather, or leaf. Footprints and the impressions of plants can also be fossils. Among the oldest known fossils are those of algae that lived in the ocean more than three billion years ago.

Most fossils formed when animals or plants died and were covered by sediment. Over time, minerals in the sediment seeped into the organisms and petrified them, or "turned them to stone." Sometimes, mineral matter replaced every body cell. In other cases, organisms were preserved intact. Insects trapped in tree resin are examples.

Studying fossils gives scientists called paleontologists clues to the ancient earth and prehistoric life. Fossils reveal what the earth was like and what kinds of plants and animals once existed on it.

SEE ALSO GEOLOGIC TIME SCALE *and* ROCK.

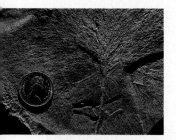

◄ *A Canadian nickel gives scale to a fossil sequoia twig found in a valley in Canada's Yukon Territory, proof that forests once thrived there in a warm climate. Now the area is cooler and the valley treeless.*

▲ *A Park Service worker chips away rock, exposing dinosaur fossils more than 100 million years old. The remains were found at Dinosaur National Monument on the Colorado-Utah border.*

FOSSIL FUEL

Fossil fuels form from the remains of plants and animals. The process that converts them into combustible, or burnable, substances takes millions of years.

Coal, oil, and natural gas are fossil fuels. They are composed mainly of hydrocarbons, chemical compounds of carbon and hydrogen. All living things are made up of hydrogen, carbon, oxygen, and nitrogen. When living things die, they decompose, or break down. If decomposition happens in the absence of oxygen—for instance, if it takes place underground or underwater—it is not complete; hydrocarbons are left behind. When hydrocarbons are ignited in the presence of oxygen, they burn.

Coal

Coal, the most abundant fossil fuel on the earth, forms from plants. Existing coal deposits developed from lush vegetation living during a time in earth's geologic history called the Carboniferous period, which began more than 300 million years ago. When plants died, many sank into swamps and other wetlands. The remains accumulated in thick, moist layers, and the lack of sufficient oxygen prevented their total decomposition. The result was brown masses of organic matter called peat, with twigs, roots, and other plant parts still visible. As water levels fluctuated, the ancient deposits of peat were covered with sand and silt, and pressure on the organic layers increased. Over time, the deposits became more compact, forming layers of solid coal.

Peat is the earliest and wettest form of coal, and it is developing in wetlands today. Peat has not been compacted into the hard substance we call coal, but when it is dried, it can be burned as a fuel. In the stage following peat, coal called lignite develops. Later it becomes bituminous coal, and finally, anthracite. In each successive stage, the level of carbon in the coal increases and the amount of moisture decreases, making the coal harder. The hardest and cleanest-burning form of coal, anthracite, is also in the shortest supply.

People discovered how to burn coal more than a thousand years ago. Extensive

coal mining, however, began only about three centuries ago, in England. By the 1800s, Great Britain was burning coal to power machinery. This use of coal helped bring about the industrial revolution, a time of radical change in production methods.

Oil and Natural Gas

Since the 1950s, oil and natural gas have been used more than coal in heating and transportation. Oil and gas are preferred to coal because they burn more cleanly and are easier to transport.

Nature's way of making oil and gas is complex. Unlike coal, which forms mostly from plants growing in swamps and in other wetlands, oil and natural gas form from the remains of marine plants and animals. Existing supplies began forming millions of years ago,

when the remains became mixed with sand, silt, and other sediments on seafloors beneath shallow ocean waters. As the waters advanced and retreated across parts of the earth's surface, layer after layer of sediment collected on top of the oil-forming materials.

As the overlying layers of sediment grew thicker, pressure helped cause slow, complex chemical reactions that transformed the materials into gas and droplets of oil. The sand and silt holding the oil and gas hardened into sedimentary rocks. Geologists call such sedimentary rocks "source rocks."

As pressure increased, the oil and gas were squeezed from the source rocks and migrated upward through porous rocks until further movement was prevented by impermeable layers of rock called caprocks. The porous rocks that hold the oil and gas are called reservoirs. In the pores of reservoir

◄Existing supplies of the fossil fuels coal, oil, and natural gas formed from the remains of plants and animals that lived millions of years ago. These fuels are the main sources of energy used today. Coal (top) is the most abundant fossil fuel. Though the Middle East has vast oil reserves (center), supplies worldwide are dwindling. Natural gas (bottom), often found with oil, is also in short supply.

► Coal takes millions of years to develop. (1) It begins forming when vegetation settles to the bottom of wetlands such as swamps. As the remains accumulate, they only partially decay, forming a spongy brown material called peat. (2) As water levels fluctuate, the peat layer is submerged and layers of silt, sand, and other sediments build up on top of it. (3) The sediments gradually harden into rock. Pressure from the overlying rock and sediments causes the peat to become more compact, turning it into solid coal. (4) The cycle begins anew when waters recede and vegetation again becomes abundant.

FORMATION OF COAL

PEAT

1

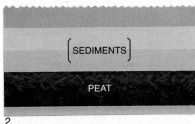

SEDIMENTS

PEAT

2

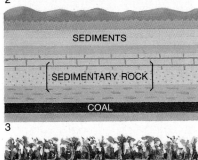

SEDIMENTS

SEDIMENTARY ROCK

COAL

3

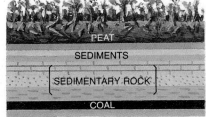

PEAT

SEDIMENTS

SEDIMENTARY ROCK

COAL

4

FORMATION OF OIL AND NATURAL GAS

1

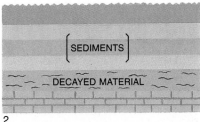

SEDIMENTS

DECAYED MATERIAL

2

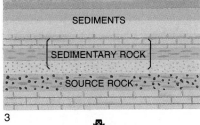

SEDIMENTS

SEDIMENTARY ROCK

SOURCE ROCK

3

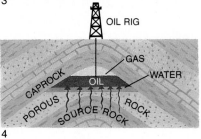

OIL RIG

CAPROCK

GAS

OIL

WATER

POROUS ROCK

SOURCE ROCK

4

◄(1) The formation of oil and natural gas begins when tiny marine plants and animals die in shallow ocean waters and their remains mix with sediments on the ocean floor. (2) The sediments containing the partially decayed organic material are buried by more sediments. (3) Over millions of years, as waters advance and retreat, many layers of sediment are deposited. Older layers slowly harden into sedimentary rock. Organic material in the rock layer called source rock is converted into gas and droplets of oil by pressure from the overlying layers. (4) The oil and gas move upward through porous sedimentary rock until they are trapped by an impermeable layer called caprock. A reservoir of groundwater, oil, and gas forms within the porous rock. This domed reservoir is one kind of reservoir that results from movement within the earth's crust.

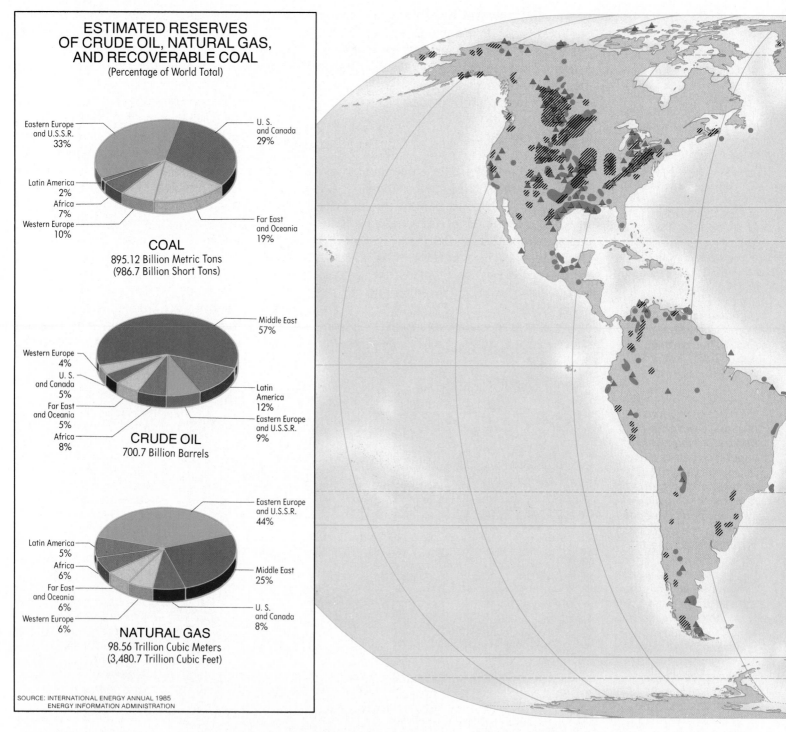

ESTIMATED RESERVES OF CRUDE OIL, NATURAL GAS, AND RECOVERABLE COAL
(Percentage of World Total)

COAL
895.12 Billion Metric Tons
(986.7 Billion Short Tons)

Eastern Europe and U.S.S.R. 33%
U. S. and Canada 29%
Latin America 2%
Africa 7%
Western Europe 10%
Far East and Oceania 19%

CRUDE OIL
700.7 Billion Barrels

Middle East 57%
Western Europe 4%
U. S. and Canada 5%
Far East and Oceania 5%
Africa 8%
Latin America 12%
Eastern Europe and U.S.S.R. 9%

NATURAL GAS
98.56 Trillion Cubic Meters
(3,480.7 Trillion Cubic Feet)

Eastern Europe and U.S.S.R. 44%
Latin America 5%
Africa 6%
Far East and Oceania 6%
Western Europe 6%
Middle East 25%
U. S. and Canada 8%

SOURCE: INTERNATIONAL ENERGY ANNUAL 1985
ENERGY INFORMATION ADMINISTRATION

▲ *The U.S.S.R., the U.S., Canada, and countries in Eastern Europe have most of the recoverable coal reserves. The Middle East has the largest concentration of crude oil. Natural gas is found primarily in the U.S.S.R., the Middle East, and in Eastern European countries.*

rocks, the gas, being lighter, rises above the oil. The oil lies atop groundwater in the reservoirs. It is from such reservoirs that oil and gas are pumped. Although frequently found together, each has been found separately. Petroleum is another name for oil in this crude state, and natural gas is the name given to the gaseous form of the hydrocarbon.

In addition to its uses as a source of heating oil and gasoline, crude oil can be used in a wide variety of products such as candles

and paints. Natural gas is also a versatile resource, though it is used primarily for home heating and cooking.

For years, oil drillers who found natural gas simply let it escape into the air or piped it out and flared, or burned, it off. Advances in technology have made it possible to capture and transport natural gas through pipelines and specially designed ocean gas tankers, though this is not done everywhere in the world. Scientists found that natural gas

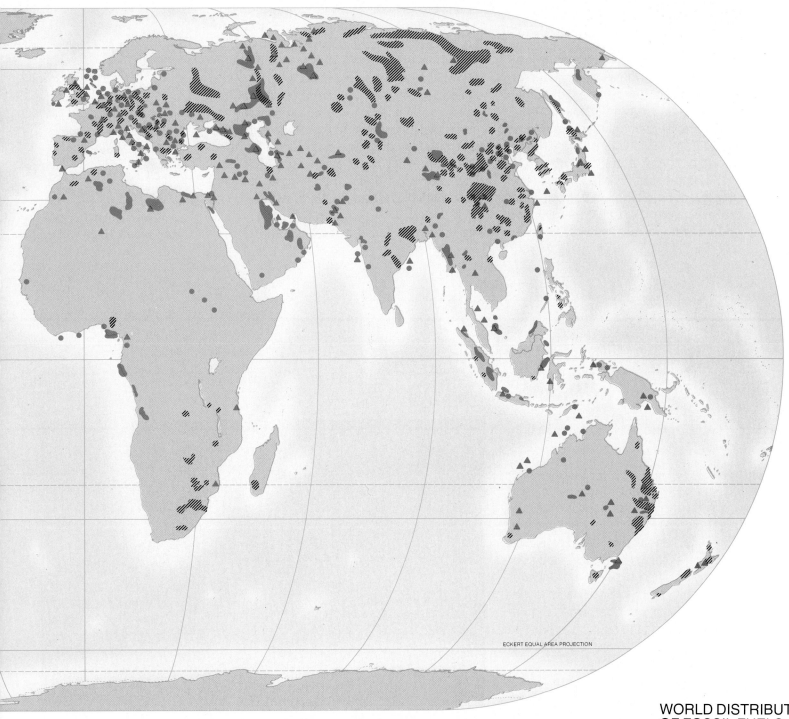

ECKERT EQUAL AREA PROJECTION

WORLD DISTRIBUTION OF FOSSIL FUELS

 COAL FIELDS

 OIL FIELDS

 NATURAL GAS FIELDS

SOURCE: Coal deposit information from *GOODE'S WORLD ATLAS*, copyright 1986 by Rand McNally, used with permission.
Oil and gas deposits from *1986 INTERNATIONAL PETROLEUM ENCYCLOPEDIA*, PennWell Publishing Company.

burned more cleanly than oil or coal, and gas became widely used.

Fossil fuels are vital to industrial societies around the world. In the late 20th century, however, supplies of all fossil fuels, especially oil and natural gas, began to shrink. Although fossil fuels are still forming, they will not be created in sufficient quantities before existing deposits run out. Because it takes so long for fossil fuels to develop, they are considered nonrenewable resources. The limited quanti-

ties of fossil fuels and the environmental damage their extraction and burning cause have helped spur the development of alternative energy technologies. Renewable energy sources such as solar power and wind power may be able to supply earth's energy needs when the fossil fuels are used up.

SEE ALSO CONTINENTAL SHELF, ENERGY, GEOLOGIC TIME SCALE, INDUSTRY, MINING, NATURAL RESOURCE, PETROLEUM, *and* ROCK.

FRONT

A front is the boundary between two air masses of different temperature and humidity. There are three basic types of fronts: warm, cold, and stationary. A warm front occurs where warm air catches up to a cold air mass. A cold front exists where cold air overtakes a warm air mass. A stationary front develops when cold air and warm air meet and neither mass moves. Sometimes a cold front overtakes a slower-moving warm front and slides underneath it, creating what is called an occluded front. Most fronts pass through the centers of low pressure areas and along the edges of high pressure areas.

Fronts often bring dramatic changes in the weather within a very short time. Most precipitation and violent weather are associated with the movements of fronts. Norwegian meteorologists were first to use the word "front" as a weather term. The turbulence in the atmosphere when cold and warm air masses meet reminded them of the raging conflicts along battlefronts during World War I.

SEE ALSO AIR MASS, CLOUDS, *and* WEATHER.

▼ *Along a cold front (left), advancing cold air forces warm air aloft. This can produce storms. Warm air along a warm front (center) rises gradually over the cold air mass. A stationary front (right) occurs when two air masses are at a standstill. Winds usually blow parallel to the front.*

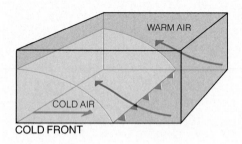

COLD FRONT

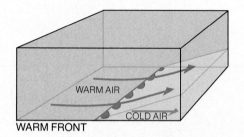

WARM FRONT

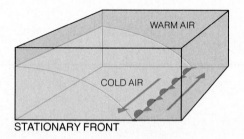

STATIONARY FRONT

FROST

Frost is the white coating of ice crystals you often see on or near the ground after a cold night. A leaf, for example, loses heat during the night. If the leaf's temperature falls below 0°C (32°F), water vapor in the surrounding air will freeze on it. This process is called sublimation. It occurs when a gas, such as water vapor, becomes a solid, or when a solid becomes a gas, without first becoming a liquid. Frost disappears when the sun's rays provide enough heat to melt the ice crystals and cause the liquid to evaporate.

Meteorologists also use the term "frost" to describe air temperatures that measure below freezing. Fruit growers are particularly concerned about "killing frosts." These are temperatures that are far enough below freezing to harm cold-sensitive plants such as orange or peach trees. Frosts occur most often in valleys because cold air is denser than warm air and thus sinks to the lowest point— the valley floor. This is why many farmers plant frost-sensitive crops on slopes, leaving colder valley floors for growing hardier plants.

SEE ALSO AGRICULTURE, DEW, *and* WEATHER.

▲ *Crystals of frost spread feathery patterns across a windshield. Frost coats objects on or near the ground as water vapor in the air changes directly into a solid. Some clouds form in the same way in freezing temperatures.*
◄ *Autumn frost layers a spray of maple leaves with ice crystals.*

G

GAP

A gap is a steep-sided opening through a mountain ridge. When a river cuts through such a ridge, the opening is called a water gap. Sometimes a river changes course after carving a gap. A gap that has no river flowing through it is called a wind gap. Glaciers, moving masses of ice, may also carve gaps.

Gaps offer gateways through mountain barriers. Some pioneers passed through the Cumberland Gap in the Appalachian Mountains on their way to the American West.

SEE ALSO GLACIER, MOUNTAIN, PASS, RIVER, VALLEY, *and* WEATHERING AND EROSION.

▲ *In South America, the Amazon has carved a gap through mountains. People often use gaps as passageways through rugged highlands.*

GEOGRAPHY

The term "geography" comes from a Greek word that means writing about or describing the earth. The study of geography begins with the perception that places on the earth differ from one another in significant ways. Just as important, people differ, and so do the ways in which they organize themselves and use the earth's resources. Geography, then, is primarily the study of places and the complex relationships between people and their environments.

There are many aspects of geography. Two broad subdivisions are physical geography and human geography. Physical geographers study natural features and the climatic, geologic, and other processes that shape our world. Human geographers focus on people and their patterns of settlement and activity. Cartography, or mapmaking, is important to geography because maps are the basic tools of geographers.

To describe and explain our world, geographers draw upon findings in many related fields—without losing sight of the whole picture. This concern with the whole picture—the interconnection of people, places, and things—is the great attraction of geography.

SEE ALSO CARTOGRAPHY, DISTRIBUTION, LOCATION, *and* MAPS AND GLOBES.

▲ *A signpost in Canada's Yukon Territory gives great circle distances in statute miles to the Arctic Circle and to places as far away as Cape Town, in South Africa.*
▼ *Mongolian students in a classroom supplied with wall maps and diagrams use a globe to explore their world.*

GEOLOGIC TIME SCALE

The geologic time scale is used by geologists to divide the earth's 4.6-billion-year history into units of time. The scale records important stages in the development of the planet's climate, life-forms, and landforms.

Geologists separate the earth's history into major units of time called eons. Though they do not always agree on the name and scope of each unit, most geologists recognize three of them: the Archean eon, the Proterozoic eon, and the Phanerozoic eon. The first two eons, often called Precambrian time, cover the history of the earth before the first complex life-forms appeared, from the time of its formation 4.6 billion years ago to about 570 million years ago. Although Precambrian time represents more than four-fifths of the earth's history, geologists know relatively little about it compared with their knowledge of the most recent eon. Physical evidence of what the earth was like in Precambrian time is meager.

Abundant remains or traces of ancient life-forms, called fossils, begin to appear in rocks that formed about 570 million years ago. Those fossils herald the beginning of the Phanerozoic eon.

Scientists separate the Phanerozoic eon into three subdivisions called eras. Just as the

▼ *Drawing on fossil evidence, scientists can speculate about the earth at different times in geologic history. In the Cambrian period, shallow seas teemed with life. The Carboniferous was a time of lush plant growth. The Triassic period saw the spread of dinosaurs. Mammals— like these ancestors of today's elephant—were abundant during the Tertiary period.*

CAMBRIAN PERIOD: 570—500 MILLION YEARS AGO

CARBONIFEROUS PERIOD: 360—290 MILLION YEARS AGO

TRIASSIC PERIOD: 240—205 MILLION YEARS AGO

TERTIARY PERIOD: 63—2 MILLION YEARS AGO

division of a person's lifetime into years, months, and days makes it easier to record events and the passage of time, these divisions make it easier for geologists to separate the changes and passage of time in the earth's history. The Paleozoic (old life) era began 570 million years ago; the Mesozoic (middle life) era began 240 million years ago; and the Cenozoic (recent life) era stretches from 63 million years ago to the present. Eras are divided into periods; periods are divided into epochs; and epochs are divided into ages.

Geologists separate the eras by the kinds of life-forms that existed during each one. During the Paleozoic era, sea life was abundant, and the first land plants, amphibians, and reptiles appeared. During the Mesozoic era, dinosaurs populated the land. The first evidence of human existence dates from late in the Cenozoic era, which scientists call the Age of Mammals.

Reading the Fossil Record

The divisions in the geologic time scale are characterized by the appearance, and then the disappearance, of certain life-forms. In the Cambrian period, the first period in the Paleozoic era, sea animals with protective shells or with other hard outer-body coverings were plentiful. During a later period, called the Silurian, the first fish with jaws appeared. The next period, the Devonian, is often called the Age of Fishes. It was a time when many kinds of fish flourished.

How do we know when these creatures existed? The answer lies in the fossils found in sedimentary rock. Sea animals buried by silt, mud, and other sedimentary deposits were preserved as fossils when the sediment hardened into layers of rock.

Over millions of years, many layers of sedimentary rock formed, with the oldest layers on the bottom. Each layer of rock holds

---

GEOLOGIC TIME SCALE TERMS

The names of geologic time units are descriptive. Some indicate regions where rocks of a particular age are well exposed or were first studied. The Cambrian period is named for Cambria, an ancient name for Wales, where fossils of early complex life-forms were first studied. The Devonian period is named for Devon, an English county. Jurassic comes from the Jura Mountains of France and Switzerland, and Permian refers to Perm, a city and a region in the U.S.S.R. The Ordovician and Silurian periods are named for peoples who once lived in regions of Wales where there are extensive fossil deposits from these time periods.

Some names, such as Carboniferous (coal-bearing) and Cretaceous (made of chalk), describe kinds of rock that formed. Others, such as Tertiary (third) and Quaternary (fourth), indicate positions in a sequence relative to other time units. One term, Triassic, means "three" in Latin and tells how many layers were deposited in Germany, where the name was first used.

Many terms come from Greek words such as *archaios* (ancient), *proteros* (first), *phaneros* (visible, evident), *zoe* (life), *palaios* (old), *mesos* (middle), *kainos* (new, recent), *eos* (dawn), *oligos* (little, few), *meion* (less), *pleion* (more), *pleistos* (most), and *holos* (complete, entire). Combinations of the words produce descriptive terms such as Phanerozoic, which means "visible, or evident, life."

---

fossils of animals that lived during the time of that layer's formation.

Early geologists noticed that fossils in one sedimentary rock layer were quite different from the fossils in layers above and below it. They recognized that each layer was a record of a particular time in the earth's history. They began the study of fossils and of the relative positions of the sedimentary rocks that contain them. The geologic time scale was developed using the relative positions as a dating technique. As technology improved, scientists began to assign absolute dates to the time units on the scale. Scientists who study fossils are called paleontologists. Over time, these experts have gathered sufficient information to reconstruct past events in the order in which they occurred. That order is shown on the following pages.

SEE ALSO EARTH, FOSSIL, GEOLOGY, OCEAN, ROCK, *and* SEDIMENT.

▼ *The geologic time scale divides the 4.6 billion years of the earth's history into eons, as shown below. The first two eons, often called Precambrian time, extend from the earth's formation to about 570 million years ago. The third and most recent eon is divided into eras on the basis of the characteristic life-forms. Sea life thrived in the Paleozoic, as did dinosaurs in the Mesozoic. Mammals are typical of the Cenozoic. The chart on pages 246–247 traces the development of life-forms during the Phanerozoic eon.*

ARCHEAN EON	PROTEROZOIC EON	PHANEROZOIC EON
4.6 billion to 2.5 billion years ago	2.5 billion to 570 million years ago	570 million years ago to present ⟶ PALEOZOIC · MESOZOIC · CENOZOIC

TIME	ERA	PERIOD	EPOCH	DEVELOPMENT OF THE EARTH	
10,000 years ago to present	CENOZOIC	QUATERNARY	HOLOCENE	Landmasses reached their present positions. The climate warmed and sea levels rose as Ice Age glaciers melted.	
2			PLEISTOCENE	The shape and position of landmasses were much as they are today. Ice covered much of the Northern Hemisphere.	
5		TERTIARY	PLIOCENE	North America and South America became connected by the Isthmus of Panama. Ice built up in the Arctic.	The five maps show earth's drifting continents from about 500 million years ago to the present. Over long periods of time, the huge landmasses come together, break apart, and come together again. They also change shape. To follow the moving continents, refer to the shapes and colors on the map above as you study the lower maps. The present-day shapes of the continents appear throughout.
24			MIOCENE	The continents were moving into their present positions. Widespread cooling occurred.	
38			OLIGOCENE	The Indian landmass joined Asia, and the Himalaya rose. During this cool and dry time, ice built up in Antarctica.	
55			EOCENE	Australia and Antarctica separated. The climate was warm.	
63			PALEOCENE	Land bridges connected North America to Europe and Asia. The climate was cool and wet.	
138	MESOZOIC	CRETACEOUS		Pangaea separated, and the Rocky Mountains began to form. Sea levels rose in this warm period.	
205		JURASSIC		Pangaea began to break apart. In this mild period, the Atlantic Ocean began to form.	
240		TRIASSIC		Pangaea drifted northward. The climate was warm and dry.	
290	PALEOZOIC	PERMIAN		The supercontinent called Pangaea formed during this period of variable climate.	
360		CARBONIFEROUS		The African landmass collided with North America. The climate was warm and wet.	
410		DEVONIAN		In this warm, dry period, there were three major landmasses: Euramerica, Asia, and Gondwanaland.	
435		SILURIAN		Europe and North America joined. The climate was warm.	
500		ORDOVICIAN		North America and Europe moved toward each other, and the Appalachian Mountains began to form. What is now the Sahara was covered with ice at the South Pole.	
570		CAMBRIAN		Most landmasses lay on or south of the Equator. The global climate was warm and wet.	

M I L L I O N S   O F   Y E A R S   A G O

DEVELOPMENT OF LIFE

Present-day life-forms became established.

Changes in plant zones occurred. Many large mammals became extinct. Humans developed.

The first humanlike beings appeared.

Grasslands were widespread. There were many more kinds of mammals than before, and grazing mammals spread.

Plants were similar to those of today. Apelike primates appeared.

Most plants resembled present-day ones. The first whales, rhinoceroses, and elephantlike mammals appeared.

Flowering plants flourished. The first rodents and primates appeared.

The first flowering plants grew. Dinosaurs became largely extinct at the end of the period. The first snakes and marsupials appeared.

Ferns and conifers were abundant. Dinosaurs ruled the land. The first birds appeared.

Ferns and conifers were plentiful. The first dinosaurs and mammals appeared.

Seed plants appeared. Many invertebrates (animals without backbones) became extinct. Reptiles spread.

Coal forests of giant mosses and ferns were widespread. The first reptiles appeared. Insects and amphibians spread.

The first trees and forests grew. The first amphibians and insects appeared.

The first land plants grew. The first fish with jaws appeared. Coral reefs were widespread.

Algae and shellfish were abundant.

Blue-green algae grew in the ocean. Sea animals with shells and external skeletons were abundant.

Time divisions and drawings are not to scale.

247

GEOLOGY

Geology is the study of the physical history of the earth, its composition, its structure, and the processes that form and change it. Geologists learn about the earth by examining its rocks. They study activities that change its surface, such as volcanic eruptions and earthquakes. Geologists also learn about the earth's history by studying fossils. With information they gather, geologists can better understand the workings of the earth's interior.

There are many specialties within the science of geology, including physical geology, the study of the processes that shape the earth's crust; petrology, the study of rocks; seismology, the study of earthquakes; and volcanology, the study of volcanoes.

SEE ALSO EARTH, FOSSIL, GEOLOGIC TIME SCALE, PLATE TECTONICS, ROCK, *and* SEISMOLOGY.

▲ *A geologist examines volcanic rock on Surtsey, an island formed in the 1960s by undersea volcanism off Iceland. Geologists learn about the earth by studying the rocks that help form it.*

GEOTHERMAL ENERGY

Geothermal energy is heat energy generated within the earth. Magma, interior rock melted by geothermal energy, sometimes lies near the surface. Rocks surrounding the magma become hot, heating groundwater. Sometimes geothermal energy is released at the surface through geysers, hot springs, or mud pots. People have long used geothermal energy; the ancient Romans enjoyed natural hot-water baths. Natural steam has been harnessed to turn turbine engines that generate electricity since 1904, when the first geothermal power plant opened in Italy. In Iceland, the heated water is tapped to warm homes. Many countries, including the United States, the Soviet Union, New Zealand, and Japan, use geothermal energy. Promising sites for future plants are near areas of volcanic activity, where magma lies near the surface.

SEE ALSO ENERGY, GEYSER, GROUNDWATER, MAGMA, SPRING, *and* VOLCANO.

GEYSER

A geyser is a hot spring through which jets of water and steam erupt. From the mouth of a geyser, a tube-like hole filled with water extends into the earth's crust. Sometimes magma, rock melted by heat generated within the earth, lies near the bottom of the hole and heats rocks surrounding the water. Water in the lower part of the hole becomes superhot, but pressure from the water above prevents it from boiling. As the surface water is heated, it begins to boil, and some of it is forced upward. This releases the pressure on the hot water below, which suddenly turns into steam and erupts, ejecting the column of water above it. Water slowly seeps back into the hole, and the process begins again. The most active geysers are in Iceland, New Zealand, and the United States. In the U.S., Yellowstone National Park's Old Faithful erupts about every 50 to 100 minutes.

SEE ALSO ENERGY, GEOTHERMAL ENERGY, GROUNDWATER, HOT SPOT, MAGMA, *and* SPRING.

▲ *Mist rises from Hot Creek in California. Geothermal heat from magma, molten rock within the earth, warms the stream's waters.*

▲ *Wyoming's Old Faithful in Yellowstone National Park is one of the few geysers that erupt predictably. Groundwater turns into steam, forcing water above it to explode from the geyser.*

GLACIER

A glacier is a huge mass of ice that moves slowly over land. The term "glacier" comes from the French word *glace,* meaning "ice." Glaciers are often called "rivers of ice."

Glaciers fall into two groups: alpine glaciers and ice sheets. Alpine glaciers form on mountainsides and move downward through valleys. Ice sheets are not confined to mountainous areas; they form broad domes and spread out from their centers in all directions.

As ice sheets spread, they cover everything around them with a thick blanket of ice, including valleys, plains, and even mountains. The largest ice sheets, which are called continental glaciers, spread over vast areas. Today, continental glaciers cover most of Antarctica and Greenland.

Massive ice sheets covered much of North America and Europe during the time geologists call the Pleistocene epoch. These ice sheets reached their greatest size some 18,000 years ago. As the ancient glaciers spread, they carved and changed the earth's surface, creating many of the landscapes that exist today. During the Pleistocene epoch, nearly a third of the land was covered by glaciers. Today, about a tenth of the earth's land is covered by glacial ice.

How Glaciers Form and Move

Glaciers begin forming in places where more snow piles up each year than melts. Soon after falling, the snow begins to compress, slowly changing from light, fluffy crystals into round granules. When new snow falls and buries this granular snow, it becomes even more compressed and recrystallizes into a dense, grainy ice called firn.

As years go by, the weight of accumulated snow on top causes more compacting and recrystallization. When the ice grows thick enough—about 50 meters (160 ft)—the grains fuse into a mass of solid ice, and the glacier begins to move under its own weight. Pulled by gravity, an alpine glacier moves slowly down a valley. An ice sheet spreads out from its center. The great mass of ice in a glacier behaves plastically; that is, it flows, oozing and sliding over uneven surfaces.

Different parts of a glacier move at different speeds. The uppermost part is a brittle, rigid section that rides on top of the flowing ice. The flowing part moves faster than the base, which grinds along its rocky bed.

The differing speeds at which parts of a glacier move cause tension to build within the brittle upper part of the ice. It fractures, forming cracks called crevasses in the topmost 50 meters (160 ft) of the glacier.

Most glaciers move very slowly—only a few centimeters a day. Some, though, have been called galloping glaciers, because at

▲ *Pools on the surface of an Antarctic glacier reflect the sky. Dirt and rocks carried by the moving ice appear as dark areas on the gray-white mass.*
▼ *A glacier crowns a mountain in Iceland. Several of Iceland's glaciers cover active volcanoes, which erupt occasionally and send floods of water, ice, and rocks over the land.*

▲ *Hubbard Glacier arrives at Yakutat Bay after moving through Canada and Alaska. In early 1986, the glacier stretched to the land at right, forming an ice dam with a lake behind it.*
► *When the dam broke in October 1986, the water gushed out, providing a rare sight: an iceberg stranded on land.*

times they have moved more than 50 meters (160 ft) a day.

Where a glacier meets a seacoast, its leading edge lifts and floats in the water, forming cliffs of ice that may be 60 meters (200 ft) high or more. Chunks of ice at the edge of the glacier break away into the water—a process known as calving. The floating chunks of glacial ice are called icebergs.

How Glaciers Change the Land

Although glaciers move slowly, they can exert enormous force. Like huge bulldozers, they plow relentlessly ahead year after year, crushing, grinding, and toppling almost everything in their paths, including forests, hills, and mountainsides.

Alpine glaciers begin to flow downhill from bowl-shaped mountain hollows called cirques. As the glaciers move downward, they widen V-shaped river valleys into broad U-shaped ones. Alpine glaciers dig deep into the terrain, forming rugged, dramatic landscapes. As ice sheets spread, however, they tend to smooth out the land beneath them.

As they move, glaciers erode, or wear away, the land by picking up and carrying great amounts of soil, rock, and clay. Some of the boulders they carry are as big as houses.

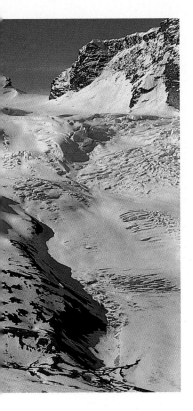

Embedded in a glacier's base, these large rocks grind against the ground like the teeth of a file or the prongs of a rake. They dig long grooves called striations in the surface. Geologists can tell in what direction ancient glaciers moved by studying striations in rock.

Glaciers eventually deposit their loads of rock, dirt, and gravel. Piles of material dumped at a glacier's end, or snout, are called terminal moraines. Many terminal moraines today are forested ridges and hills.

When the Pleistocene ice sheets began their final retreat some 10,000 years ago, they left behind hollowed-out areas. Many of these became lakes. The Finger Lakes in western New York State were excavated by a Pleistocene ice sheet. The lakes were once stream valleys that lay parallel to the southward flow of the ice sheet. Along the streams, the glacier scooped out U-shaped troughs that now contain deep lakes.

Materials deposited at the base of a glacier as it retreats over land are called ground moraines. The jumble of rock, gravel, and dirt making up the moraines is called till. Much of the fertile soil in the midwestern United States was formed from layers of till tens of meters deep left by ancient ice sheets.

Glaciers have given people not only fertile soil for growing crops but other useful resources as well. Among these are deposits of sand and gravel. Tons of these materials are used each year in making concrete.

Another important benefit from glaciers is the fresh water they provide. Many rivers, such as the Rhône and the Rhine in Europe, are fed by the melting ice of glaciers.

Glaciers have dug the basins for most of the world's lakes and carved much of the earth's most spectacular mountain scenery. The Teton Range in Wyoming, Yosemite Valley in California, and the Matterhorn in the Alps on the Swiss-Italian border were all sculptured by the moving ice of glaciers.

SEE ALSO CREVASSE, GEOLOGIC TIME SCALE, ICE, ICE AGE, ICE SHEET, ICEBERG, LAKE, LOESS, MORAINE, VALLEY, *and* WEATHERING AND EROSION.

▲ *The Gornergletsher, or Corner Glacier, plows through the Swiss Alps near the town of Zermatt. Some 15 kilometers (9 mi) long, this alpine glacier is one of Switzerland's largest.*

▼ *An alpine glacier moves downhill from a bowl-shaped depression called a cirque (1). Ice sculptured a horn (2) and an arête (3) from the mountain. A tributary glacier (4) flows in from an adjoining valley. A ridge of loose rock called a medial moraine (5) snakes through the center of the glacier, and crevasses (6) crack its surface. After the glacier's retreat, a U-shaped valley remains. The glacier cut truncated spurs (7) along the valley walls. A mountain lake called a tarn (8) fills the cirque. Where the tributary glacier met the main glacier, it left a hanging valley (9).*

GLACIATION

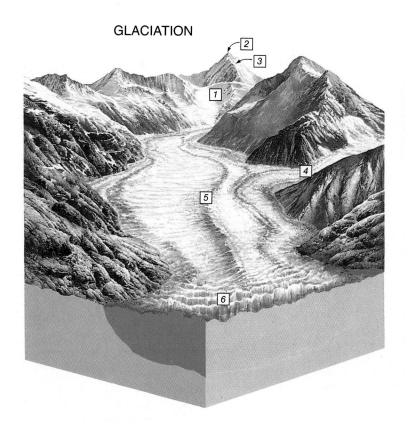

POST-GLACIATION

GLOBE

A globe is a scale model of the earth. It consists of a map of the earth mounted on a sphere of metal, plastic, cardboard, or other material. Unlike some flat maps, globes show continents and oceans in their true proportions. Distances, directions, shapes, and sizes are all accurately represented. Globes are not easy to carry around, though, and because they are limited to a very small scale, they lack detail. The first known globe was an ancient Greek one, but the oldest existing one was made in 1492 by German geographer Martin Behaim. It brought together the best geographic information of the time; its circumference, however, was too small by a fourth.

SEE ALSO MAPS AND GLOBES.

GORGE

A gorge is a deep, narrow valley with nearly vertical sides. The term comes from the French word *gorge,* which means "throat" or "neck." Although there is no sharp distinction, a gorge is usually smaller than a canyon, another kind of valley.

Gorges sometimes form in areas where streams carve channels through rock that is relatively resistant to weathering. Because the rock does not break down easily, the sides of a gorge remain steep. Other gorges may form where the rock is less resistant. Where land has been uplifted, or valleys are cut deeply as they are by glaciers, streams may carve out deep, narrow gorges.

In some gorges, a person can stretch out both hands and touch two walls at the same time. Some of the Yangtze River gorges, in China, are so narrow and treacherous that ships must pass through them one at a time.

Africa's Olduvai Gorge, in Tanzania, is famous for the fossils found there by scientists Louis, Mary, and Richard Leakey. These remains of ancient animals and plants provide clues about early humans.

SEE ALSO CANYON, FOSSIL, RIVER, VALLEY, *and* WEATHERING AND EROSION.

GOVERNMENT

Government consists of the legal, political, and administrative institutions that have authority over a political unit such as a country. Government is also the people who exercise power in the unit. Many governments base their authority on a constitution. Some governments depend on armed force for their power. A few are supported by a religion. Some accept the supremacy of a monarch.

Within a country there are usually several levels of government, and citizens are subject to all of them. The national government is generally the highest authority in a country. There are also regional governments, such as those of states and provinces, and local governments, such as those of counties and towns. In many countries, these governments administer schools, police and fire departments, and public transportation systems, and provide other direct services to citizens.

The powers of regional and local governments vary from country to country. States in the United States, cantons in Switzerland, and provinces in Canada have substantial authority to act independently. Regions and departments in France are more closely supervised by the national government in Paris. The provinces of China are under the tight control of the central government in Beijing.

▲ *A woman shows proof of identity before voting in Potosí, Bolivia. Official observers guard against fraud. Free elections are basic to democracy.*
◄ *Elected to lead the world's most powerful democracy, U.S. Presidents take the oath of office at the Capitol in Washington, D.C.*

Governments generally carry out three broad functions: legislative, executive, and judicial. The legislative function involves making laws and imposing taxes. In many countries, citizens elect representatives to a legislature, often called a parliament, congress, or national assembly. Dictators and military rulers can force a legislature to pass laws. They can also ignore the legislature or even dissolve it. Such leaders may rule by decree, a command that has the force of law.

The executive function of government includes enforcing the laws, providing for the country's administration and defense, and conducting foreign policy. Some countries, such as the United States, Mexico, and Senegal, choose their chief executives through national elections. Other countries, such as the United Kingdom and Japan, choose their chief executives through the parliamentary system. Under this system, the leader of the majority party in the legislature usually becomes the head of government, often called the prime minister. The Soviet Union has a president, but real power rests with the general secretary of the Communist Party.

Carrying out their judicial function, governments administer justice through law courts. In some countries, courts can also interpret the laws and strike down any that

◀ Thailand's king and queen watch a military parade in 1981. The power of Thai monarchs has been constitutionally limited since 1932. Their duties are now ceremonial and advisory.
▶ The River Thames flows past the Houses of Parliament in London. In the United Kingdom, the elected House of Commons enacts laws, and the leader of the majority party or of a coalition of parties serves as prime minister.
▶ Swiss citizens in the canton of Glarus vote on local issues at the annual assembly. Though rare, such meetings represent the simplest, most direct form of democracy.

violate the principles of the national constitution. A constitution consists of the basic principles and laws of a country that determine the powers of its government. In some countries, such as the United States, the government's powers are defined in a formal document. Many countries have both a written document and unwritten customs as their constitution.

Besides their traditional functions, governments today have many other duties. They may own or regulate telephone companies, postal services, television and radio stations,

▲ Carrying red flags and banners, workers celebrate May Day in Moscow's Red Square. Communist Party leaders watch from atop Lenin's tomb. The first of May—international Labor Day—is a major holiday in communist countries, where it is usually marked by officially sponsored parades.

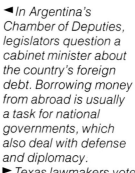

◄ In Argentina's Chamber of Deputies, legislators question a cabinet minister about the country's foreign debt. Borrowing money from abroad is usually a task for national governments, which also deal with defense and diplomacy.
► Texas lawmakers vote in the state's House of Representatives in Austin, where one raised finger means "yes" and two mean "no."

◄ Facial paint indicates rank among Kikuyu men in a Kenyan village. They act as a council to govern village affairs and settle disputes. Local governments regulate community life almost everywhere in the world.

railroads, airlines, and more. The task of protecting the environment frequently falls to governments. Government involvement in the economy varies widely, from regulation of private businesses to total state control.

Governments also represent their countries in the many international organizations that have been established since World War II ended in 1945. Such bodies include the United Nations and its agencies, and the North Atlantic Treaty Organization (NATO).

Types of Government

Monarchy, rule by a king or another royal person, was by far the most common form of government worldwide until the early 20th century. Its decline, however, was heralded by two events in the late 18th century. In 1776, thirteen colonies in North America declared their independence from the British crown and then fought successfully to win independence. The new country, the United States of America, adopted a written constitution, the oldest still in force and a model for many others. In 1789, the French Revolution began, ushering in decades of political turbulence and change in Europe.

A democratic republic, the United States was a rarity. Governments in Europe were chiefly monarchies. Tsars ruled in Russia, and emperors ruled in China and Japan. Mexico and most South American countries did not gain independence until the 1800s. Australia, Canada, and large parts of Asia and Africa were not fully independent until the 1900s.

AFRICA: A LABORATORY OF GOVERNMENTAL SYSTEMS

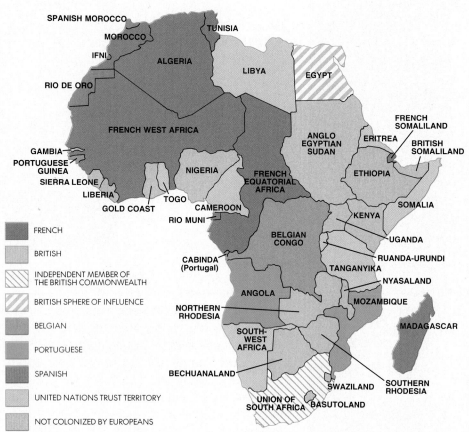

COLONIALISM IN AFRICA: 1947

Between 1885 and 1923, most of Africa was colonized by seven European powers. France, Great Britain, Germany, Italy, Belgium, Portugal, and Spain established colonies, protectorates, and spheres of influence there.

Europeans expanded into Africa primarily for economic and political gain, but scientific and humanitarian interests also played a part. Only Ethiopia and Liberia were not officially colonized.

Colonial governments ruled without the consent of the African peoples. Africans in some French and British territories were allowed to administer their own local affairs, but nowhere were Africans treated as equals by the colonists. Europeans used African land, labor, and natural resources while most Africans were barred from training in fields such as engineering, medicine, finance, and agriculture.

Germany lost its colonies after World War I, as did Italy after World War II. In 1947, these ex-colonies became United Nations Trust Territories. They were administered by other colonial powers while plans went forward for their independence. Southwest Africa (Namibia) was put under the administration of South Africa, which retained control of it against the wishes of the United Nations.

Legend (top map):
- FRENCH
- BRITISH
- INDEPENDENT MEMBER OF THE BRITISH COMMONWEALTH
- BRITISH SPHERE OF INFLUENCE
- BELGIAN
- PORTUGUESE
- SPANISH
- UNITED NATIONS TRUST TERRITORY
- NOT COLONIZED BY EUROPEANS

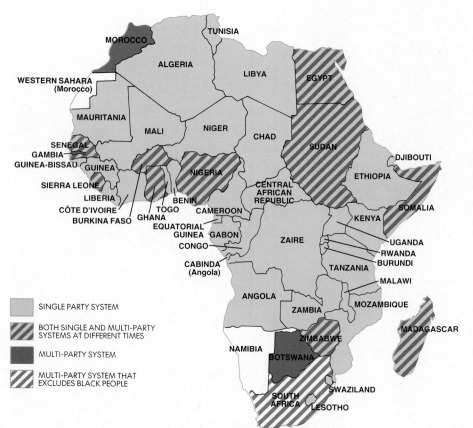

Legend (bottom map):
- SINGLE PARTY SYSTEM
- BOTH SINGLE AND MULTI-PARTY SYSTEMS AT DIFFERENT TIMES
- MULTI-PARTY SYSTEM
- MULTI-PARTY SYSTEM THAT EXCLUDES BLACK PEOPLE

POLITICAL PARTIES: 1957-1987
Single and Multi-Party Regimes

Most African states gained their independence between 1957 and 1967. Many former colonies entered the era of independence with Western-style constitutions and competing political parties. Since then, most of the former colonies have tended toward authoritarian regimes that have outlawed opposition political parties. The multi-party system often did not fit Africa's political experience, and a great deal of political experimentation has occurred.

Africans have tried to adapt both Western and African political procedures and institutions to the needs of their countries. The results have varied, but the most widespread form of government has been single-party rule. The multi-party classification used for the map excludes countries where a multi-party system failed within approximately five years after independence.

Because opposition political parties are illegal in most African countries, groups that disagree with the ruling party have often tried to overthrow the government, start civil wars, or lead separatist movements.

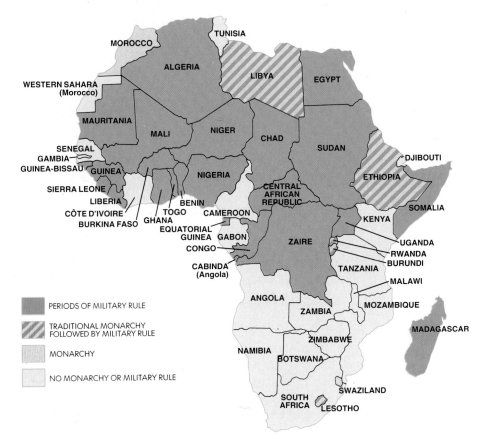

MONARCHIES AND MILITARY REGIMES: 1957-1987

Between 1957 and 1987, a few authoritarian regimes were headed by traditional monarchs such as Ethiopia's emperor and Morocco's king. Military rule, however, is the most common form of authoritarian government throughout Africa. It is usually established through a coup d'état, the overthrow of the government in power.

Economic setbacks, corruption, mismanagement, and enduring poverty provided some of the preconditions for military takeovers. Military regimes have varied from harsh, oppressive administrations to relatively benevolent, disciplined ones. Often a new military ruler brings civilians into his council—sometimes from the very government he overthrew—since the armed forces rarely possess all the complex skills needed to rule a modern state.

Military rulers sometimes set up a timetable for elections and a return to civilian rule, as happened in Egypt, Ghana, and Nigeria. In Mali, a military government was changed into a single-party regime when the former military ruler was elected as the new civilian president. In the Central African Republic, a military ruler proclaimed himself emperor, but he was later ousted.

POPULAR PARTICIPATION IN GOVERNMENT: 1957-1987

While governments have been generally authoritarian, they have experimented with a variety of ways to allow at least limited political participation. Rulers who do not provide for popular participation in the national government often permit the broad-based involvement at local levels that is traditional in most of Africa.

In a few countries with multi-party systems, such as Botswana and Senegal, people can choose among candidates from various political parties. Some single-party states, like Zambia, may present a slate for election with only one candidate for each position, which voters can approve or disapprove. Other single-party states, like Mozambique, let voters choose between candidates belonging to the same party.

In countries such as Algeria, where elections are rare, the government frequently offers referendums, asking people to vote for or against new laws or policies. A similar method called a plebiscite lets people vote for or against a change in ruler or form of government.

▼ *A police officer in New York City writes a ticket for an illegally parked car. Local governments hire police to keep order and to fight crime.*

The control people have over their government depends on whether the government is elected or imposed. Elected, or democratic, governments draw their power from the people. The most common form of elected government is a representative democracy, also called a democratic republic. It would be impractical or impossible for a large population to meet as a group and pass laws. Instead, the people choose representatives who form the legislature. Constitutional monarchies are most frequently a type of democratic government. The king or queen symbolizes national unity and may advise political leaders, but usually holds little real power. The legislature actually governs the country.

Elections are the mechanism for choosing leaders who have the confidence of the people they govern. To win an election, citizens with similar political views form or join a political party. Each party chooses candidates for office and helps fund campaigns. Most elections are held to fill political offices.

Another voting practice, called a referendum, allows a population to choose or reject a proposed law or other measure. Switzerland, for example, holds a referendum to approve any amendment to its constitution. In 1975, voters in the United Kingdom determined that their country would remain a member of the organization called the European Community. Some communities in the United States require a referendum to approve spending more money on roads or schools.

Elections are considered free when voters have a choice of candidates and do not feel pressured to vote for any particular party.

▲ *Israeli soldiers guard a border crossing in the Sinai Peninsula in 1982. All governments take measures, sometimes military ones, to secure their countries' borders.*
▼ *A lawyer in British-style attire reads evidence to a court in Nairobi, Kenya. The judicial branch of government tries civil and criminal cases and resolves legal disputes.*

Two world wars and other upheavals in the 20th century changed political boundaries and governments throughout the world. Western European countries, Canada, Australia, the United States, and Japan cooperated as industrialized democracies after World War II. Communism prevailed in Eastern Europe, the Soviet Union, the People's Republic of China, and parts of Southeast Asia. Having won independence in the 19th century, some South American countries were democracies; others were under military rule. European colonies in Africa became independent countries experimenting with different forms of government, from dictatorships to republics.

The type of government a country has depends on many factors, including the country's history, its social structure, and its particular needs and concerns. Goals such as the well-being of the people, a strong national defense, and economic prosperity may serve as guiding principles by which governments are shaped and justified.

▼ *In Bangkok, Thailand, officials count money in a commercial bank. Governments around the world regulate their countries' money supplies through central banks. This influences economic activity.*

Political leaders must abide by the election results, and elections must be free of fraud. Ferdinand Marcos had to flee the Philippines in 1986 during the upheaval that took place after voters charged that he had rigged an election to stay on as president.

Citizens with elected governments generally hold that the government's power is limited. Such a view is called constitutionalism, since a country's constitution defines the

▲ *Bulgarian soldiers graduate from military training classes. Most countries maintain armed forces to defend themselves in case of war, to assist allies, and, sometimes, to keep law and order at home.*

government's powers. A bill of rights is attached to many constitutions. Among the rights guaranteed to U.S. citizens are freedom of religion and the right to be tried by a jury if charged with a crime.

Varieties of Imposed Governments

Imposed governments are not chosen by the people. Leaders called dictators may take power after a revolution or civil war, as did Oliver Cromwell in 17th-century England and Francisco Franco in 20th-century Spain. An elected leader may become a dictator. François Duvalier, for example, took over law-making powers in Haiti and refused to permit further elections. Military governments result when the armed forces take control. This usually happens through a coup d'état, the sudden overthrow of the existing government. The military rulers, often called a junta, may appoint a single leader, govern as a group, or place military officers throughout the national and local governments. Chile, Haiti, and Uganda were examples of countries with military regimes in the 1980s.

A special category of imposed governments includes communist regimes. Pure communism is an economic system based on the idea that the members of a society should own all property together and that wealth should be distributed according to individuals' needs. In communist countries, the economic and political systems are combined.

Ownership of land or businesses by individuals is usually forbidden; all or most of the economy is directed by the government.

In 1917, revolutionaries led by V.I. Lenin overthrew the short-lived representative government that had replaced the Russian monarchy in the wake of popular uprisings. Lenin established the first communist state, known today as the Union of Soviet Socialist Republics (U.S.S.R.), or the Soviet Union. At the end of World War II, the U.S.S.R. occupied several countries in Eastern Europe and set up communist governments in them. Communism also took root in China, Vietnam, Laos, Cambodia, and Cuba.

Imposed governments may display features of elected governments, such as legislatures, elections, and constitutions, and may even call themselves democratic. For example, Soviet citizens vote in elections, but there is only one political party. In 1989, however, a new electoral system was introduced, allowing citizens as well as the Communist Party to nominate candidates.

Dictators may permit elections but control the process to ensure votes for themselves. Doing so allows them to claim popular support without risking power.

Frequently lacking popular support,

▲ A class in Harbin, China, studies English. Public education is a primary concern of governments worldwide.
◄ A woman selects a library book at a veterinary school in Siberia. Governments often fund libraries.
▼ Mount McKinley looms in Alaska's Denali National Park and Preserve. Many governments set aside lands for parks and wildlife refuges.

imposed governments often fear any possible source of rebellion or resistance. As a result, they may seek to control and direct the people, a policy called repression. Government domination of almost every aspect of citizens' lives is called totalitarianism.

An imposed government usually takes control of newspapers, television, and radio. The government may run these directly or demand to approve anything that is printed or broadcast. Religious practices may be banned, and followers of certain religions may be persecuted. Restrictions may be placed on people's movements. Citizens may not be allowed to travel widely, or they may have to be home by a certain hour. Special police may carry out the government's orders.

Governments, of course, are subject to change. Partly because of unstable economic and social conditions, some democracies have given way to military rule. This has happened in several Latin American countries. Sometimes one form of imposed government is replaced by another. In 1979, for instance, the Iranian monarchy was overthrown and a theocracy, or rule by religious leaders, was established in its place. On the other hand, some repressive governments may become less so. In the 1980s, for example, the government of the Soviet Union began permitting its citizens to express themselves more freely and to participate somewhat in public affairs.

SEE ALSO COMMUNISM, COUNTRY, DEMOCRACY, ECONOMY, INTERNATIONAL ORGANIZATION, MONARCHY, RELIGIONS, *and* TOTALITARIANISM.

▲ *A Colorado farmer collects his mail.*
◄ *A public telephone awaits users near Loch Ness, in Scotland. Governments seek to ensure that postal, telephone, and other communications systems function smoothly.*
▼ *Interconnecting highways and ramps form "Spaghetti Junction," near Birmingham, England. Maintaining an adequate road system is an important responsibility of government.*

GRAINS

Grains are the edible seeds of certain grasses. The most commonly grown grains, or cereal grains, are rice, wheat, and corn (maize). Others include sorghum, millet, rye, barley, and oats. Worldwide, grains are the most important food staples: Three-quarters of the calories that people consume come from grains. Grains also feed livestock and provide raw materials for such manufactured items as paper, paste, and cosmetics.

SEE ALSO AGRICULTURE, FARMING, *and* FOOD.

GRASSLAND

A grassland is a region where grass is the naturally dominant vegetation. A grassland occurs where there is not enough regular rainfall to support the growth of a forest, but not so little rain as to form a desert.

Most of the world's major grasslands lie in the drier portions of a continent's interior. Grasslands, which exist on every continent except Antarctica, are usually found where rainfall averages 25 to 75 centimeters (10–30 in) a year. Land that receives less than 25 centimeters of annual rainfall is too dry to support grasses and many other plants. Such arid regions have primarily xerophytic vegetation—plants that require very little water, such as cactuses. Areas that average more than 75 centimeters of rain each year are wet enough to support continuous tree growth.

Temperate grasslands exist where there are distinct seasonal variations in temperature. Summers in these grasslands are warm, and winters are cold. In the Northern Hemisphere, temperate grasslands include the North American prairie and the Eurasian steppe. The South African veld and the South American pampas are temperate grasslands of the Southern Hemisphere.

Tropical grasslands, called savannas, lie

▲ Temperate grasslands called pampas surround a ranch in Argentina. "Prairie" and "steppe" are some of the other names for temperate grasslands.
◄ Cape buffalo stampede through a savanna in South Africa's Kruger National Park. Savannas are tropical grasslands with scattered trees.

near the Equator. They lack well-defined seasons based on temperature. They are usually warm year-round, but they have distinct rainy seasons and dry seasons. The climate is generally dry, and the rainy seasons are shorter than the dry seasons.

Generally, grasslands have rich soils. Their fertility is the major reason people have altered them to a greater extent than any other vegetation region. Today, most grasslands have been converted to cropland and pasture. Some 70 percent of the earth's food is grown on former grasslands.

Temperate Grasslands

Temperate grasslands around the world are known by different names, depending in part on the language of the people who settled them. The Eurasian steppe, a grassland stretching from Hungary through the southern part of the Soviet Union to China, is the world's largest temperate grassland. "Steppe" comes from a Russian word meaning "treeless plain." Although some grasslands in North America could be classified as steppe, explorers called them prairie, which comes from the French word meaning "meadow."

Within temperate grasslands, there are

ECKERT EQUAL AREA PROJECTION

three major types of grasses. Shortgrasses, which grow where there is limited rainfall, usually measure less than half a meter (20 in) tall. Midgrasses are often half a meter to 1.2 meters (4 ft) in height, and tall grasses reach 1.5 meters (5 ft) or more.

Shortgrasses once dominated much of the Great Plains of the United States, where annual rainfall averages as little as 25 centimeters (10 in). Tallgrass prairie, the wettest of the temperate grasslands, once stretched roughly from Texas into Canada and from the edge of the Great Plains in eastern Kansas to Ohio. As many as 300 different kinds of plants may grow on a single hectare (2.5 acres) of tallgrass prairie. A grass called big bluestem dominates on rich, wet soils. It can grow more than 2 meters (7 ft) tall. Other tall grasses and many broad-leaved herbs, such as goldenrod, grow in the shadow of the bluestem. In the spring, hundreds of varieties of wildflowers turn the North American prairie into a crazy quilt of colors.

The boundary between tallgrass and shortgrass prairie was not sharply defined. A transition zone, called mixed-grass prairie, often existed between the two. It contained grasses of all three types, but was dominated by midgrasses.

▲ A prairie dog peeks out from its burrow in Wind Cave National Park, in South Dakota. Bison graze in the distance. Grassland makes up 75 percent of the park.
▼ A vast expanse of treeless steppe provides pasture for a herd of horses in Mongolia. Other animals that live on the Eurasian grasslands include cattle, sheep, goats, and camels.

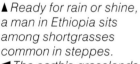

▲ Ready for rain or shine, a man in Ethiopia sits among shortgrasses common in steppes.
◄ The earth's grasslands are found primarily in the dry interior regions of continents. Grasslands flourish where there is enough rainfall to support grasses but not enough to support forests.

Tropical Grasslands

Tropical grasslands called savannas cover about 16 million square kilometers (6 million sq mi) of the earth's land. These grasslands occur in belts on either side of the Equator, where rainfall is highly seasonal. A prolonged dry season alternates with a rainy season. Savannas are areas covered with clumps of grasses and widely scattered trees. Some scientists do not classify them as grasslands because of their tree growth. Savannas are often transition zones between grasslands and forests.

Savannas cover parts of Australia, South America, and India. One-third of the African continent is savanna. The Serengeti Plain of East Africa, with its herds of zebras, wildebeests, and gazelles, and its towering termite mounds and scrubby trees, is a typical savanna. In 1940, the Serengeti National Park was set aside in Tanzania to save a sampling of its wildlife. Much of the grassland there remains in its natural state.

The Serengeti is covered with clumps of tall grasses. Shorter grasses grow between them, and scattered trees and shrubs rise above them. Baobabs, acacias, and palms are common savanna trees. Like all savannas, the Serengeti has two distinct seasons—a short wet season and a long dry season. When the rains finally come, grasses grow quickly, as much as 2.5 centimeters (1 in) in 24 hours. When the rains stop, the grasses begin to wither.

During the dry season, fires sometimes sweep savannas. By killing young trees, fires help keep forests from growing in the moister parts of savannas. Fires play an important role in the ecology of all grasslands.

Animals of the Grasslands

Countless insects live in all grasslands. It is estimated that in the spring, one hectare (2.5 acres) of grassland may contain more than nine million insects—many of them grasshoppers. The large insect population attracts many birds, such as meadowlarks, and the grasses are popular with seed-eaters such as horned larks. Birds have adapted to the lack of trees in the grasslands. Many nest on or in the ground.

▲ *Much of the native grassland on the South Island of New Zealand has been heavily grazed, but remnants of tussock grass survive along fences and roadways.*
► *Wagon wheel tracks through a prairie near Scotts Bluff, Nebraska, mark the Oregon Trail, followed by settlers in the 1800s.*

Grasslands are dominated by burrowing and grazing animals. Burrowers, such as the prairie dog of North America and the suslik, a ground squirrel of the Eurasian steppe, help grasslands by opening up air passages in the soil and mixing the soil's various components.

Grazing animals, such as bison and pronghorn on the North American prairie, wild cattle and deer on the steppes of Eurasia, and wildebeests and zebras on the African savanna, once roamed freely on vast grasslands. They did not overgraze an area, but moved on in time to allow grasses to recover. When wild animals were replaced by domestic ones, such as cattle, people confined them with fences and often overstocked the range. When there is not enough vegetation on an area of land to support the number of animals, overgrazing occurs.

The Future of the Grasslands

Little natural grassland remains today. Around the world, grasslands are lost be-cause of overgrazing, overcultivation, and urban development. Livestock such as sheep and goats can graze grass down to the roots, giving it little chance to recover. With no vegetation to protect it, the soil washes or blows away, turning grasslands into wastelands.

Millions of hectares, originally grassland, are planted with crops such as wheat, millet, and corn. The North American prairie and the Eurasian steppe have become two of the breadbaskets of the world. In the 1930s, over-use, combined with a long drought, devastated about 40 million hectares (100 million acres) of farmland in the southern part of the Great Plains in the United States. This area, called the Dust Bowl, covered parts of Colorado, Kansas, New Mexico, Oklahoma, and Texas. Crops withered, and winds swept away soil. One windstorm dumped ten million tons of soil on Chicago, Illinois. Many rural areas were left looking like deserts as strong, dry winds piled soil into deep drifts. Farms were destroyed, leaving many thousands of Americans poor and homeless. Conservation

▲ Scattered trees provide little shade for cattle grazing on a savanna in northern Argentina.
▼ An endangered black rhinoceros lives on grassland protected by Tanzania's Ngorongoro Conservation Area.

measures helped lead to economic recovery, but periodic drought still plagues the area.

There are no quick solutions to the problems of grassland destruction. Many countries cannot afford to allow arable land to lie uncultivated because they need the food and money the crops provide. When the land can no longer support crops, more natural grasslands are cultivated.

Farmers can help slow the further destruction of grasslands by using sound farming practices that will limit the effects of weathering and erosion. If the number of animals allowed to graze in an area is controlled, the grasses will be able to regenerate. The future of the earth's grasslands lies in the ability of people to recognize grasslands as a varied ecosystem valuable for its own sake as well as for its fertile soil.

SEE ALSO AGRICULTURE, FIRE, PRAIRIE, SAVANNA, STEPPE, *and* VEGETATION REGIONS.

◀ *A farmer breaks up sod in Montana's grasslands, preparing the ground for cultivation. Natural grasslands are rapidly disappearing. Many of them have become productive cropland.*
▼ *The James Woodworth Prairie Preserve, in Chicago, Illinois, is a living museum that preserves prairie land for those who might otherwise never see a natural grassland.*

GRAVITY

Gravitation is the universal attraction between two objects that causes them to pull toward each other. The more mass, or amount of material, an object has, the stronger its gravitational force. The pull between objects that are close together is stronger than it would be if the same objects were farther apart. Gravity, which is the force of gravitation on or near the surface of a celestial body, pulls mass toward the body's center.

The earth's gravity pulls everything on or near the planet toward its center. Our feet remain firmly on the earth even though our planet is spinning on its axis. Without gravity, the atmosphere, the ocean, and everything else on the earth would fly into space.

Effects of the earth's gravity are easy to see. If a flowerpot is knocked from its shelf, it does not sail away. It falls to the floor. Water, pulled by the earth's gravity, flows downhill. Every day, gravity pulls tremendous amounts of rock and soil slowly down slopes on the earth's surface. The speed of the downward movement is affected by other factors, such as water, wind, and ice.

No object has weight unless it is acted upon by gravity. The stronger the pull of gravity on an object, the more the object weighs, even though its mass stays the same. Astronauts experience weightlessness in space because they have escaped the earth's gravity. On the moon, where gravity is one-sixth that of the earth, space travelers weigh much less than they do on the earth. They are able to bound across the lunar landscape with giant leaps impossible on their home planet.

In the 17th century, English scientist Isaac Newton developed mathematical explanations for the movement of objects, including the planets. According to Newton's theory, a moving body travels in a straight line unless some outside force such as gravitation

► A combination of momentum and gravitation determine the orbital path of an object. Without the sun's gravitational force, a planet would speed through space, its momentum carrying it along a straight path away from the sun. The sun's gravitational pull, however, keeps the planet from flying outward. The gravitational forces of other objects also affect a planet's orbital path.

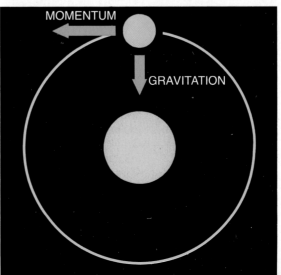

▲ Spread-eagled, a man fights the pull of the earth's gravity with the help of a column of wind generated by the propeller of a DC-4. Winds between 130 to 210 kilometers per hour (80–130 mph) hold him aloft. Spotters at the recreational facility help keep him from crashing into the metal net above the spinning blades.

tion work together to hold the planets and other celestial bodies in orbit.

Newton's theory of gravitation helped people make sense of things they saw happening every day. It explained the moon's pull on the earth's ocean waters, which helps cause the tides. Scientists applied his theory in tracing the orbits of comets and the movements of moons around the planets.

Newton's theory is adequate in explaining circumstances where gravitational fields are relatively weak, but physicist Albert Einstein improved upon that theory in the early 1900s, explaining things that Newton could not. Einstein's general theory of relativity, for example, explains circumstances in which gravitational fields become very strong, as with black holes. The gravitational pull of black holes is so powerful that not even light can escape. Einstein's theory could also be used when scientists had to work with extremely small measurements. For example, scientists found that Newton's theory could

acts on it to change its course. His work showed that each body in the solar system attracts every other with a force that depends on each object's mass and the distance between the objects.

The sun contains almost 100 percent of the solar system's mass. Its gravitational force is stronger than that of any of the planets, which are irresistibly attracted to it. It would take the mass of 333,000 earths to equal the gravitational force of the sun's mass. Without the sun's gravitational force, the momentum of each body in the solar system would carry it through space in a straight path away from the sun. Were it not for its speed and distance from the sun, each object would be pulled into the fiery ball. Instead, momentum and gravita-

▲ *Downhill movement induced by gravity is evident everywhere. Here, the roaring waters of the Niagara River plunge 60 meters (200 ft) down a steep gorge in New York State.*
► *Rock columns in Devils Postpile National Monument in California crumble as weathering and erosion weaken the natural formations. Gravity pulls the fragmented rock toward the earth's center, forming a pile of rubble.*

not explain an irregularity they had discovered in Mercury's orbit. Minute shifts in the orbit over a period of 4,000 years amounted to a distance the width of the earth's moon. The shifting path of the planet's orbit could be accounted for by using the mathematical calculations of general relativity. For everyday purposes, however, the laws of Newton are as valid today as they were when first published.

SEE ALSO EARTH, MEASUREMENT, MOON, SOLAR SYSTEM, TIDES, *and* WEATHERING AND EROSION.

▼ Gravity and rushing rainwater are the primary sculptors of these eroded hillsides in Kenya, a country in Africa. Overgrazing has denuded the area of vegetation that once helped anchor the soil.

GREAT CIRCLE

A great circle is the largest circle that can be drawn around a sphere such as a globe. More precisely, it is the circle made on the surface of a sphere by any plane, or level surface, that passes through the sphere's center. The Equator is a great circle, and every line of longitude is one half of a great circle.

The most common use of the term is in the phrase "great circle route," which means the shortest route between two points. A piece of string stretched between two points on a globe will mark a great circle route. The edge of a ruler placed between those same points on a flat map may indicate a different route that looks shorter, but only because maps distort the dimensions of the earth.

SEE ALSO EQUATOR, LATITUDE AND LONGITUDE, LONGITUDE, *and* MAPS AND GLOBES.

EXAMPLES OF GREAT CIRCLES

GREENHOUSE EFFECT

The greenhouse effect is a property of the atmosphere that allows the short-wave radiation of sunlight to pass easily to the earth's surface but makes it difficult for heat in the form of long-wave radiation to escape back toward space. Sunlight penetrates the atmosphere freely and is absorbed by the ground. The warmed earth radiates heat into the atmosphere as infrared radiation. Carbon dioxide, water vapor, and other atmospheric gases easily absorb infrared radiation. The gases, in turn, give off heat, some of it directed toward space and the rest back toward the earth.

Scientists tell us that without this "blanket," temperatures would be so cold that the earth would be uninhabitable. However, they also say that human activities may be increasing the greenhouse effect. The burning of fossil fuels, for example, releases carbon dioxide into the atmosphere. Concentrations of methane and other "greenhouse gases" are rising, too. These gases may absorb enough radiation to raise the earth's temperature 2° to 6°C (3.6°–10.8°F) within the next century. This could cause the world's climate to change dramatically, eventually causing polar ice sheets to melt.

SEE ALSO ATMOSPHERE, CLIMATE, *and* POLLUTION.

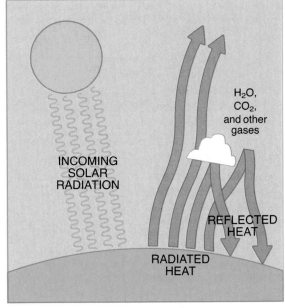

H_2O, CO_2, and other gases

INCOMING SOLAR RADIATION

REFLECTED HEAT

RADIATED HEAT

GROUNDWATER

Groundwater occurs beneath the earth's surface. It comes primarily from rain and melted snow that seep down through soil and into pores and cracks in rocks. When it encounters an impermeable layer and can move down no farther, it forms an aquifer—a zone saturated, or filled, with water. This water in the aquifer is called groundwater. At the top of the aquifer is the water table.

There is about 30 times more groundwater than there is surface water in all the lakes and streams combined. But in heavily populated areas, including some parts of the United States, groundwater is being used up faster than nature can replace it. This causes a lowering of the water table and can lead to water shortages.

In many places, chemicals from factories and farms, as well as wastes from dumps and sewers, have seeped into the earth and polluted shallow groundwater.

SEE ALSO AQUIFER, POLLUTION, WATER, *and* WATER TABLE.

GROWING SEASON

A growing season is the period of the year when crops and other plants grow successfully. The length of a growing season varies from place to place. In tropical regions, the period may last all year or it may depend on a rainy season. In temperate and polar regions, the growing season depends mostly on temperatures and can last from less than two to more than six months. Elevation also affects growing seasons: Higher elevations generally mean shorter periods, and lower elevations, longer ones. Most crops require a growing season of at least 90 days. In temperate regions, a growing season usually is figured by calculating the average number of days between the last heavy frost in spring and the first severe frost in autumn.

SEE ALSO CLIMATE, ELEVATION, *and* SEASONS.

GULF

A gulf is a portion of the ocean that penetrates into the land. Gulfs vary a great deal in size, shape, and depth. They are generally larger and more deeply indented than bays. Like bays, they often make excellent harbors.

Gulfs may be formed by movements in the earth's crust that create downfolds, or troughs, in the rock. They are sometimes connected to the ocean by one or more narrow passages called straits.

Some Major Gulfs

The Gulf of Mexico, bordered by the United States, Cuba, and Mexico, is the world's largest gulf. It has a coastline of approximately 5,000 kilometers (3,100 mi), and is more than 1,800 kilometers (1,100 mi) long and 1,300 kilometers (800 mi) wide.

The Gulf of Alaska, part of the North Pacific Ocean, has a broad mouth, and so the chemical composition and circulation of its waters are similar to those of the open sea. Glaciers have scoured fjord-like bays along the shore.

The Gulf of Carpentaria, on Australia's northeast coast, is an inlet of the Arafura Sea. Because both the sea and the gulf are shallow, the exchange of water between the two is reduced. Sediment collects at the mouth of the gulf, forming underwater barriers. The low shore is bordered in some places by mangrove swamps.

The Persian Gulf, 960 kilometers (600 mi) long, is an arm of the Arabian Sea bordered

▲ *In the shadow of the St. Elias Mountains, kayakers and fishing boats share calm waters in the Gulf of Alaska.*
▼ *Fishing boats drift in the Patraïkós Kólpos, a gulf adjoining the Ionian Sea.*

by Iran, Iraq, Kuwait, Saudi Arabia, and several other countries. It is connected through the Strait of Hormuz to the much smaller Gulf of Oman. Vast deposits of petroleum in this region make the Persian Gulf strategically important. Middle Eastern countries depend on the gulf for trade and for access to the Indian Ocean. All countries that consume oil from the region, including the United States, Japan, and countries of Western Europe, have a vital interest in keeping the gulf open to shipping.

SEE ALSO BAY, COAST, FJORD, *and* HARBOR.

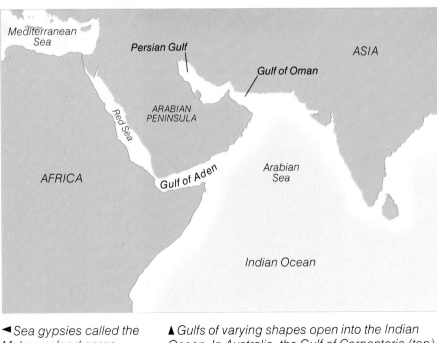

◄ Sea gypsies called the Moken unload cargo. They live on their boats, plying shallow waters in the Gulf of Thailand.

▲ Gulfs of varying shapes open into the Indian Ocean. In Australia, the Gulf of Carpentaria (top) is nearly as wide as it is long. The gulf's eastern shore was the first European landfall in Australia. Long, narrow gulfs flank the Arabian Peninsula.

H

HABITAT

A habitat is the natural environment of a plant or an animal—the place where the plant commonly grows or where the animal normally finds food and shelter. For example, a marsh is a cattail habitat. A rain forest is the habitat of three-toed sloths, which spend almost all of their lives in trees.

The habitat of a species differs from its range. The range of an animal is the part of the world it inhabits. A grassland, for example, is the habitat of the giraffe, whose range is central, eastern, and southern Africa.

SEE ALSO BIOME *and* ENVIRONMENT.

HAIL

Hail originates when colliding drops of water freeze together in the cold upper regions of a thunderstorm. As each frozen mass falls, it collides with more drops, collecting a layer of moisture. Strong updrafts lift it repeatedly; layer after layer of ice forms around it until it falls to earth as a hailstone.

SEE ALSO PRECIPITATION, THUNDERSTORM, *and* WEATHER.

▲ *Hailstones from a spring thunderstorm pelted these tulips and daffodils in England. Hailstones can be as small as peas or as large as grapefruit.*

HARBOR

A harbor is a body of water sheltered by natural or artificial barriers. Harbors can provide safe anchorage and permit the transfer of cargo and passengers between ships and the shore. A harbor is deep enough to keep ships from touching bottom and should give them enough room to turn and to pass each other. Periodic dredging keeps ship channels deep and free of silt.

Most harbors are natural ones. They are located along many types of coastline. They occur in fjords, coves, and enclosed bays, along mountainous coasts, and in lagoons. They also occur along lakeshores and in estuaries, where rivers empty into the ocean.

New York City has one of the world's finest natural harbors, with deep water, small tidal variations, and moderate currents. Other cities with outstanding natural harbors

▼ *Sailboats and other craft dock at Harbor Springs, Michigan, on Little Traverse Bay, the deepest harbor in the Great Lakes.*

include San Francisco, in California; Rio de Janeiro, in Brazil; and Sydney, in Australia.

There are artificial harbors as well as natural ones. The port at Dover, England, for example, lies behind a breakwater 1,300 meters (4,265 ft) long; the artificial barrier protects the port from the force of waves. Breakwaters were also used to create the harbor at Madras, in India, considered one of the finest artificial harbors in the world.

Harbors may serve as ports and are frequently vital to trade. When they function as ports, they often have artificial structures such as jetties, as well as lighthouses, buoys, and other aids to navigation. The large size of modern vessels requires that harbors have designated ship channels.

Harbors have played an important role in civilization ever since people began using boats and ships at sea. Some 2,000 years ago, for instance, Herod the Great had a magnificent harbor built for his city of Caesarea Maritima on the coast of what is now Israel. It set a standard for future harbors. Most harbors were not improved until the mid-1800s. As commerce increased and ships grew bigger, enlarging and deepening harbors became necessary. Modern harbors range from small enclosures to huge commercial ports.

SEE ALSO BAY, CHANNEL, PORT, TRADE, *and* TRANSPORTATION AND COMMUNICATION.

HEMISPHERE

Any great circle around the earth divides it into two equal halves called hemispheres. The earth is divided into the Northern and Southern Hemispheres by the Equator. The earth can also be divided into hemispheres along specific lines of longitude. For example, the 20° west meridian and the 160° east meridian are often used to divide the earth into the Eastern and Western Hemispheres. The Eastern Hemisphere is commonly defined as Europe, Africa, Asia, Australia, and New Zealand, and the Western Hemisphere as North and South America.

SEE ALSO EQUATOR, GREAT CIRCLE, LATITUDE AND LONGITUDE, *and* PRIME MERIDIAN.

▲ *Crossing from Manhattan to Staten Island, a ferry passes the Statue of Liberty, which has graced New York harbor since 1886.*

HERDING

Herding is the practice of caring for roaming groups of livestock over a large area. Herding began about 10,000 years ago as prehistoric hunters domesticated wild animals such as sheep and goats that naturally live and travel together in groups. The hunters learned that by controlling animals they had once pursued they could have reliable sources of meat, milk and milk products, and hides for tents and clothing.

Today, herding involves the same basic tasks that it did in prehistoric times, and some people move about with their herds as a way of life. Known as nomads, or nomadic herders, they roam in small tribal or extended family groups and have no home base. Nomads live in arid and semiarid parts of Africa, Asia, and Europe, and also in the tundra regions of Asia and Europe. Nomads of Africa depend on cattle, goats, sheep, and camels, while those of the tundra usually rely on domesticated reindeer. Other animals herded today include horses, musk-oxen, and yaks. For many nomads, herds provide meat, milk, and hides. Other supplies often come from trade.

Nomadic herding as a way of life is declining because of natural disasters such as droughts, and pressure from governments on nomads to lead a settled existence.

SEE ALSO AGRICULTURE *and* DOMESTICATION.

▲ *On a steep hillside in southern Iran, a herdsman tends goats and sheep. Nomadic tribes living here dwell in tents and move with their flocks.*

HILL

A hill is usually defined as land that rises above its surroundings and has a rounded summit. A hill is smaller and less rugged than a mountain. Many geologists classify any land with an elevation of more than 300 meters (1,000 ft) as a mountain. Whether land is called a hill or a mountain may depend on the elevation of its surroundings. For example, what is considered a mountain in the British Isles might be called a hill in North America.

SEE ALSO ELEVATION *and* MOUNTAIN.

▲ *Hikers walk a gently sloping trail along the crest of the Loess Hills in western Iowa. The hills began to form during the most recent ice age, when windblown dust left by retreating glaciers was deposited here.*
▼ *Round, cocoa-colored hills dot the island of Bohol in the Philippines. The grass carpeting these mounds turns dark brown each summer, earning them their name—the Chocolate Hills.*

HORIZON

The horizon is the line where the earth and the sky seem to meet. We can best see the horizon from a seashore or on a flat plain. In places where most people live, the horizon is often blocked by buildings or trees.

Because the earth's surface is curved, the horizon is farther away from us the higher up we are. From a beach, only the upper part of a distant ship may show above the horizon, but a view from the top of a lighthouse may include the whole ship. If you are 1.5 m (5 ft) tall, the horizon will be 4.4 km (3 mi) away when you are standing on the beach. If you look out from a lighthouse 30.5 m (100 ft) above the ground, the horizon will be 19.7 km (12 mi) away. From an airplane 10.7 km (35,100 ft) above the same location, the horizon would be 369.2 km (229 mi) away.

SEE ALSO ALTITUDE *and* ELEVATION.

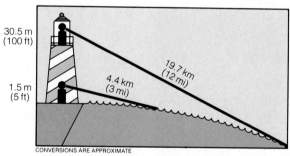

30.5 m (100 ft)
1.5 m (5 ft)
4.4 km (3 mi)
19.7 km (12 mi)
CONVERSIONS ARE APPROXIMATE

HOT SPOT

A hot spot is an intensely hot region deep within the earth. Heat from a hot spot produces a plume of molten rock called magma that rises toward the surface. A hot spot lies under Yellowstone National Park in the United States. There, heat generated by magma just beneath the surface warms groundwater, which is released periodically in eruptions of water and steam. In some places, the molten material may erupt through cracks in the crust, building a volcano. Hot-spot volcanism formed the Hawaiian Islands.

SEE ALSO GEYSER, GROUNDWATER, LAVA, MAGMA, PLATE TECTONICS, *and* VOLCANO.

HUMIDITY

Humidity refers to the amount of water vapor in the air. The most common measure is relative humidity: the amount of water vapor air contains expressed as a percentage of the maximum amount it can hold at the same temperature. For example, air at -10°C (14°F) can hold 2.2 grams of water per cubic meter. If it holds that much moisture, its relative humidity is 100 percent, and it is said to be saturated. If the same air were warmed to 40°C (104°F), its relative humidity would drop to 3.6 percent. A set of two thermometers, called a psychrometer, is used to measure relative humidity. A wet cloth covers one thermometer's bulb. Evaporation cools this thermometer below the actual air temperature, recorded on the dry thermometer. Evaporation and cooling depend on how dry the air is at a given temperature. A table can be used to determine the relative humidity from the amount of cooling.

SEE ALSO CLOUDS, THERMOMETER, *and* WEATHER.

HUMUS

Humus is the dark organic material that forms in soil as plant and animal matter decays. When plants shed leaves, or when twigs, stalks, and other plant material fall to the ground, litter accumulates. When animals die, their remains add to the litter. Over time, the litter decomposes and breaks down into chemical elements. The thick brown or black substance that remains after most of the material has decomposed is called humus. Burrowing earthworms help mix humus with minerals in the soil. Plants grow well in soil that contains humus because microorganisms that produce nitrogen, an important nutrient for most plants, thrive where decaying vegetation is found. The thick consistency of humus makes the soil structure friable, or crumbly. Water can move down easily through the loose soil. Air can circulate among soil particles, allowing oxygen to reach the roots of growing plants.

SEE ALSO SOIL.

HURRICANE

"Hurricane" is one of the names for a rotating tropical storm with winds of at least 119 kilometers per hour (74 mph). Such storms are called hurricanes when they develop over the Atlantic Ocean or the eastern Pacific Ocean. Hurricanes are identical to cyclones that form over the Bay of Bengal and the northern Indian Ocean, and to typhoons in the western Pacific Ocean. These storms

▼ *Winds of Hurricane David buffet Miami palms and pedestrians in September 1979. The storm skirted coastal Florida after causing extensive damage in the Dominican Republic.*

▼ *Tools of a hurricane watcher lie on charts that track Hurricane Elena's path. A satellite image gives data on the storm, which caused more than a billion dollars in damage on the U.S. Gulf coast in late August and early September 1985.*

occur most frequently in summer and autumn, when ocean temperatures are warmest.

Most Atlantic hurricanes are born off Africa's west coast in a region lying between 5 and 25 degrees north of the Equator. There, the trade winds of the Northern and Southern Hemispheres meet, often causing disturbances. About 100 tropical disturbances form in an average year. Of these, more than 90 percent lead to little more than thunderstorms. With energy supplied by the warm ocean, a tropical disturbance can grow into a tropical depression, characterized by thunderstorms and an organized low pressure center. The tropical depression travels across the warm ocean, drawing more energy from that heat source, as well as huge amounts of water. Eventually, as the low pressure center intensifies and the winds gain speed, the depression can build into a tropical storm.

It is easy to spot a growing tropical storm in a satellite photograph. Its spiral of clouds can measure 800 kilometers (500 mi) or more in diameter. A tropical depression becomes a tropical storm when its winds reach 63 kilometers per hour (39 mph). In an average year, six tropical storms build to hurricane strength in the Atlantic Ocean.

Water, not wind, is a hurricane's most destructive force. Nine-tenths of all hurricane-related deaths are caused by storm surges, waves that can rise about 7.5 meters (25 ft) above the ocean's surface. The greatest natural disaster in U.S. history occurred on

HYDROELECTRIC POWER

Hydroelectric power provides electricity by capturing the energy of moving water. The force of the water turns the blades of turbines. The turbines turn generator rotors to produce electricity. Rivers are the major source of hydroelectric power. Dams control the release of river water through the turbines. Hydraulic engineers have developed the technology to harness the power in waterfalls, in ocean waves, and in the ebb and flow of ocean tides to produce electricity.

SEE ALSO DAM, ENERGY, OCEAN, TIDAL ENERGY, TIDES, WATERFALL, *and* WAVES.

▲ *Grand Coulee Dam in Washington harnesses the energy of the Columbia River to produce hydroelectric power for the Pacific Northwest.*

▲ *A police officer walks a flooded road near Corpus Christi, Texas, in August 1980, during Hurricane Allen. Hurricanes pack strong winds, but storm surges cause more damage.*
◄ *A battered beach house stands on Dauphin Island, Alabama, after Hurricane Elena. Winds approaching 200 kilometers per hour (120 mph) destroyed all but the sturdiest structures.*

September 8, 1900, when a 6-meter (20-ft) storm surge inundated Galveston, Texas; more than 6,000 people drowned. An average hurricane drops more than 9 trillion liters (2.4 trillion gallons) of rain each day of its existence, causing floods that can affect an area far larger than that touched by the storm itself.

Meteorologists at the National Hurricane Center in Florida track tropical storms by satellite, weather planes, and radar. If a hurricane threatens, they warn people to leave coastal areas that might be in its path. Many communities have emergency plans so that they can be better prepared for hurricanes, among the most powerful of all storms.

SEE ALSO CYCLONE, TYPHOON, *and* WEATHER.

HYDROSPHERE

The hydrosphere consists of all the earth's water—on the surface, in the ground, and in the air. Nearly three-fourths of the earth is covered with water, most of it in the ocean. The atmosphere contains water in the form of vapor. The hydrosphere helps regulate the earth's temperature and climate. The ocean absorbs heat from the sun and distributes it around the earth in currents. Evaporation from the ocean and other bodies of water makes possible rain and other forms of precipitation that sustain life on land.

SEE ALSO ATMOSPHERE, CLIMATE, EARTH, LITHO-SPHERE, OCEAN, WATER, *and* WATER CYCLE.

I

ICE

Ice is water in its frozen, solid state. Ice often forms on lakes, rivers, and the ocean in cold weather. It occurs as frost, snow, sleet, and hail. Slightly more than 2 percent of the earth's water is frozen into ice—almost all of it in glaciers. Glaciers are huge masses of ice that can carve valleys and change landscapes. Today they are found in many mountainous areas and in the polar regions.

Water will freeze at 0°C (32°F). Near its freezing point, water begins to expand. The expansion exerts great pressure if the water is in a confined space. Because of this, freezing water can burst heavy metal pipes. If water freezes in a crack in a rock, it can break the rock apart. Thus, ice is an agent in the process of weathering and erosion. Expansion also makes ice lighter than liquid water, so that it floats. Even an iceberg weighing many tons floats easily in the ocean.

SEE ALSO FROST, GLACIER, HAIL, ICE CAP, ICE SHEET, ICEBERG, PRECIPITATION, SNOW, WATER, *and* WEATHERING AND EROSION.

ICE AGE

An ice age is a very long period of cold climate during which glaciers may cover large parts of the earth. Scientists believe there have been at least four great ice ages during the past 500 million years. The most recent began about two million years ago, and many scientists say it continues today. Since this ice age peaked about 18,000 years ago, a partial thawing has caused the ice sheets to retreat to their present positions near the Poles. Such thaws occur every 100,000 years or so during an ice age. Ice sheets may begin to advance again in the next 10,000 years.

SEE ALSO CLIMATE, GLACIER, *and* ICE SHEET.

ICE CAP

An ice cap is a thick layer of ice and snow that has formed a permanent crust over areas of land. Ice caps are found primarily in the polar regions. Some geographers use the terms "ice cap" and "ice sheet" interchangeably. Others use "ice cap" only for smaller masses of ice and snow, such as those on Spitsbergen and other island groups in the Arctic.

SEE ALSO ICE SHEET *and* POLAR REGIONS.

ICE SHEET

An ice sheet is a broad, thick layer of glacial ice that covers a large area. Like all glaciers, ice sheets are made up of layers of snow that accumulate over many years in cold regions and gradually compress under their own weight and recrystallize to form ice.

Ice sheets tend to be dome-shaped. They spread out in all directions from their thick, heavy centers. They can cover everything, even high mountain peaks. The biggest ice sheets cover land areas as large as continents and are known as continental glaciers. Today, continental glaciers are found only in Greenland and Antarctica.

Ancient Ice Sheets

About 18,000 years ago, at the peak of the most recent ice age, the earth's climate was cooler than it is today. Massive ice sheets spread out across nearly one-third of the earth's surface. Much of the planet's water became locked up in glaciers, and the sea level dropped sharply—perhaps 100 meters (330 ft) lower than it is today.

Most of the ice that blanketed the continents was contained in two great ice sheets: the Laurentide ice sheet in North America and the Scandinavian ice sheet in Europe. The Laurentide ice sheet was by far the larger. More than 3 kilometers (2 mi) thick, it spread across much of what is now Canada and reached as far south as present-day Missouri. As the ice sheets spread across the land, they greatly changed the earth's surface. In many

◄Meltwater fills furrows in the Antarctic ice sheet. Ice covers most of the frigid continent. Even Mars is sometimes warmer than the South Pole.

▼ Ice sheets have advanced and retreated repeatedly across the face of the earth during the last two million years. The ice was most extensive about 18,000 years ago. Then it began to shrink to its present extent. Another advance of the earth's ice sheets could occur thousands of years from now.

places, the moving ice scraped out basins that later became lakes. The Great Lakes in North America were shaped in this way.

The ice sheets scoured and transported huge amounts of rock and soil from northern regions to places farther south. They spread ground-up debris, called till, across the land. Leftover ridges, or moraines, of heaped debris from the glaciers form Cape Cod in Massachusetts and Long Island in New York.

Today's Ice Sheets

The Greenland ice sheet, which covers 80 percent of the island of Greenland, is a remnant of one of the huge ice sheets that once blanketed much of the Northern Hemisphere. The Greenland ice sheet covers 1.7 million square kilometers (670,000 sq mi) and measures about 3 kilometers (2 mi) thick near its center.

The world's other great existing ice sheet covers some 90 percent of the continent of

GLACIATION TODAY

PRESENT LIMIT OF MULTI-YEAR SEA ICE

LAST GREAT PLEISTOCENE ICE SHEET 18,000 YEARS AGO

Antarctica. It contains about 85 percent of all the world's ice and about two-thirds of the world's fresh water.

Scientists from all over the globe are studying the Antarctic ice sheet. They drill deep down into it and extract long cores of ice. These cores are frozen records of the past. Like rings in a tree trunk, annual layers give the ice samples a striped appearance, which the scientists can analyze to trace the climate history of the earth back for many thousands of years.

By analyzing air bubbles in samples taken from the ice sheets, experts can determine the composition of the atmosphere when the ice was formed and detect the presence of impurities such as ash from volcanic eruptions. All this information may provide clues to global climate patterns.

SEE ALSO CLIMATE, GEOLOGIC TIME SCALE, GLACIER, ICE AGE, ICE CAP, LAKE, POLAR REGIONS, SEA LEVEL, *and* WEATHERING AND EROSION.

▲ *A glacier in eastern Greenland flows off the land and into the water. The result is an ice shelf—a large mass of ice that floats on the ocean but remains attached to the coast.*

▼ *Hikers explore the edge of the Greenland ice sheet on the eastern coast of the world's largest island. Ice coats most of Greenland, which is home to only about 54,000 people.*

ICEBERG

Large chunks of ice that break off, or calve, from glaciers and fall into the sea are known as icebergs. They are formed of frozen fresh water, not salt water. In the Northern Hemisphere, most icebergs break off glaciers on Greenland. Sometimes they drift south with currents into the North Atlantic Ocean. Icebergs also calve from glaciers in Antarctica.

As little as one-eighth of an iceberg is visible above the water. The ice below the water is dangerous to ships. The sharp, hidden ice can easily rip a hole in a ship's hull. In 1912, a large British liner, the *Titanic,* struck an iceberg and sank in the North Atlantic. More than 1,500 people died. Soon after the tragedy, an international iceberg patrol was established to track icebergs and warn ships.

SEE ALSO GLACIER *and* ICE.

▲ *Off Greenland, an iceberg towers above a pair of boats. Arctic icebergs may rise 75 meters (250 ft) above sea level and extend more than a kilometer (0.6 mi). Antarctic icebergs are even larger.*
◄ *The tips of icebergs break the ocean surface near Greenland.*

IMMIGRATION

Immigration is the movement of people into one country from another for the purpose of settlement. (A related term, emigration, refers to movement out of a country.) Immigrants may seek greater economic opportunities, religious freedom, affordable land, or other goals by coming to another country. Immigrants who have fled from persecution or from disasters such as famine and war are known as refugees.

Often, large numbers of immigrants with a common national origin will cluster together in the receiving country, forming ethnic communities. This can make adjustment to new conditions easier. It also allows immigrants to maintain their own language and culture. Many cities have neighborhoods where most residents are of the same national origin. Ethnic neighborhoods in a U.S. city may include a Chinatown or a Little Italy, for example.

A few countries have been extensively populated by immigrants. The United States, in particular, received some 40 million immigrants between 1820 and 1955, more than any other country. Most of them came from Europe during the 19th and early 20th centu-

ries. Economic depression and restrictions on immigration had reduced the flow of immigrants into the U.S. by the mid-1930s. During the late 1960s and the 1970s, many refugees were admitted from Southeast Asia. Today, the chief sources of immigration into the U.S. are Mexico, the Philippines, and South Korea.

SEE ALSO EMIGRATION, ETHNIC GROUP, MIGRATION, NEIGHBORHOOD, *and* POPULATION.

▲ *Travelers from abroad wait in line to have their passports inspected at Miami International Airport, in Florida, one of the busiest ports of entry into the United States. Most immigrants to the U.S. arrive by air.*

INDUSTRY

Industry, in a general sense, is activity that produces goods or provides services. A specific industry is usually made up of companies or other groups engaged in the same business, such as mining, manufacturing, packaging agricultural goods, and banking.

Industries can be divided into three broad groups: primary, secondary, and tertiary. Primary industries gather or extract natural resources. The major kinds of primary industries are farming, fishing, and mining. Secondary industries change raw materials into finished goods. Two major secondary industries are processing—treating or packaging resources to prepare them for use—and manufacturing. Tertiary industries provide services rather than goods. Transportation, communications, and tourism are three common kinds of tertiary industries. The products of industries are called outputs.

Anything an industry needs to do its job is called a productive resource, or input. Industries require five basic inputs for production: natural resources, capital, labor, management, and technology.

Natural resources are the raw materials an industry uses to produce goods. Minerals, timber, land, and water are examples of natural resources. Goods produced by one

▲ An open pit mine in New Mexico yields copper ore. Along with farming and fishing, mining is one of the three major kinds of primary industries.
► Logs hauled by truck from a tree farm in Oregon will become lumber at a nearby sawmill.

OMAN

SOVIET UNION

TANZANIA

JAPAN

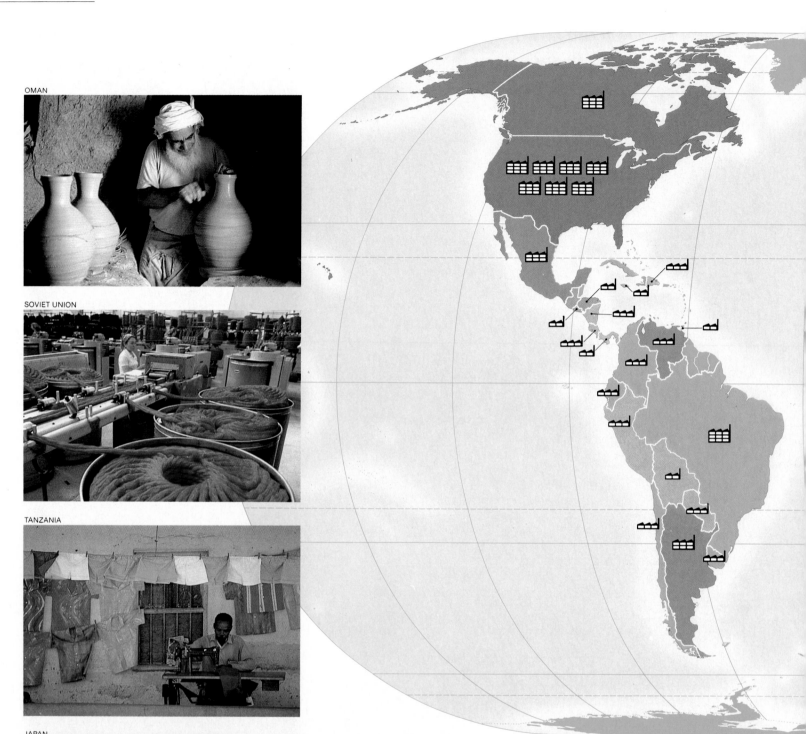

◄Skills and equipment used to produce goods vary widely. A potter in Bahla, Oman, shapes a water jug by hand. A Soviet worker operates machinery that spools yarn. A tailor in Tanzania stitches clothing on an old sewing machine. In Japan, factory workers inspect cars before their delivery to showrooms.

industry may become resources for another. Coal and iron ore are natural resources used to produce steel, which in turn can be used to make cars, ships, and many other things.

Capital may refer to a company's assets that are used in the production of goods. For example, a firm's buildings and durable equipment such as machines and trucks are capital assets. Capital may also refer to the money needed to start or expand a business. Many companies raise money from investors,

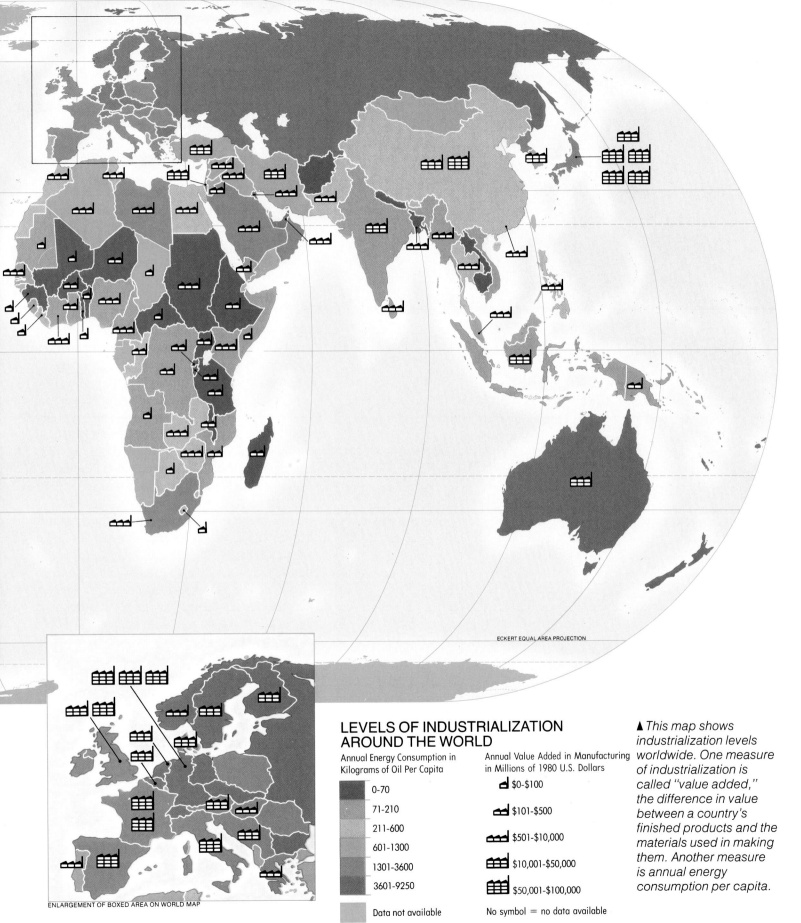

LEVELS OF INDUSTRIALIZATION AROUND THE WORLD

Annual Energy Consumption in Kilograms of Oil Per Capita

- 0-70
- 71-210
- 211-600
- 601-1300
- 1301-3600
- 3601-9250

Data not available

Annual Value Added in Manufacturing in Millions of 1980 U.S. Dollars

- $0-$100
- $101-$500
- $501-$10,000
- $10,001-$50,000
- $50,001-$100,000

No symbol = no data available

▲ This map shows industrialization levels worldwide. One measure of industrialization is called "value added," the difference in value between a country's finished products and the materials used in making them. Another measure is annual energy consumption per capita.

ENLARGEMENT OF BOXED AREA ON WORLD MAP

ECKERT EQUAL AREA PROJECTION

SOURCES: *WORLD DEVELOPMENT REPORT, 1987* AND *THE NEW BOOK OF WORLD RANKINGS*, FACTS ON FILE PUBLICATIONS, 1984.

287

◄ An Israeli shopkeeper in Jerusalem offers plastic toys for sale. The manufacture of finished products such as toys is a secondary industry.

people who buy shares in companies and often receive part of the profits.

Labor is human activity that provides goods or services. More specifically, the term refers to the services performed by workers for wages as distinguished from those rendered by owners and investors for profits. Labor is required by all industries, from small farms and businesses to large manufacturing firms such as steel companies and service organizations such as airlines.

Management is concerned with supervising and coordinating business activity. Managers decide how much a company should produce and at what cost. They decide how many workers should be hired and at what wages. They determine what the market is for the company's products and how to use resources most efficiently.

Technology includes all the ways people use tools, machines, materials, techniques, and power sources to do work and to improve their lives. Advances in technology over the past 200 years have greatly improved the quality of goods and services and have made them more readily available.

Before the late 18th century, manufacturing usually took place in homes or in small shops. Then, in the late 18th and early 19th centuries, the industrial revolution began in Great Britain, bringing radical changes. It soon spread to other European countries and to North America and Australia.

Belief in unlimited progress, different attitudes toward savings, and minimal government restriction were among the many factors that contributed to the industrial revolution. Growing populations functioned as a market. In addition, Great Britain possessed a vast empire that needed manufactured goods. Machines were invented to do work previously done by people. The most important invention was the steam engine.

As industrialization has continued in modern times, workers have become more skilled and have often needed to have more education and training. Machines have become more sophisticated.

Industrialization has not been uniform

▲ A container ship awaits unloading in Long Beach, California. Goods in large metal containers can be handled faster than loose cargo, thus reducing labor costs. Tertiary industries such as shipping provide services, not goods.
► New cars in Detroit, Michigan, have just rolled off an assembly line, where factory workers perform specialized jobs.

throughout the world. The United States, Western Europe, and Japan produce most of the world's industrial goods. Their complex economies feature a wide variety of goods and services, and conveniences such as electricity, telephones, and computers.

Developing countries produce far fewer goods and services, and often struggle to meet basic needs. Most of their resources are used to feed and house their people. They often lack the capital, skilled labor, and advanced technology needed for large-scale industries. There are wide variations among developing countries. For example, Saudi Arabia and Venezuela, which are rich in oil, are more developed than Haiti and Ethiopia, which are poor in natural resources.

Older industrialized countries have depleted many of their natural resources. They have begun to rely on less developed countries for raw materials. In addition, many American and European companies now have factories in developing countries of the Far East, where labor is much cheaper.

Industrialization has resulted in higher living standards for people in the developed world. It has also caused problems such as pollution, energy shortages, and a wide gap between wealthy and poor countries. Finding solutions has become an urgent task.

SEE ALSO AGRICULTURE, CITY, DEVELOPMENT, ECONOMY, MINING, NATURAL RESOURCE, POLLUTION, POPULATION, TECHNOLOGY, TRADE, and TRANSPORTATION AND COMMUNICATION.

◄ A welder works on a skyscraper in Dallas, Texas. The construction industry, like many others today, requires highly skilled labor.
▼ On the floor of Lloyd's of London, a famous British insurance group, underwriters insure against almost any kind of risk.

▲ Pakistani barbers serve customers at an outdoor shop. In an increasingly industrialized world, individuals still provide many goods and services.

INTERNATIONAL ORGANIZATION

When governments or private groups in different countries agree to work together for a specific purpose, they often form an international organization. Its headquarters is usually located in one of the member countries, but its activities are carried on wherever they are needed. Several thousand international organizations exist around the world. More than 300 of them are formed by governments and are called intergovernmental organizations. The biggest of these is the United Nations.

The UN was created in 1945, at the end of World War II, by governments hoping to avoid future wars. Peacekeeping remains its primary goal. Specialized agencies of the UN, such as the World Health Organization and the World Bank, try to promote international cooperation in areas that are vital to people everywhere. Most countries belong to the UN and its specialized agencies.

Many countries cluster in regional organizations with a military, economic, or political purpose. For example, the United States, Canada, many European countries, and Turkey belong to the North Atlantic Treaty Organization (NATO). They have agreed to aid each other if attacked, as have the Soviet Union and its European allies in the Warsaw Pact. The Association of South East Asian Nations (ASEAN) promotes economic growth and mutual aid among its member countries. The Organization of American States (OAS) fosters peace and understanding among countries of the Western Hemisphere.

Most international organizations are nongovernmental. They may function in a single area, like the East African Wildlife Society, or work worldwide, like the Red Cross.

SEE ALSO COUNTRY, GOVERNMENT, *and* STATE.

▲ Marked with a red cross, sacks of flour are intended for victims of famine in the East African country of Ethiopia. One of the oldest and best known international organizations, the Red Cross operates as a global network. In this case, the flour was donated by Canada.

IRRIGATION

Irrigation is the watering of land by artificial means. It is used for agriculture in places that have sparse or seasonal rainfall. In areas of erratic precipitation, the use of irrigation improves crop growth and quality.

Ancient peoples in many parts of the world practiced irrigation. The Egyptians and the Chinese built irrigation canals, dams, dikes, and water storage facilities. Some ancient farmers of North and South America used similar methods. Many civilizations developed as societies expanded through the use of irrigation.

Modern irrigation systems use reservoirs, tanks, and wells to supply water for crops. Canals or pipelines carry the water to fields, relying on the force of gravity and pumps to move it. Crops may then be irrigated by several methods: flooding an entire field; channeling water between rows; spraying water through large sprinklers; or letting it drip onto plants through holes in pipes.

In recent times, the amount of irrigated land in the world has doubled, with an estimated 18 percent of all cropland under irrigation. This expansion has occurred mainly in parts of Asia, Africa, and South America.

To help meet the world demand for food, more farmland and more irrigation will be needed. Many experts fear that the expanding use of irrigation in some areas will deplete underground water and will reduce soil fertility by depositing salts on the land.

SEE ALSO AGRICULTURE, FARMING, *and* FOOD.

▲ *Rectangular rice fields segment an African landscape. The flooding of large enclosed areas, known as basin, or flood, irrigation, is an ancient method. It is still used for watering grainfields in many parts of the world.*
▼ *Drop by drop, a young plant receives moisture directly. In trickle, or drip, irrigation, water falls from small holes in pipes.*

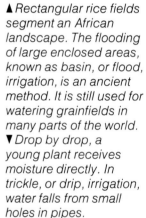

◄ *In California's Imperial Valley, sprinklers drench a field with water. The former desert became productive farmland through irrigation.*

ISLAND

An island is a body of land that is surrounded by water. Continental landmasses are also surrounded by water, but because they are so large, they are called continents rather than islands. Australia, the smallest continent, is more than three and a half times the size of Greenland, the largest island.

There are countless islands in the ocean and in lakes and rivers around the world. They vary greatly in size, in climate, and in the kinds of plants and animals that inhabit them.

Many islands are quite small, covering less than half a hectare (1 acre). These tiny islands are often called islets. Other islands are huge. Greenland, for example, covers an area of about 2,175,600 square kilometers (840,000 sq mi).

Some islands, such as Greenland, are cold and ice-covered. Others, such as Tahiti, lie in warm, tropical waters. Many islands are thousands of kilometers from the nearest mainland. Other islands, such as the Greek islands known as the Cyclades in the Aegean Sea, are found in closely spaced groups called archipelagoes.

Many islands are little more than barren rock with few plants or animals on them. Others are among the most crowded places on earth. Tokyo, one of the world's largest cities, is on the island of Honshū, in Japan. And on another island, Manhattan, rise the towering skyscrapers of New York City.

For centuries, islands have been stopping places for ships. Because of isolation and remoteness, many islands have also been homes to some of the world's most unusual and fascinating wildlife.

Kinds of Islands

There are four major kinds of islands: continental, oceanic, coral, and barrier.

Continental islands were once connected to a continent. Some of them formed as the earth's shifting continents broke apart.

Scientists believe that millions of years

► Boats dart among lush green islands in the Republic of Palau in the western Pacific. These coral islands formed on oceanic volcanoes.

CONTINENTAL ISLANDS

BARRIER ISLANDS

CORAL ISLAND

OCEANIC ISLAND

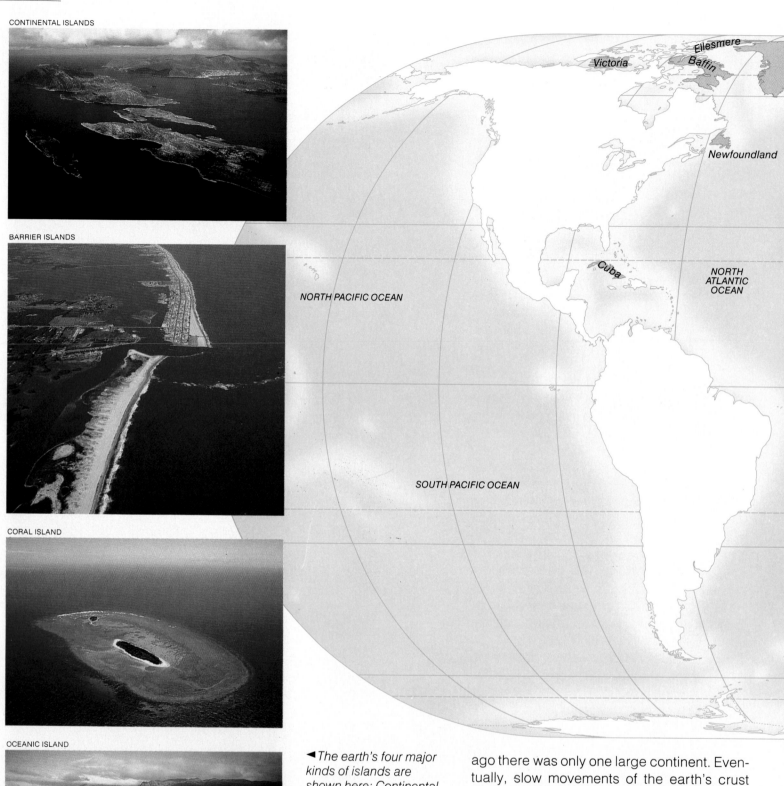

Victoria Ellesmere Baffin

Newfoundland

NORTH PACIFIC OCEAN

Cuba

NORTH
ATLANTIC
OCEAN

SOUTH PACIFIC OCEAN

◄ *The earth's four major
kinds of islands are
shown here: Continental
islands off Norway (top)
were once joined to the
mainland. Sandy barrier
islands edge the coast of
Maryland. A tiny coral
island lies near Australia.
The oceanic island of
Kauai, Hawaii, was built
up from the seafloor by
volcanic eruptions.*

ago there was only one large continent. Eventually, slow movements of the earth's crust
broke the giant continent into several pieces
that began to drift apart. When the breakup
occurred, some large chunks of land split off
along the lines of separation. These fragments of land became islands. Greenland
and Madagascar are examples of continental
islands that formed in this way.

Other continental islands formed because of changes in sea level. At the peak of

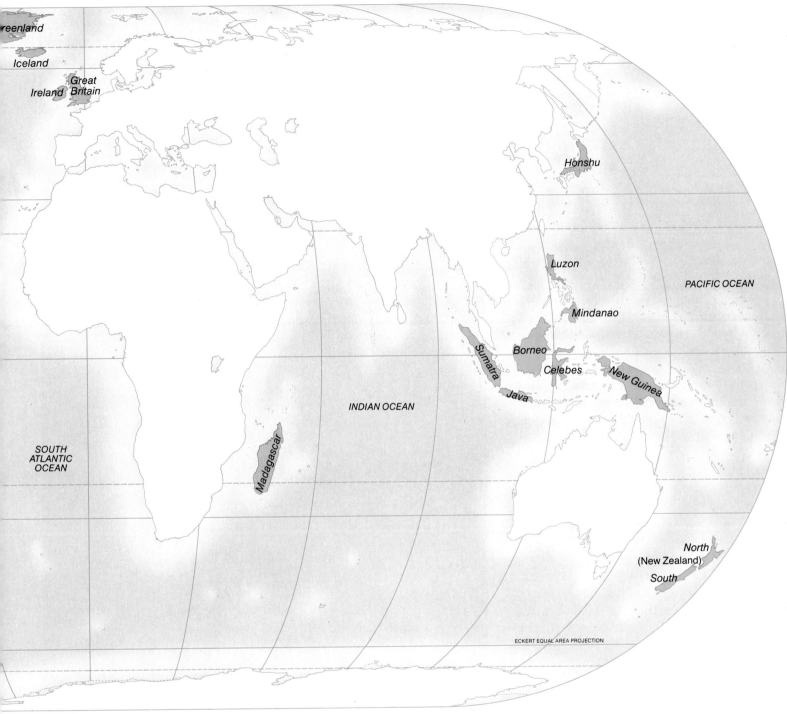

Greenland

Iceland

Ireland Great Britain

Honshu

Luzon

Mindanao

PACIFIC OCEAN

Sumatra Borneo Celebes New Guinea

Java

INDIAN OCEAN

SOUTH ATLANTIC OCEAN

Madagascar

North (New Zealand)

South

ECKERT EQUAL AREA PROJECTION

the most recent ice age, about 18,000 years ago, ice covered large parts of the earth. Water was locked in glaciers, and the sea level was much lower than it is today. As the glaciers began to melt, the sea level rose. The ocean flooded many low-lying areas, creating islands such as the British Isles, which were once part of the mainland of Europe.

Continental islands may form through the weathering and erosion of a link of land that once connected the island to the mainland.

Ocean waves or water from a river may cut across the link and wash it away. The island of Trinidad, for example, was separated from South America when the Orinoco River cut through its link to the mainland.

Oceanic islands are formed by eruptions of volcanoes on the ocean floor. As the volcanoes erupt, they build up layers of lava that may eventually break the water's surface. When the tops of the volcanoes appear above the water, they form islands such as those

▲ Countless islands dot the ocean, ranging in size from Greenland, earth's largest island, to tropical islets and keys. This map shows the 20 largest islands. Some, such as the British Isles, are home to millions of people. Many islands share both the protection and the isolation of surrounding water.

▼ *Continental islands off Maine were once coastal mountaintops. When ice age glaciers melted, the water rose around them, forming the islands.*

of Hawaii. In 1963, the island of Surtsey was born when a volcanic eruption spewed out hot lava amid clouds of steam in the ocean near Iceland.

Coral islands are low islands formed in warm waters by tiny sea animals called coral polyps. Coral polyps build up hard external skeletons. Some small coral islands are called keys or cays.

Colonies of polyps may form huge reefs of limestone. Some coral reefs may grow up in thick layers from a plateau on the seafloor until they break the water's surface, forming low islands. The Bahama Islands, which lie southeast of Florida, formed in this way.

Another kind of coral island is the atoll. An atoll is a coral reef that begins by growing in a ring around the sides of a volcanic island. As the volcanic island slowly subsides, or sinks, into the ocean floor, the reef continues to grow. Later, parts of the circular reef may be uplifted and rise above the water's surface as coral islands or islets. Atolls are found chiefly in the tropical waters of the Pacific.

Barrier islands are narrow and lie parallel to coastlines. They are made up of sediment—sand, silt, and gravel. These islands are separated from the shore by a lagoon or a sound. They are called barrier islands because they have sand dunes that act as barriers between the ocean and the mainland. The dunes protect the coast from being directly battered by storm waves and winds.

Some barrier islands form when ocean currents pile up sand in sandbars parallel to

▲ *Fair Isle, a continental island off the coast of Scotland, was isolated from the rest of Europe when glaciers melted. It is a migration stop for many species of birds.*
► *Near Finland, an islet provides an anchorage for a fishing boat. Many Finns have built summer vacation cottages on such continental islets.*

coastlines. Eventually the sandbars may rise above the water as islands.

Other barrier islands formed during the most recent ice age. As glaciers melted, the sea level rose around lines of coastal sand dunes, creating low, sandy islands. Such islands are common along the southeastern coast of the United States.

Some barrier islands were formed of materials deposited by the ice age glaciers. When the glaciers melted, they left piles of the rock, soil, and gravel they had carried. These piles of debris are called moraines. As flooding occurred along coasts after the glaciers melted, the moraines were surrounded by water. Long Island, in New York, and Nantucket, off the coast of Massachusetts, are both formed of glacial moraines.

Life on Islands

The kinds of plants and animals that live on an island depend on how the island was formed and where it is located. Continental islands have wildlife much like that of the continent they were once connected to.

Isolated oceanic and coral islands, however, have plant and animal life that may have come from other places. These islands were formed individually, often far out in the ocean and many kilometers away from other land. Plants and animals reach these islands by traveling long distances across the water.

Some plant seeds may travel by drifting in the ocean. The seeds of coconut palms, for example, are encased in shells that can float for weeks. The shells may eventually wash up on a shore. The seeds of red mangrove trees often float to new locations along a coastline.

Other plant seeds travel to islands on the wind. Many lightweight seeds, such as fluffy thistle seeds and the spores of ferns, can drift long distances in the air currents of high-altitude winds. Still other plant seeds may be stuck in mud on the foot of a bird or in its feathers and dropped on an island.

Birds, flying insects, and bats all reach islands by air. Many are blown long distances by storm winds.

Other creatures may ride to islands on floating masses of plants, branches, and soil, sometimes with trees still standing on them. These land rafts are called floating islands.

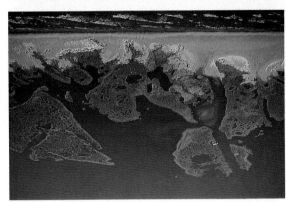

◄ Condominiums and hotels line a narrow strip of sand on Miami Beach, Florida. Building here destroyed sand dunes that used to protect the barrier island. As a result, waves and winds have eroded the beach.

◄ The Chandeleur Islands of Louisiana lie along the Gulf of Mexico. These fragile barrier islands formed centuries ago from sediments deposited by the Mississippi River.

▼ Sandy Hook stretches out from the New Jersey coast. People have built walls called groins along the beach to catch and hold drifting sand.

▶ *Tern Island, an atoll in Hawaii's Leeward Islands, supports both a wildlife refuge for seabirds and a United States Coast Guard navigation station.*
▼ *Small and crowded, a coral island rises from a reef in Indonesia. The world's largest archipelago, or group of islands, Indonesia consists of some 13,000 separate islands.*

They are usually torn out from coasts and swept away during great storms and floods. They can carry small animals hundreds of kilometers to new homes on islands. Snakes, lizards, turtles, and rodents as well as many insects may find shelter in the tree branches or among the plant leaves. Some of the best travelers are lizards, which can survive a long time with little water. Ships delivering goods also introduce new types of plants, and animals such as snakes and rats, to islands— often unintentionally.

Unusual Island Wildlife

Because plants and animals living on islands are isolated in places surrounded and protected by water, they sometimes change, or adapt, in special ways. Some island creatures multiply until their populations become enormous. This occurs because there is less competition with other species for food, and fewer diseases threaten these animals.

On the Galápagos Islands, giant tortoises developed from smaller ancestors over millions of years. Scientists believe the first tortoises probably came to the islands from the South American continent on floating vegetation. Gradually, the animals grew larger in body size, in part because there were few competitors for the plant foods they ate. Today, the tortoises may weigh as much as 272 kilograms (600 lbs) and measure more than a meter long. Sunflowers on the Galápagos Islands gradually grew larger, too, because

▲ *A diver explores a coral reef in Fiji. Reefs shelter some of the richest and most varied communities of plant and animal life in the ocean.*

there were few insects on the islands that preyed on the flowers. Eventually, the sunflowers grew as tall as some trees.

The isolation of many islands may protect some animals on them from predators and other dangers that exist on mainlands. Relatives of some animals long extinct in most parts of the world still survive on islands.

One of the most remarkable of all creatures was discovered in 1913 on the island of Komodo, northwest of Australia. Rumors of fantastic animals on Komodo had persisted over the years. When scientists arrived to investigate, they were astounded to see what looked like a living dragon. The creature was a gigantic lizard more than 3 meters (10 ft) long. Soon more of these enormous reptiles were discovered, some even larger. Named Komodo dragons, they were found to be relatives of the earth's most ancient group of lizards. The isolation of Komodo Island had preserved them.

Islands and People

How the world's most remote islands were first discovered and settled is one of the most fascinating stories in human history. The

▲ Snow-covered mountains rise around the harbor of Unalaska Island, one of the Aleutian Islands of Alaska. These islands are the tops of volcanoes that erupted and rose from the ocean millions of years ago.
◄ Tourists ride down a rocky hillside on Thíra, a Greek island in the Aegean Sea. This crescent-shaped island is part of the rim of an ancient volcanic crater.
◄ Waterfalls cascade over a lava cliff in Iceland. An exposed part of the Mid-Ocean Ridge, the island is one of the world's most volcanically active areas. Repeated eruptions have covered some two-thirds of the island with lava.

vast Pacific Ocean is sprinkled with many small islands, such as the Marquesas, Easter Island, and the Hawaiian Islands, that are far-flung and isolated from continental coasts. When Europeans began exploring the Pacific islands in the 1500s, they found people already living there. Where did these people come from?

Scientists believe the ancestors of these Pacific island inhabitants came originally from Southeast Asia. Beginning about 3,000 to 4,000 years ago, groups of these people set out in great oceangoing canoes on amazing voyages east over thousands of kilometers of ocean. Sailing without compasses, sextants, or maps, they discovered islands they could not have known existed.

Archaeologists who have studied the remains of their culture believe the ancient Pacific peoples were expert sailors and navigators who could steer by the stars and read patterns in ocean waves and swells that helped them find the islands. Some of their voyages were probably accidental, and occurred when great storms blew canoes traveling to nearby islands far off course. Yet other voyages were almost certainly intentional ones designed to expand the people's territory through colonization.

As Europeans continued to visit remote Pacific islands from the 1500s through the 1800s, they sometimes caused harm. For example, they brought devastating diseases unknown to the islanders, who had no resistance to them. Many island people perished from diseases such as measles. On their

ships the Europeans also brought animals—including cats, dogs, rats, snakes, and goats—that killed and ate many native island plants and animals and destroyed the natural ecological balance of the islands.

Since the days of the early explorers, islands have been important as places for ships to take on supplies and for their crews to rest. Later, islands became part of ocean trade routes, linking distant parts of the world. And, like stepping-stones, islands have helped people to migrate over vast expanses of ocean from one continent to another.

Today, millions of people live on islands. There are many island countries, including Japan, the Philippines, New Zealand, Cuba, and Iceland, as well as the countries of the British Isles.

Islands are now valued by people as homes for rare and endangered wildlife. Many islands where people once destroyed native species by hunting them or destroying their habitats are today maintained as national parks and wildlife refuges. On some of these island preserves, such as the Galápagos, scientists conduct research to learn more about the wildlife and how

▲ *Formed of volcanic rock, the Galápagos Islands look desolate, but they are home to many animals. Here, a plant-eating land iguana walks near a gull's egg.*
◄ *A giant tortoise lumbers along. Protected for centuries by the islands' isolation from enemies and disease, the tortoises gradually became extremely large.*
◄ *A bull sea lion patrols a beach. It will charge anything that challenges its authority to claim an area for its harem.*
► *Marine iguanas bask in the sun. The world's only marine iguanas, these Galápagos lizards feed on ocean-dwelling algae.*

▲ *Isolated on the remote Galápagos Islands, swallowtail gulls have not learned to fear humans. This pair allowed a photographer to approach.*

to protect the animals from further harm.

Many islands are known as beautiful and restful vacation spots, where people can enjoy swimming, fishing, scuba diving, and other activities. Some of the most famous vacation islands are in the Caribbean Sea and the South Pacific.

SEE ALSO ARCHIPELAGO, ATOLL, CONTINENT, CONTINENTAL DRIFT, CORAL REEF, GLACIER, KEY, MORAINE, OCEAN, PLATE TECTONICS, SEA LEVEL, VOLCANO, *and* WEATHERING AND EROSION.

ISTHMUS

An isthmus is a narrow strip of land connecting two larger land areas and separating two bodies of water. A well-known example is the Isthmus of Panama, which connects the continents of North and South America and separates the Atlantic and Pacific Oceans. Other examples are the Isthmus of Suez, which connects the continents of Africa and Asia, and the Isthmus of Corinth, which links the Peloponnesus with the rest of mainland Greece. Canals have been cut through many isthmuses, including those of Panama, Suez, and Corinth. Many thousands of years ago, isthmuses offered natural pathways for plant and animal migration between the two landmasses they connected.

SEE ALSO CANAL *and* CONTINENTAL DRIFT.

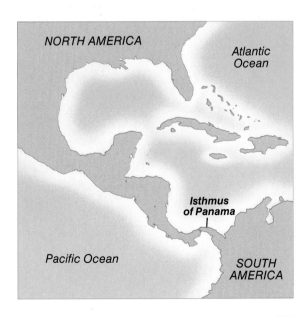

J

JET STREAM

Jet streams are currents of air high above the earth, meandering eastward at altitudes of about 8 to 15 kilometers (5–9 mi). They form where large temperature differences exist in the atmosphere. The strongest winds occur at the altitude of the tropopause, the boundary between the troposphere and the stratosphere. Jet streams blow more than 160 kilometers per hour (100 mph) in winter and blow only about 80 kilometers per hour (50 mph) in summer. They are faster in winter when the temperature differences between tropical, temperate, and polar air are greater.

At most times in the Northern and Southern Hemispheres there are two jet streams: a subtropical jet stream centered at about 30 degrees latitude and a polar-front jet stream whose position varies with the boundary between polar and temperate air. A reverse jet stream blows toward the west in tropical high altitudes during the Northern Hemisphere summer. It is associated with the thermal heating of the Asian continent and may help bring summer monsoons to the Indian Ocean.

SEE ALSO ATMOSPHERE, CLIMATE, *and* WIND.

JUNGLE

A thick, tangled mass of tropical vegetation is popularly called a jungle. A tropical rain forest is often referred to as a jungle, but there is little undergrowth on the floor of the forest's interior. The trees' continuous leafy crowns form a canopy that keeps sunlight from reaching the forest floor. Jungles do grow at the edges of a rain forest and in areas where a gap occurs in the canopy because there the sun's rays can reach the ground. Competition for sunlight results in a mass of palms, vines, orchids, and other plants. It is easy to see how a rain forest, viewed from the outside, could be thought of as an impenetrable jungle.

SEE ALSO FOREST *and* RAIN FOREST.

▲ *Jungle vegetation flourishes at the edge of a rain forest, as seen from the upper Rio Negro in Brazil.*

▼ *Palms, fernlike trees, and other tropical plants form a jungle landscape on St. Lucia, an island in the West Indies.*

K

KARST

Karst is an area of land underlain by limestone that is honeycombed with sinkholes, underground streams, and caves.

Limestone, a soluble rock, easily develops cracks, or joints. As rainwater seeps through the cracks, it slowly dissolves the limestone. Gradually, underground streams and caves form in the rock, and sinkholes develop at the surface.

The processes that form karst topography occur underground. In areas where weathering and erosion have worn away the land above, the limestone ridges, caves, and sinkholes that are characteristic of a karst region are visible.

Even where rain is plentiful, some karst looks dry and barren. In these areas, rainwater seeps through a thin layer of soil into the limestone and disappears.

The word "karst" comes from the Karst region of Yugoslavia, which is rugged and lined with caves.

SEE ALSO CAVE, GROUNDWATER, SINKHOLE, *and* WEATHERING AND EROSION.

▲ *Along the Li River in the Guilin region of China, steep karst formations shape a landscape of limestone peaks some 200 meters (650 ft) high.*

KEY

A key is a small, low island on a coral reef platform. In many parts of the world, such islands are called cays. A key appears just above the ocean surface. Its formation is constantly affected by winds and tides. Gradually, the accumulation of sand, coral, and other debris piled up by waves solidifies into rock, and the key begins to support vegetation. Keys are found chiefly in the tropics. Perhaps the best known are those off the tip of Florida and on Australia's Great Barrier Reef.

SEE ALSO CORAL REEF *and* ISLAND.

L

LAGOON

A lagoon is a shallow body of water that has an opening to the ocean but is also protected from it by a sandbar or a coral reef. There are two types of lagoons. One is a narrow stretch of water between a barrier island and a shoreline. The other is circular and is surrounded by the coral reef of an atoll. Both kinds of lagoons are often used as harbors during calm weather.

SEE ALSO ATOLL, HARBOR, *and* ISLAND.

▲ *A lagoon washes the shores of volcanic Naitauba Island, in Fiji. Coral reefs ring the island, separating the lagoon from the open ocean.*

LAKE

A lake is a body of water that is surrounded by land. There are millions of lakes. They are found on every continent and in every kind of environment—in mountains and deserts, on plains, and near seashores.

Lakes vary greatly in size. Some measure only a few square meters. Such small lakes are often referred to as ponds. Other lakes are so big they are called seas. The Caspian Sea, between Iran and the Soviet Union, is the world's largest lake, with an area of some 371,000 square kilometers (143,240 sq mi).

Lakes vary greatly in depth. The deepest is Lake Baykal, in the Soviet Union. Its bottom is 1.6 kilometers (1 mi) below the surface in places. Although Lake Baykal covers less than half the surface area of Lake Superior, it is about four times deeper and holds nearly

▲ Potholes and sinkholes dot fields in Manitoba, in Canada. Sinkhole lakes form when underground caves collapse and their outlets are clogged. Pothole lakes were left behind by ancient glaciers.

◀ *A satellite provided this image of the Great Lakes of North America. Lake Superior is at the top, with Lake Michigan below it. Lake Erie is in the lower right corner, just below Lake Huron. (Lake Ontario is not shown.) Green shades added to the image indicate vegetation.*

as much water as all five of North America's Great Lakes combined. Other lakes are so shallow that a person could easily wade across them.

Lakes exist at many different elevations. One of the highest is Lake Titicaca, in the Andes. It lies about 3,800 meters (12,500 ft) above sea level. The lowest lake is the Dead Sea, between Israel and Jordan. Its shores lie 400 meters (1,312 ft) *below* sea level.

All lakes are either open or closed. Lakes from which water leaves by an outlet or by

▲ *The basin of this lake in the Canadian Rockies was formed by a glacier that moved down the valley.*

▼ *In a high glacial valley surrounded by Rocky Mountain peaks, Colorado's Pierre Lake reflects clouds and sky.*

► A volcanic explosion in 1912 caused the top of Mount Katmai, in Alaska, to collapse. Ice melt and rainwater filled the resulting crater.
▼ Lava from a 1971 eruption built an island in a lake that fills the crater of Soufrière volcano on the island of St. Vincent.

seepage are open. Those from which water leaves only by evaporation are closed.

The water in lakes comes from rain, snow, melting ice, streams, and groundwater seepage. Most lakes contain fresh water. All freshwater lakes are open. Closed lakes usually become saline, or salty. This is because evaporation removes water in the form of water vapor and leaves behind a residue of dissolved salts. The Great Salt Lake, in Utah, is the largest saline lake in North America. Its waters are saltier than the ocean.

How Lakes Are Formed

All lakes fill depressions in the earth's surface called basins. Lake basins are formed in several ways.

Many of the lakes existing today, especially in the Northern Hemisphere, were formed by glaciers that covered large areas of land at the height of the most recent ice age, some 18,000 years ago.

The huge masses of ice gouged and scoured out great hollows and pits in the land as they moved slowly along. When the glaciers melted, water filled these depressions, forming lakes. Glaciers also carved deep valleys and deposited large quantities of earth,

---

LAKE FACTS

Lakes contain an estimated 125,000 cubic kilometers (30,000 cu mi) of the earth's water.

Lake Baykal, in the Soviet Union, and North America's Great Lakes hold about 40 percent of all fresh water in the earth's lakes and streams.

Lake Baykal, the deepest, oldest lake on the earth, is 1,620 meters (5,315 ft) deep. It holds 23,000 cubic kilometers (5,520 cubic miles) of water, making it the largest lake by volume.

The salty Caspian Sea has the largest surface area of all lakes: 371,000 square kilometers (143,240 sq mi). Lake Superior in North America has the largest surface area of all freshwater lakes: 82,100 square kilometers (31,700 sq mi).

The highest named lake in the world is Panch Pokhri, on Mount Everest, at 5,414 meters (17,758 ft) above sea level. There are unnamed glacial lakes even higher on Mount Everest, at 5,886 meters (19,300 ft).

Several times saltier than the ocean, the Dead Sea, at 400 meters (1,312 ft) below sea level, is both the saltiest and the lowest lake on the earth.

Lake Titicaca, on the Peru-Bolivia border, is the world's highest navigable freshwater lake, at about 3,800 meters (12,500 ft) above sea level.

pebbles, and boulders as they melted. These materials sometimes formed dams that trapped water and created more lakes.

Many areas of North America and northern Europe are dotted with sparkling glacial lakes. Minnesota alone has thousands. The Great Lakes, North America's largest lakes, were created in their present form primarily by the action of glaciers.

Some lake basins form where earth movements change the earth's crust, making it buckle and fold or break apart. When the crust breaks, deep cracks, or faults, may form. Such faults and folds make natural basins that may fill with water from rainfall or from streams flowing into the basin. When crustal movements occur near the ocean, an arm of the ocean may be cut off by a new block of land that has been thrust up. The Caspian Sea was formed in this way.

Many lakes form as a result of volcanoes. After a volcano erupts and then becomes inactive, its crater may fill with rain or melted snow. Sometimes the top of a volcano is blown off or collapses during an eruption, leaving a depression called a caldera. It, too, may fill with rainwater and become a lake.

Some lakes are formed by rivers. Mature rivers often wind back and forth across a plain in wide loops called meanders. During periods of flooding, a swollen, rushing river may carve out a shortcut channel and bypass a meander, leaving a curved body of standing water. It is called an oxbow lake because its shape resembles the U-shaped frame that fits over an ox's neck when the ox is harnessed to pull a wagon or a plow.

Lakes may also be created by landslides or mudslides that send soil, rock, or mud sliding down hills and mountains. The debris piles up in natural dams that can block the flow of a stream, forming a lake.

Dams that beavers build out of tree branches can plug up rivers or streams and make large ponds.

People make lakes by digging basins or by damming rivers or springs. Such artificial lakes serve as reservoirs, storing water for irrigation and for other purposes.

◄ *Lake Mead, between Arizona and Nevada, has existed since the completion of Hoover Dam in 1936. The dam holds Colorado River waters.*

The Life Cycle of Lakes

Once formed, lakes do not stay the same, but are always changing. Like people, they go through different life stages—youth, maturity, old age, and death. All lakes, even the largest, slowly disappear because their basins fill with sediment and plant material.

An increasing number of plants usually grow in a lake, slowly filling in its basin. Rain washes soil and pebbles into the basin. The remains of fish and other animals pile up on the lake bottom. Eventually, the lake becomes a marsh, a bog, or a swamp, and, finally, dry land. The natural aging of a lake happens very slowly. The aging process may go on for thousands of years.

Life Around Lakes

Lakes are important in preserving wildlife. They serve as migration stops and breeding grounds for many birds and as refuges for a wide variety of other animals. They provide

▲ The salty waters of Lake Magadi in Kenya are tinted by bacteria. Extracting and selling salt from the lake is an important local industry.

▲ Their feathers colored by bacteria in the food they eat, flamingos wade in Lake Magadi.
◄ A volcano rises beyond salty Lake Verde on the high frontier between Chile and Bolivia.

homes for a diversity of living things, from microscopic plants and animals to large fish called sturgeon that may weigh hundreds of kilograms.

Plants growing along a lakeshore may include mosses, ferns, reeds, rushes, and cattails. Small animals such as snails, worms, frogs, and dragonflies live among the plants and lay their eggs on them below the waterline. Farther from the shoreline, floating plants such as water lilies and water hyacinths often thrive. They have air-filled bladders, or sacs, that help keep them afloat. These plants shelter small fish that dart in and out under their leaves. Waterbugs, beetles, and spiders glide and skitter across and just below the water's surface.

Many kinds of water birds live on lakes or gather there to breed and to raise their young. Ducks are the most common lake birds. Others include swans, geese, loons, and kingfishers. Lakes are also home to many kinds of fish. Among them are tiny shiners, as well as sunfish, perch, bass, lake trout, pike, eels, catfish, salmon, and sturgeon. Many of these provide food for people.

Lakes are valuable resources for people in a variety of ways. Through the centuries, lakes have provided routes for travel and trade. The Great Lakes in North America, for

▲ A racing car speeds along Utah's Bonneville Salt Flats, once the bed of a vast saline lake.
◄ The largest lake in the world, the Caspian Sea in Eurasia shrinks by a few centimeters each year.

► *Great Salt Lake, in Utah, flooded several times in the 1980s. Heavy rain and snow raised the water level 2.6 meters (8.5 ft) in two years.*
▼ *In February 1987, Chicago's Lake Shore Drive was closed by floods for the first time. Storm winds drove the water over Lake Michigan's southern shore. A warm winter had melted icy barriers that usually protect the city.*

example, are major inland routes for ships carrying grain and raw materials such as iron ore and coal.

Farmers use lake waters to irrigate croplands. The effect of very large lakes on climate also helps farmers. Because water does not heat or cool as rapidly as land does, winds blowing from lakes help keep the climate more temperate. In autumn, lake winds blow warmer air over the land, extending the growing season. In spring, cool lake winds help delay the blooming of crop plants until the danger of harmful frosts is past.

Lakes supply many communities with water. Artificial lakes are used to store water for times of drought. Lakes formed by dams also provide energy from rushing water. The water is channeled from the lakes to drive generators that produce electricity. Called hydroelectric power, this energy provides enough electricity to light entire cities.

Because of their often spectacular beauty, lakes are popular recreation and vacation spots. People seek out their sparkling waters to enjoy boating, swimming, water-skiing, fishing, sailing, and, in winter, ice skating, ice boating, and ice fishing.

For some people, lakes are permanent homes. For example, Indians have lived on Lake Titicaca in the Andes for centuries. The lake supplies almost everything the Indians need. They catch fish from the lake and hunt water birds.

The Indians also use the reeds that grow in Lake Titicaca to build floating "islands" to live on. The islands are some two meters (6.5 ft) thick. On them, the Indians build reed houses and make reed sleeping mats,

▲ *Boaters on Lake Titicaca, on the border of Bolivia and Peru, use different modes of travel. Beyond the traditional Ayamara Indian canoe, an ultramodern hydrofoil skims over the water.*
◄ *Islands of tufa, a form of calcium carbonate, appear in Mono Lake, in California (far left). Its feeder streams diverted for city water, Mono Lake has dropped some 13 meters (44 ft) since 1941.*
◄ *Lake Eyre, in Australia, is usually mostly dry. Its basin fills only in times of flood.*

baskets, fishing boats, and sails. The Indians also eat the roots and the celery-like stalks of the reeds.

The Future of Lakes

Although lakes naturally age and die, people have speeded up the process by polluting lake waters. Sewage from towns and cities causes explosive growths of blue-green algae, which can choke a lake and use up the oxygen that fish and other living things depend upon for survival. Chemical fertilizers that wash into lakes from farmlands pollute lakes, as do wastes from factories.

A major threat to lakes today is acid rain. It is caused by harmful gases from factories, power plants, and automobile exhausts. The gases rise in the air and may be carried hundreds of kilometers by the wind. When the gases mix with moisture in clouds, they form strong acids, which fall in rain or snow on lakes and kill fish, plants, and other living things. Eventually, acid rain leaves the lakes sterile and lifeless.

Today, many lakes in the United States, Canada, and parts of Europe are dead or dying from acid rain. People in many countries are working to find ways to curb the pollution that causes acid precipitation.

Lakes are among the most valuable as well as the most beautiful of the earth's resources. Most experts agree that lakes must be kept clean and free from pollution if they are to continue to provide the many benefits that we receive from them today.

SEE ALSO BASIN, DAM, GLACIER, HYDROELECTRIC POWER, OXBOW LAKE, POLLUTION, RIVER, SINKHOLE, VOLCANO, WATER, *and* WETLAND.

LAND USE

The term "land use" refers to the ways people use land and the natural resources it provides. Land includes not only soil and minerals but also plant and animal ecosystems. People use land in many ways. Farming, mining, logging, establishing parks and wildlife sanctuaries, and building cities and highways are all examples of land use. People often change ecosystems to reap benefits from the land, as farmers do when they plant crops.

How land is used depends on the physical, economic, and social conditions of the area involved. Some parts of the world are rich in farmland and forests. Others have small amounts of arable land and large populations. People in countries with limited farmland tend to use it intensively, growing as much food as possible, the way Asian farmers do when they plant rice.

Land is often misused. In the southern Great Plains of the United States, for example, continuous overuse of the land for farming led to the loss of fertile soil. During a period of drought in the 1930s, much of the topsoil blew away, leaving a dust bowl.

Today, the rapid clearing of trees for firewood, farming, and grazing is damaging forests in some parts of the world. Exposed to rain and wind, the soil erodes, or wears away. Scientists worry that the destruction of forests will harm the environment in other ways, since trees play a vital role in maintaining the earth's temperature and rainfall patterns.

Strip mining coal without restoring the land, dumping toxic wastes into streams, overgrazing, and overdevelopment are other examples of land misuse.

Wise land use requires that care be taken to preserve the land for future generations. Foresters, for example, practice careful land use when they replant areas where trees have been felled. People often disagree about how land should be used. Some may be more interested in economic uses, while others may be more concerned about damage to the environment. By following land-use plans that address both economic and ecological concerns, people can fulfill their needs and still preserve the land's ability to renew itself.

SEE ALSO AGRICULTURE, CITY, CONSERVATION, FOREST, GRASSLAND, NATURAL RESOURCE, POLLUTION, POPULATION, *and* SOIL.

▲ *In a process called desertification, the nearby Kalahari Desert could expand into this rangeland in the African country of Botswana. Overgrazing by cattle has caused soil erosion by reducing protective vegetation.*

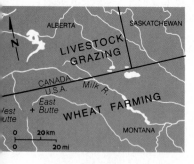

► *Colors added to a satellite image of an area along the Canada-United States border highlight the different ways the two countries use the land. Dark and light areas delineate the border. Canada devotes the dark-tinted land to livestock grazing. In the U.S., wheat is grown on the light-colored land. To the west, bright red spots mark two large buttes in an area of Montana left in its natural state.*

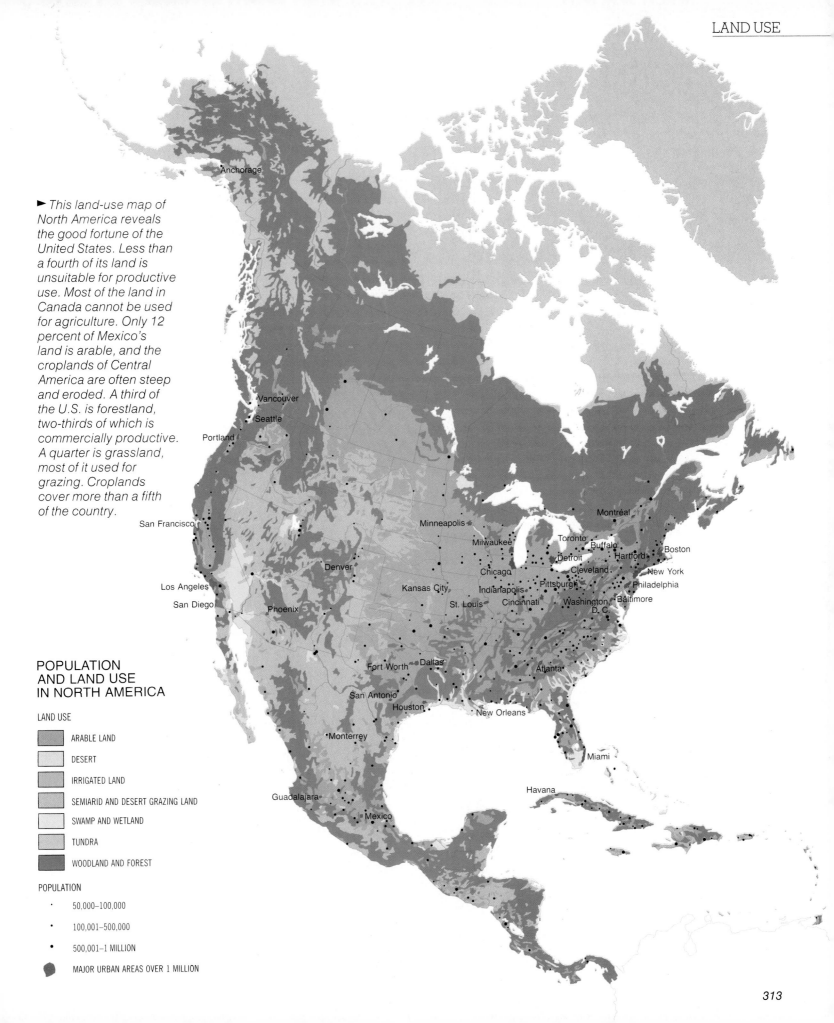

► *This land-use map of North America reveals the good fortune of the United States. Less than a fourth of its land is unsuitable for productive use. Most of the land in Canada cannot be used for agriculture. Only 12 percent of Mexico's land is arable, and the croplands of Central America are often steep and eroded. A third of the U.S. is forestland, two-thirds of which is commercially productive. A quarter is grassland, most of it used for grazing. Croplands cover more than a fifth of the country.*

POPULATION
AND LAND USE
IN NORTH AMERICA

LAND USE

- ARABLE LAND
- DESERT
- IRRIGATED LAND
- SEMIARID AND DESERT GRAZING LAND
- SWAMP AND WETLAND
- TUNDRA
- WOODLAND AND FOREST

POPULATION

- 50,000–100,000
- 100,001–500,000
- 500,001–1 MILLION
- MAJOR URBAN AREAS OVER 1 MILLION

313

LANDFORM

A landform is a feature of the earth's surface. Plains, mountains, plateaus, and hills are the four major types of landforms. Minor landforms include buttes, canyons, valleys, and basins. Landforms have great influence on the location of settlements and roads.

Tectonic activity and weathering and erosion are major forces in shaping landforms. Tectonic activity is the interaction of huge slabs of rock called plates that make up the earth's rigid shell. Plate movement may push up landforms such as mountains. Weathering and erosion wear down mountains and cut into plateaus. Sediments deposited by the processes of weathering and erosion may accumulate, producing landforms such as deltas and moraines.

SEE ALSO DELTA, HILL, LANDSCAPE, MORAINE, MOUNTAIN, PLAIN, PLATE TECTONICS, PLATEAU, *and* WEATHERING AND EROSION.

LANDSCAPE

A landscape is the part of the earth's surface that can be viewed at one time from one place. The term comes from the Dutch word *landschap,* the name given to paintings of the countryside. Geographers have borrowed the word from artists. An artist paints a landscape; a geographer studies it.

A natural landscape is made up of a collection of landforms, such as mountains, hills, plains, and plateaus. Lakes, streams, soils, and natural vegetation are other features of some natural landscapes.

A landscape that people have modified is called a cultural landscape. People and the plants they grow, the animals they care for, and the structures they build make up cultural landscapes. Such landscapes can vary greatly. They can be as different as a cattle ranch in Argentina is from a large city such as Tokyo, in Japan.

The growth of technology has increased our ability to change a landscape. Today, only about 15 percent of the earth's land is truly natural landscape—land that is unchanged

by humans. An example of human impact on landscape can be seen in the Netherlands. Water from the North Sea was pumped out of certain areas, uncovering the land. Dikes were built to keep water from these areas, now used for farming and other purposes.

Many human activities increase the rate at which natural processes, such as weathering and erosion, shape the landscape. The

◄ *A hiker wanders through narrow, rocky passages in Utah's Canyonlands National Park. Features such as these are part of the natural landscape.*
▼ *Reddish sand, scrub vegetation, and the dome-shaped Olga Mountains combine to make up this unique natural landscape in central Australia.*

LANDSLIDE

"Landslide" is a general term that describes several kinds of downward movement of rock, soil, and other materials. The movement is usually rapid and involves large amounts of material sliding downhill at a rate of many meters per second.

In high mountains such as the Alps of Europe and the Himalaya of Asia, landslides are common. Earth and rocks in a cliff may tumble into a valley after their underlying support is worn away by weathering and erosion. Spring snowmelt in the mountains can cause landslides by saturating soil and rock debris. The force of gravity and the sheer weight of the material cause it to slide downhill.

Heavy rainfall causes landslides when rushing water loosens gravel and soil supporting larger rocks, so that boulders and mud thunder down slopes. Rain may also saturate hillside layers of clay atop solid rock so that they begin to sag and slide. Landslides are often caused by earthquakes, which may shake loose blocks of rock and soil on steep hillsides and send them plunging.

A major landslide may move millions of tons of rock from a higher elevation to a lower one, damaging or destroying property and causing loss of life.

▲ *Neon signs light up Tokyo, the capital of Japan. Cultural landscapes in Tokyo and other cities often consist almost entirely of structures and objects made by people.*
▼ *In China, rice fields on hillside terraces show how people's agricultural activity can change a natural landscape into a cultural one.*

cutting of forests exposes more soil to wind and water erosion. Pollution such as acid rain often speeds up the weathering, or breakdown, of the earth's rocky surface.

By studying natural and cultural landscapes, geographers learn how people's activities affect the land. Their studies may suggest ways that will help us protect the delicate balance of the earth's ecosystems.

SEE ALSO CULTURE, DIKE, ECOSYSTEM, LANDFORM, *and* WEATHERING AND EROSION.

SEE ALSO AVALANCHE, EARTHQUAKE, *and* WEATHERING AND EROSION.

▲ *Landslide debris blocks lanes of Highway 101 in Los Angeles, California. After days of heavy rain, a large mass of earth and rock broke away from a saturated slope, uprooting trees as it collapsed.*

LANGUAGE

Language is a set of spoken sounds or written symbols that allow people to give information and express thoughts to one another. The use of language is the most common form of human communication. Some experts estimate that about 90 percent of communication occurs through speech alone.

Humans are not the only beings that use particular sounds to communicate, but they are the only ones that have developed a complicated system of sounds they can combine to give an unlimited number of meanings. With language, a person can express any idea in detail. Without it, there could be no government, science, commerce, religion, or literature, and civilization could not have reached its present stage of development. Language represents one of humankind's most significant achievements.

People of every culture use language. Children begin to learn the language of their culture in infancy. This first language is called their mother tongue. The word "language" itself comes from the Latin word *lingua*, or tongue. The study of the structure and development of languages is called linguistics.

No one knows exactly when language began. It may have started as animal-like sounds made by prehistoric hunters to accompany gestures or other body movements. Systems of speech evolved many thousands of years before the first writing was developed by the Sumerians in Mesopotamia between 4000 and 3000 B.C.

Like the cultures of which they are a part, languages are continuously changing. Grammatical structures—rules for combining words to make sentences—change through time. Pronunciations and meanings of words also change. Vocabularies expand as new ideas produce a need for new words. Most changes occur gradually as languages are passed from one generation to another. Migration has also played an important part in language change, especially in the development and spread of different languages.

About 3,000 languages are spoken today. In addition, there are some 7,000 to 8,000 dialects, or subdivisions of languages. Chinese, as a first language, is spoken by the most people. English is spoken over the greatest area. Many tongues have only a few hundred speakers, but more than a hundred languages have a million or more speakers each. About ten have more than 100 million

▼ *Colors on the map below indicate the distribution of 12 major language families. Few people—perhaps one percent of the world's population—speak languages unrelated to one of these families.*

DISTRIBUTION OF LANGUAGE FAMILIES

- INDO-EUROPEAN
- DRAVIDIAN
- URALIC
- ALTAIC
- AFRO-ASIATIC
- NIGER-CONGO
- NILO-SAHARAN
- AUSTRO-ASIAN
- SINO-TIBETAN
- AUSTRONESIAN
- KOREAN
- JAPANESE
- OTHER GROUPS

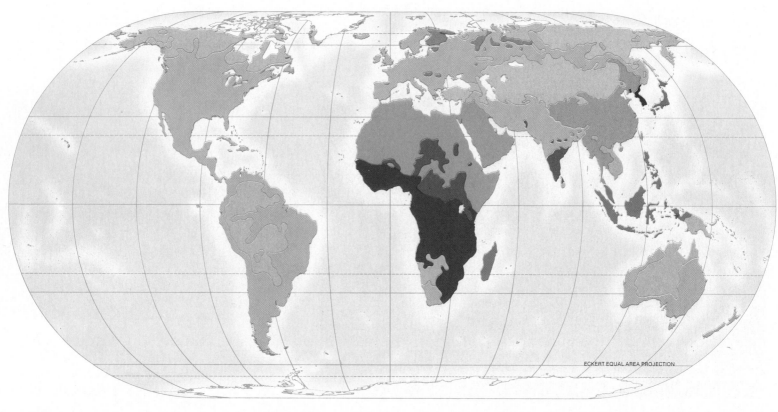

ECKERT EQUAL AREA PROJECTION

speakers—among them, Spanish, Arabic, and Russian, as well as Chinese and English.

Many linguists group languages with a common ancestry and similar words into families. Indo-European is the largest and most widespread language family. Sanskrit, used in ancient India, is the earliest known written language of this family. Though no one knows for certain, the first Indo-European speakers probably lived in eastern Europe. As people migrated, the language kept spreading and changing. Ancient peoples, such as the Romans, spread their Indo-European languages through conquest or other forms of influence. Later, Europeans took their languages to most parts of the world. Today, about half of the world's people speak a language belonging to the Indo-European family.

In the modern age of rapid communication, languages are in constant contact and borrow words freely. Science, engineering, politics, the military, and other fields use specialized words, called jargon, for quick, precise communication. Old words are often combined to form new ones—telecommunications and videotape, for example.

Language differences may present barriers to trade, national unity, and other goals. Sometimes such problems can be resolved through a lingua franca, a common language used by groups with different native languages to communicate with one another. Swahili, for example, is the lingua franca in East Africa, as are Hindi and English in India.

There have been many attempts to invent a universal language. The most successful of these, Esperanto, is based on words common to the chief European languages. It may have as many as two million speakers. Some people believe that one such artificial language, spoken throughout the world, would increase cultural and economic ties and promote better understanding among countries.

SEE ALSO ALPHABET, CULTURE, LITERACY, and TRANSPORTATION AND COMMUNICATION.

▼ *The chart below shows nine branches of the Indo-European language family. Most of them have divided again, like the branches of a tree, into some 40 modern languages. They all developed from one ancestral tongue that probably originated in eastern Europe. After about 3000 B.C., dialects of this parent language evolved into separate languages as speakers migrated to Asia and to other parts of Europe.*

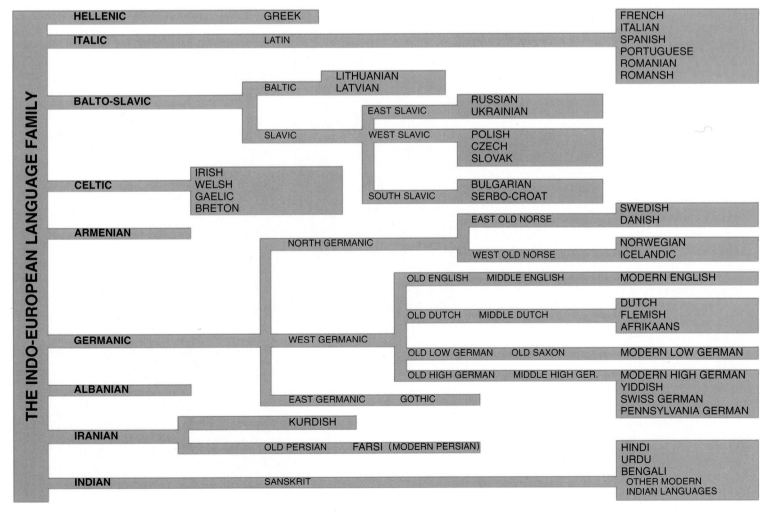

317

LATITUDE AND LONGITUDE

LINES OF LATITUDE

LINES OF LONGITUDE

Latitude is distance north or south of the Equator, and longitude is distance east or west of the prime meridian. Both are measured in terms of the 360 degrees of a circle. Imaginary lines of latitude and longitude intersect each other, forming a grid that covers the earth and helps us locate points on it.

The Equator is the line of 0° latitude, the starting point for measuring latitude. The latitude of the North Pole is 90° N, and that of the South Pole is 90° S. The latitude of every point in between must be some degree north or south, from 0° to 90°. One degree of latitude covers about 111 kilometers (69 mi).

Each line of latitude forms an imaginary circle around the earth. Because these circles are parallel to the Equator, they are called parallels of latitude. The farther the circles are from the Equator, the smaller they are; at the Poles they are simply points.

Lines of longitude, which meet at the Poles, are known as meridians. The one that runs through Greenwich, England, is internationally accepted as the line of 0° longitude, or prime meridian.

Longitude is measured in degrees east or west of the prime meridian. This means that one half of the world is measured in degrees of east longitude up to 180°, and the other half in degrees of west longitude up to 180°.

The length of a degree of longitude depends on the distance from the Equator. The greater the distance, the shorter the length of the degree is, diminishing to zero at the Poles.

For greater precision, degrees of latitude and longitude are divided into 60 minutes, and minutes are divided into 60 seconds.

Maps are often marked with parallels and meridians. The latitude and longitude of a point are called its coordinates. If you know the coordinates, you can use a map to locate any point on the earth.

SEE ALSO EQUATOR, LOCATION, LONGITUDE, MAPS AND GLOBES, *and* PRIME MERIDIAN.

LAVA

Lava is molten rock from the earth's interior that erupts from volcanoes or fissures in the earth's surface. Before the molten rock reaches the surface, it is called magma. Lava may be very fluid, moving like a fast-flowing river or spreading out in a thin layer that covers a large area. The molten material is sometimes thick and slow-moving. Lava can be so stiff that it piles up in great blocks only a short distance from where it erupted. When lava hardens, it becomes igneous rock. Igneous rocks include pumice, which may be so porous that it floats in water, and obsidian, which is a dark, glassy rock.

Many volcanoes dot the Hawaiian Islands, and people there have given names to the different forms lava takes. Geologists often use the Hawaiian names to describe lava flows. Aa (ah-ah) has a rough, fragmented surface. Pahoehoe (pa-HOY-hoy) is characterized by a ropey or gently folded surface.

SEE ALSO CONE, ERUPTION, MAGMA, ROCK, SEA-FLOOR SPREADING, *and* VOLCANO.

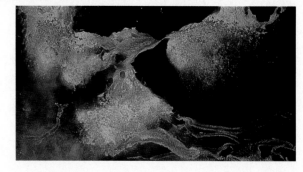

▲ *Near Kilauea, the most active volcano in Hawaii, a flow of pahoehoe lava formed a ropey mass of igneous rock as it cooled.*
▶ *Red-hot lava streams from Kilauea during an eruption. It pours over black, hardened lava left by previous flows.*

LEVEE

A levee is a ridge of sediment—gravel, silt, and other material—built up by a stream or constructed by engineers along the edges of its channel in a floodplain. The term comes from a French word meaning "raised." A natural levee is formed primarily by floods over many years. Where a river overflows its banks during a flood, the current slows down. Most of the river's muddy sediment is then deposited at the edge of the main channel, and a ridge develops.

Most natural levees rise only slightly. Along large rivers such as the Mississippi, however, natural levees rise as much as 6 meters (20 ft) above the floodplain. Because the levees are so high, the river may actually flow at a higher elevation than its floodplain.

If a river breaks through a levee during a period of high water, widespread flooding may occur. Usually, the floodplain behind a levee is poorly drained because water cannot flow up the levee and back into the river. This is why marshy areas called backswamps are often found behind levees.

To prevent flooding, people for centuries have built artificial embankments to act as levees. Along the lower Mississippi River, there are thousands of kilometers of natural and artificial levees in Louisiana alone. An artificial levee is generally much steeper than a natural one. New Orleans, on the vast Mississippi Delta in Louisiana, has floodwalls some 8 meters (26 ft) high. Portions of the city are now lower than both the levees and the river.

SEE ALSO DIKE, FLOOD, FLOODPLAIN, *and* RIVER.

▲ *Erected centuries ago on high ground, a temple perches above China's Miluo River and its levees. A rich floodplain built primarily by past floods stretches away behind the levees.*

▼ *Bordered by canals, an artificial levee in Louisiana helps prevent the lower Mississippi from flooding. Thousands of kilometers of levees have been built to keep North America's largest river within its banks.*

LIGHTNING

Lightning is the visible electrical discharge produced by a thunderstorm. The tremendous electrical power of a lightning bolt can heat the surrounding air to as much as 30,000°C (54,000°F). This is more than four times hotter than the surface of the sun. The rise in temperature makes the air expand explosively, producing the noise we call thunder. What appears to our eyes as a single lightning flash is actually many flashes along the same path, each lasting less than a thousandth of a second.

Normally the earth has a negative charge. Within a thunderstorm, an intense electrical field develops, with negative charges collecting in the lower part of the cloud and positive charges in the upper part. A negative charge in the cloud induces a positive charge on the ground for several kilometers around the storm. Lightning occurs when the two charges build up enough to overcome resistance in the air, and an electrical current flows between the two charges. Lightning can leap from one part of a cloud to another, from cloud to ground, or from tall objects on the ground to a cloud.

SEE ALSO CLOUDS, PRECIPITATION, THUNDERSTORM, *and* WEATHER.

▲ *Lightning flashes above the Maya ruins of Coba in Mexico. Lightning can leap from cloud to cloud and from cloud to ground. These bolts are ground-to-cloud, a rare kind of lightning.*

LITERACY

Literacy is the ability to read and write. Unlike speaking, which is usually learned by random observation and imitation, reading and writing are deliberately taught and consciously learned. Literacy has become widespread only since the 19th century. Before then, education and books were not available to large numbers of people.

The number of people over the age of 15 who are literate is used as one measure of the level of a country's development. Comparing the literacy rates of different countries is difficult, however, because the standards for measuring literacy vary from country to country. Wealthier, more developed countries generally have higher literacy rates than poorer, less developed ones. Some experts estimate that nearly a fifth of the world's population is illiterate—unable to read and write.

Literacy is vital to a country's well-being. It is the most important part of education, which in turn leads to social progress. For individuals, literacy allows greater choice in jobs, participation in government and society, and overall improvement in the quality of life.

SEE ALSO ALPHABET, DEVELOPMENT, LANGUAGE, and TRANSPORTATION AND COMMUNICATION.

▼ A schoolgirl of Tashkent, in the Soviet Union, writes in class. Her country claims nearly 100 percent literacy. Many others lag in educating girls. In some Muslim states, female illiteracy is almost 100 percent.

▼ Students in the Pacific island country of Western Samoa do lessons on palm-leaf mats. Most study English as well as their own language. Nearly all governments support public schools where children learn to read and write.

LITHOSPHERE

The lithosphere is the solid outer part of the earth. Scientists believe the earth consists of three main layers: the core, the mantle, and the crust. The crust and the brittle upper portion of the mantle form the lithosphere. It extends from the earth's surface to a depth of approximately 100 kilometers (60 mi). The continents and the rocky ocean basins are part of the lithosphere. Broken into huge sections called plates, the lithosphere rests on a zone in the mantle so hot that the material there may bend like red-hot iron. The plates move atop this zone, constantly interacting in a process called plate tectonics.

SEE ALSO ATMOSPHERE, BIOSPHERE, CONTINENTAL DRIFT, CRUST, EARTH, EARTHQUAKE, HYDROSPHERE, MANTLE, PLATE TECTONICS, and ROCK.

LOCATION

Location is one of the basic concepts in geography. Specifically, it means the position of a particular point on the surface of the earth. However, geographers often refer to "absolute location" and "relative location."

Giving the latitude and longitude of a point is a precise way to express its location. Together, the latitude and longitude of a point are referred to as its coordinates, and they indicate absolute location. For example, the absolute location of Mount Everest is latitude 27° 59′ N, longitude 86° 56′ E.

Relative location refers to the position of a point or place in relation to other places. Because the significance of a place is often affected by such factors as its accessibility to other places, its relative location can change. For example, to early explorers the mouth of the Chicago River was only a place along the shore of Lake Michigan. Later, however, it became the site of the city of Chicago as transportation improvements altered its accessibility and led to its development as an important commercial center and port.

SEE ALSO GEOGRAPHY and LATITUDE AND LONGITUDE.

LOESS

In some parts of the world, windblown dust and silt blanket the land. This layer of fine, mineral-rich material is called loess. Loess ranges in thickness from a few centimeters to more than 46 meters (150 ft). Extensive loess deposits occur in northern China, the central United States, central Europe, and parts of the Soviet Union. The thickest deposits are near the Missouri River in Iowa and along the Huang (Yellow) River in China.

Loess often accumulates at the edges of deserts. As wind blows across the Gobi, a desert in Asia, it picks up and carries fine particles. On the far side of the desert, moisture in the air causes the dust to settle to the ground. There, grass traps and holds the dust so that it slowly accumulates.

Loess may also consist of dust formed when glaciers grind rocks to a fine powder.

SEE ALSO DUST, GLACIER, SILT, WEATHERING AND EROSION, *and* WIND.

▶ *Loess is soft enough to carve, yet strong enough to stand in walls. Hand-dug dwellings honeycomb a loess deposit in northern China.*

LONGITUDE

Longitude is distance east or west of the prime meridian. It is represented by imaginary lines, called meridians, running north and south. They are farthest apart at the Equator, and they meet at the Poles. Near the North or South Pole, you could pass through all 360 degrees of longitude in a few minutes; but at the Equator, even the fastest commercial jet would need about 18 hours to pass through them.

The prime meridian, or line of 0° longitude, runs through Greenwich, England. Longitude is measured in degrees both east and west of the prime meridian up to 180° in each direction. Exactly halfway around the globe from the prime meridian is the 180th meridian, in the middle of the Pacific Ocean.

Longitude can be figured with a highly accurate clock called a chronometer. It keeps

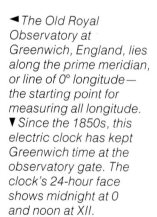

◀ *The Old Royal Observatory at Greenwich, England, lies along the prime meridian, or line of 0° longitude— the starting point for measuring all longitude.*
▼ *Since the 1850s, this electric clock has kept Greenwich time at the observatory gate. The clock's 24-hour face shows midnight at 0 and noon at XII.*

Greenwich time. Since the earth rotates 360 degrees in 24 hours, each hour represents 15 degrees of longitude. The number of hours difference between Greenwich and local time is multiplied by 15 to get degrees longitude.

SEE ALSO GREAT CIRCLE, LATITUDE AND LONGITUDE, MAPS AND GLOBES, PRIME MERIDIAN, *and* TIME AND TIME ZONES.

MAGMA

Magma is molten rock within the earth. The earth is made up of three main layers: the core, the mantle, and the crust. Magma originates in the lower part of the crust and in the upper portion of the mantle. There, high temperatures cause some rocks to melt and form magma. Magma can rise through breaks in the solid rocks of the crust and accumulate in large underground reservoirs called chambers. Heat from magma chambers warms groundwater, which sometimes rises to the surface and forms hot springs. Magma, called lava when it reaches the earth's surface, may well up through cracks in the seafloor and harden into crust. Magma erupts as lava from volcanoes. When the molten material cools, it is called igneous rock.

SEE ALSO GEOTHERMAL ENERGY, HOT SPOT, LAVA, MANTLE, MOUNTAIN, PLATE TECTONICS, ROCK, SEAFLOOR SPREADING, *and* VOLCANO.

MAGNETISM

Magnetism is the force exerted by magnets when they attract or repel each other. Evidence of this force is visible when a magnet attracts, or picks up, a nail. Magnetism is caused by the motion of electric charges.

Every substance is made up of tiny units called atoms. Each atom has electrons, small particles that carry electric charges. Spinning like tops, the electrons circle the nucleus, or core, of an atom. Their movement generates an electric current and causes each electron to act like a tiny magnet. In most substances, equal numbers of electrons spin in opposite directions, which cancels out their magnetism. That is why materials such as cloth or paper are said to be weakly magnetic. In substances such as iron, cobalt, and nickel, a majority of the electrons spin in the same direction. This makes the atoms in these substances strongly magnetic, but the substances are not yet magnets.

A magnet is surrounded by a magnetic field, the space over which a magnet can attract or repel magnetic materials. To become magnetized, a strongly magnetic substance must enter the force field of an existing magnet. This causes the north-seeking poles of the atoms in the substance to line up in the same direction. The substance is now a magnet, and the force generated by the aligned atoms creates a magnetic field.

Some substances can be magnetized by introducing an electric current. If electricity is run through a coil of wire, it produces a magnetic field like the field around a bar magnet. The field around the coil will disappear, however, as soon as the current is turned off.

The earth acts as if it contained a huge bar magnet. Scientists do not fully understand why this is so, but they think that the movement of hot liquid in the earth's core generates electric currents. The currents create a magnetic field with invisible lines of force flowing between the earth's geomagnetic poles. The geomagnetic poles are not the same as the North and South Poles, and they are not stationary. The geomagnetic poles mark the ends of the magnetic field's axis.

The shifting locations of the geomagnetic poles are recorded in rocks that form when

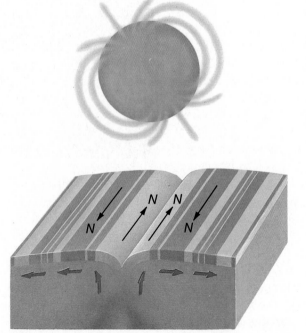

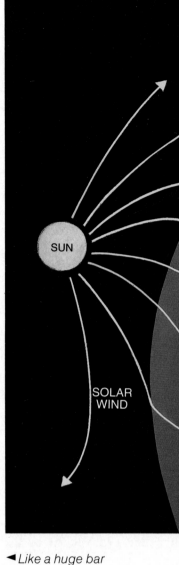

◀ *Like a huge bar magnet, the earth has invisible lines of magnetic force flowing between its geomagnetic poles. Polar reversals are recorded as lava wells up from a central rift in the Mid-Ocean Ridge and hardens into bands of seafloor (bottom). Magnetic particles in the hardening rock line up in the direction of the magnetic field at the time. When a polar reversal occurs, newly forming seafloor records the shift. As earth's plates carry the new seafloor away from the rift, the band of rock formed prior to the reversal is split.*

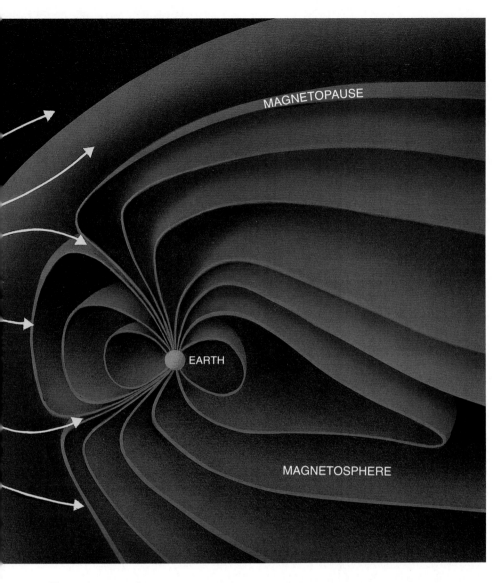

MAGNETOPAUSE

EARTH

MAGNETOSPHERE

changed into the opposite kind of pole—hundreds of times since the earth formed. The polar reversals are recorded in bands of rock running parallel to the Mid-Ocean Ridge. The ridge marks a boundary between plates that are moving away from each other. As the plates move, lava flows out of a central rift in the ridge and hardens into rock, forming a band of seafloor that records the polarity of the magnetic field at the time. When the poles reverse, the shift is recorded in new seafloor forming at the rift. The previous band is split in two as the new band showing the reverse polarity grows wider. The concept of seafloor spreading was confirmed by matching the magnetic records of rock on opposite sides of, but similar distances from, the ridge.

The magnetic field dominates a region called the magnetosphere, which wraps around the planet and its atmosphere. Solar wind, charged particles flowing from the sun, presses the magnetosphere against the earth on the side facing the sun and stretches it into a teardrop shape on the shadow side. It protects the earth from most of the particles, but some leak through it and become trapped. When they hit atoms of gas in the upper atmosphere around the geomagnetic poles, they produce light displays called auroras.

SEE ALSO AURORA, EARTH, LAVA, MAGMA, PLATE TECTONICS, POLES, *and* SEAFLOOR SPREADING.

▲ *The magnetosphere, the region dominated by the earth's magnetic field, deflects most solar wind. Some of the charged particles that make up solar wind leak into the upper atmosphere, causing colorful light displays called auroras. The magnetopause is the outer boundary of the magnetosphere, which has a teardrop shape. The side of the magnetosphere facing the sun is flattened by the force of the solar wind, and the side away from the sun stretches out for millions of kilometers.*

molten material called magma wells up through the earth's crust and pours out as lava. As lava cools and becomes solid rock, strongly magnetic particles within the rock become magnetized by the earth's magnetic field. The particles line up along the lines of force in the earth's field. In this way, rocks lock in a record of the position of the earth's geomagnetic poles at that time. The magnetic records of rocks formed at the same time, however, seem to show different locations for the poles. According to the theory of plate tectonics, which this phenomenon supports, the rocky slabs, or plates, that make up the earth's hard shell are continuously moving. Thus, the plates on which the rocks solidified have moved since the rocks locked in the position of the geomagnetic poles.

These magnetic records also show that the geomagnetic poles have reversed—

MANTLE

The earth is composed of three main layers. The middle layer of hot rock, called the mantle, is sandwiched between the inner layer, called the core, and the outer layer, called the crust. The mantle has a maximum thickness of about 2,900 kilometers (1,800 mi). It has a brittle outer boundary and is mostly solid. Rocks in its upper portion, however, are near their melting point. They are so hot that they will move or bend like red-hot iron. The upper mantle also contains molten rock that may erupt from volcanoes or through other openings in the crust.

SEE ALSO CORE, CRUST, EARTH, LITHOSPHERE, MAGMA, PLATE TECTONICS, *and* VOLCANO.

MAPS AND GLOBES

Maps and globes are among the most important tools of geographers. They help us learn about the world by showing sizes and shapes of countries, locations of features, distances between places, and distributions of things over the earth.

A globe is a scale model of the earth on which shapes, areas, distances, and directions are all accurately represented. Because it shows continents and oceans in their true proportions, a globe is an essential aid in studying the relationships among regions of the world. Globes have practical disadvantages, however. They are bulky and awkward to carry around, and they can be expensive. In addition, only part of the earth can be seen at one time on a globe, and countries appear small, with few details.

A map is a symbolic representation of all or part of the earth's surface on a flat piece of paper. Maps are useful because they present information about the world in a simple, graphic way. They can show certain distributions, such as settlement patterns, that cannot otherwise be seen, and they can show exact locations of houses and streets in a city neighborhood. Unlike globes, maps are easy to carry, easy to store, and easy to reproduce.

People use different maps for different purposes. Vacationers use road maps to plot routes for their trips. Meteorologists use weather maps to prepare forecasts. Urban planners decide where to put a hospital or a park with the help of many types of maps, including land-use and topographic ones.

The History of Mapmaking

Through the ages, maps have taken many different forms. Polynesians, for example, used networks of palm fibers to show wave patterns between certain islands in the Pacific Ocean; the islands were represented by seashells. Eskimo fishermen carved pieces of driftwood to show coastal features. The earliest maps, however, were probably

▶ Visitors to London pause in Trafalgar Square to consult a city map. With map-reading skills, they can find their location and plan their route.

sketches people made on the ground to show their surroundings. One of the oldest known maps is a small clay tablet showing an area in Mesopotamia; it is at least 4,000 years old.

The ancient Greeks are usually considered the founders of scientific cartography, or mapmaking. Greek scholars knew the general size and shape of the earth, and they developed the grid system of latitude and longitude. Eratosthenes, who lived from about 276 to 194 B.C., calculated the size of the earth using mathematics and observations of the sun. Claudius Ptolemaeus, or Ptolemy, an astronomer, mathematician, and geographer of the second century A.D., brought mapmaking to a level of precision that would not be seen again until the 15th century. He compiled all his knowledge about the world into a book called *Geography*.

The ancient Romans were concerned with managing a vast empire. This helped make them practical in their approach to cartography. They made maps of farms and other landholdings, and maps for travelers showing roads and settlements.

In Europe during the Middle Ages, cartographers drew world maps reflecting religious beliefs and legends of the time. These maps were simple and often fanciful. On some of them, the Orient was placed at the top because it was thought to be the location of Paradise; the holy city of Jerusalem was sometimes placed at the center.

In the Middle Ages, interest in scientific cartography was kept alive by the Arabs. They preserved the works of Ptolemy and translated them into Arabic. In 1154 the Arab cartographer al-Idrisi made a map of the world that was superior to the world maps the Europeans were producing. The Chinese, too, were skilled cartographers. The first map was printed in China in 1155, some 300 years before maps were printed in Europe.

The 15th century saw a rebirth of cartography in Europe. This was brought about by the rediscovery of Ptolemy's *Geography* and its translation into Latin; by the introduction of printing and engraving; and by the great voyages of discovery. Printing and engraving

▶ *Exploring space with a celestial globe, members of the Young Cosmonauts Club in Moscow learn about astronomy from their leader.*

allowed the rapid reproduction of many copies of maps that had previously been painted by hand. With the rise of navigation and exploration, sailors traveled farther and added new lands and more detailed coastlines to their maps and charts. Later, explorers brought back more detailed descriptions of the interiors of continents.

Since the 19th century, many factors have contributed to the development of cartography. They include the printing process of lithography; the development of photography and color printing; and the use of computers. Airplanes and satellites have been used to gather information about all parts of the world. Because of greater demand, many maps can now be printed less expensively.

Surveying and Remote Sensing

Cartographers rely on survey data for accurate information about the earth. Surveying, in the broad sense, is the science of determining the exact size, shape, and location of a given land or undersea area. Some surveying is still done on foot using mathematical methods such as triangulation and special instruments such as theodolites and tellurometers.

Surveying today often employs elements of remote sensing—obtaining information about an object or an area without touching it. If you stand on the top of a tall building, you will have a better view of a city than you would on the ground. Looking down on an area from a high elevation is a form of remote sensing.

One method of remote sensing is aerial photography, taking photographs of the earth from the air. Aerial photography has eliminated much of the legwork for surveyors and has allowed precise surveying of some otherwise inaccessible places. The science of taking measurements and making maps from aerial photographs is called photogrammetry.

Remote sensing by radar, which involves measuring the time it takes to send and receive radio waves, is another way to record the earth's surface features. Radar is helpful because it can be used day or night and can penetrate cloud cover.

► *One of the oldest known maps, made at least 4,000 years ago and found in Iraq, may show a river valley. Some of the lines incised in the clay tablet represent hills and a water channel.*
▼ *A Roman map, based on another from the first century A.D., shows towns, roads, and distances in France. The map emphasized east-west routes and probably fitted into a case easily carried by travelers.*

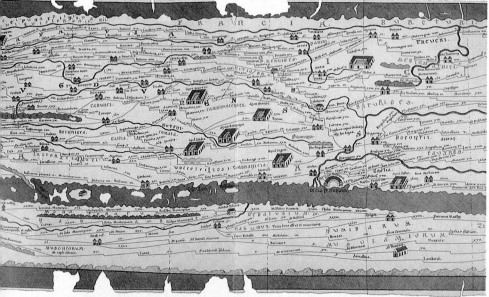

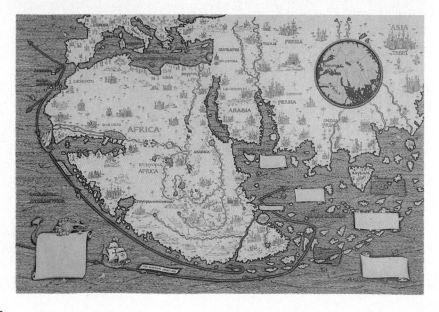

◄ *The shapes of continents reveal geographic misconceptions in this redrawing of a map made by a Venetian cartographer in the 15th century.*

Today, remote sensing is often associated with satellite images such as those from Landsat. Landsat is an unmanned satellite that orbits the earth at high altitudes about 14 times a day. It transmits huge volumes of data in the form of numbers to computers on earth. The computers translate this digital data into images that can be used to make maps.

With remote sensing devices, the earth can be surveyed in a short time, and data can be quickly assembled. Cartographers use the data to produce new maps or to correct details on old maps.

Map Projections

Imagine cutting a globe into halves and trying to flatten them. They would wrinkle and tear, and their shape would be distorted. Reproducing the spherical surface of the earth on a flat piece of paper is a major challenge for cartographers. Every map has some distortion. A map can retain either the correct sizes of countries or the correct shapes of very small areas, but not both at the same time. Maps that show true shapes of small areas are called conformal maps. Maps that show true relative sizes of all areas are called equal area maps. The larger the area covered by a map, the greater the distortion.

The process of transferring all the information from the round earth onto flat paper is called projection. Imagine a glass globe with lines of latitude and longitude etched on it. If a light shines through the globe onto paper, shadows of the grid system will be projected onto the paper. These lines can then be copied onto the paper and used to make a map.

Cartographers do not actually use this method every time they need a projection.

▼ *North and South America, though inexactly drawn, are easily recognizable on this 1587 map by Abraham Ortelius, a Flemish geographer. European voyages of discovery in the 15th and 16th centuries led to greater accuracy in mapmaking.*

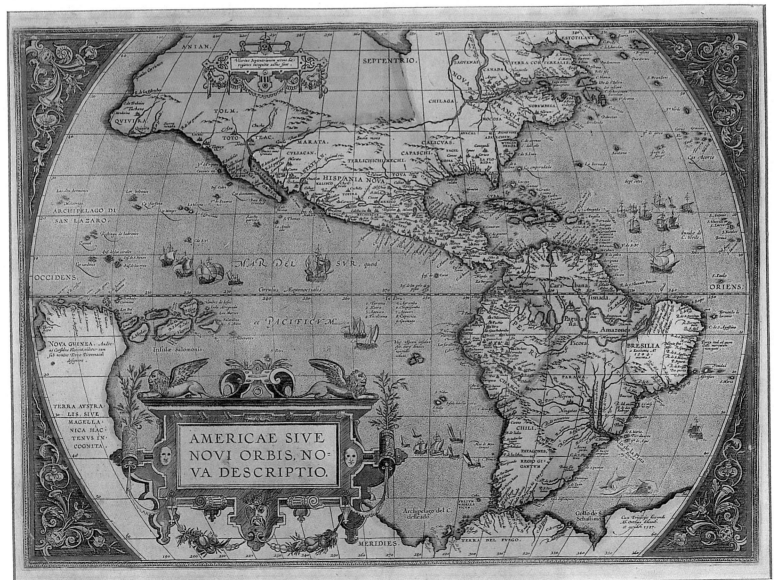

Today, most projections are made using mathematical formulas.

Several surfaces can be used to make maps. The most common surfaces are the cone, the cylinder, and the plane. The cone and the cylinder can touch the globe along one or two lines, which become the map's standard parallels. The plane surface usually touches the globe at only one point. Where the paper touches the globe is the point or line of no distortion. The projections produced on these three surfaces are known as conic, cylindrical, and azimuthal projections. The diagrams on page 330 show how these three kinds of projections might be made.

A conic projection is often made as if a cone were placed on a globe with its point directly above the North Pole. The cone touches the globe along one or two parallels in the mid-latitudes. The meridians appear as straight lines that converge toward the Poles, and the parallels are curved. This type of projection offers less overall distortion for maps of mid-latitude regions. It is useful for depicting elongated east-west areas in the mid-latitudes, such as the contiguous United States. The Lambert Conformal Conic Projection is a common conic projection.

The most common cylindrical projection is the Mercator projection. Lines of longitude on it are parallel to one another and perpendicular to the parallel lines of latitude. Introduced in 1569 by the Flemish cartographer Gerardus Mercator, the projection was a

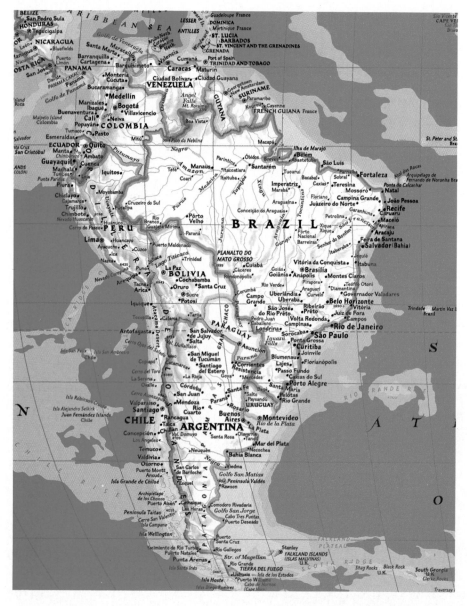

▲ A general reference map of South America gives a wealth of geographic information. It shows country boundaries as well as cities, rivers, mountains, and other features.

► Thematic maps illustrate distributions of things over specific areas. This one shows annual hours of sunshine around the world. Because of daily cloud cover, regions along the Equator have fewer hours of sunshine than do many other parts of the world.

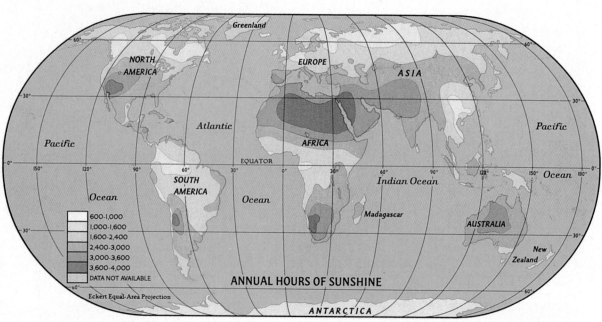

ANNUAL HOURS OF SUNSHINE

	600-1,000
	1,000-1,600
	1,600-2,400
	2,400-3,000
	3,000-3,600
	3,600-4,000
	DATA NOT AVAILABLE

Eckert Equal-Area Projection

great help to navigators. They could plot rhumb lines—lines that follow a single direction or bearing—as straight lines between any two points on the map. The Mercator projection is conformal, but because the meridians do not draw closer together and meet at the Poles as they do on a globe, there is great distortion of size in the high latitudes. On a Mercator map of the world, Greenland appears much larger than South America although it is actually about the size of Mexico.

Azimuthal projections are often used to map the polar regions. One type of azimuthal projection is the gnomonic projection. On a gnomonic projection, any great circle appears as a straight line. A great circle is the largest circle that can be drawn around a globe. The most common use of the term is in the phrase "great circle route," which refers to the shortest route between two points over the surface of the earth. Gnomonic maps are particularly useful to pilots who fly airplanes along great circle routes.

How Maps Are Made

Before making a map, cartographers decide what area they want to display, what type of information they want to present, and thus what kind of projection and scale they need. After the necessary data are gathered, work on the map can begin.

Lines of latitude and longitude are mathematically plotted on the flat surface of the paper, forming a pattern of intersecting lines called a grid. The latitude and longitude of a point are called its coordinates.

Some maps are drawn by hand with special pens and ink. Another method of drawing lines and points is called scribing. With a small pointed tool, the cartographer scrapes away the color coating from a sheet of plastic, leaving clear, sharp lines. Each kind of feature shown on the map requires a different plastic sheet. Dark shading or contour lines are sometimes added on another sheet to show the relief of the area. Contour lines join all points of equal elevation. Special type is used for all the place-names, which are pasted onto yet another plastic sheet.

When all the plastic sheets are finished, they are carefully checked and made into separate color films. The films are used in

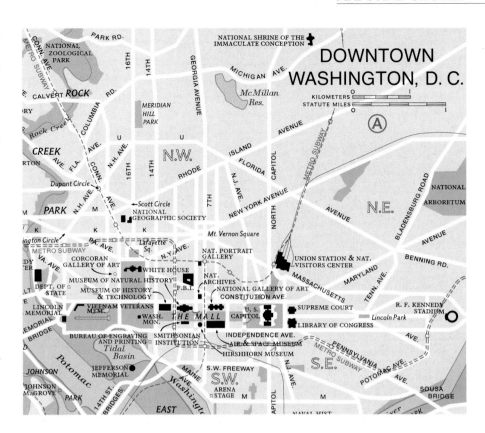

▲ A large-scale map of downtown Washington, D.C., shows important sites and main streets. A bar scale relates distances on the map to actual distances on the earth.

▼ A small-scale map shows the Washington, D.C., area, but gives fewer details. Lines indicate roads; dots, cities; airplanes, airports; and stars, capitals. All maps use symbols.

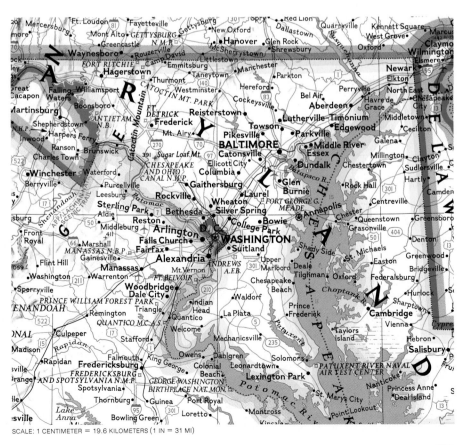

SCALE: 1 CENTIMETER = 19.6 KILOMETERS (1 IN = 31 MI)

MAP PROJECTIONS

CONIC

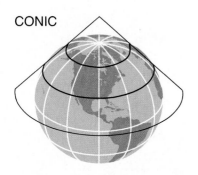

A conic projection can be made as if a cone were placed on a globe with its point directly above the North Pole. This type of projection is useful for mapping regions in the mid-latitudes.

CYLINDRICAL

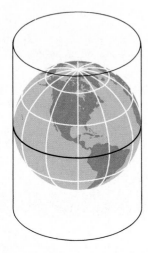
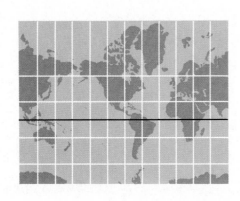

The well-known Mercator map is based on the projection of the globe onto a cylinder. This type of projection greatly distorts the sizes of landmasses in the high latitudes.

AZIMUTHAL

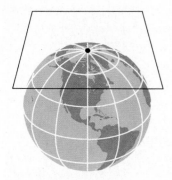
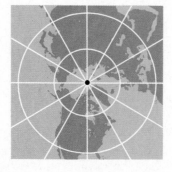

An azimuthal projection can be made by projecting the globe onto a plane surface that touches the globe at one point, in this case at the North Pole.

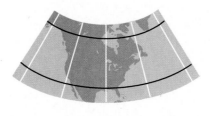

making the metal plates for the printing press that will reproduce the map.

Today, more and more mapping is done with the help of computers. The coordinates of every point are entered into a computer, a process called digitizing. By feeding new data into the computer or by deleting old data from it, map changes can be made quickly and easily. For example, colors can be changed, new roads added, or features moved slightly. The computer can print out the new map on a plotting machine much faster than a cartographer could redraw it by hand. Such new technologies not only have improved the process of mapmaking, but also have given cartographers many more options for creating and displaying all sorts of maps.

Scales and Symbols

Every map has a scale. The scale indicates the relationship between the distances on the map and the actual distances on the earth. This can be expressed in three ways: by a graphic scale, by a verbal scale, or by a

▲ Using an instrument called an alidade, a surveyor in California's Yosemite National Park records data for a topographic map.

representative fraction. The graphic scale, the most common type, is a bar scale, which looks like a ruler. The verbal scale is simply a sentence that relates distance on the map to distance on the earth. For example, the verbal scale might be "one centimeter represents one kilometer" or "one inch represents eight miles." The representative fraction does not have specific units. It is shown as a fraction or ratio—1:63,360, for example. That could mean "one centimeter on the map represents 63,360 centimeters on the earth" or "one inch represents 63,360 inches (one mile)."

The scale of a map is determined by how much detail the cartographer wants to fit onto one sheet of paper and by the size of the area covered. A map on which buildings or towns are shown in great detail is known as a large-scale map. A street map of a neighborhood is an example of a large-scale map. A map of the world or a continent is a small-scale map.

The scale of the map helps determine how many symbols the cartographer can use. The use of symbols on maps is known as symbolization. On some small-scale maps, cities are represented by small circles or dots. A circle with a star inside indicates a capital of a state or a country. Other map symbols include lines that represent boundaries, roads, and railroads; lines that indicate rivers; and a picture of an airplane that represents an airport. Colors are often used as symbols, too.

▲ *A cartographer guides a scribing tool as it cuts contour lines on a coated plastic sheet. Each curving line represents constant elevation.*
◄ *Steady hands attach a place-name to a plastic sheet. After selecting place-names, the cartographer orders the type and positions it using a lined guide. Such plastic sheets, each with a different kind of information, are made into separate color films. These are used in making the metal plates for printing a map.*

For example, green is often used for vegetation; tan for deserts; and blue for water. A map usually has a key, or legend, that gives the scale of the map and explains what the various symbols represent.

Types of Maps

Many people use maps to help them do their jobs. There are weather maps for meteorologists, road maps for drivers, and relief maps for engineers, to name just a few. Although the wide variety of maps often makes strict classification difficult, there are two broad categories: general reference maps and thematic maps.

General reference maps show general geographic information about an area, including the locations of coastlines, cities, roads, boundaries, mountains, and rivers. Some large-scale general reference maps are carefully made by government agencies such as the U.S. Geological Survey (USGS).

▲ *A portrait of the 48 contiguous states combines 569 color images made using satellite data. Most of the eastern United States appears here as an expert blends lines where two color prints join.*

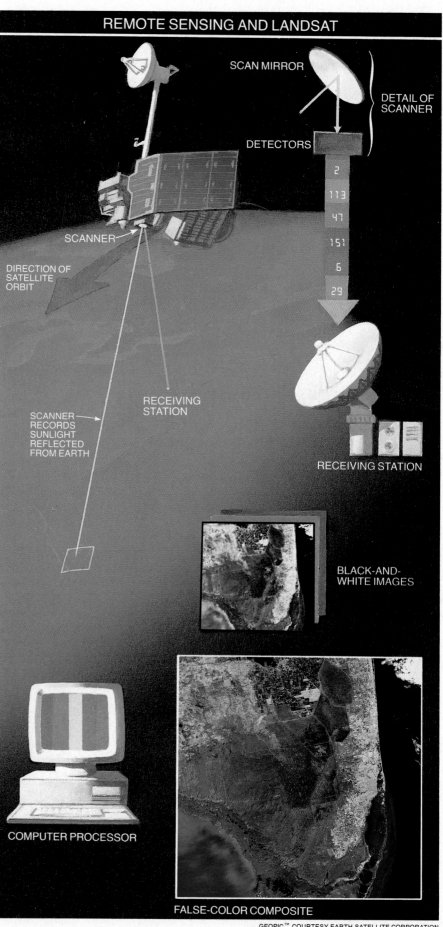

REMOTE SENSING AND LANDSAT

SCAN MIRROR

DETAIL OF SCANNER

DETECTORS

2
113
47
151
6
29

DIRECTION OF SATELLITE ORBIT

SCANNER

RECEIVING STATION

SCANNER RECORDS SUNLIGHT REFLECTED FROM EARTH

RECEIVING STATION

BLACK-AND-WHITE IMAGES

COMPUTER PROCESSOR

FALSE-COLOR COMPOSITE

◄ Landsat surveys the earth in a series of strips 185 kilometers (115 mi) wide. A scanner records sunlight reflected from the earth's surface. A scan mirror focuses the light into color-sensitive detectors. Light intensities are converted into digital numbers transmitted to a receiving station on the earth. From this data, computers produce black-and-white images. The images are combined, and a computer processor assigns colors to the numbers. This produces an image called a false-color composite. The added colors enable experts to analyze and interpret the image.
▼ At the EROS Data Center in South Dakota, a scientist studies terrain patterns on Cape Cod, Massachusetts. Satellite images stored at the center have both scientific and commercial value.

These are known as topographic maps. They use contour lines to show topographic variations. Such maps are helpful to hikers and campers because they give a detailed presentation of the topography of small areas. Engineers use them in determining where to build highways and dams. Small-scale general reference maps, such as those of countries, continents, or the world, are found in most atlases.

Thematic maps are designed to display distributions, or patterns, over the earth's surface. They emphasize one theme or topic. Examples of thematic maps include those that show distribution of population, average annual rainfall, or settlement patterns.

Maps are essential to geographers, but geographers are not the only people who use maps. Everyone needs to be able to read and interpret maps to understand a weather forecast, to get from one place to another, and to locate places in the news. Technology is changing the ways maps are produced. Many types of maps are now available to help us learn about the world of yesterday, solve the problems of today, and plan for tomorrow.

SEE ALSO AREA, ATLAS, BOUNDARY, CARTOGRAPHY, CHART, DIRECTION, DISTRIBUTION, ELEVATION, GLOBE, GREAT CIRCLE, LATITUDE AND LONGITUDE, LOCATION, *and* TOPOGRAPHY.

MARSH

A marsh is a wetland, an area of land where surface water or groundwater covers or saturates the ground for long periods of time. Marshes are usually treeless and dominated by grasses. These watery pastures support a rich variety of plants and animals.

There are three types of marshes: tidal salt marshes, tidal freshwater marshes, and inland freshwater marshes. Tidal salt marshes form a grassy fringe near river mouths, in bays, and along coastlines protected from the open ocean. Grasses such as saw grass can tolerate fluctuating tidal waters, which are too salty for most trees and bushes. Many kinds of animals, from mosquitoes to stilt-legged egrets, make up the salt marsh community. Commercially valuable fish and shellfish find food and shelter in marshes.

Tidal freshwater marshes lie farther inland than salt marshes. Although fed by freshwater streams, they are close enough to the coast to be affected by tidal fluctuations.

Inland freshwater marshes occur along the fringes of lakes and rivers where the water table is high. They vary in size from bowl-shaped depressions called prairie potholes to some of the vast watery grasslands of the Florida Everglades. Freshwater marshes are home to animals such as ducks, geese, raccoons, turtles, frogs, and snakes.

SEE ALSO WATER TABLE *and* WETLAND.

▲ An inland freshwater marsh lies on the edge of Mush Lake in Canada's Kluane National Park. Grasses dominate this kind of wetland.

MEASUREMENT

Measurement is the process of determining length, mass (weight), volume, distance, or some other quantity. This is done in units such as centimeters or inches, kilometers or miles, kilograms or pounds, and liters or quarts. Accurate measurements are important in travel, shopping, trade, weather forecasting, and many other activities. They are essential in science and engineering.

The history of measurement goes back to ancient times. One of the earliest recorded units of measurement is the cubit, used by the Egyptians; it was based on the length of the arm from elbow to fingertip. For weighing, ancient people used stones and grains of wheat or barleycorns; the grain to this day is one of the smallest units of mass. The carat, used in weighing gems, was derived from the tiny carob seed. To the Romans, a mile was 1,000 double steps, called paces, by a soldier. The emperor Charlemagne (A.D. 742–814) decreed the foot to be the length of his own foot, but in 14th-century England the foot was standardized as 36 barleycorns laid end to end. The gallon, the one in use in the United States today, was Queen Anne of England's wine gallon; it is different from the imperial gallon eventually adopted for British use.

Over the years, these measures, along with dozens of others, led to a great deal of confusion. This made people want a sensible, uniform system of measurement.

Customary and Metric Systems

Today, there are basically two systems of measurement. One is the customary system, which is still widely used only in the United States. The other is the metric system, which is standard in almost all other countries.

The customary system was adapted from the old British imperial system of measurement. Both use inches, feet, and miles; pints, quarts, and gallons; ounces, pounds, and tons. Both give temperature in degrees Fahrenheit. The systems are not identical, however. For example, the imperial system uses the same units to measure liquid and dry quantities. In the customary system, subdivisions of the gallon—fluid ounces, pints, and quarts—

measure liquids; subdivisions of the bushel—dry pints, quarts, and pecks—measure some dry quantities. There are a few other differences as well. In 1965, the United Kingdom began conversion to the metric system. Australia and Canada soon followed.

The metric system was developed in France during the French Revolution, and by 1840 its use had been made compulsory there. It is a simple decimal system based on units of ten, not on body parts or other arbitrary measures. Its principal unit is the meter.

▲ *Signs direct visitors to sections of a park in Espoo, Finland. The uppermost sign points toward a recreation area 4,100 meters (2.5 mi) away. About 95 percent of the world's people use the metric system.*
▼ *Simple methods of measurement devised centuries ago paved the way for the more exact systems of today.*

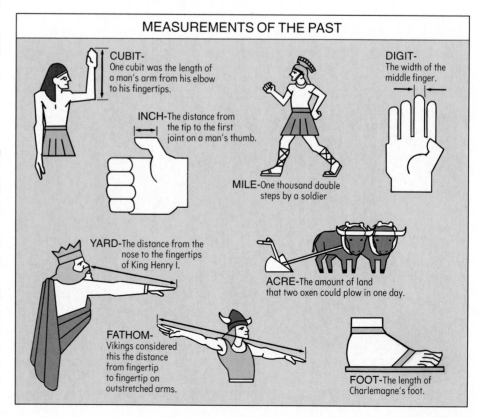

MEASUREMENTS OF THE PAST

CUBIT- One cubit was the length of a man's arm from his elbow to his fingertips.

DIGIT- The width of the middle finger.

INCH- The distance from the tip to the first joint on a man's thumb.

MILE- One thousand double steps by a soldier

YARD- The distance from the nose to the fingertips of King Henry I.

ACRE- The amount of land that two oxen could plow in one day.

FATHOM- Vikings considered this the distance from fingertip to fingertip on outstretched arms.

FOOT- The length of Charlemagne's foot.

▼ *A stone monument in Ecuador marks the Equator, an imaginary line that circles the earth and gives the South American country its name. The distance around the earth at the Equator measures 40,076 kilometers (24,902 mi).*

▼ *Customers line up to buy onions in Beijing, China. The vendor weighs a purchase on a beam scale balanced with a counterweight.*

The French National Assembly decreed that the meter was to be one ten-millionth of the length of a meridian of longitude between the Equator and the North Pole. To determine this distance, surveyors measured an arc of the meridian between Dunkirk, in France, and Barcelona, in Spain. The resulting meter was approximately 39.37 inches. From this unit of length, units of volume and mass could be calculated.

Over the years, the metric system has been modified and expanded into what is known today as SI, the abbreviation for *Le Système International d'Unités*—the International System of Units. Besides the meter for length, the system includes the liter for volume; the kilogram for mass; the second for time; the ampere for electricity; and the degree Celsius for temperature.

The metric system is easy to use because its units are related to each other by factors of ten. Prefixes are used to indicate multiples and divisions of the basic metric units. For example, deka-, hecto-, and kilo- mean 10, 100, and 1,000; deci-, centi-, and milli- mean one-tenth, one-hundredth, and one-thousandth. Thus, the meter (m) is divided into 10 decimeters (dm), 100 centimeters (cm), and 1,000 millimeters (mm); there are 1,000 meters in a kilometer (km).

After years of slow adoption, the metric system is coming into greater use in the United States. American scientists have been using metric exclusively for a long time. To operate in international markets, automobile companies and other manufacturers have converted to metric. Government agencies increasingly use metric measurements. Labels on items sold in stores often show metric as well as customary measures. In many schools, children are taught both the metric and the customary systems. By the end of the century, most experts predict, the United States will be a predominantly metric country.

SEE ALSO AREA, LONGITUDE, MAPS AND GLOBES, *and* TEMPERATURE.

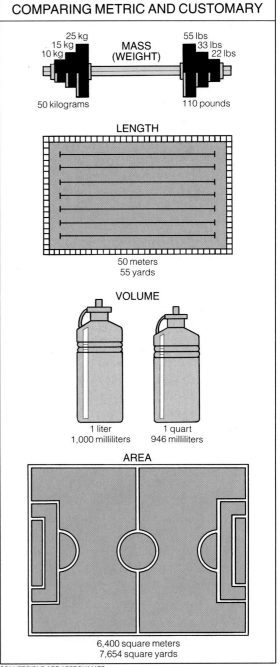

COMPARING METRIC AND CUSTOMARY

MASS (WEIGHT)
25 kg
15 kg
10 kg
55 lbs
33 lbs
22 lbs
50 kilograms
110 pounds

LENGTH
50 meters
55 yards

VOLUME
1 liter
1,000 milliliters
1 quart
946 milliliters

AREA
6,400 square meters
7,654 square yards

CONVERSIONS ARE APPROXIMATE

MESA

Mesas are broad, flat-topped landforms with steep sides. Spanish explorers of the American Southwest gave these formations the name *mesa,* which means "table," because their tops are flat like those of tables. Mesas are found in arid or semiarid regions where the rock layers that make up the landscape lie in horizontal beds.

Mesas vary in size and usually are wider than they are high. They form when streams cut through a raised area of flat land called a plateau. Geologists refer to the freestanding remnants of the original plateau—mesas, buttes, and other formations—as outliers.

Like a plateau, a mesa is topped by a layer of durable rock called caprock. Because the caprock resists erosion, the mesa stays almost the same height as it ages. But the action of rain, streams, and gravity continue to erode the exposed rock on the mesa's steep sides. Eventually the sides erode so much that the caprock breaks off. A resulting outlier, which has a smaller cap than the mesa from which it formed, is called a butte.

SEE ALSO BUTTE, PLATEAU, *and* WEATHERING AND EROSION.

METEOROID

A meteor is a streak of light in the sky produced by a meteoroid passing through the earth's atmosphere. Meteors are not stars, though some people call them "shooting stars." Usually just a few meteors are visible in an hour's time, but sometimes the sky is filled with lights that look like heavenly fireworks.

Often no larger than gravel, many meteoroids are lumps of rock or iron. They orbit the sun just as the planets do, traveling at great speed. Many were once part of larger bodies called asteroids, which orbit the sun between the paths of Mars and Jupiter in a region called the asteroid belt. Other meteoroids are debris, mostly dust-size bits, shed by the tails of comets. A meteor shower may occur when the earth passes through the orbit of a comet.

When a meteoroid enters the earth's upper atmosphere, it is heated by air resistance. The heat generated causes gases around the meteoroid to glow brightly, and a meteor appears. Earth's atmosphere protects the planet from most whirling space debris, which is usually invisible to us.

Most meteoroids that enter the earth's

▲ *U.S. marines grapple with a meteorite that slammed into the Old Woman Mountains in California hundreds of years ago. Meteorites, lumps of space debris, can weigh many tons.*

▼ Gosses Bluff formed when a meteorite fell on Australia 130 million years ago. Some meteorites have the impact of a multimegaton bomb.

▲ A meteor, at left, streaks down a starry sky in a time-lapse photograph. The meteor is part of a shower that occurs when the earth passes through debris from the tail of a comet.

▲ Gloved hands help protect a meteorite chunk from contamination. Such space debris can reveal much about the formation of our solar system.

atmosphere disintegrate into dust before they reach the ground. The pieces that do strike the earth's surface are called meteorites. Dust-size particles called micrometeorites make up 99 percent of the approximately 50 tons of space debris that fall through the earth's atmosphere each day.

The largest meteorites leave enormous holes in the ground called impact craters. The best example of an impact crater in the United States is Meteor Crater, which lies close to Winslow, Arizona. There, more than 20,000 years ago, a meteorite weighing about 270,000 tons slammed into the earth, making a hole 1.3 kilometers (.75 mi) wide and 175 meters (575 ft) deep.

SEE ALSO ATMOSPHERE, CRATER, MOON, ORBIT, and SOLAR SYSTEM.

METEOROLOGY

Meteorology is the science dealing with the atmosphere and especially the weather. Meteorologists use information from atmospheric studies to develop techniques for forecasting the weather, primarily during a period of a few days. Climatologists use meteorological data to study changes in weather patterns over long periods. Today, one goal of meteorology is to learn how human activity affects atmospheric processes, and how this activity might change weather and climate patterns in the future.

SEE ALSO CLIMATE and WEATHER.

MIGRATION

Migration is the movement of people from one place to another for the purpose of settlement. The seasonal movement of nomadic herders and migratory workers may also be considered migration. Migration can be internal, within a country, or external, from one country to another. The dominant pattern of internal migration has been from rural to urban areas. In the case of external migrations, people are said to emigrate from their country of origin and to immigrate into a new country.

Migrations can be voluntary or forced. Most people migrate by choice and do so to improve their lives. The factors that encourage people to leave their place of origin are called "push" factors. These include food or housing shortages, lack of employment, and persecution. "Pull" factors are those qualities that attract people to a new place. Economic opportunity and religious or political freedom are common pull factors. Usually, both push and pull factors play a role in migration.

Forced migration is the removal of people from their place of origin by a government or other powerful group. From the early 1500s to the late 1800s, for example, millions of Africans were forced to leave their homelands to work as slaves in the Americas.

SEE ALSO CITY, EMIGRATION, IMMIGRATION, and POPULATION.

▲ The faces of two Bantu women reflect their plight in the Ciskei homeland. Forced to migrate there under South Africa's policy of racial separation, they were refused housing upon their arrival.

MINERAL

A mineral is a solid substance found in nature. It is inorganic—formed from materials other than plants or animals. A rock is not considered to be a mineral, but many different minerals are found in most rocks. Geologists have identified more than 2,000 minerals, each with its own distinctive internal structure and chemical composition.

A mineral is composed of one or more chemical elements. Elements are substances that cannot be broken down chemically into other, simpler substances. There are more than a hundred elements, each with its own kind of atom. Atoms in minerals arrange themselves in regular, repeating patterns that form solids called crystals.

The kind of crystal structure the atoms form and the kinds of elements within a mineral help differentiate one mineral from another. Diamond and graphite, for example, are composed of the same chemical element, carbon, but their crystal structures differ. Diamond, which forms under intense pressure, has close-packed atoms, making the mineral durable, or hard. Diamonds, known as the hardest substances in nature, are used by industry for cutting and drilling. Graphite atoms, on the other hand, are bound in loose layers, making the mineral flaky and slippery. Graphite is used as a lubricant and as part of the "lead" in pencils.

A mineral can be a single element like copper, silver, gold, or graphite, but most minerals are compounds, or mixtures, of elements. The most common mineral is silicate. Silicate is a combination of oxygen and silicon, elements that make up almost three-fourths of the earth's crust.

Though a specific mineral's chemical structure is always the same, the external shape, size, or color may vary from one deposit to another. Quartz, for example, may have impurities that make it appear white, rose, or another hue.

Minerals are divided into metals and non-metals. An ore is a deposit that contains one or more minerals, usually metals, in quantities that make mining them profitable. A metallic mineral, such as copper, is usually shiny and can be easily shaped. Metals that conduct

◀ On the Guajira Peninsula, in Colombia, a mountain of salt grows ever larger as the mineral pours from a conveyor belt. The salt is left behind by evaporating seawater.
▼ A lineman inspects power lines made of aluminum. The metal is extracted from an ore called bauxite. A versatile metal, aluminum is also used in making airplanes, beverage cans, and many other products.

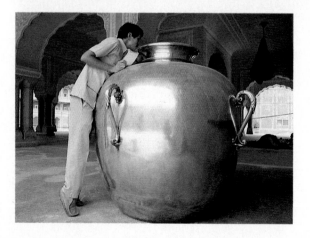

◀ Craftsmen often fashion silver, a precious metal, into useful and decorative objects, such as this gigantic water jug in Jaipur, India.

heat and electricity well are often used in building and in manufacturing.

There are various classifications of metals. Gold, silver, and platinum are classified as precious metals. Other metals may be rarer or more costly, but these three have a worldwide market, are abundant enough to serve many practical uses, and have often been employed as mediums of exchange.

Ferrous metals include iron and those metals often alloyed, or mixed, with iron to form various kinds of steel. Alloying the metal manganese with iron, for example, makes a hard, tough steel that can be used in making safes. Nonferrous metals, those containing little iron, include such metals as copper, lead, zinc, tin, and aluminum.

Nonmetallic minerals have hundreds of uses. Halite, composed of the elements sodium and chloride, is often used as table salt. Sulfur is an ingredient in some medicines. Phosphates and nitrates are used in making fertilizer. Construction cement is a mixture of nonmetallic minerals.

SOME IMPORTANT MINERALS AND THEIR USES

Mineral	Chemical Symbol	Uses	Principal Ores	Metal Extracted	Uses
COPPER	Cu	Wiring for homes, offices, and factories; plumbing pipes; roofing; coins; alloyed (mixed) with tin to make bronze and with zinc to make brass	BAUXITE	Aluminum (Al)	Containers and foil; body parts for cars, planes, ships, and trains; window frames and doors; siding for houses
DIAMOND	C	Gemstone quality for jewelry; industrial quality for drill tips, abrasives, and phonograph styluses	MAGNETITE AND HEMATITE	Iron (Fe)	Iron and steel products, such as motor vehicles, construction supplies and equipment, and household appliances
GOLD	Au	Bullion (gold in bars or ingots); jewelry and decoration; electronic parts; tooth fillings and other dental work	GALENA	Lead (Pb)	Storage batteries; additive in leaded gasoline, glass (lead crystal), paints, enamels, and glazes; chemical storage containers; X-ray shields; fishing weights; compounds used in explosives, insecticides, and rubber products
HALITE (Common Salt)	NaCl	Preservative in food and animal feed; agent in making fertilizers, soda, lye, chlorine, and hydrochloric acid; road de-icer	PENTLANDITE	Nickel (Ni)	Additive for strengthening iron and steel and for preventing corrosion; batteries; coins; used in petroleum refining
MERCURY	Hg	Batteries and other electrical equipment; thermometers and barometers; tooth fillings; compound used in Mercurochrome	CASSITERITE	Tin (Sn)	Coating for containers, paper clips, safety pins, and straight pins to prevent corrosion; solder when combined with lead; bearings and engine parts; component of pewter and bronze; ingredient of stannous fluoride in toothpaste
QUARTZ	SiO$_2$	Timing devices in clocks and watches; lenses and prisms; oscillators for stabilizing radio broadcast signals; jewelry and decorative items	SCHEELITE	Tungsten (W)	Filaments in light bulbs and vacuum tubes; alloyed with iron and steel to make tools with sharp cutting edges; compounds used in making fabrics waterproof and fire-resistant
SILVER	Ag	Photographic film; jewelry and tableware; coins; mirrors; electronic parts	URANINITE AND CARNOTITE	Uranium (U)	Fuel for nuclear reactors
SULFUR	S	Sulfuric acid, used in almost every industry, from fertilizers to petroleum, plastics, and rubber; ingredient in sulfa drugs and some shampoos	SPHALERITE	Zinc (Z)	Rust preventive coating on iron, steel, and other metals; component of brass and sometimes bronze; compounds used in cosmetics, paint pigments, plastics, printing ink, coating on color TV tubes and luminous dials on clocks

▲ More than 2,000 minerals have been identified by geologists. Diamonds (top) shine in a bed of kimberlite gravel at a mine in Kimberley, South Africa. Deposits of hematite, limonite, siderite, and taconite (center), all of which contain iron, are from a mine in Egypt. The flakes of gold (above) are from a Montana creek.

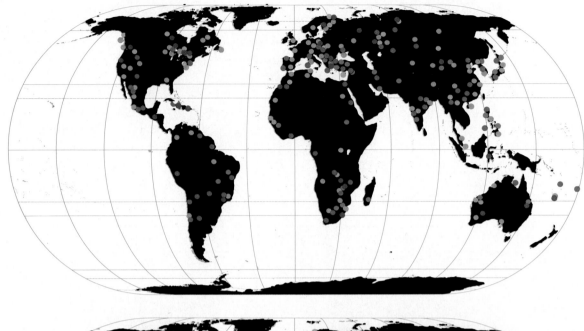

FERROUS METALS
- IRON
- MANGANESE
- CHROMIUM
- NICKEL
- COBALT

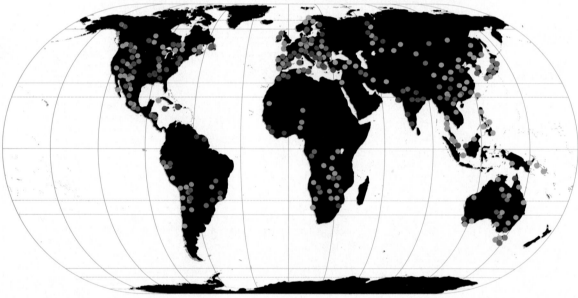

NONFERROUS METALS
- COPPER
- ZINC
- ALUMINUM
- TIN
- LEAD

▲ Coils of copper wire await shipment at a Georgia factory. Copper conducts heat and electricity well and resists corrosion, so it is often formed into tubing that carries water, gas, or oil.

Some minerals are used in making jewelry and other decorative objects. Gold has been used in art pieces for thousands of years. When some mineral crystals reflect light, they glitter. Hard, sparkling mineral crystals called gemstones are cut, polished, and set in metals, such as gold and silver, to make jewelry. Some gemstones are more valuable than others. The value usually depends on the beauty, popularity, durability, and rarity of the gemstone. Certain countries are known as sources for particular gemstones: Myanmar (Burma), for its rubies; Colombia, for its emeralds; Thailand, for its sapphires; and South Africa, for its diamonds.

Minerals are found everywhere in nature.

The first minerals crystallized as the earth cooled during its formation more than four billion years ago. Since that time, minerals have continued to form and re-form in a variety of ways. Magma, which is molten rock within the earth, forms mineral crystals when it cools. Gases and fluids sometimes escape from magma and interact with existing rock, altering the rock's mineral composition by adding new elements. The recrystallization of minerals within rocks also results from movements in the earth's hard shell. The shell is made up of thick slabs of rock called plates, which are moving continuously. Intense heat and pressure caused by interaction of the plates often change the minerals in rocks deep in the

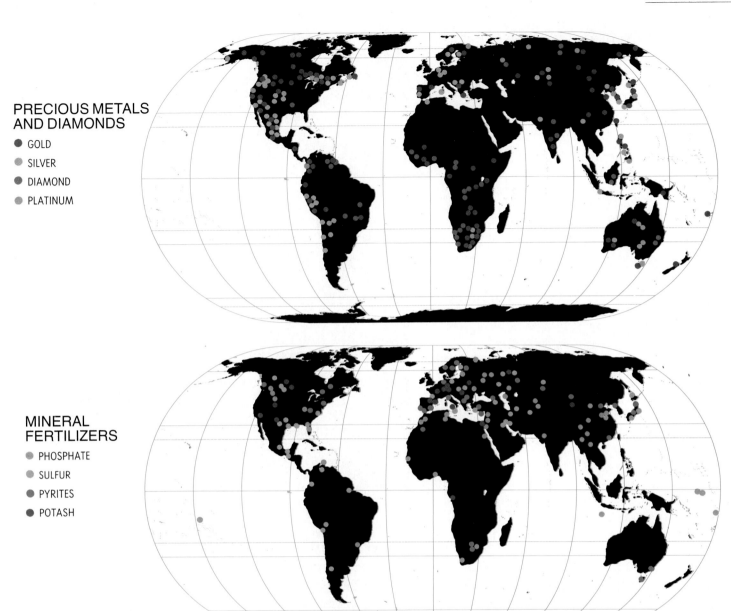

**PRECIOUS METALS
AND DIAMONDS**

- GOLD
- SILVER
- DIAMOND
- PLATINUM

**MINERAL
FERTILIZERS**

- PHOSPHATE
- SULFUR
- PYRITES
- POTASH

▲ *A wavy pattern in
a sheet of platinum
remains after shavings
are scraped away. The
metal has many uses in
the chemical industry.*

earth's crust, thus forming different minerals.

Not all minerals are buried in the earth's crust. Some lie in riverbeds, where they are deposited as sediment. Others result from evaporation. Salt, for example, is left behind when salt water evaporates. Other minerals are found on top of the earth's crust on the ocean floor. They may form when seawater enters cracks in the ocean floor and comes in contact with magma. The seawater separates minerals, such as cobalt, iron, and manganese, from the magma. As magma heats the mineral-rich water, the water is forced back to the surface of the ocean floor like a gushing hot spring. Contact between the heated water and the cold ocean water causes the minerals

to separate out and settle on the seafloor.

A mineral deposit may go through several processes in its formation. Some minerals, such as gypsum, may form in a few hours. Others take thousands of years to develop. Many of the most vital minerals are from this slow-forming group. Thus, even though some minerals are found in abundance, they are not necessarily renewable resources. Many minerals, however, can be used more than once. Conservation practices, such as recycling aluminum containers, can help make some of the earth's mineral resources last longer.

SEE ALSO CONSERVATION, MINING, NATURAL RE-SOURCE, ORE, PLATE TECTONICS, *and* ROCK.

MINING

Mining is the process of removing useful deposits from the earth's crust. Many materials are mined, including coal, minerals, sand, gravel, and building stone.

People have been mining for centuries. The 20th century, however, brought tremendous advances in mining technology. Few miners still rely on picks, shovels, and their own strength to extract materials from the earth, though these were the primary tools used as recently as the late 1800s. In the coal industry today, a machine as tall as a 20-story building scoops aside thousands of tons of earth, exposing the coal beneath.

The decision to develop a mine depends on the potential expense of mining, processing, and transporting the deposit and the price the final product will bring. Mining operations may be small, with only one worker, or they may be enormous businesses. Some mines in South Africa employ thousands of workers to mine gold.

Resources are extracted through surface mining or underground mining. The method chosen depends primarily on the location of the deposit and on the form in which it is found. Materials such as gravel and sand are often found in loose deposits in riverbeds or on the ocean floor. Metals are generally found within the earth as part of a compact mass of rock containing other mineral deposits.

▲ Placer deposits mined in Montana's Deep Creek yield gold flakes. Loose minerals that have been carried to an area by glaciers, wind, or water are called placer deposits.
► At Serra Pelada in the Brazilian rain forest, a crude open pit mine teems with workers searching for gold with picks and shovels.

▲ At a salt farm in Thailand, a woman rakes mounds of the mineral left by evaporating seawater. With this surface mining method, ocean waters are captured in shallow artificial ponds at high tide. Salt crystallizes in the ponds when the seawater evaporates.

▼ Sheer, smooth walls of limestone rise above workers in a quarry on Malta, an island in the Mediterranean Sea. The sedimentary rock, widely used for building and ornamental purposes, is cut from the earth's crust in squared-off blocks.

Surface Mining

A mining operation that extracts deposits on or close to the surface is called surface mining. Strip mining is a surface mining method used to extract coal. Giant excavating machines strip away the overburden—rocks, vegetation, and soil—by making a cut, or slice, into the ground to reach the coal. Power shovels or other machinery remove the coal exposed by the cut and load it onto trucks or railroad cars. A second cut is made near the first, and the overburden from the new cut is dumped into the first cut. This process is repeated as long as recoverable coal remains. Eventually the overburden from the first cut is used to fill the final cut.

In open pit mining, a method often used

efficient ways to mine the deep-ocean floor, which is rich in minerals.

Strip mining, open pit mining, quarrying, and dredging are some of the main surface mining methods used today. Though surface mining is effective in gathering resources, it can scar the earth's surface. Since 1977, mining companies in the United States have been required to fill the cuts left after coal is mined. The overburden, including waste rock and topsoil, must be replaced and the area contoured and planted.

Underground Mining

Underground mining is used to reach deposits below the surface. Shafts are sunk to reach coal or mineral deposits. Tunnels are dug from the shaft into the deposits. Explosives are often used to separate deposits from surrounding rock. Material from a deposit is usually taken to the shaft on conveyor belts or on powered vehicles. There, the material is hoisted to the surface. Sometimes railway cars carry it to the surface.

◄ *Trucks wind up and down the terraces of a huge surface mine on a mountainside in Austria. Iron ore has been removed from this site since the Middle Ages. Most surface mining requires stripping away overburden—overlying earth and vegetation—to expose the deposits.*
▼ *Jetting from a nozzle, a powerful stream of water loosens gravel from a bluff. This method, called hydraulic mining, separates deposits such as gold and coal from surrounding rock.*

to extract metals such as copper and iron, a pit is cut larger than the area of the deposit to ensure the stability of the slopes. The slopes are cut in steps down to a point where it becomes impractical to go deeper.

Another kind of surface mining is called quarrying. It usually involves extracting marble, limestone, and other high-quality stone used for ornamental and building purposes. The stone is cut from a pit in large blocks. Some quarries use blasting to fracture the stone from surrounding rock.

Special machines called dredges are used in surface mining called dredging. Dredges drag riverbeds and the ocean floor, removing placer deposits—loose minerals that have been carried to an area by glaciers, wind, or water. Scientists are seeking more

In many underground mines, pillars of coal or rock are left standing to keep a tunnel from collapsing. Stability is sometimes achieved by filling shafts and tunnels with waste rock. This method also allows for disposal of waste materials.

Underground mining techniques have become more complex in recent years. Machines are performing a number of the tasks once done by people. Many coal mines, for example, use continuous mining machines that cut coal from the tunnel walls and discharge it into a shuttle car for transport from the mine, all in one operation. Such machines eliminate the need for blasting the coal from the surrounding rock.

One coal-mining method, called longwall mining, relies on an enormous cutting machine that is brought into an excavated area beneath the surface. The machine moves along a face, or wall, of coal, shearing off large amounts in a single pass. Hydraulic jacks on top of the machine support the roof along the working face, keeping the rock above from caving in on the operators. As the machine moves forward, the roof above the machine may collapse behind it. Longwall mining is a highly productive form of underground mining. Where this method is practical, a greater percentage of coal often can be removed than with other methods.

Whether underground or on the surface, mining is dangerous. Ventilation is a major problem in underground mines. If a fire occurs, workers may be in more danger from asphyxiation by carbon monoxide than from the flames. Long exposure to mining dust can cause respiratory diseases such as black lung. Even with better machinery and tougher safety standards, a miner works in one of the world's most hazardous occupations.

SEE ALSO COAL, FOSSIL FUEL, INDUSTRY, MINERAL, NATURAL RESOURCE, ORE, *and* POLLUTION.

▼ *In the Mount Isa mine complex in Australia, a miner prepares the walls for blasting. Explosives set in holes in mine walls blast away rock to expose the deposits of metals such as copper, zinc, lead, and silver. Mining is one of Australia's largest industries.*

▲ *In Ireland, weary coal miners head home. Helmet lamps provide light when miners work deep in a mine.*
► *Below the ground near Williamsburg, Kentucky, miners take a brief rest. Mining is hazardous, difficult work and is considered one of the world's most dangerous occupations.*

MIST

Mist, like fog, is a cloud at ground level. If microscopic water droplets suspended in the air reduce visibility to less than one kilometer, they form fog. If visibility is greater than one kilometer, they form mist. Mist can form when relative humidity is less than 100 percent. This occurs because water vapor condenses on particles of dust, salt, or other material, called condensation nuclei. In North America, mist often refers to a fine drizzly rain.

SEE ALSO FOG, PRECIPITATION, *and* RAIN.

MONARCHY

Monarchy is a form of government headed by a king, a queen, an emperor, or another royal person. A monarchy whose power is defined by a constitution is called a constitutional monarchy. Modern monarchs usually have little political power. In the United Kingdom, for example, royalty is mostly symbolic; real power rests with Parliament. The rulers of Saudi Arabia and Qatar are among the few remaining powerful monarchs. As the two pie charts below illustrate, the percentage of countries with monarchies has declined dramatically since 1900. Most monarchies have been replaced by other forms of government.

SEE ALSO GOVERNMENT.

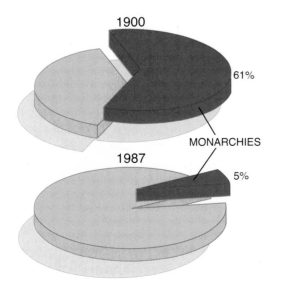

1900

61%

MONARCHIES

1987

5%

MONSOON

A monsoon is a seasonal change in the direction of the prevailing winds. The term comes from the Arabic word *mausim,* meaning "season." Monsoons cause wet and dry seasons throughout much of the tropics. The summer monsoon, which normally produces torrential rains in India, carries moist ocean air over large parts of Asia. During the Northern Hemisphere winter, monsoons bring crucial rainfall to Australia and Indonesia. Half the world's population depends on yearly monsoon rains to provide water for agriculture.

A tropical monsoon's path follows that of the intertropical convergence zone (ITCZ), where the trade winds of the Northern and Southern Hemispheres meet. In summer, when the ITCZ is north of the Equator, the Southern Hemisphere trade winds cross the Equator, are bent to the right by the Coriolis effect, and move into the rising air of the ITCZ. As the cooler, moisture-laden ocean air moves inland, it is heated by the warm Asian landmass. This causes the air to rise, shed its moisture as rain, and be replaced by cooler, heavier air moving in from the ocean.

In a normal year, the monsoon reaches Myanmar (Burma) by late April or early May and India in late May. Carrying moisture-laden air from the South Atlantic Ocean, the monsoon also brings rains to the western part of central Africa. For reasons unknown, the

▲ *Near the end of the dry season in India, herders guide lean cattle across parched, cracked land. Monsoon rains will soon turn this barren spot into a seasonal pond.*
▼ *A sudden downpour, typical of India's monsoon season, catches a boy and two shepherds in an open field. Their umbrellas offer little protection from the hard rain.*

◀ *Rice fields in Goa, India (far left), lie parched and brown in May before the monsoon arrives. In early summer, the wind direction changes, bringing monsoon rains. By August, the same fields are lush and green with the year's rice crop.*

▼ *Parts of the world affected by monsoons experience shifts of wind from dry to wet seasons. In January, trade winds blowing mostly from the northeast leave India dry, but bring rains to Australia and Indonesia. By July the winds shift, carrying moisture-laden air over southern Asia and West Africa.*

monsoon may arrive late or not at all, causing drought from a lack of rain and from the heat that builds throughout these areas.

Though monsoon rains are welcome and needed, they can become excessive. This is particularly true in northern India, where the moist air collides with the Himalayan range. Cherrapunji, a town in the foothills of the Himalaya, holds the world record for rainfall in one year. It had 2,647 centimeters (1,042 in) of rain between August 1860 and July 1861. In Bangladesh, on the Bay of Bengal, rivers swollen by monsoon rains and runoff from melting Himalayan snow regularly overflow, causing severe flooding. In August 1988, for example, water covered most of the country; thousands of people died, and millions were made homeless.

As autumn approaches, the ITCZ moves south again. By January, it sits south of the Equator, causing the winds in the Southern Hemisphere to shift direction. They deliver rain to Australia, to Indonesia, and to other areas with northeast coastlines.

SEE ALSO AGRICULTURE, CLIMATE, CORIOLIS EFFECT, SEASONS, WEATHER, *and* WIND.

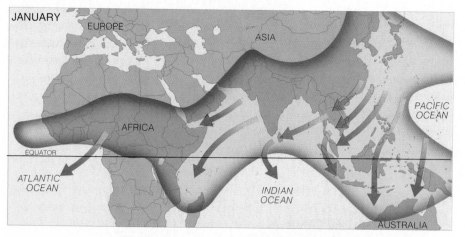

JANUARY

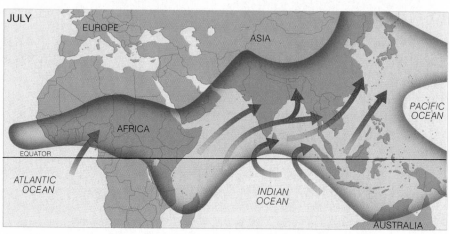

JULY

MOON

The moon, our nearest neighbor in the solar system, is the earth's only natural satellite. The earth and its moon, like dancers arm-in-arm, trace a wobbly path through space as they orbit the sun together.

Before the moon could be studied scientifically, people imagined many things about it. For the ancient Romans, the moon was sacred to Diana the huntress. For the Chinese it was home to the goddess Chang E, who fled there after she stole the secret of immortality.

People think of familiar things on the earth when they look at the moon. Large dark areas on the moon's surface, visible to the naked eye, were labeled *maria,* the Latin word for "seas," because they were thought to look like the earth's seas. As people began using telescopes, they discovered features similar to the earth's mountains, valleys, and plains and gave them names.

Scientists have learned much about the moon. The distance between it and the earth averages about 384,400 kilometers (238,900 mi). The diameter of the moon is 3,476 kilometers (2,160 mi), one-fourth of the earth's diameter. The moon's mass, the amount of material that makes up the moon, is 1/81 of the earth's

▼ Sandstone towers near Moab, Utah, frame a gibbous moon, one that is rounded but not full.

MANNED MOON LANDINGS

Apollo 11 July 16-24, 1969. Landing site: Mare Tranquillitatis. Men stepped onto the moon for the first time on July 20. The crew of the spacecraft *Eagle* brought back the first soil and rock samples and set up instruments that would conduct several experiments after they left.

Apollo 12 November 14-24, 1969. Landing site: Oceanus Procellarum. Crew of the *Intrepid* collected parts of Surveyor 3, an unmanned spacecraft that had landed more than two years earlier.

Apollo 14 January 31-February 9, 1971. Landing site: Fra Mauro hills. The crew was the first to land in the lunar uplands.

Apollo 15 July 26-August 7, 1971. Landing site: Montes Apenninus. The crew drove a wheeled vehicle on the moon. They left a television camera to transmit pictures of the lift-off.

Apollo 16 April 16-27, 1972. Landing site: Descartes highlands. Using the moon as an observatory, the crew took ultraviolet photographs of interplanetary gas, distant stars, and the earth's atmosphere.

Apollo 17 December 7-19, 1972. Landing site: Taurus-Littrow. The crew on this last Apollo mission to land on the moon spent 75 hours on the surface, more time than any other mission.

PLATO

MARE IMBRIUM

APOLLO 15 ▲

MARE SERENITATIS

▲ APOLLO 17

MARE CRISIUM

MARE TRANQUILLITATIS

OCEANUS PROCELLARUM

COPERNICUS

APOLLO 11 ▲

MARE FECUNDITATIS

KEPLER

APOLLO 12 ▲

▲ APOLLO 14

APOLLO 16 ▲

LANGRENUS

MARE NUBIUM

MARE HUMORUM

PITATUS

TYCHO

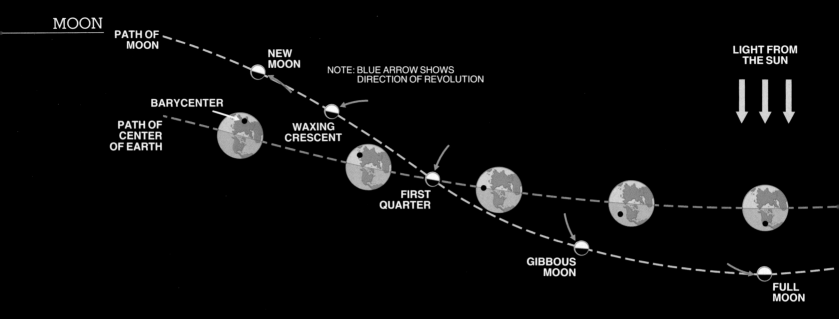

PATH OF MOON

NEW MOON

NOTE: BLUE ARROW SHOWS DIRECTION OF REVOLUTION

LIGHT FROM THE SUN

BARYCENTER

PATH OF CENTER OF EARTH

WAXING CRESCENT

FIRST QUARTER

GIBBOUS MOON

FULL MOON

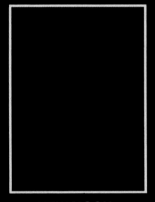

NEW MOON   **WAXING CRESCENT**   **FIRST QUARTER**   **GIBBOUS MOON**   **FULL MOON**

▲ The diagram at top traces the path of the earth and the moon through one lunar month as if viewed from a point looking down on the North Pole. The angle between the sun, the moon, and the earth determines the phases of the moon—how it appears to us. One complete cycle of phases occurs in the time between two consecutive similar alignments of the three bodies, as shown by the first and last positions in the diagram. During each cycle, different amounts of the sunlit (white) lunar surface are visible from the earth, as revealed in the photographs below the diagram.

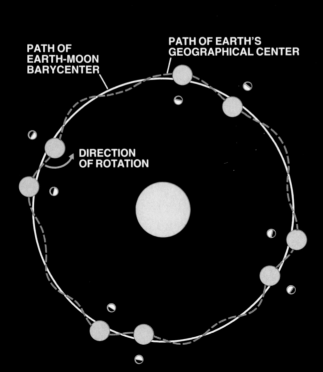

PATH OF EARTH-MOON BARYCENTER

PATH OF EARTH'S GEOGRAPHICAL CENTER

DIRECTION OF ROTATION

◄ Traveling through space together, the earth and its moon act like a double planet, joined by their gravitational attraction. If the earth and the moon were equal in mass, their common center of gravity, called the barycenter, would fall at a point in space midway between the geographical centers of the two. The earth's mass, however, is 81 times that of the moon, so the earth-moon barycenter lies deep within the earth. As the earth and the moon orbit the sun, their barycenter follows a smooth elliptical path around the sun. Because the barycenter is 4,670 kilometers (2,900 mi) from the earth's geographical center, the planet traces a curvy path along its solar orbit. That curve is greatly exaggerated at left.

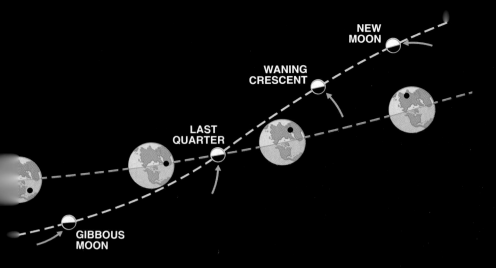

NEW MOON

WANING CRESCENT

LAST QUARTER

GIBBOUS MOON

GIBBOUS MOON

LAST QUARTER

WANING CRESCENT

► It takes the moon approximately 29½ days to complete one cycle of phases, from new moon to new moon. Although the length of a cycle can vary by as much as 13 hours, each phase occurs at predictable intervals within a lunar month.

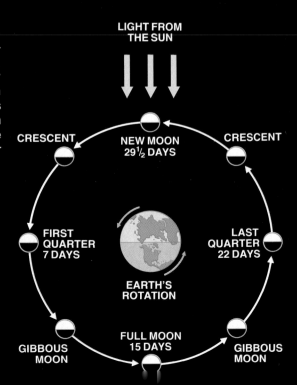

LIGHT FROM THE SUN

CRESCENT

NEW MOON
29½ DAYS

CRESCENT

FIRST QUARTER
7 DAYS

EARTH'S ROTATION

LAST QUARTER
22 DAYS

GIBBOUS MOON

FULL MOON
15 DAYS

GIBBOUS MOON

mass. Because the force of gravity at the surface of an object is a result of the object's mass and size, the surface gravity of the moon is only one-sixth that of the earth's. The force gravity exerts on a person determines the person's weight. Even though your mass stays the same, if you weigh 60 kilograms (132 lbs) on the earth, you would weigh about 10 kilograms (22 lbs) on the moon.

Tied together by gravitational attraction, the earth and the moon revolve around the sun as a double planet. The two masses are like unequal ends of a weight lifter's barbell. The common center of gravity in the earth-moon barbell is called the barycenter. It is not the earth's geographical center but is about 1,700 kilometers (1,100 mi) below the earth's surface. As the earth rotates on its axis, the barycenter is constantly changing its position with respect to the continents. The barycenter is the point around which the earth and moon turn as they move along in their wobbly orbit around the sun.

The moon's gravitational pull on the earth is the main cause of the rise and fall of ocean tides. The moon's gravitational pull causes two bulges of water on the earth's ocean, one where ocean waters face the moon and the pull is strongest and one where ocean waters face away from the moon and the pull is weakest. These are high tides. As the earth rotates, they move around it, one always facing the moon, the other directly opposite. The combined forces of gravity, the earth's rotation and other factors usually cause two high tides and two low tides each day.

Since 1958, about 50 spacecraft from the United States and the Soviet Union have flown near the moon or visited it, and those explorations have answered some questions about our nearest neighbor. There is still some question, however, about how the moon formed. The "giant impact" theory, the most widely accepted explanation, proposes that a giant planetesimal, or primitive planet, about the size of Mars struck the earth more than four billion years ago. The violent impact threw a cloud of material outward from both the earth and the planetesimal. Some of the material recombined and became the moon.

This theory seems to explain why materials taken from the moon are the same as many of the earth's materials, but are found in

◄Taking great care to avoid contaminating precious samples, planetary scientists use sterile tongs to inspect a fragment of lunar rock. Astronauts collected more than 380 kilograms (840 lbs) of lunar soil and rock during the manned Apollo missions.

different proportions. The theory also explains the lack of water on the moon; the heat from the collision would have vaporized any water released from the two planets.

The pitted lunar landscape is the work of countless meteorites that have been bombarding the moon and reshaping its surface for billions of years. Millions of years after the heaviest bombardment, lava welled up from the moon's interior into some of the largest craters left by the meteorites. Each *mare,* or sea, is actually a huge plain of hardened lava. Moon rocks were formed from cooled lava or from compacted fragments of rocks broken by the impact of meteorites.

The moon has no atmosphere to help regulate heat, so daytime temperatures may reach as high as 102°C (216°F). At night, temperatures may drop as low as -173°C (-280°F). The moon, like the planets, does not shine with its own light as stars do. It reflects light from the sun. The shape of the moon appears to change in a repeating cycle when viewed from the earth because the amount of illuminated moon we see varies, depending on the moon's position in relation to the earth and the sun. We always see the same side of the moon because the moon takes the same amount of time to revolve around the earth as it takes to rotate on its axis.

Geologically, the moon is much quieter than the earth. Instruments left behind by the United States Apollo missions have detected

◄ Apollo 11 astronaut Edwin E. Aldrin checks an aluminum panel he has planted on the moon's surface to collect particles of solar wind.

as many as 3,000 moonquakes a year, but the energy released by these tremors is only a fraction of the energy released by the earth's hundreds of thousands of tremors annually. By studying records of the moonquakes, scientists have been able to learn something about the moon's interior. Like the earth, the moon is composed of layers. A crust covers a thicker solid layer beneath. Deeper still is a layer probably made of partially melted material. It is not known for sure whether a separate core exists. This is just one of the many remaining mysteries about earth's only satellite.

SEE ALSO EARTH, GRAVITY, REVOLUTION, ROTATION, SOLAR SYSTEM, SUN, *and* TIDES.

MORAINE

A moraine is a deposit of rocks and debris left behind by a glacier. As glaciers flow, they push the rocks and debris into ridge-like moraines. Lateral moraines form along both edges of the flowing ice. When two glaciers merge, lateral moraines join into a single dark strip in the ice, called a medial moraine. Terminal moraines form at a glacier's leading edge. Ground moraines, which appear as flat plains rather than ridges, form when a moving glacier evenly spreads rock and debris. When a glacier melts and retreats, moraines remain as hills and ridges. Some trap water, forming lakes such as Italy's Lake Como.

SEE ALSO GLACIER *and* ICE SHEET.

MOUNTAIN

Mountains dominate many landscapes, rising above the ocean and landforms around them. Most geologists classify a mountain as land rising 300 meters (1,000 ft) or higher above the surrounding area. Most have a wide base and a narrowed peak or ridge. Mountains are one of the four major landforms, along with hills, plains, and plateaus.

Mountains rise on every continent and cover much of the seafloor. The earth's highest mountain is Mount Everest in the Himalaya. It soars 8,848 meters (29,028 ft) above sea level. Mauna Loa, a volcano in Hawaii, is the largest, with a volume of over 40,000 cubic kilometers (9,600 cu mi).

The Mid-Ocean Ridge

The longest series, or chain, of mountains is mostly hidden beneath the ocean. This chain, called the Mid-Ocean Ridge, circles the earth. It is more than 1,600 kilometers (1,000 mi) wide in some places and more than 64,000 kilometers (40,000 mi) long.

Some parts of the Mid-Ocean Ridge extend above the surface of the water, forming islands. Iceland, an island in the North Atlantic Ocean, and Easter Island, in the South Pacific, are the tops of mountains in the Mid-Ocean Ridge system.

A series of mountains, such as the Mid-Ocean Ridge, is called a mountain range. The Andes form the longest mountain range on land. It stretches 6,437 kilometers (4,000 mi) along the western edge of South America.

Mountain Building

The solid outer part of the earth is made up of large, rigid slabs of rock called plates. The plates slowly but constantly interact around the planet in a process called plate tectonics. In places where the plates collide, the action can cause the earth's crust to wrinkle, somewhat in the way that pushing against the edge of a flat rug will cause the rug to

▶ *A hiker enjoys a vista in the European Alps. Wreathed in clouds and crowned with snow, the Alps soar as high as 4,600 meters (15,000 ft).*

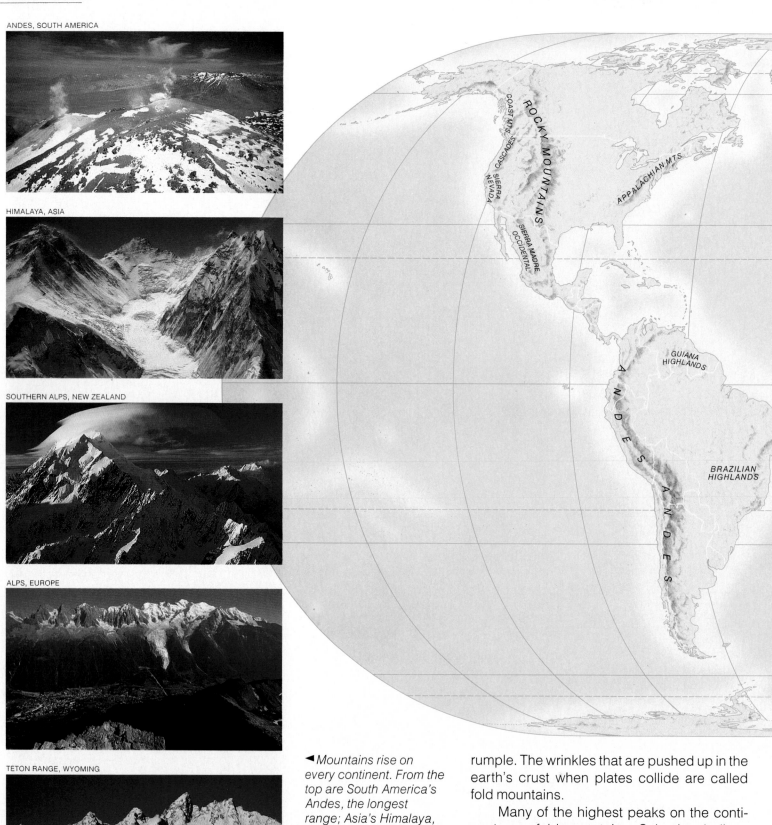

ANDES, SOUTH AMERICA

HIMALAYA, ASIA

SOUTHERN ALPS, NEW ZEALAND

ALPS, EUROPE

TETON RANGE, WYOMING

◄Mountains rise on every continent. From the top are South America's Andes, the longest range; Asia's Himalaya, the highest; the Southern Alps of New Zealand; the Alps oí Europe; and Wyoming's Teton Range.

rumple. The wrinkles that are pushed up in the earth's crust when plates collide are called fold mountains.

Many of the highest peaks on the continents are fold mountains. Scientists believe that the Himalayan range, which includes 30 of the world's highest mountains, started folding upward millions of years ago when the plate carrying what is now India collided with the Eurasian plate carrying the rest of the Asian continent. Because the slow collision of

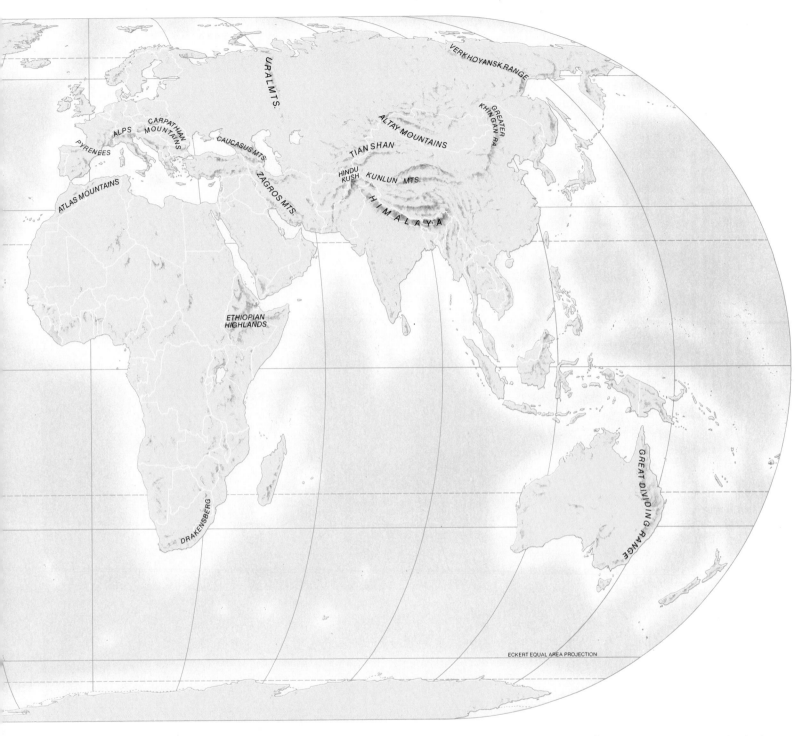

ECKERT EQUAL AREA PROJECTION

the two plates continues today, the Himalayan range is gradually growing taller every year.

Another kind of mountain is formed by movement along a fault, a break in the earth's crust. Land on one side of the fault may rise much higher than land on the other side, eventually forming a range of fault-block mountains. The rugged Sierra Nevada in western North America is a range of fault-block mountains.

A volcano is a third type of mountain.

Molten rock from within the earth erupts from volcanoes. A series of eruptions builds up lava, cinders, ash, and rock particles. The result may be a cone-shaped volcano such as Mount Peleé on the island of Martinique in the Caribbean or Mount Fuji in Japan. Volcanic mountains also form under the ocean, where repeated eruptions can make new islands.

Molten rock that rises within a continental plate may form a fourth kind of mountain—a dome or batholithic mountain. Instead of

▲ *Most mountains belong to one of three major systems. One lies along the western edge of the Americas. Another arches across Europe and Asia. Peaks in the western Pacific, eastern Asia, and Australia make up the third mountain system.*

escaping through a volcano, molten rock sometimes forms a large mass inside the earth's crust. It may grow and push up a bulge on the surface of the earth. The rock that covers this mass, called "country rock" by geologists, is then gradually worn away by weathering and erosion, exposing the igneous rock that has cooled and hardened. This exposed igneous mass is called a dome. The Black Hills of South Dakota and Wyoming, named for their dark evergreen forests, are dome mountains.

The building of fold mountains, fault-block mountains, most volcanoes, and dome mountains takes place over thousands and thousands of years. Although day-to-day changes may not be noticeable, some existing mountains are rising and new mountains are forming even now.

Weathering and Erosion of Mountains

The Himalaya, the Alps, and the Rocky Mountains appear to be indestructable. Folded mountains that began to form millions of years ago, these ranges are relatively young. They are higher and their peaks look more rugged than those in older mountain ranges.

▼ *The diagrams and photographs on these pages illustrate each type of mountain and how it forms. Scientists classify mountains as volcanic, fold, fault-block, and dome. Each type of mountain has a different shape or appearance.*

▲ *Volcanic mountains form when molten rock from deep within the earth rises and escapes through cracks in the crust. Layers of erupted lava, rock, cinders, and ash may gradually form a cone. The composite cone of a volcano called Fuego, in Guatemala (right), consists of layers deposited during eruptions over a long period.*

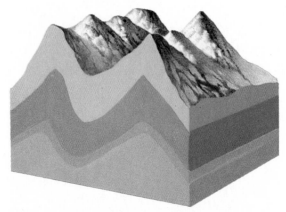

▲ *Fold mountains are formed when two of the large plates that carry the earth's crust slowly collide and compress, or when one plate gradually folds and wrinkles as a result of this action. When this happens, layers of rock may bend like the strata exposed on this cliffside in Canada's Rocky Mountains (right).*

Millions of years ago, the Appalachian Mountains of eastern North America, now gently rolling, may have stood as rugged and as tall as the Himalayan range does today. But over millions of years, exposure to air, water, and ice weathers, or breaks down, mountains. Erosion, which occurs when water, wind, or ice, along with gravity, transports weathered rock from one place to another, also changes the contours of mountains. Glaciers, for example, move large quantities of rock down valleys. Wind and water transport smaller amounts of rock down mountains.

The forces that build and wear away mountains combine in many ways. As a result, each mountain range develops its own distinctive characteristics.

Mountains and Weather

On land, mountain ranges can affect weather patterns. Coastal mountain ranges cause moisture-laden air moving in from the ocean to rise. At higher altitudes, the air cools. The moisture it contains condenses and falls to the ground as rain or snow. Most of the precipitation falls on the windward side of the mountains. The slopes on the leeward side, the side away from the wind, lie in an area known as a rain shadow and are often very

▼ Each mountain-building process is explained separately below. Over millions of years, however, a mountain range may be shaped by several of these processes. Volcanic eruptions and folding, for example, produced the Andes of South America.

▲ Fault-block mountains, such as Wyoming's Teton Range (at right), form when movement takes place along a fault, a break in the earth's crust. Rock on one side of the fault rises higher than rock on the other side. Most fault-block mountains have steep walls on one side and gentler slopes on the other.

▲ Dome mountains develop when magma and tectonic uplift push up surface rock layers, causing the ground to bulge. The magma slowly hardens into igneous rock. Weathering and erosion wear away the surface, exposing the dome formations. Those in the Black Hills of South Dakota and Wyoming (right) are an example.

dry. For example, eastern Washington State, lying in the rain shadow of the Cascades, is semiarid; the western part, on the windward side, receives more precipitation.

Life Zones

A mountain can be so high that the climate varies from the base to the summit. As elevation increases, air temperature decreases. Each marked temperature change brings about a new environment. These different environments, with different kinds of plants and animals, are called life zones. The life zone at the base of a mountain is similar to that of the land surrounding it.

When hiking up 5,895-meter (19,341-ft) Mount Kilimanjaro, in Africa, for example, a climber passes through most of the life zones that would be seen on a journey from the Equator to the Arctic. Tropical forest, with its broadleaf evergreen trees, gradually gives way to hardier evergreen forest. These

evergreen trees reach to the timberline, the upper limit of continuous tree growth. Beyond the timberline lies the alpine or tundra zone.

Alpine Plants and Animals

Plants and animals that live in the alpine or tundra zone are adapted to very cold temperatures, high winds, little available water, and a short growing season. Fierce winds may blow at more than 100 kilometers per hour (63 mph). To survive them, plants have adapted by remaining relatively small. The tallest reach only about a meter (3 ft). Root systems spread wide to collect water and to anchor plants to the ground. Many alpine plants have small, waxy leaves that hold moisture. Some plants are covered with hairlike fuzz that retains heat.

Like plants, animals have adapted to the harsh alpine environment. For example, mountain goats have thick, shaggy coats that protect them from winter storms. Their split

▼ *Bands of vegetation called life zones mark different climates on a mountain. The same trees and other plants flourish in the zone at the base of the mountain as in the surrounding countryside. As elevation increases, conditions grow colder and drier. Winds blow harder, and the growing seasons shorten. Above the timberline, alpine meadows take over. Snow caps the peak. Variations can occur because some slopes may get more sun than others, and some slopes may get more rain.*

◄ *High in the Andes of South America, an Indian tends a flock of sheep. Wool from the animals is used to weave warm clothing.*
▼ *In the mountains of Bolivia, a Chipaya Indian winnows quinoa, a hardy, high-protein grain used to make flour and cereal.*

hooves and padded toes make the animals surefooted on steep slopes. Small mammals called pikas prepare for the alpine winter by harvesting grasses and other edible plants. They pile the food in little stacks near their underground dens. During the winter, meadow mice live in tunnels in the snow, where they are sheltered from the wind and cold. The tiny animals feed on plants beneath the snow.

Eagles are well adapted to mountain environments. In half an hour, an eagle can soar from the base of a mountain to its highest alpine meadows, often a distance of several kilometers. Eagles have large, efficient lungs that help them adjust to sudden changes in elevation that most animals could not tolerate. Eagles and other birds living on mountains avoid the stormy weather that can suddenly develop there by moving to lower elevations.

Mountains and People

Because mountains often have high summits, some have inspired myths. Ancient Greeks believed their gods lived on Mount Olympus. In Viking legends, giant trolls lived in the mountains of Norway and Iceland. Other peaks have played a part in religious beliefs. The Bible says that Moses received the Ten Commandments on Mount Sinai.

Mountain ranges can act as boundaries between countries and as barriers to settlement. The Pyrenees, for example, divide France and Spain. The Appalachians hindered the pioneer settlement of western North America until the Cumberland Gap was discovered and helped open the way west.

Mountains are obstacles to some people and havens for others. Many people, such as the Tibetans, moved to mountains to escape their enemies. Mountainous terrain helped to keep Switzerland safe from invasion during two world wars that devastated much of the rest of Europe. Living in relative isolation, mountain people often develop distinct dialects and customs.

Steep slopes, intense cold, and air that contains little oxygen make life difficult at high

▼ *A Chipaya man and woman cultivate the earth. Poor soil and short growing seasons often make farming difficult in the Andes.*

elevations. The blood of Andean Indians of South America has more oxygen-carrying red cells than does the blood of lowland peoples. These Indians also have larger lungs that help their bodies function in the thin air.

Some mountain people must survive on a limited diet. Only certain crops, such as potatoes and some kinds of corn, will grow at high elevations in the Andes. Indians there terrace steep mountainsides to build fields where they can grow food. They make clothing from the wool of such animals as llamas and alpacas, and they burn animal dung to cook food and to heat their homes.

Many Tibetans rely on hardy animals called yaks. They use these shaggy animals as beasts of burden. Yaks provide milk, butter, meat, and wool. The yaks shape the way of life for many Tibetans, as the animals must be herded from pasture to pasture.

Mountain Resources

Each year, millions of people throughout the world visit mountains to enjoy the majestic scenery. Mountain climbers attempt daring ascents of the highest and most challenging peaks. In summer, hikers and campers

▲ In Kashmir, a village and terraced fields lie beneath peaks of the Karakoram Range of southern Asia.
◄ Young helpers support ceremonial trumpets for Buddhist monks at Lamayuru Monastery in India. Isolated in the Ladakh Range, these Himalayan people continue old traditions.
► A girl tends goats in the shadow of Asia's Ladakh Range. To survive in this area, the Ladakhis raise goats, sheep, and yaks, and farm small plots.

▲ *A popular ski spot, the village of Mürren, in Switzerland, perches on the edge of a cliff below Alpine pastures.*
► *Scenic lakes and mountains attract many visitors to Switzerland.*
▼ *Adorned with flowers, cows follow Swiss villagers to winter pastures in a valley. Snow will soon blanket high mountain pastures where the animals grazed in summer.*

explore mountain paths and meadows, and anglers fish in mountain streams and lakes.

For centuries, mountains have been a source of minerals. Indians of South America mined the Andes for silver and gold.

The Urals provide the Soviet Union with a rich source of iron ore. Austrians mine mountains in Salzburg for salt, one of life's necessities. Mountains hold other valuable natural resources, such as forests, clean water, and grazing land.

People can threaten mountain environments. Not even high peaks have escaped damage. Mountain climbers and hikers may leave trails of litter. Increased farming, mining, logging, and recreational use expose slopes to erosion. Then, heavy rains can cause devastating floods and landslides, damaging settlements in the valleys below.

Many people are searching for solutions to these problems. From Mount Everest in the Himalaya to Mount McKinley in Alaska, climbers lead cleanup expeditions to remove trash. Many countries are designating more and more mountain regions as parks or wilderness areas. Scientists from many countries are working to find ways to prevent the destruction of fragile mountain habitats. In these and other ways, people work to preserve the earth's precious mountain environments.

SEE ALSO CLIMATE, DOME, ELEVATION, FAULT, GLACIER, HILL, LANDFORM, OCEAN, PASS, PLATE TECTONICS, RAIN SHADOW, SEAFLOOR SPREADING, TIMBERLINE, TUNDRA, VALLEY, VOLCANO, WEATHER, *and* WEATHERING AND EROSION.

MOUTH

The place where a river enters a lake, a larger river, or the ocean is called its mouth. A river may deposit large amounts of alluvium—gravel, sand, silt, and clay—at its mouth, forming a delta. On the way to the ocean, a river may, at its mouth, enter an estuary. In an estuary, seawater washes in with the tides and mixes with the river's fresh water. Many major port cities have been built at river mouths where natural harbors have formed.

SEE ALSO DELTA, ESTUARY, HARBOR, *and* RIVER.

N

NATION

A nation is a group of people who share a common culture, language, and history. "Nation" is often used interchangeably with "country." A country, though, may contain more than one national group. A nation may be split by political boundaries. For example, the Kurds are divided by boundaries of Iran, Iraq, Syria, Turkey, and the Soviet Union.

SEE ALSO BOUNDARY, COUNTRY, CULTURE, *and* ETHNIC GROUP.

NATURAL GAS

Natural gas is a fossil fuel, formed from the remains of marine plants and animals. Supplies existing today were formed from remains that were buried under sand and other sediments millions of years ago. Pressure from overlying layers of sediment helped turn the remains into natural gas and oil, and hardened surrounding sediments into rock. Deposits of natural gas and oil are often found together in sedimentary rocks. Burning natural gas causes less pollution than the burning of the other fossil fuels, oil and coal.

SEE ALSO ENERGY, FOSSIL FUEL, *and* ROCK.

▲ *Natural gas flares from a well. Often found with oil, gas burns more cleanly than other fossil fuels.*

◄ Logs fill a pond at an old sawmill in Oregon. A versatile natural resource, timber can be used for fuel, as building material, and in making paper and many other products. Forests must be carefully managed to ensure a constant supply of timber.
► In Finland, a man in traditional dress stands amid fox pelts. In frigid regions, furs have long been used to make warm, durable clothing.

NATURAL RESOURCE

A natural resource is any part of the natural environment that people can use to promote their welfare. Some resources provide food or heat. Others are the raw materials people use in manufacturing many kinds of structures and goods, from buildings to toys.

The environment provides water to drink, air to breathe, soil in which crops grow, and fish and valuable minerals from the ocean. Beneath its surface, the earth contains not only mineral deposits but also deposits of fossil fuels—oil, natural gas, and coal—which are sources of energy. Plants and animals are natural resources. They provide us with food, and they are sources of medicine, clothing, and many other products.

Some of the planet's natural resources are renewable; that is, they can be replenished in the foreseeable future. Air, water, soil, and plants and animals are all renewable resources. The sun's radiation is considered a renewable resource because the sun will continue to exist for at least five billion years. Other resources, such as fossil fuels and certain minerals, form so slowly that they are considered nonrenewable. Once we have used current supplies, these resources will no longer be available.

The earth's natural resources are unevenly distributed. Some countries, such as the Soviet Union and the United States, have large deposits of coal. Others, including many Middle Eastern countries, possess vast reserves of oil. Canada is rich in forests, Japan in fisheries. All countries have some natural resources, but some countries are particularly lacking in important ones, and no country has all that it needs. Countries with abundant resources often grow rich and powerful. The uneven distribution of resources has led to conflict among people throughout history.

▲ On a Pennsylvania farm, two girls hug their sheep. These animals are pets, but around the world people raise sheep for their wool and meat.

Renewable Resources

The sun, the air, and water are three of the most vital natural resources. The sun is the original source of most of the energy used on earth. The air has the right combination of oxygen and other gases to sustain life. Water is necessary to all living things.

The oxygen in the air is constantly being renewed through a process called photosynthesis. During photosynthesis, trees and other green plants absorb carbon dioxide from the air and release oxygen into it. Large-scale clearing of forests and pollutants from cars and factories threaten to destroy the quality of this natural resource. Polluted air is harmful not only to people but also to other living things. In addition, it causes damage to buildings and monuments.

The earth's supply of fresh water is constantly being renewed through the water cycle. During this process, the sun's heat evaporates water from the ocean, lakes, and streams. Water vapor condenses into clouds, which release fresh water as rain and other precipitation, thus recycling the earth's water supply. Some areas, such as parts of northern Africa, do not have enough fresh water. When there is not enough to grow crops to feed a population, famine may result. As expanding populations use more and more water, the need to conserve it and to protect its quality becomes increasingly important.

▲ Waste gas flares from pipes at an oil refinery in the United Arab Emirates. At the refinery, crude oil is cleaned and processed into fuels such as heating oil and gasoline. Oil remains one of the world's most important sources of energy.

The ocean teems with more than 200,000 species of living things. Many people and other beings depend on the ocean for food. The ocean is also a major source of minerals, including common salt.

In some areas, overfishing has caused a decrease in fish populations. Some scientists have suggested that catches of certain species should be limited, giving the fish sufficient time to replenish their numbers. In areas where recommended quotas are ignored, catches are becoming progressively smaller as fish populations decline.

The soil in which crops grow is a renewable resource, but its replacement is a slow process. It can take hundreds of years for a centimeter of soil to form. Throughout the world each year, millions of tons of topsoil are carried to the ocean by wind and water. Wise land management would help conserve much of the soil now being carried away.

The earth's forests, which cover an estimated 30 percent of the land, are valuable in their natural state as well as when they are harvested. Forests shelter millions of animal and plant species, prevent soil erosion, and play a major role in the water cycle. They also help stabilize the world's climate by absorbing much of the sun's radiation. From harvested trees, people produce lumber for building and wood pulp for paper and fabrics. Wise forest management practices include replanting and selective tree-harvesting—the cutting of only certain trees in an area while the rest are left standing. Such practices not only preserve trees as a natural resource but also protect the underlying soil and plants and dependent animal life. And though they are economically more expensive, they are much less costly to the environment.

Trees and other plants give us food and products such as medicines. Cultivated plants such as rice and wheat feed much of the world's population, and many species of plants are valuable in treating diseases. Protecting the environments of known plant species and those yet to be discovered will ensure their availability to future generations.

Animals are a renewable resource. They are a source of food and are often used in agriculture and for transportation. Because of habitat loss and overhunting, many species are now in danger of disappearing. Protecting

endangered species is an important part of natural resource conservation.

Nonrenewable Resources

Minerals and fossil fuels provide the raw materials for most manufacturing, energy, and transportation needs. Most of these nonrenewable natural resources were formed within the earth's crust by geological processes that took place over millions of years.

Ever since someone first picked up a rock and used it as a tool, people have been using mineral resources. Over the centuries,

◄ Outside their cottage, an Irish couple stacks chunks of peat to be burned for heat during the winter. Formed from partially decomposed plants in swamps and bogs, peat is the first stage in the long process of coal formation.
▼ Coal loaded on railroad cars awaits shipment from a port on Hampton Roads, in Virginia. Coal is an abundant natural resource. Millions of tons are mined each year, yet huge reserves remain.

▲ A crane lifts slender aluminum columns from molds set in a factory floor in Greece. Aluminum, processed from an ore called bauxite, is one of the most widely used metals in manufacturing.

people have learned to convert fossil fuels into energy to run machines.

People are using up nonrenewable resources faster than nature can replace them. When the planet's existing deposits of nonrenewable resources run out, they will not be replenished. Many of the world's mineral and fossil fuel deposits have already been located and mapped, and many of them have already been depleted.

As the world's population grows, people will have to find ways to conserve limited supplies of natural resources. This will require a variety of wise practices, including the recycling of materials; less wasteful mining methods; substituting plentiful materials for scarce ones; and developing energy systems based on renewable resources.

The ways people choose to manage both renewable and nonrenewable resources will have a tremendous effect on the future of our planet. The relationships between living and nonliving things in the earth's ecosystem are so intertwined that people's actions can cause a chain reaction far beyond any intent. Actions based on an awareness of the fragile balance within this ecosystem will help ensure plentiful natural resources in the future.

SEE ALSO AGRICULTURE, AIR, CONSERVATION, ENERGY, FOOD, FOREST, FOSSIL FUEL, INDUSTRY, MINERAL, OCEAN, POLLUTION, SOIL, *and* WATER.

▲ *Farmers in Israel turn the soil with a horse-drawn plow. Good agricultural land is a vital natural resource. It provides the means for raising crops to feed people and livestock.*
▼ *A big catch fills the nets of fishermen in China. People around the world depend on fish from rivers, lakes, and the ocean for food. Vast fishing grounds exist in many parts of the ocean.*

NAVIGATION

Navigation is primarily the science or art of determining the position of a ship or a plane and guiding it to its destination. Position can be determined by measuring the time it takes to receive radio signals from stations of known location on the ground or aboard satellites. Position can also be determined by observing the locations of the sun, moon, planets, and distant stars. This requires a sextant, a highly accurate clock, and an almanac giving the positions of celestial bodies. Compasses, which indicate direction, are used in navigation on land, at sea, and in the air.

SEE ALSO ALTITUDE, CHART, COMPASS, DIRECTION, *and* LATITUDE AND LONGITUDE.

▲ *With a sextant, a man sights the sun's altitude just after dawn. Sailors use this navigational tool to determine latitude, which helps pinpoint location.*

NEIGHBORHOOD

A neighborhood is a residential area where people live near, and interact with, one another. Usually neighborhoods are in cities, although they may be found in rural areas as well. Their geographical boundaries are often loosely defined.

Residents of urban neighborhoods often share the same concerns and values. They generally have similar incomes as well as similar social characteristics such as education level and housing preference, and a similar sense of public order. The most familiar such unit is the ethnic neighborhood, an area where people with the same cultural background choose to cluster together to live. This strengthens their sense of community and preserves cultural traditions. Residents benefit from nearby relatives, common language, stores and services geared to their needs, and institutions important to them, such as churches and clubs. Unlike neighborhoods, ghettos historically have been areas where ethnic groups were forced to live.

SEE ALSO CITY, CULTURE, *and* ETHNIC GROUP.

NUCLEAR ENERGY

Nuclear energy is the energy that binds the nucleus of an atom together. In nuclear fission, the energy is released when the nucleus splits. In a nuclear reactor, which uses fission, atoms of uranium break apart. As they split, the atoms release particles that cause other uranium atoms to split, starting a chain reaction. The breakdown of the atoms produces heat energy. The heat warms water and creates steam, which turns turbines to generate electricity. Long-lasting radioactive wastes and the occurrence of radioactive leaks make the fission process controversial because of the danger radiation poses to life.

Nuclear fusion is a process in which the nuclei of atoms fuse, or join. Though it may be a safer process than nuclear fission, fusion is not yet a practical source of energy.

SEE ALSO ENERGY, POLLUTION, *and* SUN.

▲ *Surrounded by desert, a mineral spring in Peru supports a small oasis. The town of Huacachina grew up around this source of water, a rarity in arid lands.*
▼ *Oases come in all shapes and sizes. An aquifer supplies water for El Qasr, a city built on a large oasis in Egypt's Western Desert.*

OASIS

An oasis is an area made fertile by a source of fresh water in an otherwise arid region. Oases vary in size from a cluster of date palms around a well or a spring to a city and its irrigated cropland. Dates, cotton, olives, figs, citrus fruits, wheat, and corn (maize) are common oasis crops.

Underground water sources called aquifers supply most oases. In some cases, a natural spring brings the underground water to the surface. At other oases, wells tap the aquifer. These wells may be centuries old and are painstakingly maintained for the life-giving water they bring.

Some of the world's largest supplies of underground water exist beneath the Sahara, supporting about 90 major, palm-fringed oases in this African desert. Rivers flow through some deserts, providing permanent sources of water for large, elongated oases.

SEE ALSO AQUIFER, DESERT, GROUNDWATER, IRRIGATION, *and* WATER.

OCEAN

The ocean is the vast body of salt water that covers nearly three-fourths of the earth. It is one continuous expanse of water surrounding the continents.

Although the ocean is one continuous body of water, geographers have given it different names according to where it is divided by the continents. The main sections of the global ocean, from largest to smallest, are the Pacific, Atlantic, Indian, and Arctic Oceans.

The earth's ocean is the only one in the solar system. It contains about 1.35 billion cubic kilometers (320 million cu mi) of water, and it makes life on earth possible.

The Ocean and Climate

The ocean plays a vital role in climate and weather. The sun's heat evaporates many tons of ocean water each day, adding moisture to the air. This water vapor condenses to form clouds that release their moisture as rain or other kinds of precipitation. Without this process, nothing could live on the land.

The atmosphere receives much of its heat from the ocean. As the sun warms the ocean waters, the ocean transfers heat to the atmosphere. In turn, the atmosphere distributes the heat around the globe.

Because water absorbs and loses heat more slowly than the landmasses, the ocean helps balance global temperatures by absorbing heat in the summer and releasing it in the winter. Without the ocean to help regulate global temperatures, the earth's climate would be bitterly cold, much like that of Mars.

How the Ocean Formed

Scientists are not sure how the ocean formed. But most believe that after the earth began to form about 4.6 billion years ago, it gradually separated into layers of lighter and heavier rock. The lighter rock rose and formed the earth's crust. The heavier rock

► Surfers and swimmers enjoy the ocean near Rio de Janeiro, in Brazil. The ocean covers nearly three-fourths of the earth's surface. It is this vast supply of water that makes life on earth possible.

sank and formed the earth's core and mantle.

Many scientists believe that the water in the ocean came from rocks inside the hot new earth. As the molten rocks cooled, they released water vapor and other gases. Eventually the water vapor condensed and covered the crust with a primitive ocean. Hot gases from the earth's interior continue to produce new water at the bottom of the ocean.

Ocean water is about 3.5 percent salt, and it contains traces of all the chemical elements found on the earth. The salt in the ocean came from the rocks in the ocean floor and from the land. Billions of tons of salt continue to wash into the ocean each year. As rain falls on land, it dissolves and washes away bits of salt and other minerals in rocks and soil. The rain carries these materials into streams, many of which reach the ocean.

The Ocean Floor

People once believed that the ocean floor was smooth and flat. Then, in the 1920s, scientists began mapping it, using instruments called echo sounders that measure the ocean depths with sound waves. The sonar equipment showed that the ocean floor has dramatic physical features, including huge mountains, deep canyons and crevices, steep cliffs, and wide plains.

From the shore of a continent outward, the ocean floor is divided into several different areas. The first is the continental shelf, the submerged extension of the continent.

The continental shelf gradually descends to a depth of about 180 meters (600 ft). From there it drops off more sharply in what is called the continental slope. The slope descends steeply almost to the bottom of the ocean. Then it tapers off into a gentler slope known as the continental rise. The continental rise descends to the deep-ocean floor, which

▶ *Beneath the waters of the ocean lies a varied realm of tall mountain ranges, broad plains, deep trenches, and great canyons. This map shows the major features of the ocean floor.*

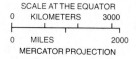

SCALE AT THE EQUATOR

0   KILOMETERS   3000

0   MILES   2000

MERCATOR PROJECTION

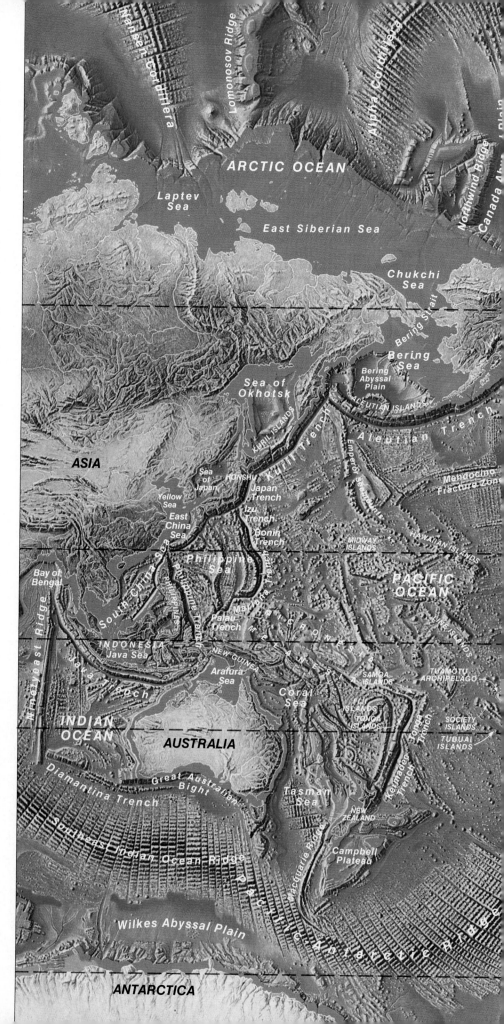

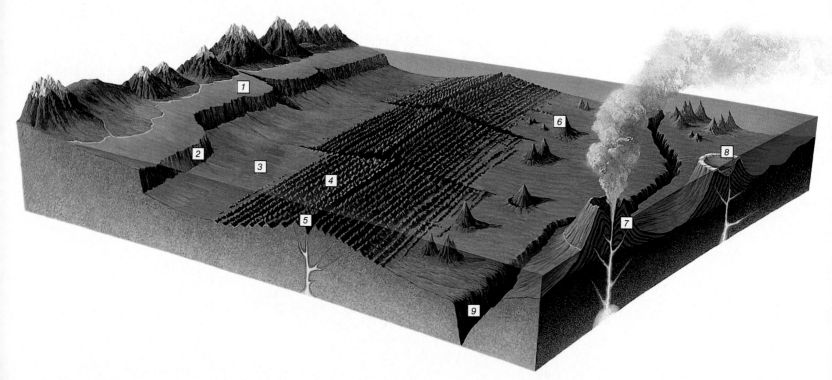

▲ *The ocean floor has several different regions. The continental shelf (1) is an underwater extension of a continent. It ends in a steep cliff called the continental slope (2). The slope descends to the abyssal plain (3). Running along the center of the ocean floor is the Mid-Ocean Ridge (4). At the crest of the ridge is a deep crack called a rift. Hot molten rock from the earth's interior wells up in the rift (5). Underwater volcanoes form seamounts (6). Some rise above the water and become islands (7). Coral reefs form around some volcanoes, which eventually submerge, leaving atolls (8). Deep, narrow depressions called trenches (9) are the deepest parts of the ocean.*

is called the abyss or the abyssal plain.

Abyssal plains are broad, flat areas that lie at a depth of about 2,000 meters (6,560 ft) to more than 6,000 meters (19,680 ft). Scattered across them are abyssal hills and underwater volcanic peaks called seamounts.

Rising from the abyssal plains in each major ocean is a huge chain of mostly undersea mountains. Called the Mid-Ocean Ridge, the chain circles the earth, stretching more than 64,000 kilometers (40,000 mi).

A major portion of the ridge runs down the middle of the Atlantic Ocean and is known as the Mid-Atlantic Ridge. It was not directly seen or explored until 1973, four years after an astronaut first walked on the moon.

Much of the Mid-Ocean Ridge is split by a deep central rift, or crack. Molten rock from the earth's interior wells up from the rift, building new seafloor.

Some areas of the ocean floor also have deep, narrow depressions called trenches. They are the deepest parts of the ocean. The deepest spot of all is the Challenger Deep, which lies in the Mariana Trench in the Pacific Ocean near the island of Guam. It is 10,915 meters (35,810 ft) below the ocean surface.

From the shoreline to the deepest seafloor, the ocean waters teem with life. Hundreds of thousands of species of living things exist in the ocean. They range in size from microscopic algae and animals to the blue whale, the largest creature known to have lived on the earth.

Ocean Life Zones

The ocean has three main life zones: 1) the shallow coastal waters from the shore to the edge of the continental shelf; 2) the shallow layer of surface water above the open ocean floor; and 3) the dark depths and bottom. Living things in all three zones are specially adapted to survive there.

In the open ocean, most sunlight reaches only the upper layers of the water. Vast numbers of microscopic algae grow there, as well as in shallower waters. Microscopic animals feed on the algae. The tiny plants and animals that drift near the surface are called plankton. Plankton provide food for fish and other animals, including giant whales.

As the ocean water becomes deeper, less sunlight penetrates it. At about 900 meters (3,000 ft), the light is very dim. Below this level is a world of perpetual blackness and cold, where food is scarce. Many animals in this zone have huge mouths, sharp teeth, and expandable stomachs that enable them to catch and eat any food that comes along in the darkness.

Many of the animals that live on the

ocean bottom feed on the remains of plankton that drift down from the surface of the water. Not all bottom dwellers, however, depend on such a food source. In 1977, scientists discovered a community of creatures on the floor of the Pacific that feed on bacteria around vents, or openings, in the seafloor. The vents, which are part of the system that forms new seafloor along the Mid-Ocean Ridge, discharge hot water containing minerals from the earth's interior. The minerals nourish the bacteria, which in turn nourish creatures such as crabs, clams, and giant sea worms.

Ocean Currents

Ocean currents are riverlike streams of water. Currents flowing near the surface transport heat from the tropics to the Poles and cooler water back toward the Equator. This keeps the ocean waters from becoming extremely hot or cold.

Deep cold currents transport oxygen to living things throughout the ocean. They also carry rich supplies of the nutrients that living things need. The nutrients come from the remains of plankton and other living things that drift down and decay on the ocean floor.

Along some coasts, winds and currents produce a phenomenon called upwelling. As winds push surface water away from shore, cold water flowing in deep currents rises to take its place. This upwelling of deep water brings up nutrients that nourish new growths of plankton. These provide food for fish. In this way, ocean food chains constantly recycle food and energy.

Some ocean currents are enormous and extremely powerful. One of the most powerful is the Gulf Stream, a warm surface current that originates in the tropical Caribbean Sea and flows northeast along the eastern coast of the United States. The Gulf Stream measures up to 80 kilometers (50 mi) across and is more than a kilometer deep.

Like other ocean currents, the Gulf Stream plays a major role in climate. As the stream travels north, it transfers heat and

▲ *The Nubble Light, a lighthouse in Maine, stands on the coast to guide ships. Since ancient times, people have used the ocean for travel and trade.*
▶ *A fisherman of Fiji, in the Pacific, brings his catch to market. The ocean provides vast tonnages of seafood. Some of it is ground into meal to feed livestock.*

▶ *A tanker loaded with oil piped from Prudhoe Bay leaves the port of Valdez, Alaska. Scientists estimate that nearly half the earth's oil and natural gas resources lie in deposits under the ocean.*

moisture from its warm tropical waters to the air above. Westerly winds carry the warm, moist air to the British Isles and to Scandinavia, causing them to have milder winters than they otherwise would experience at their northern latitudes.

People and the Ocean

For thousands of years, people have depended on the ocean as a source of food and as a highway for trade and exploration. Today, people continue to travel on the ocean and to rely on the resources it contains.

Fishermen catch more than 90 million tons of seafood each year, including more than 100 species of fish and shellfish. Minerals, especially common salt, come from the ocean, too. New techniques are being developed to mine the seafloor for valuable minerals such as copper and nickel.

Oil is one of the most valuable resources taken from the ocean today. Offshore rigs pump petroleum from wells drilled in the continental shelf. As land sources of oil grow scarce, oil under the ocean becomes more important. About one-quarter of oil and gas supplies now comes from offshore deposits.

Through the centuries, people have sailed the ocean on long-established trade routes. Today, oceangoing ships still carry most of the world's freight, particularly bulky goods such as machinery, grain, and oil.

In the future, scientists and other experts hope that the ocean will be used more widely as a source of energy. Some countries have already harnessed the energy of ocean waves and tides to power turbines to generate electricity.

Overfishing and Pollution

The ocean offers us a wealth of food and other resources. But over the last two centuries, these resources have been threatened. People have harvested so many fish and other ocean animals for food and other products that some species have begun to disappear.

► *From sunlit surface waters to dark seafloor, the ocean holds a vast array of life, as this painting indicates. These creatures are not drawn to scale and would not all be found in such a small space.*

FLYING FISH

OCEAN SUNFISH

DOLPHIN FISH

HUMPBACK WHALE

DOLPHINS

MANTA RAY

GULPER EEL

EEL-LARVA

DRAGONFISH

SPERM WHALE

LANTERN FISH

VIPER FISH

ANEMONE

OCTOCORAL

GIANT SQUID

BARREL SPONGE

TRIPOD FISH

SEA CUCUMBER

BRITTLE STAR

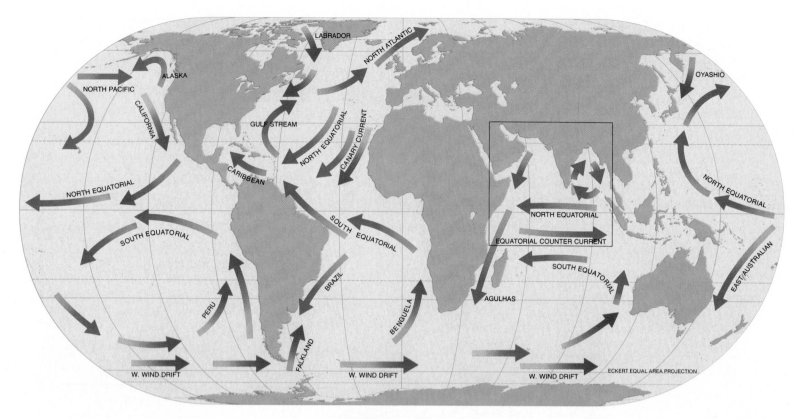

During the 1800s and early 1900s, whalers killed thousands of whales for their oil and ivory. Some species, including the blue whale, were hunted nearly to extinction. Many species are still endangered today.

In the 1960s and 1970s, catches of important food fishes, such as herring in the North Sea and haddock in the Atlantic, began to drop off dramatically. The fish were disappearing. Fishermen were using more advanced equipment, such as electronic fish finders and large trawling nets, so they could catch more fish. But the nets dragged across the seabed and in the process caught many small, young fish. This meant that there were far fewer fish left behind to reproduce and replenish the supply. In some areas, overfishing still goes on.

Another threat to the ocean and its wildlife comes from pollution. For centuries, people have used the ocean as a dumping ground for sewage and other wastes. In the 20th century, the wastes have included chemicals from factories, insoluble plastics,

▶ Sea fog rolls over the Namib, a desert on the southwest coast of Africa. A cold ocean current chills winds and prevents the formation of rain clouds. Fog results, and vegetation is scarce.

◄ *Set in motion by prevailing winds, ocean currents carry warm water (red) from the tropics to the Poles and cold water (blue) from the Poles to the tropics.*

→ WARM CURRENT

→ COLD CURRENT

INDIAN OCEAN CURRENTS DURING MONSOON SEASON

▼ *Desert land juts into the sea along the coast of Peru. The cold Peru Current cools ocean winds and inhibits rain on the coast. Yet the current also brings nutrients that support rich fishing grounds.*

oil spilled from ships, and pesticides such as DDT. These harmful substances have killed sea life and threatened the food supply.

To find ways to protect the ocean, scientists from all over the world are cooperating in studies of the ocean waters and marine life. They are also working together to control pollution. And many countries are working to reach agreement on how to manage and harvest ocean resources.

Although the ocean is vast, it is more easily polluted and damaged than people once thought. It requires care and protection as well as expert management. Only then can it continue to provide the many resources that living things—including people—need.

SEE ALSO ATMOSPHERE, BAY, BEACH, CLIMATE, COAST, CONTINENT, CONTINENTAL SHELF, CORAL REEF, CURRENT, EARTH, ESTUARY, FJORD, GULF, HYDROSPHERE, ISLAND, OCEANOGRAPHY, POLLUTION, SEA, SEAFLOOR SPREADING, TIDES, TRENCH, WATER, WATER CYCLE, *and* WAVES.

OCEANOGRAPHY

Oceanography is the systematic scientific study of the ocean. Scientists who specialize in this field are called oceanographers. They explore and investigate all parts of the ocean, from coastal shallows to the deepest depths. They do much of their fieldwork on specially designed research ships equipped with scientific instruments and laboratories.

Within the field of oceanography are several specialties. Chemical oceanographers, for example, study the chemical composition of seawater. Physical oceanographers study the physical characteristics of seawater, such as temperature and the movements of waves, tides, and currents. They also try to assess how the circulation of ocean water interacts with that of the atmosphere to regulate the earth's climate.

Marine geologists study the ocean floor and map its topography and structure. They examine its sediments for clues to the earth's history and to learn how the earth's crust is changing today. They also search for deposits of valuable metals, other minerals, and

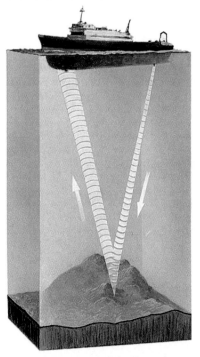

▲ *Using a process called sonar, or echo sounding, oceanographers calculate the depth of the ocean by bouncing sound waves off the seafloor. By measuring the time sound pulses take to return to the surface as echoes, the scientists can map ocean bottom features.*

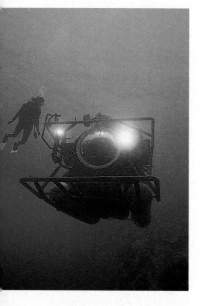

▲ *Small diving craft such as this two-person submersible help scientists obtain valuable, firsthand information about life in the ocean.*
▼ *With only its red conning tower in view, the research vessel* Alvin *bobs in the ocean off St. Croix, in the Virgin Islands. A diver who helped launch the sub in choppy waters uses a telephone to talk with scientists inside the instrument-filled craft.*

reserves of fossil fuels such as petroleum.

Marine biologists study the plants and animals of the ocean. They investigate the effects of pollution on sea life. They also study life cycles and growth patterns of fish and other marine creatures to find ways to increase their numbers to help feed the world's rapidly growing human population.

People have been curious about the ocean since ancient times. Yet scientific study of it did not really begin until the 1700s. Then, explorers began to measure ocean currents and depths. In 1872, the British ship *Challenger* set out on the first expedition devoted entirely to the scientific exploration of the ocean. During the voyage, British scientists collected thousands of specimens of sea plants and animals. The expedition marked the beginning of modern oceanography.

Since then, scientists have continued to learn about the ocean and its life, often using sophisticated technology such as satellite observation. By using small diving craft called submersibles that take them deep below the surface, oceanographers have explored the ocean firsthand. They have discovered undersea volcanoes and creatures living near chemical-spewing vents in the deep. With more discoveries still to come, the ocean remains the earth's last frontier.

SEE ALSO CLIMATE, CURRENT, GEOLOGY, OCEAN, SEAFLOOR SPREADING, TIDES, *and* WAVES.

OIL

Oil is a fossil fuel, formed from the remains of marine plants and animals. Existing supplies began developing millions of years ago when remains were deposited on the seafloor with mud and silt. Over time, pressure from overlying sediments helped convert the remains into oil. Drilling is used to reach oil deposits. Oil can be extracted from tar sands (sand mixed with oil) and oil shale (rock saturated with oil) as well, but the recovery process is costly. Crude oil, also called petroleum, can be refined into many products.

SEE ALSO ENERGY, FOSSIL FUEL, *and* PETROLEUM.

ORBIT

An orbit is the path followed by a celestial body or satellite as it revolves around a more massive object. The momentum of the revolving object and the strength of the gravitational field it moves through determine the shape of its orbit. The earth's momentum, for example, would carry the planet forward in a straight line if it were not for the sun's gravitational pull. The earth's orbit is slightly oval-shaped.

SEE ALSO EARTH, GRAVITY, REVOLUTION, SEASONS, *and* SOLAR SYSTEM.

ORE

An ore is a deposit of one or more minerals that is profitable to mine. Ore may contain pure metals, such as copper or gold. Some ores contain metals combined with silicon, sulfur, oxygen, or other elements. Metals are often associated with particular ores. Aluminum, for example, is found principally in the ore called bauxite. Rock containing ore is mined and crushed. Then the mineral is extracted by one of several methods, including smelting, which uses heat, or electrolysis, which uses acid and an electric current.

SEE ALSO MINERAL, MINING, *and* ROCK.

OXBOW LAKE

An oxbow lake forms from an abandoned bend, or meander, in a river that curved so much that only a narrow neck of land separated either side of the loop. It is called an oxbow because its curved shape looks like the U-shaped harness frame that fits around an ox's neck.

When a meandering river overflows—as it does during periods of heavy rains and flooding—it may cut through the neck of land in the oxbow curve. This opens up a new channel for the river. The crescent-shaped body of standing water left behind is known as an oxbow lake.

Oxbow lakes are often shallow and may fill up with sediment and become dry until another flood occurs. They are common on the lower Mississippi River. Other names for this type of lake are horseshoe lake, loop lake, and cutoff lake.

SEE ALSO FLOOD, FLOODPLAIN, LAKE, *and* RIVER.

◀ *Oxbow lakes develop from meanders like these that loop back and forth on the Fraser River in western Canada.*
▼ *A river in Alaska has cut a channel through the neck of land in a meander. Soon, the loop will be sealed off, forming an oxbow lake.*

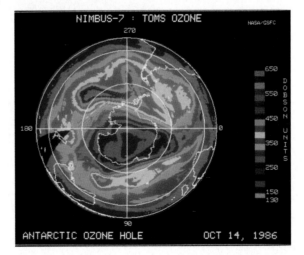

OZONE LAYER

The ozone layer is a region in the stratosphere that contains high concentrations of a gas called ozone. This bluish gas absorbs the sun's ultraviolet radiation more efficiently than does any other substance in the atmosphere. Although ozone constitutes only about one-millionth of the atmosphere, it absorbs most of the sun's ultraviolet radiation. Without the ozone layer, ultraviolet radiation would destroy all life on the earth's surface.

The oxygen molecules needed to sustain life each contain two atoms. In the stratosphere, ultraviolet light strikes these molecules, splitting each into two oxygen atoms. When one of these combines with an oxygen molecule, the result is an oxygen molecule with three atoms. Ozone is made up of oxygen molecules that contain three atoms.

An ozone molecule is very reactive: When struck by an ultraviolet ray, it falls apart to yield an oxygen atom and the oxygen we need. These recombine, though, to produce another ozone molecule. Some manufactured

◀ *A view of the earth recorded by the NIMBUS-7 satellite shows the ozone layer over the Southern Hemisphere. Antarctica, outlined in white, lies at the center. Each color represents a range of ozone concentrations. Areas of purple near the center show that the ozone layer there is very thin. This region is called the "ozone hole." Its presence may signal that certain manufactured chemicals are destroying the ozone layer. This is of worldwide concern because the ozone layer prevents harmful ultraviolet radiation from reaching earth's surface.*

chemicals stop this cycle, reducing the amount of ozone in the stratosphere. Among the worst offenders are chlorofluorocarbons (CFCs), chemicals used in refrigeration and in the production of foam plastics. A worldwide ban on CFCs, proposed in 1987, would help preserve the ozone layer. In time, it could begin to reconstitute itself.

SEE ALSO ATMOSPHERE, CLIMATE, GREENHOUSE EFFECT, *and* POLLUTION.

P

PARK

A park is an area of land set aside to preserve the special features within it. There are many kinds of parks. A park may contain unspoiled wilderness, unusual geologic features, native wildlife, archaeological finds, historic sites, recreational facilities, or a combination of these. Some parks are enormous, like Yellowstone National Park, which covers some 900,000 hectares (more than two million acres) in the western United States. Some are tiny, like the "vest-pocket parks" nestled among tall buildings on vacant lots in New York City. Parks are managed by a variety of groups, including national and local governments and private organizations.

In Europe, many parks originally were private preserves where members of the aristocracy could hunt deer, birds, or other wild animals. Gradually, many of these parks were opened to the public.

The idea of having national parks administered by the government originated in the

▲ *Boaters enjoy the Serpentine, a lake in London's Hyde Park. The large park offers city dwellers a leafy retreat from urban noise and crowding.*
▶ *On a bright winter day after a snowfall, ice skaters flock to Central Park in New York City.*

▼ *Visitors to Yellowstone National Park watch Old Faithful erupt. Extending beyond the Wyoming border into Idaho and Montana, Yellowstone contains some 10,000 geysers and hot springs.*

United States during the late 19th century. People who were concerned about the way urban and agricultural development was rapidly destroying the country's wildlands appealed to the federal government to protect some of these lands. In 1872, Congress set aside part of the Yellowstone region to preserve its spectacular wilderness. Following the establishment of Yellowstone National Park, many more parks were set aside. In 1916, the National Park Service was established to administer the country's growing heritage of protected land.

Inspired by the actions of the United States, other countries began to set aside portions of their lands as national parks, and today the interest in parklands is increasing worldwide. India maintains large areas as parks primarily for wildlife preservation. In Africa, a wide variety of animals lives in parks, where rangers strive to protect wildlife. In Kenya, these animals range from the lions of Maasai Mara to the flamingos of Lake Nakuru. A national park in Poland protects the last free-roaming population of European bison. A park movement to protect tropical rain forests has been successful in Costa Rica.

The International Union for the Conservation of Nature and Natural Resources (IUCN) has been active in promoting the global park movement. The IUCN is an environmental organization dedicated to the collection and exchange of information among countries to benefit the establishment, maintenance, and protection of parks around the world.

With more and more people living in densely populated urban areas, parks offer people the opportunity to experience and better understand natural and historical environments. Whether camping, fishing, skating, or just walking in a park, visitors can learn firsthand about nature, the past, and the world.

There are problems associated with establishing parklands. Some developing countries are reluctant to set aside land for parks because they fear that doing so would deprive them of farmland they need to grow food for their people. Some countries have found, however, that their economies are actually helped by the establishment of parklands that bring in tourist income.

The automobile has made most U.S. parks easy to visit, but it has led to overcrowding as well. Overcrowding often results in littering and other pollution and in crimes such as vandalism and theft. The National Park

PENINSULA

A peninsula is a piece of land jutting out into a lake or into the ocean. Because they are surrounded on three sides by water, peninsulas usually have long coastlines. "Peninsula" comes from two Latin words, which together mean "almost an island."

The map below shows three large peninsulas in North America. The state of Florida is bordered on three sides by the Atlantic Ocean and the Gulf of Mexico. Baja, or Lower, California, in northwestern Mexico, is a narrow peninsula 1,225 kilometers (760 mi) long. Yucatán, also in Mexico, separates the Gulf of Mexico from the Caribbean Sea.

SEE ALSO COAST.

▲ In a cloud of dust, an elephant wanders in Amboseli National Park, a vast preserve in Kenya. In Africa, the existence of elephants and other large mammals is increasingly threatened by poachers and by disruption and loss of habitat.
◄ Parks preserve history and culture as well as animals and natural environments. These cliff dwellings, built by the Anasazi in the 13th century, are the centerpiece of Colorado's Mesa Verde National Park.

Service is regulating the flow of automobile traffic into some parks. Many countries are working on ways to solve these and other problems so that parks can be protected for future generations to enjoy.

SEE ALSO CONSERVATION *and* WILDERNESS.

PASS

A pass is a gap, or break, in high, rugged terrain such as a mountain ridge. A pass forms when a glacier or stream erodes, or wears away, the land. Passes allow people to cross mountain barriers more easily. "Pass" may also refer to a channel, or deeper part of a body of water, that allows passage through otherwise shallow waters.

SEE ALSO CHANNEL, GAP, GLACIER, MOUNTAIN, *and* WEATHERING AND EROSION.

PERMAFROST

Permafrost is a permanently frozen layer below the earth's surface. It consists of soil, gravel, and sand, usually bound together by ice. Where permafrost is continuous under all surface features, it can reach depths of up to 450 meters (1,500 ft). Found in areas where temperatures rarely rise above 0°C (32°F), permafrost exists most widely in the far north.

In summer, when the top layer of soil thaws, water cannot drain through the frozen subsoil. The ground becomes muddy, and some structures built over permafrost may sink. Heat from buildings may thaw permafrost unless the site has been insulated with materials such as gravel.

SEE ALSO POLAR REGIONS *and* TUNDRA.

PETROLEUM

Petroleum is another name for crude oil. The term comes from two Latin words: *petra,* which means "rock," and *oleum,* which means "oil." Existing supplies of petroleum formed from ancient microscopic marine plants and animals. When they died, their remains were deposited on the seafloor, along with mud, silt, and other sediments. Pressure from additional layers of sediment helped convert the remains into petroleum, and compacted and cemented surrounding sedimentary materials into rocks called source rocks.

In its crude form, petroleum is not a single chemical substance, but a mixture of hundreds of substances. Jet fuel, heating oil, and gasoline are processed from petroleum. Various chemicals in petroleum are used in making products such as nylon, plastics, and drugs. Demand for petroleum has caused supplies of this limited resource to dwindle.

SEE ALSO ENERGY, FOSSIL FUEL, NATURAL GAS, NATURAL RESOURCE, OIL, *and* POLLUTION.

PIEDMONT

The term "piedmont" comes from two French words—*pied,* which means "foot," and *mont,* which means "mountain." When used to describe an area, as in "piedmont glacier" or "piedmont lake," the word tells you that the area is at the base, or foot, of a mountain. When used alone, "piedmont" sometimes serves as the proper name of a region located at the base of a mountain or mountain range—the Piedmont in Italy, for example.

Mountain streams deposit silt, sand, and other kinds of sediment on piedmont areas, improving the fertility of the soil. The Piedmont at the base of the Alps in Italy is the rich agricultural region in the northwestern part of the country. In the eastern United States, the Piedmont is the region that stretches from the base of the Appalachian Mountains to the Atlantic Coastal Plain.

SEE ALSO ALLUVIAL FAN, MOUNTAIN, RIVER, *and* WEATHERING AND EROSION.

PLAIN

A plain, one of the four major types of landforms, is a large area of relatively flat land, often covered with grasses. More than half of the world's population lives on plains, which cover some 55 percent of the earth.

Some plains are formed by the natural processes of weathering and erosion, which wear away landforms such as plateaus, mountains, and valleys. Smaller plains called floodplains result from weathering and the side-to-side erosion of meandering rivers. Rock fragments, silt, clay, and other sediments are deposited as rivers overflow onto their floodplains.

Rivers carry weathered materials to the ocean and deposit them on continental shelves—broad, sloping underwater plains. Coastal plains may form when movements in the earth's crust push up continental shelves. Other plains, in the interiors of some continents, resulted from the uplift of shallow seas millions of years ago. These are just a few of the ways in which plains form.

Deposits of rich sediments such as those found on plains in eastern China or on North America's central plains increase the fertility of many plains.

SEE ALSO ALLUVIAL FAN, COASTAL PLAIN, FLOODPLAIN, LANDFORM, SEDIMENT, *and* WEATHERING AND EROSION.

▼ *Open plains surround Garden City, Iowa. People often settle on plains, where there is fertile farmland and level ground that makes building and travel easy.*

▼ *Rough grass carpets the Great Plains near Independence Rock, in Wyoming. Too dry for farming, this area serves as pastureland for sheep and cattle.*

PLANETS

Ancient astronomers, who viewed the sky with nothing more powerful than their own eyes, noticed several "stars" that looked different from the others and appeared to move in strange ways. The Greeks called them *planetes,* which means "wanderers." Our word "planet" came from this Greek word, but today we know these wanderers are not stars.

The planets move constantly through space, each in its own orbit around the star we call the sun. They do not shine with their own light the way stars do. The planets shine with light reflected from the sun.

Of the nine known planets in our solar system, Mercury, Venus, Earth, and Mars orbit closest to the sun. Because each planet in this inner group is dense and solid like Earth, they are often called "terrestrials." Their atmospheres vary in density from Mercury's extremely thin atmosphere to that of Venus, which is thick with clouds of sulfuric acid.

Only Earth has an atmosphere with clouds composed of water droplets and ice crystals.

Many thousands of rocky fragments called asteroids form a wide belt between the inner planets and the outer planets—Jupiter, Saturn, Uranus, Neptune, and Pluto. The outer planets, except icy Pluto, are gaseous and have deep atmospheres that thicken into hot liquid reaching all the way to their cores.

Every planet except Mercury and Venus has at least one satellite, or moon, that orbits the planet as it revolves around the sun. Jupiter, Saturn, and Uranus have so many moons that they appear to be at the center of mini-solar systems of their own.

As astronomers examine the planets with the help of space probes, they hope to discover more about these wanderers, and in turn, to learn about planet Earth. Increasingly powerful telescopes may make possible the discovery of other planets and solar systems.

SEE ALSO EARTH, METEOROID, MOON, SOLAR SYSTEM, *and* SUN.

▼ *Although not to scale, this composite of photographs from the space probe Voyager 1 provides a glimpse of Saturn, its rings, and several of its moons.*

▼ *While orbiting the moon in the Apollo 10 lunar module, astronauts photographed their home planet. The moon and the Earth both shine with light reflected from the sun.*

	MERCURY	**VENUS**	**EARTH**	**MARS**
Average distance from sun	57,900,000 km (36,000,000 mi)	108,200,000 km (67,200,000 mi)	149,600,000 km (93,000,000 mi)	227,900,000 km (141,600,000 mi)
Period of revolution	88 days	225 days	365.26 days	1.88 years
Average orbital speed	48 km per second (30 mps)	35 km per second (22 mps)	30 km per second (19 mps)	24 km per second (15 mps)
Period of rotation	58.6 days	243 days	23.93 hours	24.6 hours
Equatorial diameter	4,878 km (3,031 mi)	12,104 km (7,521 mi)	12,756 km (7,926 mi)	6,787 km (4,217 mi)
Tilt of axis	0°	3°	23° 27′	25° 12′
Surface gravity (earth = 1)	0.38	0.91	1	0.38
Temperature	-170° to 430°C (-270° to 810°F)	470°C (880°F)	-50° to 55°C (-60° to 130°F)	-122° to -22°C (-189° to -9°F)
Number of known satellites	0	0	1	2

Note: The tilt of the axis is given in degrees from the perpendicular to the plane of the planet's orbit.

JUPITER

This painting shows the comparative sizes of the planets, in the order of their orbits around the sun. Satellites circle most of the planets. Distances are not to scale.

MARS

EARTH

VENUS

MERCURY

SUN

JUPITER	SATURN	URANUS	NEPTUNE	PLUTO
778,300,000 km (483,600,000 mi)	1,429,000,000 km (888,000,000 mi)	2,875,000,000 km (1,786,000,000 mi)	4,504,000,000 km (2,799,000,000 mi)	5,900,000,000 km (3,700,000,000 mi)
11.86 years	29.46 years	84 years	165 years	248 years
13 km per second (8 mps)	9.6 km per second (6 mps)	6.8 km per second (4.2 mps)	5.4 km per second (3.4 mps)	4.7 km per second (2.9 mps)
9.9 hours	10.5 hours	17.2 hours	17.9 hours	6.4 days
142,796 km (88,729 mi)	120,000 km (74,500 mi)	51,800 km (32,200 mi)	48,600 km (30,200 mi)	2,280 km (1,420 mi)
3° 06'	26° 42'	82° 06'	28° 48'	68°
2.5	1.08	0.9	1.2	0.08
-130°C (-200°F)	-185°C (-300°F)	-215°C (-355°F)	-200°C (-330°F)	-230°C (-380°F)
16	17	15	*	1

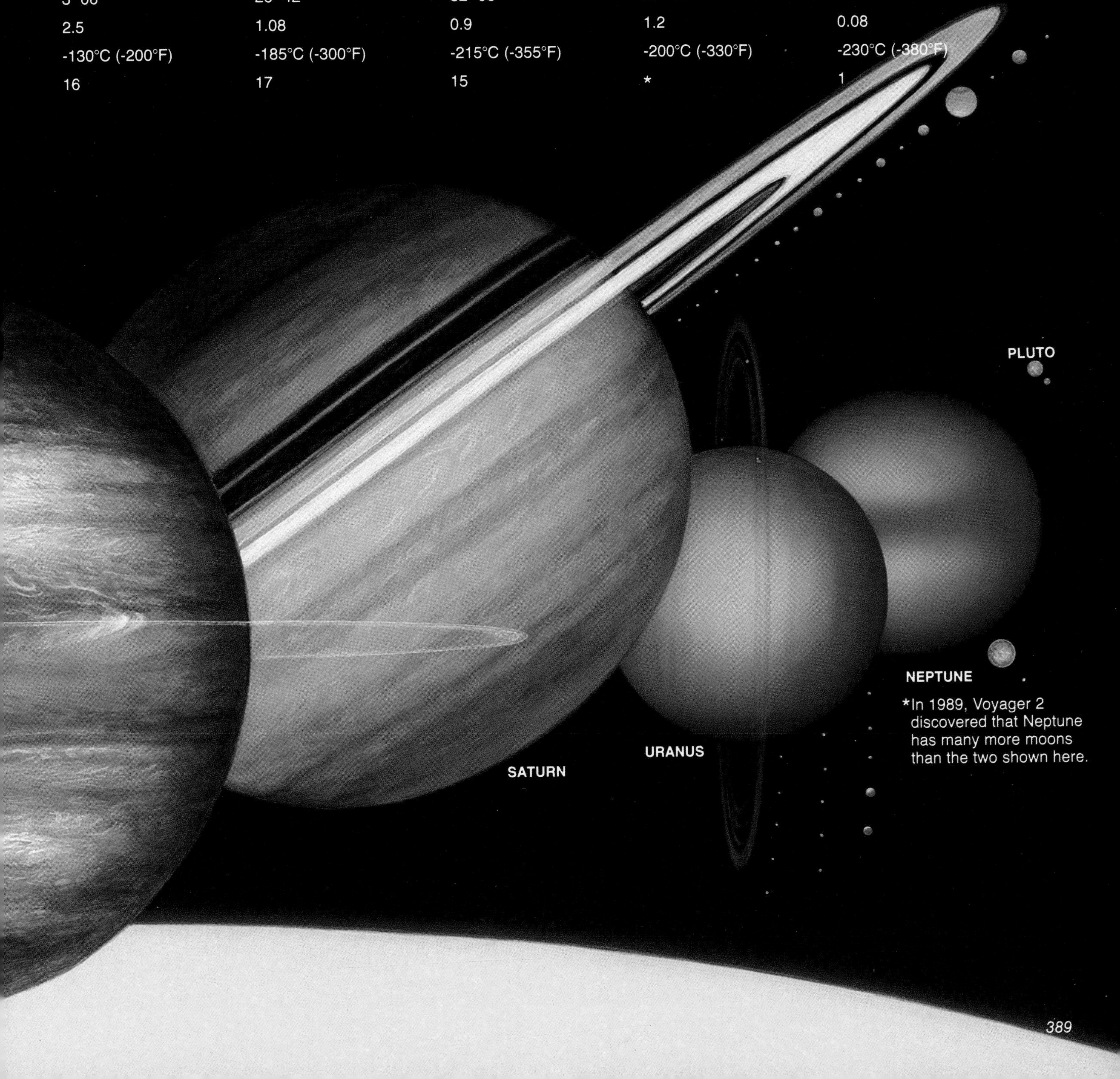

PLUTO

NEPTUNE

URANUS

SATURN

*In 1989, Voyager 2 discovered that Neptune has many more moons than the two shown here.

PLATE TECTONICS

Most of the time, the surface of the earth seems solid and still. Actually, the earth's hard shell is made up of thick slabs of rock called plates, and these plates are constantly moving. Scientists call the interaction of the slabs plate tectonics.

The huge, rigid plates hold both the ocean floor and the continents. There are several small plates and seven large ones: the North American, South American, Pacific, Indo-Australian, African, Eurasian, and Antarctic plates. Sensitive scientific equipment is able to measure the few centimeters that the plates move each year. But the movement is usually so gradual that people cannot feel it. Geologists think that the plates have been interacting for more than three billion years.

The word "tectonics" comes from a Greek word meaning "builder." As plates slowly move about the earth, mountain building occurs. Plate tectonics raised the Himalaya in Asia and pushes those mountains higher each year. Plate tectonics fuels volcanoes like Mount St. Helens, in Washington State, and reshapes land in California along the San Andreas Fault. And it constantly causes new seafloor to form along the Mid-Ocean Ridge, the massive underwater mountain system that

▲ Volcanic cones rise in Djibouti, an East African country that lies within the Great Rift Valley system. Plates are pulling apart here along a line marked by rifts, faults, and volcanoes.
► Mineral salts accumulate in Africa's Danakil Depression. Plate tectonics may someday cause a connection between this area and the Red Sea.

curves along the seafloor for more than 64,000 kilometers (40,000 miles).

Layers of the Earth

The rigid shell of the earth, broken into plates, is called the lithosphere. The lithosphere is made up of the earth's outermost

▶ *Earth's rigid shell is broken into rocky slabs called plates that are always moving. This map roughly traces the present boundaries of plates. Along these boundaries, plates interact in various ways. The places where they are pulling apart are known as spreading zones. Where they collide, the edge of one plate may slide beneath the edge of another in a process called subduction. Along transform faults, plates slide past each other.*

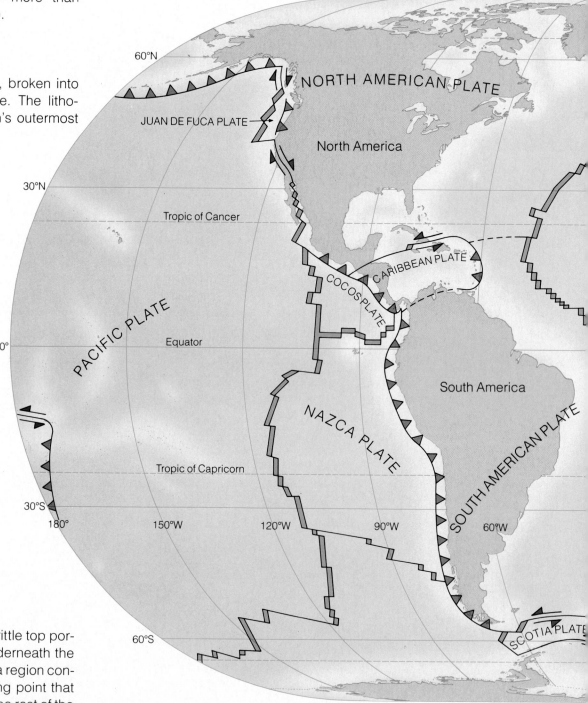

PLATE BOUNDARIES

- ⟋ SPREADING ZONE
- ▲▲▲ SUBDUCTION ZONE
- ⇄ TRANSFORM FAULT
- - - - - UNCERTAIN BOUNDARIES

layer, called the crust, and the brittle top portion of the mantle, which lies underneath the crust. Beneath the lithosphere is a region containing rocks so near their melting point that they can bend like red-hot iron. The rest of the mantle is a thick layer of mostly solid rock.

Scientists are working to determine exactly what causes the plates to move. Research indicates that the center of the earth— the core—is hotter than once thought. Some studies suggest that the core is even hotter than the surface of the sun. Geologists think that the core's intense heat causes slow movement within the mantle. Over millions of years, this circulation has affected the surface of the planet by shifting the plates. The

movement continues, slowly changing the shapes and positions of the continents and ocean basins.

Seafloor Spreading

The development of sophisticated undersea equipment has enabled scientists to explore a hidden realm: the ocean floor. What they have found there helps explain how the plates move. Oceanographers discovered

▶ *New Zealand's volcanic White Island formed in a subduction zone. In Kenya, a lake fills part of a valley in a spreading zone. On California's San Andreas Fault, a sliver of land marks an area where plates slide along a transform fault.*

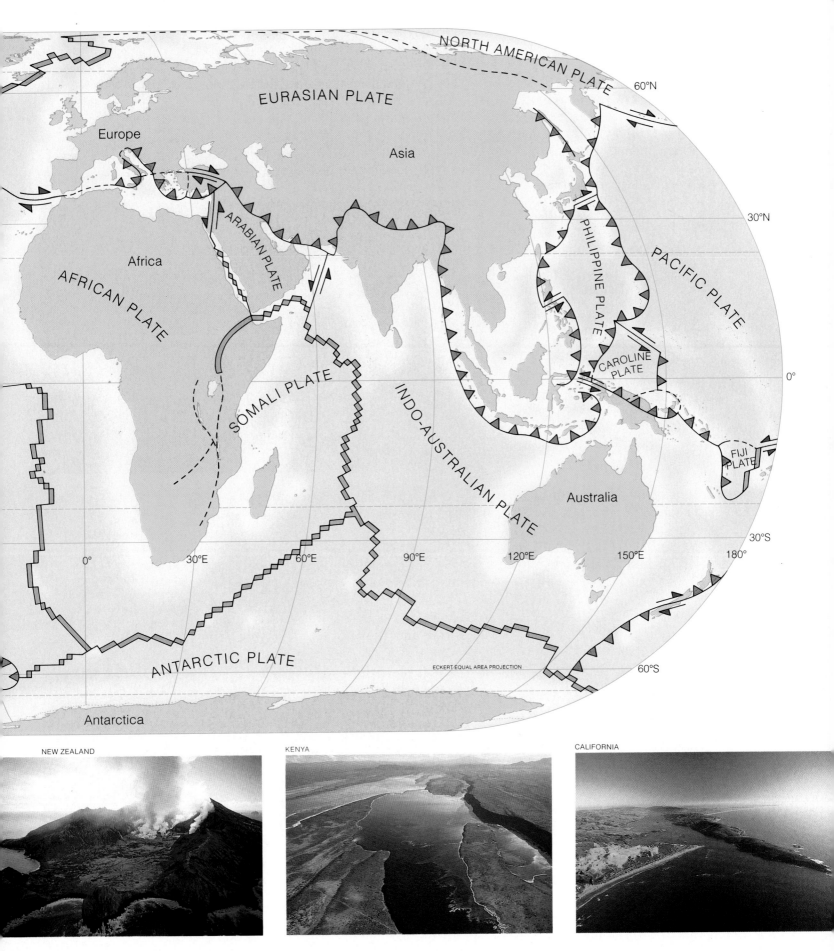

NORTH AMERICAN PLATE

EURASIAN PLATE

60°N

Europe

Asia

30°N

ARABIAN PLATE

Africa

PHILIPPINE PLATE

PACIFIC PLATE

AFRICAN PLATE

SOMALI PLATE

CAROLINE PLATE

0°

INDO-AUSTRALIAN PLATE

FIJI PLATE

Australia

30°S

0°   30°E   60°E   90°E   120°E   150°E   180°

ANTARCTIC PLATE

ECKERT EQUAL AREA PROJECTION

60°S

Antarctica

NEW ZEALAND

KENYA

CALIFORNIA

that the ocean covers the immense mountain range, the Mid-Ocean Ridge.

A deep central rift, or crack, runs along the crest of the ridge. The plates on either side of the rift move away from each other, as if carried on gigantic conveyor belts moving in opposite directions. Molten rock called magma wells up between them. The molten material is called lava when it pours out of the earth. As the plates move apart, lava flows out and hardens into crust. For 150 million years,

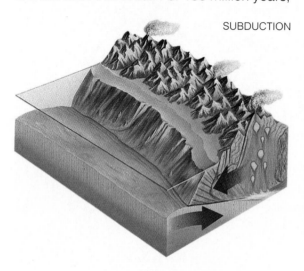

SUBDUCTION

the upwelling of magma has formed the floor of the Atlantic Ocean on either side of the Mid-Ocean Ridge crest in a process called sea-floor spreading. The activity along the ridge continuously makes new crust, and older crust moves outward.

Along Plate Boundaries

Even though new crust is constantly being formed by seafloor spreading, the earth stays the same size in the process. How is this

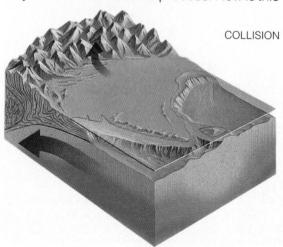

COLLISION

possible? When the leading edge of a plate that carries ocean floor meets the edge of a plate that carries a continent, something has to give. This situation exists along the western shores of North and South America. There, the plates bearing the Pacific Ocean meet those bearing the two continents. The heavier oceanic plates bend downward, diving beneath the continental plates and forming

huge underwater depressions called trenches. Deep in the earth, the rock of the oceanic plates melts.

When one plate dives under another, the process is called subduction; the plate boundaries where this happens are known as subduction zones. Some molten material produced in subduction zones rises to the earth's surface. The result: volcanoes such as

▼ As the Nazca plate subducts, or slides, beneath the South American plate, magma rises toward the surface and builds mountains such as these Andean peaks in Chile.

▼ The collision of the Indian and Eurasian landmasses millions of years ago began pushing up mountains, such as these in the Karakoram Range of India and Pakistan.

Mount St. Helens. But much of the subducted material melts and mixes with the mantle.

As molten material wells up along the Mid-Ocean Ridge crest and new crust forms, old crustal material descends into the mantle at subduction zones and melts. Eventually, the old material may be recycled, flowing out again at the Mid-Ocean Ridge and forming new seafloor. During these processes, the earth's size stays virtually the same.

Sometimes two plates collide and neither

ACCRETION

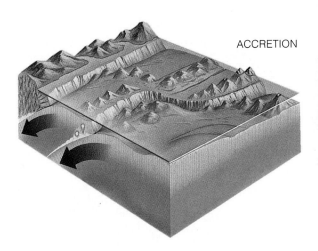

plate subducts completely. This occurs when continental crust collides with more continental crust. The landmasses push slowly against each other, and their edges crumple. The collision may push up high mountain chains such as the Himalaya in Asia. The Himalaya began to rise millions of years ago, when continental crust on the northward-moving Indo-Australian plate collided with the continental crust of the Eurasian plate. Because the plates are still shoving against each other, the Himalaya continue to rise.

SPREADING

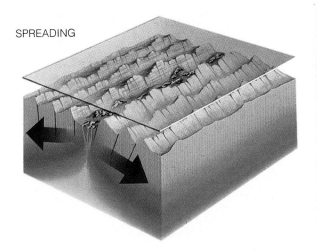

Smaller collisions of crustal material cause continents to grow outward as well as upward. Seamounts and other chunks of crust are carried along by a subducting plate until they reach a trench. There they fuse with the crust on the overlying plate in a process called accretion.

Sometimes plates meet without ramming together. Instead, they grind past each other

along transform faults. The San Andreas Fault in California is one place where this occurs. Earthquakes are common in such areas.

Not all tectonic activity occurs at plate boundaries. As a plate moves over a stationary hot spot in the mantle, magma rises into the crust. Heat from the magma may warm groundwater and produce hot springs, or lava may erupt, building a line of volcanoes.

▼ *Chunks of crust are patched together like pieces of a quilt by a process called accretion. The west coast of North America contains a variety of accretion landscapes, such as this scenic area in Alaska.*

▼ *In spreading zones, plates move apart and molten rock may well up between them. Iceland straddles a plate boundary where rifts, or cracks, open in the crust as spreading occurs.*

The Theory of Continental Drift

For many years, scientists did not believe that the earth's surface could move. In the early 20th century, when German scientist Alfred Wegener first suggested that the continents might be drifting, most experts thought his ideas were ridiculous.

Wegener developed his theory of continental drift after noticing that Africa and South America look as if they would fit together if placed next to each other. The two continents resemble pieces of a jigsaw puzzle. If you

FAULTING

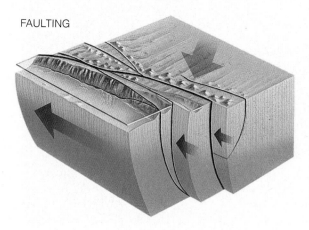

look at the world map on pages 392–393, you will notice that the bulge of Brazil could fit below the bulge of Africa. Wegener suggested that all the continents once had been joined in a single supercontinent. The large landmass is known as Pangaea, which means "all lands" in Greek. About 200 million years ago, Pangaea began to split apart. Over time, the individual continents gradually drifted to their present positions on the planet.

Although most scientists did not take Wegener seriously, some found his theory of

HOT SPOT

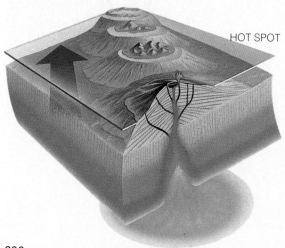

continental drift interesting. They studied the possibility that the continents were in motion. By the late 1960s, Wegener's ideas had been developed into the theory of plate tectonics.

Proving Plate Tectonics

Fossils provided some of the first evidence confirming the theory of continental

movement. Researchers had found fossils of an ancient reptile called *Lystrosaurus* in India and in South Africa. The fossils also showed up in Antarctica. How could *Lystrosaurus*, a land animal found only in warm climates, have lived in Antarctica? Scientists decided that Antarctica must once have been linked with Africa and India in a single landmass that had a warm climate. In addition, geologists found

▼ *Transform faults occur where plates slide past each other. The San Andreas Fault cuts a long scar across part of California, marking part of the boundary between the Pacific and North American plates.*

▼ *A chain of volcanic islands forms as a plate moves over a stationary hot spot in the mantle. Rising molten rock melts through the crust and lava pours out, building volcanoes such as these in the Hawaiian Islands.*

masses of rock on the eastern coast of South America that match rock masses on the west coast of Africa. Tests showed that the rock masses had formed at the same time—some 550 million years ago. The rocks on both continents must have been part of the same geologic deposit.

Geologists also noticed that a belt of mountains running along the eastern coast of North America matches a belt that exists in northern Europe, on the other side of the Atlantic Ocean. The scientists concluded that North America and Europe must have been joined at some point in the earth's history.

Studies of the ocean floor provided more evidence that the plates forming the earth's surface are moving. During the 1950s and '60s, oceanographers began to explore and map the Mid-Ocean Ridge. They took rock samples from different sections of the seafloor. Their research revealed that ocean floor rocks are even younger than scientists had thought and that new ocean floor is forming along the Mid-Ocean Ridge. As plates move away from each other at the ridge crest, the continents they carry also move.

Using lasers and satellites, scientists began to measure the rate of each plate's movement. As experts in many scientific fields gathered data, they became convinced that the theory of plate tectonics is correct. In 1987, precise measurements provided proof that the plates are moving. Observations showed that Hawaii is moving toward Japan at a rate of 8 centimeters (3 in) a year, and North America and Europe are moving about 2.5 centimeters (1 in) apart each year.

The huge plates continue to move about the planet. The Pacific Ocean is getting smaller and the Atlantic is growing. Perhaps Australia will become part of Asia, and perhaps western California will break away from North America and become an island. If you could visit the earth millions of years from now, you would find a planet with new and unfamiliar landscapes to explore.

SEE ALSO CONTINENT, CONTINENTAL DRIFT, CORE, CRUST, EARTH, EARTHQUAKE, FAULT, FOSSIL, GEOLOGIC TIME SCALE, HOT SPOT, LITHOSPHERE, MAGNETISM, MANTLE, MOUNTAIN, OCEAN, RIFT VALLEY, RING OF FIRE, ROCK, SEAFLOOR SPREADING, TRENCH, *and* VOLCANO.

▲ *Water gushes from a drill pipe aboard a research vessel. Geologists use the equipment to probe the ocean floor.*
◄ *Sliced core samples reveal seafloor age. Because of seafloor spreading, samples taken far from the Mid-Ocean Ridge are older than those taken closer.*

PLATEAU

A plateau is a large, relatively flat area that stands above the surrounding land. Rising from 90 to more than 900 meters (300–3,000 ft) high, plateaus occupy about a third of the earth's land and occur on every continent. Plateaus are one of the four major landforms, along with mountains, plains, and hills.

Plateaus form as a result of upward movement in the earth's crust. This uplift is caused by the interaction of the earth's plates—huge, moving slabs of rock that make up the earth's rigid shell. Over time, colliding plates may force sections of the crust to rise thousands of meters above sea level. A plateau may result from these collisions. Scientists estimate that the Colorado Plateau has been rising about .03 centimeter (.01 in) a year for more than ten million years. The plateau now stands almost two kilometers (1.2 mi) higher than the surrounding area.

◄Canyons scar the Colorado Plateau, a vast, raised landform that extends into the states of Colorado, Utah, New Mexico, and Arizona. Rivers carved out the canyons over millions of years.
◄Over time, the forces of weathering and erosion have sculptured mesas and buttes from the rocks of Monument Valley, an area of the Colorado Plateau in Arizona and Utah.
▼In Idaho, farmers have irrigated and planted fields atop the flat tablelands along the Snake River.

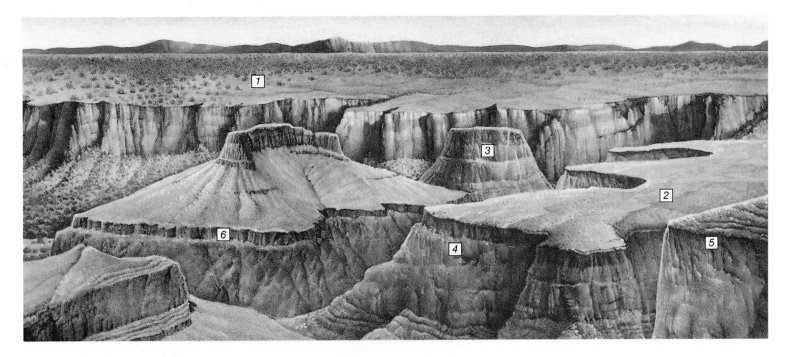

A plateau often has alternating horizontal layers of soft and hard rock. Running water on the surface and freezing water and thawing ice in the ground weather, or break down, soft rocks more easily than they do hard ones. Agents of erosion carry the weathered materials away. Gradually, weathering and erosion wear down the plateau until an especially hard or resistant layer lies exposed. This layer, called caprock, forms a durable surface that protects the layers directly beneath it.

Because plateaus have flat tops like tables, people sometimes refer to them as tablelands. In addition to their flat tops, plateaus usually have one or more steep sides, which add to their tablelike appearance. These steep sides, or cliffs, develop when rivers cut through the caprock, often producing deep valleys within a plateau. The Grand Canyon, in Arizona, formed in this way, when river waters cut through the Colorado Plateau.

Weathering and erosion sculpture plateaus in other ways. Sometimes a plateau is so eroded that it is broken up into smaller raised sections called outliers. If the outliers are wider than they are high, they are called mesas. High, thin outliers are called buttes.

In dry areas, such as parts of the south-western United States, mesas and buttes keep their basic shapes as they age. They stay roughly the same height, but erosion gradually reduces their diameter until they topple. In wetter regions, erosion rounds the edges of these tablelands, forming features such as the Catskill Mountains, in New York State, which are part of the Allegheny Plateau.

SEE ALSO BUTTE, CANYON, CLIFF, MESA, PLATE TECTONICS, RIVER, ROCK, VALLEY, *and* WEATHERING AND EROSION.

▲ *In areas where the earth's crust is gradually rising, a plateau (1) may form. Over millions of years, rivers carve the plateau into outliers called mesas (2) and buttes (3). All of these landforms have steep sides, such as an escarpment (4) or a cliff (5). A flat layer of durable rock known as caprock (6) tops the plateau.*

► *On Asia's Tibetan Plateau, herders tend yaks, which are both beasts of burden and sources of food. Here on one of the world's highest, most desolate plateaus, every resource counts.*

POLAR REGIONS

The polar regions are at opposite ends of the earth. The Poles, at the center of each region, lie at latitudes 90°N and 90°S. They are at either end of the earth's axis, an invisible line running north and south through the center of the planet and about which it rotates. The North Polar region is primarily the area encompassed by the Arctic Circle, which falls at about latitude 66½°N. The South Polar region is primarily an area within the Antarctic Circle, which is at about latitude 66½°S.

The North Polar region, also called the Arctic region, consists of ice-covered ocean almost surrounded by landmasses. The South Polar region, or the Antarctic region, consists mostly of ice-covered land—the frigid continent of Antarctica—ringed by ocean. "Antarctic" means "opposite to the Arctic."

Though located at opposite ends of the earth, the two regions are similar in many ways. Both are inhospitable, icy regions in which temperatures rarely rise above 10°C (50°F). The cold temperatures are generally a result of the location of the polar regions on the earth and in relation to the sun. Because the earth is spherical in shape, the sun's rays do not strike it uniformly. The rays hit the polar regions at a slant, which lessens their intensity; they strike the equatorial region more directly. Much of the solar radiation that does

▲ *Icebreakers face a constant challenge: keeping sea-lanes open for deliveries to Antarctica.*
► *Many Lapps in Norway are reindeer herders. The animals are valued for their meat and for their pelts, which are used for clothing and shelter.*

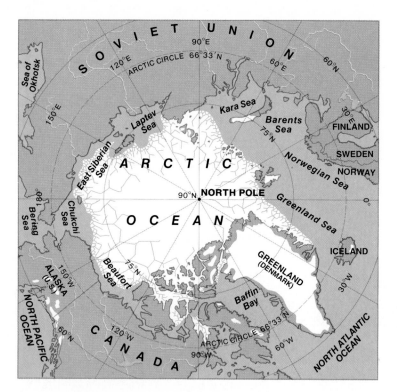

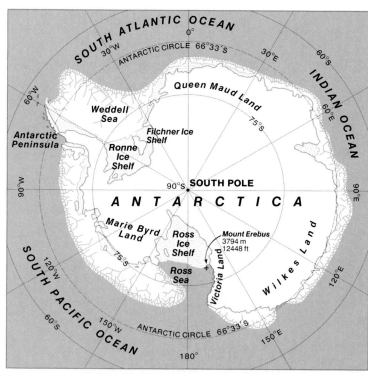

▲ *These maps show the approximate extent of the ice cover in the polar regions during late summer.*

▼ *The polar regions have long periods of daylight in summer and darkness in winter because of the tilt of the earth's axis of rotation as the planet orbits the sun. The periods are longest at the solstices. On the day of the June solstice, the North Polar region receives 24 hours of sunlight and the South Polar region is in darkness for 24 hours. The opposite occurs at the December solstice.*

reach the polar regions is reflected into space by vast expanses of ice, which act as enormous mirrors.

The number of daylight hours in the polar regions varies dramatically from summer to winter. This is because the earth's axis is tilted in relation to the earth's plane of orbit as the planet revolves around the sun. The North Pole's position on the planet is such that the sun does not drop below the horizon there during spring and summer. Thus, there are about six months of daylight. At the South Pole, it is autumn and winter during this time, and for about six months the sun does not rise above the horizon. As the earth continues around the sun, autumn and winter come to the North Pole and spring and summer come to the South Pole; the periods of daylight and darkness are reversed. Away from the Poles,

these conditions become less extreme. Those who live near the Arctic and Antarctic Circles, for example, have just one day of complete darkness and one day of continuous daylight a year.

Strong winds are common in these giant freezers at the ends of the earth's axis. Cold winds flowing from the polar regions can have an impact on weather in lower latitudes. Polar air is sometimes associated with the development of winter storms that bring heavy precipitation.

The world sea level depends on the state of the ice in both regions. If the ice sheet covering Greenland ever melted, the sea level could rise almost 6 meters (20 ft). The melting of Antarctica's ice sheet would have an even greater effect; the sea level could rise as much as 45 to 60 meters (150–200 ft).

The North Polar Region

The North Polar region includes the Arctic Ocean and its thousands of tiny islands, most of Greenland, and the northern parts of Alaska, the Soviet Union, Canada, and Scandinavia. The terrain varies from high icy plateaus and mountains to wet, poorly drained lowlands in the tundra.

Most of the Arctic Ocean, at the heart of the North Polar region, is covered by ice

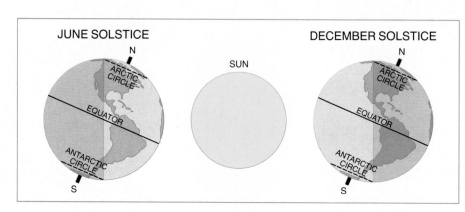

JUNE SOLSTICE

DECEMBER SOLSTICE

SUN

year-round. The second largest ice sheet in the world covers most of Greenland. Antarctica's is the largest. The Greenland ice sheet is about 3 kilometers (2 mi) thick near its center.

With the exception of Greenland, nine-tenths of the region's lands are free of ice and snow in summer. Precipitation in some parts of the North Polar region rarely exceeds 15 centimeters (6 in), less than falls on some hot deserts. Similar arid conditions exist in the South Polar region, so many scientists classify polar regions as deserts. In summer, the Arctic ground is damp in some places because permanently frozen subsoil called permafrost inhibits drainage. Evaporation is low because cool summer air does not absorb water vapor well. The average winter temperature is -34°C (-30°F).

The harsh conditions in the North Polar region limit tree growth, although some forests exist on the southern edges of the region. Some dwarf trees, small shrubs, and grasses survive in the tundra's boggy soil. Lichens grow on dry rock faces, as well as in moister areas, where mosses are found. There are about 900 kinds of hardy flowering plants in the Arctic. Flowers bloom in a brief burst of color in the short summer.

A wide range of animals lives in the severe Arctic climate, including polar bears, caribou, reindeer, foxes, hares, lemmings, snowy owls, and wolves. They have adapted to the region's harsh environment. Polar bears, for example, have thick fur that insulates them from the cold.

The North Polar region has been sparsely inhabited for centuries by Inuit and Eskimos of North America, Samoyeds and Chukchi of the Soviet Union, and Lapps of Europe. Although their cultures are varied, they have adapted in similar ways to life in the North Polar region. Many people live off of such animals as fish, seals, and reindeer. They use animal skins for some clothing. Fishing, seal hunting, and herding are still primary sources of income for some, although many have found employment at weather stations, at military bases, in mines, and with oil companies.

Important natural resources have lured developers to the North Polar region. There are large, scattered deposits of coal, iron ore, lead, and silver. The discovery of oil and natural gas in Alaska's North Slope led to the

construction of the trans-Alaska pipeline. One day it may be possible to ship oil and other bulk commodities out of the area in super-tanker submarines traveling below the ice. This method would shorten the sea route between Japan and Europe.

The South Polar Region

At the heart of the South Polar region lies Antarctica, the world's highest continent. Its average elevation is 1,830 meters (6,000 ft).

▲ Arctic tundra on Alaska's North Slope begins to turn green as grasses, sedges, and other plants come to life with the summer thaw. Meltwaters feed the Sadlerochit River as it meanders toward the Arctic Ocean.
▼ Winter has arrived in Kiana, Alaska, which means long periods of darkness each day.

An Eskimo in Greenland (top) works with his dog team. Dog-drawn sledges, once a basic means of travel in the polar regions, have largely been replaced by faster but more expensive snowmobiles. In Siberia (above), a young child bundled in reindeer fur toddles from a tent made of reindeer skins stretched over wood poles. The tent floor is made up of more skins, grasses, and bark, which provide insulation.

down from the continent's high plateau to its edges. The wind whirls off the continent at speeds of up to 320 kilometers per hour (200 mph). Great cyclonic storms circle Antarctica. Moist ocean air clashes with the cold air blowing across the land, making the waters around Antarctica some of the world's stormiest. Cold ocean currents flow from the region, cooling ocean waters and helping regulate climates at latitudes to the north.

The continent—which is about one and a half times the size of the United States—is covered by an ice sheet containing much of the earth's fresh water. The average thickness of the ice sheet, or continental glacier, is about 2 kilometers (1.2 mi), and parts of it are millions of years old. Covering almost all of Antarctica's surface, the ice sheet is occasionally pierced by steep mountain peaks. Slowly and continuously, the ice moves toward the coast, where it spreads into the ocean and forms huge ice shelves. These make the continent look larger than it really is. The Ross Ice Shelf, west of Marie Byrd Land, is larger than France.

Masses of ice calve, or break off, from the ice sheet, filling the surrounding ocean with icebergs. Resembling giant tables, the flat-topped icebergs are characteristic of the Antarctic. They can be 150 to 300 meters (500–1,000 ft) thick and up to about 130 kilometers (80 mi) long, far larger than their counterparts in the far north.

Few plants live on the cold continent, and no trees grow in the frozen ground. Some rock faces are covered by lichens and mosses. These plants must survive long periods of freezing temperatures as well as abrupt increases in temperature when the winds stop blowing and the sky is clear. The growing season may last only a few weeks.

There are few animals in the interior of Antarctica. The surrounding waters, however, are rich in squid, fish, and shrimplike crustaceans called krill that support many animals, including seals, penguins, and whales. Antarctica's once-thriving population of whales has been reduced by excessive hunting. Stocks were depleted to near extinction, but now most species are protected by international regulations. The supply of fish in these ocean waters may one day be a source of food for the world's increasing population.

Antarctica is far colder than the North Polar region and probably holds six times as much ice. Geologists have found that East Antarctica is much older than West Antarctica, which has experienced intense volcanic activity. The continent's most active volcano is Mount Erebus, which is less than 1,400 kilometers (870 mi) from the South Pole. Its frequent eruptions are evidence of hot rock beneath the icebound surface.

The climate here is the most severe in the world. The average temperature is -50°C (-58°F). The region is so cold and so high that the air does not hold much water vapor, and snowfall is light.

The desolate continent is whipped by fierce winds. Chilled by the freezing temperatures, air becomes heavier, so that it flows

▲ *A tongue of the ice sheet covering most of Antarctica moves slowly across the land. The continent contains much of the world's fresh water locked in its ice.*

▼ *A tourist ship heads for McMurdo Station on Antarctica's Ross Island. The peak season for tourism is between December and February, the relatively temperate summer months.*

▼ *Flags of many countries fly at McMurdo Station, a U.S. research center for scientists in Antarctica. Researchers from different countries share data on geology, meteorology, and oceanography.*

Many coal deposits have been found along Antarctica's coast, and oil and natural gas may lie beneath rock layers there. Exploitation of these resources, however, seems remote not only because of environmental pressures against it but also because of the staggering extraction costs.

No country owns land in Antarctica, though several countries have laid claim to territory there. In an effort to end territorial claims, to ban military activity, and to establish Antarctica as a nuclear-free zone, 12 countries agreed to the Antarctic Treaty of 1959. They set up a large-scale cooperative research project on the continent. Since then, other countries have agreed to abide by the treaty's terms. Scientists from around the world conduct research in such fields as oceanography, seismology, glaciology, meteorology, and surveying. The population consists mainly of scientists and their staffs.

The treaty comes up for review in 1991, and many people think Antarctica should then be declared an international wilderness. For now, Antarctica remains a unique land without political boundaries, where scientists from such diverse countries as China, Argentina, the Soviet Union, and the United States work side by side.

SEE ALSO AURORA, CLIMATE, CONTINENT, EARTH, GLACIER, ICE SHEET, ICEBERG, OCEAN, PERMAFROST, SEASONS, TUNDRA, VOLCANO, *and* WIND.

POLES

The North and South Poles are at the ends of the earth's axis of rotation—an invisible line through the earth's center. Nearby are the magnetic poles. A compass needle lines up with the earth's magnetic field; one end points to magnetic north and the other to magnetic south. There are also geomagnetic poles—points where the axis of the magnetic field intersects the earth's surface.

SEE ALSO AXIS, COMPASS, LONGITUDE, MAGNETISM, POLAR REGIONS, *and* ROTATION.

POLLUTION

Pollution is the introduction of harmful materials into an environment. Polluting substances, such as car exhausts, industrial wastes, and chemical pesticides, damage the quality of air, water, and land.

Many of the things that make people comfortable and provide them with goods and services contribute to pollution. The burning of coal to produce electricity pollutes the air. Industries and households generate quantities of garbage and sewage, causing waste disposal problems.

For millions of years, nature has provided an abundance of clean air, water, and land. But now, expanding populations and increasing demands for goods and services have led to the disruption of the earth's ecological balance. More wastes are going into the air, water, and land than nature can handle.

To thrive, plants and animals need clean air, uncontaminated water, and wholesome nutrients. Pollution in the biosphere—those parts of the air, water, and land in which life exists—has become a serious problem because the earth is a closed system. Its supplies of air and water are used again and again. When these resources are polluted, all life in the biosphere is threatened.

Pollution is a global problem. Although it is usually concentrated in heavily industrialized areas, it spreads all over the planet, even to remote, unpopulated places. For example,

◄Dense smog shrouds Los Angeles, causing a pollution alert. Despite strict emission control laws, exhaust given off by the city's heavy automobile traffic helps cause this dangerous form of air pollution.
► In Cubatão, Brazil, boys cover their faces to avoid inhaling fumes from a nearby fertilizer plant. Residents call this severely polluted area the "valley of death."

▲ *Oil spills into the ocean off Nantucket Island. When this tanker ran aground, it broke in half, and more than 23,000 tons of oil poured into the Atlantic. Such spills endanger sea life and damage coastlines.*

▼ *In Tierra del Fuego, a penguin tries to clean oil from its feathers. If birds swallow oil or if their feathers become soaked with it, they often die.*

concentrations of pesticides and other chemicals have been found in polar bears in the Arctic and in penguins in the Antarctic.

Ocean currents and migrating fish carry pollutants far and wide. Smoke from a factory in one country drifts into other countries. Radioactive material accidentally released from a nuclear power plant is picked up by winds and spread around the world.

Atmospheric Pollution

Sometimes air pollution is visible, as it is when dark smoke pours from the exhaust pipes of large commercial trucks, but it is often invisible. Polluted air can harm many living things. It makes eyes burn and causes headaches. It can worsen respiratory problems and increase the risk of lung cancer. Heavily polluted air not only harms life-forms but also eats away at the stone in buildings and in statues.

The primary source of atmospheric pollution is the burning of fossil fuels—coal, oil, and natural gas. When the fuel that powers cars and trucks is burned, it produces carbon monoxide, a colorless, odorless gas. The gas

is harmful in high concentrations, which are common in heavy city traffic.

Other pollutants that are causing some of the most severe air pollution are nitrogen oxide, sulfur dioxide, and hydrocarbons from vehicle and factory emissions. These chemicals react with sunlight to produce smog and other atmospheric pollution. They also mix with moisture in the air to form acid

▲ *Volunteers clean a beach in France that was fouled when the breakup of a tanker spread oil along 160 kilometers (100 mi) of coastline.*

precipitation. Though commonly called acid rain, acid precipitation can be in the form of snow, hail, sleet, fog, or even dry particles. Such deposition, which often falls far from the pollution source, can damage forest and lake ecosystems, killing trees and causing fish populations to decline or die out.

Chemicals called chlorofluorocarbons (CFCs) are depleting the ozone layer, a region in the earth's upper atmosphere. The ozone layer protects the earth by absorbing much of the sun's harmful ultraviolet radiation. CFCs are widely used—in aerosol sprays, refrigerants, and foam products. If the damage continues, exposure to increased radiation may weaken people's immune systems and increase the chance of skin cancer and eye diseases. Other living things could be affected as well. In 1978, the U.S. Environmental Protection Agency banned the use of CFC propellants in aerosol sprays. In 1987, most industrialized countries agreed to cut production of CFCs 50 percent by 1999. These cutbacks may not be sufficient, as the ozone layer appears to be thinning rapidly.

The rise in global temperatures is another environmental threat that is caused by air pollution. Atmospheric gases such as carbon dioxide absorb heat radiating from the earth. They release some of the heat into space and the rest back to earth. This causes a greenhouse effect that keeps the earth warm enough to be habitable. The greenhouse effect is increasing, and global temperatures are rising. Scientists believe this is occurring because the burning of fossil fuels and the clearing of forests have increased the amount of carbon dioxide and other heat-trapping gases in the atmosphere. If the warming trend continues, there could be widespread

▲ Floating litter piles up on a riverbank in Brunei, on the island of Borneo. A market is the source of much of the trash thrown into the river.
► Although clear, the water of this Adirondack stream is deadly to fish because of acid precipitation. Commonly called acid rain, it contains high levels of nitric and sulfuric acids from the emissions of motor vehicles and factories far away.
◄ A biologist in London checks a sample of Thames water by mixing it with chemicals that test its oxygen content. The cleanup of the Thames is an environmental success story: Fish and birds have returned to the once-polluted river.

changes in climate that would affect agriculture and natural processes all over the world.

Air pollution is not limited to the air outdoors. Indoor air pollution comes from a variety of household products, including oven and carpet cleaners and insect sprays. Radon, a radioactive gas produced as uranium decays in underground rocks, may seep into homes as natural pollution. Many scientists believe radon causes lung cancer.

Water and Land Pollution

Polluted water may look muddy, smell bad, and have garbage floating in it. Or it may look clean but be polluted with germs and chemicals you cannot see or smell. Polluted water is unsafe for drinking, bathing, and swimming. The fish that live in polluted water may be unfit for eating because poisons are concentrated in their flesh.

When hazardous wastes are dumped on the land or buried in it, they may pollute not only the land but eventually the water as well. Chemical wastes were disposed of carelessly for a long time before the practice was found to be dangerous. In 1978, people living in the Love Canal area in Niagara Falls, New York, abandoned their homes after unusually high numbers of cancer cases and birth defects were detected in the population. A toxic waste dumpsite had contaminated the area's groundwater. Mining wastes have also contributed to water pollution. If not disposed of properly, radioactive wastes from nuclear power plants can escape into the environment, destroying cells in humans and other

▲ Junked cars and old tires clutter a muddy field. In the United States, people junk some seven million automobiles each year; many of the vehicles end up in unsightly "graveyards" like this. Tires and much of the metal in car bodies could be recycled and used again.
◄ At a landfill, a worker removes bottles and cans containing toxic household products. Poisonous chemicals in the products could become concentrated in the earth and contaminate supplies of underground water.

animals and contaminating plants and water.

Pesticides are powerful poisons used to kill weeds, harmful insects, and other pests such as rats. Pesticide runoff from farms pollutes water when rain washes the chemicals into lakes and streams or causes the chemicals to seep into groundwater. In some developed countries, certain pesticides, including DDT, have been banned because they harm the environment. In some of these countries, however, DDT is still produced for export to developing countries. Foods produced where DDT is used are often shipped to countries where the pesticide has been banned.

Worldwide, solid wastes such as paper, aluminum cans, glass jars, plastic products, and junked cars and appliances mar the landscape. Many of the things now thrown away as waste products could be recycled. Recycling can reduce energy costs for processing such materials as aluminum and wood, as well as reduce the costs of waste disposal. One way of dealing with so much solid waste is to reduce the amount produced in the first place.

There are various simple ways to reduce pollution. For instance, if people protect existing forests and plant more vegetation, especially trees, carbon dioxide levels in the environment can be reduced. Advances in technology have led to means of reducing pollution. Some coal-burning industries have installed devices called scrubbers that remove from smoke those chemicals that can form acid precipitation. Many cars are equipped with devices called catalytic converters, which reduce the amount of harmful material that automobiles spew into the air.

Concern for the environment has prompted pollution reduction efforts in many countries. Fish have returned to the River Thames in England. The air in many cities in the United States has improved. Japan and several European countries recycle half their garbage.

Despite such efforts, people continue to pollute the environment at an alarming rate. Much more needs to be done if we want to restore and maintain the health of the planet and its inhabitants.

SEE ALSO BIOSPHERE, CONSERVATION, ENERGY, FOREST, FOSSIL FUEL, GREENHOUSE EFFECT, OZONE LAYER, *and* SMOG.

► *Wearing protective gear, workers draw samples of toxic material from barrels at a disposal site. They will study the samples to determine their chemical content. Leaking barrels will be removed for safer disposal elsewhere.*
▼ *Two girls struggle with a bag of empty drink cans they collected during an aluminum recycling contest at their school in Tampa, Florida.*

POPULATION

A population is the total number of people in an area. The area may be as small as a city neighborhood or as large as the world. Births, deaths, and migration—the movement of people—determine a population's size.

Every 15 seconds, the world's population increases by about 100 people. There are hundreds of thousands more people on earth today than there were yesterday. A year from now, perhaps 90 million additional people will be living on the earth. Where are they being born? How long will they live? Can their basic needs be met? Understanding population growth and distribution is critically important in planning for the future.

The study of population and related subjects is called demography; scientists who study population are called demographers.

▲ *Suburbs of Mexico City stretch to the mountains. Home to 20 million people, the Mexican capital is one of the world's fastest growing cities.*
◄ *Victims of famine and civil war, refugees from northern Ethiopia crowd a camp in Sudan.*

413

Demographers interpret statistics about large groups of people.

One of the demographer's most valuable tools is the census periodically conducted by governments. Most censuses provide a count of a place's population and often other information as well. To get an accurate picture of a population, census takers attempt to contact the entire population directly at about the same time. A census can be a complicated and expensive undertaking. In 1982, China, the world's most populous country, hired more than six million census workers to survey its population of more than one billion.

Governments may also gather information about groups of people by examining records of vital statistics, such as births, deaths, marriages, and divorces, and incomes and other data. Governments use these statistics for various purposes, and they publish them for use by the public.

The United Nations and other international organizations compile population figures from countries around the world. A few countries, however, have never counted their people; many others are unable to make an accurate count. For these reasons, published population figures sometimes vary widely.

Statistics help demographers to discover many things in addition to a population's size. They may show a country's crude birthrate, the number of births per year per thousand people. In 1988, for instance, Mexico's crude birthrate was 30, and Canada's was 15.

▲ Pallbearers lead a funeral procession in Ireland. The number of deaths per year helps determine the population growth rate of a country.
◄ Flickering oil lamps honor the dead in Greece, where both birthrates and death rates are low.

◄ Swaddled newborns fill hospital cribs in China, the world's most populous country. By the time of the 1982 census, its population exceeded one billion. Chinese policy aims to restrict births to one or two children per couple.
► Illegal immigrants await deportation from Los Angeles, California, to Mexico. Millions of foreign job seekers swell the U.S. population.
▼ In Thailand, makeshift tents become temporary homes for refugees from Cambodia. In Asia, as elsewhere, wars cause people to migrate to other countries.

Before demographers can decide what is happening to the size of a country's population, they must subtract its crude death rate— the number of deaths per year per thousand people—from its birthrate. The result, called the rate of natural increase, shows how fast a population is growing. It is expressed as a percentage. In 1988, the crude birthrate of Sierra Leone, in West Africa, was 47, much higher than Mexico's, but its death rate, or

mortality rate, was so high (29 compared to Mexico's 6) that Mexico had a greater rate of natural increase, 2.4 percent. Overall, the world's rate of natural increase that year was 1.7 percent. In a few countries, including West Germany and Denmark, populations became smaller, but the populations of many East African countries grew by more than 3 percent. These numbers do not take into account gains or losses through migration.

Knowing rates of natural increase allows demographers to calculate doubling time. This is the number of years it will take for a population to double if the growth rate remains unchanged. Death rates and other statistics are used to project life expectancy, the number of years a newborn baby can be expected to live. Infant mortality, the death rate for babies under age one, is usually figured as a separate statistic. It is often a good indicator of a country's general health conditions.

Maps and graphs of various kinds can

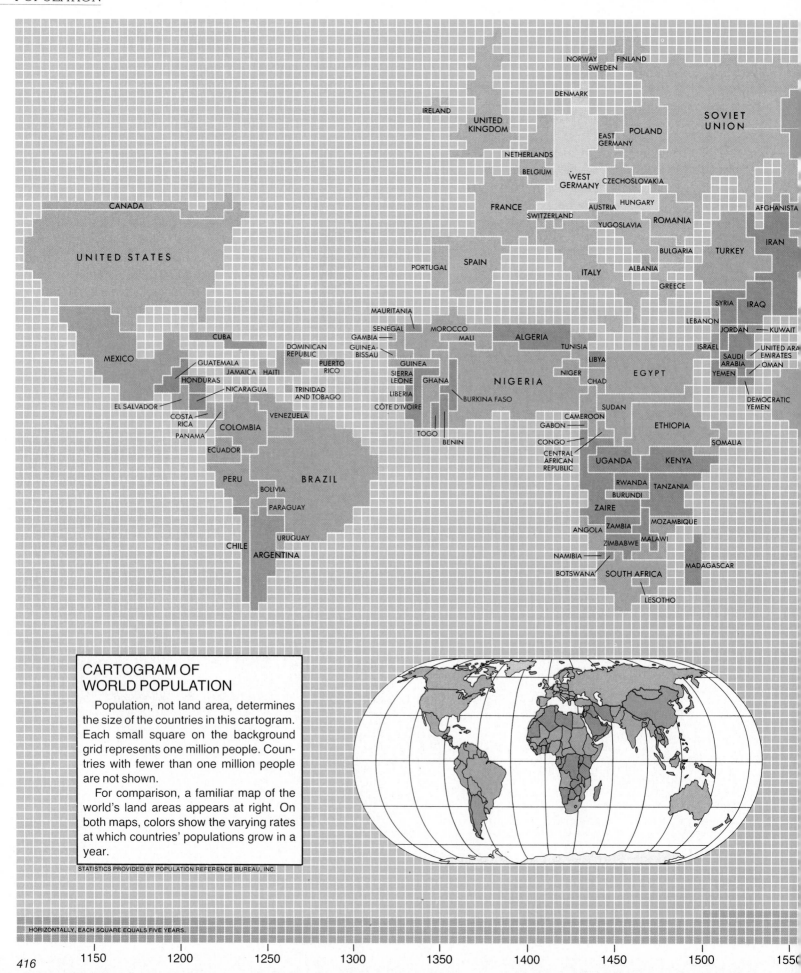

NORWAY   FINLAND
SWEDEN

DENMARK

IRELAND
UNITED   POLAND   SOVIET
KINGDOM   EAST   UNION
               GERMANY
NETHERLANDS
BELGIUM   WEST
           GERMANY   CZECHOSLOVAKIA   AFGHANISTA

CANADA   FRANCE   AUSTRIA HUNGARY
                            SWITZERLAND   IRAN
                                       YUGOSLAVIA ROMANIA

UNITED STATES   BULGARIA   TURKEY
                       PORTUGAL SPAIN
                                        ITALY ALBANIA   SYRIA   IRAQ
                                               GREECE
                                                              LEBANON
                                  MAURITANIA   JORDAN — KUWAIT
                          SENEGAL   MOROCCO   ISRAEL
                 CUBA   GAMBIA —   MALI   ALGERIA   SAUDI   UNITED ARA
                                                          TUNISIA   ARABIA EMIRATES
              DOMINICAN GUINEA-   — OMAN
MEXICO   REPUBLIC   BISSAU   LIBYA   NIGER   YEMEN
        GUATEMALA   PUERTO   GUINEA   EGYPT
        JAMAICA HAITI   RICO   SIERRA   NIGER CHAD   DEMOCRATIC
HONDURAS   LEONE   GHANA   NIGERIA   YEMEN
                 NICARAGUA   LIBERIA
EL SALVADOR   TRINIDAD   CÔTE D'IVOIRE   BURKINA FASO   SUDAN
        COSTA   AND TOBAGO   CAMEROON
        RICA   VENEZUELA   TOGO   GABON —   ETHIOPIA
PANAMA COLOMBIA   BENIN   CONGO —   SOMALIA
ECUADOR   CENTRAL
                                                  AFRICAN UGANDA   KENYA
                                                  REPUBLIC
PERU   BRAZIL   RWANDA
     BOLIVIA   BURUNDI TANZANIA
                                                  ZAIRE
     PARAGUAY   MOZAMBIQUE
                                                  ANGOLA ZAMBIA
     URUGUAY   ZIMBABWE MALAWI
CHILE   NAMIBIA —   MADAGASCAR
     ARGENTINA   BOTSWANA SOUTH AFRICA
                                                           LESOTHO

CARTOGRAM OF WORLD POPULATION

Population, not land area, determines the size of the countries in this cartogram. Each small square on the background grid represents one million people. Countries with fewer than one million people are not shown.

For comparison, a familiar map of the world's land areas appears at right. On both maps, colors show the varying rates at which countries' populations grow in a year.

STATISTICS PROVIDED BY POPULATION REFERENCE BUREAU, INC.

HORIZONTALLY, EACH SQUARE EQUALS FIVE YEARS.

1150   1200   1250   1300   1350   1400   1450   1500   1550

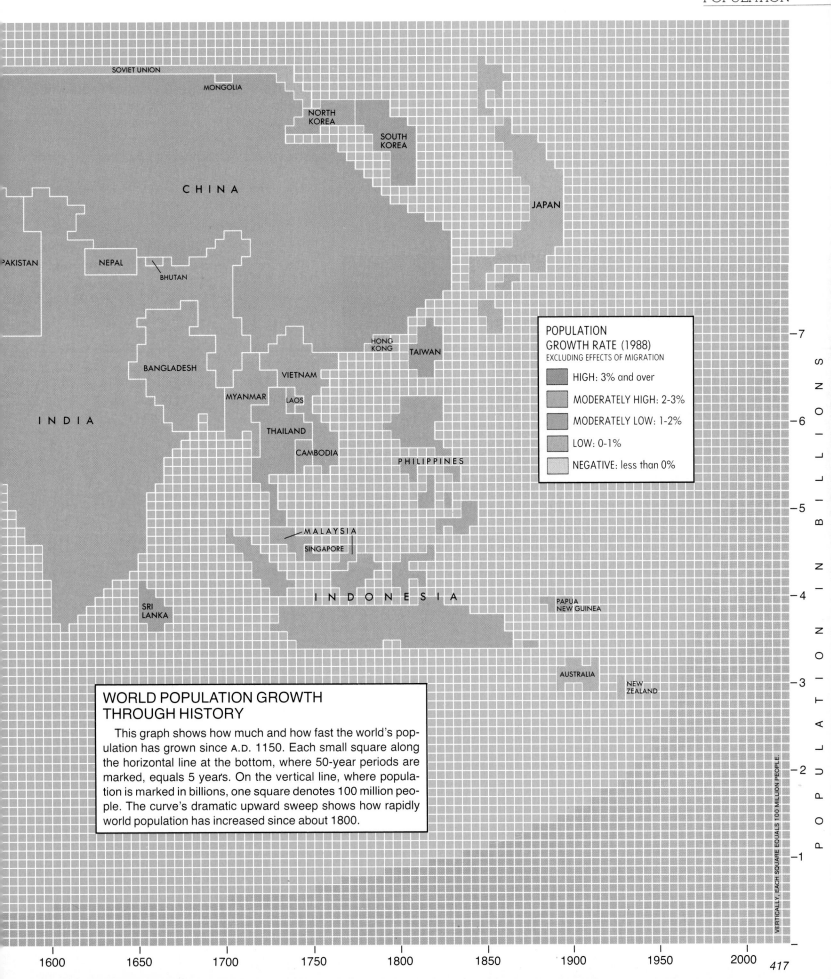

SOVIET UNION

MONGOLIA

NORTH KOREA

SOUTH KOREA

CHINA

JAPAN

PAKISTAN

NEPAL

BHUTAN

HONG KONG

TAIWAN

BANGLADESH

VIETNAM

MYANMAR

LAOS

INDIA

THAILAND

CAMBODIA

PHILIPPINES

MALAYSIA

SINGAPORE

INDONESIA

SRI LANKA

PAPUA NEW GUINEA

AUSTRALIA

NEW ZEALAND

POPULATION GROWTH RATE (1988)
EXCLUDING EFFECTS OF MIGRATION

HIGH: 3% and over

MODERATELY HIGH: 2-3%

MODERATELY LOW: 1-2%

LOW: 0-1%

NEGATIVE: less than 0%

WORLD POPULATION GROWTH THROUGH HISTORY

This graph shows how much and how fast the world's population has grown since A.D. 1150. Each small square along the horizontal line at the bottom, where 50-year periods are marked, equals 5 years. On the vertical line, where population is marked in billions, one square denotes 100 million people. The curve's dramatic upward sweep shows how rapidly world population has increased since about 1800.

POPULATION IN BILLIONS

—7

—6

—5

—4

—3

—2

—1

VERTICALLY, EACH SQUARE EQUALS 100 MILLION PEOPLE.

1600   1650   1700   1750   1800   1850   1900   1950   2000

▼ *The numbers of young and old people provide valuable information about a society. In the Solomon Islands, a western Pacific country, a bright-eyed baby gazes at his mother. High birthrates mean many youngsters for such developing countries.*

► *An elderly Chinese watches the world go by in a Shanghai park. Life expectancy, the average number of years a person might be expected to live, varies from country to country.*
► *Called "pyramids," though their shapes vary, graphs like these show the number of males and females in thousands in each age group. Fairly evenly distributed among most age groups, Sweden's population resembles those of many low-growth European countries. The West African country of Senegal has a large young population and very rapid growth.*

show this type of information vividly and are often used by demographers. On a diagrammatic map called a cartogram, the sizes of countries can be distorted according to the sizes of their populations. (A population cartogram is shown on the preceding pages.) A population pyramid is a graph that portrays a population by age and sex. If the pyramid's base is quite broad, we know the population includes many children. This points to a much larger population in the future. (Two population pyramids are shown below.)

Demographers collect information that describes a population in other ways. What kinds of work are people doing? How many people are unemployed? What percentage of the population is married? How many children go to school? The answers to these and other questions reveal characteristics of a population that are indicators of its well-being.

Where People Live

Demographers study population distribution, the way people are spread out over an area. Population distribution is very uneven over the earth. Much of Europe is densely populated. Some parts of Asia, the most populous continent, are so densely populated that crowding causes severe problems. India alone has more people than the Western Hemisphere, Australia, and Oceania (the lands of the central and South Pacific Ocean) combined. Yet very few people live in some other parts of Asia and other continents. In fact, only about 30 percent of the world's land is inhabited (see the population density map on page 422). Most sparsely populated areas are unsuitable for dense settlement.

Densely populated places usually share features that attract people to them: plenty of rainfall, moderate temperatures, level or gently rolling land, and fertile soil. These things are especially important for farming, which is how most people in the world earn their living. In Asia, the rich valleys of the Ganges in India,

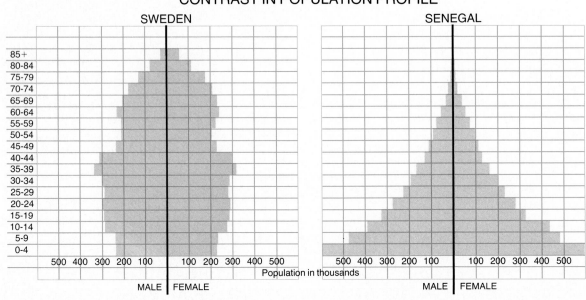

CONTRAST IN POPULATION PROFILE

SWEDEN

SENEGAL

Population in thousands

◄ Czechoslovakian newlyweds prepare to jump a rope strung with objects symbolizing their hope for children. Records of marriages and other demographic statistics are kept by local governments.

the Huang (Yellow) and Yangtze in China, and other great rivers may hold more than 1,200 people per square kilometer, or 3,000 people per square mile. Almost the entire population of Egypt lives in the fertile valley and delta of the Nile.

Populations of continents are generally densest along the coastlines, which usually have the same advantages as the great river valleys if fresh water is available. In addition, many of the world's major cities have grown up around good harbors, where trade with distant lands can flourish. Inland, however, towns have often grown into large cities because of their closeness to natural resources and transportation routes. For example, Pittsburgh, in Pennsylvania, and Essen, in West Germany, are near rivers and rich coalfields.

Population distribution can be greatly affected by migration. From about 1880 to 1920, for example, more than 23 million people emigrated from southern and eastern Europe to the United States, occasionally emptying entire villages.

Within most poor, or developing, coun-

tries, the most important change in population distribution since 1900 has been caused by migration from countryside to city. Believing that better opportunities awaited them in urban areas, hundreds of millions of people—about one-fourth of the rural populations of these countries—have migrated to cities in recent decades. The continuing redistribution of populations from rural areas to urban areas has been called the "population implosion."

▲ In a language lab, a Japanese schoolboy uses electronic equipment to learn English. Changes in birthrates may signal a need for more or fewer classrooms in a country.
◄ A factory worker uses a welding torch on an automobile assembly line in Michigan. By the year 2000, demographers estimate, another billion people worldwide will be looking for jobs.

A far more common term is "population explosion." This refers not only to the fact that there are more people than ever in the world, but also to the fact that the pace of population growth has dramatically increased in some regions since World War II ended in 1945.

How Populations Grow

During most of human history, population change has been a process of slow growth and, at times, of temporary decrease in some areas. Demographers estimate that 250 million people lived on the earth at the beginning of the Christian era, some 2,000 years ago. The world's population did not double to 500 million until about 1650. Birthrates were very high, but so were death rates. Poor sanitation and diseases that are now preventable were largely to blame. In the mid-14th century, for example, bubonic plague killed perhaps a third of Europe's population. Diseases such as measles and smallpox that Europeans introduced in the 16th century, and also malaria and yellow fever from Africa, devastated native populations in the Americas.

Wars and famines, sometimes leading to mass starvation, also kept death rates high in Asia, Africa, and Europe. But gradually, in the late 17th century, changes began to occur that brought mortality rates down. Mostly, these changes originated in western Europe and spread to other parts of the world.

The changes were so important that they are sometimes called revolutions. Some historians refer to the agricultural revolution, a series of advances that led to better farming methods, improved seeds and fertilizers, and

▲ Small compartments of a "capsule hotel" offer privacy at a modest price in densely populated Japan.

▼ Home is usually a high rise in Hong Kong, where crowding limits the building of single-family dwellings.

WHERE PEOPLE LIVE

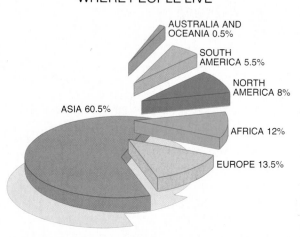

AUSTRALIA AND OCEANIA 0.5%

SOUTH AMERICA 5.5%

NORTH AMERICA 8%

ASIA 60.5%

AFRICA 12%

EUROPE 13.5%

more and better food. The biological revolution included the development of vaccines and better sanitation to prevent diseases and, more recently, antibiotics to treat them.

These revolutions were part of an even greater one, the industrial revolution. Human labor began to be replaced by power-driven machines—tractors and other farm equipment, for instance, that greatly increased crop yields. Better transportation systems made food and natural resources more accessible, and linked the world in trade. In Europe, and later elsewhere, death rates fell sharply, people lived longer, and, as a result, world population increased dramatically—to about one billion by 1800.

Doubling time for the world's population had fallen from about 1,600 years to 150 years. Since 1800, doubling time has continued to plummet. The number of people on earth doubled to two billion by about 1930,

and doubled to four billion only 45 years later.

To look at this another way, it took many thousands of years for the earth's population to reach one billion. It took just 12 years, from 1975 to 1987, for the world's population to grow from four to five billion.

The Demographic Transition

Using European countries as models, some demographers have identified certain factors that historically have made population growth look like a transitional process. Population growth rises, then falls in predictable ways as a country moves through different

▼ A family uses scrap materials for shelter in a New Delhi shantytown. The shack has no indoor plumbing or electricity. The most populous country after China, India faces crises of housing and other needs.
▼ People throng a sidewalk in Paris, France. Much of Europe is densely populated, with most of the people living in cities and towns.

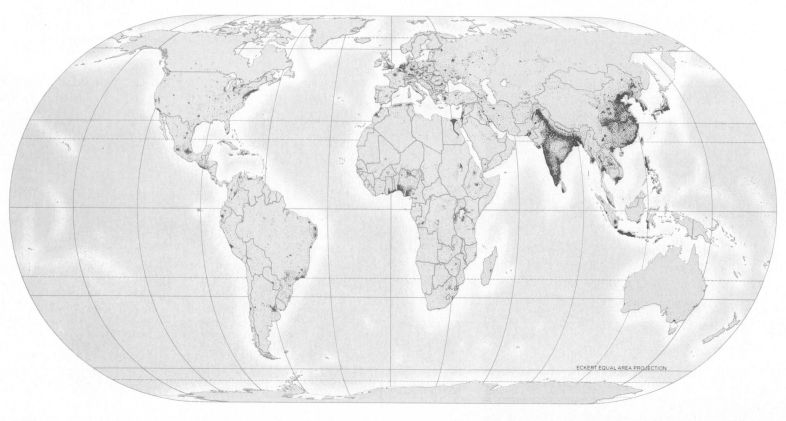

America have only recently passed from the first to the second stage of the transition.

In the second stage, death rates fall as modernization begins and health care improves. Birthrates, though, remain high, often with an average of six to eight children per woman. This happens for many reasons. One is that in countries where wages are low and schools are few, children are an important source of labor and income. They work several hours a day, whether they go to school or not. More children mean more income, or at least help, for the family. Another reason for high birthrates is that, in many countries, large families are traditionally an important part of the culture. This is so partly because of the expectation that many children will die young. Another significant factor leading to high birthrates is that people do not know about or cannot afford safe and effective methods of family planning to limit the number of children they have.

Populations grow extremely rapidly in countries in the second stage of the transition. Birthrates fall, however, as countries become more economically developed and move into the third stage. Among the reasons for this is that when women have more education and better jobs, they usually marry later and have

▲ *Pyramids of Giza rise beyond the Nile and the outskirts of Cairo, Egypt. Most Egyptians live in the river's valley and delta.*
▼ *The red dots on this map, each representing 200,000 people, show population densities. Ribbonlike clusters, mostly in Asia, shade many river valleys and coasts. Blank areas hold few people or none.*

stages of economic and social development. Demographers hope that as other countries progress through these stages, their population growth will follow the European pattern.

These different stages, five all together, make up what is called the demographic transition. In the first stage, birthrates and death rates are both very high, with slow or no population growth. This stage characterized the entire world before the industrial revolution. Just beginning to industrialize, many countries in Africa, Asia, and Central and South

ECKERT EQUAL AREA PROJECTION

▲ An orderly urban layout gives way to the sprawl of a migrant camp on the edge of Nouakchott, capital of Mauritania. Drought and overgrazing in this West African country have forced thousands of nomads to give up herding and migrate to the city.

fewer children. In the third stage, populations grow, but more slowly. A few South American and Asian countries exemplify this stage.

The United States, Canada, Australia, and New Zealand, along with Japan, the Soviet Union, and most European countries, are in the fourth stage, in which population growth becomes extremely low or ceases altogether. This is sometimes called zero population growth. Some European countries have reached the fifth stage, in which population slowly begins to decline.

The theory of demographic transition describes what has happened in the past and the different stages that countries are in now. It cannot definitely predict what will happen in the future. One of the greatest concerns for the world in the next few decades is how, or whether, the developing countries in the second stage can move on to the third. Their

▲ Commuters jam Tokyo's Shinjuku Station, the world's busiest rail hub. People who travel from outlying areas to jobs in Tokyo increase its daytime population by more than two million.
◄ Skyscrapers gleam beyond shacks and drying laundry in Bombay, India. Cities in many developing countries lack resources to cope with huge numbers of migrants from rural areas.

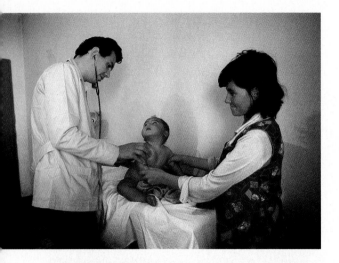

◄ Holding still for the doctor, a baby receives a checkup at a clinic in Argentina. Improvements in health care and sanitation lower death rates, especially among infants, and often lead to rapid population growth.
◄ Computer imaging allows a doctor in North Carolina to "see" the brain of a patient. In developed countries, life expectancies continue to rise as technological advances are made.
▼ A shower of corn fills a farmer's harvester in South Africa. Innovations such as high-yield crops, mechanized equipment, and agricultural chemicals have boosted food production—and lowered death rates—in many countries.

development will naturally bring birthrates down. Many social scientists, however, believe that the problems caused by the population explosion are creating crises in poor countries that will prevent development and bring about tensions with other countries.

People and Resources

At the end of the 18th century, an English economist named Thomas Malthus argued that population would grow much more rapidly than the food supply could. The result would be starvation. Soon, however, the great agricultural advances of the industrial revolution seemed to show that the situation was more complex than Malthus thought. Populations grew, but food supplies kept pace. Also, as Europe became more crowded in the 19th century, millions of people migrated to the Americas, which offered vast new croplands.

Today, perhaps 450 million of the world's people go to bed hungry every night. Millions of people starve every year, and millions more die of diseases brought on by hunger. Millions of young children suffer brain damage because they do not get enough to eat. Does this mean that some regions have become overpopulated? Not necessarily, because factors other than the size of a population may affect its food supply. Also, many social

population growth rates are high; in dozens of developing countries, nearly half the population is under the age of 15. Soon these young people will begin having children of their own. So even if fertility were to drop to a two-child family average, the point at which couples "replace themselves," the populations of these countries would continue to grow rapidly for many decades.

A few experts do not see this as a problem. They argue that larger populations help countries to develop economically and that

► *Her backyard a battleground, a young girl stands in a doorway in northern Nicaragua. Though death rates from disease have fallen in this century, many people still die in wars.*
▼ *An Iranian woman grieves at the grave of a soldier killed in her country's long war with Iraq.*

scientists say that, in terms of population concerns, there are two different "worlds."

Perhaps half the earth's people live in countries that are developed or somewhat developed and have low or moderately low rates of natural increase. These are the countries that have reached at least the third stage of the demographic transition. In them, incomes, food production, and the general standard of living are continuing to rise. Economic progress has gone hand-in-hand with demographic change. But in much of the other world, where birthrates are very high, the opposite is happening. In many of these developing countries, which were already poor, incomes and grain production have been falling as populations soar.

In Malthus's time, perhaps, overpopulation could be thought of simply as too little food for too many people. Social scientists today have begun to think of population problems in terms of people's entire environment and especially in terms of natural resources.

Land, for instance, is a natural resource. In the past, as populations grew, new farmland could be added by clearing forests. But this is usually not the case any more. In many countries, land shortages make population problems worse. Bangladesh, one of the world's poorest countries, has rich soil, but not nearly enough land for its swelling population. Millions of rural people there are too poor to own land, and most are unemployed because there are not enough jobs.

Even those in Bangladesh who do own land face another menace brought on by rapid population growth: flooding. Every year during the rainy monsoon season, the Ganges, the Brahmaputra, and other rivers overflow their banks, carrying huge loads of silt. Every year, more of low-lying Bangladesh is flooded, even though the amount of rainfall varies little. The problem begins in the mountainous areas where the rivers rise. There, on the Himalayan slopes, rapid population growth has led to the clearing of trees for

▲ *Human skulls and bones from a mass grave in Cambodia testify to genocide, the systematic murder of a people. During the 1970s, dictator Pol Pot ordered perhaps three million of his own people killed—a third of this Southeast Asian country's population. Large numbers of survivors fled to neighboring Thailand.*

firewood. With no trees to anchor the soil, rain does not soak into the ground, but instead rushes downhill, carrying tons of soil with it.

In Tanzania, Ethiopia, and some other African countries, rapid population growth is having an even more disastrous effect on the environment. People's need for firewood has caused widespread deforestation, exposing valuable soil to forces of erosion—wind and water—which carry it away. In the Sahel region of Africa, overcultivation, overgrazing, and the cutting of trees are ruining the land. The result is that every year vast tracts of land are turned into unproductive desert. Some social scientists think that in many West African countries, populations have already grown beyond the ability of their natural environment to sustain them.

Population pressures are contributing to other environmental problems that span the globe. Air pollution, for example, is a problem shared by an ever increasing number of cities. With millions of people clustering in and around cities, the effects of automobile and

factory emissions are multiplied. The result is poor air quality, smog, and, often, acid rain. Densely populated areas such as Los Angeles, California, and Athens, Greece, are struggling to deal with similar environmental crises intensified by growing urban populations.

Population growth also has a major effect on people's social environment. When growth is rapid, governments have a much harder time providing people with public health and other social services. New schools cannot be built or paid for fast enough for all the children

▲ *Children of poverty face a bleak future in Mexico City, where schools, jobs, and housing lag behind rapid population growth.*
◄ *Middle East conflict forces Palestinian children to endure hardship in a refugee camp. Perhaps 15 million people in the world, half of them children, are displaced from their homelands, most by war or by persecution.*
► *Too weak to stand, a starving man watches as a doctor examines him at an Ethiopian feeding camp. In the 1980s, famine turned huge numbers of East Africans into refugees.*

▼ *Food from a wealthy country helps sustain a child in drought-stricken Mali. The cutting of trees for firewood and the overuse of land have turned parts of West Africa into desert. In several countries there, populations have outgrown the environment's ability to support them.*

in need of education. New jobs cannot be created fast enough to employ the rising numbers of young adults. In this setting of overcrowding and poverty, social conflict threatens to erupt. Such social problems do not always remain within the boundaries of countries with fast-growing populations. For instance, in Mexico about one million more people each year need jobs, but the jobs do not exist. Many Mexicans naturally think of entering the United States to look for work.

The Demographic Crisis

Some experts believe that unless another technological revolution occurs, more and more people will starve and whole societies will break down. Developed countries have an important role to play. They can help countries with rapidly growing populations to develop new kinds of crops and to develop natural resources such as minerals, fuels, and foods from the ocean.

Developed countries should also take poorer countries' population crises into account when they make certain economic decisions. They can offer aid and assistance in many areas that affect population growth—education and health care, for example. By their laws and policies, developing countries can affect how fast their own populations grow. Local traditions and other factors,

though, may influence family size no matter what governments do.

Population experts agree that there are no easy solutions to the demographic crisis, and that, for some countries, it may be too late to prevent catastrophe. Only one thing seems certain to demographers: Population growth in many parts of the world will remain explosive for decades to come.

SEE ALSO AGRICULTURE, CENSUS, CITY, DENSITY, DEVELOPMENT, DISTRIBUTION, ECONOMY, EMIGRATION, FERTILITY, FOOD, IMMIGRATION, MIGRATION, NATURAL RESOURCE, *and* POLLUTION.

PORT

A port is a place on a coast, a river, or a lake where ships can tie up to load and unload passengers and cargo. Ports serve not only water commerce but also land regions. They are points where water transportation and land transportation meet. Ports are often classified by their function. For example, Ra's Tannūrah, in Saudi Arabia, is an oil port; Concarneau, in France, is a fishing port; and Gibraltar is a naval port. Some ports, such as Dover, in England, chiefly serve passengers. Others, such as Rotterdam, in the Netherlands, handle mostly cargo.

SEE ALSO HARBOR, INDUSTRY, TRADE, *and* TRANSPORTATION AND COMMUNICATION.

▲ *Tugboats move about the harbor of Shanghai, the busiest port in China. Some 100 million tons of goods pass through the port each year.*

427

PRAIRIE

A prairie is a temperate grassland characterized by a rich variety of grasses. Prairies occur where there are distinct seasonal variations in temperature. The term "prairie" is applied most often to the temperate grasslands of North America.

A prairie receives 25 to 75 centimeters (10–30 in) of rainfall in an average year. Tall grasses, which may reach heights of 1.5 meters (5 ft) or more, grow where rainfall is greatest. Shortgrasses dominate where precipitation is scarcer. The shortgrass prairie of North America's Great Plains, which receives as little as 25 centimeters (10 in) of rain a year, is also correctly classified as steppe.

The North American prairie is a vast rolling plain covered with grasses. Like most prairies, it harbors an enormous diversity of plant life—hundreds of species of grasses, herbs, mosses, and other plants. A thick mat of roots, called sod, reaches as deep as 2 meters (6 ft) below the surface of the ground. The dense, tangled root mat helps plants survive when fires sweep dry grassland.

Tallgrass prairie once covered more than a million square kilometers (400,000 sq mi) of North America. Only isolated areas remain. Most of the prairie and other grasslands have been converted to cropland and pasture. Breadbaskets of the world, these lands contribute greatly to the earth's food supply.

SEE ALSO GRASSLAND, SAVANNA, STEPPE, *and* VEGETATION REGIONS.

▲ *Pasqueflowers in bloom mark the start of spring in a Minnesota prairie. Horned larks nest in the tall grasses of this temperate grassland.*

PRECIPITATION

"Precipitation" is a term that covers all of the forms in which water falls to earth from the atmosphere. The main types of precipitation are rain, snow, sleet, and hail. Precipitation is life-sustaining, and the amount and distribution that a region receives play a major role in what can survive there. Yet precipitation can be harmful, too. A hailstorm, for example, can destroy crops worth millions of dollars in a matter of minutes. Too much rain can produce devastating floods, such as the ones that struck Bangladesh in 1988.

Much of the world's precipitation falls on the ocean, and what falls on land is unevenly distributed. Precipitation is barely measurable in the Atacama Desert of Chile, one of the driest places on earth; Arica, a town there, has an average yearly rainfall of .05 centimeter (.02 in). The wettest place on earth, Mount Waialeale, in Hawaii, receives on average 1,200 centimeters (472 in) of rain a year.

When Air Rises, Precipitation Falls

Precipitation falls from clouds. Both clouds and precipitation form when warm, moist air rises into cooler regions of the atmosphere. As air cools, its capacity to hold water vapor decreases to the point where it becomes saturated. Further cooling causes the vapor to turn into water or ice.

The three most common causes of rising

▲ *A large summer thunderstorm brings needed moisture to the dry Arizona countryside. A column of rain falls from the center of the cumulonimbus cloud.*

to rise. The windward side of most mountains receives more rainfall than the leeward side as a result of orographic lifting. As the air mass moves down the other side of the mountain, it warms again, reducing the chance of rain. Thus, a mountain's leeward side, the side away from the prevailing wind, is often dry. This dry area is called the rain shadow.

Air cooled to its saturation point will usually form clouds, but, as we know, it does not always rain or snow when the sky is cloudy. Clouds consist of microscopic water droplets or ice crystals too small to fall through the rising air that has produced the clouds. But

▼ *These maps show how much precipitation falls in the United States during January (top) and July (bottom) in an average year. Different areas receive large amounts of precipitation at different times of year. In January, the Northwest is wet, and the Gulf coast is dry. In July, however, the situation is reversed.*

air are the movement of weather fronts, convection, and orographic lifting. When a cold front overtakes a warm front, the warm air is forced over the heavier cold air. Clouds form and bring precipitation that can last for a day or more. In contrast, convection often produces brief but intense, even violent, precipitation such as downpours and thunderstorms. Convection occurs on sunny days. The sun warms the earth, which in turn heats the air above. A parcel of air becomes lighter when it heats up, so it rises higher into the atmosphere. As it rises, it expands and cools. If air rises and cools enough, it will reach its saturation point.

Orographic lifting takes place when a moving air mass encounters a geographic obstacle, such as a mountain. As the air mass is forced up the mountain, gaining altitude as it goes, it cools to the saturation point. Clouds form, and precipitation starts as air continues

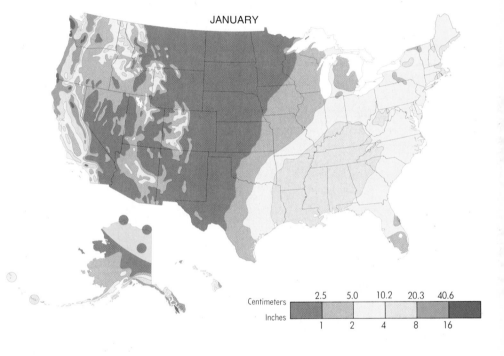

JANUARY

	2.5	5.0	10.2	20.3	40.6
Centimeters					
Inches	1	2	4	8	16

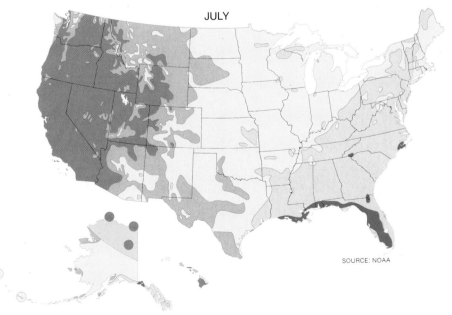

JULY

SOURCE: NOAA

◀ *Light rain falls as children in Sacramento, California, wade after a downpour.*

under favorable conditions the droplets or crystals can grow and fall to earth.

At the center of all cloud droplets lies a tiny impurity called a condensation nucleus. Salt particles from the ocean, meteoric dust, windblown sand grains, and pollutants can all act as nuclei around which water condenses to form droplets. In freezing temperatures, ice crystals form on microscopic clay particles that act as freezing nuclei. Except in the tropics, where the atmosphere is too warm for ice to form, most precipitation begins as ice crystals. The diagram at right shows ways that precipitation forms.

Precipitation grows in several stages. The first stage is nucleation. In this stage, water vapor collects on condensation nuclei and forms water droplets. This process may also start with sublimation, when water vapor changes directly into ice crystals on freezing nuclei without first becoming a liquid.

In the second stage, the droplets or crystals continue to grow through condensation or

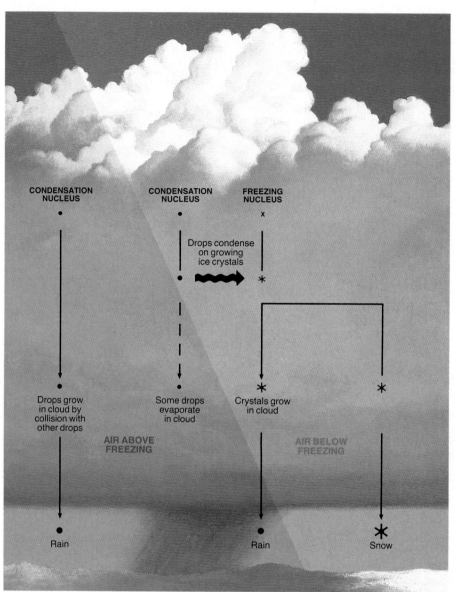

CONDENSATION NUCLEUS CONDENSATION NUCLEUS FREEZING NUCLEUS

Drops condense on growing ice crystals

Drops grow in cloud by collision with other drops

Some drops evaporate in cloud

Crystals grow in cloud

AIR ABOVE FREEZING AIR BELOW FREEZING

Rain Rain Snow

TROPICS MID-LATITUDES POLES
SUMMER ←→ WINTER

▲ Hailstones pummel a street in Colorado Springs, Colorado, during a thunderstorm. Hail damaged flowers, trees, and vegetable gardens.

HOW PRECIPITATION FORMS

Precipitation forms when warm, moist air rises in the atmosphere, and cools to below its saturation point. This occurs through the three basic processes shown here. The type of precipitation that reaches the ground depends largely on the atmosphere's temperature and the amount of moisture in the air (above).

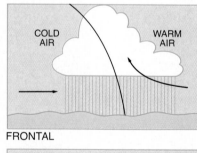

COLD AIR WARM AIR

FRONTAL

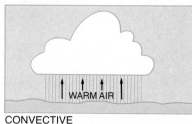

WARM AIR

CONVECTIVE

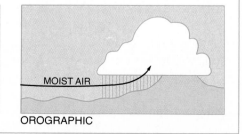

MOIST AIR

OROGRAPHIC

sublimation. Water droplets and ice crystals cannot coexist easily in the same cloud, however, because water vapor is more attracted to ice crystals. The result is that ice crystals grow at the expense of water droplets.

Condensation or sublimation occurs rapidly at this point. The process soon produces crystals that are large enough to capture smaller water droplets with which they collide. This rapid growth is called coalescence. If the crystals grow large enough, they soon begin falling to earth. When the air temperature between cloud and ground is below freezing, snow falls. If the air temperature is above freezing, the crystals melt completely and it rains. If the crystals melt while falling through a layer of warm air and then freeze in a layer of cold air near the ground, sleet forms.

Meteorologists measure amounts of precipitation with a rain gauge, which is simply a pail fitted with a ruler to measure depth. Snow, hail, and sleet are melted before the measurement is made. On average, 10 centimeters (4 in) of fresh, dry snow contains about as much water as one centimeter (0.4 in) of rain.

▲ *Windblown snow turns a man's black coat white as he trudges through a spring snowstorm in Helsinki, Finland. Like many northern cities, Helsinki receives much of its precipitation as snow.* ▼ *Light snow dusts pastures and obscures buildings in Wyoming.*

SEE ALSO CLIMATE, CLOUDS, CONDENSATION, FRONT, HAIL, MIST, RAIN, RAIN SHADOW, SLEET, SNOW, THUNDERSTORM, *and* WEATHER.

PRIME MERIDIAN

The prime meridian is the line of 0° longitude, the starting point for measuring distance both east and west around the globe. Any line of longitude can serve as the prime meridian. Countries often published maps and charts with longitude based on the meridian passing through their capital city. At an international conference in 1884, it was agreed that the meridian passing through Greenwich, England, would serve as the prime meridian. This became the international standard.

SEE ALSO GREAT CIRCLE, LATITUDE AND LONGITUDE, LONGITUDE, *and* TIME AND TIME ZONES.

PRIME MERIDIAN

PROVINCE

Countries are often divided into provinces, states, territories, counties, or other administrative units. The term "province" dates from the days of the Roman Empire, when it referred to territories outside Italy that were governed by Roman officials.

Canada has ten provinces and two territories. The Canadian provinces have a greater degree of self-government than do the territories, and they generally have more power than the states of the U.S. For example, they have full ownership of all natural resources within their boundaries. The provinces of China, on the other hand, have very little power.

SEE ALSO COUNTRY, GOVERNMENT, *and* STATE.

R

RACE

The study of genetics has led biological anthropologists to classify the world's human population in new ways. Before 1950, ideas of "race" relied heavily on physical appearances such as facial features and the color of hair and skin. This approach is now outdated. Today, scientists define a race as a population that differs significantly from other populations in its gene pool—the sum total of genetic material of all these populations. They have discovered that overall genetic differences between the so-called "major races" are not as significant as had previously been believed. Some scholars have stopped using the term "race" entirely.

SEE ALSO ANTHROPOLOGY.

RAIN

Rain is liquid precipitation. It falls from clouds as drops 0.5 millimeter (.02 in) in diameter or larger. Drizzle consists of drops smaller than 0.5 millimeter (.02 in). Most rain forms as snowflakes melt. Raindrops are more than a million times larger than the cloud droplets that combine to form them.

SEE ALSO CLOUDS, PRECIPITATION, *and* SNOW.

▲ *Persistent people endure a cold English rain to fish in London's Hyde Park. Two take shelter beneath a large umbrella hung with clear plastic.*

RAIN FOREST

A rain forest is a moist, densely wooded area usually found in a warm, tropical wet climate. Annual rainfall is about 200 centimeters (80 in) and sometimes ranges as high as 1,000 centimeters (400 in) in some tropical rain forests. The average temperature in most rain forests is 27°C (80°F). Broadleaf evergreen trees, vines, sparse undergrowth, and nutrient-poor soils are common characteristics of this kind of forest.

Tropical rain forests encircle the planet, forming an uneven green belt between the Tropic of Cancer at about latitude $23\frac{1}{2}$°N and the Tropic of Capricorn at about latitude $23\frac{1}{2}$°S. These rain forests are home to nearly half the earth's plant and animal species. Tropical rain forests once covered more than 1.6 billion hectares (4 billion acres) of the earth. Today, nearly half the tropical rain forests are gone. They now cover only about 7 percent of the earth's land, including parts of South and Central America, central Africa, and Southeast Asia. The largest continuous rain forest lies in South America, where about 6.9 million square kilometers (2.7 million sq mi) of forest cloak the Amazon basin.

Though fewer in number, rain forests grow in the temperate regions as well. Temperate rain forests have a more seasonal climate, with less constant temperatures and

▲ Mist softly envelops the interior of this protected rain forest in a national park in Venezuela.
◄ One of the world's last areas of virgin rain forest lies in northern Brazil. This forest has a wide range of tree species, a common trait of rain forests.

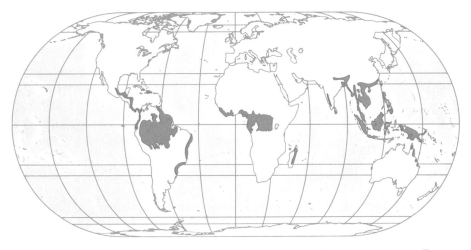

▲ *The world's tropical rain forests lie near the Equator, where a warm, wet climate allows broadleaf evergreen trees and many other plants to flourish.*

◄ *Exploding with life, rain forests are thought to contain almost half of the earth's animal and plant species. In this artist's view, some of the typical inhabitants of a rain forest are shown together. An upside-down howler monkey (1) reaches for a favorite food: fresh green leaves. A regal-looking scarlet macaw (2) watches a shaggy three-toed sloth (3) stretch lazily. A baby red spider monkey grabs a ride with its mother (4). A squirrel-size silky anteater (5), with its baby on its back, clings to a vine. A porcupine (6) anchors itself with its prehensile tail; an emerald tree boa (7) lies coiled nearby. Tapirs (8) stand nose to nose on the forest floor near a tawny ocelot (9), a wild member of the cat family. A green leaf frog (10) hangs on a vine.*

less rain, than do rain forests near the Equator. Though plant and animal life are abundant, the species are not as diverse as they are in the warmer, tropical rain forests.

Layers of Life

Viewed from the air, a tropical rain forest looks like a rumpled blanket of foliage. The crowns, or tops, of the trees form a thick canopy, the layer in which most insects and other animals live. In rain forests, canopy trees may rise 15 to 45 meters (50–150 ft) before forming a dense ceiling of branches and leaves. Less than 2 percent of the sunlight filters down through the closed canopy. The lack of light limits plant growth in the lowest layers of a rain forest.

In the warm, damp climate of the tropical rain forest, decomposition on the bottom layer, the forest floor, occurs rapidly. Insects, earthworms, and fungi help decompose plant and animal remains. Nutrients released during decomposition are quickly absorbed by trees and other plants, often leaving the floor relatively bare. Frequent rains leach, or wash away, minerals from the nutrient-poor soil.

Millions of animal and plant species live in tropical rain forests, and the discovery of new species continues. Some species can be found only in a tropical rain forest. The okapi, a relative of the giraffe, is one example. More than a thousand kinds of trees have been identified in a square kilometer of tropical rain forest. The rain forest in the South American country of Ecuador has 20,000 kinds of flowering plants. The state of California, a third larger than Ecuador, has only 5,000.

Tropical rain forests are a valuable natural resource. Millions of people live in rain forests, relying on them to fulfill their needs for food and fuel. The rest of the world relies on rain forests for such by-products as rubber, wood, dyes, oils, foods, and medicines. More than 40 percent of prescription drugs in the United States contain ingredients derived from plants, many of them from rain forests.

Rain forests play a role in recycling the earth's water. Much of the moisture absorbed by the trees transpires from the leaves and evaporates into the atmosphere to return as rainfall. The roots of the trees help anchor the soil and slow water runoff.

Vanishing Rain Forests

Clearing forestlands for farming, ranching, logging, and mining is rapidly decreasing the remaining rain forests. Some scientists estimate that an area of tropical rain forest the size of Delaware is cleared every month.

▲ *Using traditional methods, two men in Sierra Leone perch on a makeshift platform, preparing to fell a giant tree. Trees in a tropical rain forest often rely on massive buttress roots to support them in typically shallow, nutrient-poor soils.*

► *A big bite has been taken out of this rain forest in Brazil to clear land for raising cattle.*
▼ *Only a few trees are left standing in what used to be a rain forest in Rondônia, Brazil. The world's rain forests are being felled at a rapid rate. Their future depends on wise land-use practices.*

Although the land is often used for agriculture, the nutrient-poor tropical soils can support crops or cattle for only a few years. Then the land is abandoned, and people move farther into the forest. Erosion accelerates as the cleared land is exposed to torrential rains and blistering sunlight.

This destruction is no longer going unnoticed. Governments, scientific organizations, and conservationists and other citizens are deeply concerned about the loss of rain forests. They also recognize that people need the food and fuel that forests provide. The future of the earth's rain forests may depend on management plans that preserve some areas of rain forest while allowing people to cut trees selectively in other areas. Better land-use practices, education, and wiser planning may slow deforestation, but experts worry that the rain forests will be virtually gone by the time these changes can be widely implemented.

SEE ALSO CONSERVATION, FOREST, JUNGLE, SOIL, TROPICS, *and* VEGETATION REGIONS.

RAIN SHADOW

"Rain shadow" refers to the dry lands that lie on the leeward side of mountains, the side away from the prevailing wind. Rain shadows are most common in areas where mountains lie parallel to coasts. When moisture-laden winds blowing inland from the ocean encounter the windward slopes of a mountain range, they are forced to rise. This process, called orographic lifting, increases the air's relative humidity. Clouds form, and precipitation soon begins as the air continues to rise. When the air moves over the crest of the range and begins to descend, there is little moisture left. Descending air makes it difficult for clouds and precipitation to form. As the air moves down the leeward slopes, it is compressed by the weight of the air above. This warms the air, reducing relative humidity.

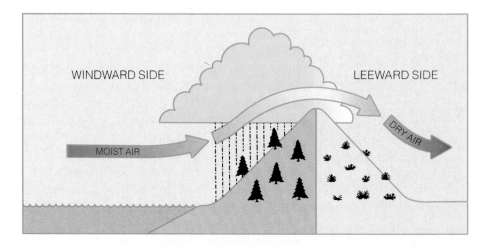

WINDWARD SIDE

LEEWARD SIDE

DRY AIR

MOIST AIR

The eastern part of Washington State, for example, lies in the rain shadow of the Cascade Range and is a semiarid wheat-growing region; the western part of the state, with ample rainfall, is heavily forested.

SEE ALSO CLIMATE, CLOUDS, *and* PRECIPITATION.

▲ *When moist air is forced over mountain barriers, it loses moisture as precipitation on the windward slopes. The descending air makes the leeward, rain-shadow side relatively dry.*

RAINBOW

A rainbow is a multicolored arc produced by sunlight striking raindrops beneath a rain cloud. Red is always the outside color and violet is always the inside color of a primary rainbow. Occasionally you will see a secondary rainbow in which the order of the colors is reversed. If you stand with your back to the sun, the rainbow will be at a 42-degree angle above the end of your shadow. The secondary rainbow will appear at a 51-degree angle, or 9 degrees higher in the sky. How high the rainbow appears in the sky depends on the sun's altitude above the horizon. When the altitude of the sun is low, the rainbow will appear higher in the sky.

Rainbows occur because of two characteristics of light known as refraction and reflection. Light refracts, or bends, when it passes from air into a water drop. Each color of light refracts a different amount: Violet bends more than blue, which bends more than green, and so on, with red refracting the least of all. If sunlight enters a raindrop at just the proper angle, it refracts and the colors spread. It then reflects off the back of the drop and refracts again as it leaves the drop. As a result, each drop projects tiny spots of different colored light in the sky. The spots from millions of raindrops merge to form the rainbow.

SEE ALSO ALTITUDE, PRECIPITATION, *and* RAIN.

▼ *A double rainbow serves as a backdrop for an ultralight aircraft. The primary rainbow is bright and has a red outer arc. In the larger, secondary rainbow, the colors are reversed and fainter.*

▼ *Sunlight scattering off a curtain of raindrops produces a rainbow over adobe houses in Santa Fe, New Mexico.*

RAPIDS

Rapids are areas of broken, fast-flowing water in a stream that is making a slight descent. The water tumbles over or around large boulders or rock ledges, or it flows quickly through a narrow part of the stream. Indians and European explorers and fur traders in North America navigated some rapids in canoes and in other small boats. Other rapids were so dangerous that the boats had to be portaged, or carried overland.

SEE ALSO RIVER *and* STREAM.

▲ *Kayakers maneuver through a long stretch of rapids as the Grande Ronde River descends from the Blue Mountains in northeastern Oregon.*

REGION

A region is an area of the earth having one or more common factors that are found throughout. Regions are the basic units of geographic study. They may be defined by human factors, such as language or government, or by physical features, climate, vegetation, or other characteristics. The Sahel, for example, is a region bordering the southern edge of the Sahara in Africa. It is characterized by a semiarid climate, poor soils, and erratic rainfall. Regions can be large, like the Great Plains, or small, like Champagne, a wine-producing region of France. Smaller regions often lie within larger ones. Most regions do not have well-defined boundaries.

SEE ALSO AREA, BOUNDARY, *and* ZONE.

RELIGIONS

Throughout the world, people's customs and ways of life vary greatly. Even so, cultural anthropologists—scientists who study the life-ways of peoples both ancient and modern—have never discovered a group that does not have some kind of religious beliefs.

No definition covers all religions, though certain things are typical of most of them. Most religions have one or more deities, or gods, and most have a system of sacred beliefs or teachings. These beliefs may explain things that are hard to understand, such as the nature of good and evil and the origins of the earth. A religion's teachings include rules of behavior in daily life. These rules and beliefs are usually written down in holy or authoritative books, or scriptures. Religions also have rituals, such as prayer, and nearly all have leaders, such as priests and rabbis.

Religion has been a part of human life for many thousands of years. Prehistoric peoples often believed that the forces of nature were

▲ Hand extended in greeting, Pope John Paul II leads Roman Catholics in Easter ceremonies.
► Age-old pageantry in Canterbury Cathedral marks the installation of a new Archbishop as the spiritual head of the Church of England.

▲ A pointed hood and an ornate cape distinguish a priest of the Armenian Apostolic Church.
▼ In a chapel adorned with frescoes, a priest celebrates Mass according to the rites of the Greek Orthodox Church. Most Christians were unified in beliefs and practices until 1054, when the Roman Catholic and Eastern Orthodox Churches formed separate branches.

spirits and that spirits inhabited trees, rivers, and other natural sites. This ancient type of religious belief is called animism, and it still survives in isolated parts of the world.

Today, most people who follow a religion practice one of the great faiths that began in Asia. Judaism, Christianity, and Islam arose in the Middle East, in western Asia. Confucianism, Taoism, and Shinto are religions of eastern Asia. Several religions began in India. Among them, Hinduism and Buddhism have the largest followings.

A common religion can provide important links between people in different lands. Yet disagreements over religion have caused wars and injustices.

Religions of India and Eastern Asia

The oldest of the major religions is Hinduism, which began in India perhaps more than 4,000 years ago. Hindus believe that many deities exist within Brahman, the supreme power of the universe. One of the most important ideas in Hinduism is reincarnation, the rebirth of a person's soul during many lives. Another is caste, a system in which people are separated into different rigid social groups. More than 650 million people are Hindus. While the other major faiths have followers in many countries, most Hindus live in India.

Buddhism, like Hinduism, began in India,

◄ A mass baptism takes place in a Virginia river. The use of water in Christian baptism signifies the washing away of sins and spiritual rebirth.

but today most of its followers—about 300 million—live in other Asian countries. Buddhism grew out of Hinduism, beginning about 2,500 years ago. Its founder was Siddhartha Gautama, a Hindu prince who became known as Gautama Buddha. (The title "Buddha" means "the Enlightened One.") Gautama Buddha taught that life always brings suffering because people have selfish desires. Buddhists believe that to achieve the blissful state of nirvana, Buddhism's goal, people must purify their lives and thoughts by following strict rules of behavior.

Buddhism spread from India through eastern and southeastern Asia. In China, it flourished alongside Confucianism and Taoism, the major native philosophies there.

Confucius lived at the same time as Buddha. Confucianism aimed to create harmony between fathers and sons, rulers and subjects, friends, and finally between earth and heaven. It defined the roles that people of different ages and ranks should play in society.

Taoism, which began around the same time, sought harmony between humans and

MAJOR RELIGIONS OF THE WORLD

- CHRISTIANITY
- ISLAM
- HINDUISM
- LOCAL RELIGIONS
- JUDAISM
- BUDDHISM
- SHINTO and BUDDHISM
- TRADITIONAL CHINESE PHILOSOPHIES
- TRADITIONAL RELIGIONS SUBJECT TO RESTRAINT

▼ This map shows in general where different faiths are practiced by a majority of the people. Only those religions with the largest followings are represented. Such a map cannot be accurate in every detail.

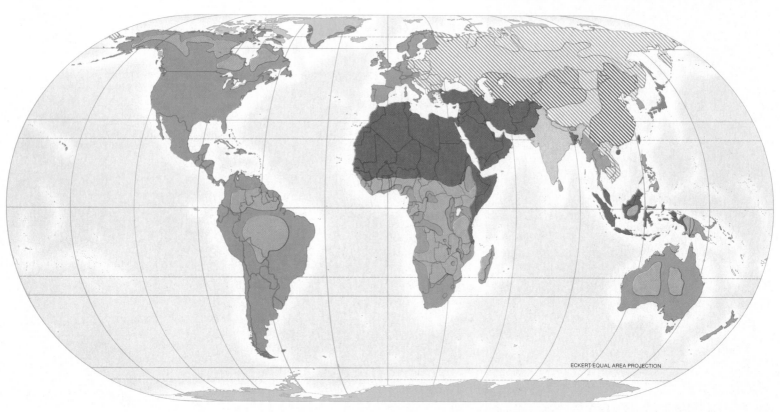

ECKERT EQUAL AREA PROJECTION

nature. It valued natural goodness and creativity above political order and social conventions, and gave rise to many works of art. Taoism acted as a balance to Confucianism, which remained the dominant philosophy. Over many centuries, elements of Confucianism, Taoism, and Buddhism blended together into a traditional philosophy that still exerts a strong influence on Chinese life.

Japan's ancient native religion is Shinto, which places importance on spirits of nature called kami. It has coexisted with Buddhism for 1,500 years. From the late 1800s to 1945, Shinto was Japan's official religion.

The Monotheistic Faiths

Judaism, Christianity, and Islam, all of which arose in the Middle East, share an important concept: monotheism, a belief in one God. Judaism is the oldest of the monotheistic religions. Both Christianity and Islam have roots in Judaism.

▲ Crowds gather at Jerusalem's Wailing, or Western, Wall, sacred to Jews. The Dome of the Rock, an Islamic mosque, gleams beyond.

▼ A rabbi in Jerusalem lifts up a Torah, the Jewish Scripture. The first five books of the Old Testament are inscribed in Hebrew on the scroll.

Judaism arose nearly 4,000 years ago. Jews believe that God made a covenant with Abraham, a Hebrew leader, agreeing to bless Abraham and his people in return for their faithfulness. Centuries later, God gave the Prophet Moses the Ten Commandments, rules governing the relationship of people with God and with one another. The history of the Jewish people has been marked by wandering and suffering. During World War II, the Nazis of Germany murdered six million European Jews. After the war, Jews were allowed to establish their own country, Israel, in the Middle East. About 3.7 million of the world's 18 million Jews live in Israel.

Christianity began about 2,000 years ago in a part of the Middle East called Palestine. Christianity centers upon the belief that Jesus of Nazareth was the son of God. During his ministry of teaching and helping others, Jesus was viewed by many powerful people as a troublemaker and a threat to the authority of Rome. He was crucified—put to death on a cross—in Jerusalem. On the third day, Christians believe, Jesus rose from the dead.

Early Christians were often made to suffer in the Roman Empire. About 300 years after Jesus' crucifixion, however, the Roman emperor Constantine was converted to Christianity and made it the empire's official religion. In the centuries that followed, Christianity became not only the dominant religion

▲ *Evening devotions absorb a Muslim woman in Jerusalem. Following a tenet of her faith, she faces toward Mecca, Muhammad's birthplace.*
◄ *In Mecca's Sacred Mosque, Muslim pilgrims create a blur of motion as they circle seven times around the draped Kaaba, Islam's holiest shrine.*

in Europe but also a profoundly important influence on Western civilization. Today, Christianity has more than 1.5 billion followers worldwide—more than any other religion.

The most recent of the major monotheistic faiths is Islam. It is based upon the teachings of the Prophet Muhammad, who was born about 570 years after Christ in what is now Saudi Arabia. Muhammad taught people to worship only one God, whom he called Allah. Like Jesus, Muhammad made many enemies because of his teachings. In A.D. 622, he fled the city of Mecca, where he lived, with his followers. Several years later, he led an army of 10,000 men to conquer Mecca. From then on, Islam spread rapidly. Today, it claims almost a billion followers, known as Muslims.

The Koran, the Muslims' holy book, calls for daily prayer, almsgiving, a month of daytime fasting each year, and at least one pilgrimage to Mecca in a lifetime. Muslims are also obliged to defend Islam from enemies. The call to holy war, or jihad, inspired the early Muslims to form powerful conquering armies. By A.D. 750, little more than a century after Muhammad's death, Muslim rule stretched from Spain to the borderlands of China.

The Spread of Religions

Throughout history, military campaigns have been one of the ways in which religions have spread. Even more important has been the role of trade routes. They were traveled not only by merchants but also by missionaries, people who work to bring others, mostly in foreign lands, into their faith by conversion. Missionaries have had a profound effect on some cultures. About one thousand years ago, for instance, Christian missionaries in Russia invented an alphabet to translate the Bible into the Russian language. This gave the Russians a written language, a form of which is used today in the Soviet Union.

▼ *In the Way of the Buddha, Sri Lankan youths wear saffron garments and shave their heads during a period of religious service. Many Buddhists in Asia spend a year or more as monks or nuns.*

▲ *A dry landscape garden of raked gravel and carefully placed rocks offers a setting for meditation at one of Japan's many Zen Buddhist temples. Emphasizing simplicity and enlightenment, Zen has inspired artists and poets for centuries.*
► *Bell-shaped monuments called stupas house statues of Buddha on Borobudur, a temple in Java. Completed in the ninth century, the shrine is a pyramid-shaped model of the Buddhist universe. The carvings on it represent the ascending stages of enlightenment.*

▶ Temple-ringed Pushkar Lake, in the Indian state of Rajasthan, draws throngs of Hindus. Immersion, they believe, purifies the soul and assures them of a place in heaven.

▼ Following Hindu custom, mourners observe the cremation of the dead on the banks of the Ganges. Burning is believed to release the soul from the body.

In the past, missionaries often accompanied or followed explorers and traders to distant lands. The first Buddhist missionaries in China traveled there from India along traders' caravan routes. Roman Catholic priests were members of nearly every Spanish expedition to the Americas in the 16th and 17th centuries. They converted hundreds of thousands of Indians, sometimes by force.

Migration is another way that religions spread to new places. When people set out for new homes, they usually take their faith with them. Sometimes the search for religious freedom itself has been the cause of migration. The Pilgrims, who in 1620 founded Plymouth Colony in Massachusetts, are a famous example of this. They felt forced to leave their homes in England after they had broken away from its official church.

Branching Paths, Shared Symbols

Along with other customs, religious practices have varied from place to place. Christianity was split apart in 1054 because of differences in doctrine. Its followers in Western Europe and in the Byzantine Empire established branches with different rituals — the Roman Catholic Church and the Eastern

Orthodox Church. Nearly 500 years later, a German monk, Martin Luther, and others broke away from the Roman Catholic Church. The Lutheran movement formed the first of various Protestant branches of Christianity, which took hold in different parts of Europe.

Even when they live in different countries, followers of a religion often share the same holy place. Muslims live in many lands, but they all face toward Mecca, Muhammad's

◀ Preparing for meditation, a sadhu, or Hindu holy man, applies white paint to his skin. Coils of jute bind his hair.

birthplace, when they pray. The city of Jerusalem is important in Judaism, Christianity, and Islam because major events in the history of all three faiths occurred there. The Ganges River, in India and Bangladesh, is sacred to Hindus, who make pilgrimages to bathe in it. Places like these are symbols that help unite the followers of a faith.

Religious buildings are also symbols. In most countries, they play an important part in the way towns and cities look. Among the most impressive anywhere are the great cathedrals built in western Europe hundreds of years ago during the Middle Ages. As symbols of Christianity, the cathedrals remind us of the importance of religion in daily life at the time they were built. In the Middle Ages, the Roman Catholic Church was more powerful in western Europe than kings were. The Church operated almost all schools, and monks made the only books that existed. During the Middle Ages and for centuries afterward, most of Europe's greatest art and music drew upon Christian themes.

Other religions have also had a powerful influence on different aspects of culture. During the Middle Ages, lands under Islamic rule made great contributions to civilization. Muslim scholars built observatories and instruments for gazing at the stars, and they published great medical encyclopedias. Partly because of their pilgrimages to Mecca, they became skilled geographers and map-

▲ Beyond a sword-bearing guard, gilded copper domes crown the Golden Temple at Amritsar, in India. The temple, in the center of the Pool of Immortality, is the holiest site for the Sikhs, who form one of India's many religious minorities.

► A torii, or gateway, leads to an ancient Shinto shrine in the mountains of central Japan. Within such sacred places, say followers of Japan's native religion, dwell kami, spirits of nature.

makers. The "Arabic" numerals and decimal system that we use were developed by Hindus in India and introduced to the Western world by a Muslim mathematician.

Ancient Religions in the Modern World

While secularism, or indifference to religion, has undermined religious belief for some people, religion continues to be a powerful force in societies. In fact, several of the most important events of the 20th century have centered on religion. Some have changed the way a map of the world looks today. The founding of Israel as a Jewish homeland in 1948 put a new country on the map. A year earlier, another new country, Pakistan, was formed out of part of India as a home for India's Muslims, who were in conflict with that country's Hindus. Religious conflict continues in other areas: between Catholics and Protestants in Northern Ireland and among rival religious groups in the Middle East.

The policies of governments concerning religion can be roughly divided into three types. In secular states, the government neither encourages nor discourages religion, and the separation of church and state is established by law. The United States is a secular state, as are most other countries.

The governments of atheistic states have discouraged the practice of religion to greater or lesser degrees. The Soviet Union, China, and some other countries, mostly communist, are atheistic. In recent years, several communist countries, including the Soviet Union and China, have permitted members of some faiths to practice their religions openly.

Religious states are those whose governments have official links to a religion or a branch of a religion. Nepal, for example, is officially Hindu, and the state churches of Sweden, Norway, Denmark, and Iceland are Evangelical Lutheran. In several Middle Eastern countries, Islam is not only the official religion but also a powerful force in daily life.

SEE ALSO CITY, CIVILIZATION, *and* CULTURE.

RESERVOIR

A reservoir is an artificial lake in which large quantities of water are stored. It may be formed from a natural lake whose outlet has been dammed so that the water level can be regulated, or it may be part of a river whose flow is controlled by a dam. In China, reservoirs have been formed by damming inlets to collect water that would otherwise run into the ocean. The stillness of the water in a reservoir allows sand, rocks, and other sediments to sink to the bottom, leaving a constant supply of clear water. Over time, however, the sediments build up, greatly reducing the volume of water in the reservoir.

Modern reservoirs are usually multipurpose, serving more than one function. They provide water for generating electricity, for irrigating farmland, and for use in homes and industries. They are also used to control flooding and for boating and other recreation.

The world's largest reservoir in terms of capacity is the Kariba Reservoir in Zimbabwe, in southern Africa. It can hold some 180 cubic kilometers (43 cu mi) of water—about one-third the volume of Lake Erie.

The dams that create reservoirs are costly, extensive engineering projects that require huge amounts of material. Hoover Dam, spanning the Colorado River on the Nevada-Arizona border, rises 221 meters (726 ft) to form the reservoir known as Lake Mead.

SEE ALSO DAM, ENERGY, *and* LAKE.

REVOLUTION

The earth and other planets revolve around the sun, each in its own orbit, or path. One complete journey around the sun is called a revolution. It takes the earth about 365¼ days to travel the 950 million kilometers (590 million mi) of its orbit.

"Revolution" may also refer to a great change, such as the overthrow of a government or a major innovation in technology.

SEE ALSO EARTH, INDUSTRY, ORBIT, SEASONS, *and* SOLAR SYSTEM.

RICHTER SCALE

The Richter scale, developed in the United States by seismologists Charles F. Richter and Beno Gutenberg in the 1930s and '40s, is used to indicate the amount of energy released at the focus of an earthquake. With an instrument called a seismograph, seismologists record and measure the seismic waves, or vibrations, a quake produces to determine its magnitude on the Richter scale.

Seismologists assign a number to express the magnitude—the larger the number, the more powerful the earthquake. An increase by one unit represents an increase in the amount of released energy by about 30 times, so the difference between magnitudes is tremendous. For example, compared with a magnitude 5 earthquake, one of magnitude 6 releases approximately 30 times more energy; a magnitude 7 quake releases 900 times more energy; and a magnitude 8 releases 27,000 times more energy.

The smallest earthquake that can be felt has a magnitude of about 2. Property damage usually occurs with an earthquake of about magnitude 5. The scale has no limits, but to date the largest quakes recorded have been between magnitudes 8 and 9. Earthquakes in this range cause massive destruction.

SEE ALSO EARTHQUAKE *and* SEISMOLOGY.

▲ *Charles F. Richter, a developer of a scale that ranks earthquakes, studies a seismogram.*

RIFT VALLEY

A rift valley forms where the earth's crust, or outermost layer, is spreading or splitting apart. This kind of valley is often narrow, with steep sides and a flat floor.

Plate tectonics causes rift valleys. Plates are the huge, rocky slabs that contain the earth's crust, and tectonics involves their movement and interaction. Where plates move apart, crust separates, forming deep cracks called rifts that may widen into valleys.

The floors of rift valleys develop in different ways. Molten rock from the earth's interior may well up in a rift and harden into new crust. This occurs along the crest of the Mid-Ocean Ridge, where a deep valley formed between plates. The rate of plate separation determines how fast the valley floor widens.

On continents, as tectonic activity splits the earth's crust, chunks of crust between long, parallel faults may sink, forming the floors of narrow valleys. The Great Rift Valley system stretches from southwestern Asia into East Africa. As the sides of the valley move farther apart, the floor sinks lower. The Red Sea fills part of the Great Rift system. Geologists think that the rest of the valley may sink enough to allow seawater to pour in, flooding the valley and splitting Africa in two.

SEE ALSO FAULT, OCEAN, PLATE TECTONICS, SEA-FLOOR SPREADING, VALLEY, *and* VOLCANO.

▲ *Kenya's Lake Magadi covers part of the floor of Africa's Great Rift Valley, a depression that formed between parallel faults in the earth's crust. The rift's walls move apart as the crust of the African continent slowly splits.*
▼ *In Iceland, a researcher peers into a rift that has appeared in the ground. The island country is part of the Mid-Ocean Ridge. If tectonic activity along the ridge widens the crack further, it could develop into a rift valley.*

RING OF FIRE

If you placed a red pin at the location of each active volcano on a map of the earth, you would need about 600 pins to mark them all. You would notice that your pins form patterns, like the red dots on the map below. The majority of the pins would be concentrated in a wide, uneven loop around the Pacific Ocean. This belt of volcanoes is known as the Ring of Fire.

Ring Around the Pacific

Looking at the map, you can follow the Ring of Fire from the southern tip of South America north to Alaska, then west to Asia, and south through Japan, the Philippines, Indonesia, and New Zealand.

The volcanoes ring the Pacific for a reason. The earth's rigid shell is made up of huge slabs of rock called plates. The Ring of Fire marks the boundary where the plates that cradle the Pacific meet the plates that hold the continents surrounding the ocean. In this zone, the edges of the Pacific plates slide un-

der the continental plates and bend down into the hot mantle—a process called subduction.

In subduction zones, friction from the grinding plate edges and heat from the earth's interior combine to melt some material in the subducting rocky plate, forming magma. The magma, which is hotter and lighter than the surrounding rock, rises through the overlying plate, where it bursts out as lava. Subduction builds volcanic islands and continental mountain chains that are characteristic of the Ring of Fire.

SEE ALSO EARTHQUAKE, MAGMA, PLATE TECTONICS, TRENCH, *and* VOLCANO.

▲ *Frequent volcanic activity around the Pacific Ocean inspired the name Ring of Fire. A dramatic eruption of Indonesia's Galunggung (left) occurred in 1982; Augustine, in Alaska, (above) erupted in 1986.*

▼ *More than half of the earth's active volcanoes lie along the Ring of Fire, shown in light green on the map. The volcanoes are fueled by a process known as subduction.*

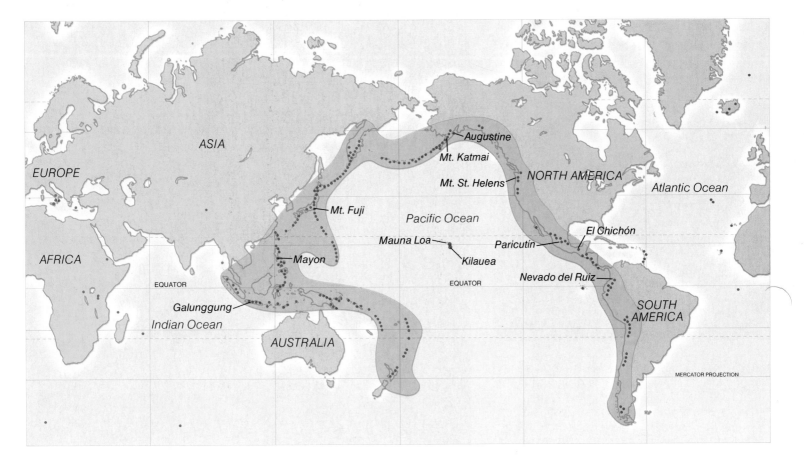

RIVER

A river is a large natural stream of flowing water. Rivers are found on every continent and on nearly every kind of land. Some flow continuously; others flow intermittently. They wind across plains, deserts, and grasslands, and through mountain valleys, canyons, and forests. A river may be fairly short, or it may span much of a continent. The Nile in Africa, the world's longest river, flows 6,671 kilometers (4,145 mi). The Amazon of South America, the second longest river, carries more water than any other.

The Importance of Rivers

Rivers are important for many reasons. One of the most vital things they do is to carry large quantities of water from the land to the ocean. There, seawater constantly evaporates. From the resulting water vapor, clouds form. They carry moisture over land and release it as precipitation. This fresh water feeds rivers and smaller streams. The movement of water between land, ocean, and air is called the water cycle. Through it, the earth's supply of fresh water, essential for many living things, is continuously replenished.

To people, rivers have always been immensely important. In prehistoric times,

▲ At dawn, a Hindu meditates beside India's Ganges River. Hindus consider the Ganges sacred and worship it as the goddess Ganga Ma.
► Swift waters of the Jari River rush and foam over a waterfall in Brazil. The Jari is one of more than a thousand tributaries of the mighty Amazon.

AMAZON RIVER

DANUBE RIVER

HUDSON RIVER

MAE KLONG RIVER

NILE RIVER

Yukon
Mackenzie
Saskatchewan
Fraser
Nelson
Columbia
St. Lawrence
Missouri
Colorado
Ohio
Allegheny
Mississippi
Tennessee
Rio Grande

NORTH ATLANTIC OCEAN

NORTH PACIFIC OCEAN

Orinoco
Negro
Amazon

SOUTH PACIFIC OCEAN

Paraguay
Parana
Río de la Plata

ECKERT EQUAL AREA PROJECTION

▲ *Major rivers of the world appear on this map.*
◄ *Rivers create fertile land such as islands in the Amazon. Rivers are passageways for barges on Europe's Danube and for a canoe on the Hudson, in New York. Women wash clothes in Thailand's Mae Klong River, and boatmen sail the Nile in Egypt.*

people settled along the banks of rivers, where they found fish to eat, as well as water to drink and to use for cooking and bathing.

Later, people learned that the fertile soil along rivers is good for growing crops. The world's first great civilizations arose in the fertile valleys of the Nile in Egypt, the Indus in southern Asia, the Tigris and the Euphrates in the Middle East, and the Huang (Yellow) River in China.

Centuries later, rivers provided routes for

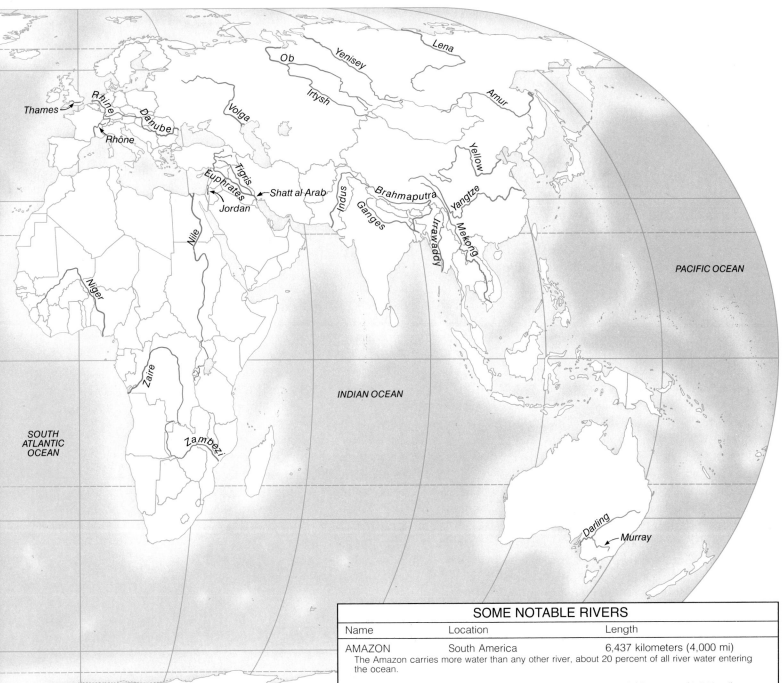

Thames · Rhine · Rhône · Danube · Ob · Yenisey · Irtysh · Volga · Lena · Amur · Euphrates · Tigris · Shatt al Arab · Jordan · Indus · Ganges · Brahmaputra · Yellow · Yangtze · Irrawaddy · Mekong · Nile · Niger · Zaire · Zambezi · Darling · Murray

PACIFIC OCEAN

INDIAN OCEAN

SOUTH ATLANTIC OCEAN

SOME NOTABLE RIVERS

Name	Location	Length
AMAZON	South America	6,437 kilometers (4,000 mi)
The Amazon carries more water than any other river, about 20 percent of all river water entering the ocean.		
GANGES	India-Bangladesh	2,478 kilometers (1,540 mi)
The Ganges is sacred to followers of the Hindu religion.		
MISSISSIPPI	United States	3,766 kilometers (2,340 mi)
The Mississippi is the longest river in the United States. Water from 31 states and two Canadian provinces drains into the Mississippi system.		
NILE	Northeast Africa	6,671 kilometers (4,145 mi)
The Nile is the longest river in the world.		
RHINE	Europe	1,320 kilometers (820 mi)
The Rhine is the busiest inland waterway in Europe.		
ST. LAWRENCE	Canada-United States	1,287 kilometers (800 mi)
The St. Lawrence connects the Great Lakes and the Atlantic Ocean, forming the St. Lawrence Seaway, an inland waterway for oceangoing ships.		
VOLGA	Soviet Union	3,685 kilometers (2,290 mi)
The Volga is the longest river in Europe.		
YANGTZE	China	6,380 kilometers (3,964 mi)
The Yangtze is the longest river in Asia.		

exploration and settlement in North America and on other continents. When towns and industries developed, the rushing water of rivers supplied power to operate machinery.

Rivers remain important today. If you look at a world map, you will see that many well-known cities are on rivers. Great river cities include New York, Buenos Aires, London, Paris, Cairo, Calcutta, and Shanghai. Rivers continue to provide transportation routes, water for drinking and for irrigating farmland, and

power for homes and industries. Large dams built on rivers harness the energy of flowing water to produce electricity. Hydroelectric power is an important source of renewable energy for many of the world's developed and developing countries.

The Anatomy of a River

No two rivers are exactly alike. Yet all rivers have many features in common and go through similar stages as they age. The photographs on this page and the painting, opposite, illustrate the main features of a river.

The beginning of a river is called its source. The source may be ice melting in a glacier, snow melting on a mountain, a lake with an outflowing stream, or a spring bubbling out of the ground. The water that feeds all these sources originates as precipitation.

From its source, a river flows downhill as a small stream. Gradually, precipitation and groundwater add to the river's flow. It is further fed by other streams, called tributaries. Together, a river and its tributaries make up a river system.

The end of a river is its mouth. Here, the river empties into another body of water—a larger river, a lake, or the ocean. Many

of the largest rivers empty into the ocean.

As it moves downhill, the flowing water of a river has great power to carve and shape the landscape. Many landforms were sculptured by rivers that have been flowing for thousands of years. The energy of flowing river water comes from the force of gravity, which pulls the water downward. The steeper the slope down which a river flows, the faster the river moves and the more energy it has to cut into the land.

In the upper course of a river that flows down a mountain or a hillside, the water can move rapidly, especially after a storm. The movement of water in a river channel is called

▲ *In the Swiss Alps, icy water streams from the Rhône Glacier (far left), source of the Rhône River. Roaring waters of the Iguaçu River rush along the Brazil–Argentina border. Rafters in Oregon shoot rapids on the Illinois River.*
▼ *Crossing North Dakota marshes, the Souris River forms meanders (far left). Barges move through the mouth of the Mississippi River. A river forms a delta as it enters North America's Lake Superior.*

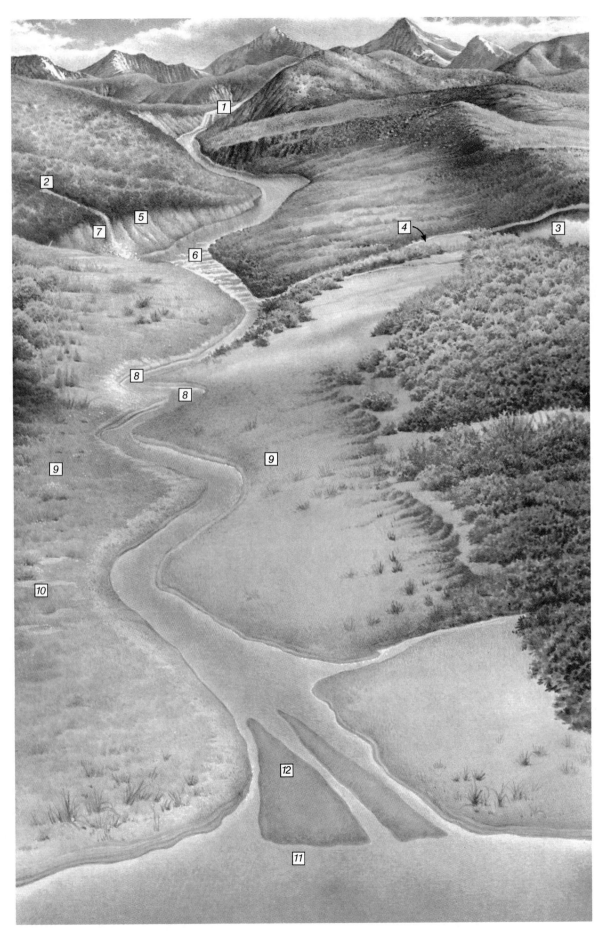

► A portrait of a river, this painting shows many of the primary features of a typical river. The river begins at a source—here, a melting glacier (1) high in the mountains. From its source, the river flows swiftly downhill, cutting a narrow valley. Smaller streams flow into the river from springs (2) and lakes (3), and are called tributaries (4). Where the river and its tributaries tumble over rocks and down steep bluffs (5), rapids (6) and waterfalls (7) occur. Farther downstream, as its slope levels out, the river begins to flow more slowly. Then it winds from side to side, forming meanders (8). It gradually widens, and builds a broad floodplain (9). As it nears the ocean, the river may form a marsh (10). Near the ocean, the river gradually drops the heavy load of sand, silt, and clay it carried from upstream. These sediments form an area of flat, fertile land at the mouth of the river (11), called a delta (12).

► *Famous for its scenic beauty, the Rhine River flows past vineyards, castles, and old villages such as this one—Bacharach, West Germany.*
▼ *Fishermen on the Volga River in the Soviet Union haul in sturgeon, source of fish eggs for caviar.*

a current. A swift current can move even large boulders. These break apart and the pieces carried in the moving water scrape and dig into the river bottom, or bed.

Little by little, a river tears away rocks and soil and carries them downstream, carving a narrow V-shaped valley. Rapids and waterfalls are common to young streams, particularly near their sources, or headwaters. The processes by which a river slowly wears away the land are called weathering and erosion.

Gradually, the river flows down to lower land. As the slope of its course flattens, the river cuts less deeply into the bottom of its channel. Instead, it begins to wind from side to side in looping bends called meanders. This action widens the river valley.

At the same time, the river begins to drop some of the rocks, sand, and other solid material it collected upstream. This material is called sediment. Once the sediment is deposited, it is called alluvium. Because alluvium may contain a great deal of eroded topsoil from upstream and from the outside banks of its meanders, a river deposits very fertile soil on its floodplain.

Near the end of its journey, the river slows and may appear to move sluggishly. It has less energy to cut into the land, and it can no longer carry a heavy load of sediment. Where the river meets the ocean or a lake, it may deposit so much sediment that new land is formed. This land is called a delta.

► *Tower Bridge spans the River Thames in London, England. The river winds past many historic buildings on its way through the ancient city, including the Tower of London and the Houses of Parliament.*

▲ *The Pearl River flows through Canton, a major port in southern China. For centuries, the busy river has been a trade route serving the city.*

Rivers of Europe and Asia

In every part of the world are rivers that have greatly influenced the lives of people. Many of these rivers have played a major role in various cultures for thousands of years.

The longest river in Europe is the Volga. It flows 3,685 kilometers (2,290 mi) across the Soviet Union and empties into the Caspian Sea. A major waterway for centuries, the Volga is used to transport many raw materials, including timber from northern forests and grain from farms along its valley, as well as manufactured goods. The river is also known for its sturgeon, large fish whose eggs are used to make a famous delicacy—Russian caviar.

The Thames in England is one of Europe's most historic rivers. Along its banks stands the city of London, with such famous landmarks as the Houses of Parliament and the Tower of London. By A.D. 100, London had already become an important Roman settlement and trading post that commanded the

▲ *At sunrise, elephants plod into the Ganges River at Sonpur, India, for a morning bath in preparation for an annual fair held along the river.*
◀ *A worshiper lights candles along the river. Millions of Hindus attend religious festivals on the Ganges each year.*

▼ *Sportsmen fish for salmon on the Upper Humber River in Newfoundland, in Canada. Recreation on a river can include canoeing and other sports.*

Thames. Because of its location on the river and near the seacoast, London became England's principal city and trade center.

Europe's busiest river is the Rhine, which runs from the Swiss Alps through West Germany and the Netherlands into the North Sea. It flows through many manufacturing and farming regions and carries barges laden with farm products, coal, iron ore, and a variety of manufactured goods.

Asia's longest and most important river is the Yangtze, in China. It flows from the mountains lying between Tibet and Qinghai Province to the East China Sea. The Yangtze is not only a highway for trade but also an agricultural river. Its valley is a major rice-growing region, and its water is used to irrigate the fields. Many Chinese live on the river in houseboats or in sailboats called junks.

The Ganges is the greatest river on the Indian subcontinent. It is sacred to the millions of followers of the Hindu religion. Since long before the time of Christ, Hindus have worshiped the river as a goddess. To them, the river is Ganga Ma, Mother Ganges. Hindus believe the river's water purifies the soul and heals the body.

Rivers of North and South America

In North America, rivers served as highways first for Indians and then for European explorers. French explorers began traveling the St. Lawrence and other rivers of Canada

▲ *Cargo ships and barges travel on the Mississippi River near New Orleans, Louisiana. Located near the river's mouth, the city is one of the world's busiest ports.*
◄ *The Chicago River flows through Chicago, Illinois. The city depends on the river for a transportation link between the Great Lakes and the Mississippi.*
► *Steep walls of the Grand Canyon rise above the Colorado River in Arizona. After millions of years, the river continues to cut its way through layers of rock, carving out the canyon.*

in the 1500s. They found an abundance of fish and other wildlife, and they encountered Indians who hunted beaver and other game. The explorers took beaver pelts back to Europe, where they were used in making hats. Soon, networks of rivers in North America were traveled by hunters in search of pelts. The establishment of trading posts along the rivers later opened the way into the continent for settlers.

The St. Lawrence River is still a major waterway. Linked to the Great Lakes by the St. Lawrence Seaway—a series of canals, locks, dams, and lakes—the river is a route into the interior of the continent for oceangoing ships.

The Mississippi is the chief river of North America. Its name, given to it by Indians, means "big river." The Mississippi flows 3,766 kilometers (2,340 mi) through the heart of the United States from Minnesota to Louisiana and the Gulf of Mexico.

Spanish and French explorers first traveled the Mississippi in the 1500s and 1600s. In 1803, the United States bought the land of the Mississippi River Valley from the French in the Louisiana Purchase. After that, the Mississippi was widely traveled by traders and settlers on rafts, keelboats, and flatboats.

With the introduction of the steamboat, a new era began on the Mississippi. Steam paddle wheelers carried trade goods up and down the river. Soon, workboats were joined by luxurious passenger vessels on which gamblers and elegant ladies and gentlemen traveled. Writer Mark Twain, who had been a river steamboat pilot, described this era in his book *Life on the Mississippi*.

Over time, the Mississippi increased in importance as a trade route. Today it carries cargo ships and barges in long lines that may extend for more than a kilometer. Large quantities of petroleum, coal, and other heavy, bulky, and nonperishable goods are conveyed on the river by massive barge trains pushed by powerful towboats.

The Colorado River is famous for forming the Grand Canyon in Arizona. For millions of years, the river has cut its way down through layers of rock to carve the canyon. Long ago, the river flowed through a flat plain. Then the earth's crust began to rise, uplifting the land. The river began cutting into the land much as a river in its upper course cuts a deep valley. The Grand Canyon is now about one and a half kilometers (1 mi) deep in one place and is as wide as 29 kilometers (18 mi).

Of all the rivers in the world, the greatest in terms of water volume is the Amazon in South America. It begins as an icy stream high in the Peruvian Andes and then flows east through Brazil to the Atlantic Ocean. The river has more than a thousand tributaries. The map on page 461 compares the area of the drainage basin of the Amazon with the area of the contiguous United States.

The amount of water flowing through the Amazon is greater than the amount carried by the Mississippi, the Yangtze, and the Nile

▲ *Canoeists paddle up the Vaupés River in Colombia. This river is a tributary of the Amazon, which drains six countries.*
▼ *Harnessed for energy, the Paraná River rushes through Itaipú Dam on the Brazil-Paraguay border. The flowing water generates electricity.*

together. The Amazon carries nearly one-fifth of all the river water in the world.

The first Europeans to see the Amazon were Spanish explorers, who traveled it in the 1500s. They encountered a group of Indians who all appeared to be women, or so the story goes. The explorers called the Indians "Amazons," after female warriors described in Greek mythology. The name "Amazon" was later given to the river.

For much of its course, the Amazon flows through the world's largest tropical rain forest. The region has abundant and unusual wildlife, including fierce flesh-eating fish called piranhas; huge fish called pirarucus, which grow to weigh more than 125 kilograms (275 lbs); and giant snakes called anacondas.

▲ Clear blue waters of the Xingu swirl into the cloudy brown Amazon where the two rivers meet in Brazil. Vegetation and suspended sediments give the Amazon its color.

► High in the Andes in Peru, the Apurímac River, headwaters of the Amazon, snakes between cloud-swept peaks. From its source, the Amazon courses 6,437 kilometers (4,000 mi) to the Atlantic.

▼ Largest river system on the earth, the Amazon drains a basin that covers an area equal to three-fourths of the contiguous United States.

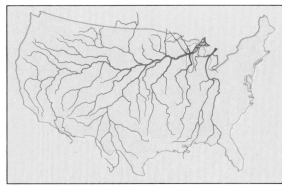

On another South American river, the Paraná, the Itaipú Dam is capable of producing an enormous amount of electricity—some 12,600 megawatts. Construction of the dam, on the Brazil-Paraguay border, required the labor of thousands of workers and cost more than 12 billion dollars. The huge reservoir formed by the dam supplies water for drinking and for irrigation.

Rivers of Africa and Australia

Africa's two largest rivers are the Nile and the Zaire, or Congo. One branch of the Nile, the White Nile, flows from tiny streams in the mountains of Burundi into Lake Victoria, Africa's largest lake. The other branch, the Blue Nile, begins in Lake T'ana. The two join at Khartoum, in Sudan. The Nile then flows through the desert lands of Sudan and Egypt, and into the Mediterranean Sea.

Along the Nile in Egypt, one of the earliest civilizations in the world developed. The ancient Egyptian civilization arose about 5,000 years ago, and its beginning was directly related to the Nile. Each year, the river overflowed, spreading rich black sediment across its broad floodplain. This made the land very fertile. Without the river and its floodplain, Egypt would have been just another barren part of the Sahara. With it, early Egyptian farmers were able to grow plentiful crops. These ancient people called their land Kemet, which means "Black Land," because of the rich black soil deposited by the river. They used the Nile as a major transportation route as their civilization flourished.

From papyrus, a tall reed that grew in the

river marshes, Egyptians made paper as well as rope, cloth, and baskets. Egyptians also built great cities, temples, and monuments along the river, including tombs for their kings, or pharaohs. Many of these ancient monuments still stand.

Today, Egyptians control the flow of the Nile with dams. The largest, the Aswan High Dam, has formed a huge reservoir that provides water for irrigating farmland and for generating electricity.

The Zaire River flows across the middle of Africa through a huge equatorial rain forest. Along parts of its course, the river is known as the Congo. In the country of Zaire, the river is the principal highway for carrying goods. Boats traveling the river range from dugout canoes to large freighters. The river supplies an abundance of fish. Fishermen use baskets and nets hung from high poles across rushing falls and rapids to catch the fish.

Much of Australia is arid. Its principal rivers are the Murray and the Darling, in the southeastern part of the continent. The Murray courses some 2,590 kilometers (1,610 mi) from the Snowy Mountains to a lagoon on the southern coast. Near the town of Mildura the

▲ Small boats sail along the Nile River near Aswan, in Egypt. Since ancient times, Egyptians have used the Nile as a travel and trade route.
◄ Waters of T'īs Ābay Falls cascade from Lake T'ana in Ethiopia, the source of the Blue Nile, a branch of the Nile.
► In Zaire, a fisherman uses baskets to catch fish at rushing Boyoma Falls on the Zaire River.

Murray is joined by the Darling, which flows some 2,735 kilometers (1,700 mi) from the highlands of the eastern coast.

By the mid-1800s, farmers had settled along both rivers and along some of their tributaries to raise sheep and cattle. Riverboats began plying the waters, and towns grew up along the banks.

Much of Australia's farmland lies within the Murray-Darling basin, where river water irrigates some 1.2 million hectares (3 million acres). The region is the chief supplier of the country's leading agricultural exports—wool, beef, wheat, and oranges and other fruit.

Polluted Rivers

For centuries, people have depended on rivers for many things. Rivers have provided waterways for shipping, building sites for cities, and fertile land for farming. Yet the extensive use of rivers has contributed to their pollution. The pollution has come from dumping of garbage and sewage; disposal of toxic wastes from factories; and runoff of rainwater containing chemical fertilizers and pesticides used in agriculture.

By the 1960s, many of the world's rivers were so polluted that fish and other wildlife could no longer survive in them, and their waters were unsafe for drinking, swimming, and other uses. Since then, stricter laws in many countries, including the United States, have helped to clean up polluted rivers. The laws have restricted the substances factories can put into rivers, banned toxic pesticides such as DDT, and required treatment of sewage to remove some pollutants.

Although the situation in some parts of the world has improved, serious problems remain. These include problems with long-lasting and extremely toxic chemicals still found in river water years after their use in industry and agriculture. In parts of the United States, Canada, and Europe, there is also the severe problem of acid rain. Acid rain develops when gases and chemicals from factory smokestacks and automobile exhaust pipes mix with moisture in the air and form acids. These acids fall in rain and other precipitation on streams and lakes, polluting water and killing wildlife.

Environmentalists and governments are

trying to understand and solve these pollution problems. Many people have come to realize that to provide safe drinking water as well as habitats where fish and other wildlife can thrive, rivers must be kept clean.

SEE ALSO AGRICULTURE, BASIN, CURRENT, DAM, DELTA, FLOOD, FLOODPLAIN, IRRIGATION, POLLUTION, RAPIDS, SEDIMENT, SOURCE, SPRING, STREAM, TRANSPORTATION AND COMMUNICATION, TRIBUTARY, VALLEY, WATER CYCLE, WATERFALL, *and* WEATHERING AND EROSION.

▲ *A riverboat chugs down the Murray River in southeastern Australia. Water from the river irrigates more than a million hectares of farmland and pastures.*
▼ *On the Australian island of Tasmania, the Gordon River curves through lush rain forests and scenic mountains, part of a wild region protected as a national park.*

ROCK

Rock is the material that makes up most of the earth. The scientific study of rock is called petrology. The scientific study of the earth is called geology. By examining rocks, geologists learn about the physical history and composition of the earth, and the processes that shape and change our planet. The study of rocks also yields information about the earth's past climates and the development of life-forms. Fossils provide important clues to the earth's past. They are the preserved remains and traces of ancient plants and animals found in some rocks.

Scientists define rock as a natural substance—of either organic or inorganic origin—composed of solid mineral matter. This matter consists of crystals, which are substances whose chemical building blocks—units called atoms, ions, or molecules—are arranged in patterns that form three-dimensional solids. Some rocks are made of just one mineral. Pure marble, for example, is made up of a single mineral called calcite. Other rocks are combinations of minerals. Granite includes the minerals quartz, feldspar, and mica.

The interior of the planet is made up mostly of rock. Ocean basins and all continents and islands are made of rock. In many places, buildings, vegetation, soil, or water cover the solid rock that underlies the landscape. It is possible, however, to find large areas of exposed rock in cliffs, in streambeds, on mountains, in stone quarries, and in road cuts.

Rock was so useful to early humans and their ancestors that the first periods of human prehistory are sometimes called the Stone Age. Overhanging rock formations often sheltered hunting camps, and rocks in their natural shapes were among the first tools and weapons. Evidence from Africa's Olduvai Gorge shows that the inhabitants shaped rocks into specialized tools by about two million years ago. For thousands of years afterward, people of many places made rocks into items such as axes, spearpoints, and knives.

► *Some of the earth's oldest rocks are exposed in the Canadian Shield at Hudson Bay. They date back more than three and a half billion years.*

In North America, a refined type of spear-point, known as Clovis, was developed around 10,000 B.C. It was one of the first major revolutions in technology because it greatly improved efficiency in hunting. Certain kinds of rock, such as flint and obsidian, were so prized that they became long-distance trade items vital to some ancient economies.

Strictly speaking, many cultures, such as the Indian tribes of the Americas, had a Stone Age technology until more advanced groups introduced metal tools. Yet those earlier people, with their dependence upon rock, developed some of the world's most complex ancient civilizations.

After farming people first began living in permanent settlements in southwestern Asia about 10,000 years ago, many groups used rock to build houses, temples, defensive walls, and other structures. Romans perfected the use of concrete, a mix of sand, stones, water, and a binding material called cement, that could be poured and shaped. The great medieval castles and cathedrals and Renaissance palaces were built of rock. And just as they do now, people valued precious gems—such as diamonds, emeralds, and rubies—that come from rock.

Today, rocks remain useful substances. Granite and marble are still favored for construction. A versatile material, concrete is often used in buildings, dams, and highways.

▼ Geologic processes form and transform rocks in a sequence geologists call the rock cycle. During a complete cycle, molten rock becomes igneous rock, which slowly breaks down into sediments. These are compacted or cemented into sedimentary rock. Heat and pressure may transform these into metamorphic rock. When this melts and hardens, igneous rock forms again. Rocks do not always move through the full cycle.

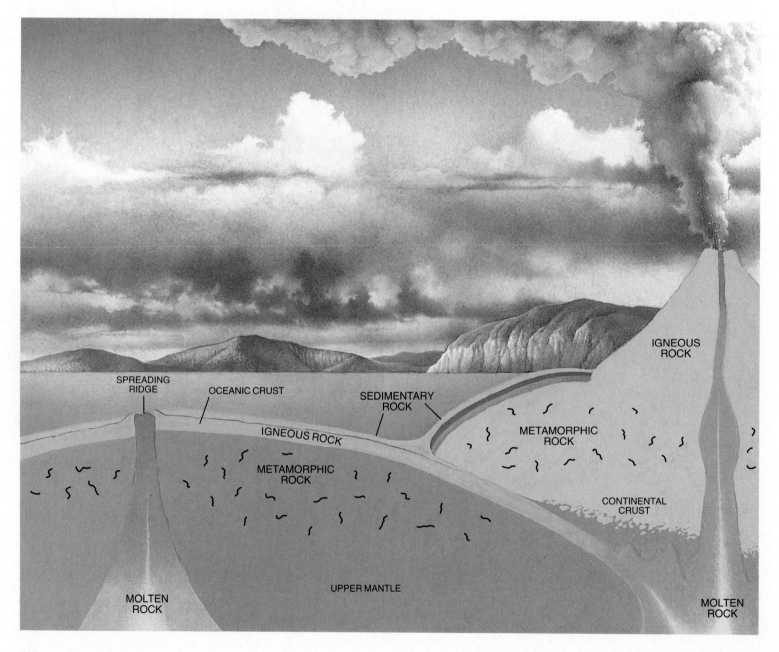

SPREADING RIDGE

OCEANIC CRUST

SEDIMENTARY ROCK

IGNEOUS ROCK

IGNEOUS ROCK

METAMORPHIC ROCK

METAMORPHIC ROCK

CONTINENTAL CRUST

MOLTEN ROCK

UPPER MANTLE

MOLTEN ROCK

Deposits of such resources as oil, coal, and natural gas are found in rock. Some rocks contain deposits called ores from which valuable and useful minerals such as tin, copper, and iron can be extracted.

The Three Kinds of Rock

Rocks are found in a variety of shapes, colors, textures, and sizes. But geologists put each rock into one of three categories: igneous, sedimentary, or metamorphic.

Rocks are classified into the three groups according to how they were formed. Igneous rocks form from molten material called magma. Most sedimentary rocks are formed from compressed or cemented particles of sand, silt, mud, and the remains of living things such as shellfish, corals, and plants. Metamorphic rocks form when igneous, sedimentary, or pre-existing metamorphic rocks are changed by heat or pressure inside the earth. The crust of the earth is made up of a mixture of these three kinds of rock.

▲ In Iceland, a waterfall plunges over a wall of igneous rock. Called organ-pipe basalt, these six-sided columns formed as a lava flow cooled. Virtually all of Iceland's rocks are volcanic.

Igneous Rocks

The term "igneous" comes from the Latin word for fire. Igneous rocks form from fiery-hot molten material that originates far below the earth's surface. The material is called magma when it is underground and lava when it reaches the surface.

Scientists theorize that billions of years ago, as the earth was forming, the rocky materials of its hot interior began to separate. Heavier materials sank. Lighter ones floated upward and cooled, gradually forming a thin crust of igneous rock.

Eventually, the earth's materials were sorted into three main layers. Scientists believe the superhot core of the planet may consist of a solid iron-rich center surrounded by an outer layer of liquid. Around the core is the mantle, a thick layer of mostly solid rock. The planet's outermost layer is called the crust.

The crust and the brittle top portion of the mantle are together known as the lithosphere, which means "sphere of rock." Geographers frequently use this term when describing the earth's physical environment. There are also spheres of water (hydrosphere), of air (atmosphere), and of life (biosphere).

Magma forms within the lithosphere. Because the molten material is hotter and lighter than surrounding rock, it tends to rise toward the surface of the earth. The rising magma may melt rocks above it, or it may flow upward into the crust. As magma moves toward the

▲ Granite blocks surround a tent beside Bighorn Lake in California's Sierra Nevada. Granite is an igneous rock. It forms when magma, or molten rock, solidifies deep within the earth. Erosion may later expose the rock, as it did here.

▲ On a volcanic island in Indonesia, a boy examines hardened lava that was ejected during an eruption of the volcano Anak Krakatau— "Child of Krakatau."

surface, it begins to cool and to crystallize into igneous rock. The rate of cooling influences the size of the mineral crystals that form. Slow cooling results in the formation of large crystals, and fast cooling allows only small crystals to form. Mineral crystals commonly found in igneous rock include sodium and potassium feldspars.

Because molten material cools at different rates, depending on whether it is underground or on the surface, the appearance of igneous rock varies widely. Granite forms from slowly cooling magma far below the surface. Its mineral crystals are large enough to be easily seen and give the rock a coarse-grained appearance. Huge areas of granite make up parts of all the continents. Granite may be exposed at the surface when layers of

other rock above it are broken down and worn away by weathering and erosion.

Rhyolite is one of several kinds of igneous rock that form from lava. Though rhyolite has the same mineral composition as granite, its appearance is quite different: It is very fine-grained. This is a result of the rapid cooling of the lava that formed it. Lava may flow great distances and cover huge areas, but it cools much more rapidly than bodies of underground magma do.

Basalt is the most common volcanic rock. It forms from very fluid lava and is the major component of volcanic islands, which rise from the ocean floor. It also forms the oceanic crust and can be found in some parts of the continental crust.

Obsidian is another kind of igneous rock

▼ *Long ago, geologic forces pushed up the Colorado Plateau, shown in cross section in the painting below. As the land rose, rain, rivers, and ice cut into its horizontal strata, exposing some of the earth's history in successive layers of sedimentary rock. In the process, spectacular landforms were carved, including Bryce Canyon (below left) and Zion Canyon (below right), both in southern Utah.*

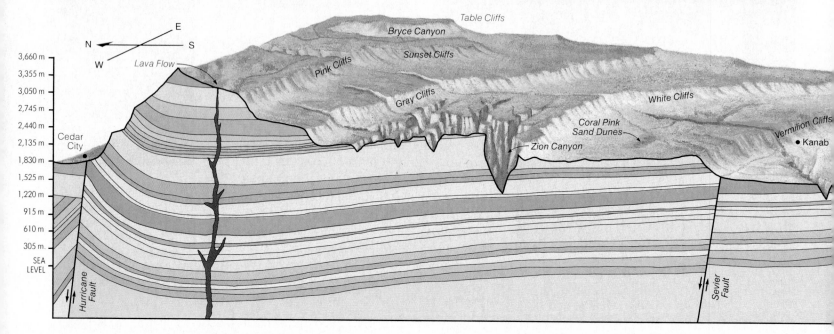

that forms when lava pours from a volcano and cools very rapidly. It is actually a kind of smooth, shiny, dark-colored glass. The rapid cooling inhibits crystal formation and causes the rock's glassy texture.

In contrast, an igneous rock called pumice forms when gases escape from cooling lava that has burst from a volcano. The escaping gases leave tiny holes, producing igneous rock that looks like a sponge and is often light enough to float.

Pluton is the general term for an underground formation of igneous rock. Plutons occur in many sizes and shapes. The largest of these masses, called batholiths, may have areas of several thousand square kilometers and form the cores of mountains.

Magma that creeps upward along deep cracks cutting across older rock layers forms sheets of igneous rock called dikes. Magma injected parallel to surrounding layers forms sheets called sills.

Batholiths, dikes, and sills may eventually be exposed by weathering and erosion. Along the western bank of the Hudson River is a line of steep cliffs called the Palisades. Extending several kilometers through southeastern New York and the northeastern part of New Jersey, the cliffs are an exposed sill about 300 meters (985 ft) thick.

Volcanic formations may also occur in several shapes. For example, very fluid basaltic lava may cool into rock formations that to some resemble coils of rope. Underwater, such lava forms pillowlike shapes. Thicker lava flows may produce rough and jagged

▼ *Lake Powell, a body of water in Utah and Arizona created by a dam, fills part of Glen Canyon (below left). Sandstone exposed in upper Glen Canyon also forms the bottom of Bryce Canyon to the west. For some ten million years, the Colorado River has been cutting deep into the plateau, sculpturing Arizona's Grand Canyon (below right). Rocks in the canyon's deepest part formed almost two billion years ago.*

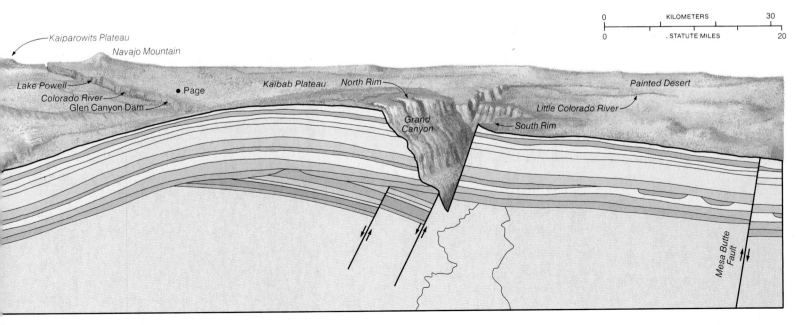

rocks. Some sills and flows of very hot lava may produce formations of column-shaped rocks. As the surface of a lava flow cools and contracts, long parallel cracks perpendicular to the surface may develop within the hardening lava. The result is a mass of tightly spaced columns, each having from five to seven sides. The usual shape, however, is six-sided. Devils Postpile, in California, formed as a result of this process.

Sedimentary Rocks

Sedimentary rocks are formed mostly of debris from the weathering and erosion of rocks on the earth's surface. During weathering, rocks are subjected to freezing and thawing, and they break down into small particles called sediment. The agents of erosion, primarily water, wind, and ice, carry the sediment, along with decayed remains of plants and animals, and distribute it over wide areas.

Sediment may be deposited in valleys and rivers and on deserts, plains, and the seafloor. Year after year and layer by layer, sediment builds up. Over millions of years, the layers harden into rock. Geologists estimate that more than two-thirds of the rock exposed at the earth's surface is sedimentary.

The layers of sediment become rock

▲ *The Seven Sisters stand along the coast of southern England. The pale cliffs are composed of chalk, a sedimentary rock formed from accumulations of tiny sea organisms that lived millions of years ago.*
▶ *Morning sun brightens limestone cliffs in northwestern Montana. Over millions of years, layers in this formation were laid down as sediments in shallow seas. Later, geologic forces uplifted the rocks, creating escarpments.*
▶ *Layers of rock called strata, or beds, are characteristic of sedimentary rock formations. A road cut for Utah Highway 95 reveals a multitude of strata.*

through two processes: compaction and cementation. During compaction, the weight of overlying layers forces air and water from among the particles of sediment, slowly squeezing them together until they form rock. Cementation occurs when certain materials carried by water filter down through spaces in the sediment. The natural materials form a cement, filling spaces among the particles and gluing together bits of sand or other material to form rock.

There are many kinds of sedimentary rock. They differ according to the material they came from. Most limestone is formed chiefly of calcite, a mineral commonly found in seawater and in the shells of some water animals. Chalk is a kind of limestone made of the hard parts of ancient microscopic sea animals and plants. Sandstone is made of cemented sand, while conglomerate rock is composed of rounded fragments larger than sand grains—pebbles and gravel. Shale, the most abundant sedimentary rock, is a consolidation of silt, mud, or clay. Sedimentary formations hold all reserves of coal, oil, and gas, and most of the earth's groundwater.

In addition to holding a wealth of natural resources, sedimentary rocks also provide a wealth of information about the earth's past. From preserved remains called fossils, scientists can develop a picture of what the earth was like long before humans walked upon it. Fossils form a record of prehistoric life. Studying them reveals what kinds of animals once lived on earth and what types of plants grew. Each layer of sedimentary rock suggests what the environment was like at the time the sediment within it was deposited.

In Arizona's Grand Canyon, layers of sedimentary rock tell a tale nearly two billion years long. One rock layer indicates to geologists that a sea once covered the area where the canyon is today. Below that layer, older rocks contain evidence that rivers of fresh water once flowed through the area. Deeper in the canyon—and farther in the past—fossil marine life appears in the rocks again and indicates an even more ancient sea.

In undisturbed layers of sedimentary

◄ In Madagascar, rock needles 30 meters (100 ft) tall formed as rainfall over thousands of years dissolved much of a limestone deposit.

471

► *Workers in Carrara, Italy, quarry marble, a metamorphic rock, from a mountain. Metamorphic rocks develop from rocks that already exist. The form and structure are changed primarily by heat and pressure deep within the earth.*
▼ *In Australia, quartz veins run through schist, metamorphic rock with a layered appearance.*

rock, the deeper a layer lies, the older the rock in it is. "Reading" layers of sedimentary rock takes skill. The layers may be tilted, uplifted, or folded by pressures originating deep within the earth so that sometimes older rock rests atop more recently formed rock.

Metamorphic Rocks

The word "metamorphic" comes from two Greek words that mean "to change shape." The third kind of rock found on the earth is formed from one of the two other kinds or from older metamorphic rock. This kind of rock is igneous, sedimentary, or previously metamorphosed material that has been changed by heat and pressure deep within the earth, so that it becomes a different rock. The metamorphosis, or change, may result from the recrystallization of minerals in the original rock material or from the development of new minerals. Most of the oldest rocks on earth are metamorphic. These include an exposure of a rock called gneiss nearly four billion years old that is in Greenland. Intense metamorphism gives gneiss its coarse-grained appearance.

Though subjected to intense heat and pressure at great depths, metamorphic rocks remain solid even as their chemical and physical properties change. If they melt, they become igneous and are no longer metamorphic. As metamorphism occurs, new crystals slowly form. These crystals may be larger or smaller than those in the original rock. Under extreme pressure, minerals may bend and fold, creating patterns in the metamorphic rock. Marble, which results from the recrystallization of limestone, may contain colorful streaks or have a veined appearance. Builders often seek out such marble for use in walls, floors, and columns.

Plate tectonics contributes to the buildup of heat and pressure that produces metamorphic rock. The earth's rigid shell, or lithosphere, consists of huge slabs of rock called plates. Plate tectonics involves the constant movement and interaction of the giant slabs. Forces deep inside the earth cause the plates to grind together, bend, or pull apart. Friction from the grinding together of rocks located at plate boundaries and along breaks in the plates generates heat, and this may cause the minerals in rocks to recrystallize. The pressure that plate tectonics exerts on rocks deep below the surface causes deformation, or changes in the size, shape, and overall appearance of the rocks.

Regional metamorphism occurs when the forces of plate tectonics slowly push up a large region of the earth's crust. This kind of metamorphism produces the most abundant metamorphic rock. Its effects are extensive, involving rocks at great depth and over a wide area. Mountain-building occurs as the crust crumples in response to tremendous pressures. As friction from the grinding together of huge masses of rock produces heat, it causes both chemical and physical changes in rocks. This results in metamorphic rocks that may have been igneous, sedimentary, or previously metamorphosed rock.

Some changes in rocks result from contact metamorphism, which affects the rocks located next to pockets of fiery-hot magma rising into the crust. The heat from the pockets of magma causes minerals in the surrounding rock to recrystallize. Even minerals several hundred meters away from the magma may be affected and changed. Over time, the magma hardens into a large mass of igneous rock. Geologists call the zone of metamorphic rock around the hardened magma an aureole—a word originally meaning "radiant light"—because it surrounds the igneous rock somewhat like a halo. Metamorphic aureoles often contain valuable metal-bearing

▲ *Some rocks are of organic origin: They contain material that once was part of living organisms. Coquina (top) is made of the cemented shells of clams and other marine animals. Coal is sedimentary rock that formed from the compressed remains of ancient swamp plants.*

ores, from which useful metals such as tin, copper, or lead are extracted.

The Rock Cycle

You may live in a community that recycles newspapers, bottles, and cans. The old materials are broken down and re-created in another form. In nature, rocks are also transformed. This process is called the rock cycle. The complete cycle takes rocks from their original igneous form, through a sedimentary stage and a metamorphic stage, and back to igneous rock again.

Here is how a rocky piece of crust might travel through the cycle, following one possible route out of many. The rock originates as part of a mass of magma deep within the crust. The magma rises, cools, and hardens into a granite batholith—an igneous rock formation below the ground.

Over time, weathering and erosion break down and wear away the surface materials,

▼ *In Arizona's Petrified Forest National Park, a visitor examines petrified wood. Ancient trees, buried in sediment, became fossilized as minerals slowly replaced the living material, cell by cell.*

exposing the granite mass. Water and ice wear down the mass, and fragments wash to the ocean, where they are deposited as sediment. Bits of rock and other sediment are cemented together, forming sedimentary rock.

Millions of years pass, and pressure builds up as tectonic plates collide. Layers of sedimentary rocks near the plate edges are compressed, broken, and folded. Mineral and structural changes occur. The sedimentary rock is now metamorphic rock.

The rock that began as magma has moved through the cycle as igneous, then sedimentary, and now metamorphic rock, but the rock cycle is not yet complete. A large mass of high-temperature magma may rise through the crust and come in contact with the metamorphic rock. The metamorphic rock then melts and hardens into igneous rock, completing a journey through the rock cycle. The same material may then move through the slow cycle of transformation once again.

It is also possible that rocks may not move all the way through the cycle. An igneous rock may become magma again. An exposed metamorphic rock may be broken down into sediment, which in turn can harden into sedimentary rock. Pressure may turn an igneous rock into a metamorphic rock. Sedimentary rocks may be melted directly into magma. It is very common for weathered and eroded sedimentary rocks to produce sediment, which in turn re-forms into sedimentary rock, which may then be broken down again.

The rock cycle began billions of years ago as earth cooled and its rocky crust formed. The surface of the earth has been changed again and again by weathering and erosion. The erosion process moves rock fragments and mineral grains. Sedimentary deposits build up and wear down. Tectonic activity changes igneous and sedimentary rocks into metamorphic rocks. Earth movements carry rocks down into the earth where they are melted. Day-to-day differences may not be visible, but the rock cycle continues.

SEE ALSO BEDROCK, CONTINENT, CORE, CRUST, DIKE, EARTH, FOSSIL, FOSSIL FUEL, GEOLOGY, LAVA, LITHOSPHERE, MAGMA, MAGNETISM, MANTLE, MINERAL, MINING, MOUNTAIN, OCEAN, ORE, PLATE TECTONICS, SEDIMENT, VOLCANO, *and* WEATHERING AND EROSION.

◄ *The Rock of Gibraltar, a limestone mass 426 meters (1,398 ft) high, towers over the Strait of Gibraltar, which connects the Atlantic Ocean and the western Mediterranean Sea. Not as solid as it appears, this well-known landmark is riddled with caves.*

ROTATION

While the earth revolves around the sun, it also rotates, or spins, on its axis, an invisible line running from Pole to Pole through the center of the planet. A rotation, one complete turn, takes approximately 24 hours.

The earth's moon, the other planets, and the stars also rotate on their axes, but at differing speeds. A single rotation equals one planetary day. A complete revolution around the sun equals one planetary year.

SEE ALSO AXIS, EARTH, REVOLUTION, and TIME AND TIME ZONES.

RURAL AREA

The term "rural area" describes a countryside used chiefly for agriculture, either now or in the recent past. The word "rural" may describe the life-styles and activities of people in such an area. For example, most people in rural areas worldwide have jobs related to agriculture. They may actually farm the land, or they may supply goods and services to those who do. Hamlets, villages, and other small settlements are considered rural places.

Usually, the difference between a rural area and an urban area is clear. But in developed countries with large populations, such as the United States and Japan, the difference is becoming less clear as more and more people move from cities to outlying areas. In the United States, settlements with 2,500 inhabitants or more are defined as urban. In Japan, which is far more densely populated than the U.S., only settlements with 30,000 people or more are considered urban.

Throughout the world, the dominant pattern of migration within countries has been from rural to urban areas. This is partly because improved technology has decreased the need for agricultural workers and partly because cities are seen as offering greater economic opportunities. Most of the world's people, however, still live in rural areas.

SEE ALSO AGRICULTURE, CITY, MIGRATION, POPULATION, URBAN AREA, and VILLAGE.

▲ Ayers Rock, a sandstone monolith in central Australia, looms over the surrounding desert. The rock is sacred to the Aborigines, the people who first inhabited Australia.
► Devils Tower, in Wyoming, is a rock tower of volcanic origin. The eroded column of solidified magma rises 264 meters (865 ft) above the countryside.
◄ Stone Mountain, in Georgia, is a granite mass that was formed underground and exposed by weathering and erosion. A memorial to Confederate heroes is carved into the rock.

S

SAVANNA

A savanna is a tropical grassland with clumps of grasses and widely scattered trees. Savannas are found in the warm, tropical regions of the world where rainfall is highly seasonal; a prolonged dry season alternates with a rainy season. The grasses and trees occur in varying proportions depending largely on the amount of rain a savanna receives. The longer and more intense the dry season, the sparser the tree growth is.

Savanna grasses are well adapted to the seasonal cycles. For example, in the rainy season the savanna region of the Serengeti Plain of East Africa is transformed from dusty brown to green as new growth springs up almost overnight. After the rainy season, vegetation above the ground withers quickly, but the parts of the plants below the ground continue to soak up any available moisture.

Fires caused by lightning or people sometimes rage across a dry savanna. Fires help maintain grasses as the dominant vegetation in savannas and in other grasslands.

SEE ALSO CLIMATE, FIRE, *and* GRASSLAND.

▲ *Acacia trees, common in tropical grasslands, are scattered throughout the African savanna in and around Tanzania's Ngorongoro Crater.*

SEA

People often use the term "sea" in referring to the ocean, the vast body of salt water that covers nearly three-fourths of the globe. To geographers, though, a sea is a division of the ocean that is enclosed or partly enclosed by land. Using this definition, there are more than 50 seas; many of them are around Europe and in the western Pacific Ocean.

Enclosed seas reach deeply into continents and are connected with the open ocean by narrow passages of water called straits. Seas of this type include the Mediterranean Sea, the Baltic Sea, and Hudson Bay. Because such seas are almost landlocked, they have a small range of tides or no tides at all. And since there is little exchange of water between an enclosed sea and the open ocean, the two may differ from each other physically, chemically, and biologically. The Red Sea, for example, is saltier than the Indian Ocean.

Partly enclosed seas are more like the open ocean, especially in the circulation of their waters. Some, such as the Weddell Sea

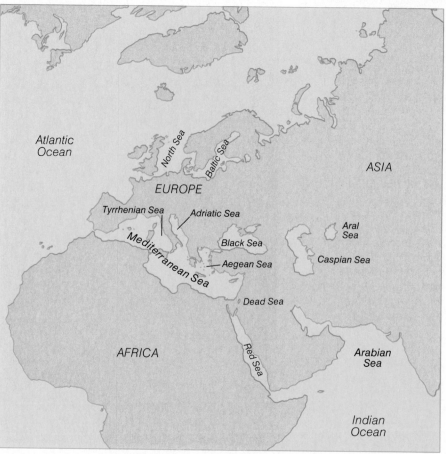

SEA LEVEL

Because the ocean is one continuous body of water, its surface tends to seek the same level throughout the world. However, winds, ocean currents, river discharges, variations in gravity, and temperatures of the different water masses prevent the sea surface from becoming level. These effects vary from one place to another and over time.

So that the surface of the ocean can be used as a base for measuring elevations, the concept of local mean sea level has been developed. In the United States and its territories, local mean sea level is determined by taking hourly measurements of sea levels over a period of 19 years at various locations and then averaging all of the measurements.

The 19-year period is called a Metonic cycle. It enables scientists to account for the long-term variations of the tides that are caused by variations in the moon's orbit. It also averages out the effects of local weather and oceanographic conditions.

Changes in Sea Level

The volume of water in the ocean may vary with changes in climate. During past ice ages, sea level was much lower because the climate was colder and more water was frozen in continental glaciers. At the peak of the most recent ice age, about 18,000 years ago, sea level was perhaps 100 meters (330 ft) lower than it is today.

If the climate becomes warmer, remaining glaciers in Antarctica and Greenland could melt, and sea level would rise. Global warming would also cause the ocean waters to expand, further raising sea level. Coastal areas around the world could be flooded.

Sea level is measured in relation to the adjacent land, which may also be rising or falling. For example, the tremendous weight of ice on land might push the land down. That same land might rise if the ice retreats and its weight is removed. Thus, local mean sea level measurements are a combination of sea level variations and vertical movement of the land.

SEE ALSO CLIMATE, ELEVATION, GREENHOUSE EFFECT, ICE AGE, ICE SHEET, OCEAN, *and* TIDES.

▲ *On Thíra, one of the Greek islands, terraced houses overlook the Aegean Sea, an arm of the Mediterranean.*
► *Picnickers enjoy the beach on the Gulf of Aqaba, an extension of the Red Sea, as ships take on cargo at Jordan's only seaport.*
◄ *Many seas touch or are contained by the continents of Europe, Asia, and Africa. Bodies of salt water completely surrounded by land, such as the Aral and the Caspian Seas, do not have access to the ocean, but still are known as seas.*

of Antarctica, and the North Sea, are linked to the ocean by a wide opening. Others, such as the South China Sea and the Sea of Okhotsk in the western Pacific, are connected with the ocean by passages between islands. All of these seas have a large range of tides.

Some bodies of salt water that are called seas are really lakes. They are completely surrounded by land and have no access to the ocean. Among them are the Caspian Sea, between Iran and the Soviet Union, and the Dead Sea, between Jordan and Israel.

SEE ALSO LAKE, OCEAN, *and* STRAIT.

SEAFLOOR SPREADING

Seafloor spreading occurs along the Mid-Ocean Ridge, an immense mountain range rising from the ocean floor. A deep central rift, or crack in the earth's surface, runs along the crest of the ridge, marking a boundary between huge rocky slabs called plates that form the earth's rigid shell. Geologists believe that the earth's plates are always moving. At the ridge, the plates are moving slowly apart, causing the seafloor to spread. Molten rock rises from the earth's interior and fills the growing gap between the plates. Seawater cools and hardens the material into a band of new seafloor, which is eventually split in two by the moving plates. Each plate carries its portion of new seafloor away from the central rift. The formation of new seafloor is balanced by the destruction of old seafloor in the ocean trenches that mark subduction zones. In these zones, the edge of one plate subducts, or dives, beneath the edge of another. The seafloor on the subducting plate may melt in the earth's hot interior.

SEE ALSO CONTINENTAL DRIFT, MAGNETISM, PLATE TECTONICS, RIFT VALLEY, TRENCH, and VOLCANO.

▲ New seafloor forms along the Mid-Ocean Ridge. Here, the rocky plates that make up the earth's shell slowly move apart. Molten rock wells up between the plates, hardens, and is carried away by the plates as if on conveyer belts.

SEASONS

Seasons are periods of the year that are distinguished by special climatic conditions. Spring, summer, autumn, and winter follow one another regularly, each with its special light, temperature, and weather patterns that repeat themselves yearly. The seasons in the Northern Hemisphere are the opposite of those in the Southern Hemisphere, and not all parts of the earth have four distinct seasons.

The changing seasons occur because the earth, tilted on its axis, orbits the sun. Thus, the plane of the Equator is tilted with respect to the plane of the earth's orbit. Since the earth is always tilted in the same direction, the latitude at which the sun appears directly overhead at noon changes as the earth orbits the sun. The sun appears to follow a yearly pattern of northward and southward motion in the sky. If the equatorial plane and the orbital plane were the same, the sun would always be directly overhead at noon to an observer at the Equator, and there would be no change of seasons. However, since the planes are tilted about $23\frac{1}{2}$ degrees from each other, the latitude at which the sun appears directly overhead at noon varies throughout the year between about $23\frac{1}{2}°$N, the Tropic of Cancer, and about $23\frac{1}{2}°$S, the Tropic of Capricorn.

Following centuries of tradition, astronomers divide the year into seasons according to equinoxes and solstices. The equinoxes occur when the earth reaches the points in its orbit where the equatorial and orbital planes intersect, causing the sun to appear directly overhead at noon at the Equator. During equinoxes, the periods of daylight and darkness are nearly equal all over the world. One equinox occurs about March 21. In the Northern Hemisphere, this is the spring equinox. In the Southern Hemisphere, this is the autumn equinox. The other equinox occurs about September 23. This is the autumn equinox in the Northern Hemisphere and the spring equinox in the Southern Hemisphere.

► People living in the earth's mid-latitudes generally experience four distinct seasons. Living things respond to seasonal variations in sunlight and temperature, but few react as colorfully as sugar maples, like these in Connecticut.

The solstices occur at points in the orbit where the sun's vertical rays reach their maximum northern or southern latitudes. The solstice occurring about June 22 is the summer solstice in the Northern Hemisphere and the winter solstice in the Southern Hemisphere. The sun's vertical rays strike the Tropic of Cancer, and the Northern Hemisphere has its longest period of daylight, and the Southern Hemisphere its shortest period of daylight. About December 22, the other solstice occurs, and the sun's vertical rays strike the Tropic of Capricorn. This is the winter solstice in the Northern Hemisphere and the summer solstice in the Southern Hemisphere.

The climate conditions that distinguish one season from another change at varying times from place to place and are not tied to the days on which solstices and equinoxes occur. Spring flowers often come and go in Savannah, Georgia, for example, long before the ice melts in Minneapolis, Minnesota. The warmest or coldest temperatures may come several weeks after a solstice. The seasonal climate changes are due in part to the earth's tilt, which causes the periods of daylight and the angle of the sun's rays to vary at different latitudes throughout the year. Wind patterns, topography, and other factors help determine seasonal climate conditions.

Areas in the mid-latitudes generally experience the most seasonal variations in climate. In the low latitudes, especially around the Equator, the seasonal changes are not as noticeable. The angle of the sun's rays year-round is more direct at these latitudes than at higher latitudes. The more direct rays help cause warm daily temperatures that change little during the year. In the tropics, the seasons may vary in amount of rainfall, a situation that is linked to the earth's position in relation to the sun. Rainfall varies greatly in some poleward parts of the tropics, so there may be just two climatic seasons: dry and wet.

Around the polar regions, the angle of the sun's rays is slanted year-round. Thus, though daily temperatures may vary greatly throughout the year, they are generally colder there than on most of the earth. The amount of daylight changes dramatically between summer and winter. Each Pole is tilted toward the sun during spring and summer. Consequently, there are about six months of daylight at

each Pole because the sun does not drop below the horizon. In autumn and winter, each Pole is tilted away from the sun. There are about six months of darkness because the sun never rises above the horizon. Away from the Poles, differences in the periods of daylight and darkness become less extreme.

SEE ALSO AXIS, CLIMATE, EQUATOR, EQUINOX, POLAR REGIONS, SOLSTICE, *and* WEATHER.

◄ *Throughout history, stargazers have found ways to mark the turn of the seasons. At summer solstice, the sun will cast the shadow of a nearby rock across the center of this spiral carved centuries ago on a stone in Arizona.*
▼ *In England, on the day of the summer solstice, the sun rises over a stone marker at Stonehenge, one of many structures scientists speculate were built to track the changing of the seasons.*

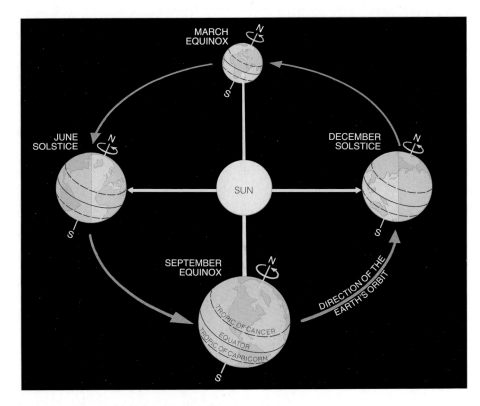

As the earth orbits the sun, the planet is always tilted in the same direction. This tilt causes the sun's vertical rays to strike different latitudes on the earth as it revolves around the sun. On the days when an equinox occurs, the earth is at a point where the plane of the Equator intersects the plane of the earth's orbit, and the sun's vertical rays strike the Equator. On solstice days, the sun's vertical rays reach their northernmost and southernmost points. At noon on the day of the June solstice, the sun appears directly overhead at the Tropic of Cancer. At noon on the day of the December solstice, the sun appears directly overhead at the Tropic of Capricorn.

SEDIMENT

Sediment is the solid matter that water, ice, and wind—the agents of weathering and erosion—transport and deposit. Sediments may contain particles of rocks and minerals, as well as the remains of plants and animals. Sediments range in size from tiny bits of clay and silt to boulders.

When the movement of water, ice, or wind slows, sediments settle out and are left behind. Where rivers overflow their banks, the sediments they are carrying are deposited in layers on the floodplain. Where a stream slows as it meets a standing body of water, such as a lake or a sea, sediments are dropped, forming a delta. Sedimentary deposits often enrich the soil, making it fertile and suitable for farming.

Over millions of years, layers of sediment may build up and harden into sedimentary rock. Among the sedimentary rocks are sandstone, shale, chalk, and limestone. Sedimentary rock covers much of the earth's surface.

SEE ALSO DELTA, FLOODPLAIN, RIVER, ROCK, SILT, *and* WEATHERING AND EROSION.

Suspended sediment creates a ribbon of color as currents carry it along a shoreline. Eventually the material may form a deposit large enough to rise above the water and extend the coastline.

SEISMOLOGY

Seismology is the scientific study of earthquakes. Geologists called seismologists study the seismic waves, or vibrations, caused by movements of rocks in the earth's solid shell. They record and analyze the waves using sensitive instruments.

When rocks under great stress beneath the earth's surface suddenly shift or break, energy that was stored in the strained rocks is released as seismic waves, which race away from the place where the movement began. The waves travel outward in all directions the way ripples move outward when a pebble is dropped into a pond. When seismic waves reach the earth's surface, they shake the ground, sometimes violently. When earthquakes shake the ocean floor, they may cause tsunami, or seismic sea waves.

Seismic waves can be recorded by an instrument called a seismograph. A seismograph is anchored to the ground. When the earth moves during an earthquake, a device suspended within the seismograph makes lines on paper or film. These lines make a record of the quake called a seismogram. The seismogram reveals how much energy was released at the quake's focus, the place where the earthquake began. Seismologists analyze seismograms to find out where an earthquake began, how strong it was, and how long it lasted.

They also use the data to learn about the internal structure of the earth. As seismic

▲ *A seismologist monitors equipment at Cascades Volcano Observatory in Vancouver, Washington. The rotating drums record seismic activity, which could signal upcoming eruptions at Mount St. Helens, a volcano in the Cascade Range.*
▼ *Along the San Andreas Fault in California, sensitive equipment detects movement of the earth. Seismologists gather important data from a device that measures changes in the tilt of the ground.*

waves move through the earth, they speed up or slow down depending on the density, or compactness, of the rock they move through. Waves move faster through dense rock than they do through less compact rock. Some waves cannot penetrate liquid rock at all. By studying a seismogram, seismologists can determine the speed of the waves and the kinds of rocks the waves passed through.

A new method called seismic tomography, a kind of earth X ray, produces images of the inside of the earth. Using seismograms and tomographic images, geologists hope to learn more about the earth's structure.

SEE ALSO EARTH, EARTHQUAKE, GEOLOGY, RICHTER SCALE, TSUNAMI, *and* VOLCANO.

SETTLEMENT

Any place where people live is a settlement. It can be a campsite, an isolated house, or a large city. Nomads set up temporary settlements as they move their herds or hunt game. Settlements can be classified as either nucleated or dispersed. Nucleated settlements have buildings grouped together, as in towns. Scattered farmhouses are examples of dispersed settlements.

SEE ALSO CITY, RURAL AREA, TOWN, URBAN AREA, *and* VILLAGE.

SHELTER

Three basic human needs are generally considered to be food, clothing, and shelter. A shelter is a place that provides protection. Shelters serve several purposes. They shield us from heat and cold, wind and rain, and also from dangerous animals and violent forces of nature. Without shelter, humans would not survive very long except in a few places where the climate is always mild. Shelters that people use as dwellings provide comfort, privacy, security, and enjoyment. They are places where family and friends gather and where possessions are stored. Our dwellings are central to our daily lives.

Bands of hunters may have built the first human shelters as long as 50,000 years ago. The shelters were dome-shaped huts made of animal bones and hides. Today, a similar type of simple, temporary dwelling made of branches, leaves, and grass shelters the San people, or Bushmen, nomadic hunters of southern Africa. As the development of agriculture encouraged settled life in some areas about 10,000 years ago, farmers built permanent dwellings for themselves, as well as shelters for livestock and for storing crops.

Often, the intended use of a building influences its size and shape. For example, kings and nobles built palaces to entertain large numbers of people and to display wealth and the trappings of power. Huge covered arenas shelter athletes and spectators during sports events. Neither type of building,

▲ *Traditional Icelandic barns use natural insulation. Set into the ground and roofed with thick sod, they give protection against cold and heat.*

▼ *Western Samoans relax in their tropical thatch-roof house. Rolled mats under the eaves can be lowered to keep out hot sun and seasonal rain.*

▲ *A domed cistern keeps water cool in hot, dry central Iran. Wind towers like those flanking the cistern are also used to cool homes. Air moving in the towers produces refreshing breezes indoors.*

though, would serve the purpose of the other.

People usually erect shelters in styles their cultures prefer. Three other factors may also influence the type and form of a building: climate, available materials, and natural hazards. We can see examples throughout the world. In some hot, dry countries of Africa, mud houses have thick walls and narrow windows to keep out sunlight. Houses in areas that receive a lot of snow usually have steep roofs so that snow will slide off. Houses in places that are often cold and windy, such as the mountainsides in Switzerland, frequently have thick walls and sturdy roofs. In parts of Yucatán in Mexico, many houses have thin pole walls to let cool breezes pass through, and thick thatch roofs of leaves or grass that give protection from heavy seasonal rains. Because of dampness, floods, and tides,

people in parts of Indonesia, India, and the Amazon basin in South America build dwellings on stilts. Tree houses in Borneo, Malaysia, and the Philippines have ladders that can be pulled up to keep out unwanted visitors and dangerous animals.

In developed countries, people do not depend entirely upon local building materials. Supplies such as wood and metal are often shipped from far away. With central heating and air-conditioning, climate does not always determine types of shelter. More often, economic means and personal tastes control such decisions. High costs of land, especially in urban areas, have made apartment buildings near work centers a practical and convenient type of dwelling.

We can learn a great deal about societies from studying the buildings that shelter them. Usually, their large structures show what is most important to them. In a primitive settlement, the house of a chief is likely to be the largest. During the Middle Ages in Europe, castles and cathedrals rose highest. Today, tall office buildings used by government and business dominate many city skylines.

SEE ALSO ANTHROPOLOGY, CITY, *and* CULTURE.

▲ *A servant sweeps the walkway of a grand Argentinian ranch house. A thriving cattle industry means luxurious life-styles for landowners here. Above, a simple mud-and-stone house typifies farm dwellings in the African country of Lesotho.*

▲ *Modern garden-style apartments built by Israelis cover a hilltop on the West Bank of the Jordan River. As populations increased over time and land became more valuable, dwelling styles changed. They generally evolved from isolated houses to homes clustered together to the dense complexes of today.*
◄ *On a bend in the Seine River, the French village of Le Petit Andeley preserves a dwelling style of past centuries. Individual houses cluster near the church and community buildings.*

SIERRA

A sierra is a high mountain range, such as the Sierra Nevada in California, with jagged peaks that resemble the teeth of a saw. The Spanish word *sierra* means "saw." Large, moving masses of ice called glaciers carved out the sharp peaks characteristic of a sierra.

A sierra begins to form when the leading edge, or head, of a valley glacier plucks tons of rock from the highest part of a mountain valley. This hollows out a bowl-shaped depression called a cirque.

In areas where glaciers carve out several cirques, high, isolated peaks called horns may be left, or a sharp ridge may form. Glaciers also sculpture jagged, knife-like ridges called arêtes. A sierra is a series of these sharp horns and ridges.

SEE ALSO GLACIER, MOUNTAIN, *and* WEATHERING AND EROSION.

SILT

Silt is a type of solid matter, called sediment, that water, ice, and wind transport and deposit. Silt is made up of particles of rock and mineral grains that are larger than clay but smaller than fine sand. Individual silt particles are so small that they are difficult to see. To be classified as silt, a particle must be less than .005 centimeter (.002 in) across. Along with clay, sand, and gravel, silt is found in soil. Soil itself is called silt if its silt content is greater than 80 percent. When deposits of silt are compressed and the grains are cemented together, rocks such as siltstone form.

Silt results when water and ice cause rocks to crumble. As flowing water transports the rock fragments, they scrape against the sides and bottoms of streambeds, chipping away more rock. The particles grind against each other, becoming smaller and smaller until they are silt-size.

Silt—along with other sediments such as sand and gravel—can change the landscape. For example, deposits of silt slowly fill in wetlands, lakes, and harbors. Floods deposit silt along riverbanks and on floodplains. Deltas develop where rivers deposit silt in the ocean. Some 60 percent of the Mississippi Delta is made up of silt. In some parts of the world, windblown silt blankets the land. Such deposits of silt are known as loess.

SEE ALSO DELTA, FLOODPLAIN, LOESS, RIVER, ROCK, SEDIMENT, SOIL, *and* WEATHERING AND EROSION.

▲ *Silt and other sediments thicken the Huang (Yellow) River, in China. This restless river often floods. It has changed course perhaps 26 times.*

SINKHOLE

A sinkhole is a hole in the ground that occurs where limestone, a type of rock that is readily dissolved by water, lies beneath the surface. Sinkholes are often funnel-shaped. Where rainfall is plentiful, water collects in cracks called joints in the limestone. Slowly, as the rock dissolves and is carried away, the joints widen, forming sinkholes. Sinkholes also form when the roofs of caves collapse.

Sinkholes vary from shallow holes about one meter (3 ft) deep to pits more than 50 meters (165 ft) deep. Water drains through a sinkhole into an underground channel or a cave. When mud or debris plugs a sinkhole, it fills with water to become a lake or a pond.

SEE ALSO CAVE, GROUNDWATER, KARST, ROCK, *and* WEATHERING AND EROSION.

▲ *Divers prepare to explore a dangerous sinkhole in Australia. The hole extends below the ground at a sharp angle, plunging 20 meters (66 ft) deep.*

SLEET

Pellets of frozen rain are called sleet. It forms when rain falls through a layer of air near the ground that is below freezing. This condition exists when warm air is forced up over cold air. Sleet is already solid when it falls to earth, whereas freezing rain does not freeze until it strikes the ground. Unlike hail, sleet freezes from the outside in. A mixture of rain and snow is sometimes called sleet.

SEE ALSO HAIL, PRECIPITATION, *and* RAIN.

SMOG

Originally the term "smog" referred to a mix of smoke and fog. Now smog includes pollutants such as ozone, sulfur dioxide, and nitrogen oxides. These are irritants to humans and other animals, and can kill plants. Smog was more common in industrial cities before governments began controlling pollution emissions. In 1952, more than 4,000 people in London, England, died from respiratory ailments aggravated by smog that covered the city for a week.

Today, smog refers to any pollution that reduces visibility. Photochemical smogs, common in Los Angeles, California, form when nitrogen oxides given off as automobile exhausts react in sunlight to produce a brown, irritating haze.

SEE ALSO FOG *and* POLLUTION.

▼ *Mexico City is barely visible through thick smog. Pollution from factories and millions of cars combines with dust to produce what may be the world's foulest air.*

SNOW

Snow is precipitation composed of ice crystals. A single snowflake is a complex ice crystal. Snow appears white because snowflakes act like prisms, scattering light in all directions. Snow crystals come in an infinite variety of types—plates, starlike shapes, columns, needles, and more. Most snow crystals are hexagonal, or six-sided, because of the way water molecules align when they freeze. Temperature and humidity in the cloud where the crystals form determine which type the snow crystals will be.

Snow forms in the extremely cold upper reaches of clouds. At the center of every snowflake is a microscopic freezing nucleus, on which supercooled water vapor can collect, freeze, and form a snow crystal. Once the crystal forms, it grows by collecting more supercooled vapor, by colliding with tiny water droplets, or by merging with other snow crystals. The flake eventually becomes heavy enough to fall to earth. If the air temperature near the ground is below freezing, snow falls. If not, the snowflakes melt and it rains. Except in the tropics, nearly all rain comes from snow that melts as it falls through warm parts of the atmosphere. The largest snowflakes form when the temperature is around freezing.

SEE ALSO CLOUDS, PRECIPITATION, RAIN, and WEATHER.

▲ Industrial pollution, windblown dust, and fog rolling in from the Pacific Ocean all contribute to the smog covering Arequipa, a city in southern Peru.

▲ Heavy snow falls on a stand of trees in Wyoming. Usually ten centimeters (4 in) of dry snow equals only one centimeter (0.4 in) of rain.

▲ Magnified snowflakes show the hexagonal shape common to most snow crystals.

SOCIALISM

Socialism is an economic system based on the idea that a government should use its power to distribute the society's wealth equally. Countries with largely socialist economies include Israel, Sweden, and Norway.

Socialism arose in Europe in the 19th century. Ever since, socialists have disagreed on how to bring about greater economic equality. Utopian socialists founded experimental communities to share wealth. Other socialists, called communists, argued that a workers' revolution was needed.

A moderate type of socialism called democratic socialism evolved in Western Europe. Its supporters advocated government ownership of industry. Socialist governments took over, or nationalized, steel mills, railroads, automobile factories, and other industries. Today, this policy is being reversed.

Democratic socialists helped secure government assistance for unemployed, disabled, and elderly people, and national health services to provide care for all citizens.

SEE ALSO COMMUNISM and ECONOMY.

SOIL

Soil is the layer of mineral and organic material that covers most of the earth's land surfaces. Though their compositions vary, soils usually contain plant roots, living animals, plant and animal remains, air, water, and minerals weathered from rock.

Soil is made by the slow, continuous physical and chemical breakdown of rock and by the decay of organisms that were once alive. Soil is dynamic. It evolves constantly as the proportions of its mineral, organic, air, and water content change. Soil provides nutrients to environments such as grasslands, croplands, and forests, which supply people and other life-forms with food and shelter. The fertility of a soil is determined by its capacity to supply plants with the nutrients they need to grow.

There are many kinds of soils. Soil scientists, called pedologists, have designed classification systems to identify the kinds of soils found around the world. A soil classification system used in the United States and increasingly in many other countries was developed by the U.S. Department of Agriculture. This system divides soils into ten major orders, or kinds. The map on pages 490–491 shows which orders predominate in different parts of the world. The chart on page 490 describes the characteristics of the ten orders. The name of each order has the same ending, -sol, which comes from the Latin word *solum,* meaning "soil."

◄ *A Costa Rican farmer plants potatoes while his companions till the earth with the help of a team of oxen. The soil in this field is enriched with nutrients contained in ash that erupted from a volcano.*
► *Plant roots play an important role in soil conservation. By helping to anchor the soil, they hinder its erosion by wind and water. Soil in turn provides nutrients that plants absorb through their root systems.*

SOIL ORDERS OF THE WORLD

ALFISOLS are commonly found in mild climates. Crops grow easily in these productive soils because alfisols contain large amounts of base nutrients—chemicals that help make soils fertile. A light-colored surface layer covers a subsurface layer of clay in alfisols.

ARIDISOLS are the chief soils of deserts and other arid lands. They cover one-fifth of the earth's land surface. Lacking plant and animal matter, they commonly have a sandy texture and are light-colored. Aridisols in some areas may be suitable for farming if irrigated.

ENTISOLS are new soils. They have not been in place long enough to develop layers. Entisols are found on recently exposed surfaces such as floodplains and sandhills. Their productivity varies.

HISTOSOLS are found throughout the world, but in limited quantities. They are usually saturated with water and do not drain well. Histosols contain partially decomposed plant matter and are acidic. The dark, water-logged soils of the Scottish moors are histosols.

INCEPTISOLS are often found on former valley floodplains and on other stable land surfaces in which soil layers are developing. These soils are starting to form a subsurface layer of clay.

MOLLISOLS are the most fertile and productive soils. In the United States, they are found mostly in the wheat and corn belts of the Midwest. Mollisols are known for their dark, mineral-rich surface layer. This thick layer has large amounts of base nutrients and is full of humus, or decomposed plant and animal matter.

OXISOLS are found mainly on weathered, or broken up, land surfaces in tropical areas. Nutrients have been leached, or washed, out of them. This kind of soil has a subsurface layer full of iron and aluminum.

SPODOSOLS, which do not hold moisture well, are infertile and acidic. Commonly found in New England, they have a pale surface layer and a dark subsurface layer in which plant and animal matter, iron, and aluminum have accumulated.

ULTISOLS have a light-colored surface layer and a reddish clay subsurface layer full of iron and aluminum. Although they are similar to alfisols, ultisols are found in warmer regions, such as the southeastern United States. With fewer base nutrients, ultisols are less fertile.

VERTISOLS contain large amounts of clay. They develop in a climate of alternating wet and dry seasons, like that of India. This kind of soil swells when wet and shrinks when dry, which causes cracking. Although they are fertile, vertisols are hard to cultivate because of their texture.

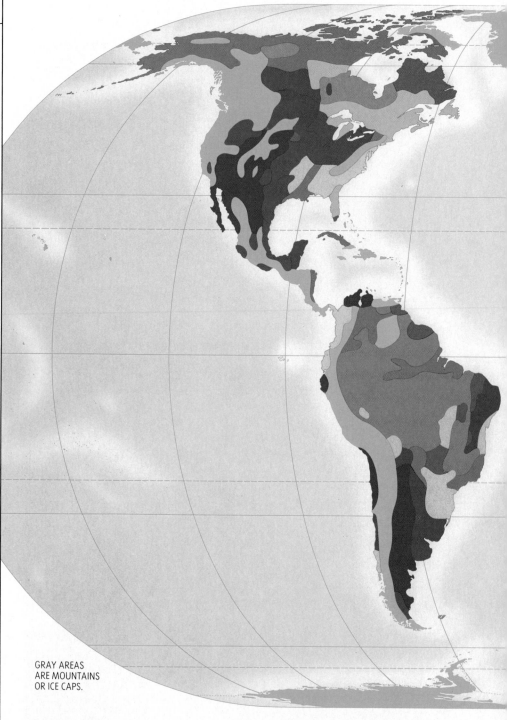

GRAY AREAS ARE MOUNTAINS OR ICE CAPS.

◀ *Soils have been classified into ten major orders according to their particular characteristics. These are determined by the parent material and the age of the soil and by climate, vegetation, and surface features such as mountains and valleys.*

Common Soil Characteristics

Soils in general are made up of four major components, or parts: minerals, organic matter, water, and air. These components are combined in a mixture of decomposing rock material and decaying plant and animal matter. The mixture contains openings called pores, which can hold water and air.

Pores make up about half of the volume of an average soil. Much of the rest of the

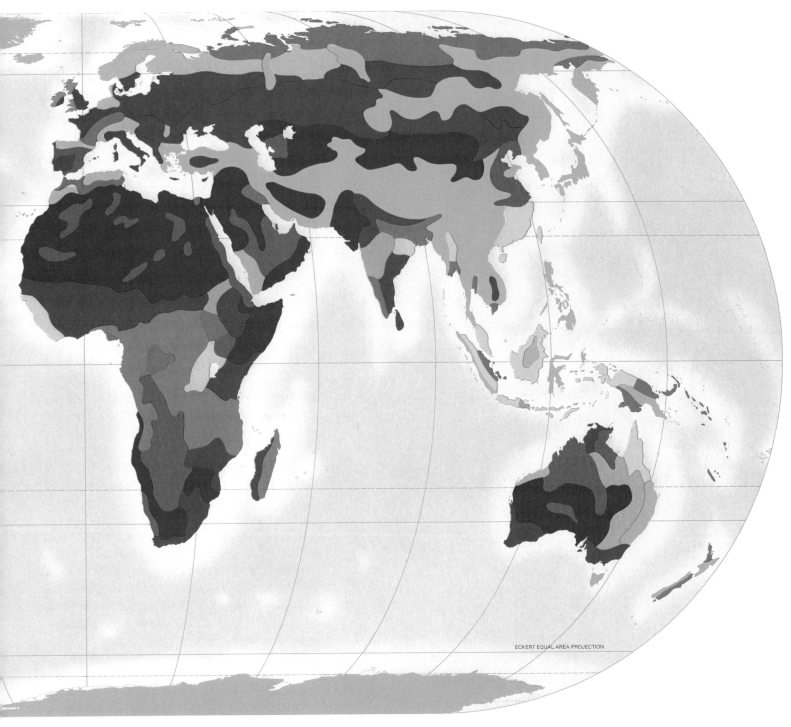

ECKERT EQUAL AREA PROJECTION

volume consists of mineral particles of varying sizes. The remainder of the soil, commonly ranging from one to twelve percent of the total volume, consists of organic matter, which includes decaying leaves, twigs, animal wastes, and the remains of dead animals, as well as a variety of living organisms.

An astonishing number of life-forms make their home in the soil. These include rodents, insects, worms, and microscopic bacteria. A single hectare (2.5 acres) of soil

may contain a million earthworms. Including billions of bacteria, the total number of organisms in one kilogram (2.2 lb) of soil is likely to exceed a hundred billion.

How Soils Differ

In classifying soils, pedologists identify ways in which soils differ. Color and texture help distinguish one soil from another. Pedologists recognize 175 color variations within

▲ This map shows the general distribution of the ten major soil orders. Aridisols are the most widely distributed. Mollisols, the most productive soils, are common to the central Eurasian grasslands, North America's Great Plains, and the pampas of Argentina.

▼ *Leaf litter tops a cross section of soil. A layer of humus, formed from the decaying remains of plants and animals, lies under the leaves. Below that is a layer of humus mixed with minerals.*

the basic soil shades of black, brown, red, yellow, gray, and white. Although color can provide clues to a soil's fertility, it can also be misleading. A dark soil often contains humus, an organic material that makes soil fertile. Infertile soil, however, like that formed from volcanic ash that is acidic, can also be dark. In some regions a red color indicates soil fertility. In other areas it may indicate leaching, the washing out of mineral nutrients, which results in an infertile soil.

The texture of a soil affects its fertility, its ability to hold moisture, and the ease with which it can be cultivated. Texture is determined by the sizes of mineral particles in the soil. Pedologists divide the particles into three groups. From largest to smallest, the particles are sand, silt, and clay. Sandy soils dry out quickly. Clayey soils are usually more fertile because they retain moisture and nutrients, but they are hard when dry and sticky when wet. Loams—mixtures of almost equal amounts of sand, silt, and clay—are fertile, retain moisture, and are easy to cultivate. In general, loams are the best soils in which to grow plants.

The age of a soil, the parent material from which it formed, climate, surface features, and vegetation contribute to differences in soils. The age of a soil—how long the soil has been forming—often affects its depth and fertility. The kind of parent material affects the chemical composition and texture of a soil. For example, when limestone is the parent material, the soil may be rich in calcium

▲ *In an idealized soil, the profile is well developed. A soil that has had time to develop all these layers is sometimes not very fertile because percolating water has carried nutrients below the reach of plant roots. Many soils have only some of the layers shown here.*

IDEALIZED SOIL PROFILE

O HORIZON The surface layer, made up of organic matter that is undecomposed or partially decomposed

A HORIZON A mineral layer, commonly called topsoil, containing an accumulation of decomposed organic matter in which most seeds germinate and grow

E HORIZON A layer consisting primarily of sand and silt particles with little clay, iron, aluminum, or organic content

B HORIZON A mineral-rich layer containing primarily clay particles, iron, and aluminum that have filtered down from the O, A, and E horizons

C HORIZON A layer beyond the normal reach of plant roots that is composed of weathered material from the underlying bedrock

R HORIZON A layer of solid rock, called bedrock or parent material, which is the basic source of all soil-forming materials

▶ *Bright-orange lichens make swirling patterns on rock in Nebraska. The plants produce acids that gradually etch tiny cracks in the rock. The development of cracks is one of the first stages in the breakdown of rock, which allows soil to form.*

and other essential elements. Shale, a fine-grained rock, can produce a smooth, clayey soil that resists penetration by water and air. Sandstone, on the other hand, can produce a loose, easily penetrated sandy soil that is low in fertility.

Climate may affect the speed with which some biological processes occur. Soil depths are usually greater, and plant growth and the decomposition of dead plants and animals often occur faster in warm, moist climates than in cool, dry climates.

Topography, or surface features, plays a role in the kind of soil that forms. On expanses of flat land, soils are usually deeper because of increased water movement through them. The water deposits minerals down through the soil, allowing soil to form at a rate exceeding that of wind and water erosion. On slopes, less water moves through the soil; erosion is greater; and soil layers remain shallower.

Soil Profiles and Soil Formation

The special characteristics of a soil are clearly visible in a vertical cut through the layers of a soil, from the surface to the underlying parent material. These observable horizontal layers are called horizons, and they make up what is called a soil profile. By examining its profile, pedologists can classify a soil.

A profile of an idealized soil would include several horizons, as shown in the illustration on page 492. The number and thickness of the horizons in a soil may vary, depending on factors such as climate, topography, and the age of the soil.

In an idealized soil, leaves, branches, and other debris on the surface of the soil make up the O horizon. After plants and animals die, they start decomposing in this layer.

The top layer of a mineral soil, called the A horizon, consists of plant roots, animals, and mineral fragments mixed with decayed organic materials. The A horizon, often called the topsoil, is the one from which plants receive most of their nutrients.

Beneath the A horizon is the E horizon. It is made up primarily of sand and silt particles. It is usually lighter in color than the A horizon because it has less organic material.

The next layer is the B horizon, which consists of mineral soil with a higher content of clay-size particles, as well as some organic matter. Some of the clay and organic matter has filtered down from the A and E horizons.

The C horizon is made up of partially weathered soil material and rock particles that have broken away from the underlying bedrock. This horizon has not yet been changed much by external weathering or by the biological activity of plants and animals.

Below the C horizon is the R horizon, where solid bedrock begins. The soil's minerals come from this parent material.

As parent material is exposed to air and the action of water, it slowly weathers, or breaks down. Bedrock may lie beneath the

▼ *A sample of Mississippi mud contains particles in the three basic sizes that give soil its texture. At the top is fine-grained clay. A mixture of large and small sand grains underlies the clay. Silt is found at the bottom.*

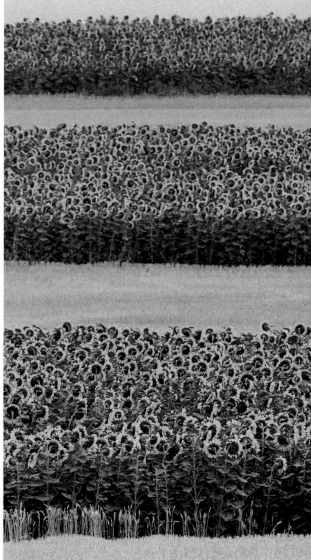

ground or protrude above the surface. Weathering produces a layer of loose rock fragments called regolith, from which a soil eventually forms. Tiny plant roots contribute to the creation of regolith by breaking up surface bedrock. The roots penetrate hairline cracks in the parent material, causing it to crumble.

The activities of living organisms contribute to soil formation. Bacteria, worms, insects, and other living things feed on organic material and excrete nutrients into the soil. After plants and animals die, their remains add still more nutrients. Their decay releases nitrogen, phosphorus, potassium, and other elements. Plants grow as they absorb these essential elements through their roots.

Organic material called humus is continuously forming from the decaying remains of animals and plants. Humus is often responsible for a soil's dark color. The crumbly texture of humus helps form the soil structure and loosens the consistency of the soil, allowing air and water to penetrate. Humus increases a soil's ability to hold water and helps cause chemical reactions that release nitrogen and other nutrients important to plant growth.

The burrowing of animals such as groundhogs, mice, termites, and especially earthworms opens up air passages in the soil. The animals' tunnels and trails provide paths for water. The animals help mix the various components of soil as they move through it.

The pull of gravity and the forces of wind, water, and ice are constantly moving soil and other surface materials from one place to another. This natural process is called erosion.

▲ *In an Ohio pasture, a farmer examines a pile of livestock droppings. Animal waste is a natural fertilizer. Plowed into the ground, it restores many nutrients such as nitrogen that help make soil fertile.*
▼ *Stone walls support terraces on a hillside in Washington State. For centuries, people have built terraces to allow farming on steep terrain. Terraces help retain water for crops and help keep runoff from removing rich topsoil.*

Some soils are deposited far from the rock that is their parent material. Volcanic eruptions, for example, may scatter ash across the land. Soils rich in sand, silt, and clay are carried by floodwaters and often are left on land when the waters recede. Many of the world's important food-producing regions, such as the Mississippi River Valley in the United States and the Ganges River Valley in India, are a result of the alluvial process, the depositing of soils by flowing water. Recently deposited soils are often very fertile because nutrients have not yet leached out of them. Not all eroding surface materials are deposited on land. Productive topsoil often washes away into the ocean.

Human Activities and Erosion

Accelerated erosion may be brought about by human activities and can cause excessive loss of topsoil. This can have catastrophic global effects. Since people first began farming, human activity has reshaped the natural landscape, making soil subject to overuse and quickened erosion. Digging mines, damming rivers, cutting forests, and plowing fields are all activities that contribute to soil erosion. The fundamental cause of such erosion is the removal of the natural vegetation that protects soil—the root systems of grasses, shrubs, and trees that anchor the soil, and the leaves and other litter that collect on the ground. Once the protective vegetation is gone, soil is quickly eroded by wind and water.

Excessive erosion can lead to choked streams and lakes, disrupting ecosystems that are homes to fish and other wildlife. When soils are depleted, crops are not as healthy. When crop yields decline, people may suffer from undernourishment or, in extreme cases, from starvation.

In cities and surrounding suburbs, soil has been lost through the construction of buildings, highways, and airports. Land tends to erode more quickly during construction, since vegetation is stripped away and natural drainage systems are disrupted.

In many developing countries, farmers often have to cultivate steeply sloping land that erodes easily. Farmers also try to grow crops in semiarid areas where plowed land

▲ Bands of sunflowers alternate with wheat on a North Dakota farm. This farming method, called strip-cropping, uses windbreaks such as trees and tall flowers to keep the wind from eroding the soil and damaging crops.
► A garden in New York City provides a floral landscape for urban dwellers. Cultivating the garden protects soil that would otherwise be blown away, paved over, or covered by rubble.

can blow away unless careful conservation methods are used. Indonesia, Ethiopia, and India are among the countries experiencing severe soil erosion. Agricultural experts estimate that India loses more than five billion tons of soil through water and wind erosion each year.

When water acts on the whole surface of a sloping field, the soil is sometimes removed in thin layers. The loss of topsoil through this process, called sheet erosion, may not be noticed by the farmer until the different-colored subsoil is exposed.

Soil Conservation

Most soils form over a long period of time. Like other natural resources, soil should be conserved so that supplies are not used faster than nature can replenish them.

Maintaining soil fertility is an important part of soil conservation. The natural fertility of a soil often changes, depending on the way the soil is used. Planting some crops year after year, for example, uses up nutrients in a soil, reducing its fertility.

Agricultural experts have developed many ways to conserve soil. In open country, farmers can plant shelter belts of trees to reduce the force of winds that blow across their fields. A shelter belt can slow strong winds

▼ Dark glasses protect a woman's eyes from windblown sand on a Texas farm (left). Wind has eroded the soil and reduced the fertility of the fields, whose furrows are filled with sand. Below, an abandoned truck sits half buried in sand. This desolate Texas landscape was once a flourishing farm. Poor land-management practices and changing weather patterns destroyed the fertile topsoil here.

to less than 21 kilometers per hour (13 mph) over a distance of up to 10 times its height. Winds below this speed do not cause erosion. Thus, winds blowing across a belt of evergreens 6 meters (20 ft) high will not erode soil for 60 meters (200 ft) on the other side.

In some areas, efforts are being made to keep farmers from plowing land that is unsuitable for crops, such as that of rain forests. When farmed, the soil in these forests rapidly loses its nutrients and becomes infertile.

To help reduce the erosion caused by mining, land can be replanted. Lumber businesses can plant cleared land quickly with grasses and trees. Grasses hold soil in place while trees begin to grow.

Reducing excess numbers of livestock grazing on grasslands helps retain vegetation and protect the soil.

Good Farming Practices

Good agricultural practices, such as planting nutrient-rich grasses, can both protect land from erosion and restore a soil's fertility. Legumes like alfalfa and clover not only anchor the soil but also transfer nitrogen from the atmosphere into the soil. Farmers can alternate a grain crop like corn with a legume from season to season so that nutrients can be returned to the soil. This practice is called crop rotation. The practice of plowing under nutrient-rich legumes and grasses before the next crop is planted is called green manuring. Adding decaying leaves and barnyard manure to a soil increases water retention.

Another effective erosion control method is contour farming—plowing, seeding, and harvesting fields across a slope instead of up and down it. Contour plowing lessens water runoff, so smaller amounts of soil are washed away during storms.

In some parts of the world, terracing is a method used in mountainous areas where farmland is scarce or rainfall is irregular. Small level patches called terraces are cut into the slopes, and walls or mud banks are built around the terraces so that water and soil can be retained. In the United States, the term "terrace" commonly refers to artificial ridges of soil that intercept surface runoff and allow excess water to drain slowly from a field.

Another practice that helps slow down

▲ Gullies scar a sloping field where water erosion has carried away valuable topsoil. Soil loss could be greatly reduced by terracing across the slope or by strip-cropping, in which alternating strips of vegetation hinder the downward flow of water.

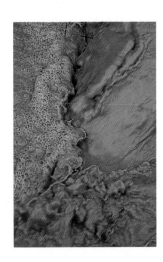

▲ Soil washed from fields colors a rushing stream a muddy brown. Water erosion can quickly remove unprotected soil that may have taken centuries to form.

▲ In Tennessee, two trees anchor a column of soil surrounded by heavily eroded land. The trees' extensive root systems preserved the soil by protecting it from the effects of wind and water.

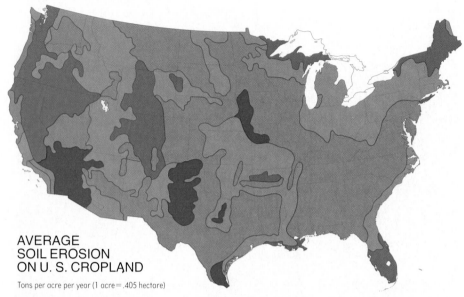

AVERAGE SOIL EROSION ON U. S. CROPLAND

Tons per acre per year (1 acre = .405 hectare)

▨	less than 2	▨	5-13.9
▨	2-4.9	▨	14+

Note: The maximum soil loss that the best deep soils can endure and still remain productive is 5 tons per acre per year. Shallower or more fragile soils may have lower tolerance levels. Severe erosion in the West is caused by wind. In the Midwest and East, it is caused by heavy precipitation.

SOURCE: SOIL CONSERVATION SERVICE NATIONAL RESOURCES INVENTORY, 1982

▲ Trash forms one layer of a Nebraska landfill. Only shallow-rooted plants such as grass grow in the soil above. The deeper roots of larger plants cannot easily penetrate the compacted trash.

erosion is called contour strip-cropping, in which alternating rows of different kinds of crops are planted across the slope of a field. This hinders the downslope flow of rainwater.

Plowed furrows can become small streams during a rainstorm, and tiny channels called rills may form. Planting close-growing crops, such as barley and wheat, can slow the erosion associated with rills and small gullies. Large gullies can be reclaimed by building dams of straw and manure or piles of brush reinforced with wire. After soil has filled in behind the dam, farmers can seed the area with grass and fast-growing shrubs and trees. In addition to anchoring the remaining soil in the gully, the vegetation provides shelter for birds and other wild animals.

Inspired by environmental groups, the United States has begun a successful effort to reduce soil erosion. During 1986 and 1987, soil erosion on U.S. cropland was reduced by 460 million tons, perhaps the largest annual reduction ever accomplished in the world. The program responsible for the savings involved converting 57 million hectares (140 million acres) of highly erodible cropland into grassland and woodland.

As more people become aware of the serious consequences of soil erosion, other programs like this one may be developed to help stop the rapid depletion of the world's soils.

SEE ALSO AGRICULTURE, CONSERVATION, DELTA, FERTILITY, FLOOD, GRASSLAND, HUMUS, NATURAL RESOURCE, POLLUTION, ROCK, SEDIMENT, and WEATHERING AND EROSION.

SOLAR ENERGY

Solar energy is created by nuclear fusion that takes place in the sun. Fusion occurs as particles of hydrogen gas collide in the sun's core. When the particles collide, they join, or fuse. Fusion occurs at extremely high temperatures and releases tremendous amounts of energy as heat and light. The sun is the original source of most of the energy used on the earth. Solar energy warms the earth, causes wind and weather, and sustains plant and animal life.

In less than an hour, enough solar energy reaches the earth to meet everyone's needs for a year. The challenge for scientists is to find ways of harnessing solar energy. In one method, the sun heats fluid stored in tubes within rooftop collector panels. As the fluid circulates throughout homes or other buildings, it radiates warmth for space heating. The fluid is also used to heat water.

Solar cells, called photovoltaics, convert sunlight directly into electricity. First used on spacecraft, photovoltaics are gaining in importance as a source of electricity on earth.

Solar energy is a promising alternative to coal, oil, and natural gas, which are considered nonrenewable resources. Solar energy is clean and comes from a source scientists say will last for at least five billion years.

SEE ALSO ENERGY, NUCLEAR ENERGY, and SUN.

▲ Solar collector panels on a rooftop in Tucson, Arizona, glitter in the sun. Heated by the sun's rays, fluid in the panels circulates throughout the house, providing heat and hot water. This method can also be used to heat swimming pools.

SOLAR SYSTEM

The sun is at the center of our solar system, a community of bodies including asteroids, meteoroids, comets, interplanetary dust, and nine known planets with their moons. All of these bodies circle the sun, the only star in our solar system.

The sun contains 99 percent of the mass in our solar system, which is mostly empty space. The planets and moons shine by the light they reflect from the sun; they do not radiate light of their own. Solar wind, made up of electrically charged particles of hydrogen and helium escaping from the sun, blows throughout the solar system.

Our solar system is part of a galaxy called the Milky Way, a vast system of stars 100,000 light-years across. A light-year, the distance light travels in one year, is approximately 9.46 trillion kilometers (5.88 trillion mi). Everything in the Milky Way, including the sun and 200 billion other stars, revolves around the galaxy's center. The Milky Way is one of many galaxies in the universe. The Large Magellanic Cloud, our galaxy's nearest neighbor, lies 170,000 light-years away.

Astronomers think that our solar system is about 4.6 billion years old. The system may have originated in an enormous cloud of gas and dust that collapsed into a spinning disk. Gravity pulled so much material toward the center that pressure and heat there lit a nuclear fire, and the sun began to shine. Other material slowly accumulated into clumps of solids and gases, which became the planets.

The Planets

There are nine known planets revolving at varying speeds around the sun. Earth is the only planet known to support life. Mercury, Venus, Earth, and Mars orbit closest to the sun. Known as the inner planets, they are all Earthlike in that they have rocky exteriors and are believed to have metal cores.

Jupiter, Saturn, Uranus, Neptune, and Pluto are the outer planets, separated from the others by a belt of asteroids. All but Pluto are gas giants. Tiny Pluto appears to be made mostly of ice. The large, gaseous planets are circled by rings of dust, ice, and other mate-

rial. All the planets except Mercury and Venus have one or more moons.

The planets orbit in the same direction; the closer they are to the sun, the faster they revolve. All but Pluto and Mercury move in nearly the same plane. Each planet rotates, or spins, on its axis. The axes of Mercury, Venus, and Jupiter are almost perpendicular to their

◄ *No one knows exactly how our solar system formed, but evidence suggests that it began when a dying star exploded violently about 4.6 billion years ago. The explosion left a vast spinning cloud of gases and dust, which developed a dense core as it contracted (top). The whole cloud rotated faster and faster until, about 10 million years later, the entire mass flattened, and its center grew intensely hot. The core became a nuclear furnace, forming a new star at the center of the rotating mass (middle). Away from the center, gases and solids accumulated and formed the planets, orbiting the star we call the sun.*

▼ *A robot arm prepares to collect soil samples on Mars. Space explorations like that of the U.S. Viking 1 mission to Mars will tell us much about the solar system's history.*

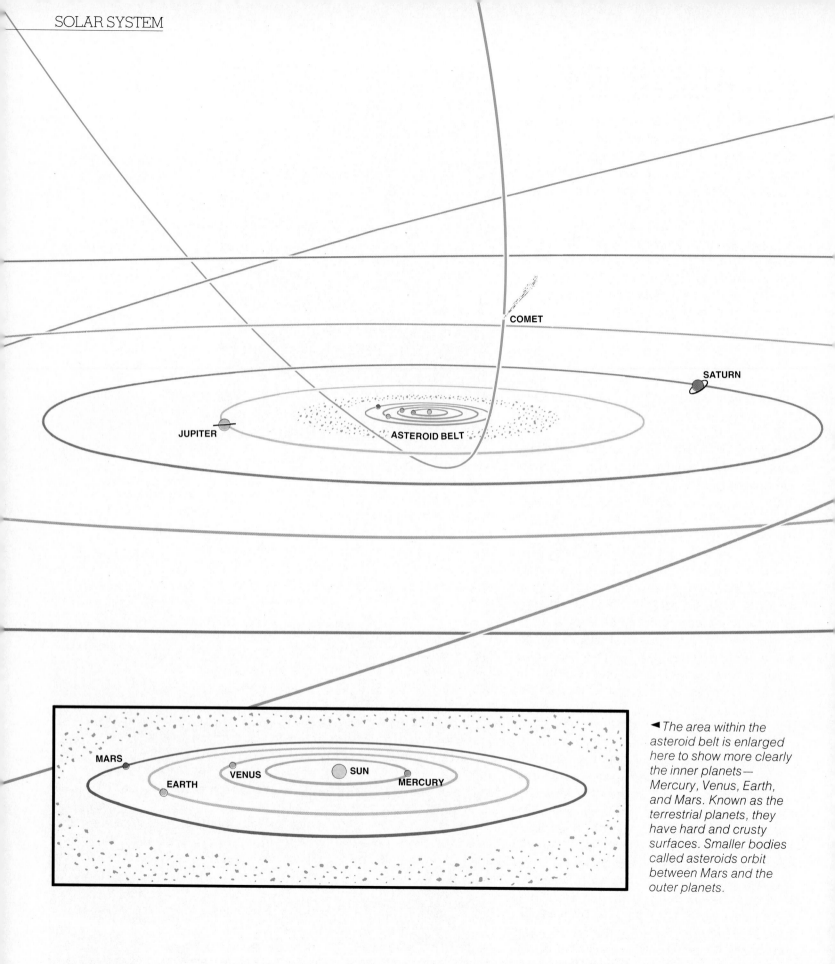

COMET

SATURN

JUPITER

ASTEROID BELT

◄ The area within the
asteroid belt is enlarged
here to show more clearly
the inner planets—
Mercury, Venus, Earth,
and Mars. Known as the
terrestrial planets, they
have hard and crusty
surfaces. Smaller bodies
called asteroids orbit
between Mars and the
outer planets.

MARS

VENUS   SUN

EARTH   MERCURY

PLUTO

NEPTUNE

URANUS

▲ *Four of the five planets orbiting beyond the asteroid belt are gas giants, much less dense than the inner planets. They need from 12 to 165 Earth years to complete one revolution of the sun. Pluto, a planet of ice, is the farthest from the sun and completes an orbit every 248 Earth years. A comet may take more than a million years to complete its orbit.*

orbital planes. The axes of the other planets are tilted to varying degrees. Earth's axis, for example, is tilted about 23$\frac{1}{2}$ degrees from the perpendicular to its orbital plane.

Each planet differs from the others in mass, gravity, and density. Mass is the measure of the amount of material that an object contains. Jupiter's mass equals 318 Earths. Earth's mass equals the mass of its moon, Mercury, Venus, and Mars together. The more mass a planet has, the stronger its gravitational pull. The density of a planet refers to how tightly its mass is packed. Two planets may have the same mass, but one will be smaller if it has a higher density.

Asteroids and Comets

Hundreds of thousands of rock and metal objects called asteroids, or planetoids, form

the asteroid belt between Mars and Jupiter. Asteroids, most of which are irregularly shaped, are usually less than a kilometer (0.6 mi) across. They can collide violently, breaking off chunks of debris that orbit on their own. The smallest chunks are called meteoroids.

Meteoroids range in size from sandlike particles to pieces of iron and nickel as large as a house. Sometimes a meteoroid passes through the earth's upper atmosphere. Friction caused by air resistance to its passage generates so much heat that gases surrounding the meteoroid glow brightly. The streak of light caused by a meteoroid is called a meteor. Most meteoroids that enter the atmosphere disintegrate before they reach the ground. Meteoroids that do strike Earth's surface are called meteorites. Scientists have studied meteorites and found they are made of material as old as the solar system.

Besides planets and asteroids, thousands of comets orbit the sun. A comet starts out as a nucleus of frozen gas and dust. As the nucleus approaches the sun, solar heat vaporizes some of the ice, creating a cloud of gas and dust around the nucleus. The cloud forms into a tail, which streams away from the sun throughout a comet's orbit. A comet's tail may extend millions of kilometers. Each time a comet passes close to the sun, it loses some of its mass. Some meteoroids are debris from a comet's tail. When Earth's orbit takes the planet through a comet's tail, a meteor shower may occur.

Some astronomers think billions of comets were flung out into a region beyond Pluto called the Oort Cloud while the sun and planets were forming. The Oort Cloud, named after the Dutch astronomer Jan H. Oort, is thought to be a collection of 100 billion orbiting comets. The cloud is about 3 trillion kilometers (2 trillion mi) away from the sun, in the farthest reaches of the solar system.

The gravitational pull of a passing star can snatch a comet from the Oort Cloud and fling it into a long, narrow elliptical orbit that brings it close to the sun. Some comets stay in this path, with one end of the long orbit near the sun and the other end in the Oort Cloud. Comet orbits extend deep into space, far beyond Pluto and the view of present-day telescopes. Some comets take more than a million years to complete one orbit.

Orbits may change as comets move through space because their paths are influenced by the gravitational forces of the planets they pass. For example, if a comet makes a close pass by Jupiter or Saturn, the gravitational tug from the planet may fling the comet out of the solar system.

Each year five to ten new comets are discovered. Comets with definitely established orbits are called periodic comets. The time it takes periodic comets to orbit the sun varies greatly, from about 3 years for comet Encke to about 150 years for comet Rigollet.

Space Explorations

Since 1957, when the Soviet Union launched the first space satellite, Sputnik 1, several countries have sent spacecraft on missions to explore our solar system and beyond. Technological advances in instruments have allowed astronomers to study other

galaxies in an effort to learn more about how our galaxy and solar system evolved. The Hubble Space Telescope will offer a view of the universe ten times clearer than was previously possible. Specialized instruments on the Cosmic Background Explorer (COBE) satellite will provide clues to the early days of the universe. Scientists hope the answers will lead to a better understanding of our planet, of the solar system, and of the universe.

SEE ALSO EARTH, GRAVITY, MAGNETISM, METEOROID, MOON, ORBIT, PLANETS, *and* SUN.

▲ *Telescopes with finely ground lenses and mirrors have expanded the power of the human eye, making it possible to explore the solar system and the universe. Simple ocular telescopes of the past evolved into powerful giants like this refractor at the Old Royal Observatory in Greenwich, England.*

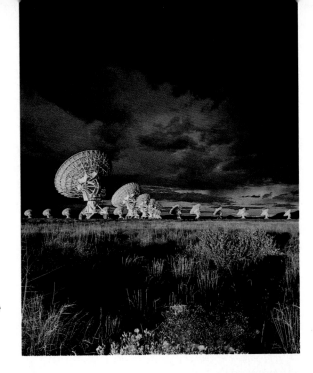

▶ *Giant antennas of the Very Large Array (VLA) radio telescope network in New Mexico have been used to study radio waves emitted from Jupiter. The 27 antennas can be moved on tracks to make the VLA equal to a single radio telescope some 30 kilometers (19 mi) in diameter.*

▼ *This sunken hemisphere is part of an astronomical observatory in India built in the early 1700s.*

▶ *The spiral-shaped Andromeda Galaxy is visible to the unaided eye but is so far away that its light takes more than two million years to reach Earth. Andromeda is believed to be similar in many ways to our galaxy, the Milky Way.*

SOLSTICE

A solstice occurs twice a year when the the sun appears directly overhead to observers at the Tropic of Cancer or at the Tropic of Capricorn. The earth, tilted on its axis, orbits the sun. Thus, the equatorial plane is tilted about $23\frac{1}{2}$ degrees with respect to the plane of the earth's orbit. The latitude at which the sun appears directly overhead at noon changes as the earth revolves around the sun (see figure on page 481). About June 22 the sun's vertical rays strike the Tropic of Cancer, at about $23\frac{1}{2}°$N. In the Northern Hemisphere, this is the summer solstice, when the period of daylight is longest. In the Southern Hemisphere, it is the winter solstice, when the period of daylight is shortest. The opposite occurs about December 22 when the sun's vertical rays strike the Tropic of Capricorn, at about $23\frac{1}{2}°$S. Then it is the winter solstice in the Northern Hemisphere and the summer solstice in the Southern Hemisphere.

SEE ALSO EQUINOX, SEASONS, *and* TROPICS.

SOURCE

The place where a river begins is called its source. Many rivers, including the Rhône and the Ganges, begin as streams in mountains or hills. As ice and snow melt, streams begin to flow downward from high mountains and from openings at the bases of glaciers.

Springs feed the sources of some rivers, such as the Danube and the Volga. A spring is a place where water in the earth, called groundwater, flows out. Some springs form when rain soaks into the ground and reaches a layer of rock through which it cannot pass. The water runs along the rock until it finds an exit, where it flows out as a spring.

Lakes with outflowing streams can become the headwaters of rivers. The Mississippi and the Amazon Rivers begin this way. The lakes may be fed by groundwater as well as water from glaciers, snow, and rain.

SEE ALSO AQUIFER, GLACIER, GROUNDWATER, LAKE, RIVER, *and* SPRING.

SPRING

A spring is a place where water in the earth flows naturally to the surface. When water from rain and melting snow soaks into the ground, it seeps into layers of porous rock that are cracked or fractured. When the water reaches a layer of rock through which it cannot pass, it flows along the top of the impermeable rock. Eventually it reaches a crack or other exit leading to the surface of the land. There, it sometimes flows out as a spring. Often springs are found where the surface of the land is uneven—on mountains, on hills, and in valleys.

Thermal springs, or hot springs, bring warm water to the surface. The water is heated as it seeps down to hot rocks in volcanic regions or deep in the earth. Many hot springs are found in Yellowstone National Park in the western United States. Mineral springs carry to the surface water that contains large amounts of dissolved minerals.

SEE ALSO AQUIFER, GEOTHERMAL ENERGY, GEYSER, GROUNDWATER, *and* WATER TABLE.

STATE

A state is a politically organized group of people occupying a specific territory. The term is often used as a synonym for "country." (In some countries, such as the United States, Brazil, and India, a state is a unit of regional government.) Usually, the territories of states are clearly defined by boundaries.

States are the building blocks of international relations. Cooperation among them is essential to military alliances, trade agreements, and efforts to control the spread of diseases and to preserve the environment.

A state whose members share a common culture, language, and history is called a nation-state. Because of migrations and boundary changes, most states today contain more than one national group. Iceland is one of the few remaining nation-states.

SEE ALSO BOUNDARY, COUNTRY, GOVERNMENT, INTERNATIONAL ORGANIZATION, *and* NATION.

STEPPE

A steppe is an area covered mainly by shortgrasses. Steppes are temperate grasslands, which means they occur where there are distinct seasonal variations in temperature. The Eurasian steppe, extending from Hungary to China, is the largest temperate grassland in the world. Many grass species cover a steppe. The grasses vary in height, but few kinds grow taller than half a meter (20 in).

A steppe typically receives 25 to 50 centimeters (10–20 in) of rain a year. While this is enough rain to support shortgrasses, it is not enough for the growth of tall grasses or trees. Annual rainfall of less than 25 centimeters (10 in) results in desert conditions.

Most people recognize "steppe" as the appropriate name for the vast grasslands of Eurasia. While not as commonly used, the term is also appropriate for the dry, shortgrass prairie of North America's Great Plains.

Many of the world's grasslands have been converted to cropland and pasture. Steppes provide grazing for cattle, goats, horses, and sheep. Overgrazing occurs when there are more animals than the land can support. Overgrazing and overcultivation can make grasslands look like deserts.

SEE ALSO CLIMATE, DESERT, GRASSLAND, PRAIRIE, *and* VEGETATION REGIONS.

▼ *Dust flies as workers plow a cornfield in the Soviet Union. Once a steppe, this and many other temperate grasslands throughout the world have been converted to cropland.*

▼ *A herder rounds up goats grazing on the shortgrasses of a steppe in Mongolia. Goats must be moved often because they will graze the plants down to their roots.*

STORM

A storm is an occurrence of severe weather indicating a disturbed state of the atmosphere that arises from uplifted air. Storms are characterized by heavy precipitation, strong or gusty winds, and often, lightning and thunder. Cyclones—low pressure systems—are often called storms. Tornadoes and hurricanes are particularly violent storms.

SEE ALSO CYCLONE *and* WEATHER.

STRAIT

A strait is a narrow passage of water that connects two larger bodies of water. It may be formed by a fracture across an isthmus, or by the ocean overflowing land that has subsided or has been eroded. One of the best known is the Strait of Gibraltar, which links the Mediterranean Sea and the Atlantic Ocean. Other famous straits shown on the map below include the Strait of Messina, which connects the Tyrrhenian and the Ionian Seas; the Dardanelles, between the Aegean Sea and the Sea of Marmara; the Bosporus, leading into the Black Sea; and the Strait of Hormuz, between the Persian Gulf and the Gulf of Oman. Historically, straits have had great strategic importance. Whoever controls a strait is likely to control the sea routes of an entire region.

SEE ALSO ISTHMUS, OCEAN, *and* SEA.

► *Ships pass through the Strait of Gibraltar, a narrow stretch of water that separates Spain and Morocco and joins the Atlantic Ocean and the Mediterranean Sea.*
▼ *The Turkish city of Istanbul lies on a strait called the Bosporus. Many straits have served as thoroughfares of travel and commerce since ancient times.*

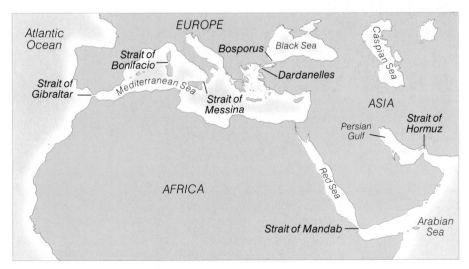

STREAM

A stream is any body of flowing water that runs from higher to lower ground in a channel under the force of gravity. Streams are fed by rain, melting snow and ice, and groundwater. They vary in size from tiny rills to larger brooks and creeks to rivers. The term is often used interchangeably with "river." Though a river may be considered a large stream, "stream" usually refers to a smaller body of water.

SEE ALSO RIVER *and* TRIBUTARY.

SUN

The sun is an ordinary star, one of more than two hundred billion in the Milky Way galaxy. Without this star, however, there would be no life on the earth. The sun, the star nearest to the earth, is the original source of most of the energy used on this planet.

Throughout history people have watched the sun and recorded their observations. It is easy to understand how some ancient peoples were so awed by the sun that they worshiped it, thinking it a divine sphere of celestial fire.

By the 16th century, scholars began to understand that the sun is at the center of our solar system. It was not until the 17th century, however, when the telescope was invented in Europe, that people were able to examine this brilliant star in detail. The sun is much too bright to allow us to study it with our eyes unprotected. With a telescope, it was possible for the first time to project a clear image of the sun onto a screen for examination. Astronomers could observe that the sun, like the planets, rotates on its axis—an invisible line through its center.

Today we know that the sun is 150 million kilometers (93 million mi) from the earth. That is 390 times the distance from the earth to its moon. The sun's energy travels to the earth as electromagnetic radiation, which can be thought of as energy moving in waves. Different kinds of waves carry varying amounts of energy and range in length from radio waves hundreds of meters long to gamma rays with wavelengths shorter than the diameter of an atom. The only waves seen by the unaided eye are those that make up visible light. Though not visible, infrared waves are felt as heat, and ultraviolet waves may burn the skin.

An optical instrument called a spectroscope, developed in the 19th century, made it possible to break light down into its various wavelengths and to identify the gases in the sun's atmosphere. Scientists learned that a large part of the sun's mass is made up of hydrogen and another gas, which was unfamiliar to them. They called the gas helium.

Twentieth-century astronomers use balloons and rockets to send sensitive instruments high above the interference of the

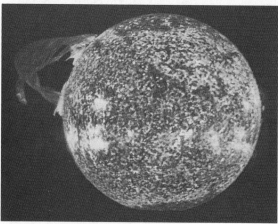

earth's atmosphere to examine the sun. Solrad 1, the first spacecraft designed for study of the sun, was launched by the United States in 1960. A number of spacecraft have followed since then. Although much information has been gathered by the instruments on these spacecraft, scientists are just beginning to solve some of the sun's mysteries.

The sun's core, more than a thousand

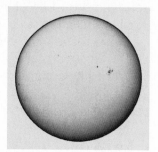

▲ Sunspots, areas of intense magnetic activity on the solar surface, appear dark (above) because they are cooler than surrounding areas. Propelled by magnetic forces, great loops of hot gas erupt from the sun (left). This photograph was taken in 1973 during the last of the NASA Skylab missions.

times the size of the earth and more than ten times denser than lead, is like a huge furnace. Temperatures within the core are thought to reach 15,000,000°C (27,000,000°F). No one knows exactly what occurs in the sun's core, but scientists believe that the great pressure and the high temperatures there cause protons from hydrogen atoms to collide so violently that they fuse, or join together. Fusion produces enormous amounts of energy as it changes hydrogen to helium. The energy released during one second of solar fusion is far greater than that released in the explosion of hundreds of thousands of hydrogen bombs.

Energy, in the form of tiny units called photons, takes millions of years to work its way to the sun's surface. The sunlight we see is made up of trillions of photons that hit each square meter of the earth every second. It is from the sun's surface, called the photosphere, that the earth receives most of its light and other energy.

The photosphere is about 400 kilometers (250 mi) thick, and temperatures there reach about 6000°C (11,000°F). Photographs show us that the surface bubbles like boiling oatmeal as gases rise from the interior through a region called the convection zone. The gases rise in cells called granules. At the surface,

▲ Shimmering sunlight frames structures at the Kitt Peak National Observatory, near Tucson, Arizona. Astronomers use the McMath Solar Telescope at right to reflect images of the solar surface for study. Sunspots are sometimes visible to the unaided eye, as they are in this photograph.
► The sun's structure is no longer a total mystery to scientists. They have learned about the star by using sophisticated telescopes and by studying information from space instruments.

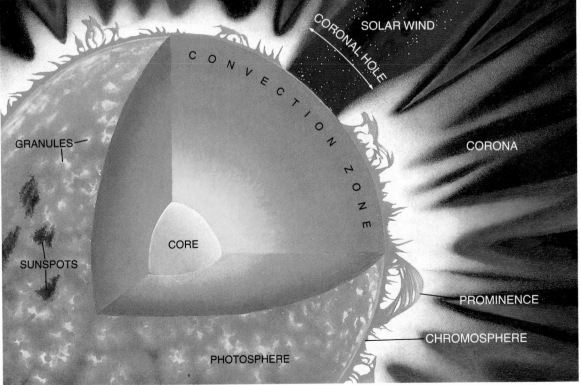

the gases cool slightly, spread out, and sink.

The turbulent gases and the way in which the sun rotates have an effect on the sun's relatively weak magnetic field. The sun rotates faster at its equator than at its poles, and the uneven rotation causes the sun's magnetic lines of force to wrap around the star like thread around a spool. Upwardly flowing gases twist the tightly wound lines, causing kinks that generate strong local magnetic fields. Where these fields block rising gases, spots may appear on the sun's surface because the areas are cooler, and thus darker, than the rest of the photosphere. These cooler, darker areas are called sunspots.

Obscured by the bright light emitted by the photosphere, the upper layers of the solar atmosphere—the chromosphere and the corona—are rarely seen without special instruments. Only during solar eclipses, when the moon moves between the earth and the sun and hides the glowing disk briefly, can these layers be seen with the unaided eye.

The pinkish red chromosphere is about 3,200 kilometers (2,000 mi) thick and is riddled by jets of hot gas called spicules. It is in the chromosphere that violent eruptions of energy called flares are seen. Caused by the same magnetic fields that create sunspots, flares are a sudden outpouring of energy and electrically charged particles.

Normally, charged particles swim about freely as a solar soup called plasma and are released by the sun each day as solar wind. Some of the particles in this solar wind slip through the earth's magnetic field and into the earth's upper atmosphere near the Poles. As they collide with atoms there, they set the atmosphere aglow with color, creating light displays called auroras.

When solar flares erupt, blasts of energy and particles are thrown outward as part of the solar wind. Flares increase the brilliance of auroras and cause geomagnetic storms that can disrupt radio transmissions on earth.

Great clouds of hot gas called prominences are another solar feature. They sometimes hang above the chromosphere, suspended in lines of twisting magnetic force. Some of these glowing geysers appear to surge upward at great speed and make graceful loops. Others float in the corona for several months.

SOLAR ENERGY BUDGET

TOTAL ENERGY REFLECTED – 30%

REFLECTED FROM ATMOSPHERE 10%

REFLECTED FROM CLOUDS 18%

REFLECTED FROM EARTH'S SURFACE 2%

ABSORBED BY CLOUDS 3%

ABSORBED BY LAND AND WATER 45%

ABSORBED BY ATMOSPHERE 22%

TOTAL ENERGY ABSORBED – 70%

Magnetic fields control the shape of the corona, the wispy outermost layer of the solar atmosphere. Where the lines of magnetic force loop from one place on the sun to another, very little plasma escapes. In these places where plasma is confined, the corona looks bright in photographs. Where the magnetic lines stretch out into interplanetary space, great streams of plasma escape into the solar system as solar wind. These places where plasma does escape are called coronal holes, which look dark in photographs.

Twentieth-century research has shown that the sun is a place of violent activity. We are just beginning to find out the ways in

◄ *The distribution of the sun's energy is called the solar energy budget. About a third of the energy transmitted to the earth is reflected directly back into space. About half of the energy is first absorbed by the earth's surface, then released back into the earth's atmosphere. The atmosphere absorbs some energy directly from the sun.*

▼ *A total solar eclipse offers a chance for people to view the sun's corona without special instruments.*

▼ *Looking directly at the sun, even during a solar eclipse, can damage your eyes. A telescope focuses an image of the moon's progress across the solar disk onto a plain, flat surface where the eclipse can be viewed without harm.*

▼ *The stages before and after a 1983 solar eclipse are shown left to right in this time-lapse photograph. The sun appears to shine brightly near total eclipse because filters blocking the sun's rays were briefly removed.*

which solar activity affects our lives. Scientists estimate that the star will shine for at least five billion more years. Improvements are continually being made in the technology for harnessing this tremendous source of energy.

SEE ALSO AURORA, CLIMATE, EARTH, ECLIPSE, ENERGY, EQUINOX, MAGNETISM, SEASONS, SOLAR SYSTEM, SOLSTICE, *and* WEATHER.

SWAMP

A swamp is an area of land permanently saturated with water and sometimes covered by it. There are two main types of swamps, both dominated by trees. Freshwater swamps are commonly found inland, and saltwater swamps usually fringe coastal areas protected from the open ocean.

Freshwater swamps form on land around lakes and streams where the water table lies at or near the surface and water runoff is slow. Rain and seasonal flooding cause water levels to fluctuate. In many freshwater swamps in the southeastern United States, cypress and tupelo trees grow. Spanish moss may hang from the branches, and tiny plants called duckweed may cover the water's surface. Alligators, frogs, and other reptiles and amphibians often live in swamps.

Saltwater swamps form on seacoasts. Mangrove trees often grow on stilt-like prop roots in sandy mud flats, where tidal waters fluctuate. The roots anchor sand and other sediments. The growth and decay of the roots increase the accumulation of soil. These swamps are home to a rich community of fish, shellfish, and water birds. Because the young of many marine animals find food and shelter in saltwater swamps, these wetlands are sometimes called the nurseries of the ocean.

SEE ALSO WATER TABLE *and* WETLAND.

▲ *Nets at the ready, fishermen in a Brazilian swamp await a catch. Freshwater and saltwater swamps are wetlands that are dominated by trees.*

T

TAIGA

Taiga is a forest of the cold, subarctic region and begins south of tundra vegetation. Many scientists call a boreal forest taiga. Some consider taiga to be the scattered forest on the northern fringes of a boreal forest. Coniferous, or cone-bearing, trees, such as spruce, pine, and fir, are common in taiga. Unlike deciduous trees—trees that are leafless for a season—these needleleaf evergreens can survive the long, cold winters and short summers of the subarctic climate. In the taiga region, which stretches across northern North America, Europe, and Asia, tree growth is thickest beside boggy depressions and lake basins formed by glaciers. Plant species are limited in this harsh climate, but many kinds of animals live in the taiga, including bears, wolves, and moose. In the Soviet Union, the world's largest taiga stretches some 5,800 kilometers (3,600 mi) from the Pacific Ocean to the Ural Mountains.

SEE ALSO FOREST *and* TUNDRA.

▲ *Taiga along Canada's Mackenzie River becomes a mosaic of forest and water during a summer thaw. Spruce and fir are the dominant needleleaf evergreen trees in taiga.*

TECHNOLOGY

Through the ages, people have looked for ways to make work easier, more efficient, and more productive. They have invented tools and machines, developed materials and techniques, and harnessed power sources such as flowing water and electricity. The term "technology" covers all the ways people use these inventions and discoveries to do work and to improve their lives.

Technology includes traditional ways of doing things, such as cooking food over a fire or tilling the soil with a hoe. Such simple technology is still common in many parts of the world. In contrast, technology in industrialized countries is often highly advanced.

Tools and machines not only help or replace human labor but also enlarge human senses and capabilities. Telescopes and satellites, for example, enable us to probe the universe. Telephones and radios let us hear over great distances. Computers permit us to make complex calculations in an instant.

One challenge for developed countries is to share technological knowledge with developing countries. Another is to solve problems that modern technology has helped cause. These include pollution, depletion of natural resources, and disposal of wastes.

SEE ALSO AGRICULTURE, INDUSTRY, *and* TRANSPORTATION AND COMMUNICATION.

▲ *A young craftsman in Bahrain shapes clay on a potter's wheel. Simple technology is still common in many places. In developed countries, though, powered machinery has largely replaced hand labor.*
▼ *High-speed trains and public telephones serve commuters at a station in Tokyo, in Japan. Advanced technology includes sophisticated systems of transportation and communication.*

TEMPERATURE

Temperature is the degree of hotness or coldness measured by a thermometer with a numerical scale. The Fahrenheit scale is widely used only in the United States. The Celsius, or centigrade, scale is standard in almost all other countries. Both scales, shown on the thermometer below, are set according to the points at which water freezes and boils. On the Celsius scale, water freezes at 0° and boils at 100°. On the Fahrenheit scale, water freezes at 32° and boils at 212°. Scientists often use another temperature scale, called the Kelvin scale, in which each unit of measurement equals one Celsius degree, and absolute zero, the complete absence of heat, is 0°. On the Kelvin scale, the freezing point of water is 273.16°.

The temperature of an object indicates the amount of heat or energy it contains. Adding heat to an object raises its temperature; removing heat lowers its temperature.

SEE ALSO MEASUREMENT *and* THERMOMETER.

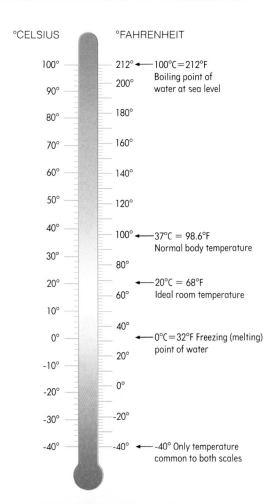

°CELSIUS | °FAHRENHEIT

100° — 212° ← 100°C=212°F Boiling point of water at sea level
90° — 200°
80° — 180°
70° — 160°
60° — 140°
50° — 120°
40° — 100° ← 37°C = 98.6°F Normal body temperature
30° — 80°
20° — ← 20°C = 68°F Ideal room temperature
10° — 60°
0° — 40° ← 0°C=32°F Freezing (melting) point of water
-10° — 20°
-20° — 0°
-30° — -20°
-40° — -40° ← -40° Only temperature common to both scales

TERRACE

A terrace is a raised formation with a level top and often a steep front that resembles a giant stair step. It either occurs naturally or is made by people. Natural terraces border rivers, lake beds, or seashores. These terraces mark old water levels or floodplains. Artificial terraces intended for use in agriculture are built onto the sides of hills or mountains. Their retaining walls or embankments are engineered to hold soil and moisture in place and to prevent erosion. Artificial terracing is probably the oldest method of soil conservation.

Both natural and artificial terraces have supported farming societies for centuries throughout much of the world. Some early civilizations developed along natural river terraces and floodplains in Egypt, China, and southwestern and southern Asia. Farming artificial terraces has produced crops for generations in such countries as the Philippines, Japan, China, and Peru.

Much labor is required to build and maintain artificial terraces, and often they are not suited to modern farm machinery. But in mountainous areas, where growing crops is normally difficult, terraces provide people with productive plots. In densely populated countries, this wise use of land may support large numbers of people.

SEE ALSO AGRICULTURE, FARMING, *and* SOIL.

▲ *Terraced paddies, or rice fields, curve along slopes in southern China. A large population and a scarcity of level land require farmers to cultivate hillsides.*
▼ *Terraces on the Indonesian island of Bali retain water needed for growing rice. Farmed intensively, these fertile fields produce several crops each year.*

THERMOMETER

A thermometer is a device that measures temperature. A common type of thermometer consists of mercury or another liquid in a glass tube and operates on the principle that the liquid expands more than the glass does when heated. For very low temperature measurements, alcohol is used, since mercury freezes at -39°C (-38°F). Thermometers are marked according to one of three temperature scales: Celsius, Fahrenheit, or Kelvin.

SEE ALSO MEASUREMENT *and* TEMPERATURE.

THUNDERSTORM

A thunderstorm is a cumulonimbus cloud, or thunderhead, that produces heavy rains and lightning. If severe, the storm may bring hail and tornadoes. More than 16 million thunderstorms occur yearly on the earth.

Thunderstorms are born from warm, rising air that carries moisture skyward. Cumulus clouds form, strengthening updrafts that carry more moisture to higher altitudes and enable the clouds to grow. At sufficient altitude, ice particles form in the towering thunderhead. As precipitation falls, downdrafts are created, bringing strong winds and rain to the earth's surface. The downdrafts eventually block the updrafts, and the storm ends.

SEE ALSO CLOUDS, LIGHTNING, *and* WEATHER.

▲ *Marked by a shaft of rain and a bolt of lightning, a dramatic thunderstorm breaks over Nebraska.*

TIDAL ENERGY

Tidal energy is produced as ocean waters surge in and out during the rise and fall of tides. The gravitational pull of the moon and the sun on the earth and the force of the earth's rotation help cause tides. During the 20th century, engineers developed ways to use tidal movement to generate electricity in areas where there is an extreme rise and fall of the tides. In the mid-1960s, the world's first tidal power plant began operation in France. A dam was built near where the Rance River empties into the English Channel. Reversible turbines in the dam allow electricity to be generated not only when powerful tides come in but also when they go out.

SEE ALSO ENERGY *and* TIDES.

TIDES

The regular daily rise and fall of the ocean waters are known as tides. Along coasts, the water slowly rises up over the shore and then slowly falls back again. When the water has risen to its highest level, covering much of the shore, it is at high tide. When the water falls to its lowest level, it is at low tide.

Causes of Tides

The major cause of tides is the moon's gravitational force, or pull, on the earth. The closer celestial bodies are, the greater the gravitational attraction is between them. Although the sun and the moon both exert gravitational force on the earth, the moon's pull is stronger because the moon is much closer to the earth than the sun is.

Orbiting the earth, the moon exerts gravitational force on all the earth's surfaces. This has little effect on land surfaces because they are solid and not flexible. But it has a great

► *At high tide, the ocean reaches to the seawall at St.-Malo, a seaport in France. At low tide (top), sunbathers enjoy a sandy shore that is exposed when the water goes out.*

effect on the surface of the ocean because water is liquid and can move about freely.

The gravitational force exerted by the moon is strongest on the side of the earth facing the moon. It is weakest on the side of the earth opposite the moon. These differences in gravitational force—in combination with the earth's rotation and other factors—allow the ocean to bulge outward in two places at the same time. One bulge occurs on the side of the earth facing the moon; the other bulge occurs on the opposite side of the earth. These bulges in ocean waters are known as high tides. In the open ocean, the water bulges out toward the moon. Along the seashore, the water rises and spreads onto the land.

One high tide always faces the moon, while the other is always directly opposite it. Between these high tides are areas of lower water levels—the low tides.

Two high tides and two low tides usually take place each day along most of the earth's

▲ At low tide, Mont-St.-Michel, a Benedictine abbey just off the coast of Normandy in France, rises above vast mud flats. At high tide, the ocean will surround the islet, leaving a causeway as its only connection to the mainland.

▲ *In a few rivers, high tide sometimes begins with a tidal bore—an abrupt front of high water—like this one moving up the Petitcodiac River near Canada's Bay of Fundy.*
▼ *St. Andrew's Wharf in the Bay of Fundy is built to accommodate the rise and fall of the world's greatest tides, with water levels that may vary more than 15 meters (53 ft).*

coastal areas. For example, when an area covered by the ocean faces the moon, the moon's gravitational force on the water causes high tide. As the earth rotates, that area moves away from the moon's influence, and the water recedes. Now it is low tide in that area. As the earth keeps rotating, another high tide occurs in the same area when it is on the side of the earth opposite the moon. The earth continues spinning; the water again recedes; another low tide occurs; and the cycle, about 24 hours long, begins again.

The vertical difference between high and low tide is called the range of the tide. Each month, the range changes in a regular pattern as a result of the sun's gravitational force on the earth. Although the sun is almost 390 times farther away from the earth than is the moon, it still affects the tides.

Because the earth's surface is not uniform, tides do not follow the same patterns in all places. The shape of a seacoast and the shape of the ocean floor both make a difference in the range and frequency of the tides. Along a smooth, wide beach, the water can spread over a large area and may rise only a few centimeters at high tide. But in a confined area, such as a narrow, rocky inlet or bay, the water may rise many meters at high tide.

Twice each month, the moon travels to a position in its orbit that makes it line up with the earth and the sun. When the sun, the

earth, and the moon are aligned in this way, the sun's gravitational force works with the moon's pull on the earth. The combined pull can cause the highest high tides, called spring tides. The name has nothing to do with the season of spring. It comes from the German word *springan*, which means "to jump."

In the period between the two spring tides, the moon moves in its orbit so that it faces the earth at a right angle to the sun. When this happens, the pull of the moon and the sun on the earth is weakened. This causes tides that rise less than usual. They are known as neap tides.

SEE ALSO COAST, GRAVITY, MOON, OCEAN, ORBIT, SUN, TIDAL ENERGY, *and* WATER.

TIMBERLINE

The timberline is the boundary above which continuous forest vegetation ends. Beyond this boundary, the climate is too severe for all but stunted tree growth. Cold temperatures, whether occurring at high elevations or at high latitudes, are the main factor in determining the timberline. Lack of precipitation, exposure to wind, and nutrient-poor soil are other limitations to normal tree growth. Timberlines are found on all continents except Antarctica, where no trees grow.

SEE ALSO CLIMATE, MOUNTAIN, POLAR REGIONS, SOIL, *and* TUNDRA.

▲ *At Imogene Pass, in Colorado, bare rock rises above the timberline, the boundary that marks the end of continuous forest growth.*

TIME AND TIME ZONES

All living things have a sense of time. Geese migrate at the same times each year, and morning glories open at dawn. Animals have a sense of time that prompts them to sleep and to wake up on a regular schedule. These are kinds of biologic time, in which physical processes are linked to repeating rhythms of the natural world.

Long ago, people relied primarily on repeating events to measure the passage of time. They doubtless counted frequent, dependable natural events, such as sunrise, to see how many times they occurred between regular events that did not repeat often.

The positions of the sun and the other stars in the sky during earth's rotation provide us with our fundamental unit of time—the day. Because the earth rotates on its axis, the sun and other stars appear to be moving westward across the sky. Scientists call the point in the sky directly overhead a zenith, and they call the imaginary line that runs north and south through a zenith a celestial meridian. Using a meridian as a reference point, they measured the time it takes a star to return to the same meridian. That amount of time is called a sidereal day, a measurement used by astronomers. The solar day, the time the sun takes to return to the same meridian, is longer than the sidereal day because during the time the earth turns on its axis, it also moves along its orbit around the sun. Thus, the earth must turn slightly more than one complete rotation for the sun to cross the same meridian. The earth does not rotate at a uniform speed, however, so the length of the real solar day varies. To set a standard, the length of all the solar days in a year were averaged to arrive at a mean solar day of 24 hours.

In a time when there was little communication among different areas, each town set its clocks by observing the sun's position. People looked up at the sky and declared the time to be noon when the sun was directly overhead. When it was noon in Washington, D.C., for example, clocks in New York City read 12:12 p.m. There was no need to coordinate local time with the time anywhere else. As transportation and communication technology advanced, however, such casualness led to confusion, and the need for a standard system of time became apparent, especially to those trying to set train schedules. The 48 contiguous United States cover approximately 60 degrees of longitude. The more communities that a railroad operated in, the more local times had to be considered.

To solve the problem, U.S. railroad officials decided at a conference in 1883 to divide the country's 60 degrees into four time zones of 15 degrees each, with the meridian through Greenwich, England, being the prime (0°) meridian. Their decision was based on the fact that during earth's rotation the noon meridian moves approximately 15 degrees each hour. The local time at the meridian in the center of the zone was to be used by all people within that zone. The time in adjoining zones differed by one hour. Political boundaries such as county lines and the areas served by the different railroads were considered before the zone divisions were made. Although lines have been changed often over the years, these four zones still broadly define the areas of today's Eastern, Central, Mountain, and Pacific time zones.

The need for international agreement on a prime meridian for marking longitude and for keeping time brought representatives from 25 countries together in 1884 for a conference in Washington, D.C. No binding agreements were reached, but resolutions were passed recommending that the Greenwich meridian be the international prime meridian and that a 24-hour day be used.

The practical outcome of the conference was the gradual adoption, country by country, of a time-zone system based on Greenwich as the prime meridian. Ideally, a global system of time zones would have 24 zones, each 15 degrees wide. The time in each zone would be the difference between the time at a zone's central meridian and Greenwich Mean Time (GMT). The map on pages 516–517, however, reflects the countless variations that developed as a time-zone system evolved. These additional zones, which exist for practical or political reasons, may vary by a fraction of an hour from adjoining zones. Generally, though, the time zones east of Greenwich

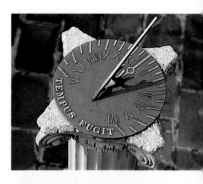

▲ The sundial (top), the sandglass (middle), and the mechanical clock in the British Parliament clock tower are all tools used to keep track of time. Timekeeping technology has made tremendous advances since the days of the primitive sundials.

have times later than Greenwich time, and those to the west have earlier times—usually a one-hour difference for each zone.

Halfway around the globe from the prime meridian, the time zone that is centered on the 180th meridian is divided into two parts to allow for a date line, the point at which one day ends and another begins. The date line roughly follows the 180th meridian. Within that zone, the time on each side of the date line is the same, but the date is one day different from one side to the other.

It was not until 1918, during World War I, that the United States passed the Standard Time Act, which authorized the establishment of standard time zones and "daylight saving time" within the United States. Daylight saving time is observed by adjusting clock time to move the daylight hours to later in the day and is not related to any astronomical changes. First instituted to help save fuel during the war, daylight saving time is authorized by state law in most of the United States and is observed in several other countries.

Using the system of time zones, people are able to determine accurately what time it is anywhere in the world. Most people today set their clocks or watches according to Universal Time (UT). UT, or earth time, is calculated by astronomical observations. Although adequate for everyday use, UT is not a very precise or consistent time system because the earth's rotation is irregular, and the planet even wobbles on its axis. Those in the telecommunications industry and in other high-technology fields require a system that can measure time consistently and accurately to a billionth of a second. They use a system called coordinated universal time (UTC), based on clocks that are more precise and reliable timekeepers than the earth.

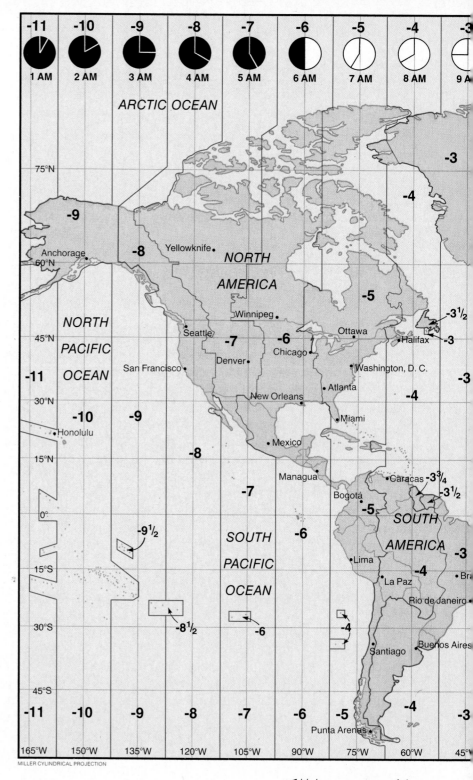

MILLER CYLINDRICAL PROJECTION

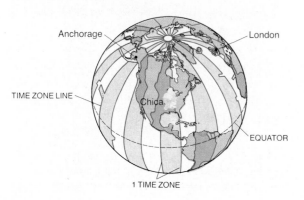

TIME ZONE LINE

EQUATOR

1 TIME ZONE

ANCHORAGE
3 A.M.

CHICAGO
6 A.M.

LONDON
NOON

◄ Using a system of time zones, people in one part of the world can calculate the time in other parts. At the moment that it is 3 a.m. in Anchorage, it is 6 a.m. in Chicago, three zones to the east, and noon in London, nine zones to the east.

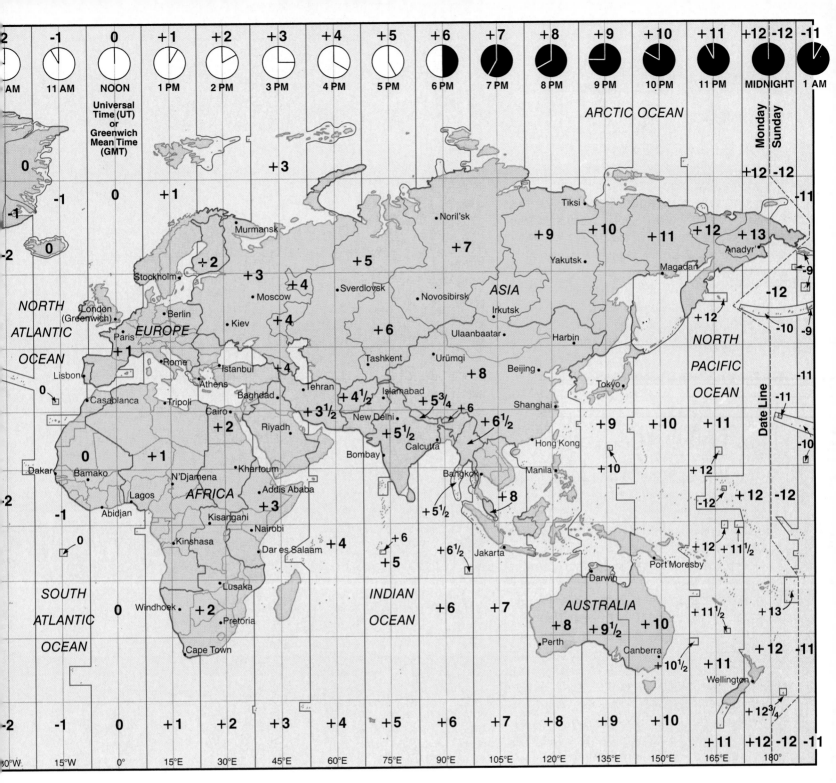

-1	0	+1	+2	+3	+4	+5	+6	+7	+8	+9	+10	+11	+12	-12	-11
11 AM	NOON	1 PM	2 PM	3 PM	4 PM	5 PM	6 PM	7 PM	8 PM	9 PM	10 PM	11 PM	MIDNIGHT		1 AM

Universal Time (UT) or Greenwich Mean Time (GMT)

ARCTIC OCEAN

Monday / Sunday

▲ *The global time zone system is based on a prime meridian running through Greenwich, England. Variations in the basic pattern of 24 time zones, indicated by the red lines and numbers on the map, have developed over the last century.*

UTC uses atomic clocks to define time accurately and quickly, and also keeps in step with earth time, or UT. The atomic clocks define what a second is by measuring time according to the vibration of cesium atoms. The mean time of atomic clocks in 28 countries is the basis for setting world time today. To keep the time shown on the atomic clocks within 0.9 second of UT, the clocks are occasionally adjusted by adding a second to the last minute of a particular day. Timekeepers around the world are told when to make the adjustments that allow the time showing on the clocks to coordinate with the earth's movement. Present systems for keeping track of time are still imperfect, however, and scientists are searching for new ways to make them even more accurate.

SEE ALSO CALENDAR, DATE LINE, EARTH, GEOLOGIC TIME SCALE, LATITUDE AND LONGITUDE, LONGITUDE, PRIME MERIDIAN, *and* SOLAR SYSTEM.

TOPOGRAPHY

Topography is the lay of the land—the shape of the surface features of a geographic area. Geographers sometimes use the word in a descriptive way, referring, for example, to the rugged topography of the Rocky Mountains or the flat topography of California's Central Valley. Or they may be more scientific and speak of the glacial topography of Wisconsin, for instance, or the karst topography of central Kentucky.

Topographic maps are important geographic tools. Contour lines are their most distinctive feature. These curving lines connect points that are at the same elevation.

SEE ALSO ELEVATION *and* MAPS AND GLOBES.

TORNADO

A tornado, also called a twister, is a violently rotating column of air that descends to the ground during intense thunderstorm activity. The average tornado is approximately 200 meters (660 ft) wide; advances at about 50 kilometers per hour (30 mph); and seldom travels along the ground for more than 10 kilometers (6 mi). Occasionally, huge killer tornadoes travel as fast as 110 kilometers per hour (70 mph), cutting a path up to 1.6 kilometers (1 mi) wide and 480 kilometers (300 mi) long.

A tornado has more concentrated destructive power than any other kind of storm. Its winds may reach 480 kilometers per hour (300 mph). That is just speculation, since no anemometer, an instrument used to measure wind speed, can withstand a tornado's force. Tornadoes move buildings, locomotives, and even bridges. They can blow the water out of a river, leaving behind a dry riverbed.

Where and When Tornadoes Occur

Argentina, Australia, India, and the Soviet Union are among the many countries that experience tornadoes, but more form in the United States than in any other place on earth. Between 700 and 1,000 are reported there each year. While they occur in every state,

▲ *Extending from a dark thunderstorm, a tornado rakes the New Jersey countryside. Its whirling funnel shape is typical of all tornadoes.*
◄ *Destruction marks the path of a tornado that hit Albion, Pennsylvania, on May 31, 1985. That day, a total of 43 tornadoes struck Pennsylvania, Ohio, New York, and Ontario, killing 87 people. Ten of the tornadoes, including this one, were classified as "maxi," the most violent type.*

A small number of tornadoes cause most of the deaths that occur from the storms.

How Tornadoes Form

The tremendous power of tornadoes makes them difficult to study, so scientists are unsure about how and why they form. Some tornadoes have one giant whirlwind; others have several smaller ones within a larger storm. They all start when cold, dry air and warm, moist air collide, producing a strong updraft. Denser cold air is forced over warm air, usually producing thunderstorms.

The rising column of air will rotate if the surrounding winds vary sharply in speed or direction from lower to higher levels. The rotating updraft is called a mesocyclone. Warm air feeding into the moving thunderstorm is drawn into the mesocyclone, intensifying its

▼ A tornado is born of wind shear in a thunderstorm. Wind shear develops when strong winds blow over weaker winds, making the air between them spin like a pencil rolling on a table. A strong updraft inside the thunderstorm can catch the wind shear, lifting it to a vertical position and twisting it at the same time. The rotating updraft is called a mesocyclone. Not all mesocyclones spawn tornadoes. When a tornado does form, upper level winds propel it forward.

Texas holds the record with an annual average of 120. That state lies in Tornado Alley, the area where twisters strike most often. The "alley" stretches from north-central Texas through Oklahoma and into Kansas.

Other states have been hard hit as well. In 1925, the deadliest tornado on record swept Missouri, Illinois, and Indiana, killing nearly 700 people. The greatest number of storms in a 24-hour period developed on April 3 and 4, 1974, when more than 140 twisters struck in a vast area from Alabama to Ohio.

In the United States, the tornado season begins in early spring in the states bordering the Gulf of Mexico, when warm, moist air moving north from the Gulf collides with cooler, dry air moving south with the jet stream. As spring advances, the jet stream swings farther north, and with it moves the tornado breeding ground. May generally has more tornadoes than any other month. April tornadoes, however, are usually more violent.

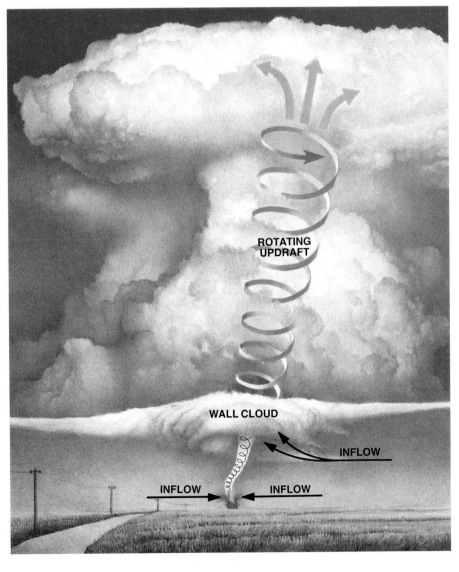

ROTATING UPDRAFT

WALL CLOUD

INFLOW

INFLOW   INFLOW

rotation. Cool air fed by the jet stream into the top and rear of the storm provides even more energy as it rushes downward.

Few things in nature are as terrifying as a whirling funnel descending from a huge thundercloud only about 1 kilometer (3,300 ft) above the earth. A funnel cloud is made up of water droplets that form from moist air spinning rapidly in the low pressure of the growing mesocyclone inside the storm cloud. As the whirlwind continues to grow, the funnel descends from the cloud, usually at the rear, rain-free side of the storm. It officially becomes a tornado when it touches the ground.

Forecasting Tornadoes

The best protection against tornadoes is to be forewarned. Meteorologists at the National Severe Storms Forecast Center in Kansas City, Missouri, constantly check atmospheric conditions in the lower 48 states. They use a computer system that gathers information from satellites, balloons, radar, and weather stations. If evidence shows that severe thunderstorms or tornadoes are likely to develop in an area, the meteorologists notify local weather offices. A computerized radar system that tracks and measures wind speeds in storms nationwide also makes tornado forecasting more accurate.

SEE ALSO CLOUDS, CYCLONE, FRONT, JET STREAM, THUNDERSTORM, *and* WEATHER.

▲ *Shaken but uninjured, a tornado survivor stands on a lawn strewn with debris from houses. The storm struck Edmond, Oklahoma, in May 1986.*
▼ *Tornadoes occur more often in some areas of the United States than in others. On this map, colors show the numbers of tornadoes in an area of 25,900 square kilometers (10,000 sq mi) in an average year. The large purple area is Tornado Alley, a region named for its frequent twisters.*

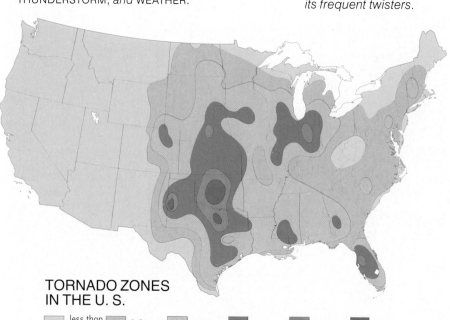

TORNADO ZONES IN THE U. S.

| | less than 1.0 | | 1.0 | | 3.0 | | 5.0 | | 7.0 | | 9.0 |

Average annual number of tornadoes per 25,900 square kilometers (10,000 square miles)
SOURCE: NATIONAL SEVERE STORMS FORECAST CENTER

TOTALITARIANISM

Totalitarianism is a political system in which the government exerts absolute control over nearly all aspects of people's lives. A totalitarian government usually outlaws any political or social institutions that oppose it. Censorship, propaganda, and police terror are among the tools it uses to smother free thought and expression. In the 20th century, Germany under Adolf Hitler and the Soviet Union under Joseph Stalin were totalitarian.

SEE ALSO GOVERNMENT.

TOWN

A town is an urban settlement generally larger, and with a greater variety of functions and services, than a village, but smaller, and with fewer services, than a city. Some geographers further define a town as having 2,500 to 20,000 residents. Towns usually have local self-government, and they may grow around specialized economic activities, such as mining or railroading. In some parts of the United States, a town or township is also a subdivision of a county.

SEE ALSO CITY, SETTLEMENT, *and* VILLAGE.

TRADE

Trade is the buying and selling of goods and services. Typical goods include wheat, candy, TV sets, and cars. Typical services include haircuts and dry cleaning; travel on buses, trains, and planes; and financial assistance, such as loans and insurance. A primary goal of trade is to give consumers the best goods and services at the best prices.

Trade is the basis of the modern money economy. Money is a medium of exchange that is acceptable to both parties in a trade. The amount of money required to purchase a good or a service is called the price. Prices can be set by a producer or a store, by a government, or by bids or offers leading to a business arrangement called a contract.

Without money, trade would have to be a direct exchange of goods, or barter. In a barter economy, a grower of wheat who wanted a

▲ Soft drink signs decorate a post office in Sur, a town in Oman. Many products of industrialized countries are traded throughout the world.

▼ Hasidic Jews shop for a chicken in Jerusalem. Buyers and sellers bargain directly in open-air markets, the economic centers of many towns.

horse would have to find a horse owner who wanted wheat. Then they would have to decide how many bushels of wheat were equal in value to one horse. In a money economy, the wheat grower simply sells his product in a marketplace and buys a horse.

The Role of Trade

Trade has played an important role throughout history. Centuries ago, caravans transported goods from Asia to buyers in Europe. In the 15th and 16th centuries, European explorers discovered new lands while seeking new trade routes to the East. In more recent times, the Suez and the Panama Canals were built to provide shorter and more economical trade routes. At all times, trade has advanced civilization through exchanges of ideas as well as goods.

Trade helps to fulfill people's needs and wants. Basic needs are food, clothing, and shelter. As their incomes rise, people tend to eat more varied and expensive food, live in better homes, and wear the latest fashions. Today, people need or want many things.

Trade makes possible specialization, or the division of labor, so that a factory can make one product, a worker can perform one job, and a farmer can grow one crop. A trading country does not have to produce everything it needs. Saudi Arabia, for example, produces petroleum but no television sets. Japan makes television sets but has almost no petroleum resources. Through trade, people in both countries can have both products.

Marketplaces

To carry on trade, buyers and sellers must be brought together in what is called a market. The oldest kind of trading place is the open-air market, where goods are exchanged through face-to-face bargaining. Such markets still exist in many countries.

In an industrial economy, producers and consumers are brought together by a distribution system. A common arrangement is for producers to sell goods to merchants known as wholesalers, who sell goods in large quantities to retailers. Retail stores sell goods in small quantities to the final consumers.

For basic commodities, such as wheat,

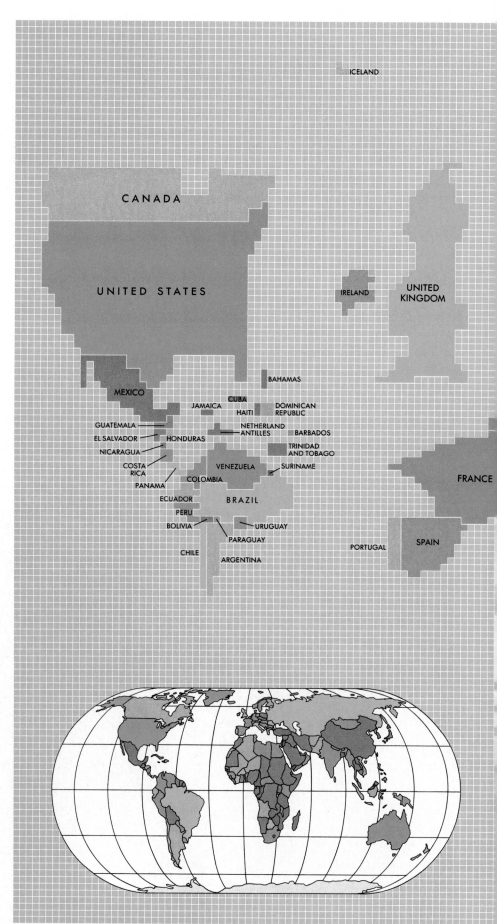

STATISTICS ADAPTED FROM THOSE USED FOR
THE NEW STATE OF THE WORLD ATLAS, 1987.

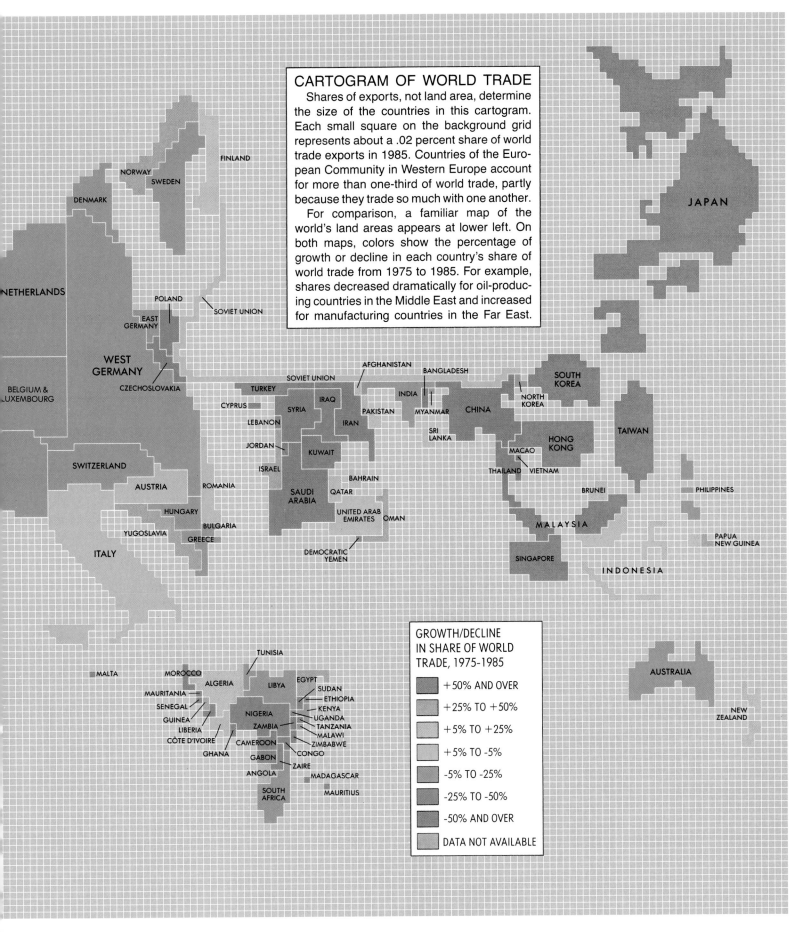

CARTOGRAM OF WORLD TRADE

Shares of exports, not land area, determine the size of the countries in this cartogram. Each small square on the background grid represents about a .02 percent share of world trade exports in 1985. Countries of the European Community in Western Europe account for more than one-third of world trade, partly because they trade so much with one another.

For comparison, a familiar map of the world's land areas appears at lower left. On both maps, colors show the percentage of growth or decline in each country's share of world trade from 1975 to 1985. For example, shares decreased dramatically for oil-producing countries in the Middle East and increased for manufacturing countries in the Far East.

GROWTH/DECLINE IN SHARE OF WORLD TRADE, 1975-1985

- +50% AND OVER
- +25% TO +50%
- +5% TO +25%
- +5% TO -5%
- -5% TO -25%
- -25% TO -50%
- -50% AND OVER
- DATA NOT AVAILABLE

A WORLDWIDE WEB OF EXCHANGE

IN BILLIONS OF DOLLARS, 1983

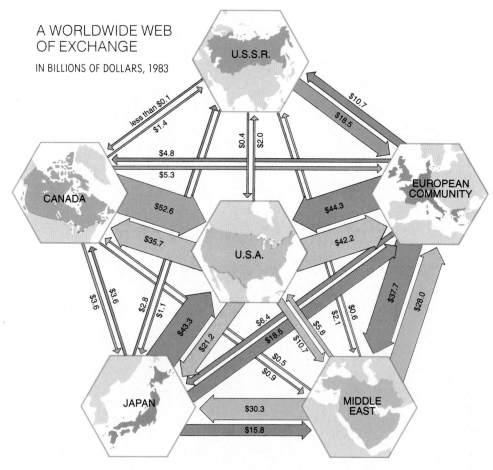

▲ *This diagram shows the volume of trade in 1983 among the United States, Canada, Japan, the Soviet Union, countries in the European Community, and countries in the Middle East (except Israel and Egypt). In some cases, a few commodities account for a strong export/import figure. For example, exports from Japan to the United States and the European Community are chiefly cars and electronic equipment. Japan and the European Community import large quantities of oil from some Middle Eastern countries.*

livestock, petroleum, and rubber, there are special marketplaces called commodity exchanges. Trading takes place through an auction system based on standard quantities and grades. Buyers bid on and purchase goods without actually seeing them. Shares of ownership in corporations are sold in a similar way on stock exchanges, such as those in New York City, London, and Tokyo.

In most countries, most trade is regulated by the government. In the United States, for example, Congress has enacted laws that forbid companies to conspire to fix prices, to advertise products that do not exist, and to use child labor. The goal of regulation is fairness to consumers and producers.

International Trade

Trade is carried on between people in different countries as well as between people in the same country. The buying and selling of goods and services between people in different countries is called international trade. International trade gives consumers a greater variety of choice in the marketplace. Also, the

competition for markets encourages manufacturers to make better products, as has happened in the U.S. automobile industry.

Purchases from another country are called imports, and sales to another country are called exports. Almost every country has its own money, or currency, used for domestic trade—trade in its own economy. In international trade, currencies are bought and sold just as commodities are. Most international trade is based on the U.S. dollar.

Many economists favor open markets between countries, or free trade. With free trade, the amount of trade most often depends on the quality and the price of the products. Free trade is often limited, however.

Barriers to free trade are erected by governments to protect their countries' producers. The most common barrier is a tariff, or duty, paid on imported goods when they enter a country, making them more expensive for consumers. Most governments impose quotas on certain goods, which means that only fixed amounts of those goods can enter a country. For example, a quota might limit the number of cars that can be imported.

Trade between countries, or among groups of countries, is regulated by negotiated agreements. Free trade is often the goal. In 1988, for example, the United States and Canada agreed to do away with tariffs. The European Community seeks free trade among its member countries.

International negotiations to open up world trade are carried out under the General Agreement on Tariffs and Trade (GATT), which covers almost all trade in goods by most countries. More than a hundred GATT countries have tariff agreements with each other and agree to some common trading rules. Agreement among all countries on trading practices is difficult to achieve, but great progress has been made.

Most international trade is carried on among industrialized countries whose borders are open to one another's goods and services. The major trading partners of the U.S. are Canada, Western European countries, and Japan. Most of the goods they trade are mass produced. Most exports from developing countries are basic commodities such as foodstuffs and minerals, though many are trying to diversify their exports.

► *A worker in an Argentine mint holds sheets of new bills. Unlike gold, paper currency has value only if sellers will accept it in exchange for goods and services.*
▼ *On the floor of the New York Stock Exchange, traders buy and sell shares of ownership in corporations. By offering shares, a company can raise needed funds.*

An important area of international trade is tourism—economic activity that depends on tourists. For many countries, such as Jamaica and the Bahamas, tourism trade is more important than merchandise trade.

Since the 1970s, important changes have occurred in the pattern of international trade. Today, no single country dominates world trade as the United Kingdom and the United States once did. Some developing countries have become exporters of products made from basic commodities. For instance, Brazil exports rubber galoshes as well as raw rubber. Because their labor costs are low, some Asian countries, such as Taiwan, have become major exporters of textile goods and electronic equipment; some, such as South Korea, have become exporters of automobiles as well. Many large companies have become "multinationals," with factories all over the world. Imports into the United States market, for example, may come from foreign factories that belong to U.S. companies.

SEE ALSO DEVELOPMENT, ECONOMY, INDUSTRY, *and* TRANSPORTATION AND COMMUNICATION.

TRADE WINDS

Trade winds are the constant winds that blow from northeast to southwest toward the Equator in the Northern Hemisphere, and from southeast to northwest toward the Equator in the Southern Hemisphere. They arise from the circulation of the atmosphere between the Equator and regions known as the horse latitudes, which lie about 30 degrees north and 30 degrees south of the Equator. Air warmed by the equatorial sun rises and moves toward the Poles, becoming cooler as it goes. At the horse latitudes, some of the air descends and circulates back toward the Equator. The Coriolis effect, which is caused by the earth's rotation, deflects the moving air toward the west.

Trade winds were important in establishing sea routes in the days of sailing ships. Columbus pioneered the southerly trade winds route across the Atlantic to the Americas.

SEE ALSO CORIOLIS EFFECT *and* WIND.

TRANSPORTATION AND COMMUNICATION

Transportation is the movement of people and goods from one place to another. Communication is the process by which people exchange information. Both are vital to the orderly functioning of society. Though the ways and means of transportation and communication vary throughout the world, people everywhere use both to achieve similar goals.

People in all countries use some form of transportation, whether it is a double-decker bus rolling through the streets of London, a trailer truck heading down a California freeway, or a camel ambling through a crowded North African market. Communication can be described as a type of transportation, too. It helps transport messages and ideas from one person or group to another.

In developed countries, communications systems often are highly sophisticated, allowing people to speak to each other from their homes, from their cars, and even from aircraft. People in less developed lands often must rely on the same simple methods of communication that were common centuries ago. In remote areas without electricity, for example, information is often passed along

▲ Chinese children ride in baskets hung from a carrying pole. Muscle-powered forms of transport are still the most commonly used worldwide.
► Guiding as many as 200 takeoffs and landings an hour, controllers at Chicago's O'Hare International Airport use radar, radios, and other means of communication that aid transportation.

only as fast as a messenger on foot or on horseback can travel.

Modern transportation and communications systems are often linked. At busy airports, for instance, air traffic controllers use computerized radar to track the flight paths of incoming and departing planes. They also use special-frequency radios to speak to pilots and guide them to runways. Imagine the confusion there would be if pilots had no reliable way of knowing when or where other planes were landing or taking off. Transportation and communications systems thus may depend on each other for success.

Getting from Here to There

Modes of transportation vary in form and complexity throughout the world. In the Asian region of Tibet, for example, long-haired oxen called yaks are sometimes used to transport heavy goods through rugged mountains. In the mountains of North America, four-wheel drives and other engine-powered vehicles are the preferred means of transportation.

Whatever their speed or range, nearly all modes of transportation attempt to move people and goods swiftly and safely.

The earliest way of traveling was on foot, and the earliest means of transporting goods was on the human back or head. People were using domesticated animals for transportation by about 4000 B.C. Perhaps the greatest advance in transportation was the wheel, first developed in Mesopotamia around 3500 B.C. Wheeled vehicles and, later, the sailing ship allowed people to travel and to transport their goods faster and farther than ever before. Tunnels, bridges, canals, and paved roads made transportation easier as well. Transportation has become even faster in relatively recent times. The steamboat, the steam and diesel locomotives, the automobile, the airplane, and the space shuttle were all developed during the past 200 years. Each has revolutionized transportation in its own way.

Today, civilization depends on many means of transportation. Without trucks or trains, for instance, how could millions of us live in cities that are hundreds of kilometers

▼ *From drums to satellites and from sledges to space shuttles, the time line below and on the following pages shows major advances in communication (upper half) and transportation (lower half) from ancient times to the present.*

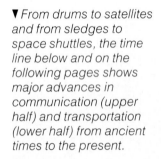

Paintings found on cave walls in Europe may represent an early form of communication.
About 20,000 B.C.

Using drums, fires, and smoke signals, people could communicate over great distances.
After 8000 B.C.

The world's first system of writing, using wedge-shaped characters for syllables and called cuneiform, was developed in Sumer.
4000–3000 B.C.

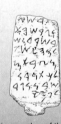

Semitic peoples of the eastern Mediterranean developed the first alphabet based on simple, one-sound consonants and vowels.
About 1500 B.C.

Paper was invented by Ts'ai Lun of the Han court in China.
A.D. 105

About 7000 B.C.
Sledges and dugout canoes were common forms of transportation in northern Europe.

By 4000 B.C.
People were using domesticated animals for transportion.

About 3500 B.C.
The first known form of the wheel was developed in Mesopotamia.

About 3000 B.C.
Egyptians probably built the first sailing ships.

About 300 B.C. to A.D. 400
The Romans constructed the most extensive network of paved roads in the ancient world.

TRANSPORTATION and COMMUNICATION

from the farms that produce much of our food? Without cars, buses, trains, or subways, how could people live in suburbs and commute to jobs in cities?

Transportation is essential to trade—the exchange of goods and services. Without supertankers, for example, Japan and parts of Europe would not receive the quantities of oil they need from the Middle East. Without freighters, Middle Eastern countries would not get the manufactured goods they require.

Advances in transportation have made the world seem smaller. Sailing ships often took months to cross the Atlantic; now, the fastest liners take five days. The same distance is traveled in less than four hours by a Concorde supersonic jet, at a cruising speed of 2,170 kilometers per hour (1,350 mph).

Although modern transportation has brought us many benefits, it has also caused problems. In urban areas, traffic jams are common during rush hours. Car exhausts pollute the air. In the United States alone, some 50,000 people die each year in motor vehicle accidents. Most engine-driven vehicles require gasoline and motor oil, and thus contribute to the depletion of the world's supply of petroleum. Some experts estimate that, at the current rate of use, the supply could be exhausted sometime during the 21st century.

Land Transportation

Of the three main kinds of transportation—land, water, and air—land transportation is by far the most common. Engine-powered wheeled vehicles are the chief form of land travel in industrialized countries. Such vehicles include automobiles, trucks, buses, motorcycles, and trains. Ever since the first practical gasoline-powered automobile was invented in Germany in the 1880s, motor travel has become increasingly popular. In the United States, millions of motor vehicles pass over the country's 6.4 million kilometers (4 million mi) of public roads each year.

In many developing countries, strained economies and rugged terrain have hindered the building of paved roads and the laying of railroad tracks. Many people in these

Chinese used movable type to produce books.
About 1040

Johann Gutenberg introduced the method of printing with movable type in Europe.
Mid-1400s

Printed, regularly published newspapers first appeared in several European countries.
Early 1600s

Louis Daguerre of France developed a process for making quick, clear photographs.
1830s

About A.D. 480
The nailed-on iron horseshoe was being used in Europe, allowing much faster and more extensive travel by horse than ever before.

1769
Nicolas-Joseph Cugnot of France invented a steam-powered, self-propelled vehicle.

1783
The first successful manned hot-air balloon flight was made in France in Joseph and Jacques Montgolfier's balloon.

1807
On the Hudson River in New York, Robert Fulton operated the first commercially successful steamboat.

1825
The first public steam railroad began service in Great Britain.

countries still rely on old forms of transportation. They walk, or they ride bicycles, and their goods are carried by pack animals or pushed along in carts and wheelbarrows.

The development of railroads in the 19th century and the mass production of automobiles in the 20th century dramatically changed society in the industrialized countries. Railroads opened new lands, influenced the growth of cities, linked towns and cities, and increased the speed and efficiency of trade. Automobiles provided travelers with greater mobility and spurred the growth of suburbs. Today, roads are being built more often than railways. Although trains still carry much of the heavy freight in developed countries, the automobile has become the most popular means of passenger travel.

Some experts predict that, with advanced technology, passenger trains could make a comeback in industrialized countries. High-speed trains are already in use in Japan and in many Western European countries. They are expected to become more popular and to compete with airlines for runs of up to

640 kilometers (400 mi) or so. Unlike centrally located train stations, many airports are some distance from the big cities they serve. Sometimes, getting to the airport can take as much travel time as the flight itself does.

Engineers are perfecting new types of high-speed passenger trains that could revolutionize rail travel. One train, called a magnetic levitation vehicle (maglev), has powerful electromagnets that lift the train 10 to 15 centimeters (4–6 in) above a single guide rail on a cushion of air instead of on wheels. This train of the future travels at speeds of up to 480 kilometers per hour (300 mph) in near silence.

Pipelines are a form of land transportation. They are used to transport petroleum products, natural gas, and some other substances over long distances. North America has the world's most extensive networks of oil and natural gas pipelines—nearly 2.4 million kilometers (1.5 million mi). Pipeline systems in the Soviet Union carry oil and natural gas from remote northern fields to centers throughout the country and to much of Eastern Europe. The Siberian system of natural gas pipelines

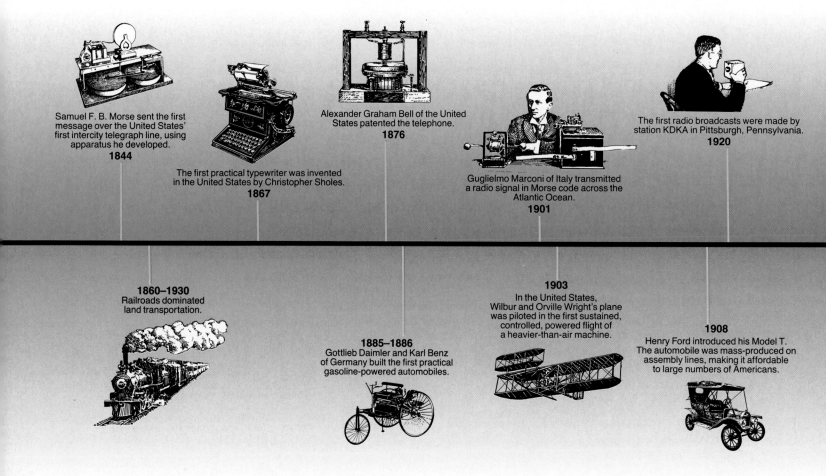

Samuel F. B. Morse sent the first message over the United States' first intercity telegraph line, using apparatus he developed.
1844

The first practical typewriter was invented in the United States by Christopher Sholes.
1867

Alexander Graham Bell of the United States patented the telephone.
1876

Guglielmo Marconi of Italy transmitted a radio signal in Morse code across the Atlantic Ocean.
1901

The first radio broadcasts were made by station KDKA in Pittsburgh, Pennsylvania.
1920

1860–1930
Railroads dominated land transportation.

1885–1886
Gottlieb Daimler and Karl Benz of Germany built the first practical gasoline-powered automobiles.

1903
In the United States, Wilbur and Orville Wright's plane was piloted in the first sustained, controlled, powered flight of a heavier-than-air machine.

1908
Henry Ford introduced his Model T. The automobile was mass-produced on assembly lines, making it affordable to large numbers of Americans.

is the largest in the world. In the Middle East, pipelines bring oil from the desert to ports on the Persian Gulf and the Mediterranean Sea.

Water Transportation

People have used water transportation since prehistoric times. Today, it remains the most important form of transportation in many parts of the world. It is one of the most economical ways to move cargo, and in many tropical areas, such as the Amazon basin in South America, it is the only way.

Accessibility to water transportation has played an important role in the development of cities and regions worldwide. For example, New York City, Buenos Aires, Rotterdam, and Shanghai are located where ships can be harbored safely, and New Orleans and Belém are near the mouths of major rivers. Steel mills are often built where water can bring iron ore and coal together, as at Pittsburgh, Pennsylvania, and at Essen, West Germany. Canals linking major rivers are vital to the economies of parts of Europe and China.

Log rafts and primitive canoes were once the quickest means of transportation, but they eventually gave way to sturdy sailing vessels first built in Egypt about 3000 B.C. Improvements in sailing vessels made possible distant voyages and the European discovery of the Americas. Water transportation has become swifter and safer over the centuries.

Until the development of commercial jet airliners in the 1950s, ships were the chief means of overseas travel. Now, most ships that sail the ocean or other large bodies of water, such as the Great Lakes, are used to carry heavy cargo. They are also important for military transport. Barges, pulled by tugboats, are used to transport heavy loads along inland waterways. Tugboats also tow ships into port for the loading and unloading of passengers and goods. Besides tugs, workboats include trawlers and other vessels used in commercial fishing worldwide.

Many kinds of boats are used to transport people and goods. Ferries, for example, are a common means of travel in Europe and Asia and in parts of North America. Log rafts,

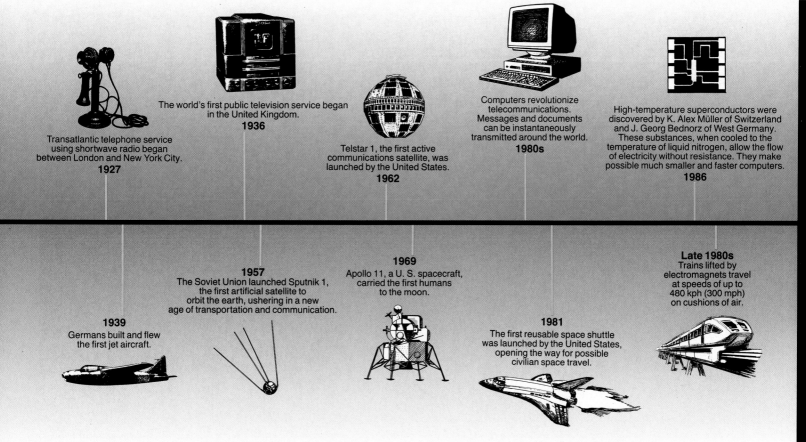

Transatlantic telephone service using shortwave radio began between London and New York City.
1927

The world's first public television service began in the United Kingdom.
1936

Telstar 1, the first active communications satellite, was launched by the United States.
1962

Computers revolutionize telecommunications. Messages and documents can be instantaneously transmitted around the world.
1980s

High-temperature superconductors were discovered by K. Alex Müller of Switzerland and J. Georg Bednorz of West Germany. These substances, when cooled to the temperature of liquid nitrogen, allow the flow of electricity without resistance. They make possible much smaller and faster computers.
1986

1939
Germans built and flew the first jet aircraft.

1957
The Soviet Union launched Sputnik 1, the first artificial satellite to orbit the earth, ushering in a new age of transportation and communication.

1969
Apollo 11, a U. S. spacecraft, carried the first humans to the moon.

1981
The first reusable space shuttle was launched by the United States, opening the way for possible civilian space travel.

Late 1980s
Trains lifted by electromagnets travel at speeds of up to 480 kph (300 mph) on cushions of air.

COMMUNICATION and TRANSPORTATION

▼ *A man leads his camel on a beach in Pakistan. Able to bear heavy loads in searing heat, camels have made desert travel possible in Asia and Africa for centuries.*

steered by paddles or poles, are used in the Pacific islands and in various tropical regions for transportation along rivers or between islands. Sailboats and motorboats are widely used for fishing and for recreation.

Hydrofoils and air-cushion vehicles quickly carry people across swamps and other bodies of water that can be hard to navigate. Hydrofoils, fitted with fins that provide a

lift as speed increases, are used, for example, on the Nile River in Egypt. Air-cushion vehicles travel above water or land on a cushion of air produced by powerful fans. Called Hovercraft in the United Kingdom, such vehicles transport people across the English Channel.

Air Transportation

On December 17, 1903, as his brother Wilbur watched, Orville Wright piloted their *Flyer* for 12 history-making seconds near Kitty Hawk, on the coast of North Carolina. Before the Wright brothers, people had flown in hot-air balloons and in zeppelins and other airships. But this was the first sustained, controlled, powered flight of a heavier-than-air machine. The Wright brothers' plane flew only about 37 meters (120 ft), a distance about the same as the wingspan of a commercial jet.

Throughout the 20th century, pilots and inventors have improved airplane design. Today's aircraft include commercial transport planes; light planes such as those used as air taxis, in spotting fires, and in rescue operations; military planes and seaplanes; and special-purpose planes such as crop dusters

▼ *Pedal power transports citizens of Beijing. Bicycles are a principal mode of travel in China, where perhaps only one person in 75,000 owns a car.*

▲ *A mule-drawn cart carries farm people along an unpaved road in Paraguay. In many parts of the world, animals are still used to haul loads.*

◄ *Overcrowding drives riders to train roofs in Cambodia. Many are traders who depend on the damaged railways of this war-torn country.*
▼ *Trolleys rumble along a street in Toronto. City dwellers in many countries rely on mass transit.*

and the vertical or short take-off and landing planes used by the military.

Airplanes are by far the quickest means of moving people and goods over long distances. Commercial jet airliners routinely fly at speeds of 800 to 965 kilometers per hour (500–600 mph). Flights originating in the United States, Canada, or Western Europe enable people to reach almost any destination in a day or less. In many developing countries and in remote areas, however, flights are much less frequent and are often limited to a single destination.

Air travel at first was prohibitively expensive. As aviation technology improved, air transportation became more economical and efficient. It is also one of the safest ways to travel. In 1987, more than one billion journeys were made by individuals on scheduled flights worldwide. Most of the world's people, however, have never traveled by air.

Science and technology, experts say, will continue to bring improvements not only to airplanes and their engines but also to the handling of aircraft within air traffic control systems. Air transportation should thus become even safer and more efficient.

In 1981, the United States launched the first space shuttle, opening the way to future

◄ *Convenience has its cost: rush-hour traffic jams for San Francisco-area commuters and for millions of other Americans who drive to work.*

transportation in space. The reusable space shuttles circle the globe, carrying experiments, satellites, and space probes, and then return to earth. Eventually, many scientists predict, advanced shuttle craft will carry workers and materials high above the earth to build the first permanent space structures. These may include manufacturing plants, laboratories, solar power stations, and, in time, the first space settlement.

The Exchange of Information

Communication is the process by which information is exchanged between individuals through a common system of symbols, signs, or behavior communicated orally or by written message. Communication can be divided into two basic kinds: interpersonal communication and mass communication. In the home, a discussion at the dinner table, a note from a parent reminding a child to wash the dishes, or a phone conversation with a faraway grandparent are examples of interpersonal communication. Communication that takes place when information is sent to large audiences is called mass communication. Books, magazines, newspapers, and radio and television broadcasts are examples of mass communication.

Many forms of communication are vital to society. The leaders of countries use both oral and written communication to learn of each other's concerns and thus avoid

▲ Steered with a pole, a small log boat with a shelter of grasses is a typical means of transport in the Ganges Delta off the Bay of Bengal.
► Travelers on the Nile crowd a felucca, an ancient type of sailboat. Since most Egyptians live near the river, water transport remains essential.

confrontations. Scientists use satellites and other advanced communications systems to monitor dangerous weather conditions such as hurricanes. Television and radio announcers broadcast storm warnings to the public.

In industrialized countries, businesses use a variety of electronic equipment to increase the speed and reliability of communication. For example, salespeople at a company's branch office often type their sales orders into a computer, which then relays the information to a computer in the main office. Customers leave messages on telephone answering machines, mail letters to companies, or transmit printed copies of important documents through facsimile machines, which use telephone lines to reproduce printed matter automatically. All of these are forms of modern communication.

Once, it took an ocean journey of several weeks to carry a message from the United States to Europe. Today, the world is linked by many communications systems. A passenger on an airplane high above the United States can use an on-board telephone service to call home. People in London, England, watched a televised broadcast of the Olympic Games in Seoul, South Korea. And doctors in Beijing, China, communicated a demonstration of spinal cord treatment to doctors in the U.S. by using telephone lines and special software to link their personal computers. While modern transportation allows us to travel almost anywhere in a day or less, modern communications systems allow us to share information around the globe in seconds.

From Drums to Telephones

Prehistoric people sometimes communicated by beating against hollow logs and tree trunks. Drum sounds enabled them to develop codes for signaling war, peace, and other news. Some societies still use drums or other instruments, smoke signals, or fire beacons to transmit important messages.

One of the earliest means of communicating over great distances was by runners who carried oral or written messages. After horses were domesticated, riders could deliver messages faster and farther. Sometimes men with strong lungs were stationed on hilltops to relay military orders to the next

▲ A hydrofoil approaches a port in Crete. As the passenger boat picks up speed, its bladelike "wings" lift the entire hull clear of the water.
◄ Loaded trucks arrive by ferry on the Mekong River in Thailand. Ferries provide vital transportation links in many parts of the world.
▼ Giant cranes load and unload freighters at Durban, South Africa. World trade depends on oceangoing vessels.

manned hilltop within shouting distance. Later, people sent messages by carrier pigeon.

Perhaps the earliest form of written communication was picture writing, or pictographs. Each picture illustrated an idea. The world's first writing system was developed around 4000 to 3000 B.C. in Mesopotamia by people called Sumerians. Known as cuneiform, the system used wedge-shaped characters for syllables. The invention of writing systems by different peoples in different parts of the world was one of the most important developments in human history. Writing provided a means of permanently recording events and ideas. It also allowed people to send messages long distances without having to rely on the memories of runners.

Before the development of printing, the small number of books that were made were copied by hand, letter by letter. Very few people could do this; most were illiterate—unable to read or write. Although movable type was used in China in the 11th century, Europeans did not begin experimenting with it until the

mid-1400s. Most historians credit Johann Gutenberg with introducing the method of printing with movable metal type to Europe. He used a special press, metal molds for each letter of the alphabet, and oil-based inks. On a press, books could be produced more quickly and with greater uniformity. People also began printing newspapers, magazines, and almanacs, and soon printed publications became the most important form of mass communication.

▲ *On fragile wings,* Gossamer Albatross *glides above the English Channel in 1979. Only the pilot's pedaling powered the ultralight aircraft on its 36-kilometer (22.5-mile) flight from England to France, which took less than three hours.*
◄ *Crewmen tether the Houston-based blimp* America *as passengers board its gondola for a sightseeing flight. Blimps fly low and cruise at about 56 kilometers per hour (35 mph). Today's airships display ads, move cargo, and serve as research stations and camera platforms.*

Until the mid-1800s, most information could be sent no faster than the quickest train or steamboat could travel. Except for "visual telegraphs"—towers in Europe where messages sent in code were viewed through telescopes and sent along to the next tower—long-distance communication depended largely on transportation. In the United States, for example, it took Pony Express riders 10½ days to carry mail from St. Joseph, Missouri, to Sacramento, California. Stagecoaches bearing news from Washington, D.C., often took 44 hours to make the 385-kilometer (240-mile) trip from there to New York City.

All of this changed after American inventor Samuel F. B. Morse sent the first message over the first intercity telegraph line, from Washington, D.C., to Baltimore, Maryland. That historic message, sent on May 24, 1844, was "What hath God wrought!" Morse's telegraph interrupted a steady battery current to produce messages in dots and dashes on an electromagnetic receiver. The dots and dashes are now known as Morse code.

At first, people were skeptical about the telegraph, but soon wires were strung up along railroad lines and in major cities across the United States. In August 1858, a telegraph cable was laid under the Atlantic Ocean to connect North America and Europe, but a month later the signals were barely readable. Not until 1866 were the continents successfully linked by cable. International commerce was stimulated, and news could be exchanged in minutes instead of weeks.

The invention that improved communications the most was the telephone. It was developed by the Scottish-born American inventor Alexander Graham Bell. His first patented telephone had a parchment drum that vibrated when sound waves reached it. On March 10, 1876, Bell transmitted the first message ever heard over a wire. "Mr. Watson, come here! I want to see you," he shouted into the mouthpiece as his assistant, Thomas Watson, listened in a room adjoining their laboratory in Boston, Massachusetts. The first regular telephone line was installed between Boston and

▲ Runway lights blur as a special camera attached to the tail of a Lockheed L-1011 TriStar records the touchdown of this wide-bodied commercial jet.
▼ Columbia's dazzling ascent in 1981 launches the era of space shuttles, which may one day link orbiting colonies to earth.

▼ *A vendor's display in Jerusalem offers newspapers and magazines in many languages. They typify one kind of mass communication.*

Somerville, Massachusetts, in 1877. Bell's invention quickly caught on, and by 1890 there were 228,000 telephones in the U.S. alone.

Today, advanced technology, including signal amplifiers, satellites, and special transmission lines, allows telephone users in developed countries to speak with friends and business associates across oceans and continents; to talk with many people at one time; and to make calls to and from automobiles on cellular mobile phones.

Radio, Television, and Computers

Building on the results of earlier experiments in electricity and magnetism, the Italian inventor Guglielmo Marconi proved the feasibility of radio communication in 1896. Later, from a transmitter in Cornwall, England, Marconi sent a message of three dots—Morse code for the letter "S"—3,540 kilometers (2,200 mi) across the Atlantic to a receiver in Newfoundland. Electricity for the transmitter was generated by a 25-horsepower oil engine, and the antenna was supported by two tall masts. The receiver was connected to an antenna supported by a kite. Marconi's experiment proved that radio waves can travel around the earth.

In 1906, a telephone circuit was attached to an early radio—then called a wireless telegraph—and an experimental program of voice and music was broadcast from Brant Rock, Massachusetts. It was heard by ship wireless operators with headphones within a radius of several hundred kilometers. Now

▲ *The postmaster stands outside the two-room post office that serves the residents of Salvo, North Carolina.*

▼ *Chinese villagers scan movie advertisements. Films are a popular form of entertainment worldwide.*

◄ Wares of a music shop in Amman, Jordan, signal the spread of information and entertainment through affordable electronic appliances.
▼ Communication serves transportation in the Traffic Control Center of the Tokyo police department. A giant wall map and television monitors enable officials to track rush-hour traffic through Japan's huge capital city.

◄ Computers perform important tasks for workers in a busy office in New York City. Capable of completing millions of calculations per second, computers have revolutionized communications, leading many experts to call the late 20th century the "information age."

voice broadcasts could reach many people at the same time.

In 1920, the first radio broadcasts were made by station KDKA in Pittsburgh, Pennsylvania. Commercial radio stations advanced communications by quickly providing news and entertainment to large audiences. No longer did people have to wait for newspapers to be printed to learn about current events.

The origins of television, once called "visual radio," can be traced as far back as 1884. In that year, German scientist Paul Nipkow invented a picture-sending device that used a "scanning disk," a rapidly spinning perforated wheel with an illuminated screen behind it. The perforations broke each image into thousands of individual dots—the basis of television transmission. In 1936, the British Broadcasting Corporation initiated the world's first public television service incorporating an all-electronic system. In 1987, there were nearly 10,000 television stations throughout the world sending out programs to more than 648 million television sets.

While radio allows information to be relayed quickly to mass audiences, it can do so only through sound. People rely largely on their imaginations to visualize the events that radio announcers describe. Television allows us to see as well as hear an event as it unfolds, often giving us a clearer, closer view of what is happening than is available to people actually at the scene. A descriptive radio report could feed our imaginations and help us experience the drama of the first landing on the moon in 1969. But only live television could take us along with the astronauts as they traveled through space and stepped onto the surface of the moon.

Like several other breakthroughs in communications, television has made the world seem a smaller place by allowing people separated by great distances to share the same experiences. With the use of communications satellites and other devices, television permits millions of people in dozens of countries to watch the same programs at the same time. In 1985, perhaps 1.5 billion viewers in more than 150 countries watched a rock music concert broadcast worldwide from London and Philadelphia. It raised more than 50 million dollars to aid victims of famine in Africa.

Most people in developing countries,

► *At Jodrell Bank, England, a giant radio telescope 76 meters (250 ft) in diameter collects and measures faint radio waves given off by objects in space.*

▼ *Television brings live coverage of important events to people around the world. During an America's Cup yacht race in 1987, an Australian ground station receives signals from cameras on boats and aircraft and beams them to INTELSAT V. The satellite relays them to a ground station in California. Another satellite picks up the signals and sends them to an East Coast transmitting station. Total time from sea to TV set: less than a second.*

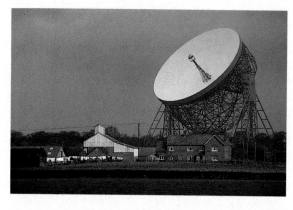

however, do not have television sets. In India, for example, there might be one set for an entire village. The people gather around it to watch a program, much as people in developed countries might go to see a movie.

One of the most significant communications developments in the 20th century was the computer. With amazing accuracy, today's computers can store, organize, and send vast amounts of information at dizzying

speeds. Advances in the design of microchips—circuits the size of a baby's thumbnail that serve as computer nerve centers—help some supercomputers perform more than 1.5 billion calculations per second. The world's first electronic computer, completed in 1946, could perform about 5,000 per second. It occupied the space of a two-car garage.

The benefits of the new machines seem endless. Economists use sophisticated computers to track economic patterns and can instantly inform financial markets of new trends. High-technology businesses use computers to monitor and control communications satellites that ride many thousands of kilometers above the earth. And personal computer users who link their machines to telephone lines can make simple financial transactions through their local banks. They can also communicate with other computer users around the world. Computers have put much of the world's knowledge at our fingertips.

Advances in communications continue to occur rapidly. Today, for example, the use of fiber optics is revolutionizing the telephone industry. Fiber optics are hair-thin strands of very pure glass that can carry many thousands of telephone conversations over high-capacity light beams.

Communications experts predict that larger satellites will be sent into orbit to relay thousands more television, telephone, and other signals to the earth. Microcomputers, telephones, and televisions will all be linked to home communications systems.

Advances are also being made in cellular mobile phone systems. Soon we may be able to buy pocket-size phones that will enable us to reach others, and be reached by them, on the street, in the market, or almost anywhere else we go.

We have come a long way in both transportation and communication since the days of dugout canoes and fleet-footed messengers, sailing ships and hand-copied books. Today, people and places around the world are linked in ways undreamed of in past centuries. Recent changes in transportation and communication have been swift, and, experts say, there are many more changes to come.

LIVE TELEVISION TRANSMISSION FROM AUSTRALIA TO THE UNITED STATES

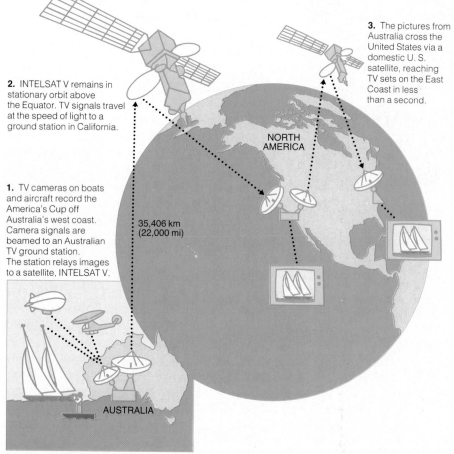

2. INTELSAT V remains in stationary orbit above the Equator. TV signals travel at the speed of light to a ground station in California.

1. TV cameras on boats and aircraft record the America's Cup off Australia's west coast. Camera signals are beamed to an Australian TV ground station. The station relays images to a satellite, INTELSAT V.

3. The pictures from Australia cross the United States via a domestic U. S. satellite, reaching TV sets on the East Coast in less than a second.

NORTH AMERICA

35,406 km (22,000 mi)

AUSTRALIA

SEE ALSO ALPHABET, BRIDGE, CANAL, DEVELOPMENT, LANGUAGE, TECHNOLOGY, *and* TRADE.

TRENCH

A trench is a long, deep depression in the ocean floor. Some trenches are adjacent to continents. Others are found near chains of volcanic islands, such as the Aleutians, Japan, and the Philippines.

Trenches occur where plates—huge rocky slabs that hold the earth's crust—are colliding. Forces within the earth cause the plates to move constantly. Sometimes when two plates collide, the edge of one dives beneath the other in a process called subduction. The deep depression this forms is called a trench.

The rock of the subducting plate may melt as it descends. When this occurs, some of the molten material can rise through the overlying plate and erupt, forming volcanoes. The volcanoes often build mountain ranges or long chains of volcanic islands that lie parallel to the trench.

The earth's lowest known spot is the Challenger Deep, at the bottom of the Mariana Trench, which drops about 11,000 meters (36,000 ft) below the ocean's surface near Guam, an island in the western Pacific.

SEE ALSO OCEAN, PLATE TECTONICS, RING OF FIRE, SEAFLOOR SPREADING, *and* VOLCANO.

TRIBUTARY

A tributary is a stream that feeds, or flows into, a larger stream. The smallest tributaries are tiny trickles of rainwater known as rills. As these flow downhill, they join other rills to form larger streams, which may feed into bigger streams. The larger streams, or rivers, may also be tributaries. The Ohio and Missouri Rivers, for example, are two major tributaries of the Mississippi River. A trunk river and all its tributaries are known as a river system. Some rivers have few tributaries, while others have many. The Amazon, which carries more water than any other river system in the world, has more than a thousand tributaries.

SEE ALSO LAKE, RIVER, SOURCE, *and* STREAM.

TROPICS

The line of latitude about 23½ degrees north of the Equator is called the Tropic of Cancer. The line of latitude about 23½ degrees south of the Equator is called the Tropic of Capricorn. "Tropics" is used most often to describe the region that lies between these two parallels. The tropics encompass 36 percent of the earth's land, including parts of North America, South America, Africa, Asia, and Australia. The subtropics are the zones between 23½ degrees and about 40 degrees north and south of the Equator.

The tropics are generally warm year-round, with monthly temperatures averaging from 25°C to 28°C (77°F–82°F). The warm temperatures are primarily a result of the position of the tropics on the earth as it orbits the sun. This region receives the sun's rays more directly than the rest of the planet does.

The amount of precipitation in the tropics, however, varies greatly from one area to another. Some areas have a tropical wet climate. Rain forests, with their wide variety of plant and animal species, are common there. Other parts of the tropics have a tropical wet and dry climate, which results in three main seasons: cool and dry, hot and dry, and hot and wet. Life in these regions of the tropics depends on the wet season's rains.

SEE ALSO CLIMATE, EARTH, *and* SEASONS.

EASTERN HEMISPHERE

WESTERN HEMISPHERE

▲ *About a third of the world's people live in the tropics, the region between the parallels of latitude called the Tropic of Cancer and the Tropic of Capricorn.*
▼ *Java islanders scale coconut palms, which thrive in Indonesia's tropical climate. Most places in the tropics have warm temperatures year-round.*

TSUNAMI

Tsunami are ocean waves triggered primarily by movement of the ocean floor during strong earthquakes. Volcanic eruptions in or near the ocean may also cause them. The waves radiate from the site of a disturbance in widening circles, often traveling great distances. Many people mistakenly call them tidal waves, but they have nothing to do with tides—the regular rise and fall of the ocean's surface. The waves are also different from ordinary waves caused by wind. They are properly called seismic sea waves or tsunami, from a Japanese word, now used worldwide, meaning "great harbor wave."

Seismic sea waves race through the ocean at speeds that may exceed 800 kilometers (500 mi) an hour. In deep water, tsunami are less than a meter high, but when they arrive in shallow areas along coasts, the waves pile up into walls of water that may tower as high as a ten-story building. The masses of water surge ashore, hitting land with tremendous force. Powerful tsunami can cause great destruction.

Throughout history, tsunami have been responsible for thousands of deaths, especially in coastal areas of the Pacific Ocean. Today, the Pacific Tsunami Warning System, with centers in Hawaii and Alaska, detects tsunami and warns people of their approach.

SEE ALSO EARTHQUAKE, OCEAN, SEISMOLOGY, VOLCANO, *and* WAVES.

▲ *When earthquakes or volcanic eruptions trigger tsunami, a series of low, broad waves races through the ocean. As the waves approach land and reach the shallows, they slow and climb. Sometimes they are preceded by a sudden withdrawal of water from the shore (top). Then the whole mass of water surges inland (bottom).*

TUNDRA

Tundra is a cold region characterized by low vegetation. There are two kinds of tundra: the alpine tundra of high mountain ranges in lower latitudes and the Arctic tundra of the landmasses around the polar seas in the far north. The two kinds share some characteristics. For example, plant species in both are limited in number. The plants have adapted to short growing seasons and cold temperatures. There are, however, significant differences between the two kinds of tundra.

Alpine Tundra

The cold of the alpine tundra is associated with high elevation rather than with high latitude. With its strong winds, snow, and cold and widely fluctuating temperatures, the alpine tundra is a harsh environment for plants. Alpine tundra is the zone on mountaintops above the timberline, the boundary above which continuous tree growth ends. There are some 10 million square kilometers (4 million sq mi) of this kind of tundra, mostly in the northern temperate latitudes.

Unlike Arctic tundra, which experiences long periods of sunlight in summer but is deprived of sunlight during the long Arctic winter, alpine tundra receives daily doses of solar

▲ A gray wolf in Canada's Northwest Territories pauses on a carpet of white heather, a plant adapted to the harsh climate of the Arctic tundra.
◄ Freezing and thawing form a pattern of polygons in the tundra of Alaska's Flaxman Island.

radiation. The growing season lasts 50 to 180 days. The pattern of vegetation in the alpine tundra depends largely on the distribution of moisture and the amount of wind exposure an area has. In the highest windswept areas, only tiny plants called lichens may cling to the rocks. Below the lichen growth, cushion plants tend to grow together in rock depressions, forming a solid mat that helps protect them from biting winds. The structure of the plants helps them trap heat. In more protected areas of the alpine tundra, sedges and flowering plants may cover the ground. In well-drained soils, meadows may exist. Only in wet meadows or bogs are soil conditions similar to those of the damp Arctic tundra. Most alpine plants are perennials; that is, they survive for more than one growing season.

Animal life in alpine tundra regions includes mountain goats, sheep, marmots, and a number of bird and insect species.

Arctic Tundra

Arctic tundra encompasses an area equal to about a tenth of the earth's land—15 million square kilometers (6 million sq mi). It exists primarily in extreme northern latitudes, between the northern margins of forests and the Arctic Ocean. In the Southern Hemisphere, ice-covered Antarctica does not have areas of well-developed tundra, though mosses and lichens do grow there.

Summer temperatures in the Arctic usually remain below 10°C (50°F), and the growing season lasts 50 to 60 days. Permafrost, a layer of permanently frozen ground beneath the earth's surface, is mainly a characteristic of Arctic tundra, although it does occur in alpine tundra in the far north or at very high elevations. Permafrost consists of soil, sand, and gravel, usually frozen together in a solid mass. It can reach depths of 450 meters (1,500 ft). When the surface layer above it thaws in summer, the water cannot drain through the frozen subsoil. Puddles, lakes, and bogs, on which some well-adapted plants flourish during the short Arctic summer, form at this time.

Lichens are more widespread in Arctic tundra than they are in alpine tundra. In the Arctic, lichens cover not only rocks but wood and ground as well. The Arctic tundra's

waterlogged soil supports only plants with shallow roots, such as grasses and small flowering plants. Permafrost, cold temperatures, strong winds, and other factors keep trees from developing fully.

Much of the vegetation in Arctic tundra is perennial. Plants have adapted to the harsh climate. They have living tissue or roots that remain in frozen ground for most of the year. When summer arrives and the ice melts, they often bloom in a matter of days. Some species

► *Arctic tundra encircles the Arctic Ocean. Alpine tundra exists at very high elevations on mountain ranges worldwide.*
◄ *Drummond's dryas are hardy evergreen plants common in tundra near the Arctic Circle. The small, creeping plant is also found on top of high mountains farther south.*
▼ *Lupines and other wildflowers bloom briefly in the tundra of Alaska's Arctic National Wildlife Refuge. The growing season is short in tundra regions.*

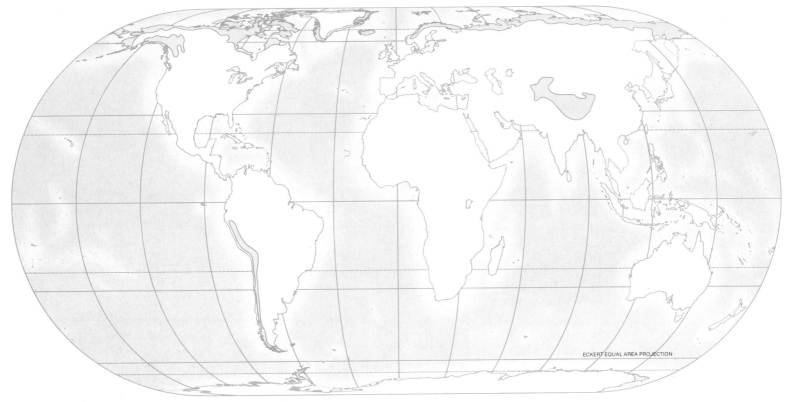

have unusually large leaves that tilt toward the sun so that they catch as much light as possible. Some have hollow stems that retain heat, and some grow protective coverings. The woolly lousewort, for example, is encased in a mass of fine fibers.

Arctic tundra formed relatively recently—geologically speaking—when glaciers began to retreat after the peak of the most recent ice age about 18,000 years ago. Today, the tundra landscape continues to be shaped by ice and has a number of unusual-looking landforms, including pingos and polygons. Pingos, small hills with icy cores, form when groundwater is locked in by permafrost and freezes. As the ice expands, it forces up the overlying layer of earth and gravel. Some pingos spread 550 meters (1,800 ft) and rise as high as 45 meters (150 ft). Polygons form when freezing and thawing of the soil cause it to expand and contract, opening up cracks in the tundra's surface. The cracks fill with water from snowmelt, which freezes into vertical ice wedges. The interlocking polygons form a honeycomb pattern in the ground.

Animal life in the Arctic tundra, which includes foxes, polar bears, gray wolves, caribou, and musk-oxen, is more plentiful than is life in the alpine tundra. Millions of birds

PERMAFROST

▲ In this cross section of tundra soil, the blue area represents permafrost, a layer of ground that remains frozen year-round. In the summer, the soil's top layer thaws and becomes saturated with water. Permafrost prevents the water from draining. Only plants with shallow roots can live in tundra soil. Such plants include grasses, lichens, and mosses.

545

► *Millions of barrels of oil cross Alaska's tundra regions yearly inside the trans-Alaska pipeline.*
▼ *To avoid melting the permafrost, engineers elevated parts of the pipeline on steel supports to keep it above the tundra's fragile soil.*

inhabit the region in summer, feeding on fish and on insects such as flies and mosquitoes.

Some animals live in the tundra region year-round; others migrate there only in summer. The animals have adapted in various ways to life in the tundra. The musk-ox has a shaggy coat and a woolly undercoat that protect it from the cold. Caribou have large, concave hooves that prevent them from sinking into the snow or into damp soil.

Lemmings, small mouselike creatures, are common tundra animals. The furry lemmings eat twice their weight in food each day. Their digestive systems are inefficient, so almost 70 percent of this food is excreted back onto tundra soil, where it helps nourish the plants. Lemmings clear away snow and dead plants to reach tender shoots of new growth. This speeds up the cycle of plant decay and renewal and adds nutrients to the soil.

Natural resources such as coal, oil, and natural gas have attracted people to the Arctic tundra. At first, people were unaware of the fragile nature of the ecosystem. They removed the soil layer covering the permafrost, which soon began to thaw. Structures placed over permafrost sank or collapsed. Heavy vehicles destroyed vegetation and left deep tracks on the land. Through weathering and erosion, some tracks deepen into gullies, then widen into ravines. Destruction of the permafrost threatens the existence of tundra vegetation. Oil spills have killed vegetation and penetrated the natural drainage system. Air

pollution from North America, Europe, and the Soviet Union has spread a haze over the Arctic. With little precipitation, the pollutants are not easily washed away.

Efforts are now being made to protect the tundra. To keep permafrost from thawing, building sites are covered with a thick layer of gravel, or buildings are placed on pilings with an insulating air space below. Hot-water lines and parts of the trans-Alaska pipeline are elevated on steel supports above the surface. The future of the Arctic tundra, whose ecological balance is easily upset, will depend on how people interact with the fragile region.

SEE ALSO CLIMATE, MOUNTAIN, PERMAFROST, POLAR REGIONS, *and* POLLUTION.

► *Oil workers use special equipment to help them locate petroleum deposits beneath Alaskan tundra without unnecessary drilling. Companies often locate potential oil fields by first surveying an area using ultrasonic and seismic instruments.*

TYPHOON

"Typhoon" is one of the names for a rotating tropical storm with winds of at least 119 kilometers per hour (74 mph). Such storms are called typhoons when they occur in the China Sea and in the western Pacific Ocean. They are identical to the hurricanes that form over the eastern Pacific and the Atlantic. Typhoons occur most frequently between June and December, when ocean temperatures are warmest. There is typically a lull during July and August, when strong easterly winds at high altitudes disrupt developing tropical cyclones in the western Pacific.

Typhoons can be extremely destructive. In December 1944, during World War II, a typhoon severely damaged a U.S. naval fleet that was to help invade the Philippines. Three ships sank and almost 800 sailors perished. Six months later, another typhoon struck the U.S. fleet, killing six men and damaging 33 ships. Japan was hit hard by three typhoons in the 1950s. The worst was Typhoon Vera, which in September 1959 caused nearly 4,500 deaths, destroyed 40,000 dwellings, and left more than a million people homeless.

SEE ALSO CYCLONE, HURRICANE, *and* WEATHER.

URBAN AREA

"Urban" means "characteristic of a city." An urban area is a built-up area where most inhabitants have nonagricultural jobs. The term covers small towns and their surrounding areas, as well as large cities and their suburbs. The latter are often called metropolitan areas, or "greater," as in Greater New York or Greater London. When two or more metropolitan areas grow until they combine, the result may be known as a megalopolis.

SEE ALSO CITY *and* RURAL AREA.

V

VALLEY

A valley is an elongated natural depression in the earth bordered by higher land. It may be narrow or wide. Valleys occur more frequently than any other land formation. They are found in high mountain ranges, in hills, in lowlands, and on the ocean floor. The movement of water, ice, or the earth's crust leads to the formation and development of valleys.

River Valleys

Streams produce most valleys. As water flows in a stream, it moves sand and gravel along the bottom, carving a channel. As the water, laden with abrasives, cuts deeper and deeper, the walls of soil and rock it leaves form the sides of a valley.

In some areas, almost vertical valley walls are formed, consisting of durable rock that does not wear away easily. These steep-sided valleys are called canyons. Narrow canyons are known as gorges.

In other areas, valley walls consist of softer rock that weathers and erodes—breaks down and wears away—more easily from the action of water, ice, and temperature changes than does harder rock. Rain and snow help move soil and rocks from the top of the valley walls down to the valley bottom, or floor. The force of gravity pulls soil and rocks down the slopes and into the water below. The top of the valley, most exposed to weathering and erosion, gradually widens. A valley formed in this way usually has a V shape.

Over time, the downward cutting action of a stream slows, and the stream begins to cut sideways. The water flows around boulders and other obstacles instead of over them. The path of the stream begins to meander, or curve from side to side, as the lower Mississippi River does. Following a snakelike path, the water cuts into the valley walls, causing soil and rocks to collapse and fall into the water. This process slowly widens the valley floor until it becomes a flat plain. Sometimes a stream floods, flowing over its banks onto the valley floor. The part of the floor

◄ Immense Dezadeash Glacier winds through the Coast Mountains in Canada's Yukon Territory. Moving masses of ice, glaciers carry loads of rock and other debris that enlarge valleys and sculpture the land as the ice flows forward. After the glaciers melt, U-shaped valleys remain.

▲ *West Germany's Mosel Valley cradles the village of Cochem. Vineyards have flourished in the area since Roman times. For almost 2,000 years people have shipped their goods on the Mosel River. Such valleys provided settlers with fertile soil, abundant water, and convenient transport and travel.*

on either side of a stream that is sometimes covered by floodwater is called a floodplain.

Glacial Valleys

The movement of ice leaves its mark on valleys. When masses of ice called glaciers flow through high mountain valleys, they move rocks and boulders down the valley floors and scrape along the sides. This eroding action of the moving ice straightens and enlarges V-shaped valleys, making them U-shaped. Yosemite Valley in east-central California has the U shape that is typical of a glacial valley.

Sometimes smaller glaciers feed into a main glacier. The smaller glaciers do not erode valleys as deeply as the main glacier does. After the ice melts, the floors of these shallower tributary valleys stand high above the floor of the main glacial valley. Where the valleys join, the troughs carved by smaller glaciers seem to hang high on the main valley walls. They are called hanging valleys. When a stream tumbles from a hanging valley to the valley floor below, it becomes a waterfall.

▼ *The Great Rift Valley stretches some 8,000 kilometers (5,000 mi) from Asia into Africa. A rift valley forms where slabs of the earth's crust pull apart along two parallel lines. Land between the cracks sinks, forming the valley.*

Yosemite Falls, one of the world's tallest waterfalls, cascades from one hanging valley to another before reaching the floor. The total drop measures some 740 meters (2,425 ft).

Rift Valleys

Movements of the earth's crust, or outer layer, produce rift valleys. The crust is the top part of rigid slabs of rock called plates. Movement of plates sometimes causes the crust to separate or split apart. Chunks of crust may sink between two parallel faults, or cracks. The sunken flat area becomes the floor of a steep-sided depression called a rift valley. As the valley widens, molten rock from inside the earth may well up in the rift, forming new floor. Many rift valleys continue to widen. The Great Rift Valley, a rift system in East Africa and Asia, ranges from about 30 to 50 kilometers (20–30 mi) wide. Its width is increasing about a millimeter each year.

Bodies of water often occupy rift valleys. Many lakes occur in the Great Rift Valley system. The Red Sea also fills part of it. The Rhine River in Europe flows through a rift valley. The largest rift valley system, along the crest of the Mid-Ocean Ridge, circles the earth beneath the ocean.

Valleys and People

Rivers flowing through valleys supply people with water. When the rivers flood, the water may deposit nutrients on valley floors and floodplains, increasing their fertility. Wetlands in river valleys provide food for people as well as for birds and other wildlife.

Many rivers serve as travel and trade routes. Waterways in valleys have been avenues of transportation for thousands of years. People often have found it easier to build roads that wind through valleys than to establish routes across high mountains.

Because river valleys are sources of water and food, and are convenient for travel, people in many parts of the world settled in them thousands of years ago. Farmers tilled the Nile Valley in Egypt, and land near the Tigris and Euphrates Rivers in Mesopotamia. In India, China, and the Americas, ancient peoples also established flourishing cultures in river valleys. As a result, many valleys have become known as cradles of civilization.

SEE ALSO CANYON, FLOODPLAIN, GLACIER, GORGE, PLATE TECTONICS, RIFT VALLEY, RIVER, *and* WEATHERING AND EROSION.

◄ *Icelanders stroll through a rift on their island, which sits atop the Mid-Ocean Ridge. The floor of the rift formed when molten rock from inside the earth welled up as the rift gradually widened.*

VEGETATION REGIONS

The world's vegetation can be divided into four broad categories: forest, grassland, tundra, and xerophytic (desert) vegetation. Climate helps determine the vegetation of a region. If you compare the world climate map on pages 108–109 with the map of vegetation regions below, you will see that there is a relationship between the two. Soil, drainage, and slope are among the other factors determining the kind of vegetation in a region.

Forest Vegetation

Every continent except Antarctica has forest vegetation. A forest is defined as a large area covered with trees grouped so that their foliage shades the ground. This kind of continuous tree growth usually requires an average annual rainfall of at least 75 centimeters (30 in). Trees, the dominant vegetation in forests, are sometimes categorized by how often they lose and grow leaves. Deciduous trees lose their leaves for a season. Evergreen trees constantly shed and replace some leaves while remaining green all year. Deciduous and evergreen trees are further classified as broadleaf or needleleaf.

Many systems are used to categorize kinds of forests. One system classifies forests by their climate and the kinds of trees found most often in them. The five kinds of forests in this system are tropical rain forests, containing broadleaf evergreen trees; tropical deciduous forests; temperate deciduous forests; temperate evergreen forests; and the needleleaf evergreen, or boreal, forests of the subarctic region. Forests with both evergreen and deciduous trees are called mixed forests.

▲ *Alpine tundra on the Sawtooth Mountains of Idaho begins at the timberline, the upper edge of forest growth.*

VEGETATION REGIONS

- Forest Vegetation
- Grassland Vegetation
- Tundra Vegetation
- Xerophytic (Desert) Vegetation
- Ice Sheet (No Vegetation)

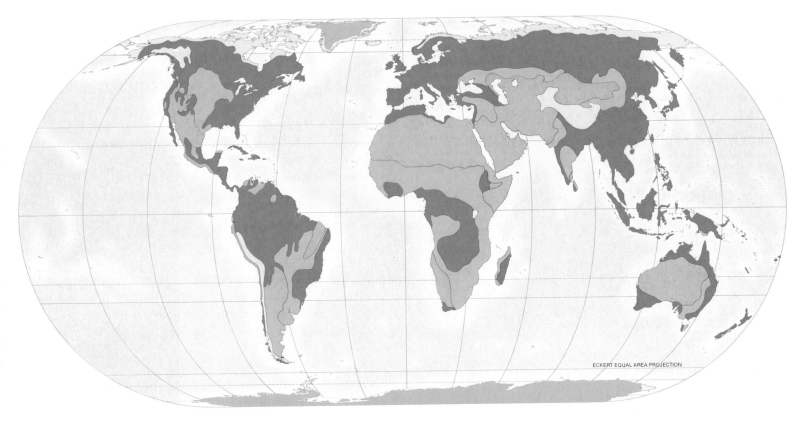

ECKERT EQUAL AREA PROJECTION

Grassland Vegetation

Grasslands, flat or rolling open areas where grasses are the natural vegetation, occur on every continent except Antarctica. Grasses are the dominant vegetation in areas where annual rainfall averages 25 to 75 centimeters (10–30 in). Scientists recognize two types of grasslands: temperate and tropical.

Temperate grasslands exist where there are distinct seasonal variations in temperature: summers are warm, and winters are cold. In most temperate grasslands, such as the prairies of North America, the steppes of Eurasia, and the veld of South Africa, scant precipitation falls year-round.

The climate in tropical grasslands called savannas is usually warm year-round, and a prolonged dry season alternates with a shorter, distinct rainy season. With their clumps of grass and scattered tree growth, savannas are often considered transition zones between grasslands and forests.

Tundra Vegetation

Tundra vegetation is classified as Arctic or alpine. Arctic tundra lies primarily between the northern margins of forests and the Arctic Ocean. Alpine tundra exists at very high elevations on mountain ranges. It usually begins

► Ambling across temperate grasslands in northern China, a pregnant mare and a pony search for forage. Dominated by shortgrasses, these grasslands are called steppe in Eurasia.

at the timberline, the boundary that marks the end of continuous forest. In both, plant species are limited and are able to survive short growing seasons and cold temperatures.

Permafrost, a subsurface layer of permanently frozen earth, is common in Arctic tundra. During the short Arctic summer, only a shallow surface layer of ground thaws. Hardy plants such as shortgrasses, mosses, and lichens grow in the thin, thawed layer of waterlogged soil, but trees cannot develop fully.

Permafrost is not generally found in alpine tundra. Only in meadows or bogs in the alpine tundra are soil conditions similar to those of the damp Arctic tundra.

Xerophytic (Desert) Vegetation

Xerophytic vegetation dominates in desert regions, where average annual precipitation is 25 centimeters (10 in) or less. Xerophytes are plants that have adapted to low levels of precipitation. In xerophytic vegetation regions, plants are widely scattered, taking in water from as large an area as possible. Cactuses and other xerophytes have special ways of getting water and of using it sparingly. Long roots, small leaves, stems that store water, and spines that discourage grazers are common adaptations of such vegetation.

Classifying Natural Environments

The primary emphasis of the vegetation region concept is on the plant community. Human activity greatly affects vegetation. People have converted vast forests to grassland. Grasslands are used for grazing and plowed for cultivation. Cities and towns cover portions of every vegetation region. Broad classifications of vegetation regions, however, generally do not take these changes into account, and the natural world is viewed as if it were unchanged by human intervention.

SEE ALSO BIOME, BIOSPHERE, DESERT, ECOSYSTEM, FOREST, GRASSLAND, PRAIRIE, RAIN FOREST, SAVANNA, STEPPE, TAIGA, and TUNDRA.

▲ Xerophytic vegetation, such as these shrubs in a West African desert, adapts in several ways to the limited water supply in arid lands.

▲ Loggers in Alaska survey stumps of felled evergreen trees. Some kinds of forest vegetation are able to regenerate quickly in cleared areas because seedlings benefit from full sunlight.

VILLAGE

A village is a small settlement usually found in a rural setting. It is generally larger than a hamlet but smaller than a town. Some geographers further define a village as having 500 to 2,500 inhabitants. In most parts of the world, villages are nucleated settlements of people engaged in primary activities such as farming, fishing, and mining. They provide some basic goods and services for their inhabitants and for people in surrounding areas. They function as trading centers and, often, as units of local government.

Agricultural villages are the predominant form of rural settlement throughout most of the world. In much of North America and Australia, however, the most common form is the isolated farmstead.

Today, many villages in developed countries are no longer oriented toward primary activities. Economic and other factors have encouraged residents to seek other occupations or, in some cases, to migrate. In addition, some urban residents have moved to villages and commute to jobs in larger places.

SEE ALSO CITY, SETTLEMENT, *and* TOWN.

▲ *Beehive houses cluster along a narrow street in the Italian village of Alberobello. Their steep roofs direct rainwater to underground cisterns.*
▼ *The inhabitants of this village in Zimbabwe live in thatch-roof dwellings plastered with mud. They work together to farm the surrounding land.*

▼ *A rainbow seems to reflect the hues of heather, saxifrage, bearberry, and other wildflowers in Alaska's Arctic tundra.*

VOLCANO

Long ago, people in many parts of the world thought that the terrifying powers of volcanoes belonged to gods. They explained the awesome mountains through religious beliefs and folklore. The Romans thought that Vulcan, their god of fire and metalworking, kept his forge beneath a fire-breathing mountain on an island near Sicily. The island was named Vulcano for the god. Over the years, all such fiery mountains have come to be called volcanoes. The science that deals with them is known as volcanology.

Scientists who study volcanoes are called volcanologists. They have learned much about these geographic features since the days of the Romans. These experts explain that the earth's rigid shell, or lithosphere, is made up of several huge slabs of rock called plates. The movement and interaction

▲ Steam and ash fill the sky above Galunggung, an Indonesian volcano that is part of the Ring of Fire, a volcanic zone rimming the Pacific Basin.
► Piton de la Fournaise spews red-hot lava. Rising from a volcanic island in the Indian Ocean, the peak is one of the earth's most active volcanoes.

of these plates are responsible for most volcanic activity. The plates drift on the zone in the earth's mantle, or middle layer, where rocks are near their melting point. The rocks are so hot that they will move or bend like red-hot iron. Pockets of molten rock called magma are also located there. Scientists speculate that movement within this extremely hot zone may cause the plates to shift. As the plates move, their edges collide, slide under or past each other, or pull apart.

Where the edge of one of the huge plates slides under or pulls away from the edge of another, magma may rise toward the surface of the earth. When the molten material reaches the surface, it is called lava. It often comes out through volcanoes. Volcanoes are windows in the earth that allow us to discover things that happen inside. Through them we can learn more about the structure, composition, and internal processes of our planet.

Zones of Volcanic Activity

At times, the edges of two plates grind together, and the edge of one plate slides under the edge of the other. This process is called subduction. Friction, combined with heat from deep within the earth, melts some of the rock in the descending plate, forming magma. The magma, hotter and lighter than the surrounding rock, rises through the overlying plate. In some places on the earth's surface, it bursts out and gradually builds a volcano. Hundreds of such volcanoes rise in subduction zones around the Pacific Basin. They formed where the plates that cradle the Pacific meet the plates that hold the continents surrounding the ocean. This wide band of volcanoes encircling the Pacific is known as the Ring of Fire.

Volcanism also occurs at spreading centers. These are zones where the earth's crust is spreading or splitting apart because of plate movement. Most of this kind of volcanic activity occurs along the Mid-Ocean Ridge, a broad mountainous region extending along the seafloor for more than 64,000 kilometers (40,000 mi). There, as plates move away from each other, molten rock wells up between them and hardens into new seafloor. In places along the ridge, piles of lava have formed volcanic islands such as Iceland.

◄ *Fiery lava pours from Kilauea, a volcano in Hawaii, and streams across previous flows now hardened into black volcanic rock. Kilauea's repeated eruptions have built up a shield volcano, so named because its shape, that of an overturned saucer, resembles a warrior's shield. Some of the world's largest volcanoes are in this category.*

◄ *The nearly symmetrical cone of Mount Fuji towers 3,776 meters (12,388 ft) in Japan. It formed gradually from layers of ash and rock alternating with layers of lava flow. The volcanic material erupted from a central vent, or opening in the earth. Mount Fuji's narrow summit and wide base mark it as a typical composite volcano.*

◄ *In Arizona's San Francisco volcanic field, a dark cinder cone rises above an old lava flow. Many such cones dot this bleak landscape, which was a training ground for astronauts before their Apollo moon missions. Cinder cones build up as lava fragments ejected from a vent settle into a steep-sided pile. This cone probably formed about 70,000 years ago.*

SOME FAMOUS VOLCANOES OF THE WORLD

NAME AND LOCATION	ELEVATION (ABOVE SEA LEVEL)	TYPE	INTERESTING FACTS
COTOPAXI, ECUADOR	5,897 m (19,347 ft)	Composite	Cotopaxi, one of the world's highest active volcanoes, has erupted more than 50 times since its first recorded eruption in 1532.
ETNA, SICILY, ITALY	3,323 m (10,902 ft)	Composite	One of Europe's most active volcanoes, Etna has had more than 200 recorded eruptions.
KILAUEA, HAWAII, U.S.A.	1,243 m (4,078 ft)	Shield	A spectacular lava fountain during a 1959 eruption from Kilauea Iki vent soared 580 meters (1,900 ft), a record for a Hawaiian eruption.
KRAKATAU, INDONESIA	813 m (2,667 ft)	Composite	The great eruption of 1883 was heard 4,700 kilometers (2,900 mi) away. Enormous sea waves called tsunami killed 36,000 people.
MAUNA LOA, HAWAII, U.S.A.	4,169 m (13,677 ft)	Shield	Mauna Loa, the world's largest volcano, rises more than 9,000 meters (30,000 ft) from the ocean floor and has a volume of more than 40,000 cubic kilometers (9,600 cubic mi).
MOUNT KATMAI, ALASKA, U.S.A.	2,047 m (6,715 ft)	Composite	In 1912, an enormous flow of ash from Novarupta vent formed the Valley of Ten Thousand Smokes.
MOUNT PELÉE, MARTINIQUE	1,397 m (4,583 ft)	Composite	A 1902 eruption killed more than 28,000 people and incinerated the city of St. Pierre in minutes.
MOUNT ST. HELENS, WASHINGTON, U.S.A.	2,550 m (8,366 ft)	Composite	The force of a 1980 eruption tore off nearly 400 meters (1,300 ft) of the volcano's top and flattened more than 600 square kilometers (230 sq mi) of surrounding forest.
PARICUTÍN, MEXICO	2,740 m (8,990 ft)	Cinder cone	The first volcano to be scientifically observed from its earliest stage of formation, Paricutín began as a small fracture in a farmer's field in 1943.
STROMBOLI, ITALY	926 m (3,038 ft)	Composite	Stromboli, an island volcano, has erupted almost continuously for at least 2,000 years, hurling up bits of glowing lava every few minutes or hours, on average.
SURTSEY, ICELAND	173 m (568 ft)	Cinder-cone and lava-flow island	Underwater eruptions created the island of Surtsey, which appeared above the surface of the sea in 1963. Surtsey now has an area of more than 2.8 square kilometers (1.1 sq mi).
TAMBORA, INDONESIA	2,851 m (9,354 ft)	Composite	Tambora's 1815 eruption, the largest in modern history, released 80 times more ash and other material than did Mount St. Helens in 1980.
VESUVIUS, ITALY	1,281 m (4,203 ft)	Composite	The famous eruption in A.D. 79 destroyed the cities of Pompeii, Stabiae, and Herculaneum.

Spreading centers may also develop within continents, forming new plate boundaries and triggering volcanic activity along them. The spreading process may have formed the Great Rift Valley in East Africa. There, volcanoes rise where lava has flowed from deep cracks, or rifts, in the valley area.

Not all volcanoes are located at plate boundaries. Hot spots, unusually hot regions deep within the earth, cause intraplate volcanism. As magma rises from a hot spot, heat from the molten rock may warm groundwater and produce hot springs such as the ones in Yellowstone National Park in the United States. If the molten rock flows out through openings in the earth's surface, it can build a line of volcanoes and even chains of volcanic islands as a plate moves over a hot spot. The Hawaiian Islands were formed this way. The islands mark the northwesterly passage of the Pacific plate over a stationary hot spot in the mantle. The most recently formed island lies atop the hot spot at the southeastern end of the chain. There, volcanoes continue to erupt.

INTRAPLATE VOLCANISM

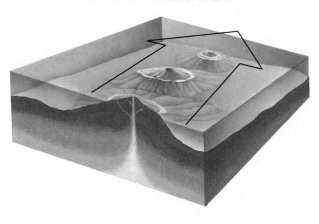

◄ *Intraplate volcanism is triggered by an unusually hot region deep within the earth. Molten rock rises from this hot spot and pours out as lava, erupting through cracks in the earth's surface. As a plate of the earth's crust slowly moves across a hot spot, the buildup of lava may create a series of volcanoes, one after the other. Such hot-spot volcanoes continue to form in several locations around the world.*

SPREADING CENTER VOLCANISM

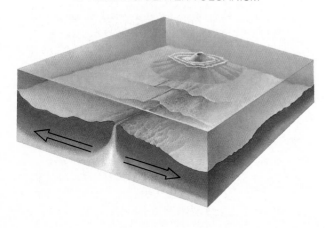

◄ *Spreading center volcanism occurs where plates move away from each other. This occurs most often along the Mid-Ocean Ridge. Molten rock wells up, fills the gap between plates, and hardens into seafloor. As plates move and the process continues, older seafloor is carried away from the spreading center. The rock can eventually build peaks that rise above the surface of the ocean.*

SUBDUCTION ZONE VOLCANISM

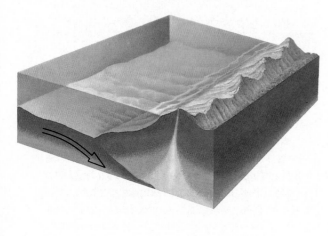

◄ *At some places where the earth's plates meet, subduction zones develop. During the subduction process, the edge of one plate slides under the edge of another plate. Heat melts some of the rock in the descending plate, forming magma. This molten rock rises through the overlying plate and erupts, gradually building volcanoes.*

In Wyoming, algae grow in water warmed by a hot spot under Yellowstone National Park.
◄ Snow tops a cinder cone on Mauna Kea, a hot-spot volcano in Hawaii. Scientists have determined that it last erupted more than 3,500 years ago.

▲ Mount Kilimanjaro is one of several volcanoes in a spreading zone that runs through East Africa.
◄ In Iceland, fountains of lava gush higher than a 25-story building. These fissures opened along a spreading center on the Mid-Ocean Ridge.

▲ Oregon's Crater Lake formed after the explosion of a subduction volcano nearly 7,000 years ago.
◄ Nevado Sajama, a volcanic peak that formed as magma rose in a subduction zone, lies in Bolivia, about 160 km (100 mi) from the Pacific coast.

The oldest islands are in the northwest, having passed over the hot spot several million years ago.

Types of Volcanoes

Not only do volcanoes occur at different types of locations (subduction zones, spreading centers, and above hot spots), but they also vary in their composition and structure. The composition and structure of a volcano determine whether it is a shield, a composite, or a cinder cone volcano.

Mauna Loa on the island of Hawaii is a shield volcano, shaped like an overturned saucer. Its distinctive shape results from rapid flows of fluid lava that spread out easily and cool, forming smooth, gentle slopes as they harden. Mauna Loa erupts with streams of fiery lava every few years and can send out steam and other gases even when lava is not flowing. It is the world's largest volcano.

When eruptions of ash, cinders, and rock fragments alternate or combine with lava flows, the material forms what is called a composite cone. Some volcanoes considered to be the most beautiful in the world are composite cones. Snowcapped Mount Fuji in Japan is an example of this type.

Composite volcanoes are also known for their violent and explosive eruptions. Mount St. Helens in the Cascade Range in Washington State is such a volcano. The mountain had not erupted in more than a century, when early in 1980, earthquakes shook the area, and clouds of ash shot into the sky. Volcanologists also noticed a huge bulge forming on the north slope. Then on May 18 an earthquake loosened the bulge and sent tons of rock and ice sliding down the mountain. Explosions sent clouds of ash and pulverized rock into the sky. Ice and snow, melted by the intense heat, poured down river valleys in swift, gray floods. After the eruption, about 60 people were dead or missing; millions of trees were flattened; and bridges, roads, crops, and homes were destroyed.

In 1943, an eruption in Mexico began to form a kind of volcano known as a cinder cone. From a crack that appeared in a farmer's cornfield, a new volcano, Paricutín, grew rapidly, pouring out lava and piling up huge amounts of ash and cinders. Paricutín is a

typical cinder cone volcano, with most of its cone made up of ash and cinders.

Extinct Volcanoes

A volcano that has been active in historic times is usually classified as an active volcano. When a volcano is in a temporarily inactive phase, it is said to be dormant. Some volcanoes have never erupted during recorded history. Scientists call them extinct volcanoes. Diamond Head in Hawaii, for example, is an extinct volcano.

Today there are no active volcanoes in the British Isles. But geologists know that volcanic activity occurred there millions of years ago. The evidence? Igneous rock that formed from magma as it cooled and hardened. The rocky remains of ancient volcanoes loom over the city of Edinburgh, Scotland.

Harm—and Help

Volcanoes can be terrifying and destructive. If an eruption occurs suddenly in a heavily populated area, or in a remote area where residents cannot be warned or evacuated quickly, large numbers of people may die. Clouds of ash and gases from volcanic eruptions can even affect world climate.

But volcanoes bring benefits as well as destruction. The areas around volcanoes often yield rich deposits of minerals. The ash layer that some eruptions deposit on a landscape is rich in minerals and adds fertile soil for growing crops. Lava flows can build new land, as they have in Hawaii and Iceland. Durable igneous rock can be used in construction. Volcanoes contribute pumice, a light, gritty material used in industry.

One of the useful by-products of volcanism is geothermal energy. In Iceland, buildings are warmed by pipes carrying natural hot water. Geothermal energy can also power electric generators. People are developing new ways to put volcanic power to work.

SEE ALSO ASH, ATOLL, CALDERA, CONE, CRATER, ERUPTION, GEOTHERMAL ENERGY, HOT SPOT, ISLAND, LAVA, MAGMA, MANTLE, MOUNTAIN, OCEAN, PLATE TECTONICS, RIFT VALLEY, RING OF FIRE, ROCK, *and* SEAFLOOR SPREADING.

▲ *When Mount St. Helens in Washington State erupted in 1980, it gave scientists a rare opportunity to study a volcano in action. This geologist gathers data inside the crater.*
▼ *A year after the eruption, avalanche lilies bloom amid the volcanic ash on the slopes of Mount St. Helens.*

◄ In Iceland, near the Arctic Circle, bathers enjoy the warmth of outdoor swimming pools—even in January. Volcanic activity heats groundwater, springs, and water pipes, which Icelanders use to warm greenhouses, schools, homes, and pools.

▲ Workers weigh baskets of sulfur taken from the crater of an Indonesian volcano. Sulfur is one of the useful materials that come from volcanoes. It is used in making such products as medicines, paper, and gunpowder.

W

WATER

Water is the most common substance on the earth and the only substance necessary to all forms of life. It covers about three-fourths of the earth's surface and is also found underground. Water fills streams, lakes, and the ocean. It occurs as precipitation and in masses of ice called glaciers. It is present in the atmosphere as water vapor.

Every drop of water is made up of millions of tiny particles called molecules. Each molecule consists of even smaller particles called atoms. Because one molecule of water contains two atoms of hydrogen (H) and one atom of oxygen (O), the chemical symbol used for water is H_2O.

Water can exist in three different forms: liquid, solid (ice), and gas (water vapor or steam). Water is the only substance that can be found in these forms in the average range of the earth's temperatures. Rain (liquid), hail or snow (solid), and water vapor (gas) may all occur in the same area at the same time during a severe storm.

Water vapor is the invisible gas that water turns into when it evaporates. It can be felt in the air on humid days. Steam is a form of water vapor. When it collides with cooler air,

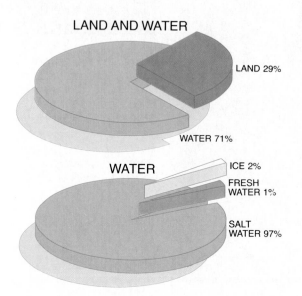

LAND AND WATER

LAND 29%

WATER 71%

WATER

ICE 2%

FRESH WATER 1%

SALT WATER 97%

▲ *Women in Pushkar, India, obtain water from a well. Necessary to all life, water is a vital natural resource.*
◄ *In rounded figures, these charts compare the earth's water and land areas (top), and show how much of the water is salty, fresh but frozen in glaciers, or fresh usable liquid.*

water vapor condenses and forms water droplets in a cloud or mist that is visible.

When water freezes, it does not contract like most substances. As it nears its freezing point of 0°C (32°F), it begins to expand. Expansion makes ice lighter than liquid water, so that it can float.

Water can absorb a great deal of heat without becoming extremely hot itself. This makes the ocean a major regulator of climate. Winds blowing from the ocean bring cooler air in summer and warmer air in winter.

Water has the ability to dissolve many

other substances exposed to it. Bit by bit, it can break down even the hardest rocks. This property makes water a universal solvent, and a primary force in shaping the earth's surface.

Earth's Water Volume

The earth's total volume of water—ice, liquid, and vapor—is about 1.4 billion cubic kilometers (336 million cu mi). This probably has remained nearly constant since the ocean formed. About 97 percent of the earth's water is in the ocean. Ocean water is salty and cannot be used for drinking, farming, or for many other purposes.

Only about 3 percent of all the earth's water is fresh—not salty. More than two-thirds of the fresh water is frozen in glaciers and polar ice sheets. That leaves less than one percent of the total volume for homes, factories, and farms, and for wildlife requiring fresh water. Most of this fresh water is underground; it is called groundwater. Only a tiny fraction of the fresh water on the earth is found in streams and lakes.

In the United States, people consume some 1.5 trillion liters (400 billion gal) of water every day. Why do we require so much water?

At home, people use water for drinking, cooking, washing clothes and dishes, bathing, brushing their teeth, flushing toilets, watering lawns and gardens, and washing cars. In cities, workers use water to fight fires, clean streets, pump away wastes, and operate sewage-treatment equipment that helps purify waste water.

Huge amounts of water are consumed in industry to manufacture goods and in agriculture to grow food crops. In the United States, for example, it takes 240,000 liters (63,000 gal) of water to produce a ton of steel, and it takes 435 liters (115 gal) to grow enough wheat to make one loaf of bread.

By far the biggest use of water, in the United States and throughout the world, is for irrigation. Because rain does not fall evenly on the earth, some lands are too dry for cultivation. Water used for growing crops in such dry areas often must be brought up from groundwater sources through deep wells or transported from distant lakes and rivers.

In many parts of the world, people suffer

▲ In the Pacific, Samoan boys prepare to go spearfishing. Most of the earth's water is the salt water of the ocean.
▼ Brazilian sailors paddle through Atlantic surf. Salty ocean water is recycled into fresh water through the water cycle.

from constant water shortages because the earth's total supply of fresh water is unevenly distributed. Millions of people lack dependable sources of clean drinking water and water for agriculture. In some places, hundreds of centimeters of rain may fall each year, but other areas, such as the Atacama Desert in Chile, may receive almost no rain for years.

The driest regions include parts of southern Australia and much of central Asia, northern Africa, and Antarctica, the world's driest continent. During some years, even less precipitation than usual falls on these lands.

Severe dry periods, called droughts, sometimes occur in lands that normally have enough precipitation, as does most of the United States. These droughts occur when weather patterns change temporarily, bringing less than normal rainfall.

Conserving Water

When water becomes scarce where it had been abundant, people often worry that the earth's supply is running out. Yet the total amount of water now is about the same as it was during the days of the dinosaurs. This is because fresh water is a renewable resource. It is constantly recycled as the sun evaporates water from the ocean and other bodies of water, often forming clouds. They, in turn, release fresh water as rain and other precipitation, replenishing the earth's supply.

Today, the demand for fresh water is

▲ Cooling off, people in inner tubes float down the Comal River in Texas. Most of the United States has abundant fresh water in streams and lakes.
◄ Women use nets to catch fish in the Nam Mae Kok, a river in Thailand. Many rivers provide not only fish to eat but also water for drinking, for washing, and for irrigating crops.

increasing as populations grow. Developed countries use the most water, sometimes inefficiently. For example, clean water is wasted every time household faucets are allowed to drip or city water pipes are allowed to leak. To meet future needs, all countries should conserve their water resources.

Another way to ensure the future supply of fresh water is to prevent pollution. Pollution from sewage, and from chemicals used in factories and on farms, has poisoned many streams, lakes, and groundwater sources. When water is badly polluted, it cannot be used safely.

Water conservation alone cannot help the driest parts of the world where rainfall is always scarce. There, only technology can relieve some water shortages. Such technology includes extensive irrigation projects, deep wells to tap water sources far underground, and desalting equipment. This equipment can remove salt from seawater to provide more fresh water in coastal areas.

Many of these ways of obtaining water are very expensive. Developing countries that need to obtain their water through such methods may require the help of other countries and international organizations.

SEE ALSO AQUIFER, CLOUDS, CONDENSATION, DROUGHT, GROUNDWATER, HYDROSPHERE, ICE, IRRIGATION, LAKE, OCEAN, POLLUTION, PRECIPITATION, RAIN, RIVER, STREAM, WATER CYCLE, WATER TABLE, *and* WEATHERING AND EROSION.

▼ *Scientists from the Norwegian Polar Research Institute measure water density and the thickness and temperature of ice near Greenland. More than 2 percent of earth's water occurs as ice.*

WATER CYCLE

The endless movement of water between the atmosphere, the ocean, and the land is called the water cycle. About 97 percent of the earth's water is in the ocean; more than 2 percent is frozen in glaciers and ice sheets; and less than 1 percent is in streams, in lakes, and under the ground. The atmosphere contains only .001 percent of the earth's water at any given time, yet it serves as the key hydrological channel between the ocean and the land. Water enters the atmosphere through evaporation and returns to the earth by condensation and precipitation. Most precipitation that falls on land evaporates. Much of the rest returns to the ocean through streams.

The water cycle transports excess heat from the earth to the atmosphere. The sun's energy changes liquid water into water vapor. When vapor condenses, it releases the energy in the form of heat.

SEE ALSO ATMOSPHERE, EVAPORATION, HYDROSPHERE, OCEAN, PRECIPITATION, *and* WATER.

WATER TABLE

When water on the surface of the land seeps down through the soil under the force of gravity, it reaches a zone where the pores in rocks and sediments are saturated, or filled with water. The water table is the area where the saturated and unsaturated zones meet.

The water table is not level like a household table. As the diagram shows, the water table follows the general slope of the land above it. In some places, the water table intersects the land surface, and springs, marshes, ponds, lakes, or even rivers may occur. In many arid regions, however, the water table may lie far below the surface.

The depth of the water table fluctuates from season to season and from year to year. The water table is constantly affected by variations in climate and by the amount of precipitation a region receives. The water table rises in rainy periods and falls in dry ones.

The texture of the soil and the nature of the terrain also affect the level of the water table in an area. Coarse soil allows easy seepage of water into an aquifer. On steep land surfaces, there is greater runoff and less seepage into an aquifer.

Human activities can affect water table levels. Farmers often build drains or drill wells to lower the water table so that they can grow crops in swampy soils. In some arid regions, including parts of the southwestern United States, increased demand for water has sometimes caused groundwater to be withdrawn faster than nature can replenish it. This lowers the water table and reduces the amount of groundwater available for use.

SEE ALSO AQUIFER, GROUNDWATER, WATER, *and* WETLAND.

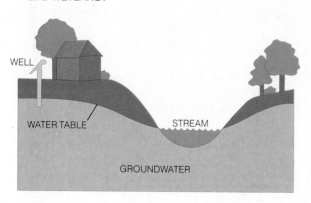

WELL

WATER TABLE   STREAM

GROUNDWATER

WATERFALL

A waterfall is a steep descent of a river over a rocky ledge. The water of a steep fall often causes some erosion at the base. Stones and pebbles carried by the water act as abrasives, wearing away the rock.

Sometimes a waterfall will occur where a river flows from hard to softer rock. The softer rock is easily eroded, or worn away, by the river. A ledge develops over which the river falls.

A waterfall may occur across a fault, or crack in the earth's surface. A number of waterfalls may develop along a fall line—a line along which parallel rivers plunge over a ridge as they flow from uplands to lowlands. A waterfall may spill over the edge of a plateau. Falls also plunge from hanging valleys in areas where glaciers have sculptured the landscape. Hanging valleys are found high up on the walls of U-shaped glacial valleys.

Some waterfalls are spectacular. At Victoria Falls, in the African countries of Zimbabwe and Zambia, the Zambezi River plunges 107 meters (350 ft) over a ledge of lava rock.

Widest of all waterfalls are the thundering waters of the Iguaçu River, on the boundary between Brazil and Argentina. These mighty falls stretch more than 3 kilometers (2 mi) from edge to edge.

Angel Falls, the world's tallest waterfall, plummets 979 meters (3,212 ft) into a remote canyon in a rain forest in Venezuela.

The Niagara River has two falls, one in New York State and one in Ontario, Canada. Each is less than 60 meters (200 ft) tall, but together they are more than a kilometer wide.

Niagara and many other falls with large volumes of water are used to generate hydroelectric power. A tremendous volume of water flows over Niagara Falls—as much as 5,525 cubic meters (195,000 cu ft) per second.

Because waterfalls are barriers to navigation, canals are sometimes built to get around them. Niagara Falls, for example, blocks passage between Lake Erie and Lake Ontario on the Niagara River. In the 19th century, the Welland Canal was built to make passage between the two lakes possible.

SEE ALSO CANAL, FALL LINE, GLACIER, HYDROELECTRIC POWER, RIVER, *and* VALLEY.

WATERSHED

A watershed is an entire river system or an area drained by a river and its tributaries. Some watersheds are sharply defined by the crest of a high ridge or by a continental divide. Precipitation that falls on opposite sides of this type of watershed flows in different directions. Watersheds in low or gently rolling areas may be poorly defined, but can be identified by the flow of the rivers.

A prominent watershed in North America roughly follows the crest of the Rocky Mountains. Runoff water from another large watershed, in the midcontinental United States, drains into the Gulf of Mexico through the Mississippi River system.

SEE ALSO DIVIDE *and* RIVER.

WATERSPOUT

A waterspout is a column of rotating cloud-filled wind that descends from a cumulus cloud to the ocean or a lake. Waterspouts are similar to tornadoes but are usually smaller and less intense. The average spout is perhaps only 50 meters (165 ft) in diameter with wind speeds of 80 kilometers per hour (50 mph). Waterspouts are most common off the Florida Keys and over coastal waters in the Gulf of Mexico. They occur most often in summer, when water temperatures are high.

SEE ALSO CLOUDS *and* TORNADO.

▲ *A waterspout drops from a cumulus cloud to the ocean surface off Baja California, in Mexico.*

▲ *Iguaçu Falls tumbles over a broad ridge along the Brazil-Argentina boundary. These falls, the widest in the world, consist of hundreds of cascades separated by rock ledges and tree-covered islands.*
◄ *Slickers protect visitors from the spray of the 52-meter (172-ft) Bridal Veil, part of mighty Niagara Falls on the border of the United States and Canada.*
► *Unknown to the outside world until 1935, Angel Falls, the world's highest waterfall, plunges 979 meters (3,212 ft) into a canyon in Venezuela.*

WAVES

The surface of the ocean is constantly moving. The up-and-down motions seen in ocean water are called waves. Most waves are caused by wind, but some are triggered by earthquakes and volcanic eruptions in or near the ocean.

The highest point of a wave is called the crest, and the lowest is called the trough. A wave's length, measured from one crest to another, is known as the wavelength.

Waves move through water at different speeds. Average ocean waves travel about 30 to 85 kilometers per hour (20–50 mph).

How Waves Form and Move

The wind makes waves by first ruffling the surface of the ocean. Even a slight breeze makes ripples form when the ocean is calm and smooth. Ripples are the smallest kind of waves. They provide surfaces for the wind to push against.

When the wind blows harder, it pushes the waves into steeper and higher hills of water. The size of a wave depends on three things: the speed and strength of the wind, the length of time the wind blows, and the distance over which it blows in the open ocean. If this distance, called the fetch, is long, and if the wind is strong and steady, huge waves may develop.

Waves vary greatly in height from crest to trough. Average ocean waves are about 1.5 to 3 meters (5–10 ft) high. Waves whipped up by storm winds may tower 15 to 20 meters (50–70 ft) or more. In 1933, the crew of the U.S.S. *Ramapo* spotted an enormous wave in the Pacific Ocean. Calculations based on the crew's observations determined that the wave was 34 meters (112 ft) high—the highest wind wave ever reliably measured at sea.

In the open ocean, water appears to move forward with the waves. However, particles of water in a wave actually travel in circles. The water does not move forward; only the waves do. The visible movement is the wave's form and energy moving through the water, making it rise and fall. The energy contained in the wave comes from the wind.

When a wave enters shallow water near shore, it slows down. The regular up-and-down motion of the wave is disrupted. The shallower the water is, the more slowly the wave moves. As it nears the shore, its crest grows higher. The crest surges ahead of the rest of the wave, traveling faster than the trough. This surge carries the water onto the shore. The wave curls forward, topples over, and breaks apart. The water rolls up onto the beach, then stops and rolls back out to sea again. Waves that break along the shore are called breakers. The zone where they break is called the surf.

Because a wave's energy is released so quickly in the short space where the wave breaks, the release is often explosive. Like a giant hammer, the force of pounding breakers on a rocky shore can batter rock and eventually crush it into grains of sand. Waves may cut steep cliffs or carve out arches and caves in a wall of solid rock. They may wear away entire sections of rocky coast. Waves may also build up the land by dumping vast amounts of sand along the shore.

Tsunami

The most awesome waves are caused not by wind but primarily by underwater earthquakes. These waves may be huge and tremendously destructive when they hit land. Many people mistakenly call them tidal waves, but they are properly called seismic sea waves or tsunami, a Japanese word meaning "great harbor wave."

Tsunami are different from wind waves. They have much longer wavelengths and can travel at more than 800 kilometers per hour (500 mph).

SEE ALSO BEACH, COAST, OCEAN, TSUNAMI, WEATHERING AND EROSION, *and* WIND.

▲ A huge wave curls toward shore at the Banzai Pipeline, the place where surf breaks off Ehukai Beach Park on Oahu Island in Hawaii.
◄ A churning breaker releases its energy off Rarotonga Island, one of the Cook Islands in the South Pacific.

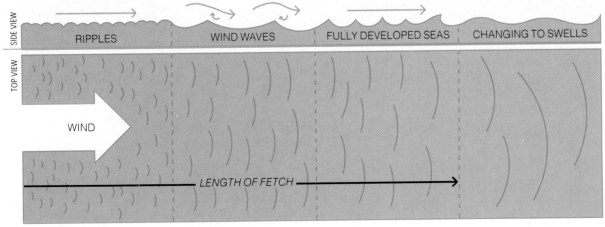

SIDE VIEW

RIPPLES · WIND WAVES · FULLY DEVELOPED SEAS · CHANGING TO SWELLS

TOP VIEW

WIND

LENGTH OF FETCH

◄ *Wind sets waves moving through the ocean. The fetch is the distance over which the wind blows. First the wind sets ripples moving up and down through the water. Stronger wind makes wind waves, then steep waves known as fully developed seas. When the wind diminishes, the water becomes rounded and smooth, forming swells.*

WEATHER

One of the first things you probably do every morning is look out the window to see what the weather is like. Your observations, coupled with what you may have learned from weather reports, determine what clothes you will wear and perhaps even what you will do throughout the day. If the weather is sunny, you might visit the zoo or go on a picnic. A rainy day might prompt you to visit a museum or stay home and read.

The weather affects us in many ways. Day-to-day changes in weather can influence our moods and the way we look at the world. Severe weather, such as tornadoes, hurricanes, and blizzards, can have a disruptive effect on our lives and the lives of people in our community and our country.

The term "weather" refers to the momentary conditions of the atmosphere. We usually think of the weather in terms of the state of the atmosphere in our own part of the world. The weather in any one area, however, may eventually influence, or be influenced by, the weather a great distance away. Weather usually changes from hour to hour or from day to day. Over many years, certain conditions are characteristic of the weather in an area. The average weather in an area, as well as its variations and extremes over many years, is called climate. Like weather, climate can change too, but much more slowly.

Components of Weather

Weather has six main components. They are temperature, atmospheric pressure, wind, humidity, precipitation, and cloudiness. Together, they describe the weather at any given time. These changing components, along with the knowledge of atmospheric processes, enable meteorologists—scientists who study weather—to forecast what the weather will be in the near future.

"Temperature" refers to how hot or how cold the atmosphere is as measured by a

◄ A massive storm rolls past people strolling the East Sussex cliffs beside the English Channel. The clouds formed over land, but were blown offshore by a cool northwest wind.

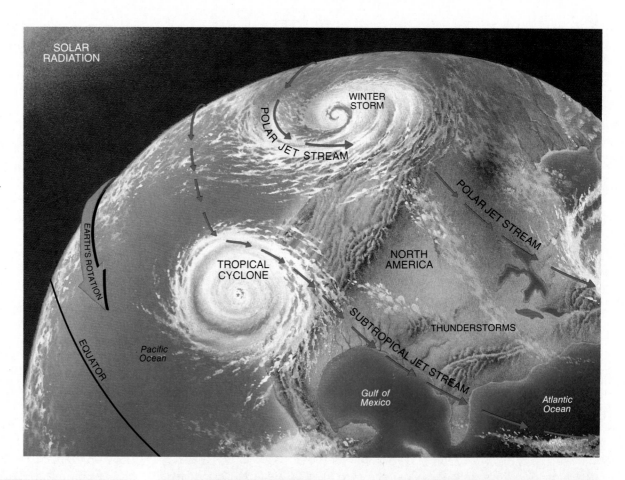

► The earth's weather develops because the sun warms the Equator more than it does the Poles. This sets in motion air circulation patterns, or winds, seen in the flow of storms and other clouds in this painting. These winds are twisted by the Coriolis effect, caused by the earth's rotation. This never ending wind pattern is responsible for passing highs and lows that cause constant weather changes in the mid-latitudes.

▼ Children in Helsinki, Finland, play hockey on a cold winter's day. The cloudless sky allows heat to escape, keeping temperatures cold.

thermometer. Meteorologists report temperature in two common scales, Celsius (C) and Fahrenheit (F). Temperature is a relative measure. A 21°C (70°F) afternoon, for example, would seem cool after several days of 35°C (95°F) heat, but it would seem warm after temperatures around 0°C (32°F).

Atmospheric pressure is the weight of the atmosphere overhead. Changes in atmo-spheric pressure signal shifts in the weather. Meteorologists express atmospheric pressure in millibars or inches of mercury. Average atmospheric pressure at sea level is about 1,013 millibars (29.9 in). A typical high pressure system, or anticyclone, usually reaches 1,030 millibars (30.4 in), and an average low pressure system, or cyclone, measures about 995 millibars (29.4 in).

▲ Cumulus clouds move beneath cirrus clouds over England. Cumulus clouds form during sunny days as warm moist air rises. Some may grow into cumulonimbus clouds that produce towering thunderstorms.

Wind is the movement of air. It arises because of differences in temperature and atmospheric pressure between nearby regions of the earth. Winds tend to blow from areas of high pressure to areas of low pressure. Powerful jet streams, at altitudes of 8 to 15 kilometers (5–9 mi), blow from about 80 to more than 160 kilometers per hour (50 to more than 100 mph). These upper-atmosphere winds help push weather systems around the globe.

"Humidity" refers to how much water vapor the air contains. It is usually expressed as relative humidity, or the percentage of the maximum amount of water air can hold at a given temperature. Cool air holds less water than warm air. At a relative humidity of 100 percent, air is said to be saturated. Clouds and precipitation occur when air cools below its saturation point. This usually happens when warm, humid air cools as it rises.

Clouds come in a variety of forms, and not all of them produce precipitation. Wispy cirrus clouds, for example, usually signal fair weather. Other kinds of clouds can bring rain or snow. A blanketlike cover of nimbostratus clouds produces steady, extended precipitation. Enormous cumulonimbus clouds, or thunderheads, release heavy downpours; often they produce thunderstorms and sometimes tornadoes as well. Clouds can also affect the amount of sunlight reaching the earth's surface and the amount of heat lost from the atmosphere. Cloudy days as a rule are cooler than clear ones. The opposite is true at night because clouds act as a blanket, keeping the earth warm.

Weather Systems

The painting at the top of page 572 shows two spiral cloud systems and several distinct bands of clouds stretching across North America. These cloud patterns indicate the presence of weather systems, which produce most of the weather in the earth's midlatitudes. The spirals are cyclones, and the bands are fronts.

Cyclones have a spiral shape because of winds rotating about an area of low pressure. Such systems are also called lows. Anticyclones, or highs, rotate around high pressure areas; they are not visible in cloud photographs because they generally bring clear

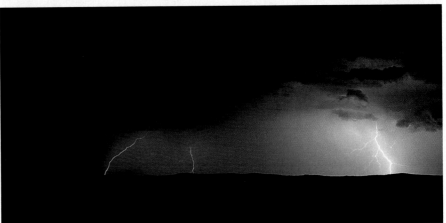

▲ Sunset glows beneath a thunderstorm sweeping across hills in northern California. The storm was part of a larger weather system moving inland from the Pacific Ocean.
▲ Brilliant bolts of lightning strike the earth during a thunderstorm. About 2,000 storms are in progress somewhere at any given time.
◄ Skiers pause during a snowstorm in the Japan Alps. Because temperature drops as elevation increases, more snow falls on mountains than on nearby lowlands.

skies. Highs and lows continually pass through the mid-latitudes, producing the ever changing weather patterns of those regions. Areas of clouds and precipitation are usually associated with cyclones. As air streams converge and rise near the low's center, the air cools and expands, often resulting in clouds and precipitation. In contrast, anticyclones usually bring more settled weather and clear skies. The sinking air of a high pressure system keeps moisture from rising into the atmosphere and forming clouds.

Fronts are features of weather systems. A front is a narrow zone across which temperature, humidity, and wind change abruptly. Along a front, the atmosphere is often unstable and severe storms can break out.

A front exists at the boundary between

▼ *An infrared view from a weather satellite in May 1986 shows severe thunderstorms over the central United States. Each color represents a different temperature and cloud height.*

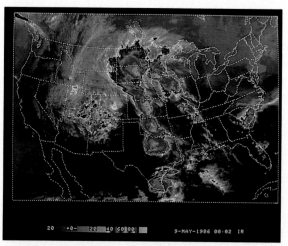

▲ *Unusual mammatus clouds over Kansas indicate an unstable atmosphere. They can occur in severe weather.*
◄ *The funnel cloud of a tornado touches down on North Dakota farmland. Tornadoes pack more power for their size than any other phenomenon of the atmosphere.*
► *Scientists hurry to set the Totable Tornado Observatory, or* TOTO, *in the path of an oncoming tornado. Named for the dog in* The Wizard of Oz, TOTO *was designed to withstand powerful twisters while recording scientific data from inside the storms.*

two air masses. An air mass is a large volume of air that is mostly uniform in temperature and moisture content. Air masses can extend great distances along the ground. When a moving warm air mass displaces a cold air mass, the boundary between them is called a warm front. When a cold air mass displaces a warm air mass, the boundary is called a cold front. A stationary front develops when warm air and cold air meet and the boundary between the two does not move. When one front overtakes another, the front that may form is called an occluded front. Most fronts pass through the centers of low pressure areas and along the edges of high pressure areas.

Forecasting the Weather

With increased knowledge of how the atmosphere functions, meteorologists would be able to make more accurate forecasts of changes in the weather from day to day or even from week to week. Making such forecasts, however, would also require knowing the temperature, atmospheric pressure, wind speed and direction, humidity, precipitation, and cloudiness at every point on the earth. Though this is impossible, meteorologists do have some tools that give them enough information to make reasonably accurate forecasts for a day or two in advance on a fairly regular basis. But because the atmosphere is constantly changing, detailed forecasts for more than a week or two in advance will never be possible.

Since the late 1930s, the primary tool for

◄ Signal flags in Corpus Christi, Texas, warn of Hurricane Allen's approach in August 1980. High water is a result of strong winds combined with the low atmospheric pressure that is characteristic of all hurricanes.
▼ Hurricane Allen's powerful winds drive huge waves against the Texas coast. Wind, waves, and heavy rains are ways that a hurricane unleashes deadly force and sometimes causes extensive damage.

▲ A satellite image shows Hurricane Allen swirling toward Texas and northern Mexico. Such images help scientists predict a hurricane's path.
◄ Meteorologists at the National Hurricane Center in Florida monitor storms in the Atlantic Ocean, the Caribbean Sea, and the Gulf of Mexico.

▶ A weather observer in
Virginia prepares to
release a weather
balloon equipped with
radiosonde. As the
balloon rises, the
radiosonde sends
atmospheric data about
temperature, wind,
humidity, and pressure.
When combined with
readings from more than
1,000 other radiosondes
released at the same
time worldwide, the data
will be used to help
forecast the weather.

▲ A weather observer
measures the amount of
precipitation collected in
a rain gauge during a
storm in Virginia. To her
right, an aerovane,
a type of anemometer,
measures wind speed
and direction. The white
box in the distance holds
thermometers that
measure minimum and
maximum temperatures.

observing general conditions of the atmosphere has been the radiosonde balloon, which sends information needed for forecasting back to earth. It contains instruments that gather information about temperature, pressure, humidity, and wind up to very high levels in the atmosphere. Twice each day, radiosondes are released to rise into the atmosphere from about a thousand locations around the world. The U.S. National Weather Service alone sends up radiosondes from more than 90 weather stations spread evenly across the country. Meteorologists feed the radiosonde data to computers and use the data to map atmospheric winds and jet streams. The computers calculate how weather systems are moving and predict how they might change over several days.

This type of forecasting is called synoptic (a general view over a large area) forecasting. It relies on the fact that in certain atmospheric conditions, particular weather conditions are usually produced. For example, a meteorologist knows that when a cold front approaches a warm air mass with high relative humidity, rain is likely where the two meet. Similarly, a low pressure system sitting over Arizona in winter will bring warm, moist air from the Gulf of Mexico toward Colorado. Heavy snows

may result when that air mass rises against the Rocky Mountains. Synoptic forecasting is important for predicting local weather events, such as rain showers and gusty winds.

Computerized forecasting, also known as numerical forecasting, got its start in the 1950s, a decade when computers were a new invention. Scientists developed mammoth computer programs, requiring millions of calculations, that could mimic the most important physical processes that occur in the atmosphere. The computers digest data from

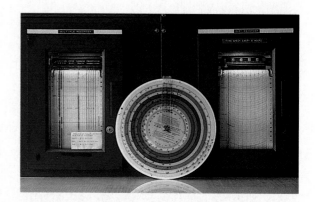

▲ The instrument on the left records wind
direction, speed, and minutes of sunshine. It also
measures precipitation. A gauge on the right
charts wind gusts. The wheel is a slide rule used
for calculating dew point and relative humidity.

radiosondes, as well as temperature, humidity, pressure, and wind information recorded at ground level. Within hours, they produce forecasts for the next 12, 24, 36, 48, and 72 hours. These forecasts do not include small-scale weather events, however, and the computers cannot yet accurately predict the movements of fronts.

Satellites and Radar

A new era in weather forecasting began on April 1, 1960, when the first weather satellite, TIROS 1, went into orbit. TIROS 1 was little more than an orbiting television camera, but it gave meteorologists their first detailed overhead view of cloud formations. With images from TIROS 1, they could track hurricanes and other cyclonic systems moving across the globe. Today's satellites contain special remote sensing instruments that take temperature and moisture readings of the atmosphere below them. Computer programs can analyze cloud movements in the satellite images to calculate wind speeds. In this way, satellite data complement data from radiosondes. Radiosonde instruments are more accurate than those on satellites, but satellites provide greater coverage of the globe,

particularly valuable over the ocean and other areas lacking weather stations. Satellite data have increased the accuracy of forecasts generated by computers, especially in the remote areas of the world that lack other sources for collecting weather information.

Radar is another major tool of weather observation. It is used primarily to observe clouds and rain on a local scale. A new type of radar, called Doppler radar, is being installed at weather stations throughout the world. Doppler radar operates on the same principle as a police radar gun. It enables meteorologists to "see" wind velocity by measuring the

◄ Scientists of the
National Weather Service
in Maryland watch a
thunderstorm from their
office window. Even with
the advanced technology
available to forecasters,
visual observation is still
one of their best tools.

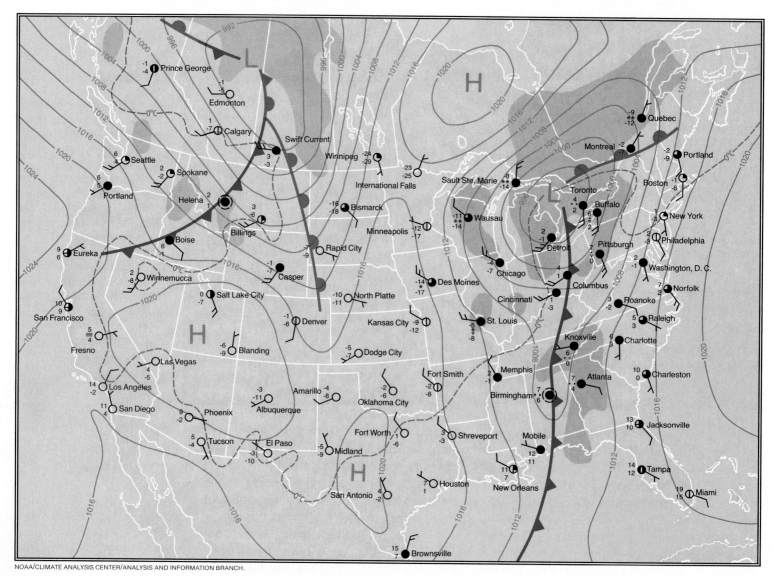

NOAA/CLIMATE ANALYSIS CENTER/ANALYSIS AND INFORMATION BRANCH.

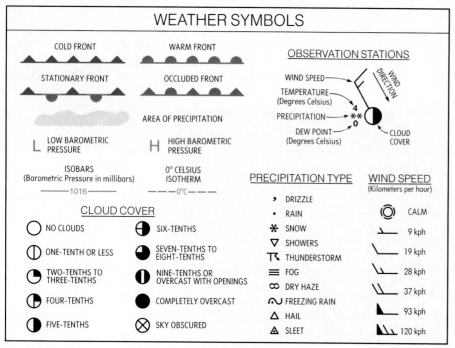

WEATHER SYMBOLS

COLD FRONT

WARM FRONT

STATIONARY FRONT

OCCLUDED FRONT

AREA OF PRECIPITATION

L LOW BAROMETRIC PRESSURE

H HIGH BAROMETRIC PRESSURE

ISOBARS
(Barometric Pressure in millibars)
——— 1016

0° CELSIUS ISOTHERM
— — 0°C — — —

OBSERVATION STATIONS

WIND SPEED
WIND DIRECTION
TEMPERATURE (Degrees Celsius)
PRECIPITATION
DEW POINT (Degrees Celsius)
CLOUD COVER

CLOUD COVER

NO CLOUDS	SIX-TENTHS
ONE-TENTH OR LESS	SEVEN-TENTHS TO EIGHT-TENTHS
TWO-TENTHS TO THREE-TENTHS	NINE-TENTHS OR OVERCAST WITH OPENINGS
FOUR-TENTHS	COMPLETELY OVERCAST
FIVE-TENTHS	SKY OBSCURED

PRECIPITATION TYPE

- ˒ DRIZZLE
- • RAIN
- ✳ SNOW
- ▽ SHOWERS
- ⟅ THUNDERSTORM
- ≡ FOG
- ∞ DRY HAZE
- ∿ FREEZING RAIN
- △ HAIL
- ⧖ SLEET

WIND SPEED
(Kilometers per hour)

- ◎ CALM
- 9 kph
- 19 kph
- 28 kph
- 37 kph
- 93 kph
- 120 kph

speed of windblown precipitation. It provides information on wind speed and direction within a radius of 230 kilometers (143 mi) when clouds and precipitation exist; conventional radar can only show existing clouds and precipitation. With Doppler radar, meteorologists are able to forecast when and where severe thunderstorms and tornadoes are developing in time to issue severe-storm warnings.

Doppler radar has made air travel safer. It enables air traffic controllers to detect severe local conditions such as microbursts. Microbursts are powerful downdrafts that originate in thunderstorms. They are among the most dangerous weather phenomena a pilot can encounter. If an aircraft attempts to land or take off through a microburst, the suddenly changing wind conditions can cause the craft to lose lift and crash. In the United States alone, airline crashes accounting for more than 600 deaths have been attributed to microbursts since 1964.

To produce a weather forecast for a particular area, meteorologists use a computer-generated forecast as a guide. They combine it with additional data from current satellite and radar images. They also rely on their own knowledge of weather processes.

If you follow the weather closely, you, too, can make reasonable forecasts. Radar and satellite images showing precipitation and cloud cover are now common on television. In addition, you will probably see weather maps similar to the one on the opposite page. Such maps show the locations of highs and lows, as well as fronts. Warm fronts are represented by bars with semicircles pointing in the direction in which each front is moving. Cold fronts are indicated by bars with triangles. Weather maps usually show isotherms and isobars, too. Isotherms are lines connecting areas of the same temperature, and isobars connect regions of the same atmospheric pressure. The maps also include information about cloudiness, precipitation, and wind speed and direction.

More Accurate Forecasts

Although weather forecasts have become more reliable, there is still a need for greater accuracy. Better forecasts could save industries across the world many billions of dollars each year. Farmers in particular would benefit. Better frost predictions, for example, could save U.S. citrus growers millions of dollars each year. More accurate forecasts of rain would enable farmers to plan timely irrigation schedules.

Imperfect weather forecasts cause construction companies to lose both time and money. A construction foreman might call his crew in to work only to have it rain. An unexpected cold spell could ruin a freshly poured concrete foundation. Power companies lose money when they misjudge the need for power. This occurs when they expect extreme temperatures, and therefore heavy demand for heating or air-conditioning, only to have the weather turn out to be moderate.

Small businesses, too, would benefit from better forecasts. An ice cream store owner, for example, could save her advertising funds for some time in the future if she knew the coming weekend was going to be cool and rainy.

Responding to such needs, meteorologists are working to develop new tools and new methods that will improve their ability to forecast the weather.

◄ *Symbols on a weather map indicate weather conditions nationwide. Each site shows temperature, dew point, wind direction, cloud cover, and precipitation. When combined with other data, fronts, precipitation areas, and high and low pressure zones can be mapped.*

▲ *An air traffic control specialist checks weather charts while video monitors display satellite and radar images. The specialist informs pilots of weather during flights.*
► *A television meteorologist is filmed in front of a blank chroma-key screen while a second camera films a weather map. He knows where to point on the map by watching nearby monitors. The combined image appears on the TV screen at front.*

SEE ALSO AGRICULTURE, AIR MASS, ANTICYCLONE, ATMOSPHERE, ATMOSPHERIC PRESSURE, CLIMATE, CLOUDS, CYCLONE, DEW, FRONT, HUMIDITY, METEOROLOGY, PRECIPITATION, TEMPERATURE, THUNDERSTORM, TORNADO, *and* WIND.

WEATHERING AND EROSION

The earth is undergoing slow but constant change. Weathering and erosion are natural processes; together they transform the earth's surface.

Geologists define weathering as the breaking down of rocks by water, ice, mild acids, plants, and variations in temperature. Erosion transports weathered material.

No rock exposed on the surface of the earth is hard enough to resist the forces of weathering and erosion. Together, they wear down mountains such as the Appalachians in eastern North America, carve canyons such as the Grand Canyon in Arizona, and sculpture rock towers and pinnacles like those in Utah's Bryce Canyon National Park.

The combined actions of weathering and erosion would eventually wear the surface of the earth into a smooth, featureless plain if it were not for the movement of the earth's plates. The plates—rigid slabs of rock that make up the earth's hard shell—constantly move and interact, building mountains and shifting the land in many ways.

Weathering and erosion are also at work beneath the earth's surface. Soil is constantly forming underground as rock is broken apart by spreading tree roots, burrowing animals, and the action of acidic solutions, or liquid mixtures, that occur naturally.

The processes of weathering and erosion can affect artificial surfaces. Potholes in roadways and crumbling curbs and sidewalks are signs of weathering and erosion at work. These forces may wear away the features of outdoor statuary or blur and dull inscriptions on buildings, making them illegible.

Weathering

The action of weathering wears away exposed surfaces over time. It smooths sharp, rough areas on rocks. Weathering can be either a mechanical or a chemical process. Usually these two types of weathering are working together.

Mechanical, or physical, weathering causes rocks to crumble. Sometimes water seeps between mineral grains underground, or into cracks in rocks. If the temperature then drops low enough, the water freezes and expands, exerting tremendous pressure on the rocks and widening the cracks. The ice works as a wedge, prying cracked rocks apart.

A growing tree may also work as a wedge. The seed of a tree may sprout in soil that has collected in a cracked rock. As the roots grow, they widen the cracks, eventually breaking the rock into pieces. Over time, trees can break apart even large rocks.

Chemical weathering changes the materials that make up rocks and soil. Chemicals in water may combine with mineral substances in rocks, making a solution. When the

◄ Flowing in the Colorado and Green Rivers, water—the major agent of erosion—carved a maze of canyons, mesas, buttes, and gorges in Utah's Canyonlands National Park.
► Rocks in Arizona, shaped by weathering and erosion, resemble giant sculptures. Flash floods swirl gritty sand through this gorge, wearing away the rock. Wind also blows sand against the walls, carving them even more.

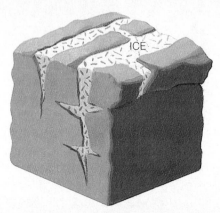

▲ Water spills over boulders in Montana's Glacier National Park. Glaciers can move rocks weighing thousands of tons. When the ice melts, the rocks remain behind.
◀ Ice is an agent of mechanical weathering. In cold weather, water may freeze and expand in cracked rocks, splitting them apart.

solution washes away, it carries the dissolved rock with it. Sometimes carbon dioxide from the atmosphere or from decaying matter combines with water. Then a weak acidic solution is produced that can dissolve limestone and certain other kinds of rock. When the solution seeps underground, it may open up cracks or hollow out vast networks of caves such as those of Mammoth Cave, in Kentucky, and Carlsbad Caverns, in New Mexico.

Rocks are made of minerals. Some rocks contain iron compounds, and they rust just as the metal itself does. The process of rusting is known as oxidation. The rust expands. As it does, it helps to break up, or weather, iron-bearing rocks.

In addition to plant and animal remains, soil consists of mineral particles produced by weathering. Both mechanical and chemical weathering help form soil.

Erosion

Erosion is the movement of weathered material from one place to another. Water, ice, and wind—together with gravity—are the agents of erosion.

When water, ice, and wind are in motion, they move rock fragments and particles of soil from the places where they were weathered. When the water, ice, and wind slow down or stop moving, they deposit the materials in other locations. The materials, called sediments, may range in size and may include boulders as well as fine grains of sand, silt, and clay. These deposits eventually build up new features that change the landscape.

Like weathering, erosion helps form soil. Erosion also transports soil. Water moves soil onto floodplains, where it can be used for farming. When rivers overflow, they deposit rich sediment along their banks. For many centuries, before the Aswan High Dam was built, floods deposited fertile soil along the banks of the Nile River in Egypt.

In some parts of the world, wind has deposited thick layers of fine-grained silt and dust known as loess. The deposits have built up over the centuries. Much of the loess came

◀ Slabs of granite in California's Yosemite National Park show the effects of a glacier's passage and the force of mechanical weathering.

from silt and clay washed out of melting glaciers thousands of years ago. Deep deposits of loess are found in the middle latitudes of China, the United States, the Soviet Union, and Argentina. Loess soils are not only some of the most fertile but also some of the most easily eroded.

Erosion by Water

Moving water is the major agent of erosion. Rain carries away particles of soil and slowly washes away rock fragments. Muddy water is a sign that erosion is taking place. The muddy color indicates the presence of bits of rock and soil suspended in the water.

Deposition of eroded rock may form alluvial fans near the bases of mountains. Alluvium—gravel, sand, and other weathered materials—is carried by water rushing down steep mountainsides. When the water reaches a valley or plain, it spreads out, slows, and drops the alluvium. These deposits accumulate in a fan-shaped arrangement.

Water transports weathered material in streams. Laden with sediment, streams scour the land, cutting channels or valleys by a process called abrasion. Over time, sediment-laden water can break down and wear away valley walls until a plain is formed. This happens as the sides of newly formed valleys become so steep that they cave in. The valleys gradually widen, and the currents of the rivers that flow through them slow down.

As rivers slow, they drop the heaviest rocks they carry. The water begins to flow around boulders in the streambed instead of rushing over them. Eventually, some rivers begin to form broad loops called meanders. Meandering rivers widen valleys still more. As they meander, rivers deposit sediments along their floodplains.

Carried by rivers, huge quantities of sediment finally wash into the ocean. It may take thousands of years for a specific particle of soil to journey all the way from a mountain to the ocean. Yet each year rivers deposit millions of tons of sediment into ocean waters, where new land may form.

At the mouth of a river—the place where it widens and joins another body of water—the river deposits its load of weathered material. Bits of rock and grains of soil may build

► A mole emerges from its tunnel. Such burrowing animals contribute to the weathering process, which helps form soil.
▼ Growing in cracks, tree roots widen openings in rocks. Over time, tree growth can break apart even massive walls of rock like this one.

up at a river's mouth, forming a deposit of sediment known as a delta.

Erosion by water changes the shapes of coastlines. Waves constantly crash against shores, often with tremendous force. The waves pound rocks into pebbles and reduce pebbles to sand.

Water may transport sand away from beaches. For example, on the Outer Banks, a series of barrier islands off the coast of North Carolina, the ocean has eroded most of the beach where the Cape Hatteras Lighthouse stands. When it was built in 1870, the lighthouse stood nearly a thousand meters (3,300 ft) from the ocean. Now the lighthouse is

► *After a storm, sediment muddies a stream in Arizona. Flowing water carries silt, clay, and other materials from one place and drops them in another. The deposits build up on floodplains.*
▼ *Heavy rain rushes down a cliff in Nevada, carrying rock fragments with it. The pounding rain erodes large amounts of rock and soil.*

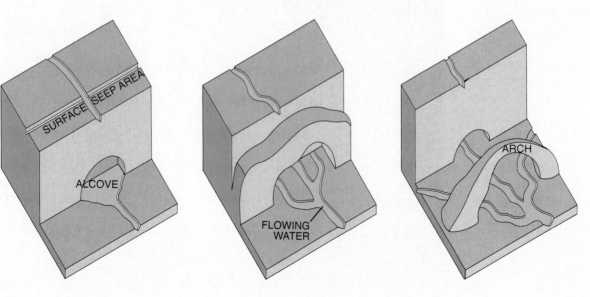

◄ *When sandstone weathers unevenly, natural arches sometimes develop. A cave-like opening forms where water dissolves softer rock at the base of a cliff. At the same time, weathering and erosion enlarge a crack running along the top of the cliff. As the crack widens, a slab of stone becomes separated from the cliff. Weathering rounds the arch into a graceful span.*
► *Delicate Arch, 26 meters (85 ft) high, is one of some 300 such formations in Utah's Arches National Park.*

less than 60 meters (197 ft) from the water.

Waves can build up beaches as well as wear them away. The currents generated by waves can move sand from the ocean floor back onto shore. This process, which is occurring on Cape Cod in Massachusetts, extends existing beaches.

In seaside cliffs, the battering of ocean waves may bore holes that develop into caves. Water sometimes breaks through the back of a cave, leaving an arch. The relentless pounding of breaking waves may cause the top of the arch to fall, leaving only columns called sea stacks.

Over time, rock that crumbles from arches is ground into sand and may be transported and deposited somewhere else along the coast. There, a beach will build up or a sandbar will develop.

Erosion by Glaciers

Ice, too, erodes the land. At the peak of the most recent ice age, some 18,000 years ago, vast glaciers called ice sheets blanketed large portions of the earth's surface, including parts of northern Europe and North America.

As these masses of ice moved, they picked up soil and rocks and covered everything in their path. The ice sheets scraped huge amounts of soil from central Canada. They carried the soil southward and deposited it on the central plains of the United States.

The ice sheets also gouged out basins that would become lakes—including the Finger Lakes in western New York State. Their basins were carved by ice sheets that moved down a set of parallel stream valleys and scooped out deep troughs.

When a glacier melts, it deposits its load of soil and rock. The deposit, which may include large boulders, is called a moraine. In some places, moraines may act as dams, plugging up valleys and forming areas where water can collect into lakes. In other places, piles of glacial debris form long ridges of land. Long Island in New York State and Cape Cod in Massachusetts are moraines.

Huge glaciers still cover much of Antarctica and Greenland. Most of today's small glaciers, however, form high in mountains. There, snow builds up from year to year and turns into ice. As these glaciers creep

downward, they sculpture sharp divides, called arêtes, between U-shaped valleys. Where such glaciers reach the ocean, they may form deep inlets called fjords.

Erosion by Wind

Wind carries dust, sand, and volcanic ash, and sculptures land surfaces. Wind works together with the other agents of weathering and erosion to carve cliff faces and to build hills of sand called dunes.

In arid areas, windblown sand can blast against rocks with tremendous force. Areas of softer rock are worn away, and more resistant rock is carved into unusual formations.

Unlike water, wind can move sediments uphill as well as downhill. This ability makes it possible for the wind to build dunes.

Dunes are found along coasts and in some deserts where large deposits of sand accumulate. There are vast fields of dunes in the Middle East and North Africa. Dunes also may develop along the sandy shores of some rivers and lakes. This has happened along

the banks of Lake Michigan and Lake Superior in North America.

Dunes constantly move and change as winds pick up and transport sand. Dunes may move so far that they bury vegetation and settlements in their path. They take on a variety of changing shapes, including hills, curving ridges, and crescents. Shifting wind patterns may even pile sand into star-shaped dunes.

Dunes that develop along barrier islands

▲ In Australia, the Finke River winds onto a plain. Where a river cuts through the land, hard, resistant layers of rock stand out in relief.
◄ Tinted by minerals, Utah's San Juan River rushes over rocks. Laden with sediment, the water gradually cuts back the ledge. Over time, the waterfall will move upstream.
► A river of ice, part of the Columbia Glacier, winds through the Rocky Mountains in Canada. As glaciers advance, they sharpen peaks, move rocks, and carve valleys.

and beaches can help protect inland areas from erosion. Along many beaches, people work to preserve dunes by planting them with beach grasses and other plants. The deep, spreading roots of the grasses and the creeping stems of the other plants help stabilize dunes by anchoring some of the sand.

Human Impact

The processes of weathering and erosion occur naturally. Sometimes they are speeded up by the actions of people. The results are often harmful. Certain kinds of air pollution can increase the rate of weathering, and certain farming, mining, and building practices make the land more vulnerable to erosion by wind and water.

As people burn coal, gas, and oil, chemicals such as nitrogen oxide and sulfur dioxide are released into the atmosphere. When these pollutants combine with sunlight and moisture, they change into acids that fall with rain and other precipitation.

This kind of precipitation is commonly called acid rain. Building stone and paint exposed to acid rain weather more rapidly than they would naturally. Acid rain is blamed for the rapid deterioration of many historic stone structures, such as the Parthenon in Greece.

People need soil to grow crops, but erosion can carry valuable soil away. For example, rain and floods may strip topsoil from fields and winds may blow it away. Certain farming practices increase the rate at which soil erosion occurs.

When farmers plow dry areas, wind can quickly carry away the exposed topsoil. When farmers plow their fields up and down the slope of the land rather than across the slope, water can more easily strip away topsoil. Heavy rainfall may cause landslides that destroy fields and villages.

Deforestation—the clearing of forests by cutting down or burning trees—also speeds soil erosion. When forests are cleared, the soil they once anchored tends to erode easily. Landslides may occur. In addition, water rushes over the exposed soil instead of soaking into it, leading to floods. In Bangladesh, for example, floods have become more frequent as whole forests in the foothills of the Himalaya have been cut for firewood and to make room for fields and dwellings.

Strip mining is a method of surface mining for coal in which the removal of rocks, soil, and vegetation leaves the land bare. Without covering vegetation to anchor and protect soil, strip-mined land is easily eroded. Mudslides are common in such areas, especially during periods of heavy rainfall.

Flooding and soil erosion also occur in urban areas. As cities grow, more land is covered by pavement, which does not absorb water or slow down its flow the way plant-covered soil does. During rains, heavy runoff

can cause flooding. During excavation at building construction sites, erosion by wind and water can cause substantial loss of soil.

Damage Control

Many countries around the world are trying to reduce the damage that is caused by weathering and erosion.

Scientists are studying acid rain and its effects on lakes, plants, and stone. They are trying to reduce the amount of pollutants released into the atmosphere and to repair the damage caused by acid rain.

Some governments are setting up soil conservation programs. They encourage farmers to practice a method of cultivation known as contour plowing. Using this method, farmers plow across the natural slope of a field. This practice can help slow erosion. So can strip-cropping—a method of planting different crops in parallel rows. Alternating rows of alfalfa with rows of corn is an example of

strip-cropping. The low-growing alfalfa tends to impede the flow of water between the rows of corn, helping to prevent the soil from being carried away.

Farmers are also being urged to plant rows of trees as well as grasses and other deep-rooted plants. The trees act as windbreaks, helping to prevent erosion by wind. The plants, grown between harvests, carpet the soil. They anchor it to the ground, helping to prevent it from washing or blowing away.

▲ *In Syria, a dust storm sweeps across the desert toward a rider. Wind can transport dust for thousands of kilometers. Accumulations of windblown dust and drifting sand blanket some deserts.*
◄ *Holes pit a rock in the Namib Desert in Africa. Water easily penetrates the softer minerals in the rock and washes them away, leaving holes. Scientists call this process differential weathering because various parts of the rock break up at different rates.*

▲ *Surf crashes on a shore in southern Africa. As the breakers wash back into the ocean, they leave behind sand and gravel. These deposits accumulate to build up beaches.*

▶ *A sea arch and a column of rock called a sea stack stand in the Bay of Fundy on the east coast of Canada. They formed as waves, sand, and pebbles whittled away both sides of a rock wall that extended into the water. Weak areas in the rock gave way, leaving holes. When an arch collapses, sea stacks remain.*

Mining companies try to reclaim strip-mined land by replacing topsoil and replanting these areas. Their efforts are intended to restore the land as nearly as possible to its original condition.

Natural Wonders

While weathering and erosion can be damaging, they can also produce spectacular landforms that many people value as wilderness and recreational areas. Governments sometimes establish national parks to protect these scenic places, and millions of visitors enjoy them annually.

Over millions of years, weathering and erosion have sculptured many natural wonders on the Colorado Plateau in the southwestern United States. Among them are the sandstone cliffs of Canyonlands National Park and the towers of Bryce Canyon in Utah, the buttes and mesas of Monument Valley in Utah and Arizona, and the stone logs of Petrified Forest National Park and the magnificent expanse of the Grand Canyon in Arizona.

SEE ALSO AGRICULTURE, ALLUVIAL FAN, BUTTE, CANYON, CAVE, CLIFF, COAST, CONSERVATION, DELTA, DESERT, DUNE, DUST, EROSION, FJORD, FLOODPLAIN, GLACIER, GORGE, ICE SHEET, KARST, LANDSLIDE, LOESS, MORAINE, MOUNTAIN, PLATEAU, POLLUTION, RIVER, ROCK, SEDIMENT, SILT, SINKHOLE, SOIL, STREAM, TERRACE, VALLEY, WATER, WAVES, *and* WIND.

WETLAND

A wetland is an area of land that is covered by water or that is saturated with surface water or groundwater for long enough periods to support vegetation adapted to wet conditions. A wetland is usually covered by water at least part of the year; the depth and duration of the flooding varies. Wetlands are transition areas: They are neither totally land nor totally water; they have characteristics of both.

Wetlands exist in many kinds of climates and on every continent except Antarctica. They vary in size from isolated prairie potholes to huge salt marshes. They are found along coasts and inland. Some wetlands are flooded woodlands. Others are more like watery grasslands. Still others are choked by mosses and similar vegetation.

People have called wetlands by many names, such as swamps, peatlands, sloughs,

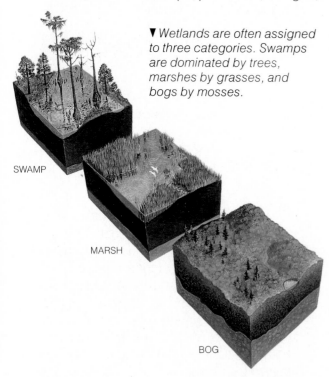

▼ Wetlands are often assigned to three categories. Swamps are dominated by trees, marshes by grasses, and bogs by mosses.

SWAMP

MARSH

BOG

marshes, muskegs, bogs, fens, potholes, and mires. Most scientists consider swamps, marshes, and bogs to be the three major kinds of wetlands.

Swamps

A swamp is a wetland permanently saturated with water and dominated by trees.

Scientists are not sure what purpose knees serve. They may simply provide support, or they may transport oxygen to the roots.

Tiny water plants called duckweed often form a green cover on the surface of the water. Alligators and water moccasins may swim among the plants. Reptiles and amphibians thrive in many swamps because they are adapted to the fluctuating water levels.

Saltwater swamps are often found along tropical coastlines. Formation of these swamps begins with bare flats of mud, sand, or sandy mud that are deposited and thinly covered by seawater during high tides. Plants such as mangrove trees that are able to tolerate tidal flooding begin to grow and soon form thickets of roots and branches. Like cypresses, mangrove trees are rooted in water, but unlike cypresses, they can tolerate salt water and low oxygen levels.

Mangrove trees are easily recognizable because of their stiltlike roots, which hold the small trunks and branches of the trees above

▲ Paddling through floating duckweed, a man guides his skiff along a wetland canal in western France. Canals are regularly dug in this area to drain the land.
◄ Weathered stumps are all that remain of once-giant cypress trees in this part of the Atchafalaya, a Louisiana swamp. Many years ago, logging destroyed these trees, but several kinds of aquatic plants still flourish.

There are two main types of swamps: freshwater swamps and saltwater swamps. Freshwater swamps are common in inland areas; saltwater swamps fringe coasts protected from the open ocean.

Freshwater swamps often form on flat land around lakes or streams, where the water table is high and water runoff is slow. Seasonal flooding and rainwater cause the water level in such swamps to fluctuate. In the wet soil, water-tolerant vegetation grows and helps maintain a swampy condition. Cypress trees often grow out of the still waters of these swamps. Spanish moss may hang from the tree branches. Willows and other shrubs may grow beneath the trees. Sometimes poking as much as 4 meters (13 ft) above the water are angular knobs called cypress knees. They are outgrowths of the trees' root systems.

▲ Punting past cypresses and tupelos in the Okefenokee Swamp in Georgia, a park guide from the wildlife refuge there tells two children about the ecosystem's rich plant and animal life.

► Teeming with life, a tidal salt marsh forms a transition zone between land and ocean. A low-lying area of sand and mud, the salt marsh is periodically flooded by seawater. This illustration shows just a few of the many species of plants and animals that typically live in this type of wetland. A marsh wren (1) perches on a branch at the water's edge. It builds its nest among the reeds and cattails. From the plankton-rich water, an egret (2) catches a tiny killifish. A fiddler crab (3) burrows into the marsh's muddy bank. Other killifish (4) swim in the shallow waters near a blue crab (5). A great blue heron (6) keeps its eyes on the fish below while two gulls (7) circle overhead. A raccoon (8) emerges from the grasses and heads for the water, where it finds much of its food. Many other creatures live in or near tidal salt marshes: mosquitoes, dragonflies, mussels, ducks, frogs, turtles, rabbits, and deer. Many of the world's commercially valuable fish species spawn in these coastal waters. Once considered wastelands, tidal salt marshes today are recognized as one of the richest ecosystems on the earth.

water. These roots anchor sediment and help soil accumulate through their growth and decay. Among these prop roots live animals that feed on fallen leaves and other material. Crabs, conchs, and other shellfish are abundant in mangrove swamps. The swamps are also home to a huge variety of birds, whose droppings help fertilize the swamp.

Marshes

North and south of the tropics, saltwater swamps give way to tidal salt marshes. These wetlands form a grassy fringe near river mouths, in bays, and along coastlines protected from the open ocean. They are dominated by grasses and are alternately flooded and exposed by the movement of the tides. Tidal creeks carrying fish and tiny plants crisscross them.

Of the ecosystems available for human use, saltwater marshes are among the richest in plant and animal life. The grasses provide food and shelter for shellfish, fish, amphibians, and other animals. Wading birds and other animals feed on the vegetation and abundant insects. Tidal salt marshes make ideal nurseries for the young of many animals that live in the ocean as adults.

Tidal freshwater marshlands are farther inland than salt marshes, but are still close enough to the coast to be influenced by tides and brackish waters. They are dominated by grasses and broadleaved aquatic plants.

▲ Fresh water and salt water flow through a marsh along the East Coast's Chesapeake Bay. Marshes and other wetlands act as giant filters, removing pollutants from waters that pass through them.

Inland freshwater marshes often develop around lakes and streams where the water table is high. Many freshwater marshes lie in the prairie pothole region of North America, the heart of which extends from central Canada through the eastern Dakotas and into western Minnesota. The potholes are bowl-shaped depressions left by chunks of glacial ice buried in the soil during the most recent ice age. When the ice melted, water filled the potholes. Rich soil and a temperate climate make these marshes some of the lushest in the world.

Freshwater marshes form much of the Everglades, a wetlands region in southern Florida. Water from Lake Okeechobee passes through the Everglades on its way to the ocean, and saw grass grows along its path. This region, best known for its diversity of wildlife, contains hundreds of species of wading birds, along with alligators, deer, and many other animals.

Bogs

Swamps and marshes are generally found in warm climates, but bogs are more common in the cooler climates of northern

North America, Europe, and Asia. Bogs are often called moors in Europe and muskegs in Canada. Like many wetlands, bogs develop in areas where the water table is high. They often begin in glacial depressions called kettle holes, which are deeper than prairie potholes. Kettle holes, which initially were filled by glacial meltwater, are fed by groundwater and precipitation. Drainage is usually poor.

A bog forms as a kettle hole lake gradually fills with plant debris. As the lake becomes shallower, mosses and other plants growing along the edges extend into the water. They form a loose, floating layer of tangled vegetation. These water plants are followed by grasses and sedges. As plants die, some of their remains float with the surface layer, and other partially decayed matter sinks to the bottom. Soon the water is choked with vegetation and hardly moves at all. The partially decayed vegetation forms a thick, spongy mat called peat as it combines with overlying mosses. Some bogs can support a person's weight. They are called quaking bogs because the surface quakes when a person walks on the peat.

The amount of acid in the soil and water

▲ Cowboys herd wild horses across a marsh on Île de la Camargue, in southern France. The island, a wildlife sanctuary, is in the Rhône Delta, which is covered by marshes and lagoons that dwindle during the summer.

▲ Low tide in a salt marsh on Georgia's Jekyll Island reveals roots of salt grass anchored in the wet sediment. Salt grass is one of the most widespread saltwater-tolerant grasses.

◄ Water lilies grow in a freshwater marsh in Canada's Point Pelee National Park, in Ontario. Hundreds of thousands of migrating birds arrive at this birdwatcher's paradise each spring.

of bogs is generally higher than that of swamps or marshes, and the supply of nutrients, especially nitrogen, is lower. Only certain kinds of plants, such as sphagnum moss, pitcher plants, and sundew, can grow there. Because of the limited species of plants, bogs sometimes do not have the diversity and numbers of wildlife common in other types of wetlands. Bogs, however, produce more peat than swamps and marshes do because of the predominance of sphagnum moss.

Some people living near bogs cut and dry squares of peat and burn them for heating and cooking or use them to insulate their homes. In Ireland, commercially harvested peat supplies a portion of the country's electrical energy. In the United States, peat moss has been used primarily in mixtures of potting soil and as a general soil conditioner.

Vital Ecosystems

Wetlands are among the most valuable ecosystems on the earth. They act like giant sponges or reservoirs. When heavy rains cause flooding, wetlands absorb the excess water, moderating the effects of the flooding. Wetlands also protect coastal areas from storms that can wash away fragile coastline. Saltwater swamps and tidal salt marshes help anchor coastal soil and sand.

The wetland ecosystem also acts as a water treatment plant, filtering wastes and purifying water naturally. When excess nitrogen and other chemicals wash from farms into wetlands, plants there absorb and use the chemicals. Chemicals not absorbed by plants slowly sink to the bottom and are buried in sand and other sediment.

Wetlands, especially marshes and swamps, are home to a wide variety of plant and animal life. Many ocean species enter

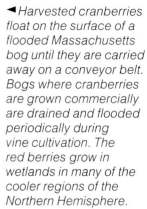

◄Harvested cranberries float on the surface of a flooded Massachusetts bog until they are carried away on a conveyor belt. Bogs where cranberries are grown commercially are drained and flooded periodically during vine cultivation. The red berries grow in wetlands in many of the cooler regions of the Northern Hemisphere.

▲ Water buttercups, white heather, rushes, sedges, and other plants flourish in an Alaskan muskeg, a bog that is dominated by sphagnum moss.
◄Visitors hear an insect symphony as they cross a New Hampshire bog near the Appalachian Trail. The bog's still waters are excellent breeding grounds for mosquitoes, flies, and other insects.

coastal wetlands to spawn. Fish swim into salt marshes to lay their eggs. When the eggs hatch, the young find plenty of food and some protection in the grasses or among the tree roots. Other species spawn in the ocean, and the young swim into the wetlands and live there until they mature. Two-thirds of the fish and shellfish that are commercially harvested worldwide are linked with wetlands.

For most of history, wetlands were looked upon as wastelands and as homes for insect pests such as mosquitoes. People thought

► *Cultivated fields of grain border Tule Lake, a national wildlife refuge in California. The marshlands and nearby grain attract many migrating birds.*
▼ *Environmentalists in the 1970s won a battle to halt construction of this jetport. It would have impeded the flow of water into Florida's Everglades region.*

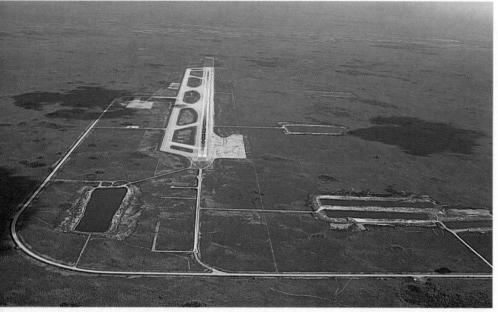

wetlands were sinister and forbidding. In the United States, filling or draining these lands was once accepted practice. Almost half of the U.S. wetlands were destroyed. Other countries have done damage through the unrestricted harvesting of peat. Commercially valuable fish species that depend on wetlands have become rare. Many wetland species are threatened with extinction.

In the early 1970s, governments began enacting laws recognizing the enormous value of wetlands. In some parts of the world, including the United States, it is now against the law to alter or destroy wetlands. Through management plans and stricter laws, people are trying to protect remaining wetlands and to re-create them in areas where they have been destroyed.

SEE ALSO BOG, ECOSYSTEM, FOSSIL FUEL, LAKE, MARSH, SWAMP, WATER, *and* WATER TABLE.

▲ *Supported on stilt-like aerial roots, a red mangrove invades an expanse of saw grass and rushes in Florida's Everglades. The roots trap sediment and cause an island of soil to build up around the mangrove.*

WILDERNESS

A wilderness is a natural environment that has remained essentially undisturbed by human activities. Wilderness areas preserve the earth's natural beauty and shelter numerous animal and plant species. They offer scientists a laboratory for the study of how ecosystems function in the absence of human intervention. Though wilderness areas are protected in many parts of the world, vast tracts of wildlands are being threatened. In 1964, the U.S. government established a National Wilderness Preservation System, which now includes much of the country's remaining wilderness. In these areas, the number of visitors, their activities, and the length of their stay are subject to strict controls. Visits to wilderness areas may be prohibited at certain times of year. Parts of Sweden's Muddus National Park, for example, are off-limits during the breeding season to protect bird life.

SEE ALSO CONSERVATION, ECOSYSTEM, ENVIRONMENT, NATURAL RESOURCE, *and* PARK.

WIND

Wind is the movement of air caused by the uneven heating of the earth by the sun. It does not have much substance—you cannot see it or hold it—but you can feel its force. It can dry your clothes in summer and chill you to the bone in winter. It can be strong enough to carry sailing ships across the ocean and rip huge trees from the ground. It is the great equalizer of the atmosphere, transporting heat, moisture, pollutants, and dust great distances around the globe.

Global Wind Patterns

There are three large-scale wind patterns in each hemisphere, as shown on the diagram at right. The sun warms the Equator more than it does the rest of the globe. The warm equatorial air rises higher into the atmosphere and migrates toward the Poles. At the same time, cooler, denser air moves over the earth's surface toward the Equator to replace the heated air. The process of warm air and cool air trading places is the main driving force for wind.

At about 30 degrees latitude, most equatorial air cools and sinks. Some goes toward the Equator, and some moves toward the Poles. At about 60 degrees latitude, polar air heading toward the Equator collides with the mid-latitude air, forcing that air to rise.

Generally, winds blow east and west rather than north and south. This happens because the earth's rotation generates what is

▲ Laundry flutters in a brisk October wind. The wind itself is invisible, but we can "see" the wind by noticing how it affects the things around us.

▼ The average wind movement over the earth is known as the general circulation of the atmosphere. This illustration shows general wind patterns as they would exist when averaged over the course of a year. These wind patterns shift north and south seasonally, along with the intertropical convergence zone, which moves with the sun back and forth across the Equator.

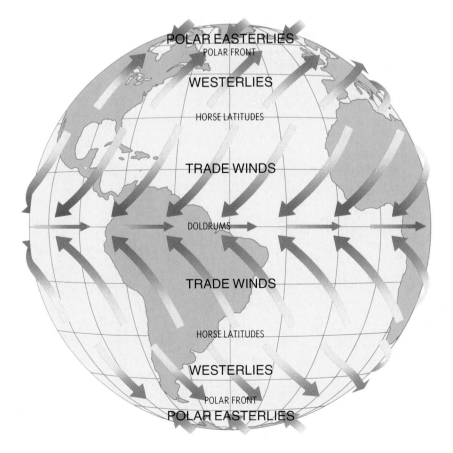

SOME WINDS AROUND THE WORLD

CHINOOK A warm, dry wind that blows down the eastern slopes of the Rocky Mountains of North America.

BURAN A strong northeasterly wind in Siberia and central Asia. In winter it is a fierce blizzard.

BRICKFIELDER A hot, dusty wind blowing south from central Australia. It is so named because of the dust the wind raised in brickfields near Sydney.

MISTRAL A violent wind blowing south to the Mediterranean coast of France, most often in winter and spring. It can prevail for a hundred days annually.

NORTHER A cold, strong wind bringing fast-falling temperatures across Texas and the Gulf of Mexico. In Mexico and Central America it is called *El Norte*.

PAMPERO A dry, bitterly cold wind that sweeps the pampas, or grasslands, of Uruguay and Argentina.

SIROCCO A hot, usually springtime wind blowing from the Sahara in Africa to Mediterranean coasts.

known as the Coriolis effect. The Coriolis effect makes winds twist to the right in the Northern Hemisphere and to the left in the Southern Hemisphere. For example, Northern Hemisphere air moving south in the tropics is turned to the west, generating the easterly trade winds that carried sailing ships to North America. The place where the trade winds of the two hemispheres meet is called the intertropical convergence zone, the ITCZ. Because winds are weak in this region, sailors named it the doldrums. When the ITCZ moves away from the Equator, which it does seasonally, the trade wind patterns shift and help bring on a phenomenon known as a monsoon.

Differences in atmospheric pressure generate winds. Wind speed and direction help determine weather and climate. In the mid-latitudes, high and low pressure systems help determine wind speed and direction. Winds try to blow directly from high pressure areas to low pressure areas. The Coriolis effect, however, causes winds to travel along

▲ *A massive dust storm sweeps toward the desert town of Alice Springs, in Australia. In arid or drought-stricken areas, a strong wind can easily lift tons of soil into the air.*
◄ *In darkness, an Inuit hunter near Canada's Hudson Bay seals an igloo's blocks with snow. The igloo will shelter him from the Arctic wind.*
▼ *The windchill equivalent temperatures given below represent how cold the air feels when the wind blows at different speeds.*

the edges of two pressure systems. These are called geostrophic winds. In 1857, Dutch meteorologist Christoph Buys Ballot formulated a law about geostrophic winds: When you stand with your back to the wind in the Northern Hemisphere, low pressure is to your left.

The fastest surface wind on record blew at 371 kilometers per hour (231 mph) on Mount Washington, in New Hampshire, on April 12, 1934. Powerful high altitude winds, called jet streams, can blow 480 kilometers per hour (300 mph). They are often used in air travel to save time and fuel.

SEE ALSO BEAUFORT SCALE, CLIMATE, CORIOLIS EFFECT, JET STREAM, MONSOON, TRADE WINDS, WEATHER, *and* WEATHERING AND EROSION.

WINDCHILL EQUIVALENT TEMPERATURES

		AIR TEMPERATURE (Degrees Fahrenheit)										
		50°	40°	30°	20°	10°	0°	-10°	-20°	-30°	-40°	-50°
WIND SPEED (miles per hour)	5	48°	37°	27°	16°	6°	-5°	-15°	-26°	-36°	-47°	-57°
	10	40°	28°	16°	3°	-9°	-22°	-34°	-46°	-58°	-71°	-83°
	15	36°	23°	9°	-5°	-18°	-31°	-45°	-58°	-72°	-85°	-99°
	20	32°	19°	4°	-10°	-24°	-39°	-53°	-67°	-81°	-95°	-110°
	25	30°	16°	1°	-15°	-29°	-44°	-59°	-74°	-88°	-103°	-118°
	30	28°	13°	-2°	-18°	-33°	-49°	-64°	-79°	-93°	-109°	-125°
	35	27°	12°	-4°	-20°	-35°	-52°	-67°	-82°	-97°	-113°	-129°
	40	26°	11°	-5°	-21°	-37°	-53°	-69°	-84°	-100°	-115°	-132°

		AIR TEMPERATURE (Degrees Celsius)										
		10°	4°	-1°	-7°	-12°	-18°	-23°	-29°	-34°	-40°	-46°
WIND SPEED (kilometers per hour)	8	9°	3°	-3°	-9°	-14°	-21°	-26°	-32°	-38°	-44°	-49°
	16	4°	-2°	-9°	-16°	-23°	-30°	-37°	-43°	-50°	-57°	-64°
	24	2°	-5°	-13°	-21°	-28°	-35°	-43°	-50°	-58°	-65°	-73°
	32	0°	-7°	-16°	-23°	-31°	-39°	-47°	-55°	-63°	-70°	-79°
	40	-1°	-9°	-17°	-26°	-34°	-42°	-51°	-59°	-67°	-75°	-83°
	48	-2°	-11°	-19°	-28°	-36°	-45°	-53°	-62°	-69°	-78°	-87°
	56	-3°	-11°	-20°	-29°	-37°	-47°	-55°	-63°	-72°	-80°	-89°
	64	-3°	-12°	-21°	-29°	-38°	-47°	-56°	-64°	-73°	-82°	-91°

WIND ENERGY

Wind energy is produced by the movement of air. A sailboat running before a brisk breeze relies on wind energy to push it forward. A windmill captures wind energy to turn its blades. Traditionally, the spinning blades have been used to rotate a millwheel for grinding grain or pumping water. By the turn of the century, however, windmills also were being used on a small scale to generate electricity in Europe and in the United States.

Today, concern about dwindling fossil fuels and the pollution they produce when burned has led to a renewed interest in using wind energy as a clean source of electricity. Scientists have developed new, more sophisticated technology to harness this unlimited energy source. The wind pushes the blades of a wind turbine, causing them to turn the shaft of a generator, which produces an electrical current. Scientists estimate that as wind passes through a turbine, about 35 to 40 percent of its energy can be captured.

In some places, wind turbines can generate power efficiently enough to compete with other energy systems. Today, thousands of wind turbines on California "wind farms" are used to generate electricity. Among developing countries, India and China are showing particular interest in wind-power technology.

SEE ALSO ENERGY and WIND.

▼ *Still used in some areas, traditional windmills like this one in Finland run on wind energy. The blades power devices that grind grain or pump water.*

▼ *Wind turbines crowd a hillside at a "wind farm" in California, which produces most of the wind-generated electricity in the U.S. Local utilities buy the electricity to supply homes and businesses. Wind power is a cleaner source of energy than fossil fuels.*

WOODLAND

"Woodland" is another name for forest. Some people use the term to describe a forest with an open canopy. The canopy is the highest layer of foliage in a forest. It is made up of the crowns, or tops, of the trees. The density of a canopy varies from one kind of forest to another. An open canopy allows full sunlight to enter. A closed canopy keeps most of the sun's light from reaching the forest floor.

SEE ALSO FOREST and RAIN FOREST.

▲ *Visitors ride through a scenic woodland in Camel's Hump State Park, in Vermont.*

Z

ZONE

A zone is an area separated from others in some artificial or natural manner. Time zones are artificial divisions of the earth made to help standardize time worldwide. Transition zones exist where boundaries are not sharply defined between one region and another, such as the transition zones between major types of vegetation or climates.

SEE ALSO AREA, CLIMATE, REGION, TIME AND TIME ZONES, and VEGETATION REGIONS.

The 334 encyclopedia entries and their page numbers appear in **boldfaced** type.

ACKNOWLEDGMENTS

The Special Publications Division is grateful to the following individuals and organizations for their generous assistance during the preparation of this book: Hal Aber, Kevin P. Allen, Kristen Allen, Maria Vincenza Aloisi, Wallace H. Andrews, Philip S. Angell, Robert C. Averett, Alex Bacho, David B. Barrett, Eddie N. Bernard, Barry C. Bishop, Osa Brand, Michael D. Buckley, Don Burgess, Richard Cahall, Joseph Caravella, Charles F. Case, Claire Monod Cassidy, Richard J. Cook, Ted Dachtera, Pete Daniel, Christopher L. Delgado, Michael J. Devine, LeRoy Doggett, John F. Dorr, Sylvia A. Earle, Brian M. Fagan, Richard W. Fenwick, Henry R. Frey, Herbert Friedman, Richard Furno, Charles Gardner, Mike Gentry, A. R. Ghosh, Chester Gillis, Frank I. Gonzalez, Thomas O. Gray, M. Grant Gross, Hildegard B. Groves, Ted Gull, Carl Haub, Heinrich D. Holland, Jodi Jacobson, Constant H. Jacquet, Larry Jones, Kenneth M. Kavula, Charles D. Kearse, Melvin Kranzberg, Miles Lawrence, Nicholas Lenssen, Richard Logan, Gail S. Ludwig, Robert Lystad, Nancie J. Majkowski, Mapping Specialists, Ltd., Stephen P. Maran, Nicholas C. Matalas, James McCraken, John McDermid, Laurence C. McGonagle, Judith S. McGuire, Jill McKelvie, Garry D. McKenzie, Max E. Miller, Christine Morin, Joe Morrison, James P. Murray, Asher Namenson, Roland R. Nichols, Jessica P. Norton, Marina S. Ottaway, B. Marie Perinbam, Craig Phillips, Wayne D. Rasmussen, Nicholas Raymond, Martin Reuss, Cathy Riggs-Salter, David A. Ross, Stephen A. Rubin, Jeremy A. Sabloff, Christopher L. Salter, William Schauffler, Wolfgang Scherer, P. Kenneth Seidelmann, Elliott Sivowitch, John P. Snyder, Daniel Sober, T. Dale Stewart, Michael Streitz, Anthony J. Thompson, Ellen Thompson, Tibor G. Toth, John R. Treiber, Albert R. Trost, Tony Trujillo, Barbara Twigg, G. T. Underwood, U. S. Department of Agriculture, U. S. Geological Survey, Richard M. Vogel, Thomas E. Vollmann, Peter Webb, Robert H. Weck, Jr., Stephen P. Wells, John H. White, David Woodward, Worldwatch Institute, Robert S. Yuill, Leo B. Zebarth.

ADDITIONAL READING

The reader may wish to consult the *National Geographic Index* for related articles and books. The following may also prove useful: Richard A. Anthes et al., *The Atmosphere;* Arco Publishing, Inc., *Energy, Forces and Resources;* David Attenborough, *The Living Planet: A Portrait of the Earth;* Alan Backler and Stuart Lazarus, *World Geography;* Roger G. Barry and Richard J. Chorley, *Atmosphere, Weather and Climate;* Robert L. Bates and Julia A. Jackson, editors, *Glossary of Geology;* John H. Baynes, *How Maps are Made;* Firman E. Bear, *EARTH: The Stuff of Life;* Mitchell Beazley Publishers Limited, *The Mitchell Beazley Atlas of World Resources;* Bureau of Mines/U.S. Department of Interior, *A Dictionary of Mining, Mineral, and Related Terms;* Doris Coburn, *A Spit is a Piece of Land: Landforms in the U.S.A.;* David Crabbe and Simon Lawson, *The World Food Book: An A-Z, Atlas and Statistical Source Book;* Howard J. Critchfield, *General Climatology;* Delwyn Davies, *Fresh Water: The Precious Resource;* Harm J. de Blij and Peter O. Muller, *Geography: Regions and Concepts;* Robert Decker and Barbara Decker, *Volcanoes;* Dorothy W. Drummond and Robert R. Drummond, *People on Earth: A World Geography;* Lee Durrell, *State of the Ark: An Atlas of Conservation in Action;* Alyn C. Duxbury and Alison Duxbury, *An Introduction to the World's Oceans;* Ernest G. Ehlers and Harvey Blatt, *Petrology: Igneous, Sedimentary, and Metamorphic;* Don L. Eicher et al., *The History of the Earth's Crust;* Edward B. Espenshade, Jr., editor, *Goode's World Atlas;* Brian M. Fagan, *People of the Earth: An Introduction to World Prehistory;* Food and Agriculture Organization/UN, *FAO Production Yearbook, The State of Food and Agriculture,* and *A Guide to Staple Foods of the World;* Herbert Friedman, *Sun and Earth;* Stanley David Gedzelman, *The Science and Wonders of the Atmosphere;* David Greenland and Harm J. de Blij, *The Earth in Profile: A Physical Geography;* R. Kay Gresswell and Anthony Huxley, editors, *Standard Encyclopedia of the World's Rivers and Lakes;* Herbert H. Gross, *World Geography;* W. Kenneth Hamblin, *The Earth's*

Dynamic Systems: A Textbook in Physical Geology; Francis P. Hunkins and David G. Armstrong, *World Geography: Peoples and Places;* The International Institute for Environment and Development/The World Resources Institute, *World Resources 1987;* Terry Jennings, *The Young Geographer Investigates Rivers;* John C. Kammerer, *Largest Rivers in the United States;* Jack Knowlton, *Maps and Globes;* Dorothy Farris Lapidus, *The Facts on File Dictionary of Geology and Geophysics;* Luna B. Leopold, *Water: A Primer;* Tom L. McKnight, *Physical Geography: A Landscape Appreciation;* Albert Miller and Richard Anthes, *Meteorology;* F. J. Monkhouse, *A Dictionary of Geography;* W. G. Moore, *The Penguin Dictionary of Geography;* Marie Morisawa, *Streams: Their Dynamics and Morphology;* Norman Myers, *GAIA: An Atlas of Planet Management;* Esko E. Newhill and Umberto La Paglia, *Exploring World Cultures;* Frank Press and Raymond Siever, *Earth;* Laurence Pringle and the editors of Time-Life Books, *Rivers and Lakes;* Rand McNally, *Encyclopedia of World Rivers;* Reader's Digest, *North American Wildlife;* Helen Dwight Reid Educational Foundation in association with the American Meteorological Society, *Weatherwise* magazine; Arthur N. Strahler and Alan H. Strahler, *Elements of Physical Geography;* Walter Sullivan, *Landprints;* Edward J. Tarbuck and Frederick K. Lutgens, *The Earth: An Introduction to Physical Geology;* Glenn T. Trewartha and Lyle H. Horn, *An Introduction to Climate;* Darrell Weyman, *Tectonic Processes;* David and Jill Wright, *The Facts on File Children's Atlas;* Jerome Wyckoff, *Rock, Time, and Landforms.*

ILLUSTRATIONS CREDITS

The following abbreviations are used in this list: (T)=Top; (B)=Bottom; (R)=Right; (L)=Left; (C)=Center; NGP=National Geographic Photographer; NGS=National Geographic Staff.

COVER: (T,L) Tim Thompson; (T,C) Rebuffat/RAPHO; (T,R) George F. Mobley NGP; (C,L) Jean-Paul Ferrero/EXPLORER; (C,C) R. Ian Lloyd/THE STOCK MARKET; (C,R) Paul Chesley; (B,L) Charles W. Friend/SUSAN GRIGGS AGENCY; (B,C) Emory Kristof NGP; (B,R) James L. Stanfield NGP. **FRONT MATTER:** 16-17 Row 1: NASA, Robert L. Gibson; George F. Mobley NGP; James P. Blair NGP; Christopher Johns; Paul Chesley/PHOTOGRAPHERS ASPEN. Row 2: George F. Mobley NGP; George F. Mobley NGP; Bryan and Cherry Alexander; Annie Griffiths Belt; Georg Gerster/Zumikon, Switzerland; Jonathan T. Wright/PHOTOGRAPHERS ASPEN. Row 3: Robert Frerck/ODYSSEY PRODUCTIONS; James P. Blair NGP; Jonathan T. Wright/PHOTOGRAPHERS ASPEN; ©Gary Braasch; Steve Raymer NGS. Row 4: Leonard Freed/MAGNUM; David Hiser/PHOTOGRAPHERS ASPEN; Eric Williams; Loren McIntyre; Loren McIntyre. Row 5: Vince Streano, STREANO/HAVENS; Annie Griffiths Belt/DRK PHOTO; Gustav Lamprecht; Paul Chesley. **A:** 36-37 Nicholas DeVore III/PHOTOGRAPHERS ASPEN; Jim Brandenburg/DRK PHOTO. 41 Tor Eigeland. 42 ROBERT HARDING PICTURE LIBRARY LTD., LONDON. 44(T) Sarah Leen; Steve Raymer NGS. 45(L) Paul Chesley/PHOTOGRAPHERS ASPEN; Jim Brandenburg/DRK PHOTO. 46 Gordon W. Gahan. 47(T&B) James L. Stanfield NGP; Mark E. Gibson. 48(T to B) Georg Gerster/Zumikon, Switzerland; ROBERT HARDING PICTURE LIBRARY LTD., LONDON; James L. Stanfield NGP. 49(L) David Alan Harvey; (R) Nicholas DeVore III/PHOTOGRAPHERS ASPEN; (B) Loren McIntyre. 50-51(L to R) Cosmo Condina/INDEX STOCK INT'L; David S. Boyer; Annie Griffiths Belt. 52-53 H. Edward Kim. 54-55(C) James L. Stanfield NGP; 55(B) Gordon W. Gahan; (R) Loren McIntyre. 56 NOAA. 57 Nicholas DeVore III/PHOTOGRAPHERS ASPEN. 58-59(L) Katia Krafft/EXPLORER; Loren McIntyre. 62(L) Georg Gerster/Zumikon, Switzerland; Gustav Lamprecht. 63(T) Mel Edelman/BLACK STAR; L. A. Frank & J. D. Craven/University of Iowa. 64-65(All) David Cupp. **B:** 66-67(All) David Hiser/PHOTOGRAPHERS ASPEN. 68-69(T,L) David Hiser/PHOTOGRAPHERS ASPEN; (B) Dewitt Jones; (T,R) Steven J. Krasemann/DRK PHOTO; (B,R) C. C. Lockwood/BRUCE COLEMAN INC. 70-71(T,L) David Alan Harvey; (B) James L. Amos. (T,R) Bruce Dale NGP. 72(T) David Thompson/OXFORD SCIENTIFIC FILMS; Jodi Cobb NGP. 74-75 (L) Steven J. Krasemann/DRK PHOTO; (R) Robert P. Carr/BRUCE COLEMAN INC. (C) James L. Stanfield NGP; (T&B) Paul Chesley/PHOTOGRAPHERS ASPEN. 76(T) Robert W. Madden NGS; (L) Loren McIntyre; (R) O. Louis Mazzatenta NGS. 77(L) David Alan Harvey; Tom Bean. **C:** 78-79(L) Art Resource; (T) Thomas Hooper; (B) James Hester, Ph.D. 80-81(L to R) Paolo Koch/RAPHQ; F. Le Diascorn/RAPHO; Robert W. Madden NGS. 82(T,L&R) George F. Mobley NGP; Tor Eigeland. 83(L) George F. Mobley NGP; (T&B) Georg Gerster/Zumikon, Switzerland; (C) James P. Blair NGP. 84-85 (L&T,C) James P. Blair NGP; (T,R) Steve Raymer NGS; (B) Tom Bean. 86(T) James P. Blair NGP; Gordon W. Gahan. 87(T) Joseph H. Bailey NGP; Jodi Cobb NGP. 88-89(L) Mark M. Laurence/THE STOCK MARKET; Chip Clark. 90-91(T) Emory Kristof NGP; Paul Chesley/PHOTOGRAPHERS ASPEN. 92-93(L) Paul Chesley; Loren McIntyre. 94-95(T,L) Ph. F. Huguier/EXPLORER; Alex Webb/MAGNUM; (C) Georg Gerster/Zumikon, Switzerland; (T) Jodi Cobb NGP; (B) William Albert Allard. 96(L) Georg Gerster/Zumikon, Switzerland; (T) Mark Godfrey; (B) James P. Blair NGP. 97(T) Georg Gerster/Zumikon, Switzerland; (C) Gordon W. Gahan; (R) William Albert Allard. 98-99(L) Annie Griffiths Belt; (C) David S. Boyer; (T) Robert W. Madden NGS; (B) Dewitt Jones. 100-101(L) William Albert Allard; (R) Larry Lee/WEST LIGHT; (T,C) Paul Chesley; (T,R) Alex Webb/MAGNUM; (B) Loren McIntyre. 102-103 (L) John Lawler/AFTER IMAGE, INC; (C) Paul Chesley; (T) Jodi Cobb NGP; (B) George F. Mobley NGP. 104(T) Raghubir Singh; Alex Webb/MAGNUM. 105(Both) Georg Gerster/Zumikon, Switzerland. 106-107(T) Nicholas DeVore III/PHOTOGRAPHERS ASPEN; David Hiser/PHOTOGRAPHERS ASPEN. 108(T to B) Loren McIntyre; George F. Mobley NGP; ©Jim Brandenburg; David Hiser/PHOTOGRAPHERS ASPEN. 110(L) Sebastiao Salgado/MAGNUM; David Hiser/PHOTOGRAPHERS ASPEN. 111(T) Steve McCurry; Anthony Edgeworth, Inc./THE STOCK MARKET. 112(T) Nicholas DeVore III/PHOTOGRAPHERS ASPEN; ©Jim Brandenburg. 113(T) ©Englebert/SUSAN GRIGGS AGENCY; Melinda Berge/PHOTOGRAPHERS ASPEN. 114(L) Paul Chesley/PHOTOGRAPHERS ASPEN; (R) Wendell Metzen/BRUCE COLEMAN INC; (B) J. C. Carton/BRUCE COLEMAN INC. 115(T to B) David Cavagnaro/DRK PHOTO; Georg Gerster/Zumikon, Switzerland; Wayne Lynch/DRK PHOTO. 116(L) Art Wolfe/ALLSTOCK; (R) B.&C. Calhoun/BRUCE COLEMAN LTD; (B) ©Jim Brandenburg. 117(L) José Azel; (R) ©Jim Brandenburg; (B) Nicholas DeVore III/PHOTOGRAPHERS ASPEN. 118(T) Robert Frerck/ODYSSEY PRODUCTIONS; (L) Tor Eigeland; (R) Pierre Boulat. 119(T) Anne B. Keiser; ©Jim Brandenburg. 122-123(L) Bruce Ando/INDEX STOCK. (C) Gordon W. Gahan; (B) Bates Littlehales. 124-125(L) George Herben; (T) Steven C. Wilson/ENTHEOS; Georg Gerster/Zumikon, Switzerland. 126-127(L) Tom Myers; (R) James P. Blair NGP; (T,C) Steve Raymer NGS; (B,C) John Johnson/DRK PHOTO; (T,R) Bohdan Hryrewych/STOCK.BOSTON; (B,R) Loren McIntyre. 128(L,&B,R) James L. Amos; (T,R) Nicholas DeVore III/PHOTOGRAPHERS ASPEN. 142 Nicholas DeVore III/PHOTOGRAPHERS ASPEN. 144-145(T&C) Georg Gerster/Zumikon, Switzerland; Adam Woolfitt/SUSAN GRIGGS AGENCY. 146-147(L) Gordon W. Gahan; (R) Jane Shaw/BRUCE COLEMAN INC; (T,C) Doug Perrine/DRK PHOTO. 150(T) Steve Raymer NGS; François Gohier/EXPLORER. 151(T) Tom Bean; Jonathan T. Wright/PHOTOGRAPHERS ASPEN. 152-153(T) Steve McCutcheon; Tom Myers. 154 Thierry Boccon-Gibod/BLACK STAR. **D:** 155(T) James L. Stanfield NGP; Loren McIntyre. 156-157 José Dupont/EXPLORER. 158-159 Georg Gerster/Zumikon, Switzerland. 161(T) E. G. Friesen; Kevin Schafer. 162(Both) Georg Gerster/Zumikon, Switzerland. 163(T) Bruce Dale NGP; J. J. Scherschel. 164(T) Michael E. Long NGS; Loren McIntyre. 165-166(All) Georg Gerster/Zumikon, Switzerland. 167(T to B) Tor Eigeland; Marc & Evelyne Bernheim/RAPHO; Georg Gerster/Zumikon, Switzerland. 168(T) Georg Gerster/Zumikon, Switzerland; Steve McCurry. 169(T) Tom Till; Patrick Ward/NETWORK. 170-171(C) Jim Brandenburg/DRK PHOTO; (B) Georg Gerster/Zumikon, Switzerland; (R) Dean Conger NGS. **E:** 172-173 NASA/APOLLO 17. 174-175 Katia Krafft/EXPLORER. 176-177 ROBERT HARDING PICTURE LIBRARY LTD, LONDON; Klaus D. Francke/PETER ARNOLD, INC. 178(L) Peter R. Dickerson/SUSAN GRIGGS AGENCY; (T,R) Wilbur E. Garrett NGS; (B,R) Robert W. Madden NGS. 179(Both) Otis Imboden. 180-181(L) Los Alamos National Laboratory/University of California; (C) Dewitt Jones; (T,R) James L. Stanfield NGP; (B,R) Georg Gerster/Zumikon, Switzerland—"Isle of California" painted by the Los Angeles Fine Arts Squad: Victor Henderson, Jerry Schoonhoven, 1972. 182(T to B) Paul Chesley/PHOTOGRAPHERS ASPEN; James Balog; James L. Stanfield NGP. 183(All) Herman Heyn. 184-185 Leonard Freed/MAGNUM; Jodi Cobb NGP. 186(T to B) David Hiser/PHOTOGRAPHERS ASPEN; James P. Blair NGP; James L. Stanfield NGP; P. Zackmann/MAGNUM. 188(T to B) Georg Gerster/Zumikon, Switzerland; Nicholas DeVore III/BRUCE COLEMAN LTD; Christopher Johns. 189(L) James L. Stanfield NGP; (R) Georg Gerster/Zumikon, Switzerland; (B) Ted Spiegel/BLACK STAR. 190(L) Dean Conger NGS; (R) Kate Bader; (B) Jodi Cobb NGP; 191(L) Robert Azzi/SUSAN GRIGGS AGENCY; (R) Sepp Seitz/SUSAN GRIGGS AGENCY; (B) Paul Chesley/PHOTOGRAPHERS ASPEN. 192-193(L) Nicholas DeVore III/PHOTOGRAPHERS ASPEN; Christopher Johns. 194-195(L) Ted Spiegel/SUSAN GRIGGS AGENCY; Paul Chesley/PHOTOGRAPHERS ASPEN. 196(T to B) Harvey Lloyd/PETER ARNOLD, INC; Michael St. Maur Sheil/SUSAN GRIGGS AGENCY; Thomas J. Abercrombie NGS. 198 Tom Myers. 199(T) Georg Gerster/Zumikon, Switzerland; ©Gary Braasch. 200 Georg Gerster/Zumikon, Switzerland. 201(T) Win Parks; Paul Chesley/PHOTOGRAPHERS ASPEN. 202(T) Tony Arruza/BRUCE COLEMAN INC; Robert Frerck/ODYSSEY PRODUCTIONS. 203(T) M. Sherman/BRUCE COLEMAN INC; Jonathan Blair. 204-205(T) ©Jim Brandenburg; (B,C) Dewitt Jones; (T,R) Michael Quearry; (B) Robert S. Patton NGS. 206(T) James L. Stanfield NGP; Annie Griffiths Belt/WEST LIGHT. **F:** 207(T) Goldwater/NETWORK; Steve Raymer NGS. 208(Both) James L. Stanfield NGP. 209(T) James L. Stanfield NGP; Frans Lanting. 210-211(T,L) ©Jim Brandenburg; (B) ©Gary Braasch; (T,R) Nicholas DeVore III/PHOTOGRAPHERS ASPEN; (B,R) Tor Eigeland. 212(T) Michel Baret/RAPHO; P. J. Griffiths/MAGNUM. 213(T) Richard Olsenius; Don & Pat Valenti/DRK PHOTO. 214(T) Cary Wolinsky/STOCK.BOSTON; Adam Woolfitt/SUSAN GRIGGS AGENCY. 215(L) Wilhelm Braga/RAPHO; James L. Amos. 216-217 Steve Raymer NGS; James P. Blair NGP. 218(T to B) David L. Arnold NGS; Jodi Cobb NGP; James L. Stanfield NGP; James P. Blair NGP; Thomas J. Abercrombie NGS. 220(T to B) Paul Chesley/PHOTOGRAPHERS ASPEN; Steve Raymer NGS; Jonathan T. Wright/PHOTOGRAPHERS ASPEN. 221(T to B) Jeff Simon/BRUCE COLEMAN LTD; WWF Fredy Mercay/BRUCE COLEMAN LTD; Leonard Lee Rue/BRUCE COLEMAN LTD; Dr. Eckart Pott/BRUCE COLEMAN LTD. 222 (Clockwise, from T) D. Cavagnaro/DRK PHOTO; Terrence Moore; James L. Stanfield NGP; O. Louis Mazzatenta NGS; Ian Yeomans/SUSAN GRIGGS AGENCY. 223(Clockwise, from T) George F. Mobley NGP; James L. Stanfield NGP; David Alan Harvey; Holt Conter/DRK PHOTO; Lois Ellen Frank/ALLSTOCK. 224(T) H. Edward Kim; (L) Richard Kalvar/MAGNUM; (R) Mark E. Gibson. 225(L) David L. Arnold NGS; (R) Win Parks; (B) Leonard Freed/MAGNUM. 226(T) David Alan Harvey; (L) Robert W. Madden NGS; (R) Raymond de Seynes/RAPHO. 227(T) James L. Stanfield NGP; James Nachtwey. 230-231 David Alan Harvey; Dean Conger NGS. 232 Christopher Johns. 233(L) Gordon W. Gahan; (R) William T. Douthitt NGS; (B) James L. Stanfield NGP. 234(T) Gordon W. Gahan; Paul A. Zahl, Ph.D. 235(T to B) Bruce Dale NGP; George F. Mobley NGP; James P. Blair NGP. 236-237(All) James P. Blair NGP. 238(L) George F. Mobley NGP; (B,L) James L. Amos; (T to B) Vince Streano, STREANO/HAVENS; Emory Kristof NGP; Steve Ogden/TOM STACK & ASSOC. 242(T) Nicholas DeVore III/PHOTOGRAPHERS ASPEN; José Azel. **G:** 243(L) Loren McIntyre; (T,R) George F. Mobley NGP; (B) Dean Conger NGS. 248(L) James A. Sugar; (T,R) Galen Rowell/MOUNTAIN LIGHT; (B,R) James L. Amos. 249(Both) Georg Gerster/Zumikon, Switzerland. 250-251(T) ©Ric Ergenbright; (Both) Christopher Johns. 252-253 Joseph H. Bailey NGP; Loren McIntyre. 254(L) Steve Raymer NGS; (T to B) O. Louis Mazzatenta NGS; Paolo Koch/RAPHO; Gordon W. Gahan. 255(T,L) James P. Blair NGP; (B) Robert Frerck/ODYSSEY PRODUCTIONS; (R) Gordon W. Gahan. 258-259 (T) Nicholas DeVore III/PHOTOGRAPHERS ASPEN; (B) Robert Frerck/ODYSSEY PRODUCTIONS; (T,C) Jodi Cobb NGP; (L) James L. Stanfield NGP; (R) Paul Chesley/PHOTOGRAPHERS ASPEN. 260(T to B) ©Jim Brandenburg; Dean Conger NGS; Steve McCutcheon. 261(T to B) Nicholas DeVore III/PHOTOGRAPHERS ASPEN; ©Jim Brandenburg; Annie Griffiths Belt/DRK PHOTO. 262-263(Both) James P. Blair NGP. 264-265 John Bulmer/SUSAN GRIGGS AGENCY; (T) ©Jim Brandenburg; (B) Dean L. Conger NGS. 266(T) José Azel; David Hiser/PHOTOGRAPHERS ASPEN. 267(T) Loren McIntyre; George F. Mobley NGP. 268(T) Terrence Moore; ©Jim Brandenburg. 269 Peter Menzel. 270-271(L to R) Dan McCoy/RAINBOW; Mark E. Gibson/THE STOCK MARKET; Mark N. Boulton/BRUCE COLEMAN LTD. 272-273(L) Otis Imboden; (T & B) Steve Raymer NGS. **H:** 274-275(L) Heather Angel; (T) Rob Kendrick; (B) James L. Amos; (R) Roland Michaud. 276(T) Phil Schermeister; S. Summerhays/BIOFOTOS. 277 J. Scott Applewhite. 278-279 (T & B) Paul Chesley/PHOTOGRAPHERS ASPEN; (C) Annie Griffiths Belt/DRK PHOTO; (R) Steve Firebaugh/ALLSTOCK. **I:** 280-281 Georg Gerster/Zumikon, Switzerland. 282(T) Tony Martin/OXFORD SCIENTIFIC FILMS; George F. Mobley NGP. 283(T to B) George F. Mobley NGP; Otis Imboden; Alex Webb/MAGNUM. 284-285(L) Adam Woolfitt/SUSAN GRIGGS AGENCY; ©Gary Braasch. 286(T to B) Thomas J. Abercrombie NGS; Gordon W. Gahan; Emory Kristof NGP; Bruce Dale NGP. 288 (T to B) James L. Stanfield NGP; Vince Streano, STREANO/HAVENS; James L. Amos. 289(L) James L. Stanfield NGP; (T) David Alan Harvey; (R) O. Louis Mazzatenta NGS. 290 Rémi Berli/RAPHO. 291(T & B,R) James L. Stanfield NGP; George F. Mobley NGP. 292-293 David Hiser/PHOTOGRAPHERS ASPEN. 294(T to B) Paul Chesley/PHOTOGRAPHERS ASPEN; James P. Blair NGP; R. Woldendorp/SUSAN GRIGGS AGENCY; Steve Raymer NGS. 296(L) Steven J. Krasemann/DRK PHOTO; (R) ©Jim Brandenburg; (B) Jodi Cobb NGP. 297(T & B) David Alan Harvey; (C) Georg Gerster/Zumikon, Switzerland. 298(T) Jonathan Blair; (B,L) Georg Gerster/Zumikon, Switzerland; (B,R) David Hiser/PHOTOGRAPHERS ASPEN. 299(T to B) Christopher Johns; James P. Blair NGP; ROBERT HARDING PICTURE LIBRARY LTD., LONDON. 300 (L & B,R) Nicholas DeVore III/PHOTOGRAPHERS ASPEN; Frans Lanting. 300-301 Nicholas DeVore III/PHOTOGRAPHERS ASPEN; (B) Frans Lanting. **J,K,L:** 302-303(T) Loren McIntyre; ROBERT HARDING PICTURE LIBRARY LTD., LONDON. 303(L) James P. Blair NGP; Georg Gerster/Zumikon, Switzerland. 304-305(L) Bates Littlehales; (C) Environmental Research Institute of Michigan; (T) Georg Gerster/Zumikon, Switzerland; (B) Nicholas DeVore III/BRUCE COLEMAN INC. 306(T) Tim Thompson; Nicholas DeVore III/PHOTOGRAPHERS ASPEN. 307 George F. Mobley NGP. 308(T) Georg Gerster/Zumikon, Switzerland; (L) Loren McIntyre; (R) George F. Mobley NGP. 309(L) Georg Gerster/Zumikon, Switzerland; David S. Boyer. 310(T) Georg Gerster/Zumikon, Switzerland; (C) Carl Hugare/Chicago Tribune; (B) Nicholas DeVore III/PHOTOGRAPHERS ASPEN; (R) David Austen/SUSAN GRIGGS AGENCY. 311 Loren McIntyre. 312(T) Anthony Bannister; Environmental Research Institute of Michigan. 314(T) David Hiser/PHOTOGRAPHERS ASPEN; David Austen/

SUSAN GRIGGS AGENCY. 314-315(T) David Alan Harvey; (L) Georg Gerster/Zumikon, Switzerland; (R) Jodi Cobb NGP. 318(T) Paul Chesley; James L. Amos. 319(L) George F. Mobley NGP; (R) Georg Gerster/Zumikon, Switzerland; (B) Walter Hodges/ALLSTOCK. 320(T) Gordon W. Gahan; David Hiser/PHOTOGRAPHERS ASPEN. 321(T) Lowell Georgia; (C&B) Jodi Cobb NGP. M: 324-325(Both) Steve Raymer NGS. 326(T to B) Harvard University/Semitic Museum; Joseph H. Bailey NGP; Adapted by NGS artist W. N. Palmstrom and J. W. Luthers from the Mappemonde by Fra Mauro, 1459. 327 Courtesy John J. P. Johnson. 330 Keith Gunnar/BRUCE COLEMAN INC. 331(T) Bianca Lavies; Breton Littlehales. 332 Joseph H. Bailey NGP. 333(L) James P. Blair NGP; George F. Mobley NGP. 334 Jodi Cobb NGP. 335(T) Loren McIntyre; Dean Conger NGS. 336 Albert Moldvay. 336-337 John Sanford/SCIENCE PHOTO LIBRARY, P. R. 337(T) Georg Gerster/Zumikon. Switzerland; (L) James L. Amos; (R) James P. Blair NGP; Fred Ward/BLACK STAR. 339(T to B) James P. Blair NGP; Thomas J. Abercrombie NGS; Bruce Dale NGP. 340 Alan Bolesta/INDEX STOCK INT'L. 341 James L. Amos. 342-343(L) Bruce Dale NGP; James P. Blair NGP. 344-345(T) Steve Raymer NGS; (B) Adam Woolfitt/SUSAN GRIGGS AGENCY; (C) Walter M. Edwards; (R) Steve McCutcheon. 346(L) Adam Woolfitt; (T,R) David R. Austen/AUSTRALIA; (B,R) Stacy Pick/STOCK.BOSTON. 347-348(All) Steve McCurry/MAGNUM. 349(T) John Eastcott & Eva Momatiuk/DRK PHOTO; Fiske Planetarium/Univ. of Colorado, Boulder. 350-351 Lick Observatory (except Full Moon—Fiske Planetarium/Univ. of Colorado, Boulder). 352-353 NASA; Dan McCoy/RAINBOW. 354-355 George F. Mobley NGP. 356(T to B) Loren McIntyre; Nicholas DeVore III/PHOTOGRAPHERS ASPEN; Gordon W. Gahan; Paul Chesley/PHOTOGRAPHERS ASPEN; David Alan Harvey. 358(T) Reflejo/SUSAN GRIGGS AGENCY; Georg Gerster/Zumikon, Switzerland. 359(T) Peter Cole; David Hiser/PHOTOGRAPHERS ASPEN. 361(All) Loren McIntyre. 362(T) George F. Mobley NGP; (L) Robert Frerck/ODYSSEY PRODUCTIONS; (R) Gerald Cubitt. 363(All) Jodi Cobb NGP. N,O: 364-365(L) Lowell Georgia; (C) Robert W. Madden NGS; (T) Jodi Cobb NGP; (B) William T. Douthitt NGS. 366-367(L) Robert Azzi/SUSAN GRIGGS AGENCY; (T) Adam Woolfitt; (B) Louis Psihoyos; (R) James P. Blair NGP. 368(T) Jodi Cobb NGP; (L) Bruce Dale NGP; (R) Robert deGast/PHOTO RESEARCHERS, INC. 369(T) Loren McIntyre; Georg Gerster/Zumikon, Switzerland. 370-371 Nicholas DeVore III/PHOTOGRAPHERS ASPEN. 375(T to B) Vince Streano, STREANO/HAVENS; David Hiser/PHOTOGRAPHERS ASPEN; Steve McCutcheon. 378-379 Anthony Bannister; Loren McIntyre. 380(T) M. Timothy O'Keefe/BRUCE COLEMAN INC; Emory Kristof NGP. 381(T to B) Jim Brandenburg; George Herben; NASA. P: 382-383(L) Patrick Ward/NETWORK; Nicholas DeVore III/PHOTOGRAPHERS ASPEN. 384-385(L) Paul Chesley/PHOTOGRAPHERS ASPEN; (B,R) Tom Myers; (T) George F. Mobley NGP. 386(T) Craig Aurness/WEST LIGHT; David Hiser/PHOTOGRAPHERS ASPEN. 387(T) ©NASA/PHOTO RESEARCHERS, INC.; ©NASA/BLACK STAR. 390-391(L) Emory Kristof NGP; Georg Gerster/Zumikon, Switzerland; (R) James P. Blair NGP. 393(L to R) José Azel; Georg Gerster/Zumikon, Switzerland; Dewitt Jones. 394(T) Loren McIntyre; Galen Rowell/MOUNTAIN LIGHT. 395(T) Steve Raymer NGS; Paul Chesley/PHOTOGRAPHERS ASPEN. 396(T) James Balog; James L. Amos. 397(Both) Kenneth Garrett. 398(T to B) George F. Mobley NGP; Ric Ergenbright; David S. Boyer. 399 Jeffrey Aaronson. 400-401(L) Georg Gerster/Zumikon, Switzerland; Bryan & Cherry Alexander. 403(T) Steve Kaufman; David Alan Harvey. 404(T) Bryan & Cherry Alexander; Dean Conger NGS. 405(L) Georg Gerster/Zumikon, Switzerland; (R) Kevin Schafer; (B) M. P. Kahl/DRK PHOTO. 406-407(Both) Ted Spiegel. 408(T) Cary Wolinsky/TRILLIUM; (L) François Gohier/AGENCE NATURE; (R) Mark Antman/THE IMAGE WORKS. 409(L) Steve Raymer NGS; (T,R) Gerald Cubitt; (B,R) Ted Spiegel/SUSAN GRIGGS AGENCY. 410(T) Barry Lewis/NETWORK; Fred Ward/BLACK STAR. 411(T) Fred Ward/BLACK STAR. 412-413 Goldwater/NETWORK; Stephanie Maze. 414(T) ©Jim Brandenburg; (L) James L. Stanfield NGP; (R) Nicholas DeVore III/PHOTOGRAPHERS ASPEN. 415(T) Jodi Cobb NGP; Wilbur E. Garrett NGS. 418(L) Curto/RAPHO; Bruce Dale NGP. 419(T) Nathan Benn; (B) James L. Amos; (R) David Alan Harvey. 420 Paul Chesley. 420-421 Paul Chesley/PHOTOGRAPHERS ASPEN. 421(T) Steve Raymer NGS; William Albert Allard. 422 Thomas J. Abercrombie NGS. 423(L) Georg Gerster/Zumikon, Switzerland; (R) Paul Chesley; (B) P. Menzel/STOCK.BOSTON. 424(T&B) James P. Blair NGP; (C) Joseph H. Bailey NGP. 425(L) Golestan/NETWORK; (R) James Nachtwey; (B) David Alan Harvey. 426(T) Barry Lewis/NETWORK; James L. Stanfield NGP. 427(L, Both) Goldwater/NETWORK; (R) James P. Blair NGP. 428-429(L) ©Jim Brandenburg; (R) Tom Myers; (T) Georg Gerster/Zumikon, Switzerland. 430 Nancy Adams/TOM STACK & ASSOC. 431(T) Jodi Cobb NGP; Jonathan T. Wright/BRUCE COLEMAN INC. R: 432-433(L) Patrick Ward/NETWORK; (Both) Loren McIntyre. 435 Jean Gaumy/MAGNUM. 436(L) Loren McIntyre; James P. Blair NGP. 437(L,Both) Otis Imboden; (R) David Barnes/ALLSTOCK. 438 James L. Stanfield NGP. 438-439 Ian Yeomans/SUSAN GRIGGS AGENCY. (T) Jodi Cobb NGP; (B) James P. Blair NGP. 440 David Alan Harvey/SUSAN GRIGGS AGENCY. 441(T) James L. Stanfield NGP; Jodi Cobb NGP. 442-443 Mehmet Biber; Jodi Cobb NGP. 444(L) George F. Mobley NGP; (R) Melinda Berge/PHOTOGRAPHERS ASPEN; (B) Dean Conger NGS. 445(All) George F. Mobley NGP. 446-447(L) A.J. Dean/BRUCE COLEMAN LTD.; Galen Rowell/MOUNTAIN LIGHT. 448(T) Emory Kristof NGP; (L) Charles O'Rear; (R) Katia Krafft/EXPLORER. 449(L) Katia Krafft/EXPLORER; Steve Kaufman. 450-451(L) Jonathan T. Wright/PHOTOGRAPHERS ASPEN; Loren McIntyre. 452(T to B) Loren McIntyre; Adam Woolfitt/SUSAN GRIGGS AGENCY; David S. Boyer; Tim Thompson; Steve Raymer NGS. 454(T,L) Blondeau/PITCH; (B,L) James P. Blair NGP; (T,C) Carlos Sanuvo/BRUCE COLEMAN INC.; (B,C) Matt Bradley/BRUCE COLEMAN INC.; (T,R) ©Gary Braasch; (B,R) Georg Gerster/Zumikon, Switzerland. 456(L) Jonathan T. Wright/PHOTOGRAPHERS ASPEN; (R) D.&J. Heaton/COLORIFIC!; (B) O. Louis Mazzatenta NGS. 457(T) James P. Blair NGP; (B, Both) George F. Mobley NGP. 458(T) Bianca Lavies; (B) Robert Frerck/ODYSSEY PRODUCTIONS. 458-459 Nathan Benn. 459 Wilbur E. Garrett NGS. 460(B) Goldwater/NETWORK. 460-461(All) Loren McIntyre. 462(T) Tim Thompson; (L) John Bulmer/SUSAN GRIGGS AGENCY; (R) Georg Gerster/Zumikon, Switzerland. 463(T) David R. Austen/SUSAN GRIGGS AGENCY; Jean-Paul Ferrero/EXPLORER. 464-465 David Hiser/PHOTOGRAPHERS ASPEN. 467(T) Dewitt Jones; (L) Paul Chesley/PHOTOGRAPHERS ASPEN; (R) Dave Johnson. 468(Both) Dewitt Jones. 469(L) Bruce Dale NGP; James P. Blair NGP. 470(T) Adam Woolfitt/SUSAN GRIGGS AGENCY; Tom Bean. 470-471 Paul Chesley/PHOTOGRAPHERS ASPEN. 471 Frans Lanting. 472(L) David Hiser/PHOTOGRAPHERS ASPEN; Anthony Edgeworth/THE STOCK MARKET. 473(T to B) Steve Adams; W. Perry Conway/TOM STACK & ASSOC.; Tom Bean/ALLSTOCK. 474 (C) Boutin/EXPLORER; Georg Gerster/Zumikon, Switzerland. 474-475 Otto Rogge/THE STOCK MARKET; Galen Rowell/MOUNTAIN LIGHT. S: 476 George F. Mobley NGP. 476-477(T) Gordon W. Gahan; Jodi Cobb NGP. 478-479(All) Bill Binzen/PHOTO RESEARCHERS, INC. 480-481(T) Tom Bean/DRK PHOTO; (B, Both) Georg Gerster/Zumikon, Switzerland. 482(T) Tim Thompson; Charles O'Rear/WEST LIGHT. 483(T) WWF Fredy Mercay/BRUCE COLEMAN LTD.; (L) Georg Gerster/Zumikon, Switzerland; (R) David Hiser/PHOTOGRAPHERS ASPEN. 484-485(T,L) James P. Blair NGP; (B,L) Nicholas DeVore III/PHOTOGRAPHERS ASPEN; (B,R) David Arnold NGS; (T,C) James L. Stanfield NGP; (R) George F. Mobley NGP. 486-487(L) David Doubilet; (T) Loren McIntyre; (B) David Hiser/PHOTOGRAPHERS ASPEN. 487(L) Jonathan T. Wright/PHOTOGRAPHERS ASPEN; John Shaw/TOM STACK & ASSOC. 488-489 Nicholas DeVore III/PHOTOGRAPHERS ASPEN; Steven C. Wilson/ENTHEOS. 492 Lanceau/AGENCE NATURE. 493(Both) Steven C. Wilson/ENTHEOS. 494(Both) Steven C. Wilson/ENTHEOS. 494-495 Annie Griffiths Belt. 495 Steven C. Wilson/ENTHEOS. 496-497(All) Steven C. Wilson/ENTHEOS. 498(L) Steven C. Wilson/ENTHEOS; James L. Stanfield NGP. 499 Jet Propulsion Lab. 502 Gordon W. Gahan. 503(T) Peter Menzel; Otis Imboden; Jet Propulsion Lab. 504(T) Steve Raymer NGS; Dean Conger NGS. 505(T) Bruno Barbey/MAGNUM; James L. Stanfield NGP. 506(L) NASA; (R) National Optical Astronomy Observatories. 506-507 Jack W. Dykinga. 508(T) National Optical Astronomy Observatories; Jonathan T. Wright/PHOTOGRAPHERS ASPEN. 509(L) Greg Davis/BLACK STAR; James P. Blair NGP. T,U: 510(T) Steve Raymer NGS; (L) David Alan Harvey; (R) Paul Chesley. 511(T) Georg Gerster/Zumikon, Switzerland; Nicholas DeVore III/PHOTOGRAPHERS ASPEN. 512-513(L) David Hiser/PHOTOGRAPHERS ASPEN; (C, Both) Sestor/PITCH; (R) Georg Gerster/Zumikon,

Switzerland. 514(T & B) Georg Gerster/Zumikon, Switzerland; (R) George F. Mobley NGP. 515(T to B) Hartman/BRUCE COLEMAN INC; Pat Lanza Field/BRUCE COLEMAN INC; Larry Lee/WEST LIGHT. 518-519(T) E. R. Degginger/BRUCE COLEMAN INC; Joseph H. Bailey NGP. 520 Christopher Johns. 521(T) Thomas J. Abercrombie NGS; James L. Stanfield NGP. 525(T) James P. Blair NGP; Lois Ellen Frank/ALLSTOCK. 526-527(L) Jodi Cobb NGP; Paul Chesley. 532(L) James L. Stanfield NGP; (R) O. Louis Mazzatenta NGS; (B) Dean Conger NGS. 533(L) David Alan Harvey; (R) Robert W. Madden NGS; (B) Bruce Dale NGP. 534(L) Gerald Cubitt; Anne B. Keiser. 535(L) Steve Raymer NGS; (R) James P. Blair NGP; (B) Gerald Cubitt. 536(T) Otis Imboden; George F. Mobley NGP. 537(T) Bruce Dale NGP; Wilbur E. Garrett NGS. 538(L) Jodi Cobb NGP; (R) David Alan Harvey; (B) James P. Blair NGP. 539(T to B) Jodi Cobb NGP; Bruce Dale NGP; Leonard Freed/MAGNUM. 540 James P. Blair NGP. 541 Dean Conger NGS. 542-543 Steve McCutcheon; Steven J. Krasemann/DRK PHOTO. 544-545(T) Steven J. Krasemann/DRK PHOTO; Steve Kaufman. 546-547(T,Both) Steve McCutcheon; Steve Kaufman. V: 548-549(L) George F. Mobley NGP; Larry Lee/WEST LIGHT. 550(T) Emory Kristof NGP; Paul Chesley/PHOTOGRAPHERS ASPEN. 551 David Stoecklein/WEST STOCK. 552 Christopher Johns. 552-553(T to B) Réne Burri/MAGNUM; Goldwater/NETWORK; ©Jim Brandenburg. 553(T) O. Louis Mazzatenta NGS; James L. Stanfield NGP. 554-555(L) Katia Krafft/EXPLORER; Steve Raymer NGS. 556(T to B) Robert W. Madden NGS; Georg Gerster/Zumikon, Switzerland; Tom Bean/DRK PHOTO. 558-559(T to B) Robert W. Madden NGS; Sigurdur Thorarisson; Loren McIntyre. 559(T & B) Georg Gerster/Zumikon, Switzerland; (C) George F. Mobley NGP. 560(T) ©Gary Braasch; John Marshall. 561(L) Randy Hyman; ©David Robert Austen. W–Z: 562 George F. Mobley NGP. 563(T) David Hiser/PHOTOGRAPHERS ASPEN; Loren McIntyre. 564(T) Gordon W. Gahan; Steve Raymer NGS. 565 Otis Imboden. 566 James P. Blair NGP. 566-567(T) Nicholas DeVore III/BRUCE COLEMAN INC.; (L) Loren McIntyre; (R) C. Allan Morgan. 568-569(L) Gordon W. Gahan; Tony Arruza/BRUCE COLEMAN INC. 570-571 ROBERT HARDING PICTURE LIBRARY LTD, LONDON. 572(L) Jodi Cobb NGP; ROBERT HARDING PICTURE LIBRARY LTD, LONDON. 573(T to B) Lee Foster; Jonathan T. Wright/PHOTOGRAPHERS ASPEN; George F. Mobley NGP. 574(T, L, & R, Both) Christopher Johns; (B,L) Edi Ann Otto. 575(L) Paul Chesley/PHOTOGRAPHERS ASPEN; (T to B) Michael Yada; Annie Griffiths Belt; National Earth Satellite Service/NOAA. 576-579(All) Cindy Yamanaka. 580-581 ©Ric Ergenbright; Paul Chesley/PHOTOGRAPHERS ASPEN. 582(T) Nicholas DeVore III/PHOTOGRAPHERS ASPEN; Joseph H. Bailey NGP. 583(T) Barrie E. Watts/OXFORD SCIENTIFIC FILMS LTD; Dewitt Jones. 584-585(L) Bob McKeever/TOM STACK & ASSOC.; (T) E. R. Degginger/BRUCE COLEMAN INC; (B) John Gerlach/DRK PHOTO. 586(T) Georg Gerster/Zumikon, Switzerland; George F. Mobley NGP. 587(L) Paul Chesley/PHOTOGRAPHERS ASPEN; (R) Galen Rowell/AFTER IMAGE INC; (B) ©Jim Brandenburg. 588(T) Martel/RAPHO; Georg Gerster/Zumikon, Switzerland. 589(T) Anthony Bannister; Robert Frerck/ODYSSEY PRODUCTIONS. 590-591(T) Doisneau/RAPHO; (B) John Eastcott, Eva Momatiuk/DRK PHOTO; (R) Joseph H. Bailey NGP. 593 Tom Bean/DRK PHOTO. 594(T) H. W. Silvester/RAPHO; (L & R) Steven J. Krasemann/DRK PHOTO. 595(L) Fred J. Bavendam; (R) ©Gary Braasch; (B) Sam Abell. 596(L) Georg Gerster/Zumikon, Switzerland; (R) Frans Lanting; (B) Dewitt Jones. 597 Jonathan T. Wright/PHOTOGRAPHERS ASPEN. 598(L) David Hiser/PHOTOGRAPHERS ASPEN; ROBIN SMITH PHOTOGRAPHY PTY. LTD. 599(L) Thomas J. Abercrombie NGS; (R) James P. Blair NGP; (B) Tom & Pat Leeson/ALLSTOCK.

ART CREDITS

The following abbreviations are used in this list:
PA—Publications Art; RCHL—Ross Culbert Holland & Lavery, NYC.

38-43 PA; 51 PA; 52 PA; 53 PA; 54 PA; 56 RCHL; 57 (left) RCHL; (right) PA; 60 Robert Hynes and PA; 61 Robert Hynes; 64 PA; 65 PA; 66 RCHL; 68 RCHL; 71 PA; 73 Robert Hynes; 89 (both) Robert Hynes; 91 National Oceanic and Atmospheric Administration; 108-109 RCHL; 120-121 Robert Hynes; 129-141 Tibor G. Toth (paintings) and PA; 143 Cartographic Division, Atlas of North America; 144 Robert Hynes; 145 Robert Hynes; 147 PA; 148-149 PA; 154 Robert Hynes; 156 RCHL; 157 Robert Hynes; 160 RCHL; 173 PA; 174 David Meltzer, Children's Universe Atlas; 175 PA; 180 Mark Seidler, Our Violent Earth; 183 PA; 186-187 RCHL; 192-193 RCHL; 196 PA; 197 RCHL; 204 PA; 208 PA; 215 PA; 218-219 RCHL; 228-229 PA; 230 Robert Hynes; 232 RCHL; 239 PA; 240-241 RCHL; 242 PA; 244 Robert Hynes; 245 PA; 246-247 PA; 251 Robert Hynes; 256-257 RCHL; 264 RCHL; 269 PA; 271 (both) PA; 273 RCHL; 276 PA; 281 RCHL; 286-287 RCHL; 294-295 PA; 301 RCHL; 302 PA; 312 PA; 313 Cartographic Division, Atlas of North America; 316 RCHL; 317 PA; 318 PA; 322 Paul M. Breeden; 322-323 PA; 328-329 Cartographic Division; 330 PA; 332 PA with photo inserts by Earth Satellite Corp.; 334-335 PA; 340-341 RCHL; 347 PA; 348 RCHL; 350-351 PA; 358-359 Robert Hynes; 360 U. S. Dept. of Interior, illustrated by Robert Hynes; 372-373 Cartographic Division, National Geographic Atlas of the World, 5th ed.; 374 Lloyd K. Townsend, The Mysterious Undersea World, 376-377 Robert Hynes; 378-379 RCHL; 379 Lloyd K. Townsend, Our World; 385 RCHL; 388-389 Ludek Pesek, Our Universe; 392-393 RCHL; 394-396 Susan Sanford, Planet Earth; 399 Robert Hynes; 402 (both) PA; 416-417 PA; 418 PA; 420 PA; 422 RCHL; 429 RCHL; 430 PA; 431 PA; 434 Robert Hynes; 435 RCHL; 436 PA; 440 RCHL; 444 RCHL; 452-453 PA; 455 Robert Hynes; 461 RCHL; 466 Robert Hynes; 468-469 PA; 476 RCHL; 478 Robert Hynes; 481 PA; 490-491 RCHL; 492 Robert Hynes; 498 RCHL; 499 Robert Hynes; 500-501 PA; 505 RCHL; 507 Robert Hynes; 508 PA; 511 PA; 516-517 PA; 519 Robert Hynes; 520 RCHL; 522-523 PA; 524 PA; 528-531 PA; 540 PA; 541 PA; 542 Robert Hynes; 545 (top) RCHL; (bottom) Robert Hynes; 551 RCHL; 558 Robert Hynes; 562 PA; 565 Robert Hynes; 566 PA; 569 PA; 572 Robert Hynes; 578 PA; 582 PA; 584 PA; 590 John Dawson, NATIONAL GEOGRAPHIC 3/87; 592-593 Robert Hynes; 597 RCHL; 598 PA.

Composition for this book by the Typographic section of National Geographic Production Services, Pre-Press Division. Printed and bound by R. R. Donnelley & Sons, Willard, Ohio. Color separations by Graphic Art Service, Inc., Nashville, Tenn.; Lanman Progressive Company, Washington, D.C.; Lincoln Graphics, Inc., Cherry Hill, N.J.; and NEC, Inc., Nashville, Tenn.

Library of Congress CIP Data

Exploring your world.

Includes bibliographical references.
Summary: A general encyclopedia of physical and human geography containing 334 alphabetically arranged entries and more than 1000 illustrations, including photographs, maps, and charts.
1. Geography—Dictionaries, Juvenile. [1. Geography—Dictionaries] I. National Geographic Society (U.S.). Special Publications Division.
G63.E97 1989   910.3   89-13099
ISBN 0-87044-726-2
ISBN 0-87044-727-0 (library edition)
ISBN 0-87044-728-9 (deluxe edition)